P9-BJL-535

Back, Miss Anna Boije, Fritz Schoultz (seated), Matt Ovington, Carl Pfeil, Gustaf Wicklund, Miss Anna Pfeil and Mrs. Anna Pfeil (seated),
Gunnar Sahlin
Front, Mrs. Ottilie Myhrman, Wilhelm Schoultz, Mrs. Amelie Wicklund

THE
SWEDISH THEATRE OF CHICAGO
1868-1950

By

HENRIETTE C. K. NAESETH

ROCK ISLAND, ILLINOIS
AUGUSTANA HISTORICAL SOCIETY
AND
AUGUSTANA COLLEGE LIBRARY
1951

AUGUSTANA LIBRARY PUBLICATIONS
NUMBER 22

DONALD O. ROD, *General Editor*

AUGUSTANA HISTORICAL SOCIETY PUBLICATIONS
VOLUME 12

COPYRIGHT, 1951, BY
AUGUSTANA HISTORICAL SOCIETY

F
536
.A96
.V.12

37,525

[PRINTED IN U·S·A]

AUGUSTANA BOOK CONCERN
Printers and Bookbinders
ROCK ISLAND, ILL.

In memory of my parents
Christen Andreas Naeseth
and
Caroline Mathilde Koren Naeseth

CAMROSE LUTHERAN COLLEGE
LIBRARY

The publication of this volume has been made possible in large part by the generous financial aid of

MR. D. L. ESTERDAHL, Moline

MR. HERBERT R. HEDMAN, Chicago

THE SWEDISH CLUB OF CHICAGO

Foreword

A HISTORY of the theatrical activities of the Swedes of Chicago on the scale of this book may require some justification. Theirs was never a professional theatre with regularly established companies of actors for whom the stage was a means of livelihood, as were the French and German theatres in New York, the French theatre in New Orleans, and the German theatre in Chicago and other centers of German population. These foreign language theatres have received considerable recognition. Their story has been told in special studies and included in general theatrical histories, such as Odell's *Annals of the New York stage.* Little attention, however, has been given to the theatrical enterprises of smaller national groups or of those whose native drama is less widely known. This neglect, which has been the lot of the Swedish theatre in the United States, has characterized not only general theatrical history, but local histories as well, and the records of the national groups themselves.

In the many books and articles in which writers of Swedish birth or descent have recounted Swedish achievements in America, interpreted the problems and described the way of life of Swedish Americans, every other aspect of cultural and organizational life has been dealt with more fully than the theatre. Explanations readily present themselves: the opposition of the church; the tendency, even among those interested in the theatre, to regard it merely as passing entertainment, not calling for a permanent record; the fact that the Swedish theatre, though persistently active for long periods in many so-called Swedish colonies, had little continuity of organization, and did not attain professional status; and, finally, the problems involved in collecting and organizing the materials of theatrical history.

Changing concepts of history and the perspective of time have, however, brought new recognition of the importance of this phase of immigrant life which has been so largely disregarded in the past. Recent decades have seen increased emphasis on social and cultural history, and a rapid growth of interest in the immigrant as a factor in that history. In the literature of the immigrant that has come into being, historian and sociologist alike have stressed two points: the contribution made by the immigrant to the American cultural heritage, and the problem of transition the immigrant faced in reconciling the claims and cultures of his two worlds.

Admirable studies of national groups—their settlements and their institutions, such as the church and the press—have been written from these points of view; immigrant documents have been published and interpreted. But, students of immigration agree, much remains to be done. For the history of immigration to be written "on the broad and impartial lines that its place in our national development deserves," Dr. Marcus L. Hansen pointed out, hundreds of studies are needed—of life and culture in township, village, and city ward, of singing societies and reading circles, of "the city theatres promoted by every alien group." When these studies have been made and compared, "we can more confidently say what each group has contributed to the cultural possessions of American society."[1]

The importance of the foreign language theatre as one of the institutions serving the needs of the immigrant has been called to our attention by other historians also. In Dr. Carl Wittke's immigrant saga, *We who built America*, the story of many of these developments is sketched.[2] Dr. Theodore C. Blegen, in *Norwegian migration to America. The American transition*, calls the foreign language theatre a typical immigrant phenomenon, and sees in the efforts to create a Norwegian American stage in Chicago and Minneapolis a means of effecting a "transition of Norwegian culture to the world of the immigrants and their descendants."[3] That such theatres were typical immigrant phenomena their number testifies. A study of 1925 could point to professional or amateur companies maintained over varying periods, not only by French and German groups, but by Finns, Hungarians, Italians, Jews, Lithuanians, Poles, and Ukrainians.[4] Each of the Scandinavian national groups had active theatrical companies, with striking parallels in development.[5]

The Swedish theatre in Chicago may, then, be considered to some degree representative of the foreign language theatre of America in general. To a far greater extent, of course, it is representative of the Swedish theatrical enterprises that existed wherever there were sizeable Swedish settlements. This fact makes the limitation of this history to the theatre in one city less regrettable than it might at first thought appear.

Deserving of record, certainly, are the histories of these other Swedish acting groups. San Francisco Swedes were presenting plays as early as 1863, and the San Francisco Swedish Dramatic Club established what seems to be an unrivalled record when it was able to celebrate a thirtieth anniversary. Minneapolis began its Swedish performances in the 1870's, and had a long history of successful companies and productions. New York city activities dated from the 1860's and continued for more than six decades. In the Eastern states, Brooklyn and Jamestown, New York, and Worcester, Massachusetts, maintained Swedish companies. Besides Minneapolis and Chicago, St. Paul and Duluth in Minnesota, Kansas City and Detroit, and Moline and Rockford in Illinois were Middle Western communities that supported the Swedish theatre, Rockford over a considerable period. In the far West, Seattle was another center for Swedish theatricals. Interchange of personnel and occasional tours by Chicago companies and by Eastern and other Middle Western groups will give some impression of this wider field of Swedish theatrical activity, though these phases of the Chicago history must of necessity be given limited consideration. As a matter of fact, interesting and comparable (and at times, perhaps, superior) as the achievements of these other theatres were, the history of each would in general duplicate that here given, in repertoire and in situation.[6] The long and generally unbroken record of the Chicago Swedish theatre, the quality of its productions, and the position of Chicago as the center of Swedish America make Chicago a reasonable choice for the history of a Swedish theatre in an American community.

Because of the importance of the Swedish theatre as a social institution, much material not ordinarily a part of theatrical annals has been presented in this study. Conditions in Chicago's Swedish colony, the backgrounds and occupations of the actors, the nature and tastes of the audience; the institutions and organizations with which the theatre had relations, friendly and unfriendly; slight theatrical efforts and fiascos as well as ambitious and successful productions; anecdotes unimportant in themselves but indicative of attitudes—all these have their place in such a story. In the main, however, the materials and emphases are those of theatrical history. The chronological record of performances, facts about plays, productions, and casts are as full as sources permit. The Swedish weekly newspapers published in Chicago have provided basic facts but have been supplemented by valuable materials obtained from persons connected with the theatre, and by their reminiscences. Of special value also were studies and accounts of Swedish America and the Chicago Swedish colony by Swedish and Swedish American writers, largely available in the Linder and Swan collections in the library of Augustana College, Rock Island, Illinois.

The plan of the book is chronological, after a first chapter that presents background material concerning the Chicago Swedish colony and the theatre of Sweden, as well as a preliminary historical sketch of the Chicago Swedish theatre. Five chapters cover successive periods, representative of changes in trends and personnel. For Chapters II through V, this general plan is followed: theatrical and social characteristics of the periods; actors; repertoire; chronological account. A chronological table at the close of each chapter includes plays performed, dates, companies and sponsoring organizations, and places of performance, and makes possible omission of many of these facts in the chronological account within the chapter. Biographical data for actors are normally part of the discussion of personnel in the period when an actor begins his activities in Chicago. Synopses are given for plays of unusual popularity or significance, or to indicate popular types, usually in connection with the first performance of the play, but occasionally in the general discussion of repertoire for the period when it was first acted. Chapter VI, the concluding chapter, differs somewhat in plan from Chapters II through V. Performances which were a continuation of earlier developments in personnel and repertoire and those given by newer companies and representing newer trends are considered successively, in spite of some chronological overlapping; and the three new groups mainly considered are discussed in terms of repertoire and general achievement instead of in chronological narrative. To give a better view of the main developments of the period, the chronological table following this chapter omits a large number of minor performances and performances by travelling companies. These performances are, however, given in a supplement to the chapter: an alphabetical list of plays with dates of performances, companies, and known authors for plays not otherwise acted.

An alphabetical list of all other plays known to have been performed is the first item in the general appendix that follows. This main list of plays includes known information as to author, type of play, date, publication, and the year or years when the play was acted in Chicago. There follows an alphabetical list of all known Swedish or Swedish American authors who wrote or adapted plays presented by Chicago Swedish actors, or who wrote works on which the plays were based, with known dates of birth and death. Local and other Swedish American authors are indicated by asterisks, and for each author reference by number to the main list of plays and to the plays listed in the supplement to Chapter VI indicates plays which he wrote or in which he had a part. A similar list of non-Swedish authors completes section two. Section three of the Appendix is an alphabetical list of theatres, halls, and other places used for performances, with locations, and with seasons when plays were presented at each place. All available casts, in chronological order, constitute section four. Performances for which casts are given are indicated by asterisks in the chronological tables for Chapters II through VI. A list of the chief acting companies, with references to chapters dealing with their activities, concludes the Appendix.

Bibliography, Notes, and Index complete the volume. The notes cover all sources used with these two exceptions: newspaper sources for the basic record of performances; plays that have been read, which are listed in the Bibliography, III, B. In references to newspapers the following abbreviations are used: *F.—Fäderneslandet; H.—Hemlandet; N.S.A. —Nya Svenska Amerikanaren; S.A.—Svenska Amerikanaren; S.A.H.— Svenska Amerikanaren Hemlandet; S.A.T.—Svenska Amerikanaren Tribunen; S.K.—Svenska Kuriren; S.N.—Svenska Nyheter; S.T.—Svenska Tribunen; S.T.N.—Svenska Tribunen-Nyheter; S.V.—Svenska Världen.*

Swedish play titles and Swedish names of dramatic and social organizations have been generally though not exclusively used, because, wisely or not, it was felt that the original language and the names by which organizations were long best known give a better sense of the Swedish nature of the theatrical and social activities than would translations. Translations are given at the time of first mention as a rule, and titles of plays that are not referred to in the text have not been translated. Apparent inconsistencies and errors in the spelling of Swedish words and names are accounted for by a number of factors: by the differences in spelling in old and modern Swedish; by the inaccuracies and inconsistencies in spelling in the Chicago Swedish newspapers that are often the only sources; by occasional dialect forms; and by a tendency to Americanize spelling, seen particularly in names of Chicago Swedes and in titles of plays written in Chicago. There has been no effort to make spelling conform to a single system, but practice as here explained has, it is hoped, been consistent. For play titles and for Swedish words used in identifying characters the original spelling has been used whenever certainly known. Swedish bibliographical sources do not always agree as to spelling, and at times, as with material from Chicago sources only, it has been necessary to make an arbitrary choice of the form to be used. In referring to the Chicago Swedish newspapers, articles have been omitted, as they are incorporated in the names of the papers as case endings. In names of organizations, theatres of Sweden, etc., the article has ordinarily been used with the basic Swedish form; and organization names have been italicized when they are phrases or include case endings, but not when they are single proper names such as Freja and Svea. Finally, it may be noted that in alphabetical lists the three letters, å, ä, and ö, in that order, conclude the alphabet, as in Swedish usage.

Acknowledgments

MY debts of gratitude for help and encouragement in preparing this book are many. A grant from the Council of Social Studies assisted me in my early research. The Augustana Historical Society approved of the project at its inception, and has now assumed a large share of the responsibility for publication. I have received valuable support and help from members of the Society: from my colleagues, Professor O. L. Nordstrom, its long time president, and Dr. O. Fritiof Ander, for whose many services in connection with the final stages of the work I am particularly grateful. The Honorable Carl R. Chindblom of Chicago gave me my first opportunity to meet some of the leaders of the Swedish theatre, which I appreciate as I do his recent interest. The present Board of Directors of the Historical Society, and its president, Dr. G. Everett Arden of the Augustana Seminary, have given time and thought as well as the Society's financial support. To the organizations and individuals whose help is acknowledged by the editor I wish also to express my personal gratitude for the interest they have shown in the story of the Chicago Swedish theatre.

Mr. Donald O. Rod, head librarian of Augustana College, who has edited the volume on behalf of the Historical Society and the Augustana College Library Series, has by his unflagging interest and his labor in connection with the innumerable details involved in seeing it through the press made this part of my task a most happy one. I am indebted also to Mr. Oscar G. Ericson of the Augustana Book Concern for the patience and care with which he has helped us in matters of form and accuracy. Dr. Arthur A. Wald, head of the various Swedish activities at Augustana College, has been called on for much assistance in translations from the Swedish, which I gratefully acknowledge, while assuming responsibility for undoubted shortcomings in this respect. And I wish to thank most especially Dr. Conrad Bergendoff, president of Augustana College, for all he has done in enabling me to carry on this work in connection with my college duties, for often manifested interest, and for his part in making publication possible.

In helping me search through the collections of Swedish Chicago newspapers and the many other Swedish and Swedish American materials in the library of Augustana College, the members of the staff have been invariably kind and cooperative. Dr. Ira Nothstein, archivist, and Miss Drusilla Erickson, periodical assistant, in particular, have performed many services beyond the line of duty. Varied assistance has come also from Miss Ingeborg Sylvander of Chicago, as secretary of the Swedish Pioneer Association, from the American Swedish Historical Museum of Philadelphia, and from the libraries of the University of Minnesota, of the Minnesota State Historical Society, and of the University of Chicago. To Miss Winifred Ver Nooy, reference librarian at Harper Memorial Library, the University of Chicago, I am particularly indebted. The study began at the University of Chicago, as part of the inclusive records of the theatre of Chicago compiled there under the direction of Dr. Napier Wilt, chairman of the Department of English; and he has followed its progress with advice and encouragement that I greatly appreciate.

Without the help of the men and women of the Swedish theatre of Chicago this book could not have been written. To them I owe more than I can say, for facts and materials, for the understanding of the Swedish theatre they gave me, the cordial welcome with which they received me in their homes, and the many enjoyable hours I spent in talking with them. For the period of the 1880's I am greatly indebted to Mrs. Gustaf Wicklund, now of Minneapolis, the only surviving participant from those early days. She has shared her memories with me, and has made a generous contribution of pictures and of her husband's manuscripts. An invaluable collection of programs, clippings, and photographs was sent me by Mrs. Alex Engström, the daughter of Carl and Anna Pfeil, leading figures of the late 1880's and 1890's, and herself a child favorite on the Chicago Swedish stage.

For the late 1890's and the period through the early 1920's, Mrs. Werner Melinder of Milwaukee gave me not only unique manuscripts and photographs, but particularly helpful information, derived from her familiarity with the activities of her father, Christopher Brusell, over that long period, and the extensive acting careers of both herself and her husband. Through her, also, I was able to obtain the assistance of many other persons prominent in the plays. Of special interest were interviews with Mrs. Ida Anderson-Werner and Mr. and Mrs. Carl Milton, long outstanding as character actors. From Mrs. Knut Schröder I received a splendid gift of manuscript roles and photographs from the collection of her husband. Mr. Ernst H. Behmer, now of Denver, who for many years shared with Mr. Brusell in leadership of the Chicago Swedish theatre and whose activities were to continue for additional decades, has given me programs and posters as well as much help in the matter of records, facts of authorship, and general conditions. Mrs. Anna E. Nylund, daughter of Mrs. Hanna

Hvitfeldt, and Arthur Donaldson, star of the American and Swedish American stage, graciously responded to my requests for information and pictures. Facts and insights were obtained also from Mrs. Ebba Kempe, Mrs. Ernest Lindblom, Mr. John Ternquist, Mr. and Mrs. Frithiof Burgeson, and Mr. G. Patrick Warner, all of whom were connected, directly or indirectly, with the 20th century plays. Mr. Warner's personal files of *Svenska Amerikanaren* were hospitably placed at my disposal. Leaders from the most recent period of the Swedish theatre have also been very friendly and cooperative: Mr. Carl Stockenberg, who began his career in earlier companies, and who has provided me with many pictures as well as with published materials about Chicago organizations; Mr. Arvid Nelson; and Mr. Paul Norling, who, among numerous services, secured for my use *Svenska Folkteatern* programs belonging to Mrs. Elna Lilnequist Kronberg.

I cannot hope to have presented the picture of the Chicago Swedish theatre in a way that will seem satisfactory or at all times properly interpreted to those who have shared in or were responsible for the activities of that theatre and who have been so kind in assisting me. I hope, however, they will welcome this record as recognition of efforts that, unselfishly undertaken and often unrewarded, became cherished memories for actors and audiences and are a significant part of the story of Swedish America.

HENRIETTE C. K. NAESETH

July 16, 1951
Augustana College
Rock Island, Illinois

Contents

Illustrations

Fritz Schoultz in an unidentified role

Knut Lindstrom, probably as Peter Klubbman in *Vår förening*, May 5, 1883 Central Hall

Mrs. Erika Hopp in an unidentified role

Robert Olson as immigrant Kalle Karlson in
Kronjuvelerna på Nordsidan, December 16, 1883,
North Side Turner Hall

THE SWEDISH THEATRE OF CHICAGO
1868-1950

CHAPTER I

THE CHICAGO SWEDISH THEATRE AND ITS BACKGROUND

Several years before the great fire of 1871 Swedish plays were being acted in Chicago's North Side Swedish colony. In the 1940's Swedish groups on both the North Side and South Side of the city were still entertaining themselves and the public with plays in Swedish. And in 1946 a down town theatre housed a full scale Swedish production which brought back memories of the heyday of the Swedish theatre in Chicago earlier in the century. The play was *Vermländingarne*, F. A. Dahlgren's folk play, then celebrating its 100th anniversary in Sweden as one of the country's most beloved theatre pieces. In Chicago, too, it had held the foremost place among hundreds of Swedish plays; and it was, inevitably, the play selected for the two 1950 performances which—though presented in high school auditoriums, not city theatres—constitute the only major theatrical effort of the Chicago Swedes since 1946.

For almost every season of the long period from 1868 to 1946 there are records of theatrical activity among the Swedes in Chicago. Many of the plays were slight farces amateurishly performed by club and lodge groups at festive meetings. Always, however, there were productions by able and experienced actors, interested in establishing a Swedish theatre. They did not succeed in placing that theatre on a professional basis, but their efforts made performances of standard Swedish repertoire a regular and important phase of the life of the city's Swedish colony for at least six decades. Church disapproval, the relatively small proportion of Chicago Swedes who had been accustomed to theatre-going in Sweden, and the expenses involved in ambitious productions were some of the obstacles faced by the men and women of the Chicago Swedish theatre. They were unable to depend upon the theatre for a living, but they found in it an outlet for the interests which the routine of the business world did not provide, and they devoted their free time and risked their limited financial resources to bring theatrical entertainment to their countrymen.

Scanty records tell of a succession of companies that acted in the 1860's and 1870's, welcomed by the element in the Swedish settlement that had begun its first social organization, Svea, in 1857. Svea itself sponsored the first company for which performances are known. By the close of the 1870's earlier groups were being supplanted by actors long

1

to be prominent, and the North Side Turner Hall had replaced German Hall as the home of Swedish theatricals. The 1880's, however, saw the real birth of the Swedish theatre in Chicago, with the formation, on the initiative of Fritz Schoultz, of the first company to continue through several seasons. A lively group of young people, largely from journalistic circles, they performed their own plays as well as a varied Swedish repertoire. A growing Swedish population supported as many as eleven plays in the 1889-1890 season; and in 1890 the first production in a city theatre was ventured at Hooley's, by Carl Pfeil, a professional actor from Sweden, who had come to Chicago with his actress wife, Anna Pfeil, in 1888. A long continued custom of visits to Illinois communities had begun in 1870. More ambitious tours to Minnesota were undertaken in 1888, 1889, and 1890; and the following decades, too, found Chicago companies playing in Minnesota cities.

Further expansion of theatrical activities marked the 1890's. With new companies and new talent providing rivalry, with city performances and visiting actors giving increased prestige, and the Swedes on the South Side making a second audience, the seasons became more varied and extensive, and the quality of the productions improved. Swedish organizations in general multiplied in these years, and, as in later periods, they frequently turned to the theatrical groups for entertainment at annual celebrations and summer excursions.

By the turn of the century, the Chicago Swedish theatre had advanced to the period of its greatest stability and its most ambitious ventures. The young *Svenska Teatersällskap* (Swedish Theatre Society), a joint enterprise of Christopher Brusell and Ernst H. Behmer, attained a leadership that the two men were to maintain, in joint or rival activity, for more than two decades. Outlying halls still housed plays given by a variety of small groups as well as by the *Svenska Teatersällskap* and the *Svenska Dramatiska Sällskap* (Behmer's company in his independent productions), but a series of performances in city theatres by one or both of these major companies constituted the main theatrical seasons through the first dozen years of the century. Actors with extensive experience made up the nucleus of the companies, and not infrequently they were joined by leading performers from Sweden. Old plays continued to be the mainstays, but in repertoire, too, this was the most noteworthy period for the Chicago Swedish theatre.

Gradually, however, city performances became fewer. By the 1917-1918 season, one or two city productions annually, with a variety of minor performances, had become the norm that was to continue into the early

2

1920's. The older actors were disappearing, the familiar plays were losing their appeal, and the competition of the moving picture was becoming more acute. It was not surprising that, in spite of the persistent efforts of Behmer and Brusell, the days of the Swedish theatre in Chicago seemed to be numbered. Then, remarkably, in the late 1920's and 1930's, it experienced a rebirth. There were still occasional traditional performances; but younger people recently come from Sweden were largely responsible for the resurgence of interest that brought about the formation of numerous small theatrical groups and of one prominent company, *Svenska Folkteatern* (Swedish Folk theatre). Over a span of fifteen years that rivalled the record of earlier leading groups, *Svenska Folkteatern* won popular success with comedies and revues fresh from Sweden, as well as with original works by its members. In 1941 the company acted for the last time, but its members did not give up easily, and as the decade drew to a close, eighty years after Swedish plays are first known to have been acted in Chicago, they were sponsoring dramatic entertainments reminiscent of those early days.

Through the years, the leaders responsible for the Swedish plays had often reiterated the hope that they might establish a professional theatre in Chicago comparable to that of the Germans. Surely, they argued, Swedes in Chicago were sufficiently numerous to support regular performances. Was not Chicago the second Swedish city of the world, outranked only by Stockholm? And there was justification for their attitude, in spite of the fact that the Germans in Chicago far outnumbered the Swedes.[1]

Since 1860, when Swedish immigration was about to assume large proportions for the first time, Chicago had been its clearing house and center. Many of the immigrants went on to farms and to other communities, but always many stayed in Chicago, and in general the growth of its Swedish colony corresponded to the rise and fall of Swedish immigration.[2] By 1870, there were 6,154 Swedes in Chicago, and from 1880 to 1884, in the period of greatest increase in Swedish immigration, the Swedish population grew from 12,930 to 23,755. By 1890, persons of Swedish birth in Chicago totalled 43,022, in a city population of 1,099,850. In 1900, 48,836 persons of Swedish birth and 95,883 of Swedish parentage together made up 8.4 per cent of the total city population of 1,698,573.[3] Minnesota and Minneapolis were increasingly attractive to the Swedish immigrants, and the Swedes in Minneapolis eventually constituted a larger percentage of the city population than did the Swedes in Chicago. But the Chicago colony remained the largest. In 1910, for instance, compared to

3

its nearest rivals, Chicago had 63,035 native born Swedes, New York 34,952, and Minneapolis 26,478.[4] The 1920 census showed a drop of nearly 5,000 for the native born Swedes in Chicago, but in 1930 a high point was reached, with 65,735 native born Swedes. Persons of Swedish parentage then numbered 75,178, and in a city that had passed the three million mark, the two groups made up 4.1 per cent of the population.[5]

Traditionally, the North Side has been the home of the Swedes in Chicago. Other centers have developed on the South Side and West Side, but since the first small party of Swedish settlers arrived in 1846, the chief colony has always been on the North Side. When Swedish plays were first being acted, a general northward movement was under way in the Swedish section between Kinzie Avenue (400 North) and Chicago Avenue (800 North); and by 1871, two-thirds of the Swedes in Chicago were living in a settlement of which Chicago Avenue had become the southern boundary, and which extended north to Division and North Avenues (1200 and 1600 North). The Swedes had been moving west also, from near Clark Street (ca. 100 West) to Larrabbee (600 West) and beyond. The region devastated by the 1871 fire thus included the main Swedish colony; of the 50,000 who were left homeless, it was estimated that 10,000 were Swedes, and their loss was set at close to a million dollars. Nevertheless, they re-established themselves in the same general area,[6] gradually continuing their expansion toward the north. By the 1890's the Lake View section, of which Belmont Avenue (3200 North) may be considered the center, had taken on the Swedish character it has retained, in spite of further northward moves. By 1930, Swedes were concentrated also along Lawrence (4800 North) and Bryn Mawr (5600 North), between California and Crawford (2800-4000 West), with another settlement due east, between Halsted and Damen (800-2000 West). The South Side center was then mainly in the Englewood district, along 59th, between Halsted and Racine (800-1200 West).[7]

Though the Swedish theatre achieved a status that, by the 1890's, was taking more and more of its main performances to city theatres, the majority of the plays throughout its history were given within Swedish neighborhoods. The most popular of these places of performance present in themselves a picture of the shifts in Swedish population that, taken with the city productions, leaves no question as to the extent to which the theatre became a part of the life of the Chicago Swedish colony.

The first plays were acted at German Hall, at 94 N. Wells (200 West), convenient to the Swedish settlement. The Svea Society Hall at

4

the corner of Wells and Superior (732 North) was used occasionally in the 1870's. In 1871 a Swedish play was for the first time performed at the North Side Turner Hall, then 259—later 826—N. Clark (100 West). With the 1877-1878 season, the hall began to be used regularly, becoming the chief home for Swedish plays—except for a brief period in the 1890's when the Criterion Theatre at 274 Sedgwick (400 West) housed a series of productions—until city theatres supplanted it for major performances. By the 1890's performances on the South Side were fairly frequent. Of a number of halls in the same general locality, near 3000 South and State (base line), the South Side Turner Hall was much used from 1893 until it burned in 1914. On the North Side, the northward movement was reflected by 1896, with the beginning of a period of popularity for Phoenix Hall, at 344 E. Division (1200 North). Numerous places of performance in the 20th century mark the development of the Lake View district (though the North Side Turner Hall continued in use into the 1925-1926 season). Some of these halls, with the years when they were first used, were: Spelz Hall (later Belmont Hall), 3205-3207 N. Clark, 1896; Svithiod Singing Club Hall, 624 Wrightwood (1600 North), 1901; Lake View Hall, 3143 N. Clark, 1911; Viking Temple, Sheffield (3300 North) and School (1000 West), 1911; *Svenska Klubben* (later the Swedish Club), 1258 N. La Salle (150 West), 1913; International Order of Good Templars Hall, 1041 Newport (3424 North), 1915. The German Theatre, variously called the Victoria and the Vic, at 3143 Sheffield, was used in the late 1920's and 1930's, and Lincoln Auditorium, 4219 Lincoln (200 West), and the North Side Auditorium, 3730 N. Clark, housed the majority of the *Svenska Folk-teatern* plays of the 1930's. Still farther north, at 5015-5017 N. Clark, was Verdandi Hall, where minor performances were given from the 1910-1911 season on. Growing settlements on the South Side brought plays to new halls, principal among them being the Good Templar Hall at 10156 Avenue M. (3528 East), from the 1922-1923 season on, and the South Side Viking Temple, at 6855 S. Emerald (734 West), beginning with the 1928-1929 season. There were sporadic performances also in the Swedish neighborhood to the west, as at Holter's Hall, 633 N. Cicero (4800 West), in the 1930's.[8]

The geographic unity of the early Swedish colony in Chicago was in marked contrast to the conflicting attitudes that split the immigrants of that period into two groups—the pietistic church group and, opposed to it, the unchurchly and those affiliated with more liberal churches. Though it died down with time, and understanding and cooperation between the groups increased, the conflict influenced the entire social development within the colony. For the Swedish theatre, particularly in its first decades, the division meant that the support of a large section of the colony was lacking.

The conflict had its roots in Sweden, where a growing protest against the Lutheran state church had expressed itself both in rejection by rationalistic and liberal groups and in a pietistic free church movement. Two American Swedish church bodies, much of whose early history was associated with Chicago, represented the pietistic movement that opposed the state church as worldly and autocratic. The Augustana Synod, founded in 1860, was, like the state church of Sweden, Lutheran, but in social attitudes, general democracy of organization, and relative absence of ceremony, it departed sharply from the state church. Even more strongly pietistic, and closely related to the lay preacher movement in Sweden, were the Mission Covenant churches. The Swedish Evangelical Mission Covenant was organized as a church body in 1873, but its Chicago history dates from 1869. Two other Swedish church bodies, Methodist and Baptist (the former having origins in Sweden), were also factors in the religious life of the Chicago colony.

Principal among the Swedish churches in Chicago for a long period were the Immanuel and St. Ansgar congregations. The Immanuel, founded in 1853, was the first Augustana church, and owed much of its position to the vigorous leadership of its first pastor, Erland Carlsson. In contrast to the pietistic churches was St. Ansgar's. The earliest church of the colony, it was founded in 1849 through the efforts of another noted pioneer pastor, Gustaf Unonius. It was Episcopalian in affiliation and liberal in social attitudes. Many Swedes active in the theatre belonged to the St. Ansgar church, and were welcomed participants in bazaars and other "worldly" entertainments it sponsored.

Despite all the endeavours of the various Swedish churches (and of American churches with which a considerable number of Swedes affiliated), a large number of Swedish immigrants remained outside the church. Many brought with them from Sweden opposition to the church. And, as Stephenson says in his study of the religious aspects of Swedish immigration, new scenes and new conditions weaned many of them away from the church.[9] Active hostility within this group was directed largely against the Augustana Synod, and in Chicago against Carlsson and his congregation. The Synod was attacked both as a continuation of the state church and as a church that denied freedom of thought and was narrowly puritanical in its condemna-

6

tion of drinking, dancing, and the theatre. The conflict was, in fact, one of two ways of life as well as of rationalistic reaction against fundamentalism and dogma.[10]

Much of the battle was fought in the Swedish press. The Augustana Synod was represented by a weekly newspaper, *Hemlandet*, moved to Chicago from Galesburg, Illinois, in 1859. In 1869 it passed into the ownership of two Augustana laymen, one of whom, Johan A. Enander, was to become a leading figure in Chicago as well as in the church at large. Under his direction *Hemlandet* gradually became secularized, but until almost the end of its existence, in 1914, its attitudes were close to those of the Synod. The first of the secular weeklies was *Svenska Amerikanaren*, founded in 1866 as an organ for liberal ideas. Others followed, among them *Nya Verlden* in 1871. It was consolidated with *Svenska Amerikanaren* (which had become *Nya Svenska Amerikanaren* in 1873) as *Svenska Tribunen* in 1877; a second *Svenska Amerikanaren* and the short-lived *Fäderneslandet* began publication in 1877 also. And in 1888 *Svenska Kuriren* entered the scene. These papers joined in opposing *Hemlandet*, but within their ranks were disagreements as violent as the attacks upon the common foe. The newspaper to which one subscribed indicated one's allegiance in the church and anti-pietistic conflict. Though attitudes eventually mellowed, in the 1860's, said a pioneer newsman, the worth of a paper was judged by the vigor with which it presented its views, and the editor who could scold the loudest, in coarse language, was considered the most successful.[11]

The number of Swedish weekly newspapers continued to increase through 1904, when *Svenska Världen* began a brief existence. The following years, however, brought a series of consolidations, of which the last joined the two oldest secular papers, *Svenska Amerikanaren* and *Svenska Tribunen*, as *Svenska Amerikanaren Tribunen*, the one Swedish newspaper in Chicago today.[12] A disunifying influence in its first turbulent period, the Chicago Swedish press has throughout its history served its public well, providing extensive news of both Sweden and the United States and historical and literary materials from both countries, in *feuilletons* and premiums as well as in the newspapers themselves. The Chicago news sections acquainted the Swedes with the affairs of the city and led them to participation in its general activities as well as in those of Swedish groups. Despite their language and their emphasis upon Swedes and news of Sweden, these were American papers, performing the function of the foreign language press in general as they helped their readers make the transition from immigrants to Americans.

7

To the Chicago Swedish theatre the secular Swedish press was an invaluable ally. Condemned by the conservative church, the plays were from the beginning publicized and supported by the newspapers critical of the church. Reviews, brief in the small papers of the early years, often running into columns after the first decades, were prominent features of the local news page. Pictures of actors and of scenes from plays accompanied advance "puffs" and reviews, and outstanding productions were the subject of front page feature stories. The degree of the reviewers' knowledge of the theatre varied widely, and, to a corresponding degree, the value of the criticism. Though a reviewer occasionally wearied of patience and displayed his powers of satire, the reviews were as a rule kindly, with due consideration for amateur actors and recognition of the ability of the more experienced. When audiences were small, the public was chided, and urged to give the plays the support they deserved. The values of the Swedish theatre as a factor in the cultural life of the colony, as a means of reviving fond memories of the homeland, and as entertainment were constantly reiterated themes.

Not only in general attitudes were the Swedish theatre and these newspapers closely related. In their early decades the newspapers and a series of short-lived humorous periodicals offered the chief opportunity outside the church for congenial, if not always financially secure, occupation to the educated Swedish immigrants. These men welcomed the opportunity to participate in the plays as well as to see and to write about them. As actors and authors, several newspapermen were among the prime movers of the Swedish theatre of the 1880's and 1890's, and in later years also actors not infrequently came from the newspaper circles.

There is general agreement that the Swedes adapted themselves to life in the new American environment more readily than did most immigrants. Particularly during the early period of immigration, economic hardships and class distinctions in Sweden contributed to the immigrants' readiness to respond to a more democratic America, and to transfer their interest to their new home. In a considerable number of Swedes these tendencies were so strong that all Swedish ties—names, customs, and associates—were rejected. The eagerness to become Americanized that expressed itself in name changes is a commonplace in Swedish American fiction—Anders Karlson becoming Andrew Clancy, Gustaf Bokstrand, Gus Bookshore, and Lotta Grönberg, Lottie Greenburg.[13]

The Swedish immigrants in general, however, shared the problems of other immigrant groups: the difficulties created by a barrier of language, the consequent limitations in opportunities for work, and a measure of social isolation. Exploitation by immigrant "runners" was a serious hazard for the newcomers in Chicago in the first years of extensive immigration. As to jobs, the Swedish immigrant, even if he escaped the "runners," could not be particular. Tradesman, bookkeeper, and university graduate had often to say farewell forever to their old occupations and become railroad workers and factory hands.[14] The educated were in the minority, as the names given by the Swedes to Chicago Avenue indicate. It was *Store Bondegatan* or *Smålandsgatan*—the big street of the farmers or of people from the rural Småland district. Here most Swedes "took their first hesitant steps on the thorn-strewn path of Americanization," wrote Otto Croelius, in one of the many fictional sketches that describe the life of the Swedes in Chicago; and here the men, at least, lived for a while. The girls went almost at once to the palaces on Prairie Avenue or Lake Shore Drive, where work as maids was plentiful, and learned to speak English "before the men mastered Swedish-American."[15] Still, besides the country people and workers, skilled and unskilled, who made up the chief body of Swedish immigrants, there was a fairly sizeable group from more privileged circles, representatives of the so-called *bättre folk* (better people). Not all the men and women active in the theatre came from this class, but, specially in the early years, these immigrants played a considerable part in theatrical ventures.

The situation of the *bildade* (cultured) immigrant was a favorite topic of writers on Swedish America. More often than not, the men were ne'er-do-wells and misfits who had come to America for refuge or adventure or had been sent by families whose patience they had exhausted. In America their lot was not an easy one. The social distinction that a university education or successful matriculation as a *student* carried in Sweden meant little, and the education did not prepare for the vocations open to the immigrants. The *student* would be likely to know German, French, and the ancient languages, but not English. And, wrote the newsman and humorist, Ninian Wærner, in describing his first days in Chicago, in America one does not speak Latin—one sews trousers or mends shoes. Typical sketches depicted a university man dying penniless in a saloon brawl or drowning at his work as a stevedore.[16]

Complaints that there was no place for educated Swedes in America unless they were willing to be farm hands were common. America was not always blamed, however. Magnus Elmblad, Chicago newspaperman and poet of the 1870's and 1880's, with a wisdom he was not able to

9

practise in his own life, wrote of the successful Swedes in all sorts of professional and responsible positions; the point was, not to have *been* something, but to *be* something.[17] Another Swedish American journalist wrote in the same vein: if Chicago was a polyp that lived by sucking in people and casting out the worthless, the impractical and the class conscious were among the worthless.[18]

The majority of the Swedes were neither impractical nor class conscious, but industrious and thrifty. As the years passed, and the growth of the colony brought more opportunities, they stood high in standards of living, and in percentage of home owners. A tendency to drinking, which had been a problem in Sweden and was aggravated by loneliness and strangeness in America, decreased. The rank and file of the Swedes in Chicago prospered—as skilled workers, as tailors, in the building trades, as owners of small businesses. The number of Swedes in the professions became proportionately larger. Openings awaited the trained immigrant, particularly in such fields as engineering. In the larger life of the city there had long been leaders of Swedish birth and background. Public careers and business success on a large scale became more and more common. Gradually, in short, the Swedes established themselves as an integral and respected part of the civic, industrial, and economic life of Chicago.

Important as the church, the press, and improved economic opportunities were in the progress to the present favorable situation of the Swedish immigrant and his descendants, they were hardly more important than the social organizations that have been a characteristic feature of their life. For many of the Chicago Swedes, the church, with its varied clubs, charitable enterprises, and musical activities, has been the center of social life, but it was the secular organizations that were significant in the development of the Swedish theatre.

Many of the organizations outside the church were formed to provide protection from exploitation and poverty, and established funds for times of sickness and death, or, in the later years, fraternal insurance. But an equally potent motivating force, perhaps, was the desire for companionship and entertainment. A sense of strangeness, a dislike of loneliness, the handicap of an alien language—all were certainly vital factors in the rise of the numerous social clubs, singing groups, reading rooms, and lodges— and in the long history of the Swedish theatre.

Ville Åkerberg, one of the "carefree children of Stockholm" in the Chicago newspaper circles of the 1880's and 90's, caught something of the spirit that existed in these groups in his verses, *Här ä' vi* (Here we are).

10

Here we are, he wrote, come from all parts of Sweden for all sorts of reasons, into a world of ups and downs.

> Now on a tailor's table sewing vests
> Sits a man who was destined for a judge's desk.
> He who owned horses on his own land
> Now drives and tends them for another man.
> One whose lot was digging ditches
> Here is transformed to a musical star,
> And mama's boy, *sans façon,*
> Devours the free lunch at a beer-salon.

> But cotters and students alike,
> Blacksmiths and offshoots of noble houses,
> And Stockholm misses and country girls
> Drink *du-skåls*—without wine.
> In the new world we are all alike,
> Old class distinctions must disappear.
> At last the dollars start coming in
> And we start to prosper—in a small way.

> Yes, just look happy, and laugh, and sing.
> Here there are countrymen from every corner,
> Both from Skara and Uddevalla,
> From Landskrona and Piteå,
> And Swedish girls and Swedish boys.
> . . . .
> And yes, just think, we have Swedish beer
> And Swedish theatre and Swedish *Kurir.*[19]

In large measure, a natural desire to be "happy, and laugh, and sing" was responsible for bringing the Chicago Swedes together in their many societies. Preservation of the Swedish language and culture and fostering of a nationalistic spirit were not prevalent motives. National festive days were observed, it is true—Gustaf Adolf's Day, Midsummer's Day—but largely as occasions for fun and companionship. The popularity of speeches celebrating Sweden's glorious history that were long a standard feature of the Swedish festivities, banquets and picnics alike, was, in the opinion of some writers at least, accounted for by the fact that they fostered a sense of national pride comparable to that which the Swedish immigrants had found in Americans, and counteracted the sense of inferiority likely to be present in any alien minority group.[20] There were, of course, leaders who were primarily interested in the organizations as means of keeping the Swedish language and culture alive, but their aim was to create among their countrymen a recognition of the value of their heritage, not to prevent Americanization. Actually, the varied societies were, like the press, a medium of Americanization. They were "schools for citizenship," giving practise in democratic procedure. American conditions, American politics were subjects of speeches and discussions. Help was extended to the old homeland when it was needed, but activities and interests normally centered around Swedish American and American affairs. And all the activities helped to make the Swedish immigrants feel themselves a part of America, to make their new land a new home.[21]

Svea was the first and, for a long period, the only prominent Swedish organization of the non-pietistic element in Chicago. It was founded in 1857, as a liberal society, its purposes to provide "elevating and ennobling" entertainment, and to establish a library. To carry out these ends, it supported a varied program, including, besides regular meetings, lectures and debates, plays, concerts, picnics, and bazaars. It acquired an extensive library, including a Swedish newspaper, subscribed to at an annual cost of $56.00. A sick fund was early established, and an immigrant home was built that was for a number of years the society's chief project.[22] In 1875 there was an effort, strongly supported by Editor Enander of *Hemlandet,* to establish the *Svenska Förbund* (Swedish Association), a society with aims similar to those of Svea, but expressly forbidding lotteries, the playing of cards and billiards, dancing, drinking, and "immoral and offensive" theatrical presentations. Nobody can deny, said those who urged the need for such a society, that Svea has been more notable in respect to what the *Svenska Förbund* forbids than in what it attempts to achieve.[23] The new society was, however, like a good many less ambitious organizations, short-lived, and Svea continued to flourish.

The pioneer singing society among the Swedes was Freja, begun in 1869, and shortly appearing in a series of welcome concerts. Another early musical organization, the *Svenska Sångförbund* (Swedish Song Association), began a period of activity in 1875, sharing honors for a time with a Scandinavian chorus. The Swedish lodges were, in general, later developments, but the first Swedish Odd Fellows Lodge was formed in 1877, and a principal Swedish lodge, Svithiod, which began as a club of young men in 1875, was formally organized in 1880.

The year 1882 brought into existence the most important of the private clubs, the present Swedish Club. Founded as *Svenska Klubben,* it was an outgrowth of Freja and other temporary groups. In 1882, also, began the long and active history of the Illinois Grand Lodge of Good Templars, though not all the Templar groups supported by the Chicago Swedes were affiliated with the lodge. A singing society first active in the 1880's, *Nordstjernan* (North Star), was destined to live for more than half a century. In this period, too, were founded two prominent musical clubs that are still active: in 1882, the Svithiod Singing Club, originally affiliated with the Svithiod Lodge; and, in 1887, the Swedish Glee Club, for a time connected with the Swedish Club.

New developments in the 1890's mark this decade as the culminating period of Swedish organizational activities in Chicago. The fast growing Independent Order of Vikings was found in 1890, and earlier lodges continued to expand. As secret societies with religious ritual, they were opposed by the conservative church, but more and more they drew membership from its ranks. Other societies showed a gradual breaking down of the division line that had earlier been so sharply drawn. The organization of the *Svenska Sångarförbund* (later the American Union of Swedish Singers) in Chicago in 1892 marked an important development in musical activities. At its national meetings there were concerts on a grand scale that brought to Chicago and other centers some of the finest singers in America and Sweden. The national chorus made its first and very successful appearance at the 1893 Chicago fair, and an 1897 tour to Sweden was another high point in its history.

Two organizations that served as unifying influences in the Chicago Swedish colony developed in the 1890's. These were the *Svenska National Förbund* (Swedish National Association) and the *Svenska Föreningarnas Centralförbund* (Swedish Societies' Central Association), both organized in 1894. On Christmas Eve, 1893, occurred an event that aroused the entire Swedish population of Chicago, the murder of a young Swede, Swan Nelson, by two Irish policemen. The extensive efforts and projects undertaken to provide a fund for action against the murderers brought a realization of the need for a general organization that would help Swedes who were victimized or in need. For such purposes the Swedish National Association was founded. Supported largely by a series of concerts and plays, it not only provided such assistance, but maintained for many years a Free Employment Bureau. The Swedish Societies' Central Association had as its original aim alleviation of the sufferings of Chicago Swedes in the hard times following the 1893 fair. Gradually, however, the association concentrated on the project of a Swedish old people's home, and in 1908 became the Swedish Societies' Old People's Home Association. By 1900 its efforts

13

had built an old people's home in Park Ridge, which was supplanted by a larger one in Evanston in 1912.

General growth of lodges (the last prominent Swedish lodge, the Vasa Order, did not come to Chicago until 1908, though it had existed in the East since 1896); new clubs, independent and connected with lodges; new societies like the *Svenska Kulturförbund* (Swedish Cultural Alliance) characterized the social development of the following years. Halls were acquired, club houses and lodge "temples" built. New musical organizations joined the ranks—Orphei, Harmoni, Bellman, *De Svenske* (The Swedes) among them. As the 20th century advanced, continuing immigration and a natural interest in meeting with those who shared one's particular background accounted at least in part for the rise of a new type of organization—the *hembygd,* or home community, society. Supplementing rather than supplanting societies already active, more than twenty such *hembygd* groups had been founded by 1933, most of them in the 1920's. Labor groups that placed considerable emphasis on social activities, and study clubs, often affiliated with other organizations, were prominent in the 1920's and 1930's also, but were not a novel development. New folk dance societies, too, were successors to similar organizations in earlier periods.[24]

Besides being closely linked with these multiplying social organizations throughout its history, the Swedish theatre was in itself a social institution. During the many years when the plays were most commonly given at the North Side Turner Hall, dances followed the theatrical performances and were an important drawing card upon which the promoters of the plays depended for good attendance. Rarely could the directors announce that there would be no ball, that the play was the thing. The custom continued for many of the lesser performances of later years also; and even in the 1930's the *Svenska Folkteatern* plays concluded with dances, in order to attract a youthful audience. Conducive to social enjoyment also, if not to appreciation of the plays, was the sale of beer and light refreshments—a practice long followed at the North Side Turner Hall and elsewhere, and often deplored by reviewers. The dance and bar, and the fact that performances frequently took place on Sunday evenings were, naturally, important targets for the criticism directed by the church and its adherents against the theatrical evenings.

There can be little doubt that to the majority of the men and women who saw these plays they were simply one phase of a social occasion. The audience was not, in the main, a cultivated one, and lacked the earlier acquaintance with the theatre that would make for appreciation of dramatic

14

art (another source of dissatisfaction for the reviewers). Obviously farcical, but pertinent nonetheless is the picture of incidents at a Swedish play given in a sketch, *På teatern,* by "Onkel Ola," Frans A. Lindstrand, and originally published in 1894 in his *Svenska Amerikanaren.* The reviews, he said, would give proper honors to the actors, who played *Nerkingarne,* and did their duty well. His tale concerned the audience. The North Side Turner Hall was so packed that the spectators, in spite of being sober, got into difficulties. A man who had never before seen a play climbed up on a table to get a better view, and was told by an irate waiter that the tables were to be used for drinking—"Schnapsen—Aber das ist alles, dein dummer Schwede." Jealous girls got into a fight and another fight resulted when an actor was accused by a man in the audience of wearing his boots, and a friend came to the actor's defense. The denouement took place in the police court the next day.[25] This was a far cry from the later years, when more sophisticated and experienced audiences were seeing Swedish plays in bona fide theatres, but social pleasure continued as part of the attraction.

For actors as well as audiences, the social side of their productions was important. The rehearsals were social affairs, offering opportunities for companionship. Dramatic companies had parties at the beginning and close of seasons, arranged parties to honor their directors, to celebrate holidays. And many were the romances that grew out of associations in theatrical groups. It is not unusual for reviews to show that Miss— has become Mrs.—, the wife of a fellow actor. Devotees of the theatre as most of the chief actors and directors were, an essential factor in maintaining the Swedish theatre in Chicago in eight successive decades was the fun they got out of their activities. To this fact many persons associated with the plays and representing all periods except the 1870's have borne enthusiastic witness.[26]

One may doubt, however, if the theatre would have survived or developed to the extent that it did without the support and interest of the numerous organizations. Minor performances were habitually given at meetings of lodges and clubs, and at their bazaars and other entertainments. An established dramatic company or part of its personnel might be engaged for such occasions, or the organization's own members, experienced or inexperienced, might perform. In themselves, these performances were usually of little importance, but they helped to create a taste for the theatre and to develop an audience appreciative of more ambitious undertakings. Some of the most successful theatrical productions were sponsored by singing clubs, and these clubs often cooperated in the "plays with song" that were standard in the repertoire. The *Svenska National Förbund* for many years promoted elaborate city performances, for some time in a cooperative arrangement with a major company, and was an important force in making the theatre a recognized part of the life of the Swedish colony. Almost every organization, large and small, had its summer excursion, sometimes in celebration of Midsummer's Day, Bellman's Day, or another traditional holiday. In the 1890's and the following decade, outdoor performances of plays were popular features of these affairs, and in the 1930's the custom was revived in a series of successful productions.

In its more impressive developments, the Chicago Swedish theatre was, nevertheless, chiefly a matter of individual enterprise. Its progress was the achievement of men and women to whom it was of major importance, many of whom would have liked to give their lives to the stage, but had to be satisfied to give it their leisure.

As a rule, the leaders and mainstays in the Chicago companies brought with them from Sweden their interest in the theatre; many of them brought stage experience as well. Such experience was attributed to at least three of the actors of the 1870's. Fritz Schoultz, a moving spirit of the company that dominated the early 1880's and one of the theatre's most helpful supporters in later years, had been a pupil at a well known acting school for children in Stockholm. Also in the 1880's, two sisters with professional Swedish background, Mrs. Louise Nordgren and Mrs. Hanna Hvitfeldt, began Chicago acting careers. The leaders and popular favorites, Carl and Anna Pfeil, came to Chicago in 1888 from stage careers in Sweden and Finland. Not long afterward, Albert Alberg began a long period of varied service in the Chicago Swedish theatre. As a young boy he had left Sweden for an extensive career in England as actor, playwright, and adaptor, and had for a time headed a company in Stockholm. Two young actors from Sweden, Olaf Colldén and John Liander, were briefly prominent in Chicago plays of the 1890's also, until they returned to Sweden, where Liander continued his stage career with considerable success.

Neither Christopher Brusell nor Ernst H. Behmer, who succeeded the earlier leaders of Chicago Swedish companies, had acted professionally, though their interests and ambitions in the theatrical field had developed in their youthful days in Sweden. Some of their chief actors, however, had had the advantage of experience with provincial Swedish companies—character actors Ida Anderson-Werner, and Augusta and Carl Milton. Ida Östergren, a young leading lady from 1906 to 1908, had experience

16

on the Swedish stage. John Lindhagen and Knut Sjöberg came from Stockholm theatres; and a leading figure in the Chicago musical world who frequently appeared in Chicago plays, John Örtengren, had been a member of the Royal Theatre Dramatic and Opera Companies. In *Svenska Folkteatern* of the 1930's, too, there were men who had acted in Sweden, Thore Österberg and Paul Norling.

A few actors came to the Swedish plays from the American stage; and one young American born Swedish girl, Hilma Nelson, went from the Chicago Swedish theatre to Augustin Daly's famed company, of which she was a member from 1892 to 1899. The Swedish plays of New York were a proving ground for the musical comedy star, Arthur Donaldson, who acted with well known American companies for many years, and was a stellar attraction in Chicago Swedish plays of the 1890's and later. In the 1890's, too, Knut Schröder, a Chicago Swede who had belonged to American light opera and comedy troupes for a decade, was welcomed to the Swedish plays; and Wilma Sundborg-Stern, whose long career included several engagements with American companies, then first acted in Chicago's Swedish theatre.

The maintenance of that theatre depended, of course, on the continued interest of men and women living in Chicago, not on visiting actors, but the visitors were a stimulus both to a high level of performance and to public interest. Of particular significance in both respects were the singers and actors from Sweden who appeared with local companies in Chicago and other Swedish centers, sometimes in the course of extended tours.

It was not until the 20th century that tours by Swedish artists became frequent, but the Göteborg comedian, Otto Sandgren, acted in Chicago in the 1880's, and Emil von der Osten, a German actor who was a favorite in Sweden, in the 1890's. Madame Lotten Dorsch, a leading member of Stockholm's Royal Theatre and other prominent companies, appeared in Chicago during the 1893-1894 season. Among the later visitors, one of the most renowned was Madame Anna Hellström of the Royal Opera; and light opera stars included Emma Meissner and Anna Lundberg, the latter appearing in plays directed by her actor husband, Otto Lundberg. In the 1911-1912 season, one of Sweden's successful comedians, Elis Olson, entertained Chicago Swedes in plays and "ballad evenings." A number of women who presented this popular type of entertainment were starred in musical plays. The 1920's brought an appearance by Siri Hård of the Royal Theatre, and a series of productions under the leadership of Carl Barcklind, a well known musical comedy hero, who was to win further fame in Sweden as a character actor with major companies. But unquestionably the most noted and significant of the Swedish visitors who played in Chicago was August Lindberg. He directed and acted the leading role in Strindberg's *Gustaf Vasa* in January 1912, as part of the extensive celebration of the dramatist's 63rd birthday. This occasion marked also the debut of Lindberg's son Per, who was to become a leading figure in the development of the recent theatre in Sweden.

Though many circumstances combined to prevent the Swedish theatre of Chicago from attaining professional status, it cannot be properly designated as amateur. The nucleus of capable and experienced actors in the main companies of various periods provided performances that could be approved by professional standards in the plays that constituted a real theatre: the full evening programs of plays or the full length plays seriously undertaken, as distinguished from the little comedies presented as a relatively minor feature of a social evening. For lesser roles there had always to be dependence on amateurs who had no merit beyond interest, though a number of the novices had genuine talent and attained professional competence. The mainstays of the 20th century companies, acting together season after season, were able to achieve a level of performance remarkable in view of the inadequate rehearsals that were an unavoidable handicap for actors whose days were given to earning a livelihood or keeping house.

The Swedish theatre reached its highest development in the period of performances in city theatres, but a new prestige and improved facilities did not mean absence of the problems with which its leaders had always to contend. City theatres were in general available on Sundays only, at times only on Sunday afternoons; and matinée performances were not popular with Swedish audiences. Rehearsals were difficult to arrange and expensive. Rentals were, of course, a major item, running into hundreds of dollars. There were stage hands and musicians to be paid. And admission prices could not be raised correspondingly. Through most of the theatre's history, the standard admission price at the North Side Turner Hall and similar places was, for both play and dance, fifty cents. At the city theatres, the top price long remained $1.00. Not until the 1920's were charges of $1.75 and $2.00 fairly common. By the time of *Svenska Folkteatern,* rentals for the city theatres had become prohibitive, and the company normally played at two large North Side halls and at the North Side German theatre, with admission prices of seventy-five cents and $1.00.

For city performances and full scale productions at the larger halls, the producers had to depend on a large attendance, if they were to meet expenses or make a profit. When the North Side Turner Hall was the chief home of the Swedish plays, capacity houses of 2,000 were not a rarity, and audiences of well over 500 were common. City theatres were frequently well filled; on occasion, even the largest of them, the Auditorium, attracted crowds of 4,000. But many times newspapers noted with regret that a play—in the city or in an outlying hall—was not as well supported as it deserved, perhaps because of bad weather or a rival attraction. At every period of the Swedish theatre's existence the plays represented a financial risk for the producers. Sizeable profits were the exception, though large sums were occasionally realized for charities. Producers could hope to make money or at least not to incur losses. The actors could hope to be paid; the common practice from the 1880's on was for the producer to pay the actors. But of the motives that kept the Swedish theatre alive, the expectation of making money was certainly the least important.

Adequate production of plays requiring elaborate settings was not limited to the city theatres. Many of the halls much used after the 1880's had small stages and few facilities, but the North Side Turner Hall and the halls used by *Svenska Folkteatern* were large and had reasonably good equipment. As a matter of fact, economy sometimes necessitated inappropriate and ineffective settings in the regular theatres. In both settings and costumes, however, the Swedish productions benefited greatly by the continued interest and cooperation of Fritz Schoultz, the earlier theatrical leader, who became the proprietor of one of the country's principal costume supply houses. For the many folk plays and historical dramas, "excellent costumes from Schoultz" were the rule.

The folk plays, historical plays, and comedies that were the standard repertoire of Sweden's leading theatres in the 1840's, 1850's, and 1860's were the main reliance of Chicago's Swedish theatre through the chief period of its development. In Sweden these old plays had by the 1880's been relegated largely to the provincial and touring companies, and to Stockholm's lesser theatres, where they maintained their popularity; but the principal theatres were turning to them for occasional revivals only. Familiar trends continued in the repertoire of the capital's leading companies, but were being modified by influences from the continent, from Ibsen, and from Strindberg, as he gradually established himself as Sweden's leading dramatist. Contemporary plays became increasingly a part of the Chicago repertoire, but they rarely reflected these newer literary developments; though seven plays by Strindberg were acted, only *Gustaf Vasa* was given a major city performance in Chicago. Not surprisingly, most members of the Swedish audience in Chicago were not interested in the drama as literature, or in modern Swedish literature. They wanted to see the old and familiar, that which was a part of the Sweden they had known. And they wanted to laugh. The new plays they welcomed were comedies, whether of Swedish or local authorship, or, in the 1930's, the musical revues that were a fashion both in Sweden and the United States.[27]

Whatever their own interests, the directors were necessarily guided by public taste. Accessibility and economy, however, were perhaps equally important in determining the choice of repertoire. Fortunately, the majority of the plays that Chicago audiences were most willing to see again and again were also those most readily and cheaply obtained. Many of them were published in two popular and inexpensive series: *Bibliothek för teatervänner* (Library for friends of the theatre) and *Svenska teatern* (The Swedish theatre); or they were available in standard editions of authors' works. Around 1900, thirty frequently acted plays, chiefly one-act comedies, selling at from ten to sixty cents, were published in Chicago as *Teater-Biblioteket*. In the later 20th century, Swedish series of plays for amateurs were also used extensively by the smaller acting groups. Contemporary plays not included in a popular series were occasionally brought to Chicago by actors or other new arrivals, or they might be secured through agents or personal connections in Sweden. Rights of performance were sometimes arranged, and agents were, of course, paid, but stories are told of "pirated" plays, written down from memory by those who had seen them or acted in them in Sweden. Individual roles were long written laboriously by hand— another way of saving expense. Not until *Svenska Folkteatern* began playing popular successes in the 1930's, it would seem, were royalties normally paid for the Swedish plays produced in Chicago.

The Chicago repertoire included the best of Sweden's traditional drama and was to a remarkable degree representative of the popular trends that developed in Sweden. But Sweden could boast no Shakespeare or Sheridan, no Molière or Racine, no Holberg. The history of the Swedish theatre dates from 1782, when Gustaf III established a monopolistic theatre with operatic and dramatic companies. Its repertoire was, however, foreign— largely the comedy and sentimental drama of Pixérécourt, Scribe, and Kotzebue. Not until 1842 was there opportunity or encouragement for native dramatists. In that year, Anders Lindeberg dared to defy the hampering Royal Theatre monopoly and open the *Nya Teater* (New Theatre). Soon the example of Lindeberg and his successors in modernizing the repertoire and welcoming the work of Swedish dramatists was being followed by the

Royal Theatre. Other theatres opened their doors in the capital, provincial and touring companies multiplied, and both theatre and drama entered into a period of expansion and popularity.

The romantic interest in the past and the liberal patriotism that were prominent in the general literature of Sweden in this period expressed themselves also in the young Swedish drama. Two of its chief types were the historical drama and the folk play; and two of the most popular examples of these types appeared in 1846: F. A. Dahlgren's *Vermländingarne* (The people of Vermland), the folk play that has remained un-rivalled in the affections of the Swedish—and Swedish American—public; and August Blanche's *Engelbrekt och hans Dalkarlar* (Engelbrekt and his Dalecarlians), an historical picture in which a folk hero, folk traditions, and the liberalism of the day combined for public appeal. Closer to closet drama were the pseudo-Shaksperean verse tragedies of Joan Börjesson, whose *Erik den fjortonde* (Erik the fourteenth) also was first performed in 1846. In 1848 came one of the most successful of the historical dramas, and one of the best, from the point of view of dramatic structure, poetry, and effect. This was *Regina von Emmeritz,* the work of the Finnish historian, novelist, and dramatist, Zacharias Topelius.

Popular dramatists carried on these fashions, Frans Hedberg's *Bröllopet på Ulfåsa* (The wedding at Ulfåsa) of 1865 being one of the most notable of the later historical romances, and his *Valborgsmesso-aftonen* (Walpurgis-night) of 1854, a frequently played example of the folk play genre. The later *Nerkingarne* (The people of Nerke), by Axel Anrep, was another long-lived folk play. Both histories and folk plays were generally character-ized by romantic contrasts of character and romantic idealization in patri-otic themes and country pictures. Spectacle—processionals, battle scenes, and sieges—was prominent in the historical dramas; and in the folk plays, folk songs and dances and farcical comedy types were chief sources of pop-ular appeal. In spite of naiveté and obviousness when judged by later literary standards, and in spite of the artificiality with which they used the old theatrical devices of the soliloquy and aside, the best examples of these types have both literary and technical merits above much of the general dramatic literature of the period.

The chief theatrical activity of August Blanche was limited to the years from 1843 to 1850, but within that period he wrote not only *Engelbrekt och hans Dalkarlar* but a rapid succession of plays that made him the virtual creator of Swedish comedy. His comedies were of the French vaude-ville pattern, with intrigue generally borrowed from French and German

21

originals; but they were, as Henrik Schück says, of, for, and about Stockholm. Blanche transformed his foreign materials into authentic Stockholm pictures and characters, in which the delighted audiences could recognize actual models. Eccentric character roles, absurd and lively action, and witty songs gave his most popular comedies, like *Hittebarnet* (The foundling), *Rika morbror* (Rich uncle), *Herr Dardanell och hans upptåg på landet* (Mr. Dardanell and his country adventure), and *Ett resande teatersällskap* (A traveling theatre company), popularity and longevity. Characteristically Swedish pictures also were the best features of his sensation novels—*Jernbäraren* (The iron bearer) and *Flickan i Stadsgården* (The girl in the City Yard)—which were popular in dramatized form.

If the popular Swedish drama before Strindberg became an accepted influence did not have high and lasting literary value, it was generally good "theatre." The most successful and prolific playwrights, and a host of minor writers and adaptors, were practical men of the theatre—actors, directors, men attached to the theatre in the capacity of *litteratörer,* to read plays submitted for production, make translations and adaptations, as well as write original pieces.[28] These men knew the needs and possibilities of the theatre, and they knew public taste. Most of the repertoire was written to be successful on the stage, without much consideration of literary quality or reputation.

Many comedies and a series of tearful and didactic domestic dramas were the work of Johan Jolin, a favorite actor at the Royal Theatre from the 1840's through the 1860's. One of his prolific contemporaries was an actor and director largely active in the provinces, J. H. Lundgrén, known as Uller. Comedy was his forte, and he wrote an unusual number of Swedish "originals." Literally dozens of actors and actresses adapted and translated comedies from the French, the German, and Danish, and less frequently from the English. These were largely one-act pieces, more or less localized, with improbable and farcical action centering in jealousy and all sorts of romantic, social, and financial difficulties.

No career among the playwrights and adaptors rivalled that of Frans Hedberg (1828-1908), whose lifelong activity carried him from the period of his *Valborgsmesso-aftonen* and *Bröllopet på Ulfåsa* into the years of Strindberg's established reputation. Beginning his career as an actor at the Royal Theatre, he became both instructor in its school of acting and *litteratör.* With this background of experience, he produced an almost constant succession of plays and adaptations—Blanche type comedies, more realistic comedies of everyday life, and domestic dramas, some of which reflected the newer trends toward social themes. His later translations ranged from *Gamla Heidelberg* (Old Heidelberg) to Sudermann's *Ära* (Honor). He was also a devoted student of theatrical history, and wrote extensively if not too critically in that field.

Closest to Hedberg in extent and variety as well as in popularity of dramatic output was the younger Frans Hodell (1840-1890). As actor and *litteratör* he was associated with various theatres, but in his later career shifted to journalism. For a good many years, his *Andersson, Pettersson och Lundström* (1866)—a combination of allegorical fantasy, folk comedy, and song from a German source—almost matched *Vermländingarne* as a popular favorite.

Outside of comedy, the foreign influence was notable in the popularity of French romantic drama and dramatized French novels (sometimes coming by way of Germany, as in Charlotte Birch-Pfeiffer's version of George Sand's *Fanchon*). In the 1860's the Offenbach operas made an immediate success in Stockholm theatres, and began a taste for light opera often deplored by serious critics. On the whole, visiting dramatic companies from Germany, France, and from the other Scandinavian countries served to make Swedish theatrical offerings cosmopolitan, besides exerting an influence on native playwrights.

Two significant developments in repertoire the Swedish stage owed largely to the actor and director August Lindberg: acceptance of Ibsen and acquaintance with Shakespeare. Lindberg played Ibsen throughout Scandinavia in the 1880's, when his plays were still generally feared as scandalous and morbid.[29] A few of Shakespeare's plays had been acted occasionally since the 18th century, and a new interest had been stimulated by C. A. Hagberg's excellent translations into Swedish of all the plays, and by subsequent performances by Edwin Swartz in the 1850's. But it was Lindberg's numerous appearances as Hamlet, highly controversial as his interpretation was, and his other Shakespearean productions and readings that first made Shakespeare important in Swedish repertoire.[30]

In the gradual recognition of Strindberg, August Lindberg played a similar if less vital role. Strindberg's significance was by the beginning of the 20th century generally understood. His new historical dramas were given splendid productions at leading theatres. The *Intima Teater* was founded in 1907 largely to present his naturalistic works. And his plays from the 1880's, like *Mäster Olof* and *Lycko-Pers resa,* were entering into their period of extensive performance.[31]

23

Except for Strindberg, however, the last decades of the 19th century and the first of the 20th did not produce much noteworthy Swedish drama. The group of young "80ists" who espoused the new realism were represented by Charlotte Edgren Leffler, who wrote some slight plays in addition to her novels, and by Gustaf af Geijerstam, also better known as a novelist, who made a stage success with traditional comedy and with rural comedies that were somewhat realistic and satiric in tone. A continuing interest in folk lore expressed itself mainly in fiction and collections, but a chief worker in the field, August Bondeson, wrote a popular rural comedy, *Smålandsknekten* (The soldier from Småland), in 1894. In the unpretentious comedies of the 20th century, farcical and exaggerated pictures of country life became staple materials. In the first decades of the century the career most significant for the Swedish drama and theatre was that of Tor Hedberg (1862-1931). The son of Frans Hedberg, he carried on his father's interests, was director for a time of the Royal Theatre Company, and for many years a leading critic in dramatic and literary fields. In his own plays, which were linked with Ibsen as much as with Strindberg, he made a substantial contribution to Swedish repertoire.

The appearance of new and interesting dramatists and experimentation in stage techniques made the 1920's and 1930's a vital period in the history of the theatre in Sweden, but neither these new developments nor the plays of Tor Hedberg became a part of the Chicago Swedish theatre. It was the farcical comedies and revues from the theatres of Sweden specializing in such entertainment that were brought to Chicago.[32]

On the whole, however, the repertoire of the Chicago Swedish theatre compares favorably with the popular repertoire of Sweden for the same periods. Newer movements had not found ready acceptance in Sweden, and the Chicago directors made some efforts to introduce them to their audiences. Strindberg was represented by eight plays, among them some of his most popular and most characteristic, and at least two of the Chicago performances may be considered American premières.[33] There were productions of Ibsen and Sudermann—later than in Sweden, but noteworthy attempts nevertheless. Such contemporaries of Strindberg as Charlotte Edgren Leffler, Geijerstam, and Bondeson were also acted. The interest in Shakespeare was reflected in an ambitious production of *The taming of the shrew* in 1904. *Hamlet* had been less seriously undertaken in the 1880's. Danish plays included the 18th century comedy of Ludwig Holberg, *Jeppe på bjerget* (Jeppe of the mountain); and there were examples

24

of more recent foreign fashions, like the operettas and the romantic French dramas.

The first decades of native Swedish drama that provided plays for the majority of the Chicago performances were represented by much that was trivial, but few of the most significant and popular plays of the period were not presented. All the historical dramas and folk plays that have been mentioned, as well as other representatives of the types, had repeated performances. Blanche comedies were favorites in Chicago as in Sweden. Sensation dramas by Blanche and others, comedies and dramas by Jolin, the comedies of Hedberg and Hodell, of Uller, the Swedish "originals" and adaptations that made up so much of the standard repertoire in Sweden were similarly depended upon in Chicago. *Vermländingarne* and *Andersson, Pettersson och Lundström* were perennially welcomed by both native and immigrant audiences.

When all the circumstances are considered, the repertoire of the main Chicago companies over the years cannot be judged less than impressive. It bore out in general, certainly, the claims made by Chicago reviewers and supporters for the cultural values of the Swedish theatre and for its importance as a means of acquainting audiences with the drama of their fatherland—claims emphasized also by the few writers on Swedish America who recognized the existence of a Swedish immigrant theatre.[34]

To an audience not primarily concerned with cultural values, however, the plays were more important as links between the old and the new. The Swedish immigrants, if they did not generally have strongly nationalistic feelings about Sweden, were lovers of home, of its language and of its songs. Their recollections of home were, to begin with, said an early Swedish Chicagoan, the light side of the present; then, gradually, these recollections receded into the background, where they were kept, like pictures in an art gallery, beautiful and beloved, to be turned to when there was need of renewed inspiration for the daily battle.[35] Such pictures the plays from Sweden supplied. Above all else, a reviewer wrote in 1892, folk dramas like *Vermländingarne* had the power of maintaining love for the fatherland; they brought laughter and tears, and sent the audience home to dream of their home province.[36]

The audiences liked laughter better than tears, and they liked to laugh at themselves. They enjoyed the pictures of Sweden—sentimental, patriotic, comic—and they also enjoyed the comedies of local authorship that pictured the adventures of the immigrant in America, and, particularly, in Chicago. The green country boy and girl on *Store Bondegatan*, the pitfalls of boardinghouse life, the pretensions of the snob, the clubs and taverns, and newspapers and rivalries—all the elements of their life in the Chicago Swedish colony were in the plays written there in the 1870's and 1880's and 1890's, as were their counterparts in the local revues of the 1920's and 1930's. These pictures of Americanization were light-hearted, abounding in the songs and witty verses Swedish Chicago audiences always liked. And the plays pictured the Chicago Swedes—sometimes recognizable individuals—as Americans. If *Vermländingarne* revived memories of Sweden, so a grand finale showing the Linné monument, gift to Chicago of its Swedish citizens, stirred pride in their achievement in America. Whether the plays pictured the old world or the new, whether they were modern comedies or old folk plays, they gave the audiences happy hours— and that was not the least of the values of the Swedish theatre in Chicago.

CHAPTER II

"TEATER OCH BAL." 1867-1868—1877-1878

The story of the Swedish theatre in Chicago in its earliest known period can be but incompletely told. The two comedies that were acted by the *Svea Teatersällskap* at the German Hall on March 7, 1868, must be counted as beginning this history, but a number of facts make it reasonable to assume that there were earlier performances of which no record has survived. In 1866, with the founding of *Svenska Amerikanaren*, there was for the first time a newspaper that reported Swedish theatrical activities. *Hemlandet* had been published in Chicago since 1859, but, as the organ of the Augustana Synod, it ignored the theatre when not attacking it. Files of *Svenska Amerikanaren*, for all practical purposes, do not begin until 1868 (and after that date, also, and after it became *Nya Svenska Amerikanaren* in 1873, many issues are missing, sometimes over long periods). It was a small newspaper, in those early days, and, though sympathetic to the plays, often dealt with them briefly. Still, the absence of fanfare with which the 1868 plays were announced and the way they were discussed suggest that they were not a novelty. It seems likely, moreover, that this was not the first time the Svea Society, which was in its eleventh year of activity in 1868, had turned to plays for entertainment.

The most extended hiatus in the *Svenska Amerikanaren* files begins after the fire of 1871 and continues through 1875. When the North Side section where most of the Chicago Swedes lived was destroyed in the fire, their normal activities were, of course, interrupted. Not many months elapsed, however, before concerts and meetings were resumed; new halls gradually replaced those that had burned. Though we cannot know when plays again were given or how many there were, there can be little doubt that there were dramatic performances in the seasons for which *Svenska Amerikanaren* is missing, as there were in the preceding and following seasons. For 1875 there is at least one bit of evidence of the Swedes' continued interest in the theatre, in mention of a play that by some oversight slipped into the columns of *Hemlandet*.

Few as the performances were in comparison with later seasons—six being the greatest known number for any one season from 1867-1868 through 1877-1878—the theatre of these early years anticipated to a remarkable degree its later characteristics: in repertoire, made up chiefly of comedies, but including also other popular Swedish types; in actors, including professionals as well as amateurs; in sponsorship by organizations and by individuals; in performances for charities and as personal benefits. The types of places where plays were given, performances in neighbouring communities, a visiting company from New York—all had their later parallels. By the 1878-1879 season, when the personnel of a newly organized company marked the beginning of a second stage in the development of the Swedish theatre in Chicago, much of the pattern of that development had been established. And the attitude of *Svenska Amerikanaren* was that of the secular press in following years.

At the time of Svea's first known plays, in the spring of 1868, the conflict between the group represented by the society and that represented by *Hemlandet* was being aggravated by the young *Svenska Amerikanaren*. The newspaper, Svea Society, and the Swedish Episcopalian congregation worked together against the Augustana Synod, wrote Editor T. N. Hasselquist in *Hemlandet* in 1867.[1] In turn, Editor Herman Roos of *Svenska Amerikanaren* objected to the narrowness of the church in condemning the theatre.[2] That condemnation had been made clear shortly before, in a *Hemlandet* article objecting to state support of the theatre in Sweden, partly because funds thus used were needed for worthy purposes, but also because the theatre encouraged vanity and carnal lusts—not to say worse.[3] Years passed before this attitude was modified, as another newspaper debate of 1877 bears witness. This time it was *Skandia,* of Moline, Illinois, that ventured a defense of the theatre. The theatre, *Skandia* maintained, should be respected as one of the fine arts; moreover, a moral lesson impressively presented on the stage had been a turning point in the life of many a slave to vice. To see an historical drama was an experience that could be both elevating and educational. Comedies, also, could have moral values, besides furnishing needed relaxation. In general, not to admit the value of a *good* play was a sign of a perverted view of life.[4] *Hemlandet* published an answer by *Veritas.* How many plays, he asked, were good? And on what basis should they be judged, that of Christianity or that of art? Could the theatre do what the law and gospel had been unable to accomplish?[5]

In spite of the opposing points of view of the two groups, amicable relations and cooperation were not entirely lacking. Johan A. Enander, editor and co-owner of *Hemlandet* from 1869, reported all the activities of Svea except its plays, generally in a friendly spirit, and gave much attention to Swedish musical organizations, regardless of their affiliation. In 1870 —largely through the efforts of the national minded Enander—cooperation was achieved in a grand welcome tendered to the Swedish singer, Christina Nilsson. Looking back from 1900, when the earlier divisions were no longer sharply felt, the veteran editor pictured the difficulties involved in pleasing both elements on this occasion. The church group attended the banquet, but left before the dance; even so, the ministers who participated were attacked for supporting a worldly affair, and were accused of drinking to excess of the wines that they declined.[6]

Svea and other friends of the theatre appear on the whole to have taken the attacks of the church lightly. The bad weather interfering with attendance at the May 1, 1868, plays, *Svenska Amerikanaren* ironically observed, was doubtless caused by the displeasure of a higher being at so sinful an affair.[7] A record breaking crowd at a play the following spring called forth expressions of amazement that these Swedes were so morally degraded as to be attracted to the "worldly instead of the spirituous (no— apologies), spiritual" on a Saturday night. Was this the spirit of the age or a passing epidemic? But man proposes and God disposes, or "in plain Swedish 'presten spår och Gud rår.' " After all, *Svenska Amerikanaren* concluded, the Swedes are a pleasure loving people.[8]

Saturday evening was the normal time for plays, with occasional performances on Friday or Sunday. A custom frequently followed later began in these years, the presentation of plays as part of a holiday celebration, as on May Day or New Year's Day, with "national tableaux" also marking the occasion. After the plays there were dances that lasted, sometimes at least, far into the night, and that were an added offense to the critical. Refreshments were served—probably the beer and sandwiches that were the rule in the following period—and, to the dismay of the reviewers, they were served during the performance itself.[9]

If the plays were social occasions, catering to the Swedes' love of pleasure and of worldly entertainment, they also served purposes to which nobody could object. Svea's May 1, 1868, comedies were part of a program arranged to raise money for the immigrant home that the society was later able to build. The May 1 entertainment the following year, in which Norwegian actors cooperated, and which included a play in Norwegian, was a benefit on behalf of the Swedish Women's Emigrant Aid Fund. These were projects that attempted to meet problems of exploitation and economic hardship recognized as vital by every group in the Swedish colony.

Actors of this period were usually referred to as "well known amateurs" and left unnamed. Individuals were first mentioned in connection with the plays given February 27, 1869. One Knut Erickson signed the

29

advertisement, with Reinhardt Strömberg and "other well known amateurs."[10] But the stars of the evening, who may have been making their
Chicago debuts, were Erick Fahlbeck and Alba Enbom. Miss Enbom was
said to have had a professional career in Sweden. Mr. Fahlbeck was spoken
of then and later as having belonged to Sweden's chief theatrical company,
that of the Royal Theatre in Stockholm, and was presumably the most
notable of the early actors. As to his occupation in Chicago, the only clue
is a remark that his art had not been affected by the daily routine of business.[11] Three amateurs were mentioned in the February 1869 review—
Mr. Lood, Miss Eklund, and Charles Eklund—the two latter as playing roles
of some prominence. Mr. Eklund later appeared in a play of his own
writing, and is one of the few persons acting in this period of whom something is known. He was a leading member of Svea and an initiator of its
immigrant home project (and probably of its theatrical enterprises). In
general, he became known as a supporter of charitable undertakings and,
in the years after the fire, as a link between the two groups in the Swedish
colony. He had come to Chicago in 1868, at the age of thirty-five, and subsequently engaged in various businesses, being at one time a cigar manufacturer.[12]

Fahlbeck made a second appearance in April 1869, with Knut Erickson again signing the advertisement. In the 1869-1870 season Miss Enbom
presented two plays, and Fahlbeck acted at least once, with the *Svenska
Dramatiska Förening* (Swedish Dramatic Society) which offered the play
by Eklund and another comedy on January 1, 1870. Companies acting in
these years cannot be clearly identified by name; in fact, for years a
variety of names was used in referring to the same company. With the
actors unnamed, there is, therefore, no way of knowing whether the *Svenska
Dramatiska Förening* was distinct from the *Svenska Dramatiska Sällskap*
that appeared December 18, 1869, and later in the season. Nor is it any
more clear what group took plays to Princeton and Galesburg, Illinois, in
the spring of 1870, or what, if any, relations Svea had with the majority
of the plays acted after the spring of 1868. There had, at any rate, been
two companies before the fall of 1870, for at that time a newly formed
company was commended for uniting the two earlier companies.[13] The new
company included both Miss Enbom and Mr. Fahlbeck, as well as Mr.
Strömberg, who was now also credited with being a professional actor.[14]
One other actress, Euphemia Ivendorff, is known to have appeared in
these years; her name was emphasized in advertisements for two plays

acted by the *Svenska Dramatiska Sällskap* on April 22, 1870, without further information.[15]

After the records resume in 1875, there is no mention of any of these actors, with the possible exception of Mr. Strömberg; and of the amateurs who presumably made up the acting personnel, only one, Miss Anna Hagström, is known to have continued in the plays after 1876.[16] She acted with Svea, now sharing the field of theatricals with the newly organized Svithiod Club (not yet a lodge), the Swedish Odd Fellows Lodge, and Orpheus, evidently a musical group whose history has not survived. The few persons named in connection with performances by Svea were, besides Miss Hagström, Mr. Holm, Miss Svensson, Mrs. Söderholtz, and Mr. Söderberg. Possibly the last named was John Söderberg, who had come to America in 1867, after being educated at a military school in Stockholm, and had later settled in Chicago, where he worked as a bookkeeper.[17] The first Chicago Swede to become an actor on the American stage, Alfred Johnson, made his one appearance at a Swedish play as part of a Svea theatrical evening in 1876, acting, however, in an English language skit of his own authorship, *The colored tragedian,* with both American and Swedish supporting actors. Johnson had come to Chicago as an infant in 1850, and had early turned to the stage, winning success as a comedian. He was later manager of the West Side Lyceum and the Criterion theatre.[18] His was not the only performance in English in connection with a Swedish play in this period, the witches' scene from *Macbeth* having been presented in 1871 by the "famous young actor, Mr. D. Barron of London."[19]

The beginning of 1878 brought new, though temporary, leadership, with a company headed by P. W. Nelson, His name, said *Svenska Tribunen,* was a guarantee against humbug—and one wonders if such guarantees had at times been needed. Of Mr. Nelson it is known that he had left agricultural studies in Sweden in 1866, and by 1872 had begun a successful business as a shirt manufacturer.[20] Associated with him in the 1876 company was C. F. Ekholm; and a Mrs. Hazalius was of sufficient importance to be the recipient of a benefit April 10, 1878, "in gratitude for her participation" in the plays.[21]

The 1878 plays were given at the North Side Turner Hall, at what was then 259 N. Clark Street.[22] There for the next two decades the majority of the Swedish plays were acted, and there Swedish plays were seen into the 1920's. For the Swedish actors who went on to play in the down town theatres, the hall was their old stamping ground, remembered with nostalgia. Something of the earlier enthusiasm was lost, they recall, when

31

the plays moved to grander surroundings. The North Side Turner Hall offered, as a matter of fact, good facilities: a large stage, excellent acoustics, fair scenery, and gas footlights. The main floor, with its serving tables, and the surrounding balconies had together a seating capacity of 2,000.[23]

Before it was destroyed by the 1871 fire, the earlier North Side Turner Hall at the same location had been used for one Swedish play. All the other plays of those early seasons had been acted at German Hall, at the corner of Wells and Indiana, built in 1856. It, too, burned, but was not rebuilt. Throughout its existence it housed German plays and was a center of varied Swedish activities. There the meetings of Svea were held until the society got its own hall in 1868; and German Hall was the scene of the gala welcome for Christina Nilsson. It was an elegant and commodious place, Enander wrote in that connection. Svea lost its first hall in the fire also, but in 1872 obtained new quarters at Clybourne and Larrabbee, where its plays of the late 1870's were given.[24]

Fifty cents was the regular admission price for plays (and dances) throughout these years. Occasionally there must have been satisfactory profits, for crowds of 700-800 were mentioned in 1869, 1875, and 1878.[25] But a phrase often employed in later years—a smaller attendance than the play deserved—occurred in this period also. Usually bad weather was suggested as the reason for a small crowd, but sometimes there were good crowds when the weather was unfavorable.

Comedy was the usual offering of these early Swedish groups. As *Svenska Amerikanaren* often observed, audiences in Chicago liked to laugh; and comedy, especially the kind of one-act farce most frequently presented, could be easily staged and was entertaining even when not expertly acted. Even in its beginnings, however, the Chicago Swedish theatre was not without the historical drama and folk play that had established themselves as popular types when the native Swedish drama was first developing in the 1840's. August Blanche's *Engelbrekt och hans Dalkarlar* and Johan Börjesson's *Erik den fjortonde,* two of the plays that marked the arrival of the historical genre, first represented it in Chicago. There were typical folk play materials as well in the Blanche drama—country pictures, music and dances—as there were in the "dramatic idyll with song" acted in Chicago in 1869, *En midsommarnatt i Dalarne* (A midsummer night in Dalarne). *En Majdag i det gamla hemmet* (A May day in the old home), presented as part of a theatrical program in 1868, undoubtedly also had the appeals of the folk play. It may have been a tableau or a locally written sketch; in these years there were, at any rate, some local plays, interesting in their anticipation of the type as it later developed.

For the most part, the comedies used in this early period were the work of popular Swedish playwrights of the 1850's and 1860's. Of the twenty-six comedies from Sweden known to have been acted in the first eight seasons, five were by Uller (Johan F. Lundgrén) and eight by Frans Hodell. One of the comedies that were the chief contribution of Blanche to the Swedish drama was acted, *Rika morbror*. Surprisingly, the prolific Frans Hedberg, so extensively played in Chicago in the following years, was missing. Many of the comedies now introduced were to be popular with Chicago actors and audiences over a long period. *Rika morbror*, for instance, was given ten more performances, the last in 1935; and one of the plays from the first Chicago program, Uller's *Bättre aldrig än sent* (Better never than late), was played six times, from 1868 to 1911. Leading the rest, however, was the one full length comedy acted in these years, Hodell's *Andersson, Pettersson och Lundström*. From 1869 to 1935, it was presented in full at least thirty-two times, achieving a record surpassed only by the folk play, *Vermländingarne*.

The comedies that were combined to make up an evening's program, whether they were adaptations from the French or German or whether they were Swedish "originals," generally had common characteristics: a complicated farcical plot, eccentric character types as a background for young lovers, and songs, witty or sentimental. Typical in materials and intrigue were two comedies by Uller, *En menniskovän* (A friend of mankind), played in 1869, and *En svartsjuk tok* (A jealous fool), acted in 1878. The fool in the latter is an old husband whose suspicions of his young wife lead to frantic pursuit of a strange young man and the sweetheart of the family servant. In *En menniskovän* the adventures revolve around a bluestocking who refuses her niece permission to marry a young man because of his unromantic name, and is tricked into approval by means of a deaf servant disguised as a refugee nobleman.

1868-1869

It was the Stockholm actor, Erick Fahlbeck, who ventured a departure from such theatrical fare, and presented an act of Börjesson's tragedy, *Erik den fjortonde*—accompanying it, however, with a typical comedy, *Tre friare och en älskare* (Three suitors and one lover). Given as a benefit for Fahlberg on February 27, 1869, and advertised as the best Swedish performance offered Chicago Swedes, the affair attracted a crowd

33

of unprecedented size, a fact which, as has already been noted, *Svenska Amerikanaren* reported with unholy rejoicing.[26] Fahlbeck, of course, played King Erik, and Alba Enbom was his devoted commoner queen, Katrina Månsdotter. Charles Eklund was the king's villainous brother, Duke John, and Miss Eklund the Duke's wife, Katrina Jagellonica. The amateurs of the company could not be heard, the reviewer objected— except for Eklund, who, "in accordance with his nature," spoke *ur skägget* (loudly and aggressively; literally, out of his beard). To Miss Enbom and Mr. Fahlbeck higher critical standards could be applied, and they measured up splendidly, in both acting and appearance. The dramatic meeting of the brothers, after the king had released the duke from prison in hope of a reconciliation, achieved true impressiveness in the opinion of the reviewer. But, he said, the audience did not share his enthusiasm. The general public had little interest in the beauty of Börjesson's poetry, in which the merit of the play so largely consisted. The poetic tragedy was, in short, a poor choice, for when Scandinavians go to the theatre they want "to laugh until their stomachs hop, and then to hop in dance."[27]

Börjesson's plays are heavy and solemn, with long, elaborately rhetorical speeches, and they lack the suitability for performance that characterized the popular historical drama of the time. They did not remain long in the repertoire in Sweden, and it is not surprising that the excerpt given in 1869 did not appeal to the audience. In later years, however, *Erik den fjortonde* was given one full performance in Chicago and one other of Börjesson's dramas was acted.[28]

1869-1870

For his second presentation of historical drama, nearly two years later, Fahlbeck chose *Engelbrekt och hans Dalkarlar,* a play that Chicago audiences did enjoy. In the interim, there were the usual one-act comedy offerings, varied in the 1869-1870 season by *Andersson, Pettersson och Lundström* and by *En midsommarnatt i Dalarne,* which was twice presented by Miss Enbom. This was originally the work of Erik Bögh, a Danish playwright much seen in Swedish adaptations.

The actors who performed *Andersson, Petterson och Lundström* on December 18, 1869, surely did not suspect that in bringing Hodell's recent adaptation of Nestroy's *Lumpaci Vagabundus* to Chicago they were introducing what was long to be the favorite comedy of its Swedish audiences.[29] And a remarkable mélange it offered. There was folk play material; there were elaborate scenes in the realm of the trolls and fairies, with spectacular

34

appearances and vanishings. There was satire—of social pretensions and snobbishness, of the workings of democratic government. There were popular songs, there were sentiment and morality as well as laughter and folly, and numerous character types—in short, there was something for every taste. Still, the picturesque trio of name characters was probably the main attraction, and furnished many Chicago actors with popular roles.

The adventures of Andersson, Pettersson, and Lundström, journeyman joiner, tailor, and shoemaker, respectively, grow out of difficulties in the realm of trolls and fairies. Infernalis, the guardian spirit of frivolity, has been corrupting the subjects of His Majesty, Hocus Pocus. The goddess Fortuna is upset by the power of the goddess of true love, Amorosa, over her daughter, and joins Hocus Pocus in testing the power of their enemies by bestowing fortunes upon three mortals—who are, of course, the poverty stricken but carefree journeymen. As a consequence, Andersson is able to win his longed for bride, Fiken, the scene of the romance being a country festival which introduces one of the popular characters in the play, the pedantic and conceited Schoolmaster Pluggstedt. Tailor Pettersson is tricked out of his money as he plays the gentleman in the city. Lundström remains happy-go-lucky, and spends his money traveling about a world that he momentarily expects will be destroyed by a comet. Finally Andersson, who is happy and industrious in his marriage, is able to help his friends; in the kingdom of Hocus Pocus, Infernalis is banished, Amorosa is made queen, and a closing tableau shows that Pettersson and Lundström have also been supplied with wives, in accordance with the moral that concludes the play, "Without true love—there is no true fortune."

An early repetition of *Andersson, Pettersson och Lundström* indicates its success, but it was not reviewed. Nor was it one of the plays taken shortly afterward to Galesburg and Princeton, perhaps by the same company. These plays included, besides the *Bättre aldrig än sent* earlier acted in Chicago, two one-act comedies for which there is no record of Chicago performance: *Malins korgar* (Malin's baskets) and *Grannarne* (The neighbours), the latter by August Blanche. The plays were enthusiastically received, the actors reported in *Svenska Amerikanaren;* what they emphasized, like the actors who enjoyed later tours, was the social side of the reception and trip.[30] No report indicates whether or not Chicago audiences received with equal cordiality a New York company that visited there the same spring.

The first play certainly of local authorship acted by Chicago Swedes was *En nyårsnattsdröm i Chicago* (A New Year's night dream in Chicago), concocted by Calle Dunkel for New Year's Day performance in 1870.

The pseudonym did not hide the identity of Charles Eklund, who also, it seems, acted the role of Mr. Arlekin, a man "who would not be employed" by *Svenska Amerikanaren*. Possibly the paper resented satire directed against it. At any rate, the play was severely handled, and Mr. Eklund advised that if this was the best he could do "he had better get off the track at once." The people laughed, of course, "but they will laugh at anything." As for the opening farce, it was a complete fiasco; one of the actors should never again be permitted to step on the stage. The society would have to do better if it was to maintain the reputation for ability it had gained in its short existence.[31]

1870-1871

Svenska Amerikanaren usually greeted the plays with encouragement and praise, but when a company uniting the Swedish theatrical forces gave *Engelbrekt och hans Dalkarlar* on December 19, 1870, the reviewer had recourse to superlatives. The advertisements, too, struck a modern Hollywood note. The "immortal and glorious historical drama in five acts, with choruses, melodramas, folk dances, and above all the extraordinary war march" would make this one of the greatest theatrical events of the Swedes in Chicago. With a cast of forty, the assistance of the Swedish singing society,[32] and an Engelbrekt who had played in the drama in Stockholm, there was justification for these claims. The entire performance was judged notable, and high praise given to Fahlbeck's artistry as Engelbrekt and in another unidentified role. Sharing chief honors was Alba Enbom, who played Queen Philippa with expected grace and dignity.[33]

There were to be other gala performances of *Engelbrekt och hans Dalkarlar* in Chicago, and its popularity is not difficult to understand. Blanche made good use of his opportunities in depicting the 15th century peasant hero who won freedom for the Swedish people when they were suffering from Danish oppression under the rule of Erik XIII. The play is long and loosely knit, but its central story is presented in a series of effective scenes: the appearance of Engelbrekt and his companion, Sven Ulfsen, before the king, with their gift of a loaf of bread made from brick symbolizing the sufferings of the peasantry; the flight of Engelbrekt and Sven, aided by sympathetic Queen Philippa; Engelbrekt's refusal of the crown offered him after his triumph; and his treacherous slaying. Interwoven with this story is an elaborate net of minor actions that concern mainly deeds of violence growing out of conspiracies, and the love story of Engelbrekt's daughter Ingeborg and Abilard, son of the Danish oppressor.

36

Their love is blessed by the dying Engelbrekt, to close the play on a note of unity and pathos. Probably the favorite scene of the Chicago audiences, at least the one most publicized, was that of the great processional march with which his followers honored Engelbrekt. The language of Blanche was that of rhetoric rather than poetry, and he developed his theme of resistance to tyranny in terms of the contemporary liberal movements in which he was active, but a tone of authenticity and sincerity lends impressiveness to the portions of the play depicting Engelbrekt and to the country scenes that gave it the appeal of the folk play.

Not until *Vermländingarne* was first played in Chicago in 1884 was there another play demanding dramatic ability of the Swedish actors,[34] but the remaining seasons of this first period included two-act comedies more ambitious than those that had been staple entertainment, and local writers made some contributions to the repertoire with a characteristic immigrant in America theme. How European "big bugs" get along in Brother Jonathan's country was the subject announced in order to attract the public when *Emigration 1871,* a "transformation" in three parts, with local references and songs, was twice played in January 1871.[35]

1874-1875

Two local plays of which even less is known are of interest, in part because of their connection with Magnus Elmblad. Attached to *Svenska Amerikanaren* for much of the period he spent in America, 1871-1884, he gained a reputation both for his poetic talents and for his drinking and escapades. No available newspaper tells of Elmblad's *Samhällsdanaren* (The society organizer), but his colleague, Ernst Skarstedt, recalled that it was acted in the 1870's, and the title suggests local satire. A tempting conjecture is that it pictured Editor Enander of *Hemlandet* when he was pushing the *Svenska Förbund* as a rival to Svea in 1875.[36] The one play known to have been given in 1875 is linked with Elmblad mainly because its title, *Herr Petter Jönsons resa till Amerika* (Mr. Petter Jönsons's journey to America) is practically identical with the title of his immigrant ballad, called both *Petter Jönsons* and *Petter Jönsingens resa till Amerika.* The play was given as part of the first May Day festival of the Svithiod Club, an occasion for which Elmblad wrote a poem. The verses about Petter Jönson are said to have been published in Sweden in 1872, and to have become immediately popular. Undoubtedly they were known in Chicago at that time also. They were later published in the two small collections of Elmblad's poetry printed in Minneapolis and in Sweden,

37

and in the 1930's were reprinted in one of Sweden's newspapers and in a collection of emigrant songs published in Sweden.

As to the play or skit, whether by Elmblad or by some one else, it must have capitalized on the popularity of his song; and the stage Petter Jönson, like the Petter Jönson of the song and like many immigrants later celebrated in rhyme and play, must have had high hopes for life in

> the great land in the West
> Where no king or scolding pastors are found.
> Where one may sleep and eat pork and potatoes
> And then use the fat to shine one's shoes gratis.
>
> Where no official dares bully a farmer
> And first-rate brandy costs six *stiver* a can.
> Where there is more money than there are rats in Trosa.

But the journey put an end to Petter Jönson's hopes. Discouraged by storms, sea sickness, and wretched accommodations, he sold his chest and belongings to a Jew at Castle Garden, and set out again for Sweden.

> And the sun's edges will crack asunder
> Before on the Atlantic Petter Jönson will venture.[37]

1876-1878

Several comedies of lasting popularity were among the offerings of 1876 and 1878. At Svea Hall, *Mot beräkning* (Contrary to expectation), with a Box and Cox situation involving a baker, a seamstress, and their landlady, was twice acted; and there Hodell's *Familjen Trögelin* (or *Lustresan från Skåne*—The vacation trip from Skåne) had its Chicago première. Nelson's company introduced *Bror Jonathan, eller Oxhandlaren från Småland* (Brother Jonathan or The cattle trader from Småland), and *Kärleken på sommarnöje* (Love on a summer holiday), another Hodell play, in which the action centers in a summer house used by young lovers for secret meetings and by servants for an unauthorized residence. In *Bror Jonathan*, the country hero was, in the 1878 performance, brought to Chicago instead of to Stockholm, to visit his merchant brother. Through the years, Chicago audiences were to enjoy the contrast of Jonathan's homely virtues and his brother's affected sophistication, and the Småland dance with which Jonathan and his wife upset an elegant city party.[38] The Nelson company also brought Chicago its first comedy by August Blanche, *Rika morbror.*

38

The gay songs for which Blanche was famous and his usual Stockholm pictures enliven the story of the penniless sailor, Job, whom his wealthy and snobbish brother-in-law receives, believing him to he rich. Job's supposed benefactions to his niece enable her to marry her poor suitor, and finally only her father and a love-sick governess remain disappointed.

In the fall of 1876, *Svenska Amerikanaren* had congratulated Svea on plans for a theatrical season (not to be fully carried out), and had discussed the difficulties with which the Swedish companies were faced— lack of stage resources, the problem of finding capable actors. It was unfortunate, but not surprising, the writer concluded, that there were so few opportunities to see Swedish plays in Chicago.[39] In 1878 the same things could have been said, and the situation was to continue. But, in spite of opposition and difficulties, the Swedish theatre had made a beginning. Its actors had played a varied and representative repertoire, and had found a public welcome. And new actors were soon to begin careers that would give the Swedish theatre a more assured place in the life of the Swedish colony of Chicago, more extensive and continuous activity.

The following abbreviations are used in the chronological tables: D. F. for *Dramatiska Förening* (dramatic association); D. S. for *Dramatiska Sällskap* (dramatic society); T. for *Teatersällskap* (theater society); S. D. S. and S. T. for *Svenska Dramatiska Sällskap* and *Teatersällskap;* N. S. T. H. and S. S. T. H. for North Side and South Side Turner Halls. Halls are so designated but theatres are listed by name only. When separate acts were performed, the act or acts given are indicated by Roman numerals. When a company acted for another organization, both groups are listed, when known.

Performances, 1867-1868 through 1877-1878

Date	Play	Company	Place
	1867-1868		
Mch. 7, 1868	*Bättre aldrig än sent*	Svea T.	German Hall
	Husvill för sista gången		
Apr. 18, 1868	*Husvill för sista gången*	Svea T.	German Hall
	Min hustrus affärer		
May 1, 1868	*Min hustrus affärer*	Svea T.	German Hall
	Bättre aldrig än sent		
	En Majdag i det gamla hemmet		
July 4, 1868	*Sockenskräddaren*	Svea T.	German Hall
	"I tjenst åstundas"		
	En Stockholms-mamsell		
	1868-1869		
Feb. 27, 1869	*Erik den fjortonde, II*	Fahlbeck Co.	German Hall
	Tre friare och en älskare		
Apr. 3, 1869	*Punkt för punkt*	S. D. S.	German Hall
	En liten satunge		
May 1, 1869	*Han hyr rum af sin betjent*[40]	For S. *Frun-*	German Hall
	En liten satunge	*timmerans*	
		Emigrant-	
		hjelp	
	1869-1870		
Oct. 30, 1869	*De båda direktörerna*	Enbom Co.	German Hall
	En midsommarnatt i Dalarne		
Nov. 20, 1869	*En menniskovän*	Enbom Co.	German Hall
	En midsommarnatt i Dalarne		
Dec. 18, 1869	*Andersson, Pettersson och Lundström*	S. D. S.	German Hall
Jan. 1, 1870	*Hans tredje hustru*	S. D. F.	German Hall
	En nyårsnattsdröm i Chicago		
Jan. 8, 1870	*Andersson, Pettersson och Lundström*	S. D. S.	German Hall
Feb. 3, 1870	*Mamsell Sundblad vill gifta sig*	*Thalias Vän-*	Houston
	Arfvinge till en million	*ner i New*	Street Hall
		York[41]	
Apr. 22, 1870	*En friare i lifsfara*	S. D. S.	German Hall
	Aftonsången		
Apr. 30, 1870	*Obrottslig tystlåtenhet*	*Thalias Vän-*	Houston
	Hans tredje hustru	*ner i New*	Street Hall
		York	

Date	Play	Company	Place
	1870-1871		
Dec. 19, 1870	Engelbrekt och hans Dalkarlar	S. D. S.	N. S. T. H.
Jan. 13, 1871	Ett rum för resande	S. D. S.	German Hall
	Emigration 1871		
Jan. 14, 1871	Ett rum för resande[42]	S. D. S.	German Hall
	Emigration 1871		
Jan. 28, 1871	Ett rum för resande	S. D. S.	German Hall
	1871-1872		
	1872-1873		
	1873-1874		
	1874-1875		
May 1, 1875	Herr Petter Jönsons resa till Amerika	Svithiod Co.	Central Hall
	1875-1876		
Jan. 22, 1876	Ett rum att hyra	Svea Co.	Svea Hall
Feb. 19, 1876	Mot beräkning (as Lotte)	Scandinavian Co.	Svea Hall
Feb. 20, 1876	Fäktaren i Ravenna[43]	Orpheus Co.	Aurora T. H.
Mch. 25, 1876	Mamsell Garibaldi	Swedish Odd Fellows Lodge	Svea Hall
	1876-1877		
Oct. 21, 1876	Mot beräkning	Svea T.	Svea Hall
Dec. 2, 1876	Lustresan från Skåne (as Familjen Trögelin)[44]	Svea T.	Svea Hall
	1877-1878[45]		
Jan. 27, 1878	Rika morbror	P. W. Nelson	N. S. T. H.
	En svartsjuk tok	Co.	
Mch. 3, 1878	Tre friare och en älskare	P. W. Nelson	N. S. T. H.
	Bror Jonathan, eller Oxhandlaren från Småland	Co.	
Apr. 14, 1878	Kärleken på sommarnöje	P. W. Nelson	N. S. T. H.
	En Söndag i det gröna	Co.	

CHAPTER III

NORTH SIDE TURNER HALL; THE BOHEMIANS. 1878-1879—
1890-1891

The period that began in 1879 with the formation of a youthful
company calling itself the *Svenska Amatör Sällskap* was unquestionably
the most colorful in the history of the Swedish theatre in Chicago. The
leaders of this society and of its immediate successors were as gay and carefree as they were talented and versatile. Naturally, they did not always
take their theatrical activities seriously, and their plays included ludicrous
fiascos as well as able and ambitious productions. But their interest was
nonetheless genuine. After Carl Pfeil and his wife Anna came from professional careers in Sweden to join forces with them in 1888, performances
became more frequent and regular, and the repertoire more varied and
pretentious. Successful tours were also adding to the prestige of the
theatre. And by 1890 there existed for the first time a company and an
audience that made it possible to climax a season with plays given at a
"regular down town" theatre instead of at the North Side Turner Hall.

In the 1880's the Chicago Swedish population was growing rapidly.
It had increased from 6,154 in 1870 to 12,930 in 1880, but by 1890
it was a sizeable colony of 43,032.[1] A few of those who were now active in
the theatre had come to America in the 1870's, but most of them were a
part of this new immigration. It brought an unusual number of men whose
interests were literary and artistic, and, often, convivial. These immigrants
had to turn their hands to all sorts of jobs, but many of them naturally
found places in the Swedish newspapers, some as writers and editors, others
in the offices or as agents.[2] There were increasing opportunities in this
field, for in 1877, when *Nya Svenska Amerikanaren* became *Svenska
Tribunen,* a new *Svenska Amerikanaren* also began publication, and there
were other short-lived papers. Largely as a result of the gifts and interests
of the newcomers, humorous periodicals also began to spring up. Some
of them died within a few issues, and none survived more than a few
years, but in the 1880's and the 1890's they were a lively feature of the
Chicago Swedish world.

The life of the journalist was, in general, a hand to mouth affair.
Pay was irregular and small. Editors worked for $6.00 and $12.00 a week,
and starved, so the story goes, for three weeks in order to buy a ninety

42

cent pair of shoes. Those were the Bohemian days in the Swedish news-paper world (always excepting *Hemlandet*), many reminiscences agree, with Bacchus the highest protecting god of editorial office and press room, and more than one promising talent ruined by follies and dissipation.[3]

Not all the "Bohemians" were employed by the newspapers and periodicals, but those engaged in other occupations were not, as a rule, in these early years in Chicago, more prosperous. In general they were not immoderate in their pleasures, and they were more fun-loving than un-conventional. Even the most reckless and improvident of those who have been written of and remembered did not lose their essential goodness of nature in dissipation, and their follies were marked by wit and imagina-tion. If they were Bohemian, it was not only in their way of life, so largely dictated by poverty, but in their interests as well. Music, literature, art, and the theatre were their dominant interests. The newspapermen wrote, and with little hope of profit, beyond the line of duty—fiction, poetry, plays. Much of what they wrote was trivial and broadly comic, but they gave the Swedish colony a literature in which it could recognize itself. They formed literary clubs, they collected books and works of art, they gave concerts, and *soirées,* with programs of music and readings. And they gave plays.

It was a young group that contributed so much to the pleasures of the Swedish public. Most of the men prominent in the 1880's were in their twenties. Certainly they turned to the theatre for the fun it gave them, for its social side, but they were motivated also by a love of acting and of the drama—and by the hope of adding to their incomes.[4] The audience, too, was young and fun-loving. The interests of most of the people who attended the plays were not those of the actors, but if the fine points in drama and acting were not in general appreciated, the plays were enjoyed, as well as the dances that followed them. The spirit at the per-formances was one of informality and fun, for actors and audience alike, with the informality sometimes interfering with the success of the actors. Crowded conditions and the habit of serving beer and food during the play occasionally resulted in inattention and disorders so marked that reviewers devoted their columns to demands for reform rather than to the play.[5] From time to time, however, they were able to note with satisfaction the presence of a goodly number of the "stable and respectable" citizens of the colony. Not until the late 90's was the gap between the theatre and the Augustana group bridged, but among the actors of this period affilia-tion with the Episcopalian St. Ansgar church was common, and they often appeared in its concerts and entertained at its fairs.

43

This was the heyday of the North Side Turner Hall, as far as the Swedish plays were concerned. A growing settlement of Swedes on the South Side led to some performances there as well, and the first outdoor summer productions came at the end of the 1880's. But ordinarily, when *"Svensk Teater"* was announced in a Swedish newspaper, it was hardly necessary to add *"på Nord Sidans Turner Hall."* Saturday night was still the most popular night for the plays, and the price, for play and dance, was still normally fifty cents. Some elaborate productions brought the innovation of reserved seats for seventy-five cents and a dollar, with the lowest price tickets twenty-five cents. A good house of 1,000 and a crowded one of 2,000 assured profits for the promoters. Occasionally it was the man in charge of the bar who paid the rent and hired the actors, or some organization might hire a company. More often the company or individual actors took the initiative and responsibility. Ernst Lindblom reports in his *Svenska teaterminnen från Chicago* that a crowded North Side Turner Hall with tickets at fifty and seventy-five cents at the first performance of a play he wrote and produced in 1890 brought him enough money to pay the actors and all costs of production for two performances, including rentals of $100.00.[6] Often, however, the expenses were large, the attendance was small, and those in charge were lucky if they escaped without losses.

In the early 1880's, *Svenska Tribunen,* on which one must mainly rely for records of this period, gave the theatre only spasmodic attention. Personal and journalistic rivalries, or, perhaps, the rather haphazard management characteristic of the Swedish newspapers of the time may have been responsible. The attitudes expressed, however, continued to be encouraging: the public was urged to appreciate the values of the plays and the efforts of the actors to provide them with a Swedish theatre. And as the decade progressed, plays were more consistently and more fully reviewed.

Svenska Tribunen reviews were, it seems, generally written by Valdemar Torsell, who was the paper's locals editor for most of the 1880's, and was one of the personalities in a day of personalities. A witty, satirical young man, strikingly tall, and with overtones from a Boston stay making his elegant Stockholm manner even more imposing, Torsell was considered a first-rate newspaperman. He had the "true reportorial instinct," and engaged in many strange adventures to obtain news and feature stories. Coming from a family prominent in musical and theatrical circles in Sweden, he was known as an excellent music critic; his friend Ernst Lindblom also credited him with translating American plays for the Chicago Swedish stage. *Tribunen's* caustic attacks on the plays on grounds of inadequate rehearsal, lack of talent, and vulgarity of language bear out Torsell's reputation for a style "peppered and salted" with wit. Usually, however, the wit was good humored and the reviews were appreciative.[7]

Of the people associated with the 1879 *Svenska Amatör Sällskap,* one, at least, is known to have acted earlier. This was Anna Hagström, who had married W. Oscar Lundgren, manager of the company. Ernst Lindblom wrote of her in terms of glowing praise: with her adorable appearance, her splendid voice, and her genuine inspiration, she might have adorned the stages of Stockholm's leading theatres. In the soubrette roles that were her forte, she seemed a worthy successor to Anna de Wahl, mother of the famed actor, Anders de Wahl. Anna Hagström had, before she married, intended to return to Sweden for a stage career. She died after some two years of marriage, to the great loss of the Chicago plays. Her mantle was inherited, wrote Lindblom, by Erika Hopp, wife of Hjalmar Hopp, and the one actress of merit to appear in the plays for a number of years.[8] Both Mr. and Mrs. Hopp continued their acting over a considerable period, and have been remembered as able and well liked. Mr. Lundgren was the manager of the *Svenska Amatör Sällskap* for two seasons, and then disappears from the theatrical records. The company treasurer for these seasons was Herman Hagström, a young man in his twenties who had been in Chicago since 1872. Both he and a Mr. A. Hagström who appeared with him became successful business men. Praised in a performance of *Andersson, Pettersson och Lundström* was a Mr. Strömberg who took the Lundström role, and it is possible he was the man who had acted with Fahlbeck before 1870. But nothing more is heard of him, or of a Miss Strömberg who was mentioned as acting upon occasion. Long well known in theatrical circles, on the other hand, was *Svenska Amatör Sällskap* actor Knut Lindstrom. Not until 1889, when he became the proprietor of a popular Clark Street hotel and restaurant, the Viking, did he cease his active participation in the plays.[9]

Regissör (director) and a leading actor of the *Svenska Amatör Sällskap* in the fall of 1879 was young Fritz Schoultz, sometimes called von Schoultz—now first heard of in connection with the Swedish theatre of Chicago, but destined to play an important part in its development. Through the 1880's he continued as a prominent actor and director, and in the decades that followed he was an indispensable supporter of Swedish theatrical enterprises.

Early in the 1880's Schoultz was joined in his theatrical activities by

Gustaf Wicklund and Christopher Brusell, and these three were the moving spirits of the *Svenska Dramatiska Sällskap* that emerged in 1885. In the spring of 1888, Carl and Anna Pfeil became a part of that group and quickly assumed positions of leadership. All of these leaders from the 1880's were, in varying degrees and ways, significant in the continuing history of the theatre. The careers of a number of the supporting actors also carried on into later years. Members of the *Svenska Dramatiska Sällskap* now appeared not only in company productions, but in performances initiated by visiting Swedish actors and in scattered plays under other auspices. Progress of Chicago's Swedish theatre was not steady, but the developing continuity was an important asset in its growing achievement and reputation.

The men most actively associated with the theatre in these years were not typical immigrants but remarkable examples of the fact that there were a good many immigrants who were not typical. It was the lesser figures who were the most Bohemian, but Schoultz, Wicklund, and Brusell belonged to the Bohemia of Chicago's Swedish colony in so far as their interests and their struggles to become established were concerned; and, like the more erratic Bohemians, Schoultz and Wicklund were men about whom legends gathered.

Certainly the facts of Schoultz's life lend themselves to legend. A lover of the theatre and of art throughout his life, he became also a highly successful business man—in a field closely related to his chief interests. The theatrical costume company that he and his wife began in 1888 developed into one of the largest in the country, with a clientele including prominent New York dramatic companies. Its success enabled Schoultz to become a collector and patron of the arts, and a leader and benefactor in many Swedish enterprises. His hospitable home was a "temple of art," filled with books, paintings, and objets d'art gathered in part during several European trips, which furthered both his business and aesthetic interests. As the responsibilities of his business increased, he gave up direct activity in the Swedish theatre, but he continued to give support. The high standards in settings and costuming, particularly in historical plays, that the theatre was able to maintain were largely due to his generous terms and cooperation.

Schoultz was born in Copenhagen, December 2, 1856, and was sometimes regarded as a Dane, but his mother was descended from an old French emigré family, and his father seems to have been of German and Swedish ancestry. He grew up in Stockholm, and there his interest in the

46

theatre developed, and he became a pupil in the successful children's theatre of Anders Selinder, a well known actor and ballet master. At twenty Schoultz came to America, and found work of the kind he had done in Sweden, in newspapers and printing offices. After stays in Moline, Illinois, and Salina, Kansas, he settled in Chicago, probably at about the time he began acting there, and worked at various jobs, on newspapers and at the Field, Leiter store. He did not have much money, his friends later recalled, but the initiative that was to mark his career was evident, and he always had connections through which he could secure things at wholesale. He was able to make a trip to Europe in the summer of 1882, and while there rejected an opportunity for a theatrical engagement in Denmark.[10] It was some time after his return that he married Emelia Veth, an actress with a German stock company in Chicago, who shared his interests and was of great assistance to him in the business which they shortly established, and which has continued under his name also since his death in 1931.[11]

The youthful Schoultz was a collector—and a prankster. He was, in spite of his youth, totally bald, even without eyebrows, as the result of illness and quack doctoring, and he wore a dark, curly wig. More than once when friends who were visiting him were examining his curios they were startled by the sudden apparition of a pale skull-like face atop a long, slender, draped figure. To their further amazement, the face seemed to be alive. Gradually, the visitors realized that the apparition was their host, who, with the help of a little powder and some props, had given them a dramatic revelation of his baldness. Dime museums, he confessed, had offered him a livelihood as a freak. Wicklund, one of the men thus entertained, later countered with verses celebrating Schoultz's bald head as offering ample room for laurels.[12]

Of this early group, it was Wicklund who was most closely associated with Schoultz, a friendship maintained also in the years when Wicklund lived in Minneapolis. Like Schoultz, Wicklund had acquired his love of the theatre during his early years in Sweden. He was born at Gifle, in 1852, and lived as a young man in Upsala and Stockholm, where he moved in literary and theatrical circles. From 1879, when he came to the United States, until 1882, he found opportunities only in farming, bookkeeping, and tailoring, but, as he says in an amusing semi-autobiographical poem entitled *So near—and yet so far,* "from pressing iron and needle to the press he went."[13] His first newspaper position was with *Svenska Amerikanaren,* from which he went to *Kurre,* a humorous periodical which he and Ninian Wærner edited from 1884 to 1887.

In January 1888 *Kurre* became a weekly newspaper, *Svenska Kuriren,* with a political bent; two months later Wicklund's association with it ended, and he left Chicago for Minneapolis. It was the Swedish theatre that took Wicklund to Minneapolis, he himself has explained. "Fritz Schoultz was getting together a theatre company with which he meant to invade the North West. Now I had gone off and married at Christmas, with the expectation of getting the great sum of $200.00 back pay due from my employers. My family was starving; so was Ninian's. My wife and I therefore took engagements. We played in Moline, St. Paul, and Minneapolis, Red Wing, etc., for full houses, ate well, lived at $2.00 hotels, and each got $15.00 a week. [In Minneapolis] I succeeded in winning the interest of *Svenska Folkets Tidning,* so they hired me, though strictly speaking they did not need me."[14]

In 1893 Wicklund was again in Chicago, where for five years he successfully edited another humorous periodical, *Humoristen,* and then spent two years with *Svenska Tribunen.* For the last five years of his life he was the editor of *Svenska Amerikanska Posten* in Minneapolis, where he died in 1905.

Though Wicklund acted and headed acting groups in the 1880's, his chief contribution to the Swedish theatre was in the plays he wrote and translated. He is the one figure in that theatre who can be considered a playwright. A handful of comedies at the beginning of his connection with the theatre, an admirable translation of *Pinafore* that was one of the real successes of the Chicago Swedish stage,[15] a translation of *Lilla helgonet* (*Mam'zelle Nitouche*), and an original comedy about Bellman, *En afton på "Tre Byttor,"* published in Sweden and played in Stockholm as well as in Chicago, earned Wicklund the title of the Hodell of the American Swedish theatre. Unfortunately, many of his papers were lost in a fire at the *Svenska Amerikanska Posten* building, but manuscripts of his translation of *Pinafore* and a piece of dramatic hackwork survive. A collection of his verse, both humorous and serious, *Gnistor från rimsmedjan* (Sparks from the rhymer's forge), published after his death, contains some of the verses from his dramatic sketches and some of the occasional verses with which he refurbished such familiar plays as *Andersson, Pettersson och Lundström.* Wicklund was a leader in musical organizations both in Chicago and Minneapolis, and in Minneapolis he and his wife continued their participation in Swedish theatricals. He was without question one of the best liked and most admired, as well as one of the most talented of the Swedish journalists and men of the theatre. Genial and modest as well as witty and gay, he was a loyal friend to those who were less stable than he.[16]

Christopher Brusell made his Chicago debut in Wicklund's early comedies, and soon, by reason of his interest, his ability as an actor, and his excellent voice, became a prominent member of the theatrical circle. His most significant contribution to the Swedish theatre, however, was made in later decades, after an absence in Racine, Wisconsin, from 1888 to 1892. Brusell, like Schoultz and Wicklund, had brought with him from Sweden his interest in the theatre. He grew up in Stockholm, where he was born July 26, 1861, his father the prosperous owner of the Kungsholm brewery. The failure of that business interrupted his education and his studies with Anders Willman, a prominent singer at the Royal Opera, and sent him to work in a mercantile house. Only his mother's disapproval prevented young Christopher Brusell from attempting a stage career in Sweden, and soon after coming to Chicago in 1882 he turned to the amateur stage. To make his living, he worked as foreman and factory manager in a number of clothing and cleaning establishments and in office positions with the Marshall Field Company. Except for the Wisconsin interval and a visit to Sweden in 1904, Brusell remained in Chicago until 1922. Then for a time he lived in St. Paul, Minnesota, with his daughter and her husband (also long prominent in the Chicago Swedish plays). In this period of absence, however, he acted in Chicago, and he returned to Chicago before his death in 1925. Though he was well known as a singer and was interested in varied social groups, the stage was the focus of his life. His position in the 20th century Chicago Swedish theatre, as director, head of dramatic companies, and actor was unrivalled except by that of Ernst H. Behmer, with whom, from the late 1890's, he was intermittently associated.[17]

Lines by Gus Higgins—artist, actor, singer, and sometime versifier—express the philosophy of a circle that furnished a number of actors to the Chicago Swedish stage of the 1880's and 1890s.

> I live and have fun,
> I thrive best in the sun,
> I find joy without bounds
> In a life without system.
> But respectable persons
> Shrug their shoulders and think
> That cannot be happiness,
> And brand me "Bohème."[18]

49

Of all those who earned the reputation, none were so determinedly and joyously Bohemian as Higgins himself and his inseparable fellow-actor, Ville Åkerberg; and none were the subject of more tales bearing witness to their gifts and escapades. Typical is the account of Åkerberg, "bankrupt of all but his good nature," earning a few dollars by writing a wedding poem, and spending it all on a pair of elegant patent leather shoes.

Ville Åkerberg was, like Magnus Elmblad, a poet and journalist, and, like Elmblad, he came from an excellent family.[19] But, again and again, he turned his back on opportunities in Sweden. He interrupted studies at the University of Upsala to come to Chicago in 1885. Twice he returned to Sweden to obtain inheritances, which quickly vanished, and during an 1891 visit he briefly published a humorous magazine, *Utkiken* (The lookout) in Stockholm. It was after this that he and Higgins published in Chicago their humorous magazine, *Söndags-Nisse* (Sunday-Brownie), which ceased with the death of Åkerberg in 1894. His death at twenty-nine was not surprising, wrote *Svenska Kuriren;* his was a happy child-like nature, doomed to go under in life's sea. His weaknesses were as marked as his gifts, but one could not stay angry with him.

Åkerberg had in his earlier Chicago period worked for *Svenska Kuriren,* and he had also served as editor of *Humoristen* for a year. Poetry— sentimental, witty, and Anacreontic—was his true forte, but he also wrote a variety of prose, with particular success in descriptions of Swedish nature scenes. For the Swedish stage of Chicago he wrote *Nationaldagen, eller Den importerade älskaren* (The national holiday, or The imported lover), and he was a popular actor throughout his years in Chicago.[20]

Gus Higgins was unique among the Chicago Swedes, and not only for the Irish name he made famous (the story of how Gustaf Lindstrom became Gus Higgins he told in a dozen different ways).[21] He was a gifted and successful artist—an artist "from head to foot," said *Broder Lustig* in 1896, rhapsodizing about his "shaggy hair, broad forehead, and sparkling eyes, his pincenez and flowing tie, his mouth ever ready to break into a smile."[22] But he was also "Professor Gus Higgins . . . poet, verse singer, actor, editor, fun-maker, Bellman admirer, and Bacchi devotee, one of the most genial and incorrigible sons of Stockholm ever met in our petty everyday and crassly materialistic milieu." He was spendthrift of his talents and of his money, indulging his tastes for both works of arts and dissipation. The only time Higgins was concerned about money, an acquaintance recalled, was when $48.00 in payment for drawings for the special 1893 World's Fair issue of *Svenska Amerikanaren* was given him so late at night that he had to wait until morning to spend it.[23]

Higgins was the son of a clergyman who encouraged his artistic development by taking him on a tour of Germany and by providing lessons with a well known Stockholm teacher. But dreams of a free life in primitive surroundings brought the restless lad of sixteen to Chicago in 1879. He was quickly disillusioned, but he secured work with an engraving company, mastered English, and before long had become a successful cartoonist and illustrator for various American newspapers—the *Journal, Graphic, Inter-Ocean, Globe, and Tribune.* Studies under Philippoteaux, painter of battle pieces, led to a good deal of work in the grand manner. Satire and caricature were, however, his particular bent—and one that got him into difficulty on occasion, as when a picture of an army major trying to ride a wild foal with the help of a pair of crutches led to his dismissal by the *Tribune.*

It was the limitation of opportunities in the newspaper field after the development of photographic processes that made Higgins active in the Swedish circles of Chicago. By the late 1880's and 1890's few of the newspapers, almanacs, collections of folk songs and of fiction that were being published by Swedish companies there were without their *gubbar* (old fellows, types) by Higgins, or his sketches of local scenes and scenes from Swedish life and history. He illustrated, of course, the periodicals he and Åkerberg published, and wrote for them as well. His artistic output included portraits, altar pieces—and murals for the North Side saloons. Not only temperament, but a too facile and versatile talent prevented the significant career of which he was believed capable. And the death of Ville Åkerberg, it was said, was a blow that crushed any remaining serious ambition, though a third friend who had shared their notoriety became his companion until he, too, died, in 1897. The last few years before Higgins died in 1909 he spent in McKeesport, Pennsylvania, where friends among the Good Templars helped him to a more steady life.[24] That he lived to be forty-six was proof of his good constitution, said a frank obituary notice.[25]

In the Swedish theatre Higgins was known as an excellent comedian and as a painter of scenery, and he also wrote a dramatic skit, *Sax, taylor på dekis* (Scissors, tailor on the downward path). Often he beguiled the audience during the long waits between acts with his "specialties"—a mixture of cartoons, music, and vaudeville entertainment—and with the songs of Bellman. Higgins had lived in the section of Stockholm associated with the 18th century poet, song writer, wit, and celebrator of Bacchus, Carl Michael Bellman, who was the patron saint of this theatrical group as a whole. And Higgins was Bellman risen from the dead, said his friends, ranking him with the best of the Bellman singers in Sweden.[26] None of the tales associated with his name is more amusing than that told by Lindblom of Higgins commandeering an express wagon to carry them off to Chinatown, where the artist entertained his baffled but courteous Chinese friends by singing Bellman songs and representing Bellman as the Swedish Confucius.[27]

Of the men associated with the Chicago Swedish plays who came to America "with two empty hands and book learning" Otto Pallin had, perhaps, the most variegated career. "I have been concert singer, grocery clerk, bartender, actor, and cook," he wrote. "For several years it seemed I was born under the sign of the Ram, and pursued by misfortune whenever I managed to get a foothold in any of the various fields I entered. But I suppose the Norns willed that after I had won experience and knowledge of the world in labor's hard classes, I should at last find my rightful place in an editor's chair."[28] "Palle" might have added that he had served as pharmacist and emergency doctor in remote Indiana and Illinois communities, making use of the medical studies at Lund and Upsala universities that he had left to come to America. Varied newspaper experience also preceded his editorial position with *Svenska Kuriren* in 1888, a position to which he returned after further excursions into business, before his death in 1904. Otto Pallin was born in Karlstad, Värmland, in 1848, and was accounted a true son of that traditionally warm-hearted, romantic province. He was not only one of the most faithful and gifted of the actors, but was equally well known as a singer, being credited with bringing to life in Chicago Gunnar Wennerberg's famous student songs, *Gluntarne* (The school boys).[29]

Two other lively figures from the Swedish American press, Ninian Wærner and Ernst Lindblom, had shorter connections with the Chicago Swedish plays, both of them returning to Sweden for their main careers. Ninian Wærner was Wicklund's editorial associate during most of his stay in Chicago, from 1884 to 1890, and acted in plays of that period. Positions in Minneapolis and Denver preceded his return to Sweden in 1895, where he continued his editorial work, but gained recognition largely through the Artemus Ward type of humor in letters written under the pseudonym of C. A. Tollén. These letters and the sketches he wrote about his life in Swedish America, as well as memories of his Falstaffian figure and humor, kept his fame alive in the journalistic and theatrical circles that had known him.[30]

Ernst Lindblom, generally called *Limpan* (the loafer), was in Chicago from 1885 to 1894, writing successively for *Svenska Tribunen* and *Humoristen;* he then returned to Sweden, but was in Chicago for some months in 1896 and 1897, as representative for a Swedish exposition. He enjoyed his years in Chicago to the utmost, to judge by his *Svenska teaterminnen från Chicago* (Swedish theatre memories from Chicago), which he published in Sweden in 1916. The lapse of years between the events and the writing and his propensity for making the most of a story make his tales of theatrical figures and of the newspaper and entertainment world of that time suspect in detail, but, in spite of exaggerations, his general picture agrees with other accounts. Lindblom had a fluent pen and ready wit, and was an able journalist, said *Svenska Amerikanaren* at the time of his death in 1925, but he was erratic in temperament, and unsuited to routine work. In Sweden he was a correspondent for a number of press services and a versatile and prolific free lance journalist. For the Chicago Swedish theatre he wrote and produced two plays—the first and more successful, *Pelle Pihlqvists Amerika-resa* (journey to America), in 1891; the second, *Alderman Swanson,* in 1896.[31]

Less known—by reason of their more conventional conduct and pursuits—were a number of men who played regularly with the main acting groups during the 1880's. Prominent roles were frequently in the hands of Matt Ovington, whose tall, lanky figure was a particular asset in comedy. There is no clue as to his Chicago occupation, but in later years he worked as a makeup man in Hollywood.[32] Fred Littche, a successful artist for engraving firms, began acting soon after he came to Chicago in 1882, and was a reliable performer also in the next decade.[33] (Another artist—and cabinet maker—Axel Lundgren of Pullman, headed a single theatrical venture in 1884.)[34] A mainstay of the early Schoultz-Wicklund group who acted until 1899 was Gunnar Sahlin, a business man. He was, Mrs. Wicklund recalls, both talented and handsome. Albin Smith, too, was a public favorite, and the loss of his talents was lamented when he died in 1892, en route to Sweden for his health, at the age of twenty-seven.[35]

The late 1880's brought to the Chicago Swedish theatre not only Carl and Anna Pfeil, but two men who, if less prominent, nevertheless contributed much to its popularity. Ernst Schycker was to have one of the longest careers in that theatre, continuing as a leading comedian until a few years before his death in 1922. He was thirty-two and had won some recognition as a singer in Sweden when he came to Chicago in 1888; and he had theatrical connections in Sweden through his brother, Birger Schyc-

53

ker, later a well known actor. For a living, Ernst Schycker managed and owned a series of restaurants and hotels, but with a lack of financial success for which his generosity to his friends was held responsible.[36] The acting career of Max Hedman (Carl Maximus Hedman) was more limited, but for well over a decade he found much favor in young hero and singing roles. Like Fritz Schoultz, he was to make an outstanding business success, and, like Schoultz also, he retained his earlier interests, looking back with pleasure to his acting days and continuing active in the Swedish Glee Club. His education in technical institutes in Stockholm and Copenhagen stood the young Hedman in good stead in Chicago, where, after success in several positions with electric companies, he climaxed a series of independent enterprises with a company established in 1913 to manufacture a check writer of his invention. One of the foremost businesses of its kind, it continued under the presidency of his son after Mr. Hedman's death in 1924.[37]

Carl and Anna Pfeil's thirty years of joint activity give them a place in the annals of the Swedish American theatre that may safely be called unique. From New York to Seattle and in Canada as well they acted in Swedish plays. Their period of Chicago leadership, which began soon after their arrival in the spring of 1888, continued until after the turn of the century. During these years and later they gave Swedish performances in various Middle Western centers, and they had some engagements with American companies. Mrs. Pfeil's difficulty with English, however, kept them mainly on the Swedish stage. By 1905 they had settled in Seattle; and there Mrs. Pfeil left her retirement in 1911 to act for the 500th time her most popular role, that of Anna, the heroine of *Vermländingarne*.[38] It was Anna, also, that she came from Seattle to play in her last Chicago appearances, in 1908.

In 1871 the eighteen year old Carl Pfeil had made his first journey from Sweden to America, staying in the East, and acting with Swedish companies there. His professional debut, however, was made in Sweden—in 1875, if his 25th anniversary celebration in 1900 looked back to that event. Until he came again to America in 1885, he acted with provincial and touring companies in Sweden and Finland; he and Anna Åkerholm of Åbo, Finland, had married and begun their long theatrical partnership in 1883. Together they won a favorable reputation with Swedish companies in the Eastern states before coming to Chicago.

Always Mr. Pfeil devoted much of his energy to the theatrical and entertainment world—as singer, actor, promoter, and concocter of plays— but he, like his co-workers in the Swedish American theatre, had to support himself in other fields. His various occupations indicate his versatility: he was a printer, restaurant manager, travel agent, labor organizer, and inventor. In Chicago, he and Gus Higgins managed to publish three issues of *Teater-Nisse* before it succumbed.[39] Financial and temperamental difficulties made his career one of ups and downs, but shortly before his death in 1924 an invention had brought him prosperity.

His scientific bent often served him well in stage effects and entertainments, and it had been the means of one of his early successes. The incident—recalled after Carl Pfeil's death—occurred at Vasa, Finland. A new railroad was to be dedicated, and Pfeil, using the very limited materials available, almost miraculously devised an entertainment of free fireworks that was the chief feature of the celebration. Consequently the Schörling Dramatic Company became the Pfeil Company, and Pfeil won "much honor but little money." He was, the reminiscence concludes, a man who could get on with people of high and low estate, and every inch a gentleman. Written forty-three years after the event, the picture is one representative of Pfeil and his fortunes through those years.[40] And much honor but little money might, indeed, stand as the motto for other leaders of the Swedish Chicago stage as well, though honor, too, was sometimes scarce.

Carl Pfeil's roles ranged from historic Swedish monarchs to the farcical vagabonds of *Andersson, Pettersson och Lundström,* a type of comic role in which he was markedly successful. His wife also played a wide variety of parts. Singing roles were her particular forte, but whether she was the sentimental and pathetic Anna, a gamin, or a queen, she was a public favorite. She was the steadying force in their partnership, and, besides her talents, her loyalty to her husband in times of difficulty won her the admiration of her associates. Mrs. Pfeil died in 1933, at Whidby Island, Washington, in the home of her daughter, Betty Engström (Mrs. Alex Engström). Betty or "Little Anna" Pfeil acted with her parents in the West, and as a child was the pet of Chicago audiences, appearing in plays and in the musical and dramatic entertainments of the Pfeil Trio.[41]

Besides Mrs. Pfeil, two other women who were prominent in the plays of this period had acted professionally in Sweden: Mrs. Louise Nordgren and her sister, Mrs. Hanna Hvitfeldt. Mrs. Nordgren had been a member of Stockholm's popular *Södra Teater* company. Her Chicago career began in 1884 and ended only with her death in 1892. Mrs. Hvitfeldt was born Hanna Holmquist in 1849, and left her native Stockholm at the age of sixteen to play with the Rohde stock company in Göteborg. Engagements in Stockholm, with the Wiberg and Hjalmar Sjöberg companies, followed, and she was a favorite in ingenue and servant girl roles until her marriage to Robert Hvitfeldt. His death brought her and her three children to Chicago in 1888, and there she soon established herself as a principal interpreter of mother and *grande dame* roles. Soon afterwards Mrs. Hulda Feltskogh began to appear in similar roles. She continued to act until 1917, but in 1904 Mrs. Hvitfeldt's career, like that of her sister, was cut short by death.[42]

Mrs. Hvitfeldt's son Robert was one of many sons and daughters of actors who appeared in the Swedish plays. Romances, too, made the plays family affairs. Anna Almgren, popular ingenue of this period, married Matt Ovington; Anna Palmberg became Mrs. Christopher Brusell; Gustaf Wicklund and Amelie Peterson acted together before their marriage in 1887. Ottilie Mörk and Gustaf Myhrman had roles in a few plays. As Mrs. Othelia Myhrman she was to become widely known for her work as director of the employment bureau maintained by the *Svenska National Förbund*, and as a leader in the Good Templar movement. Though she did not continue to act, she was for years an energetic impressario for the Swedish plays, and one of the people most responsible for their success in the first decades of the 20th century. Anna Almgren Ovington was active in the Swedish theatre through the early 1890's, and is said to have acted professionally in Hollywood, but the other women appeared less frequently after marrying.

In general, Mrs. Pfeil was the only one of these actresses whose position was comparable to that of the men prominent in the Swedish theatre. Young American born Hilma Nelson, however, who played her first leading role in 1891, was destined for a brief period of stardom in Swedish plays sponsored by her father, and for a later career on the American and Scandinavian stages.

Visiting actors from Sweden were almost commonplace in later years, but a rarity in the 1880's. Otto Sandgren, a comedian from *Stora Teatern* of Göteborg, visited Chicago in 1887 and headed several popular productions. It is possible, also, that "actor A. Lindeberg," who sponsored a farewell performance in 1884, was a professional actor from Sweden.[43] Fredrik Hedlund, actor and director at Stockholm theatres, cut quite a swath in juvenile roles, according to Behmer's history, and Lindblom tells of Hedlund's presenting *Vermländingarne* to full houses when in Chicago as a member of the McCaull Opera Company. But available newspapers make no positive references to appearances by Hedlund, nor do they mention another Swedish actor, G. Collin, who, says Behmer, achieved a Chicago reputation in character roles during these years.[44]

No man associated for any length of time with the Chicago Swedish theatre had so long and varied a professional background as Albert Alberg, who came to Chicago in 1891. He was then fifty-two years old, and he had acted and directed companies in both England and Sweden, had written, translated, and adapted plays in Swedish and English, and had taught acting in England. Besides his theatrical activities, he had lectured, and written and translated books for young people.

At the age of twenty, Alberg had left his native Sweden and settled in Glasgow. Within seventeen months he had mastered English so well that he was able to lecture successfully and write for publication. He then studied acting, and in 1862 made his professional debut. Except for an engagement at the Royal Theatre of Stockholm in 1865 (where Othello was one of his roles), he continued in the English theatres until 1876. He had been disillusioned by the jealousies and rivalries of the Swedish stage and discouraged by Swedish preference for a more restrained style of acting than was popular in England, but he returned to Stockholm in 1876, and for three years maintained his own company at the Djurgården Theatre. Then, once again he returned to England, where he taught acting and wrote.[45] In 1889 he came to America, hoping to make money by readings and lectures, but was, he said, tricked by a dishonest impressario. It was after this experience that he came to Chicago. For a number of years he frequently served its Swedish theatre as actor and director, and contributed original and translated works to its repertoire. He acted at least once on the American stage, taking the role of a Texan at the People's Theatre in 1892,[46] and also produced Scandinavian plays in his English translations. More and more, however, he devoted himself to writing, a prophetic philosophic book absorbing much of his interest.

In 1905 Albert Alberg returned to Sweden, where he lived until his death in 1925. Near the end of his life, in the vain hope of securing a publisher for his philosophic book and other manuscripts, the old man issued a pamphlet, listing his writings and the facts of his theatrical career. He had, the pamphlet states, acted in England two hundred minor roles and seventy leading roles on twenty-five provincial and eleven London stages; in Sweden, fifteen roles; and in the United States, fifteen roles in Swedish. In all, he had staged fifty productions and acted in fifty-four theatres. The long list of plays in which he had a hand includes his original *The street Arab*, first played in Birmingham, in 1866; versions of *Vanity Fair* and

57

Deborah, acted in the United States and in Australia; and a number of translations and original works presented by Swedish groups in Chicago.

To conclude his pamphlet, Alberg described himself with words borrowed from *Hamlet*—"a man whom fortune's buffets and rewards has taken with equal thanks [*sic*]."[47] For many years there had been more buffets than rewards. As early as 1898 he had called upon "patient resignation" when he was unable to rejoin his family in England.[48] In Chicago he was unquestionably a valuable asset to the Swedish theatre, and he was much admired for his aristocratic bearing, his majestic Oscar II appearance, and his gentle, poetic nature; but he was not, in spite of his experience and reputation, uniformly successful as actor and director.[49]

Gradually, with the increase in acting ranks, came expansion of theatrical seasons and more extensive and varied repertoire. The productions of the *Svenska Amatör Sällskap,* begun in 1879, never exceeded three or four plays a season, but there were five or six plays in the mid-80 seasons, and in 1888-1889 a record number of fourteen productions was reached. That record was not always maintained in the following seasons, but it was generally exceeded. In the thirteen seasons from 1878-1879 through 1890-1891, plays were certainly given on seventy occasions, and a total of at least fifty-five plays was presented.[50] One-act comedies of the type given earlier were still much played, but they were being relegated to lodge or club festivities, and there were only fourteen programs made up of more than one play. With increasing frequency the dramatic companies were turning to full length plays for their main productions.

Varied types of comedy dominated the repertoire, but an expanding Swedish stage brought new prominence to the folk play and historical drama, with repetitions of *Engelbrekt och hans Dalkarlar* and *En midsommarnatt i Dalarne,* and Chicago premières of plays destined for long histories. A. F. Dahlgren's *Vermländingarne* was introduced and began to establish itself as a favorite in this period. But with five performances it could not yet match Hodell's *Andersson, Pettersson och Lundström,* played nine times in these thirteen seasons. Far behind them in total number of performances throughout the years, but *Vermländingarne's* closest rival of the folk play type, was Axel Anrep's *Nerkingarne,* given in 1888 the first of its twenty-one Chicago performances. These years also brought to Chicago a well known folk play by Frans Hedberg, *Valborgsmesso-aftonen,* and two of the most notable examples of the Swedish historical drama before Strindberg: Hedberg's *Bröllopet på Ulfåsa* and Topelius's *Regina von Emmeritz. Bröl-*

lopet på Ulfåsa was given twelve performances in Chicago, the last in 1922, and the Topelius play was acted eight times, last in 1927.

The dramatists responsible for the most popular repertoire in Sweden in the preceding decades were still those most acted in Chicago, with Blanche, Hedberg, and Hodell furnishing the largest number of plays. New to Chicago were three famous Blanche comedies: *Ett resande teatersällskap, Hittebarnet,* and *Herr Dardanell och hans upptåg på landet.* Blanche was also represented by a type of play not before part of the local Swedish theatre, his dramatization of his sensational and sentimental novel, *Jernbäraren.* Two comedies by Hedberg and seven by Hodell were added to the repertoire, among them Hedberg's *Det skadar inte!* (It does no harm) and Hodell's *En brottslig betjent* (A guilty servant), which were to be staple entertainment for many years.

Despite their reliance on these and other plays from the standard Swedish repertoire of earlier years, the Chicago actors were beginning to offer their audiences plays that were more recent and that represented newer trends—a development for which the Pfeils and Alberg were largely responsible. A popular comedy from the German that was also a feature of later seasons, *Sabinskornas bortröfvande* (The rape of the Sabine women), was seen in Chicago within a few years of its Swedish première. The spectacular Jules Verne *Jorden rundt på 80 dagar* (Round the world in 80 days), a Swedish success in the 1870's, was a popular departure from the usual repertoire. And the operetta fashion that developed in Sweden in the 1860's was reflected in *Drilléns operett* (Drillén's operetta) and *Den lilla sångfågeln* (The little song bird).

Older musical pieces provided variety also: Von Weber's *Preciosa,* and one of the Bellman skits of which the Chicago audiences were always fond, *Ulla skall på bal* (Ulla is going to the dance). *Hamlet* was attempted —one of two Shakespeare plays acted in Swedish in Chicago. More to the popular taste were comedies by the Chicago journalists and actors. Not until the 1930's were local authors again responsible for so large a proportion of the repertoire.

1878-1879

The *Svenska Amatör Sällskap* made its first appearance in January 1879 with *Andersson, Pettersson och Lundström.* It proved a wise choice, drawing an attendance of nearly 900. Critics shared the audience enthusiasm they reported: even in Sweden, the Lundström of Strömberg could hardly be equalled, and *da capo* was the general sentiment. A repeti-

59

CAMROSE LUTHERAN COLLEGE
LIBRARY

tion "by general request" was equally successful.[51] A somewhat smaller house greeted Blanche's *Herr Dardanell och hans upptåg på landet,* the novelty offered by the society as its third and closing performance of the season, and the actors were hampered by the collapse of some scenery. But, as on several later occasions, the audience enjoyed the involved and farcical adventures of Herr Dardanell and Baron Lejonkula in their rival efforts on behalf of the play's young lovers; and Mrs. Fox, a middle-aged widow, and her stupid son Agapetus were considered particularly comic.[52]

1879-1880

Announcements of several plays in rehearsal and general encouragement by the press heralded the second season of the *Svenska Amatör Sällskap,*[53] but again there were but three performances. *Rochus Pumpernickel,* the opening play, was, however, taken to Moline in February. A small but enthusiastic audience saw the old comedy in Chicago, and the newspapers took the occasion to warn the public that lack of support might deprive them of entertainment that, with such talented actors, should be an "ornament to our nation in Chicago." There should be appreciation for a group of young people who, after the day's hard work, devote themselves to "this noble art."[54] But the papers themselves were to neglect these efforts through the rest of the season, except in connection with the journey to Moline. A lively account of the Moline performance provides the first cast for a play given by the Chicago Swedes and permits identification of the actors who had been approved when it was presented in Chicago. Anna Hagström Lundgren played Babette, undoubtedly a soubrette role, and Hjalmar and Erika Hopp were a Herr von Berthal and his daughter. And now for the first time Fritz Schoultz was named in an account of the Swedish plays, winning high praise for his success as director and for an excellent performance as Rochus Pumpernickel, the son of a wealthy squire.[55]

From February 1880 until the fall of 1881 there seem to have been no Swedish performances, but in September 1880 *Andersson, Pettersson och Lundström* was acted in Chicago in an English translation, an event not known to have been duplicated, and interesting in a number of ways. The translation was made by Mrs. Louise Thieleman, "aged widow of the late Colonel Thieleman," and part owner of the Thieleman Theatre on Clybourne Avenue; and the play was produced "with no expense spared" by her son Milo, head of the Thieleman Novelty Company, for a week's performance at the Olympic Theatre. Besides Milo Thieleman, the company included Alfred Johnson, the Swedish born Chicago actor who had appeared earlier in a Swedish entertainment; and Roland Reed, popular actor of the American stage, now remembered also as the father of actress Florence Reed, had one of the leading roles.[56]

1881-1882

When the resumption of Swedish theatricals was announced the following fall, the Chicago Swedish papers were already complaining that *Andersson, Pettersson och Lundström* was gray-bearded and *ausgespielt,* and were demanding novelties.[57] The comedies that were presented at the four performances of the 1881-1882 season were new to Chicago at least, and one of them, the one-act *De båda döfva* (The two deaf ones), was to remain popular. The main feature of the season was Blanche's *Ett resande teatersällskap.* Though a reworking of a French adaptation of Scarron's *Le roman comique,* it had the genuinely Swedish characteristics of all Blanche's comedies, and it has often been suggested that there were Swedish originals for the two leading characters, the bombastic theatre director, Sjövall, and the "half genius, half idiot" actor, Ölander. Wicklund made his debut as an actor as Ölander, according to Lindblom. *Svenska Tribunen* reported a masterly performance by Schoultz as Sjövall, but named no other actors. Schoultz was long remembered in the role, but the play was given in Chicago only once more, in a minor production.[58] The company for all four performances was made up in part of *Svenska Amatör Sällskap* members, and for the spring plays used the company name.

1882-1883

In February 1882 the *Svenska Amatör Sällskap* had given a benefit for Schoultz, in honor of his forthcoming trip to Europe. His return in September was hailed as the signal for renewed theatrical activities,[59] but he did not act in the two plays that made up the 1882-1883 season. They were presented by the *Nordstjernan* and *Sjustjernan* societies, whose talented young members naturally turned to dramatic entertainment. One of them, Gustaf Wicklund, was making his debut as an author with *En överraskning* (A surprise) and *Vår förening* (Our society). Christopher Brusell and Otto Pallin were seemingly beginning their acting careers, and Wicklund himself and Knut Lindstrom of the *Svenska Amatör Sällskap* were among the actors. Chicago success was followed by a February performance of *En överraskning* in Moline, which provided a gay outing,[60] and a third Wicklund play, acted by a company under his direction, opened the 1883-1884 season.

Characters and situations typical of Chicago Swedish life were the materials of these plays, as they were for the majority of those locally written. Few later plays, however, rivalled Wicklund's in wit and imagination. The surprise parties and societies that loomed large in the social life of the growing colony provided starting points for amusing satire: in *En överraskning,* satire of the present menial positions of men of rank and professional success in Sweden, with characters ranging from prize fighters and coachmen to a misunderstood poet and Lundström of *Andersson, Pettersson och Lundström;* and in *Vår förening,* satire of the rivalries and projects of a club of newspapermen and artists.[61]

1883-1884

Wicklund's third work was more elaborate and fantastic, being divided into "four agonies and a catastrophe." The catastrophe of *Kronjuvelerna på Nordsidan* (The crown jewels on the North Side) was a masked ball at which the immigrant types—tailor, book agent, Kansas farmer, painter of frescoes, all with names beginning with K and therefore O.K.— were metamorphosed into Mephistopheles, the admiral from *Pinafore,* Mother Hubbard, and other illustrious and non-Swedish characters. For this momentous event, advance publicity announced that Matthew Arnold, El Mahdi, Egypt's false prophet, a Chinese field marshal, and the Swedish playwright, Frans Hodell, had taken a box incognito. Schoultz returned to the Swedish plays in his friend Wicklund's production, and Lindstrom and Brusell were prominent in the cast. An audience of 1,200 was naturally delighted with a play about a masquerade, a favorite type of diversion among the Chicago Swedes. Author and actors were showered with applause, laurel wreaths, and flowers. A review pronounced *Kronjuvelerna på Nordsidan* witty, well acted, and splendidly costumed; and photographs from the play suggest an elaborate and amusing performance.[62]

The orchestra director for this play, and on many other occasions, was Emil Becker. He had held a similar position at *Södra Teatern,* Stockholm, and now found congenial companions in Chicago, though not at all times suitable professional opportunities.[63]

The 1883-1884 season was, in general, one of individual enterprises. *Ett sätt att fria* (A way of wooing), an occasional skit by L. Drowtey, an otherwise unidentified Chicago man, was performed. Actor A. Lindeberg produced Hodell's *Syfröknarna* (The seamstresses)—folk scenes in seven tableaux, with, as often, a song written in Chicago. On this occasion it was supplied by J. B... n, undoubtedly the well known newspaper man and

★ NORDSTJERNAN ★

→← GIFVER →←

Lördagen d. 1:sta Maj, 1886,

Å Central Hall, 22d Street & Wabash Ave.,

★ ★ ★ STOR ★ ★ ★

MAJ-FEST!

→←PROGRAM:→←

I.

1. FESTMARCH..Nordstjernans Musikkår

2. FESTTAL...F. A. Lindstrand

3. ARIA ur "DEN ONDES BESEGRARE".................... * * *
   Herr Otto Pallin.

4. POTPOURRI, O, Fair Dove! O, Fond Dove!................... * * *
   Fröken Carlström, Herr Nyström och Mr. Tapp.

5. "EN SOMMARQVÄLL"..S. R. Thomas
   Herr C. Brusell.

6. MUSIKNUMMER...Nordstjernans Musikkår

7. ROMANS (duett för 2 Barytoner)...................................Mendelsohn
   Herrar Pallin och Brusell.

8. SOLO SÅNG..
   Fröken Annie Carlström, accompagnerad af O. H. Olofson.

→← 5 MINUTERS PAUS. →←

II.

"PÅ FÖRSTA MAJ."

Tillfällighetsskämt med Kupletter i en akt,

AF
GUST. WICKLUND.

HALLMAN, gammal enkling...............................spelas af Herr Fritz Schultz

ANNIE, hans dotter...Fröken A. Peterson

SHARP (Hallmans boardare) Liktornsoperatör (Corn Doctor)......Herr Otto Pallin

KALLE FRISK, Handelsexpedit...Herr C. Brusell

Handlingen försiggår i Hallmans hem å Wentworth Ave., Chicago.

Denna pjes uppföres för första och sista gången i afton.

Derefter STOR BAL!

Dörrarna öppnas klockan 7.   Festen börjar klockan 8.

Christopher Brusell as Mefistopheles from *Faust* in Masked Ball, *Kronjuvelerna på Nord-sidan*, December 16, 1883, North Side Turner Hall

Matt Ovington ir an unidentified role

poet, Jakob Bonggren. Adequately rehearsed, and with a cast of experienced favorites, Lindeberg's "long-awaited *soirée*" was well received.[64] And Brusell took a step forward in his theatrical career when he concluded the season with the Chicago première of *Hittebarnet,* the comedy by Blanche most frequently acted in Chicago. Konjander, the gay, middle-aged bachelor who discovers a foundling on his bed, is generally considered Blanche's most popular creation, and the play has had a long history in Sweden. A succession of adventures involving Konjander's neighbours and their family skeletons ends happily with the identification of the baby as the son of his dead nephew; and a merry christening party, complete, of course, with songs, concludes the play. In Brusell's production, Knut Lindstrom as Konjander was supported by Schoultz and Wicklund, and as Konjander's housekeeper Mrs. Louise Nordgren may have made her Chicago debut. Some 700 persons saw *Hittebarnet* played "as seldom in Europe, Asia, or America" *Svenska Tribunen* reported.[65]

1884-1885

The season that followed was, if not the longest or most impressive, one of the most remarkable in the history of the Chicago Swedish theatre. It began with the première of *Vermländingarne* in November 1884, and closed with a production of *Hamlet,* played by the actors who were to carry on in the fall of 1885 as the *Svenska Dramatiska Sällskap.* The season also included an amazing local play, and the first Chicago performance of Blanche's sentimental drama, *Jernbäraren.* Lindstrom and Mrs. Louise Nordgren headed the Blanche production, and Brusell made a strong impression in his first dramatic role, as Axelson, the noble iron bearer who murders the seducer of his daughter and ultimately gives himself up after her death.[66]

Much fanfare prepared the public for the *Vermländingarne* performance, and even with advanced prices and reserved seats at $1.00, 2,500 people strained the capacity of the North Side Turner Hall to welcome Sweden's most popular folk play. The management apologized for selling tickets to more people than the hall could accommodate, and promptly arranged to repeat the play in December.[67]

As *Vermländingarne* was played season after season through the following years, its every character, every episode and song and dance became familiar, anticipated, and the subject of comparison, favorable or unfavorable, with earlier presentations. Audiences were particularly fond of its songs, and of the folk dances that are a feature of the Midsummer festival early in the play and of the wedding celebration with which it closes. They probably enjoyed the comedy of the country servants, Stina and Per, as much as the romantic love story of the hero and heroine, Erik and Anna. And they had an unfortunate habit of laughing at the most pathetic scenes.

Vermländingarne tells a Romeo and Juliet type of story, but with a happy ending. Anna is the daughter of the poor cotter, Jan Hansson, who has antagonized the proud and wealthy farmer, Sven Ersson, by bearing witness against him in a matter of property in which Sven was in the wrong. Erik is Sven's son, and the love between him and Anna has developed in their childhood days together at the home of the leading man of the community, the *brukspatron* (proprietor of iron works), who has befriended them and educated them with his children, Wilhelm and Lotta. Sven Ersson is, of course, enraged by Erik's wish to marry the humble Anna, and at the height of the Midsummer festival at his home he announces the betrothal of Erik and Britta, the arrogant and shrewish daughter of another prosperous farmer, Ola i Gyllby. Erik rebels, and is sent away by his father, over the protests of the *brukspatron*.

One of the dramatic scenes that ensue occurs outside the rural church, after Sven has had the banns read for Erik and Britta. Anna falls in a swoon and immediately loses her mind; but Sven's heart remains hard, even when he is opposed by the *provst* (clergyman, dean). After some pathetic scenes picturing Anna's madness (in the Ophelia tradition), and the suffering of her parents, Jan and Annika, the climactic action develops. The *provst* yields to Anna's fancy and takes her out in a boat. Soon Erik appears and calls to her, and Anna, unconscious of danger, jumps out of the boat and into the water. Erik attempts to rescue her, and their lives are in peril long enough to permit the arrival and repentance of his father. The *brukspatron* is also near at hand, and it is he who rescues the lovers.

The fathers are, of course, reconciled, and the play ends on a note of happy romance, folk festival, and comedy. A popular character is introduced in the wedding scene, the old wanderer and teller of tall tales, Löpare-Nisse. In this scene, also, Erik and Anna sing the play's best known melody, *Vermlands Visa*. There have been songs earlier, by Erik and Anna, by Sven's servants, Stina and Per, by Anna's father, and by his loyal servant, the unselfish Anders, who loves and serves Anna even though she rejects him. Comedy is furnished chiefly by Per and Stina and by Löpare-Nisse, but Anna, too, is seen in playful mood early in the play, as she teases Anders about seeing the supernatural creatures of the country side—a preparation

64

for her later delusion that it was *Neckan,* the water spirit, that she was to marry, and that does not answer her call.

The 1884 *Vermländingarne* was not one of the many good productions given the play in Chicago. Axel Lundgren, the Pullman artist who produced it and undertook the role of Erik, was not a bad director, scenery painter, and ballet master, *Svenska Tribunen* admitted, but he was not an actor. The performance as a whole was neither smooth nor effective, though a number of minor roles were taken by experienced actors. Brusell, who eventually was seen in almost every male role of the play, was the *brukspatron;* Littche was Anders, and Ovington, Bengt på Åsen, a country fellow whose chief contribution is a dance. Ottilie Mörk was Stina, and Anna Palmberg, Lotte. The second performance showed some improvement. Miss Palmberg, who had then become Mrs. Brusell, played Lisa (Erik's mother), and Schoultz replaced Littche as Anders. And *Tribunen* noted approvingly that the dances were more lively and the coarse language not in the original play had been eliminated.[68]

Seldom was a Chicago Swedish play greeted with such harsh words as were used to describe *Allt för guld* (All for gold), acted May 9, 1885, and advertised as the work of A. B. Holson, "an intelligent young countryman." It was, said the irate *Tribunen* critic, an example of *Rudolf, or the Bloodbath of Sicily* school at its worst, a box on the ear for every intelligent, decent, right-thinking person, and, in all, the worst trash ever offered the Chicago Swedes.[69]

Strangely, the manuscript of *Allt för guld* was found among Gustaf Wicklund's papers, written in his hand. Mrs. Wicklund could not solve the mystery, but a solution is given in Ernst Lindblom's *Svenska teaterminnen från Chicago.* No doubt Lindblom embroidered the facts, but the manuscript of the play corresponds in general to his description of it—a typical sensation drama, set in Sweden, with a large Newfoundland dog and a six year old child in the principal roles. A. B. Holson was, Lindblom tells, the coachman of the prominent Swedish business man and civic leader, Robert Lindblom. But Holson had other ambitions.[70] He had evolved the plot of a play, and approached Wicklund with the proposition that he should write it out—not all the parts, necessarily, but fully enough so the actors could say the appropriate things. Wicklund refused, and tried to persuade the stage-struck coachman that the task was not so simple. Finally, however, when Holson offered a payment of $25.00, Wicklund accepted the offer, and spent a night writing *Allt för guld.*[71]

As a burlesque, *Allt för guld* is amusing, and there are a few scenes of local color which, though incongruous or irrelevant, suggest Wicklund's talents. One such scene is a conversation about the nobility of the Swedish peasant class that takes place, ironically, as little Maria Berg, daughter of the guests at a country Christmas celebration, is being kidnapped by another member of that class (seemingly she has been left at home to make the kidnapping possible). As a further incongruity, the celebration follows a scene in which Maria's father, expecting ill health to lead to an early death, has named as her future guardian the villain, Sjöberg, who kidnaps her in order that his son may later marry her and get her father's gold. A scene introducing a visitor from America, who brags of Chicago, its high water tower and the size of the Palmer House, offers typical local appeal. Lively but even less related to the plot is an episode depicting rough sailors at a sea-side saloon, their amorous conquests and yarns.

The main story is that of the child, Maria, and of the university student who loves her and who, after the passage of years, is accused of murder, flees, with her help, and is believed dead. Actually, he escapes to America, to return at last with a fortune, and to track down the murderer, an accomplice of the villainous Sjöberg. The student finally wins the hand of his faithful Maria, and she is reunited with her parents, who are still well and prosperous, but hardly deserve to regain their child, if we are to judge by their earlier feeble efforts to find her. In short, absurdity is piled on absurdity, sentiment on sentiment, and the clichés of melodrama prevail. Maria once manages to escape from her foster parents, a kind forester and his shrewish wife, but is next seen living with them, as if nothing had happened. Sjöberg's son, with democratic nobility, defies his father to marry the servant girl he loves. The villain forgives his son and kills himself. He has learned at last the folly of his motto, "All for gold." As to the dog, he is Maria's childhood pet, and in a second appearance comes dangerously near bringing about a premature reunion with her parents.

This time, surely, the reviewer was justified in his criticism, though the profanity and coarse language to which he raised objections are not a marked feature of the manuscript version. That Wicklund agreed with the reviewer as to the merits of *Allt för guld* cannot be doubted.

Lindblom is the dubious authority for the story that Holson was so encouraged by the plaudits of his lodge brothers that he undertook to back a performance of *Hamlet*. If we believe Lindblom, this was a disillusioning experience, for Holson found the play so dull that at one point he waved the actors aside and performed a jig, "to liven up the audience a bit." And he had to part with some of his horses to cover the costs.[72] Other tales of the performance have also, perhaps, grown with the years—of Ninian Wærner playing the ghost and punctuating the revelation of murder by spitting at regular intervals; of the slain Laertes being left outside the curtain, and crawling under it to join the other corpses, leaving his wig behind him. The grave-yard scene provided another amusing story. The lights went out, and the first clown, asking the second clown (Schoultz) where he was, was answered in sepulchral tones that reached the audience, "On the other side of the grave."[73]

Svenska Tribunen found little good to say for the first and only Swedish Hamlet in Chicago. The attempt itself was incomprehensible, and members of the audience who had not looked too deeply in their glasses recognized that this time the amateurs had ventured beyond their depth. The one exception was Brusell as Horatio; even under the unfavorable circumstances, his talent and his splendid voice made the role impressive. Poet Ville Åkerberg played Hamlet, and the reviewer admitted that he showed aptitude for the stage. Mrs. Wicklund remembers him as good, and her recollections as a whole suggest that the performance was better than these humorous and satirical accounts make it appear. Mrs. Brusell was Ophelia, and Ottilie Mörk, Queen Gertrude. Contradicting Lindblom's story of Holson's backing, the advertisements announced the play as by the Svenska Dramatiska Sällskap, for the benefit of its treasury. Schoultz was director and Wicklund manager of the company, now first named, that became the main source of Swedish plays the following season and assumed renewed importance later in the decade. Hamlet was but sparsely attended (perhaps because it was given on the South Side)[74] and cannot have brought the young society profits, even if Holson's horses were not sacrificed in the cause of art.[75]

1885-1886

For the 1885-1886 season, the Svenska Dramatiska Sällskap turned to time-tested Swedish comedy, with Andersson, Pettersson och Lundström and the folk play, En midsommarnatt i Dalarne, as their main productions. The pieces were said to have been splendidly costumed, and Pallin's Lundström was a great success; but critics objected, as they often objected later, to inappropriate dialects (expecting more than was reasonable, perhaps, of amateurs from varied provinces and cities of Sweden). Wicklund's new verses for Andersson, Pettersson och Lundström were very well received, and the Svenska Amerikanaren and Svenska Tribunen writers agreed that

67

only Schoultz and Wicklund were capable of achieving anything worthwhile in the Swedish theatre.[76]

Wicklund also returned to dramatic authorship this season, with a little sketch given, as the playbill said, its "first and last performance," at a *Nordstjernan* May Day festival. *På första Maj* (On the first of May) presented Schoultz in the role of an old widower who kept a boarding house on Wentworth Avenue. Amelie Peterson, later Mrs. Wicklund, was Annie, the widower's daughter, and the boarders were Shark, a corn doctor, played by Pallin, and Kalle Friks, a travelling man, played by Brusell.[77]

1886-1887

Not until the fall of 1888 was the *Svenska Dramatiska Sällskap* again active as a company, but its members presented a number of plays in the two intervening seasons. Schoultz's name was considered a guarantee of quality when he produced *Vermländingarne* in the fall of 1886,[78] but the newspapers gave little attention to it or to the second Chicago performance of *Engelbrekt och hans Dalkarlar* that opened the season. That same fall *En natt i Falkenberg, eller Min hustru* (A night in Falkenberg, or My wife), a characteristic one-act comedy much used by Chicago dramatic groups, was introduced by Schoultz and Wicklund in a performance for the Linnea Society. Its two characters, forced to share the same room at an inn, discover they have married the same shrewish wife. Each tries to pawn her off on the other until they learn she is dead and there is a question of inheritance, but they agree to share the money equally and celebrate this happy solution with the customary song.

The spring of 1887 was given over to three productions by Otto Sandgren of *Stora Teatern,* Göteborg, with him as the star. Familiar amateurs appeared with him, and his programs of comedies, mainly by Hodell, drew full houses, with a good representation of "the best element of the Swedish public." Not for long, *Svenska Tribunen* somewhat disloyally stated, had there been such an opportunity to see Swedish plays really well acted.[79] Lindblom called the fat and jovial Sandgren "the hippopotamus," and described with lively detail his first informal appearance before a Chicago public, when, as the guest of Lindblom and Valdemar Torsell of *Svenska Tribunen,* he sang for Irish policemen in an Irish saloon.[80]

1887-1888

The single production of the fall of 1887 was a lodge performance of von Weber's *Preciosa,* which was left unreviewed; but the new year

68

brought announcement of a new dramatic group with a new name, Figaro. Former *Svenska Dramatiska Sällskap* actors Pallin, Lindstrom, and Brusell were its most prominent members. Figaro appealed for the support of the stable, respectable Swedish public, assuring orderly conditions on the stage and in the audience, and promising to avoid the long intermissions and delays usual in North Side Turner Hall productions.[81] A masquerade given to raise money was followed by a moderately successful performance of Hedberg's *Det skadar inte!*[82] but one more play ended Figaro's history. The interests of the Chicago Swedes were at this time centering on the eventually successful efforts to raise funds for a statue of Linné, the eminent Swedish botanist, in Lincoln Park; and Figaro proposed to give a third production as a benefit for the project. But its director was unenthusiastic, and the actors, being afraid that they might be left "holding the bag," dropped the plan.[83] Brusell's moving to Racine, Wisconsin, in 1888 may have been a factor in the company's early demise. There had been praise for its second performance. The play, *Bror Jonathan,* was pretty thin stuff, said *Tribunen,* but Pallin was uproarious as the country visitor, and Mrs. Feltskogh (then new to the Chicago plays) excellent as his arrogant sister-in-law. This company, unlike another in the city, did not try to pull the audience by the nose.[84] The company so slightingly referred to may have been that with which Schoultz had appeared in a February performance of *Den ondes besegrare* (The devil's vanquisher). This originally Danish play about a young wife who thwarts the devil's efforts to make her husband jealous was to be well received on other occasions, but the Danish-Swedish company that introduced it in 1888 evidently gave a slovenly performance.[85]

In April 1888 Carl and Anna Pfeil came from New York, and made the first of their many Chicago appearances in an operetta and a Hodell comedy. Schoultz and Wicklund were in the supporting company, Wicklund contributing also some of his popular lyrics. The professional visitors lived up to their advance publicity, and *Svenska Tribunen* welcomed them with a "bravo," but devoted most of its review to an attack on the vulgarity evident both on the stage and in the audience. Profanity made the plays objectionable, and the children and the noisy beer-thirsty patrons of the bar were an insult to the actors. A September announcement that there would be no serving in the *salon* during the performance suggests that this blast did not go unnoticed.[86]

Majbruden, (The May bride), a second May Day piece by Wicklund, brought the 1887-1888 season to a close, Svithiod lodge members acting the skit as part of their holiday program. *Svenska Tribunen* credited it with

Wicklund's usual wit, and noted as a high point the comic song of the celebrants when, with empty tankards, they marched funereally around the May Pole.[87] Wicklund himself had left with Schoultz and the Pfeils, on the tour to Moline, Illinois, and Minnesota cities that was to take him to a position in Minneapolis and temporarily end his connection with the Chicago theatre. The tour brought the young actors the profits they needed, as well as much pleasure—$1,000.00 to be divided among them, Mrs. Wicklund remembers.[88]

1888-1889

The association of Pfeil and Schoultz continued in the fall with a revived *Svenska Dramatiska Sällskap* of which Schoultz was manager and Pfeil director. Their plan of fortnightly performances for which the North Side Turner Hall had been rented proved over ambitious, but with eleven productions by the company and two by the Pfeils independently, the 1888-1889 season was one of unprecedented activity.

The response to the *Svenska Dramatiska Sällskap* performances varied widely, both as to public support and critical appraisal. There was a good house for the opening play, *Preciosa,* and the review in *Svenska Tribunen* was laudatory. A smaller public at the October première of *En komedi* was blamed on a street car strike, but *Tribunen* gave high praise to Pfeil's interpretation of the famous role in which Johan Jolin had made his debut as both actor and playwright in 1845. As Kalle Wallin, the young university student who undertakes a variety of successful impersonations to win his father's approval of a stage career, Pfeil had an excellent opportunity to display his versatility. Perhaps it was a jibe at the reviewer inserted in the play by Pfeil that was responsible for the changed tone of the next review: Swedish actors would have broken out in a cold sweat if they could have seen how the "little pearl," *Drilléns operett,* was vivisected; and Pfeil, shabbily clad in all the colors of the rainbow, made Drillén, the Stockholm music teacher, a mere circus clown. Furthermore, if Emil Biorn's orchestra appeared again, it would be advisable for the management to follow the example of the Colorado mining camps, and post a sign asking the audience not to shoot the musicians, who were doing their best. Pfeil was moved to write in defense of the orchestra and of his own interpretation, which was, he said, in the best tradition of the Swedish stage.[89]

Such an exchange was, of course, good publicity. In general, as the season progressed, attendance increased, and the reviews, though sarcastic upon occasion, became more favorable. The reviewer's ire was aroused by the

70

substitution of new songs for old favorites and by the reference to a Chicago strike in the November production of Hedberg's *Det skadar inte!* "Let the play remain what it is, Swedish," he thundered.[90]

The audience, at least, was as ready to welcome the local as the authentically Swedish. Certainly it enjoyed Pfeil's own composition, *Chicago nattetid* (Chicago night time), a January offering, which *Svenska Tribunen* called a hodgepodge of incongruities, with the one good feature among its local skits and familiar dramatic fragments the excepts from Offenbach's *Prins Pippi och Fröken Fiffi* (Miss Fiffi).[91] This was one of three plays seen by Ernst Skarstedt, the eccentric, gifted journalist and author, during a visit to Chicago; and he, too, thoroughly enjoyed it—particularly the impersonation of three of his fellow journalists. Pfeil, as Snillén, was Ninian Wærner; Schoultz, as Pillén, was Otto Pallin; and most masterly of all was the elongated Ovington as Skålander—so like the *Svenska Tribunen* critic, Valdemar Torsell, that even Torsell's wife said the only noticeable difference was in the shades of their beards. Never, said Skarstedt, did he see anything funnier than when Ovington's long body shot up from the prompter's box to call out a direction to the actors or orchestra, and the puzzled audience looked from Ovington to the critic in the *salon,* trying to see which was which. Pfeil himself appeared in six roles, and Higgins made his public debut as a singer.[92]

One of Swedish Chicago's favorite folk plays, *Nerkingarne,* was well received when first acted in November, 1888. The prompter did not drown out the actors, *Svenska Tribunen* conceded; the country dances went smoothly, and were, of course, popular features of the Midsummer and harvest festivals that opened and concluded the play. In the comic role of the young suitor, Lasse, Pfeil distinguished himself; and Mrs. Pfeil was excellent as always as the romantic heroine, Ingeborg, whose identity as the daughter of the *brukspatron* instead of the apparently humble country girl provided a central thread of action. Her sweetheart, Sven, was played by one Hedlund, who tried to out-sing her.[93] A favorite role with which Ovington was long associated he created on this occasion, that of the lovesick old governess, Mamselle Bom; and he played it with a commendable absence of exaggeration, *Tribunen* noted appreciatively.[94]

The first Pfeil *Vermländingarne,* announced for November 18, was unaccountably neglected by *Svenska Tribunen,* but later references indicate that it was acted. Pfeil's first *Andersson, Pettersson och Lundström* was given as a New Year's attraction, a precedent often followed. The play scored a genuine triumph, and in the role of Lundström, with which he was as much identified as was his wife with Anna, Pfeil himself was inimitable. He made Lundström an excellent portrait of a happy soul, in welcome contrast to the usual interpretation as a delirious drunkard. On this occasion, the reviewer took a more tolerant attitude toward local references, commenting only that Ville Åkerberg as an editor should have announced more loudly that Saturday was publication day for *Svenska Tribunen*.[95] Another success, repeated the following season and in later years, was *Sabinskornas bortröfvande*, in a première that closed the regular *Svenska Dramatiska Sällskap* season. It is the play from the German that was popular on the American and English stages as *A Night Off*—the farcical story of the performance by a down and out touring company of an absurd melodrama about the rape of the Sabine women, and the family difficulties of the professor-dramatist.[96]

Looking back, the *Svenska Tribunen* critic pronounced the completed season creditable, and wished the Pfeils good fortune on their April tour.[97] Their touring company of twelve probably included the actors who had played most frequently during the season—Ovington, Åkerberg, Albin Smith, Mrs. Feltskogh, and Mrs. Hvitfeldt (in her first Chicago appearances). By May, the Pfeils were back in Chicago, performing at two social events and in the joint production with which the *Svenska Dramatiska Sällskap* and Eolus celebrated Bellman's birthday in July. This was the first of a succession of Bellman Day outings that included a play with Bellman characters and songs. Again in 1891 the sketch about Bellman and his sweetheart called *Ulla skall på bal* (Ulla goes to a dance), was given, with the assistance, naturally, of Bellman devotee Gus Higgins.

1889-1890

For the 1889-1890 season, Carl Pfeil took over the *Svenska Dramatiska Sällskap,* and its nine productions were acted by the "Pfeilska" Company. This was an encouraging season, and one which, because of the daring and successful step with which Pfeil concluded it, is of special note in the development of the Swedish theatre in Chicago. For his final productions, he moved from the North Side Turner Hall to Hooley's, a leading city theatre;[98] and he offered, appropriately, the two plays most prominent in the Chicago Swedish repertoire throughout the years, *Andersson, Pettersson och Lundström* and *Vermländingarne*. Both of them had been played earlier in the season, and the season as a whole was one of familiar plays.

One of the season's two novelties was a part of the Pfeil company's opening production—Ville Åkerberg's *Nationaldagen, eller Den importer-*

ade älskaren. Like many of the Swedish plays written in Chicago, it was built around the adventures of a Swedish immigrant. Pfeil played Åkerberg's hero, the green country boy; Mrs. Pfeil, the Chicago girl who had fallen in love with his picture; and Sahlin, the snobbish brother who claims the newcomer is a stable boy imposter. The patriotic note called for by a National Day celebration was furnished by a chorus of Swedish ancestors, "pretty well preserved considering they came here 251 years ago." The reviewer's reference to a recognizable *folktalare* (patriotic speaker) almost certainly indicates that *Hemlandet* editor Enander was burlesqued in the play, and suggests that it was this play Skarstedt remembered and listed under the title of *Folktalaren,* rather than a second play by Åkerberg. In this play, too, "little Miss Pfeil, aged five years and fourteen hours," made her debut, and was voted "as sweet as her mother."[99]

Anyone knowing theatrical conditions in Sweden must judge the Pfeil company as far superior to its touring companies, wrote *Svenska Tribunen* after the next play, a successful repetition of *Sabinskornas bortröfvande.*[100] Pallin, Ovington, Anna Almgren, and Mrs. Hvitfeldt were the experienced actors who, in addition to the Pfeils, played most regularly in the company. Now Carl Pfeil was ready to turn for the first time to serious drama, and in November he presented in its Chicago première the chief contribution of the Finnish Topelius to Sweden's historical drama, *Regina von Emmeritz.*[101]

More than a month was given to preparation for a large scale production, with a chorus of forty-two from the Svithiod and *Nordstjernan* singing clubs, and 200 historical costumes supplied by Schoultz. A note Mrs. Pfeil wrote beside the review of the play pasted in her scrap book indicates how she regarded this undertaking: "It was the first time we played this piece and I did not yet have the courage to play Regina."[102] The role was taken by Mrs. Grönquist, nor otherwise known, but accounted capable. In a January repetition, Mrs. Pfeil did play Regina, and succeeded in a "fiery" characterization.[103]

A crowd of 2,000 packed the North Side Turner Hall for the first performance—a welcome sign that the Swedish public could appreciate heavy drama, wrote *Svenska Tribunen.* Only an inadequate orchestra marred an artistically successful production. Carl Pfeil made a noble and stately Gustaf Adolf, and his wife was splendid as Bertil, the king's young Finnish follower. Åkerberg and Mrs. Hvitfeldt had important roles as the Jesuit, Hieronymus, and the old nurse, Dorthea, who together incite Regina to kill the Swedish king who is invading Germany in the cause of

Protestantism. Pallin played an old Swedish soldier, Larson, one of the play's well drawn characters.[104]

Topelius's play is powerful melodrama, if not tragedy, building up through scenes in the home of Prince von Emmeritz the conflict between Gustaf Adolf and those that conspire against him. In a climactic battle field scene, Regina dies, having hidden in her bosom the poisoned letter intended for the king, whose nobility of character, displayed on his visit to her father, has transformed her thoughts of holy murder to a self-sacrificing devotion. The king's arch-enemy, Hieronymus, is killed, and in a sentimental close typical of the drama of the period, Gustaf Adolf and Regina's father, with the dead girl at their feet, are reconciled. Topelius's poetry is superior to that of his contemporaries in the drama and gives the play some literary quality, but it was probably its effectiveness as "theatre" that continued to make it welcome to Chicago audiences.

Of this performance Ernst Lindblom told a story for which—if not for all its details—there is verification. Never, he wrote, had a Swedish actor been applauded on the Chicago stage as was Carl Pfeil when he appeared in the last act after the successful storming of the German fortress. Ammunition thundered and resounded, and the noise on the stage and in the audience could hardly have been equalled by the Thirty Years War. But behind the scenes, that first night, there had been equally dramatic episodes. As Gustaf Adolf was resting between acts, police arrived to attach the evening's income on behalf of his creditors. Surprisingly, there was no cash to be found, and Carl Pfeil and his gallant soldiers routed the police—a fact which later came to the ears of the actor's public and made him doubly popular. Pfeil, in the meantime, was lamenting the disappearance of the money, as much of a mystery to him as to the police. His wife teased him: "Are *you* a king? Though you can fight, you are an idiot." Then, as evidence of her forethought, she disclosed that she had given orders for the ticket money to be brought to her whenever it totalled $5.00. The money was all hidden in her stockings. The king pronounced her an angel, kissed her heartily, and in accordance with his principles, thanked God for the victory. How Carl Pfeil managed to thwart the police on their return a few days later is another story, said Lindblom, and left it untold. *Hemlandet,* however, reported the appearance in court of Pfeil, sculptor John Holmes, and C. A. Sirbom on charges of disorderly conduct at North Side Turner Hall November 3. Pfeil pleaded self-defense and was supported by many witnesses, but he and his colleagues were given $5.00 fines.[105] The situation as a whole was by no means unique, though the financial difficulties did not usually lead to open conflict.

In February 1890 the Pfeil company appeared in *Andersson, Pettersson och Lundström* and *Vermländingarne.* Theirs was the second *Andersson, Pettersson och Lundström* of the season, a New Year's performance (one of two plays of the season with which the Pfeils were not associated) having been given by a number of actors from the company. In the holiday production, Pallin, Higgins, and Schycker played the name roles, and the usual new lyrics were contributed by Pallin and Åkerberg.[106] Pfeil's Lundström attracted a smaller audience than usual; perhaps, it was suggested, because the play was given at a new and unfamiliar South Side "opera house."[107] The February plays introduced new actors to the public: Hilma Nelson, who won immediate recognition for her beauty and natural gift for the stage as well as for the excellent Swedish she spoke, though American born; and Max Hedman, who made a romantic Erik besides having the voice for the part. In *Vermländingarne,* Pfeil's roles were Anders and Löpare-Nisse, and Mrs. Pfeil, of course, was Anna. Miss Nelson probably played Stina to Ovington's Per. The other actors mentioned in reviews of the season's productions of *Vermländingarne* were Sahlin as Sven, Mrs. Hvitfeldt as Lisa, Anna Almgren as Britta and Annika, Schycker as Jan Hansson, and Higgins as Ola i Gyllby. Ovington also doubled as the *provst.*[108]

Improved acting after some weeks on tour, with almost daily performances, was noted when the company played *Nerkingarne* in March, but inadequate publicity had limited the audience.[109] The next month there were no such sins of omission. On Sunday, April 20, *Vermländingarne* was to be acted at Hooley's; it would be "a memorable day for Swedish dramatic art in America," said *Svenska Tribunen,* the first performance by a Swedish company at one of Chicago's larger American theatres, and in a play thoroughly Swedish. And the paper gave much space to grateful recognition of Pfeil's efforts to "cultivate and elevate" the Swedish drama.[110]

The review was equally congratulatory. It was a joy for a Swedish paper to say that *Vermländingarne* was played at Hooley's, and in a fashion that did honor to all concerned. The public could not know what difficulties such a project had to overcome, but showed appreciation in its support and enthusiasm. There was a full house, at prices from twenty-five cents to a dollar, and flowers for the actors as befitted the occasion. The cast won the same admiration as before, only some inappropriately coarse language and Ovington's lack of dignity as the *provst* being criticized.[111]

Popular request, said the publicity, now demanded that the imperishable *Andersson, Pettersson och Lundström* be acted under the same favorable circumstances; and, given at Hooley's, in its third performance of the season, it also drew a full house, and received its quota of praise. This was a farewell appearance for Carl and Anna Pfeil, who were about to join an American company for a tour that would take them through the states of the far West. *Svenska Tribunen* wished them well but lamented their departure and what it might mean for the fate of the Swedish theatre in Chicago.[112]

1890-1891

The absence of the Pfeils was to be temporary, but in the meantime *Svenska Tribunen's* fears for the Swedish theatre proved unfounded. The *Svenska Dramatiska Sällskap* resumed its activities and gave an 1890-1891 season of nine successful performances. Who headed the company does not appear in the records, but regular performers were such old-timers as Schoultz, Littche, Åkerberg, Ovington, Smith, and Anna Almgren, and such relative newcomers as Schycker, Hedman, Mrs. Hvitfeldt, and Hilma Nelson. For their concluding play, another of Sweden's best known historical dramas, they were joined by Albert Alberg. Not until Brusell and Behmer's *Svenska Teatersällskap* attained prominence in the early 1900's was there to be another season so dominated by a single company. Rival companies as well as ever increasing activity characterized the following decade.

Andersson, Pettersson och Lundström was one of the two plays earlier acted in Chicago included in the 1890-1891 offerings. And even that perennial was enhanced by what *Svenska Kuriren* called the crazy idea of playing the last act *Mikado* fashion, with the trolls and fairies in Japanese costume—interesting evidence both of the popularity of Gilbert and Sullivan and of the freedom with which the Swedish plays were frequently treated.[113]

Ville Åkerberg wrote new songs for *Andersson, Pettersson och Lundström,* but the chief contribution by a Chicago writer to this season was the first of Ernst Lindblom's two ventures into dramatic authorship. Customary gusto marks his narrative of the production of his *Pelle Pihlqvists Amerikaresa.* Certainly he believed himself the most distinguished of dramatists— in Chicago, at least; and it was intoxication—with happiness—that made him tumble down the prompter's trap door at one of the two November performances of his masterpiece.

76

The play was written for Hilma Nelson. About her beauty Lindblom is so rapturous that one is not surprised at his "right-thinking" mother-in-law's tearing up the photograph of her she found lying on his desk. But, he says, it was replaced by one even more beautiful.[114] His praises are echoed in the Svenska Tribunen review, with a prophecy, soon to be realized, of a successful professional career. Like the Pfeils, but with more success, Hilma Nelson turned to the American stage. She first acted professionally and in English the following March in The fugitive, at Jacob's Clark Street Theatre.[115]

Lindblom had devised a timely situation for his immigrant characters, the staple material of the Chicago Swedish playwrights. The young dandy, Pelle, a "perpetual undergraduate" from Upsala University, could win the hand of the Chicago merchant's daughter on only one condition: the completion of the Linné monument in Lincoln Park. In anticipation of the successful conclusion of that project in the spring of 1891, a spectacular unveiling of the monument made the play's climax, and, of course, a happy ending for the lovers. Chief honors went to Ville Åkerberg in the "not easy" role of Pelle, and to Hilma Nelson, but all the actors were commended—Schoultz as the director of the Linné monument association, Albin Smith as the father, Anna Almgren as a servant, Ovington as an author from Stockholm, and Higgins as a saloon keeper. The play itself was called amusing, and the songs, set to melodies from the operetta Boccaccio, well-turned and witty. More than 2,000 people turned out for the first performance, and the second, with the added feature of a prologue commemorating the death of Charles XII, was well attended.[116]

For its 1891 New Year's Day performance, the Svenska Dramatiska Sällskap introduced a play that had been popular in Sweden, but was far different from the characteristically Swedish plays commonly offered the Chicago Swedish public. This was Jules Verne's Jorden rundt på 80 dagar. Albert Alberg was not mentioned in connection with this performance or a February repetition, but, by his own account, supplied the play. As director of the Djurgården Theatre of Stockholm, he had in 1876 given Jorden rundt på 80 dagar its Swedish première, himself acting the role of Phineas Fogg—and, he lamented, he had lost all the profits the next year with another Verne piece, På hafvets botten (At the bottom of the sea). Alberg regarded Jorden rundt på 80 dagar as trash,[117] but it delighted the Chicago audiences as it did those of Stockholm. This was a magnificent production, the Svenska Tribunen reviewer reported; and a company of 100 with costumes by Schoultz, new settings by Drake of the Criterion Theatre, and a ballet by Professor Lester Rea of the America Theatre bear him out. The elephant's snout was out of order in the first performance, but that was a minor flaw, and the whole gave evidence of careful preparation. The principals were effective: the Misses Almgren and Nelson in the feminine leads, Max Hedman as Passepartout, Ovington as Phineas Fogg, and Åkerberg as Detective Fixit. And, with a change of heart, *Svenska Tribunen* said that Biorn's orchestra was "as always" good.[118]

Valborgsmesso-aftonen, Hedberg's folk play, had opened the 1890-1891 season, and his most popular historical drama, *Bröllopet på Ulfåsa,* was to close it (except for a summer Bellman piece). *Valborgsmesso-aftonen* had all the ingredients for winning favor with a Chicago audience —comic types, romance, and national costumes and dances. A carefully rehearsed production with skilful actors made it a solid success when it was first played, as on later occasions;[119] but no such fanfare accompanied its première as introduced *Bröllopet på Ulfåsa.* For the second time, said the announcements, a Swedish theatrical season was to close with a play at Hooley's that would be a treat comparable to the best the first class theatres had to offer in English. Sweden's 13th century hero, Birger Jarl (Birger the Earl) was to be played by no less famous and experienced an actor than Albert Alberg, in his first Chicago appearance. His reputation alone guaranteed that this would be a landmark in Swedish American theatrical history. Now, too, the public would have the chance to hear the Söderman *Wedding March* in the setting for which it was composed and to see the hall of the knights of Ulfåsa in appropriate splendor.[120]

The Söderman march played for the wedding procession of Sigrid the Fair and Bengt Lagman to her father's ancestral home, Ulfåsa, was one of the play's most popular features, and Sigrid, daughter of Knut Algotson, one of the favorite heroines of Swedish drama. She loves Bengt Lagman when she thinks him a simple soldier; and when his identity as the younger brother of Birger Jarl, her father's enemy, is revealed, she is torn between her love and her duty to her father. In order to win her hand, Bengt becomes the enemy of his powerful brother, and the happy wedding festivities that follow are interrupted by an insulting gift from the Jarl, that is as insultingly returned. The Jarl is not to be dissuaded by his wife or his faithful follower, Härved Boson, and rushes away to seek Bengt. But, unlike *Regina von Emmeritz, Bröllopet på Ulfåsa* has a happy ending. At Ulfåsa, Sigrid, hiding her identity, conquers Birger Jarl with her charms and virtue, and Sigrid's father ceases to oppose the great earl under whose rule Sweden was to be united. Sentimental debates about love, duty, and honor character-

Gus Higgins

John Örtengren

Albert Alberg

Otto Pallin

John Liander

ize much of the play, but the wedding spectacle, a secondary romance, and the adroit maneuvering of Prior Botvid in the cause of peace give it variety.

In its first performance, *Bröllopet på Ulfåsa* was something of a disappointment, mainly because Albert Alberg did not live up to his reputation. Critical opinion was that his mishandling of the difficult metrical text would surely have made it unrecognizable by the author, and that his lapses of memory affected the entire production. Hilma Nelson was a charming Sigrid, and the other amateurs, left unnamed, gave varying degrees of satisfaction. Costumes and settings were, according to promise, splendid, but not altogether authentic.[121]

The public was less critical, and welcomed a second performance—at the Grand Opera House, Hooley's not being available. The time was well chosen, for the preceding day, May 23, the Swedish Chicagoans' gift to their city, the Linné monument, had at last been unveiled, and visitors for that occasion were urged to attend the play. Mellowed, perhaps, by the festival mood attending the Linné ceremonies, the *Svenska Tribunen* critic now found the performance very acceptable, and anticipated only success for the company in its forthcoming appearance in Minneapolis. The play itself was praised as the most significant ever offered the Chicago Swedes: its literary and historic merits were matched by the nobility of its sentiments, impressively epitomized in the line with which Birger Jarl closed the play, "Before the power of a beautiful and virtuous woman, all things must bow."[122] Whether their reasons were or were not those of *Svenska Tribunen,* Chicago Swedish audiences did not soon tire of the romantic story of Sigrid the Fair and young Bengt Lagman.

Asterisk following a play title indicates that the cast is given in Appendix, IV.

Performances, 1878-1879 through 1890-1891

Date	Play	Company	Place
	1878-1879		
Dec. 29, 1878	....	....	N. S. T. H.
Jan. 25, 1879	Andersson, Pettersson och Lundström	S. A. S.[123]	N. S. T. H.
Mch. 9, 1879	Andersson, Pettersson och Lundström	S. A. S.	N. S. T. H.
Apr. 19, 1879	Herr Dardanell och hans upptåg på landet	S. A. S.	N. S. T. H.
	1879-1880		
Nov. 22, 1879	Rochus Pumpernickel*	S. A. S.	N. S. T. H.
Jan. 4, 1880	....	S. A. S.	N. S. T. H.
Feb., 1880	Majorens döttrar	S. A. S.	N. S. T. H.
	1880-1881		
	1881-1882		
Nov. 20, 1881	"I tjenst åstundas" Ett resande teatersällskap	....	N. S. T. H.
Dec. 5, 1881	"I tjenst åstundas"	....	N. S. T. H.
Feb. 26, 1882	De båda döfva I klädlogen	S. A. S.	N. S. T. H.
Apr. 29, 1882	De båda döfva*	S. A. S. for Svithiod	N. S. T. H.
	1882-1883		
Nov. 19, 1882	En överraskning*	Wicklund & Co., for Sjustjernan	N. S. T. H.
May 5, 1883	Vår förening*	Wicklund & Co., for Nordstjernan & Sjustjernan	Central Hall
	1883-1884		
Dec. 16, 1883	Kronjuvelerna på Nordsidan*	Wicklund & Co.	N. S. T. H.
Jan. 12, 1884	Värfningen Ett sätt att fria	Swedish Social Club	Binz Hall
Jan. 20, 1884	Syfröknarna*	Lindeberg Co.	N. S. T. H.
May 18, 1884	Hittebarnet*	Brusell Co.	N. S. T. H.
	1884-1885		
Nov. 16, 1884	Vermländingarne*	Lundgren Co.	N. S. T. H.
Dec. 21, 1884	Vermländingarne	Lundgren Co.	N. S. T. H.
Feb. 1, 1885	Jernbäraren* En brottslig betjent*	Lindstrom & Nordgren Co.	N. S. T. H.
May 9, 1885	Allt för guld	Holson Co.	N. S. T. H.
June 27, 1885	Hamlet	S. D. S.	Baum's Pavilion

Date	Play	Company	Place
		1885-1886	
Dec. 13, 1885	Andersson, Pettersson och Lundström	S. D. S.	N. S. T. H.
Dec. 26, 1885	Jag känner till politiken, jag*	Court Vega	N. S. T. H.
	En midsommarnatt i Dalarne	Pleasure Club, No. 33, I. O. F.	
Feb. 14, 1886	Andersson, Pettersson och Lundström	S. D. S.	N. S. T. H.
May 1, 1886	På första Maj*	S. D. S. for Nordstjernan	Central Hall
May 9, 1886	Lustresan från Skåne (as Familjen Trögelin) Den vildsinte Mexikanaren	S. D. S.	N. S. T. H.
		1886-1887	
Oct. 24, 1886	Engelbrekt och hans Dalkarlar	. . . .	N. S. T. H.
Nov. 6, 1886	Vermländingarne	Schoultz Co. for Götha Lodge, K. & L. of H.	N. S. T. H.
Nov. 20, 1886	En natt i Falkenberg	Schoultz & Wicklund	S. Chi. Opera House
Jan. 23, 1887	Den hvita halsdukan Mjuka tjenare!	Sandgren Co.	N. S. T. H.
Mch. 6, 1887	De båda direktörerna Herr Larssons resa till landtbruksmötet	Sandgren Co.	N. S. T. H.
Apr. 3, 1887	De båda direktörerna Herr Larssons resa till landtbruksmötet	Sandgren Co.	N. S. T. H.
		1887-1888	
Nov. 24, 1887	Preciosa	Götha Lodge, K. & L. of H.	N. S. T. H.
Feb. 5, 1888	Det skadar inte!	Figaro	N. S. T. H.
Feb. 19, 1888	Den ondes besegrare	Danish-Swedish Co.	N. S. T. H.
Mch. 11, 1888	Bror Jonathan, eller Oxhandlaren från Småland Sparlakanslexor	Figaro	N. S. T. H.
Apr. 8, 1888	Exekutionsbetjenten-poet Den lilla sångfågeln	Pfeil Co.	N. S. T. H.
May 5, 1888	Majbruden	Svithiod	N. S. T. H.
		1888-1889	
Sept. 23, 1888	Preciosa	S. D. S.	N. S. T. H.
Oct. 7, 1888	En komedi*	S. D. S.	N. S. T. H.
Oct. 13, 1888	Alpflickan Drilléns operett	S. D. S.	N. S. T. H.
Nov. 4, 1888	Det skadar inte!	S. D. S.	N. S. T. H.
Nov. 18, 1888	Vermländingarne	S. D. S.	N. S. T. H.
Dec. 16, 1888	Nerkingarne	S. D. S.	N. S. T. H.

81

Date	Play	Company	Place
Dec. 26, 1888	*Min hustrus affärer*	Baltic Society	Grand Crossing T. H.
Jan. 1, 1889	*Andersson, Pettersson och Lundström**	S. D. S.	N. S. T. H.
Jan. 13, 1889	*Chicago nattetid*	S. D. S.	N. S. T. H.
Feb. 24, 1889	*"Det har jag gjort en visa om" Mot beräkning*	S. D. S.	N. S. T. H.
Mch. 24, 1889	*Direktör Striese* (as *Sabinskornas bortröfvande*)	S. D. S.	N. S. T. H.
May 4, 1889	*Bildning och natur*	Pfeil Co. for Svithiod	N. S. T. H.
May 25, 1889	*Hans tredje hustru**	Pfeil Co. for 8 societies	N. S. T. H.
July 28, 1889	*Balen på Gröna Lund* (as *Ulla skall på bal*)*	S. D. S. & Eolus	Hillinger's Park

1889-1890

Date	Play	Company	Place
Sept. 14, 1889	*Nationaldagen, eller Den importerade älskaren Drilléns operett*	Pfeil Co.	Freiberg's Opera House
Sept. 22, 1889	*Direktör Striese* (as *Sabinskornas bortröfvande*)	Pfeil Co.	N. S. T. H.
Nov. 3, 1889	*Regina von Emmeritz*	Pfeil Co.	N. S. T. H.
Dec. 29, 1889	*Andersson, Pettersson och Lundström*	....	N. S. T. H.
Jan. 12, 1890	*Regina von Emmeritz*	Pfeil Co.	N. S. T. H.
Feb. 2, 1890	*Andersson, Pettersson och Lundström*	Pfeil Co.	Freiberg's Opera House
Feb. 9, 1890	*Vermländingarne*	Pfeil Co.	N. S. T. H.
Mch. 24, 1890	*Nerkingarne*	Pfeil Co.	N. S. T. H.
Apr. 20, 1890	*Vermländingarne*	Pfeil Co.	Hooley's
Apr. 27, 1890	*Andersson, Pettersson och Lundström*	Pfeil Co.	Hooley's
May 17, 1890	*Det skadar inte!*	S. D. S.	Kensington T. H.

1890-1891

Date	Play	Company	Place
Oct. 18, 1890	*Valborgsmesso-aftonen*	S. D. S. for Götha Lodge, K. & L. of H.	N. S. T. H.
Nov. 2, 1890	*Pelle Pihlqvists Amerika-resa**	S. D. S.	N. S. T. H.
Nov. 30, 1890	*Pelle Pihlqvists Amerika-resa*	S. D. S.	N. S. T. H.
Jan. 1, 1891	*Jorden rundt på 80 dagar*	S. D. S.	N. S. T. H.
Feb. 22, 1891	*Jorden rundt på 80 dagar*	S. D. S.	N. S. T. H.
Apr. 11, 1891	*Andersson, Pettersson och Lundström*	S. D. S.	N. S. T. H.
May 10, 1891	*Bröllopet på Ulfåsa*	S. D. S.	Hooley's
May 24, 1891	*Bröllopet på Ulfåsa*	S. D. S.	Grand Opera House
July 26, 1891	*Balen på Gröna Lund*	S. D. S.	Hillinger's Park

CHAPTER IV

BUFFETS AND REWARDS

1891-1892—1900-1901

In each of the ten seasons of the Chicago Swedish theatre from 1891-1892 through 1900-1901, more than one dramatic company was active, and there were several seasons when three of four companies were offering plays. A new *Svenska Teatersällskap*, promoted by Hilma Nelson's father, was the leading company for the first two seasons. The *Svenska Dramatiska Sällskap*, though it lost its earlier prominence, appeared intermittently, and its members sponsored individual performances and short-lived companies. For part of the period, Carl Pfeil, at times with the *Svenska Dramatiska Sällskap* but more often heading his own performances, returned to something of his earlier position. Albert Alberg tried and tried again, but the companies he headed existed for brief periods only. And theatrical activities were being stimulated by professional actors from Sweden, some of them temporary residents of Chicago who not only acted with other leaders but directed their own companies.

In general, this was a time of shifting fortunes as well as of shifting leadership, of divided efforts and rivalries rather than constant progress. The first half dozen seasons brought the Swedish audiences more plays than ever before, with city performances no longer limited to the end of the season. The Auditorium, Chicago's largest theatre, first housed a Swedish play in May, 1892. That season and the next, the Criterion, a conveniently located North Side theatre with good facilities, was being regularly used. But there were discouraging failures as well as successes. The energetic Mr. Nelson ceased his activities. Gradually the number of performances dwindled, city performances became infrequent, and the use of the North Side Turner Hall again common. Growth in Swedish settlements on the South Side was, however, bringing an increasing number of performances in various halls there, and by the mid-90's it was becoming a usual practice to present a play on successive evenings or on successive Saturdays or Sundays at the North Side Turner Hall and the South Side Turner Hall.

Of chief importance for the future of the Swedish theatre were the new talents that were being added to its forces, the new leadership that was rising out of the confusion and ups and downs of the 1890's. Actors of ability came and went during these years, but gifted and experienced men

83

and women who were to give Chicago's Swedish plays a new continuity came and stayed. And by the end of the 1900-1901 season another *Svenska Teatersällskap*, which had been organized in the fall of 1899 by Christopher Brusell and Ernst H. Behmer, was giving evidence of what these directors were to accomplish in the following decades.

As the Swedish colony continued to grow—though more slowly than in the preceding decade—it became more highly organized, and, at the same time, more unified in spirit and activities. Of particular significance for the theatre was the organization in 1894 of the *Svenska National Förbund* (Swedish National Association), to unite the charitable efforts of the colony as a whole. Many clubs and lodges turned to the theatrical companies for entertainment or gave their own plays, but the *Svenska National Förbund* was to become the most important as a sponsor of theatrical productions. To the advantage of the theatre also was the gradual narrowing of the gap between its supporters and the Lutheran groups, a development which was in part the result of such organizations as the *Svenska National Förbund*. In 1893, the Englewood district was still considered a poor location for Swedish plays because so many churchly Swedes lived there;[1] but *Hemlandet* had begun to review plays occasionally in 1891, and by the end of the period there was clear evidence of changing attitudes within the church group. Not only did the city's most prominent Lutheran clergyman speak at a performance of *Regina von Emmeritz* at the Auditorium in 1898, but when an historical drama was presented there in 1900 the editor of *Hemlandet* was numbered among the actors. In general, the element of the Swedish population that had been "repelled by the hubbub of the beer halls"[2] was giving increasing support to a theatre advancing in quality and reputation.

Even the enlarged audience, however, could not—or would not—support adequately more than one dramatic company in a full season of performances. Again and again, newspapers reported half empty houses or attendance smaller than the play deserved, and counselled cooperation in one company "that would be of much service in raising the cultural level in the Swedish colony" and in developing its feeling of unity. Artistically as well, they pointed out, union was desirable. With the best actors scattered in a number of companies, quality suffered, and with it public interest. For one good company there should be the support that would put it on the stable basis enjoyed by the German theatre in Chicago.[3] Each newly formed company brought renewed hope that such a situation could be achieved, but

84

the leaders had hard sledding, particularly during the depression that followed the 1893 fair.

The newspapers that had traditionally supported the theatre—*Svenska
Amerikanaren* and *Svenska Tribunen,* and, since 1888, *Svenska Kuriren*—
were joined in 1898 by *Svenska Nyheter.* All plays were not publicized or
reviewed by every paper, but in general reviews were longer and publicity
was more extensive than before. The press was generous with encouragement for "what should be ranking entertainment for Swedes in Chicago,"[4]
and it was generous with advice. The inconsistency of its advice as to
repertoire must have been annoying to the actors, if taken seriously, but
ordinarily any publicity was regarded as good publicity. Small attendance
was often blamed on the failure to provide new plays, but when new plays
failed to draw, the company was scolded for not offering familiar favorites.
Unfamiliar French plays, it was said, could not be expected to appeal to a
Swedish audience;[5] but *Andersson, Pettersson och Lundström* was damned
as a mossy old play against which even the patient Swedish audience re-
belled.[6] Directors who supplied the novelties of more literary quality for
which critics clamored were told that they could not expect to get audiences
for solemn plays and historical dramas in verse—the youthful audiences
came to the theatre to be entertained.[7] At the same time that audience was
berated for its inability to appreciate serious drama and for its unreceptive-
ness to the new.

The old complaints of disorderly audiences continued, but occasionally
there was a sympathetic picture, of the kind given by *Svenska Tribunen's*
"Pelle Person":

> How respectable, well-dressed, and prosperous they look, and
> still all are laborers, their wives and daughters. One cannot help
> comparing their present circumstances with those from which they
> came. Now, instead of poverty and limited opportunities, they can
> enjoy life's pleasures. Here increasing culture and taste are evident.
> It is impossible to recognize them as farm boys and girls. This is said
> in pride and satisfaction with the Swedish people, not to slander old
> Sweden.[8]

The importance of the theatre from the point of view of "culture
and taste" was more than ever a theme of the press, but what the theatre
meant as one of "life's pleasures" for an immigrant audience was ordinarily
assumed rather than discussed. But that it was recognized an article in
Svenska Amerikanaren of April 28, 1892, also indicates. The Swedish theatre
is, it pointed out, a means of "reconciling us to life and shortening the long
work days that many of us, especially the brave girls in service in American

families, must spend in loneliness. It is, in short, the best remedy in the world for the 'blues.' "

Many of the men and women who had been mainstays of the *Svenska Dramatiska Sällskap* and the Pfeil companies were prominent in this period, in both the old and new companies—for it was the leadership rather than the supporting actors that distinguished one company from another. Mrs. Nordgren and Albin Smith died in 1892 and Ville Åkerberg in 1894. Lindstrom and Schoultz now rarely acted, though Schoultz continued to promote plays. In cast after cast, however, appear the names of Ovington, Pallin, Sahlin, Higgins, Littche, Hedman, Schycker, Anna Almgren, Mrs. Hvitfeldt, and Mrs. Feltskogh. Mrs. Hedman and Mrs. Schycker were new additions to the group. Upon his return to Chicago in 1892, Brusell resumed his earlier importance in the theatre; and in 1896 Wicklund was in Chicago again, acting only occasionally but making a valuable contribution to the repertoire in plays and songs.

The young favorite of the *Svenska Dramatiska Sällskap* of 1890-1891, Hilma Nelson, was the most publicized of the actors until she went on to a career on the American stage in 1892. It was, in fact, largely to further the career of his nineteen year old daughter that her father, L. P. Nelson, founded the *Svenska Teatersällskap* in the fall of 1891. He presented her in English as well as in Swedish productions, and she also made some appearances with Danish groups. Hilma Nelson was attractive and gifted, and she won the interest of America's most famous director, Augustin Daly. In the summer of 1892, he gave her a three year contract, and she remained in his company until his death in 1899, touring the West, appearing for two seasons in London, and then in New York. Occasionally she returned to Chicago and acted in Swedish plays before audiences that were naturally proud of her success. She did not have major roles with the Daly Company, but took a number of dramatic parts, and appeared as a singer and dancer.[9]

In 1899 the American born actress reversed the usual order, and went to Scandinavia. She made a success in Stockholm appearances, acting once, at least, opposite Birger Schycker, the brother of Ernst Schycker. Further successes in Denmark were followed by marriage in Copenhagen. There her father joined her in 1910, and continued his remarkable career until he died in 1927, at the age of eighty-three. In Chicago, Lars Peter Nelson was known as Greenbacks-Nisse, because the socialist newspaper, *Svenska Arbetaren* (The Swedish Laborer), that he published in 1887 supported the Greenbacks Party. He was a self-educated man, known for his insatiable thirst for knowledge and culture and his interest in Utopian schemes. He wrote extensively for newspapers in Sweden and in the United States, and in 1918 published a book, *En upptäcktsresa genom Sverige* (A journey of discovery through Sweden), descriptive of Sweden as he found it on his return. His brochure discussing the Ford Peace Ship venture, in which he participated, was widely distributed, both in the original Swedish and in English translation.[10] L. P. Nelson's daughter Anna attracted less attention than her father and sister, but Chicago knew her as a singer, and from time to time, in the 1890's and later, she appeared in Swedish plays.

Immigration brought to Chicago in the 1890's a considerable number of men and women who were quickly recognized as valuable acquisitions for the theatre. Several of these newcomers, a number with professional experience in Sweden, were to become the "old guard" of the following decades, when only Brusell, Schycker, and Mrs. Feltskogh represented the acting group of the 1880's. To the majority of the "Bohemians" of the 1880's, the years brought stability and a measure of success, and the new arrivals were, with a few exceptions, responsible, able, and hard-working. There were professional musicians among them, and there were men from the Swedish newspapers, but most of the men made their living in the business world. In every field, the situation of the Swedes in Chicago was more favorable to success than before, and these new actors made good use of their opportunities. They did not make fortunes, but they established themselves and, on the whole, prospered. Their love of the theatre, of music and literature and the arts, was as real and persistent as that of the actors whose ranks they joined. Possibility of financial loss did not deter the theatrical leaders, and the actors, old and new, were not attracted primarily by the promised pay—which they knew would not always be forthcoming.

Of the new actors, Ernst Hugo Behmer, Brusell's colleague and competitor, made the greatest contribution to the Swedish stage in Chicago. Almost unrivalled in his ardor, he was to outlive other leaders, and to occupy at last a unique position as the "dean" of the Chicago Swedish theatre. Behmer came to Chicago in 1891, at the age of nineteen, and began his association with the Swedish plays as Träckling in *Andersson, Pettersson och Lundström* in October 1893—a minor role, as was fitting and proper, he noted in looking back over his first twenty-five years of acting.[11] He was born in Grödinga Socken, Södermanland, but grew up in Stockholm, receiving his education at the *Norra Latinläroverket*. In Chicago, he held positions with a number of business firms, among them the American Radiator Company. Mr. Behmer left Chicago for the West in 1944, to make his home with his daughter Lisa, and he now lives in Denver, Colorado. His activities in the Chicago Swedish theatre did not end, however, with his move from the city; the 1946 performance of *Vermländingarne* under his direction, in which he acted as well, was a fitting climax to his career. His cultural interests extend beyond the theatre, and in the 1930's and 1940's, when the older Swedish theatre was becoming largely a memory, he assumed a prominent role in the Western Division of Chicago's *Svenska Kultur Förbund* (Swedish Cultural Association). Probably more than any of the other directors, he thought of his theatrical activities in terms of their artistic and cultural values, and he worked untiringly for professional standards.[12]

The year 1893 marked the beginning not only of Behmer's career, but of valuable services to the Chicago Swedish theatre by two women—Augusta Nyström and Ida Anderson-Werner (Mrs. Werner Anderson). It was as Augusta Milton that Miss Nyström became well known, however, for in 1894 she married Carl Milton. He, too, had a long acting career, though his wife appeared more consistently, and generally in more prominent roles. The Miltons and Ida Anderson-Werner came to Chicago from Norrköping, and had acted there with the Norrköping *Arbetarförening* (Labor society) company. Mrs. Anderson began a promising career at the age of fourteen, and acted for eight years, but was not permitted by her father (a machinist at *Stora Teatern*) to take engagements offered her by travelling companies. She married in 1884, and she and her family came to Chicago in 1892. She was then thirty, some ten years older than the Miltons and most of the newcomers to the stage during this period. Mrs. Anderson adopted her stage name, Ida Anderson-Werner, at the suggestion of Albert Alberg, and made it one of the best loved names in the Chicago Swedish theatre. She alone among Chicago's Swedish actors escaped adverse criticism, and in 1926 her long series of successes was crowned with a celebration of her fifty years on the stage. Both Mrs. Anderson and Mr. Milton died in 1945, and Mrs. Milton in 1948.[13]

Few other women were forming associations with the Chicago Swedish stage that were to continue for any length of time. Madame Hanna von Toyra, who had appeared with Swedish groups in the East, was in Chicago for a five year period, and, besides acting, occasionally initiated performances. Mrs. Anna Francke was enjoyed in singing roles, having, according to Mr. Behmer, "a beautiful well-trained singing voice." She was, however, criticized for inadequate Swedish.[14] Ellen Graf and Sara Nordstrom had longer careers. Mrs. Graf's specialty was dancing; as an actress, she was on the whole more decorative than talented, if one of the many reminiscences of her fellow actors provides a fair judgment. She protested to Albert Alberg, it seems, against being so frequently assigned to servant roles. And Alberg answered her question, "Do I look like a servant?" with "No, you look like a princess, but you cannot act like one." Sara Nordstrom was the daughter of a Chicago music teacher, Mrs. Sara Nordstrom, who also appeared in a number of plays. Miss Nordstrom, often spoken of as "Sweet Sara," and praised for her blond Nordic prettiness, studied voice and dancing in Chicago and New York preparatory to engagements with the Hammerstein Opera Company and dancing troupes. In New York she occasionally acted with Swedish companies, and on visits to Chicago returned to its Swedish plays.[15]

Of the talented men who joined the Swedish colony in Chicago in these years, the most experienced actor was John Lindhagen. He had left a career at Stockholm's *Nya Teater* to come to Chicago in 1894. Like other gifted immigrants of excellent background, John Lindhagen was hampered by habits of dissipation, which he did not succeed in conquering in the new environment; and in 1909, at the age of fifty-one, he ended his life. He had played many major roles with great success, and his weaknesses were viewed sympathetically by the directors—even when, as the story goes, he had to be locked up to assure his appearance. He was the son of a noted Swedish jurist and liberal legislator, Claes A. Lindhagen, and his brother, Carl Lindhagen, was a famous mayor of Stockholm, who instituted liberal reforms and was widely known for his participation in world peace movements.[16]

A new arrival in Chicago toward the end of this period was a young man who was to be one of the most successful and popular of the Swedish actors—Carl Liljegren. He was said to have acted professionally in Sweden, and he provided at least one play for the repertoire, which, it is told, he wrote from memory. Versatile, but with a particular aptitude for comedy, he acted regularly until he moved to Seattle some dozen years before his death in 1928. He had made his living in Chicago as a painter. Liljegren's was not, like Lindhagen's, a tragic life, but he gave the directors some of the same problems for the same reasons. Typical of the stories told of him is the "locals" item about his being mistakenly arrested but easily proving his identity by taking the policemen to the nearest saloon.[17]

There were other picturesque figures among the new actors also, but more characteristic of the Swedish theatre as it was to develop was such a man as Fred Bolling, for many years a reliable performer in comedy and character roles. Recently retired from his position as business manager of *Svenska Amerikanaren Tribunen,* Mr. Bolling has long been a leader in the Swedish American world of Chicago, and is a recipient of the Swedish Order of Vasa. His work in business offices of Swedish newspapers began soon after he came to Chicago in 1891, and in 1908 he became the business manager of *Svenska Amerikanaren.* Activity in musical and folk dance groups went hand in hand with his services in the theatre. From 1924 through 1933, he was president of the American Union of Swedish singers, and headed its chorus on their 1930 tour to Sweden.[18]

Leopold Chellman (also spelled Kjellman) and Ernst Ekberg, whose theatrical activities continued after most of their contemporaries had given up, were also engaged in business. Both of them were good comedians, both did some writing for the stage, and both presented plays and varied entertainments. Mr. Chellman had been a member of semi-professional companies in Sweden, and was more consistently associated with the main Chicago companies than was Mr. Ekberg. He died in 1940. Mr. Ekberg celebrated his 75th birthday in 1946, having in the preceding years displayed the versatility so often found in the men of the Swedish theatre. After an automobile accident had made regular positions impossible for him, he turned artist, painting with considerable success.[19]

The customary cooperation between Swedish musical organizations and the Swedish theatre continued in this period. Choruses not only gave their own plays on occasion, but appeared in other plays and between acts. And leading singers were pressed into service as actors. Two professional singers and teachers, however, formed more than such casual connections with the acting groups. They were Ernest Lindblom (not to be confused with the journalist of similar name) and John Örtengren. Lindblom was born in Stockholm in 1869, the son of a Baptist minister, and received a musical education there. Not many years after he emigrated in 1891, he was appearing in Chicago in English opera as well as in numerous concerts. He became a well known music teacher, and served as director of various musical organizations, among them the American Union of Swedish Singers. For more than two decades he was a regular member of theatrical companies, and was accounted a delightful comedian and an excellent actor. Mr. Lindblom died in 1924.[20]

John Örtengren was in Chicago from 1889 to 1910, and for most of that period was the undisputed leader of Chicago's Swedish musical circles. He was the director of the American Union of Swedish Singers from its foundation in 1892 until 1910. That year, after the singers made a second successful tour of Sweden, Örtengren remained in Stockholm, to continue, as business manager of the Royal Opera, a long and fruitful career. He was born in 1862, into a distinguished family of military background, and lived until 1940. Before coming to America, he had studied music in Sweden and in Paris and had been a pupil in the acting school of the Royal Opera; he had sung with the Royal Opera; and he had acted with the Royal Theatre Dramatic Company, of which his brother, Albion Örtengren, was long to be a member. In Chicago, John Örtengren was a member of the Chicago Musical College faculty, and as one of his activities directed the Swedish Glee Club. He had a splendid baritone voice, and appeared frequently in concerts. In the plays, he appeared most often in musical roles, and with his aristocratic appearance and impressive personality, he was welcomed, though his acting inclined to the stiff operatic style. As musical director, he contributed perhaps even more to the Swedish theatre.[21]

For a short period the Swedish plays also benefited by the assistance of another man from the Royal Opera—John Ringenson, ballet master and dancing teacher. From 1892 to 1897, folk dances under his direction were an important feature of a series of Chicago productions.[22]

It was experience on the American stage as well as his natural talents as a singer and actor that made Knut Schröder an asset to the Swedish plays in which he appeared intermittently for some fifteen years. Ushering at the Auditorium had supplemented young Schröder's income in his first Chicago years, and had helped to keep alive the interest in the theatre he had felt since childhood. By 1893, he was singing in choruses for the Abbey-Grau Company, and in 1900 he left a position in the *Svenska Kuriren* office to act with the Dearborn Company, in Chicago and on tour, until 1904. He first appeared with a Swedish group in 1897. After his marriage in 1911, the prosperous massage business which he and his wife established occupied him increasingly, and prevented active participation in the plays, though not the continuation of the interest in the theatre, music, and other arts which they shared with many of their associates in the Swedish theatre.[23]

Two other actors more briefly associated with the plays in this period carried on the traditional relation of the Swedish theatre and the newspapers. One was Ludwig Lundgren, popularly called Sigyn. He was a representative of the earlier type of newsman, with the versatility of a Pallin and the *joie de vivre* of an Ernst Lindblom . . . and he was in the middle of the newspaper wars that were still flourishing.[24] Lundgren came to Chicago from Göteborg in 1892, at the age of twenty, and soon became editor of a labor newspaper, *Figaro*. But he also found it necessary to carry on his earlier trade as a baker, and was instrumental in organizing a bakers' union. In 1910, he wrote of those days:

I worked three nights a week at a bakery; Saturday and Sunday nights I acted, and at times drove a bakery wagon. Many people will remember how, after they had laughed at me on the stage, they found me selling my baskets of bakery goods outside, and how, out of sheer pity, and also as a joke, they bought, laughed, and ate. But in this country, anything is possible for a newspaper man.[25]

He might have added that his play, *Anna Carlson, Stina Johnson och Lova Petterqvist,* was acted in Chicago in 1894. Another and probably more serious play, *Strejkbrytaren* (The strike breaker), may belong to his Pennsylvania period. In 1895, after travelling briefly for *Svenska Tribunen,* he moved to McKeesport, Pennsylvania, and edited *Pennsylvania Posten* until 1898. His later activities included work for the Good Templars (he told an amusing tale of Higgins and the Good Templars),[26] inventions, and business projects. When he died in 1931, he was the president of the Air Transport Exchange Company of Youngstown, Ohio.[27]

The changing situation of the Swedish immigrant is strikingly illustrated by the career of Edwin Björkman, for, unlike the earlier Swedish journalists, he was able to make English his medium, and not only succeeded in the American press but eventually made significant contributions to literature in English. In 1891, shortly after he arrived in this country, with eleven dollars and little English, he was in Chicago writing for *Svenska Amerikanaren.* He appeared in only a few plays, but won unusual acclaim. Then, in 1892, he moved to St. Paul, Minnesota, to take a position on *Minnesota Posten.* After some years, he shifted to the American press in Minneapolis, where he again acted with a Swedish group. In 1897 he moved to New York. Positions with the *Journal* and the *Sun* were followed by a variety of journalistic work, including the directorship of the League of Nations News Bureau. At the same time, he was producing a long and varied series of literary works: poems, novels, plays (at least one of which was acted by the Provincetown players); literary criticism, including a book dealing mainly with Scandinavian writers, *Voices of tomorrow;* and numerous translations, largely from the Scandinavian. His translations of twenty-four Strindberg plays are probably his major achievement.[28]

Of particular interest in connection with the Swedish and Swedish American theatres is the second of Björkman's autobiographical novels, *Gates of life.* It tells of his two years (1888-1890) on tour with August Lindberg, the famous Swedish actor later seen in Chicago, and describes vividly the difficulties of the company and the personality of Sparrgren, or

Lindberg. A year at the Royal Theatre followed, but a discouraged Björkman, who had earlier found business positions uncongenial, now tried
journalism, as a reporter on the Stockholm *Afton-Bladet*. Then, only twenty-
five, he set out for America.

One of the members of the Lindberg company described by Björkman
had found some success on the American stage and wanted to return to
America—to act, but also to establish an elegant saloon and make his
fortune. Fictional or not, this character provides an interesting commentary
on the situation of the Swedish immigrants with theatrical aspirations.

> Bob made no bones about his career out there. It had not been
> a waltz on roses. He had starved at times. He had tried many trades.
> Most of the time he had worked as night clerk in a hotel . . . But he
> possessed a neat little voice and liked to use it. And he was crazy
> about the stage ever since his cousin scored her first sensational suc-
> cess. His theatrical career began with amateur performances among
> his Swedish-American countrymen. Gradually these grew in pre-
> tentiousness. Encouraged by these successes, Bob tried for the pro-
> fessional stage and landed . . . in the gay chorus of "The Four
> Thieves," where he was discovered by the erratically famous Corinne
> Gary. When he had reached this far, his great cousin thought it was
> time for him to return to his native country.
> "But I think I'll go back to America," Bob said. "Of course, I
> think I can make good on the Swedish stage beyond all I can hope
> for out there. But there are other things to be considered . . ."[29]

And the thoughts of the young man leaving for America, with which
the book closes, must surely express what many of the men and women
of the Swedish theatre felt and hoped.

> He didn't know a thing about what his going would bring him
> out there. But . . . it meant the opening of another gate . . . the
> passing of another hampering wall . . . forever.
> It meant a new start . . . new horizons . . . and new restrictions,
> new obstacles, he supposed . . . but of these he had seen nothing as
> yet. He was merely on the way . . . to the land of work, of youth, of
> the future . . . and it might bring him also a little real love.
> Suddenly he rose . . . another of those quick decisions had taken
> shape in his mind. He was going to America to stay there . . . to
> become a part of it . . . to take root there.
> If that country was good enough to go to, as he was going, then
> it must also be good enough to stay in . . . until the future of which
> he had dreamt so long in vain was won.[30]

In 1891 John Liander, another young man who had been disappointed
in his theatrical ambitions, came to Chicago to seek his fortune. He, however, returned to the Stockholm stage for a long and successful career. He
was included in the 1902 volume, *Skådespelarne har ordet* (The actors have

the floor), made up of articles by many of Sweden's prominent actors. Liander's contribution is an amusing account of his adventures during his five years in America.

It was disappointment because his efforts as first lover (directors, he says, think that as soon as a novice begins to look somewhat human on the stage he is ready to play first lover) did not impress a visiting director at Stockholm's *Folk Teatern* that caused him to leave an ungrateful Sweden. He arrived in Chicago with twenty-six dollars and could not find a job. For a few days he attempted to adjust himself to work on a farm some ninety miles away, where conditions were completely primitive. He then spent some time in Minneapolis, and welcomed an opportunity to act in Swedish plays "under very favorable circumstances." In 1892 he was again in Chicago, and now he was able to get a kind of work he had done in Sweden, painting scenery. But "one who has given himself to Thalia finds it hard to break away," and Liander accordingly hunted up the impressario of a Swedish company [L. P. Nelson] and was easily persuaded to join its forces. Success led to work as a director, and for a time, with the backing of Schoultz, his own company. Ernst Lindblom recalled that Liander was more successful as scene painter and director than as actor,[31] but he usually won praise in all capacities.

Liander presents sympathetically the problems and achievements of the Swedish theatre in America. As its handicaps he cites infrequency of performance, the difficulty of obtaining good theatres, and the competition of the American stage. Nevertheless, with able and experienced amateurs and half a dozen genuine talents, this was a brilliant period for the Swedish plays in Chicago. In general, Liander concludes, though his stay in America did not bring him much money, he would never regret it; such an experience in the realities of life might benefit many a young actor.[32]

According to all reports, Olaf Colldén also had been an actor in Sweden, but the publicity that introduced him to Chicago Swedish audiences in the fall of 1891 included no facts; nor is it known whether or not he continued on the stage after he returned to Sweden in 1893. In Chicago he was admired both as actor and director, and for most of two seasons was one of the moving spirits in the Swedish theatre. During the 1892-1893 season, however, he dropped out of the picture, and when a benefit concert was announced in connection with his departure in October 1893, he was said to have "suffered more than most in America." Ludwig Lundgren, accurately or not, remembered him as a broken-down actor who was Pfeil's errand boy at the *Humoristen* office.[33]

Arthur Donaldson in *The Prince of Pilsen*

Hilma Nelson

Carl Pfeil as Gustaf II Adolf

Anna Pfeil as Regina von Emmeritz

Regina von Emmeritz, November 3, 1898, Auditorium

The half dozen genuine talents referred to by Liander must surely have included Arthur Donaldson, with whom he acted in 1893 and 1894, in Donaldson's first appearances in Chicago Swedish plays. Already Donaldson had begun the career on the American stage that was to lead to long years of stardom in light opera and musical comedy, and ultimately to successful pioneering in both silent and talking pictures. His actress mother had carried him on the stage for his first appearance at the age of thirteen months; before he was seven, his talents having come to the attention of director Åbjörnson of *Stora Teatern* in Norrköping, Arthur Donaldson had made his debut at that theatre. Some years of study under Åbjornson and at the Royal Theatre school followed. In 1882, the thirteen year old boy came to New York with his mother and a brother; there he worked as a typographer and watchmaker, and acted in Swedish plays while learning English, to prepare himself for the American stage. His first engagement, with the Duff Opera Company, and a concert tour with Emma Thursby preceded his Chicago debut. Then, after a short period as head of a Swedish company in New York, he devoted himself to the American theatre.

In 1899 and 1900 Donaldson played the name roles in the Swedish dialect comedies, *Ole Olson* and *Yon Yonson,* but he appeared mainly in musical productions. His greatest public success was as the hero of Henry Savage's 1903 operetta, *The Prince of Pilsen,* in which he achieved a record of 1,345 performances. Other musicals in which he had roles included *The runaway girl, Sweet Anne Page,* and *The blue moon.* He sang in grand opera and in Gilbert and Sullivan, and was a member of the Bostonians company; he acted under William Brady and David Belasco and for the Shuberts. From 1910 to 1912, he was in Sweden, appearing in Stockholm theatres and making some pictures. Among his American film roles was that of George Washington in David Wark Griffith's *America,* and in 1926 he made Dr. Lee De Forest's first talking picture. In all, Donaldson's record includes more than 350 roles, on stage and screen, in addition to the direction of some one hundred productions and the authorship of two plays, *Alpine glow* and *The goddess.*

A true matinée idol—tall and handsome, with an excellent baritone voice and an engaging personality—Arthur Donaldson was proudly claimed by the Chicago Swedes, and welcomed whenever he acted with them, both before and after he became well known. And they recalled those earlier days with interest when his 80th birthday was celebrated in New York

95

in April, 1949, and the actor, still youthful in spirit and interests, was presented King Gustaf's Pioneer Centennial Medal.[34]

The career of Wilma Sundborg (from 1904, Wilma Sundborg-Stern), another occasional visitor and star in Chicago's Swedish plays in this and later periods, in several respects paralleled that of Donaldson, though far less successful. She was a native of the Värmland province, and had studied at Ludvig Josephson's dramatic school in Stockholm, and acted at the Djurgården Theatre there, with the Fröberg Company. In the fall of 1888, she came to the United States as a member of a Swedish Ladies Octette. She, too, had acted with Swedish groups in the East before appearing in Chicago in 1898. Later she secured engagements on the American stage, first with the *Ole Olson* company, but later with Otis Skinner, and in more congenial roles in New York. She was an able actress, much interested in the theatre "as a cultural force," according to an interview she gave in 1938. She was then living in Seattle, teaching acting, doing radio work, and trying to interest Swedish audiences in Strindberg's plays.[35] Her brother, Oscar Sundborg, and his wife, Therese, shared her interest in the theatre, and in 1900 began an intermittent activity in the Chicago Swedish plays.

Actors famous in Sweden lent luster to the Chicago performances of this period—Madame Lotten Dorsch and Emil von der Osten. A third visitor, Ernst Svedelius of the Stockholm Royal Opera, appeared chiefly in concerts, but was also several times seen as an actor. Madame Dorsch was one of Sweden's most eminent actresses, and the most highly regarded of those who acted in Chicago. She had begun her career in 1867, at the age of eighteen, after studying at the Royal Theatre school of Stockholm. Some years with travelling companies and at Finland's Helsingfors theatre followed. In 1875, she returned to Stockholm, and until a year before her death in 1908 she was a leading actress in the chief theatres of the capital —from 1898 on at the *Dramatiska Teater*. From 1874 to 1889 she was the wife of a well known director, Axel Bosin, who was one of Albert Alberg's associates at the *Djurgården Teater*. Determined and self assured characters and tragic roles were her particular forte, and she won much recognition in Ibsen plays and as Lady Macbeth and Portia. "Untoward circumstances" made her months in Chicago an unhappy experience, but her one appearance in the fall of 1893 was a high point in its Swedish theatrical history.[36] Oscar Ekelund, a young colleague who accompanied her to Chicago, acted on several occasions, and with popular success. Emil von der Osten was a German actor much seen in Sweden in the 1880's and 1890's. Stockholm's critics thought him too noisy and exaggerated, and

96

would not grant him first rank, but he was a public favorite and had been honored with a decoration of the Vasa Order. He was especially successful in *Othello, Uriel Acosto,* and in *Edmond Kean,* which was the play in which Schoultz presented him to the Chicago Swedish public.[37]

In Chicago, Madame Dorsch did not act Shakespeare or Ibsen, but Topelius—the old, familiar *Regina von Emmeritz.* The majority of the plays that the Swedish actors presented in these years were still from the early decades of Sweden's drama: at lodges and club entertainments, old farces and one-act comedies; at the full length performances by the dramatic companies, folk plays, historical dramas, and characteristically Swedish comedies. *Vermländingarne* was acted at least eighteen times in these ten seasons,[38] and *Andersson, Pettersson och Lundström,* its only close rival, fourteen times. But if the plays ordinarily given were old, many of them were new to Chicago. In all, eighty-one plays were presented, at 160 performances; and fifty of the plays were new, and were seen in seventy-odd of the performances.[39] Clearly the directors were making an effort to provide variety. It was economy and accessibility as much as the well known fondness of the audiences for the old-fashioned comedy and folk play that sent the actors to Blanche and Topelius and Dahlgren and to the popular playwrights of the 1860's and 1870's.

Blanche was the dramatist represented by the greatest number of plays. Eleven of his plays were acted, three of them being new to the Chicago repertoire: *Döden fadder* (Death the godfather); *Positivhataren* (The hand organ hater); and *Magister Bläckstadius.* Five Hedberg plays were performed, of which three were new: his "originals," *Carl XII* and *Hin och Smålandingen* (The devil and the man from Småland), and an adaptation from the French, *En odåga* (A good for nothing). There were no new plays by the third of the popular trio, Hodell, but with *Andersson, Pettersson och Lundström* one of his three plays that were used, he was hardly neglected. Historical dramas included Börjesson's *Erik den fjortonde,* earlier seen only in part in 1869, and an old *Gustaf Vasa,* in its only performance. Not many of these plays were repeated after this period, and none with any frequency. A few of the slight comedies that were introduced continued to hold the stage, but mainly in minor performances—*Sparlakanslexor* (Curtain lectures), *En domares vedermödor* (A judge's tribulations), *Hon både sparkas och bits* (She both kicks and bites)—and Uller's three-act comedy, *Kärlek och upptåg* (Love and pranks). On the other hand, most of the twenty-nine plays carried over from earlier seasons were played, if not extensively, in the 20th century. Then, as in the 1890's, they were supplemented by plays of the same types but not before acted in Chicago as well as by modern plays which, as the theatre became more firmly established, made up a larger proportion of the performances.

The 1890's brought Chicago only five Swedish plays from that and the preceding decade, but three of these are of considerable interest: the first Strindberg play and two comedies by Gustaf af Geijerstam, who had won a literary reputation as one of the realistic novelists of the "80ist" movement. Strindberg's *Lycko-Pers resa* (Lucky-Per's journey) of 1882 was produced by Albert Alberg, and Nelson's company was responsible for the première of Geijerstam's light comedy of 1888, *Svärfar* (Father-in-law). Geijerstam's country life comedy of 1894, *Per Olsson och hans käring* (Per Olsson and his woman) was introduced by Brusell and Behmer's *Svenska Teatersällskap*. Hedberg's *Hin och Smålandingen* was also a recent play, and Henrik Molander's *Kapten Crona*, acted in 1897, dated from 1893. Only *Per Olsson och hans käring* had a long history in Chicago, becoming a popular repertoire piece in the later days when rural farce was the fashion.

Not all of the new plays were characteristically Swedish. Chicago as well as Stockholm saw French romantic drama and operettas—*The Count of Monte Christo, Edmond Kean*, a version of *Don César de Bazan*, and *Prins Pippi och Fröken Fiffi*, one of the Pfeils' favorite operettas. Local authors contributed adaptations in addition to a goodly quota of original works. Of two versions of *Mam'zelle Nitouche* entitled *Lilla Helgonet* (The little saint), the second was by Gustaf Wicklund. Far more successful, however, was his translation of *Pinafore*, one of the few works from the English acted by Chicago Swedish companies. The other translation from the English now presented, *Sällskapsglaset*, from *The social glass*, by T. Trask Woodward, marked the entrance of the Good Templars and the temperance theme into the Swedish theatre picture. There was a local temperance play also, *Gästgifvarmor* (Innkeeper mother), by Bruno E. Höckertt, a successful pharmacist and journalist who was active in Good Templar work.[40] *Jeppe på bjerget* (Jeppe of the mountain), one of the notable satirical comedies of the Norwegian-Danish classical dramatist, Ludwig Holberg, was several times acted in Alberg's translation. Chicago newspaper man Theodore Sjöquist was credited with adapting an operetta, *Doktor Dulcamara*, from the German. And a much publicized feature of the 1899-1900 season was the opera, *Frithiof och Ingeborg*, by composer Carl F. Hanson of Worcester, Massachusetts, performed by a visiting company.

En afton på "Tre Byttor" (An evening at "Three Buckets") by Gustaf Wicklund dates from this period, though it was written before his return to

Chicago. This Bellman piece stands alone among the dramatic works written by men associated with the Chicago Swedish theatre, both in Chicago revivals and in the recognition it received in Sweden. It was published in Sweden in 1893, and on the centennial anniversary of Bellman's death, February 11, 1895, had its Stockholm première, followed by month of successful performances.[41] The majority of the locally written plays were variations on the old theme—the adventures of the immigrant in a Chicago setting—though Alberg took his immigrants farther afield in the Spanish-American War piece, *Svenskarne på Cuba* (The Swedes in Cuba). The most ambitious efforts were Ludwig Lundgren's *Anna Carlsson, Stina Johnson och Lova Petterqvist*, Ernst Lindblom's second play, *Alderman Swanson*, and *Anna Stina i Chicago*, by Ernst Behmer, with which he and Brusell ushered in the first season of their *Svenska Teatersällskap* in 1899. Pfeil's old *Chicago nattetid* was revamped, also, for performance as *Nattetid* in 1895.[42]

1891-1892

There was real rivalry, not merely expansion of theatrical activity, in the fall of 1891. The *Svenska Dramatiska Sällskap* and Nelson's new *Svenska Teatersällskap* opened their seasons the same evening, and the next week again gave competing performances. Nelson could boast the prestige of McVicker's—and the comfort of its seats. The *Svenska Dramatiska Sällskap* was at the North Side Turner Hall. An added attraction at the first McVicker's production was the Swedish Glee Club under the direction of John Örtengren; but the next week the *Svenska Dramatiska Sällskap* countered with the Svithiod Singing Club. The veteran company could advertise favorite actors: its leaders—Schoultz, Ovington, and Smith—and Sahlin, Mrs. Nordgren, and Anna Almgren. But Mr. Nelson, to balance such unknowns as Mr. Thimgren, Mr. Walter, and Miss Stäckig, had not only his beautiful young daughter, Hilma, the famous Albert Alberg, and Mrs. Hvitfeldt, but a director from the Swedish stage, Olaf Colldén. As to the plays acted early in the season, there was not much to choose between them. Neither company offered anything substantial, but there were new comedies as well as old, some of them destined for popularity.

In spite of a flood of publicity for the *Svenska Teatersällskap*, neither company attracted good houses. The newspapers (except for *Kuriren*, which chose to ignore the new company) were stern in their admonitions. Chicago Swedes could not support two companies. If quarrels accounted for the division of forces, both sides were at fault, and to persist in rivalry would simply defeat the cause of the Swedish theatre in Chicago. There was a show of neutrality: the prospect was that first one company and then the other would be more successful, for artistically they were on about the same level. But on the whole the newspapers beat the drums for Mr. Nelson. His were not, they reiterated, free shows, but carefully rehearsed performances, serious efforts to give the public something worthwhile and full value for its money.[43]

After its second appearance the Svenska Teatersällskap temporarily ended the rivalry by going on a tour in Illinois and Wisconsin, but the Svenska Dramatiska Sällskap did not persist. Except for an October comedy, it acted only once before the summer première of Wicklund's Bellman piece. The Nelson company did not resume regular activities until spring, but seems to have been distinguished only in name from the Svenska Skådespelare Sällskap (Swedish Actors Company) that gave a series of plays in South Side halls during the fall and winter. With Colldén as director and Hilma Nelson as star, the company was generally successful. Colldén was approved as the bachelor Konjander in Hittebarnet, and in Brusell's former role in Jernbäraren, ironbearer Axelson. Andersson, Pettersson och Lundström i Chicago, the seventh act added by Ernst Lindblom to their Christmas Andersson, Pettersson och Lundström, was also joyfully received.[44] On New Year's Day the North Side Swedes were offered the same play in its usual form by the "old, well known Svenska Dramatiska Sällskap." An excellent performance drew a house of 800, Svenska Kuriren reported, the largest at the North Side Turner Hall for a long time; but so small a crowd for this play was lamentable evidence that the public had lost its taste for the Swedish theatre.[45]

Competition in the form of performances in English was coming from the leaders of the Swedish theatre themselves. In January Mr. Nelson presented his daughter in a program of translated Swedish and Danish plays at McVicker's, and in February in an English version of a Danish play at the Chicago Opera House.[46] February brought also a similar venture by Albert Alberg, a performance at the South Side Auditorium of his translation from the Norwegian, A business man, by Björnstjerne Björnson; but his projected English version of a Topelius play, Fifty years after, was not acted, probably because of poor attendance (laid to limited publicity) at the Björnson play.[47] These efforts were in general encouraged by the Swedish papers, but Hilma Nelson was not greeted with the usual enthusiasm. She did not act badly, and of course she looked sweet, danced gracefully, and spoke English well, said Svenska Amerikanaren, but it voiced agreement with Tribunen, that to make her a star prematurely merely hindered her true progress. "Dear Mr. Nelson, take things easy, and do not rush matters so frantically."[48]

There was no such faint praise for the *Svenska Teatersällskap's* series of spring plays at Hooley's and the Criterion, and at the Auditorium, a "first" for the Swedish plays. Crowds turned out to see the old plays— *Vermländingarne, Nerkingarne, Jernbäraren,* and *Bröllopet på Ulfåsa*— and the new Geijerstam comedy that concluded the season. There was, to a degree, a union of the divided forces. Ovington played his popular role, the three-yard long Mamselle Bom, in *Nerkingarne,* and Anna Almgren, Sahlin, Schycker, Higgins, and Hedman of the *Svenska Dramatiska Sällskap* now acted with Nelson's company. By April, when Mr. Nelson was celebrating his fourth successful performance of *Vermländingarne* with souvenir programs, the critics were expressing pleasure and amazement at what he and Mr. Colldén had achieved. If such success had been prophesied three months before, the prophet would have been called crazy, but now it had been proved that the Swedish public would patronize Swedish drama given in respectable theatres by a company that made an effort to give the public its money's worth.[49]

A performance of *Vermländingarne* in Pullman was the occasion of an ecstatic account of the company by *Svenska Tribunen's* "Pelle Person." What a happy family they were, as they enjoyed the journey together: Anna—the beautiful and intelligent Hilma Nelson; Per—Higgins with his artist's shock of black hair; Anders and Löpare-Nisse—Colldén, serene and strong-featured, doing one's heart good with his ringing laughter; Sven—the lively young newspaperman, Björkman; Mor Lisa—the able Mrs. Hvitfeldt; and, of course, Father Nelson himself. Like the season's other performances of *Vermländingarne,* this one was highly praised, though there was some objection to Thimgren, as Anna's father, for spoiling her mad scene with comedy.[50]

For his Auditorium venture, Nelson chose *Bröllopet på Ulfåsa* and was able to attract a good house. The production was called excellent, and Alberg considered much better than the preceding season, but both in advertisements and review the play was overshadowed by the between acts appearance of the Swedish Dragoon Regiment from Englewood that was preparing to do the Swedes honor in the World's Fair parade.[51]

No disappointment attended the première of Geijerstam's *Svärfar,* though the author's reputation and tales of 250 performances in Sweden had raised high hopes. The action was lively, the characters were well drawn, and the main roles were superbly acted was the judgment of *Svenska*

101

Tribunen. For Edwin Björkman in the title role and his last appearance in Chicago, *Svärfar* was a particular triumph, bearing out the promise he had shown in *Vermländingarne* and as Knut Algotson in *Bröllopet på Ulfåsa.* A varied artistry imbued his portrayal of the middle-aged zoology professor and his rebellion against the idea of becoming a father-in-law. Hilma Nelson was pleasing as his daughter Elizabeth, who transfers her affections from a lieutenant to an artist and ultimately succeeds in making her father accept the laws of nature and approve her marriage. Higgins made the artist entertaining, but he was criticized for not portraying an artist "as he normally behaves." Hanna Hvitfeldt, however, ranked with Björkman in the demanding role of Cecilia, the professor's wife, whose jealous fears are aroused by the artist's young and beautiful model. It is easy to believe that this performance of *Svärfar* gave the audience a merry evening, for the play is a happy blend of conventional farce and witty characterization.[52]

A typical summer Bellman Day celebration, sponsored by the *Svenska Dramatiska Sällskap* and the Eolus Singing Club, introduced Wicklund's *En afton på "Tre Byttor"* to Chicago, on July 24, 1892. A crowd of 1,500 gathered at Ogden's Grove to see fireworks and balloons "measuring 20 by 30 feet" as well as the play, acted in "a specially constructed outdoor theatre." The Pfeils and Brusell came from their homes in Wisconsin to take the main roles, but after only one evening's rehearsal gave rather disappointing performances. And, with less excuse, the Chicago actors and singers failed to do justice to the witty pictures and songs Wicklund had provided. Nevertheless, the audience enjoyed itself, and the play was rightly judged a "neat and entertaining trifle." Pfeil played Father Bergström, whose birthday is being celebrated at the "Tre Byttor" tavern, one of the favorite haunts of Bellman and his circle. Brusell was Bellman, and Anna Pfeil was his sweetheart, Ulla Winblad, who fears he will marry in his own higher social class. The action centers about Bellman's escape from pursuing bailiffs. He evades them long enough to appease Ulla's fears, but is about to be carried off to prison for debt when his friend, Gustaf III, opportunely appears, on an incognito visit. The genial monarch settles the poet's debts, is recognized when Bellman inadvertently calls him "Your Majesty," and the play concludes with songs in his honor—the last of a series of songs to Bellman melodies that are the central feature of Wicklund's contribution to Bellman legend.[53]

1892-1893

The dominance of the Nelson company was not often challenged during the 1892-1893 season. His *Svenska Teatersällskap* had a stellar attraction in Hilma Nelson when she was not busy with Daly—for its first two plays, *Vermländingarne* and *Bröllopet på Ulfåsa*, and for the *Vermländingarne* that closed its Chicago season. Its two popular fall performances of *Andersson, Pettersson och Lundström* presented two pillars of the *Svenska Dramatiska Sällskap*, Schoultz and Brusell, in addition to Schycker, in the title roles. In February, Nelson brought Anna Pfeil from Minneapolis to act in *Nerkingarne,* and as a final coup he engaged Arthur Donaldson as actor and director for a revival of *Den ondes besegrare* and the spring *Vermländingarne.*[54]

The company was said to have given twenty-one performances, but only twelve were recorded for Chicago, unless one adds the production of Alberg's earlier postponed *Fifty years after,* presented at Hooley's by "Nelson's American Players," also called the English branch of the *Svenska Teatersällskap.*[55] Two performances in Moline followed the last Chicago play, and presumably there were other visits to nearby communities. The Rockford performances Liander describes in his reminiscences of Chicago were in all likelihood part of this season. The visits were carried out in style, with publicity which was costly and typically American. Hired carriages would await the company's arrival, and, four actors to a carriage, the horses draped with white cloth emblazoned with the name, The Swedish Theatre Company, the procession would drive to the hotel via the Swedish sections of the largely Swedish city. Then there would be, or so Liander said, three or four evenings of successful performances in an opera house with a seating capacity of 4,000.[56]

For seven of its Chicago performances, the *Svenska Teatersällskap* used plays that were familiar there, but a new historical play was a fall feature, and later *Jeppe på bjerget* had its première and three repetitions. Again the company acted at good theatres—Hooley's, the Criterion, and the Columbia—and again it journeyed to Pullman, this time with *Jeppe på bjerget.* Nelson had made performances at the North Side Turner Hall old-fashioned, *Svenska Amerikanaren* proclaimed, and for the time being that was true.

All was not cooperation this season, however. The *Svenska Dramatiska Sällskap* hazarded three performances at the North Side Turner Hall, the first a traditional New Year's *Andersson, Pettersson och Lundström.* It was well received, and, surprisingly, the company's spring *Vermländingarne,* under the leadership of Hedman, was more popular than that of the much touted *Svenska Teatersällskap* a month later. Arthur Donaldson's presence in the North Side Turner Hall cast may have had something to do with

103

a crowd so large that people had to stand between tables in the *salon*. The newspapers regretted that Donaldson was not the Erik, for "like Saul he was higher than any of the people."[57] The cast was probably much the same as that for a February *Vermländingarne* acted on the South Side, the only production of a company headed by Schycker and Hedman that called itself the *Svenska Teatersällskap* Columbia. Hedman then played his usual role of Erik; Mrs. Francke was Anna; Brusell, Sven; and Schycker, Anders and Löpare-Nisse. Mrs. Hedman also appeared in an unidentified role.[58]

Close on the heels of this *Vermländingarne* came the season's one performance by the *Svenska Skådespelare Sällskap*, again directed by Colldén. On the same evening *After fifty years* was acted by Nelson's American Players. The result was, of course, mediocre houses for both companies. Colldén's play was Blanche's *Positivhataren*, with Colldén in the leading role of the tavern owner obsessed by a hatred of hand organs which his daughter's suitor must pretend to share. Swedish Glee Club songs against a background of Stockholm's Djurgården, complete with its bust of Bellman, were naturally a popular feature of the evening.[59] *Positivhataren* was not again acted in Chicago, and after this play Colldén's name is absent from the records, except for the announcement of a farewell benefit in the fall of 1893. A week after *Positivhataren*, the *Svenska Teatersällskap* presented *Nerkingarne,* but it was not the expected drawing card. And once more the companies were advised to unite. Plays every two weeks could be properly supported, but two or three within a week or so could not expect to draw adequate audiences.[60]

The *Svenska Teatersällskap* did attract adequate audiences for most of the 1892-1893 season. Its chief effort of the fall, Hedberg's *Carl XII,* was well attended and the play politely commended for its literary merits, but it was not repeated. *Carl XII* is loosely constructed and lacks the dramatic effectiveness of the author's *Bröllopet på Ulfåsa,* and its historical period was considered less familiar and appealing. There was, however, real enthusiasm for the Swedish Dragoon Regiment that first tasted action in the battle of Narva scene that is the play's final climax. Schycker played Carl XII, and with fair success, though his soft voice and gentle manner were not thought appropriate for the hero's determined nature. As Stina Leuwenhaupt, the girl whom the young king loves, Hanna von Toyra made her first appearance, and was admired but warned against being excessively emotional. Most generously praised were Alberg as the stern, prophetic church leader, Jesper Svedberg; Hanna Hvitfeldt as the strong-willed dowager queen, Hedwig

104

Eleanora; and Anna Almgren as Greta Wrangel, Stin's young friend and confidante.[61]

There was no doubt that the *Svenska Teatersällskap's* January play, *Jeppe på bjerget*, was a popular success. The translation was Alberg's, but Holberg's witty and satirical comedy had long been known in Sweden in many versions. The public welcomed it for its comedy and the critics for its literary qualities, but, surprisingly, there were no real reviews. Advertisements emphasized third act songs by the Swedish opera singer, Svedelius, but neglected to state who was to play the dominant central role of Jeppe, the peasant who finds in drink his chief refuge from a shrewish wife and her ever ready cudgel, "Master Erick." At any rate, the Chicago Swedes had ample opportunity to enjoy the famous adventures encountered by a bemused Jeppe, when he is picked up by a lighthearted baron and his friends, dressed as a nobleman and convinced of his changed estate, only to be made drunk again and returned to his earlier situation.

Presenting *Jeppe på bjerget* for a third successive week, however, proved too optimistic—unfortunately for the Independent Order of Vikings and its hopes for a free reading room. The episode is described in the lodge history, *Runristningar*. Representatives of the company came to the January 21 meeting of Lodge Vikingarna No. 1 and offered to play a benefit for the project on January 29, and to repeat the benefit annually, "provided the reading room would be arranged in a respectable way, with no liquor served, and with ladies as well as gentlemen having the opportunity to enjoy good reading and genteel treatment." The offer was accepted, with gratitude for its liberality. But, though intentions were good, losses were great; and as to the annual benefit—the next year the company no longer existed.[62]

Such catastrophes were too common to discourage the intrepid devotees of the Swedish theatre. The next month the company was playing *Nerkingarne* at Hooley's, with Svedelius and Mrs. Pfeil as special attractions. Soon Donaldson was to take the public "by storm" as the evil spirit Asmodeus in *Den ondes besegrare*. But the season's last play, *Vermländingarne*, which was delayed until May 21 to enable Hilma Nelson to appear as Anna, was a disappointment. It had been anticipated by the *Svenska Dramatiska Sällskap* performance of the play, nicely timed for the evening before the opening of the World's Fair. By May 21, the Swedish public was occupied with plans for the first big concert of the Union of Swedish Singers and other events of the Fair's *Svenskarnas Dag* (Swedes' Day). Donaldson lived up to expectations in his Chicago debut as Erik, and the cast as a

105

whole was strong, with such new talents as Augusta Nyström as Britta and Mor Annika, John Liander as Anders and Löpare-Nisse, and Ludwig Lundgren as Per. The press chided an ungrateful public and lavished praise on the performance and on Mr. Nelson's "tireless efforts on behalf of the Swedish theatre."[63]

1893-1894

"Papa" Nelson was soon to weary of those efforts. Three productions in the fall of 1893 and a play presenting Hilma Nelson in her last Chicago appearance a year later brought his theatrical activities to a close. He opened the 1893-1894 season with a production of *Bröllopet på Ulfåsa* at Hooley's that promised to be a gala event. Donaldson was to be seen for the first time as Birger Jarl, and both Hilma Nelson and Madame Dorsch were announced. Perhaps the public learned that neither actress was to appear, or perhaps the reviews were right in thinking the play was too serious and too "mossy with age" to attract an audience. At any rate, the theatre was only half full. Donaldson was pronounced masterly, the Schoultz costumes "utterly elegant," and the dances directed by Ringenson brilliantly performed. Augusta Nyström, who had stepped into the demanding role of Sigrid the Fair, was treated kindly. But Director Alberg's Härved Boson was soundly rated. As on other occasions, the veteran actor stumbled through a half-memorized role. To make matters worse, the orchestra sounded "like a congregation of yowling cats." After this near fiasco and two little publicized productions at the Criterion, the *Svenska Teatersällskap* left the field.[64]

Already the company had been eclipsed by the production of *Regina von Emmeritz* in which Madame Dorsch gave her one Chicago performance. The presence of the famous actress had aroused much interest, and the newspapers prophesied, not without reason, the best Swedish performance ever given in Chicago. Carl Pfeil and his wife came from Minneapolis to play with Madame Dorsch, Pfeil in his former role as King Gustaf Adolf, and Mrs. Pfeil as the "charming, sweet, and naive chamber maid," Kätchen. The play proved a triumph for Madame Dorsch and for the cast as a whole, *Svenska Tribunen* reported enthusiastically. Every word, tone, and movement revealed the Stockholm actress as a complete artist. Her colleague, Oscar Ekelund, was considered superb as her father, Prince von Emmeritz, and the scene between father and daughter "left hardly a dry eye in the audience." Pfeil gave a powerful characterization, and Donaldson as Captain Larson was another star in a brilliant cast. There was praise also for

106

Mrs. Hvitfeldt and Littche as Dorthea and Hieronymus. An audience filling the Criterion showed its appreciation of this "artistic treat" by applauding madly; in fact, the calls for Pfeil were so lusty that they were mistaken as warnings of fire, and for a moment there was danger of panic.[65] In spite of this enthusiastic reception, plans for Madame Dorsch's appearance in Ibsen's historical drama, *Kämparne på Helgeland* (Warriors at Helgeland) were dropped, and she did not make the tour for which she had hoped to find a supporting company in Chicago. Her second and last public appearance was in a concert with Arthur Donaldson, and in May she returned to Sweden to rejoin the Royal Theatre Company.[66]

The season's other productions were not very encouraging, but men from the 1880's kept the theatre alive, with the assistance of Donaldson and the two actors from Sweden, Liander and Ekelund. Carl Pfeil stayed in Chicago, to begin another period of leadership, but his main effort of this season was a New Year's Day *Andersson, Pettersson och Lundström* at the North Side Turner Hall. It was successfully acted for a large crowd, said *Svenska Tribunen*. *Svenska Amerikanaren* reported a small house, and protested against such a bald-headed and unsavory old piece, but agreed that the performance was spirited. And a bright spot also was Wicklund's new version of Lundström's song depicting his travels, a song usually identified by its *dudelandej* refrain, and generally provided with up to date local verses. This 1894 Lundström had visited the World's Fair, we learn from one of the fourteen stanzas in the *Lundströmkupletter* published in Wicklund's *Gnistor från rimsmedjan:*

> I stopped to peek at the exposition,
> Emptied many a potent glass at "Fyllan."
> Life and hubbub aplenty there was,
> Especially up at the Midway Plaisance.[67]

A *Svenska Dramatiska Sällskap*, directed by Arthur Donaldson, had succeeded with fall performances of both *Andersson, Pettersson och Lundström* and *Vermländingarne*. As Lundström, Donaldson, too, had new songs—by Ville Åkerberg. With Brusell and Ekelund as Andersson and Pettersson, and Ovington in one of his popular roles as the pedantic Pluggstedt, the old play pleased a large audience. Ernst Behmer made his debut in this production, without attracting particular attention, and made his second appearance as Wilhelm in *Vermländingarne,* this time to be chided because he forgot to take off his student cap in the last act, when all heads were bared. Donaldson as Erik now attracted a more numerous public than when he had first played the role for the *Svenska Teatersällskap* the preceding spring. The Anna was the same, Mrs. Francke. Brusell played her father, and a relatively new recruit, Ernst Schycker's wife, "Maja," was Stina.[68]

It was during this season that the Swedish colony was roused by the killing of the young Swede, Swan Nelson, and the apparent escape from punishment of the two Irish policemen who had murdered him.[69] The many benefits and meetings that were promoted to raise funds for their prosecution included theatrical performances by a South Side Good Templar group. With Brusell as director, they presented a temperance melodrama, *Sällskapsglaset,* that was very popular in its original English. The company was a good one, leading roles being taken by Ekelund, Liander, and Augusta Nyström. Reviewers granted their ability and the value of the play as an example, but had no illusions about its quality. Its story of villainy and murder, ruin and repentance was correctly termed implausible, exaggerated, and illogical.[70]

Another novelty of which the reviewers were contemptuous, but which pleased audiences, was *Lasse-Maja,* twice presented by a company of which Schoultz was business manager and Liander director. It was a combination of sensation drama and folk play, with Ernst Schycker in the title role of the famous Robin Hood type thief. The versatile Donaldson was admired as Quartermaster Blix in *Lasse-Maja*[71]—and again as Engelbrekt in a revival of *Engelbrekt och hans Dalkarlar* with which the same company brought the regular season to a close. The old Blanche drama was given on April 22nd, 1894, at Hooley's, and the audience was as discouragingly small as it had been for Nelson's *Bröllopet på Ulfåsa* at the same theatre the preceding September. This time the performance left nothing to be desired; costumes, settings, dances, actors were excellent. The actors were those who had been most seen during the season—Ekelund, Brusell, Liander, Ludwig Lundgren, Augusta Nyström, and Mrs. Hvitfeldt. But Schoultz received small thanks for his pains and expenditure, said an irate *Svenska Kuriren* reviewer. It could not be expected that he would continue his worthy endeavours on behalf of the Swedish theatre in Chicago.[72]

1894-1895

Schoultz did try again the following spring, with the season's one city production, but not much better response; and in February 1895 he also made one of his now rare appearances on the stage, acting with his old friends Wicklund and Pallin in Pfeil's production of *Andersson, Pettersson*

108

och Lundström. Pfeil had been the secretary of a *Svenska Dramatiska Sällskap* formally organized in October, with Ludwig Lundgren as president, Brusell as treasurer, and Liander as director. The company gave four plays before Pfeil struck out for himself with *Andersson, Pettersson och Lundström,* and only one more performance was given under the *Svenska Dramatiska Sällskap* name during the 1894-1895 season. The season as a whole brought an upswing in support, but few notable productions. Good crowds welcomed Hilma Nelson, even in the heat of August, when she presented the operetta, *Lilla helgonet,* for her two final Chicago appearances. For these occasions she used the old company name, *Svenska Teatersällskap,* but it was *Svenska Dramatiska Sällskap* actors who supported her.[73]

Liander gained new prominence as actor and director in the fall *Svenska Dramatiska Sällskap* plays, his Lasse being a chief feature of the opening production, *Nerkingarne.* He had played the role at the Stockholm *Folk Teater* hundreds of times with brilliant success, the advertisements claimed, with characteristic exaggeration.[74] As Death, in the première of Blanche's *Döden fadder,* he shared honors with Carl Pfeil, who played the collier turned quack doctor "with a skill that would have surprised Garrick himself," according to *Svenska Amerikanaren.* The play was liked, but a prologue and speech presented in connection with a Gustaf II Adolf tableau were objected to as dull fare for a thousand Swedish young people who came to be entertained. There was the old complaint, also, of incongruous local references; certainly mention of the Market Street gang and South Bend did not belong in a Swedish setting.[75]

The company also presented, with popular success, a play by its president, Ludwig Lundgren—*Anna Carlson, Stina Johnson och Lova Petterqvist.* This was a remarkable but entertaining hodgepodge, with action in Sweden and melodramatic episodes added to the usual immigrant comedy and local settings. The action involved the ruin of a Stockholm girl, Lova Petterqvist, and her final reclamation in America; the pursuit by a Swedish baron of country-bred Anna Carlson, who has married an upright Minnesota farmer; and the marriage of Stina Johnson to an American millionaire whose opportune death permits her to reward the faithful suitor waiting in Sweden. Much enjoyed American settings included a Chicago Avenue saloon, the World's Fair, and a Swedish farm in Minnesota. For further variety, guests at an elegant masquerade ball were seen passing through a Dearborn Street kitchen, an episode that gave an opportunity for a touching song by Anna Pfeil, as a Swedish servant. And there was a grand finale, with the costumes forming a Swedish flag. Pfeil played the farmer, and Gus Higgins, in an unidentified role, was considered particularly comic. This was one of several occasions when *Svenska Tribunen* expressed gratitude to Gus Colliander, who was in charge of the bar, for his diligence in keeping order during the performance.[76]

Other locally written plays of the season included Pfeil's revival of his *Chicago nattetid,* one of the two plays he presented at both the North Side and South Side Turner Halls. Whether as *Nattetid* it still presented local individuals is not clear, but at any rate Pfeil played a Stockholm soldier who encounters robbers and police in Chicago and ultimately takes the hero's role in the excerpt from *Prins Pippi och Fröken Fiffi* that was a feature of his earlier version also. *Nattetid* was accounted hilarious and Pfeil himself incomparable.[77] A comedy with a Swedish setting, *Fias rivaler,* which was the work of Chicago journalist Edward Holmes, was acted three times by a small company under his direction, but was pronounced beneath criticism.[78] More fortunate, and doubtless more deserving, was Theodore Sjöquist of *Svenska Kuriren,* whose operetta adapted from the German, *Doktor Dulcamara, eller Konsten att af basar göra tenorer* (The art of making tenors of basses) was twice performed by the Swedish Glee Club, with general approval.[79]

Pfeil and his former *Svenska Dramatiska Sällskap* associates had collaborated in his *Andersson, Pettersson och Lundström,* but as the season drew toward a close rivalry developed. In March Brusell and Liander advertised the new Hedberg play, *Hin och Småländingen,* for April 7. The performance took place as announced, but only after Pfeil had made strenuous efforts to prevent it. The story is told in the Swedish papers and in Liander's reminiscences of Chicago. Rehearsal was proceeding peacefully, Liander wrote, undisturbed by the presence of two strangers who were presumably looking over North Side Turner Hall with the intention of renting it. One of them came to the stage and asked for the director. Liander identified himself—and in the wink of an eye the man snatched the manuscript of the play and threw it to his companion in the *salon.* The actors were mystified, but, as they knew their parts, went on with the rehearsal. According to *Svenska Tribunen,* Pfeil secured an injunction, claiming to have the rights to the play. But Brusell and Liander had bought the rights, and had a letter from Hedberg to that effect with which they were able to prove their case to the judge. Liander did not name the rival director, but said he wanted to prevent their obtaining a good box office piece, and hired detectives to trick them.[80]

Front row, center, Christopher Brusell as Captain Corcoran, Anna Pfeil as Little Buttercup, Margaret Dahlstrom as Hebe, Knut Schröder as Sir Joseph Porter, Ida Linn as Josephine, Gust Lindquist as Ralph Rackstraw, Fred R. Franson as Dick Deadeye, Little Anna Pfeil as Tom Tucker

Pinafore, January 10, 1897, McVicker's Theatre

Christopher Brusell as Captain
Corcoran

Pinafore, 1896-1897

Anna Pfeil as Little Buttercup

Knut Schröder as Sir
Joseph Porter

From the whole affair *Svenska Kuriren* drew the familiar moral: though Chicago is a giant city, it cannot support two Swedish dramatic troupes. The disputed play was a popular success, with Liander as the country lad and John Lindhagen as the devil (a role he had played in Stockholm "almost a hundred times," and, in addition, costumes from Schoultz, and scenery painted by Liander and Higgins. And the disagreement blew over. When these actors, as the *Svenska Dramatiska Sällskap*, concluded the regular season with *Vermländingarne,* the performance was a benefit for Mrs. Pfeil in her best liked role. Local interest if not dramatic illusion was increased, on this occasion, by the crowning of a popularly elected May Queen during the Midsummer festivities of the first act.[81]

Fritz Schoultz's efforts to promote "really worth while Swedish drama" by presenting Emil von der Osten at Hooley's in April brought him only a sizeable loss; the public preferred "to run like mad to see outworn trash at Turner Hall." There was, however, no lack of critical appreciation for von der Osten. In a role with which he was closely identified, the sailor hero of *Edmond Kean,* he fulfilled all expectations. His fellow actors from Chicago were thought to be inspired by his example, and Carl Pfeil, at least, was not overshadowed by the famous visitor.[82]

1895-1896

Two Criterion performances of *Hin och Småländingen* began the 1895-1896 season. They were farewell benefits for John Liander, soon to return to Sweden, and were considered triumphs both for him and for John Lindhagen—whose *Hin* must surely "have made his Satanic Majesty green with envy." The cast was made up largely of actors who were to be the old reliables of the following decades—Brusell, Behmer, Ida Anderson-Werner, and Augusta Nyström Milton. Hedberg himself would have given their performances a nod of approval, *Svenska Amerikanaren* proudly asserted.[83]

The group continued as the *Svenska Dramatiska Sällskap,* under the direction of Carl Pfeil, giving eight performances that constituted the main theatrical season. Since they acted at both the North Side and South Side Turner Halls, they used only four plays, and two of these were the time-tried *Andersson, Pettersson och Lundström* and *Vermländingarne.* *Sabinskornas bortröfvande* was a successful revival, and there was one novelty, a version of *Don César de Bazan* called *Kungen och Gatusångerskan* (The king and the street singer). The audience was as well satisfied with the old plays; Pfeil made a good king in *Don César,* but funnier and more Swedish plays were what the public preferred.[84]

The rest of the season offered little occasion for enthusiasm. Donaldson headed one production, but his choice of play, Blanche's *Jernbäraren,* was criticized. Its morals were always applicable, of course, but no matter how well acted such a *tendens* drama seemed old-fashioned.[85] The Good Templars gave two plays, one of them by Chicagoan A. B. Höckert. *Nordstjernan,* the society that had played Wicklund's first pieces, acted Gus Higgins's one known contribution to the Chicago Swedish repertoire. Wicklund had to deny authorship of another local play, *Nyårsnatt på Hotell Svea.* Behmer remembered it as a disgraceful work, probably the product "of a small coterie of would-be literary saloon-bums, who infested the Swedish colony of Chicago's North Side at that time."[86] Albert Alberg produced one play at the North Side Turner Hall, as a benefit for himself. That fact and the occasion rather than the merits of the performance probably account for the kindness with which it was received. The play was *Gustaf Vasa,* though which of several old plays by that name there is no indication; and it was presented April 26, 1896, as part of the general celebrations of the 400th anniversary of Gustaf Vasa's death. Alberg yielded the role of the king to Brusell, who gave his customary able performance; and there was praise also for Mrs. Feltskogh as the heroic wife of the peasant traitor, Anders Persson. On the debit side were Lindhagen's "indisposition," thus politely designated, and a backdrop depicting Washington crossing the Delaware for a scene occurring in the valleys of Sweden.[87]

1896-1897

As early as August, 1896, advertisements were appearing for the play that was to inaugurate the 1896-1897 season. Ernst Lindblom, in Chicago for a brief stay, was attempting to repeat his success with *Pelle Pihlqvists Amerika-resa* with a second local comedy, *Alderman Swanson,* Higgins had pictured the alderman, complete with silk hat, boutonnière, and cigar, and the prospective audience was given a taste of his song,

> Jeg är en al, en der, en man
> [I am an al, a der, a man]
> En alder-alder-alderman
> En alderman.

Politicians and their families were invited to occupy reserved seats in the first rows. Perhaps they did, and perhaps the play was both successful and amusing, but the papers ignored it, and it does not figure in Lind-blom's memoirs.[88]

The newspapers were giving their attention to Albert Alberg's efforts to provide the long hoped for Swedish stock company. On September 22, the *Nya* (New) *Svenska Teatersällskap* announced formal organization, with attorney P. W. Nelson as president and Alberg as director. The secretary was a musician, John Anderson, and the orchestra director was Mr. Jennings, of *Stora Teatern* Opera Company, Stockholm, and *Nya Teatern*, Göteborg. Optimistically, Alberg had rented the Criterion theatre for Sunday performances over a three year period, and made plans for intervening trips to nearby cities.[89] The personnel of the company was promising, with such gifted and experienced actors as Carl and Anna Pfeil and their daughter, Carl and Augusta Milton, Ida Anderson-Werner, Matt Ovington, and John Lindhagen. A relative newcomer in the group was Ellen Graf; and Max Hedman and Mrs. Hvitfeldt acted with them occasionally, at least. Unusually careful preparation was given their productions, Mr. and Mrs. Milton recalled, for disappearance of jobs in the post World's Fair depression permitted daytime as well as evening rehearsals.

Though the weekly schedule was not strictly adhered to, the *Nya Svenska Teatersällskap* achieved the remarkable record of eleven performances in Chicago in two months, all but one at the Criterion. Projected out of town performances were carried out also. But in December the enterprise came to an abrupt close.

The beginning was successful. Plays were not new, but crowds were large, and reviews laudatory. Carl Pfeil and his wife scored as Herr Dardanell and the stupid Agapetus in the old Blanche favorite, *Herr Dardanell och hans upptåg på landet,* and in succeeding roles. The Blanche comedy was given in Rockford and Elgin between October 4 and 8, and again in Moline and Galesburg the 14th and 16th.[90] Lindhagen was a particular success in *Bellman på Gröna Lund,* Ellen Graf if anything too young and adorable as Gustaf III.[91] Not until November was a critical note allowed to appear in reviews. Then the excellent *Vermländingarne* was praised for having overcome the unevenness of earlier performances, while at the same time it was criticized for over emphasis on comedy in the serious scenes and for the way the Värmland dialect was mangled.[92]

On Saturday and Sunday evenings November 14 and 15 the *Nya Svenska Teatersällskap* gave its first new play, *Grefven af Monte Christo,* but it was overshadowed by the Svithiod Singing Club's *Pinafore.* The next week *Herr Dardanell och hans upptåg på landet* was repeated, and

113

performances on December 5 and 6 ended the three year project. What play was given on December 5 and 6 the newspapers did not state, reporting only the fracas that occurred at the final performance, with actors and constables tearing each other's hair, as the constables tried to seize the December 5 proceeds on behalf of a plumbing company. A mysterious correction of this version of the incident stated that the janitor of the theatre and certain other people could tell the true story.[93] Whatever the truth was, the company acted no more.

The fall had brought the final Chicago performance of *Jeppe på bjerget* also. It was acted at the North Side Turner Hall on October 18, in competition with Alberg's *Valborgsmesso-aftonen* at the Criterion. Hanna von Toyra headed the *Jeppe* company, and Ernst Behmer starred in the title role. His later colleague, Brusell, was in the cast, as well as Leopold Chellman, who may have been making his Chicago debut.[94] Seemingly there was an audience for both plays, but this group did not make a second attempt, unless it was responsible for a little publicized *Andersson, Pettersson och Lundström*, a spring production credited to the *Svenska Dramatiska Sällskap*.

Unquestionably the chief events of the theatrical season were the two performances of *Pinafore*, the first major dramatic project of the Svithiod Singing Club. Brusell directed the operetta, and made Captain Corcoran one of his most successful roles. Anna Pfeil proved a delightful Little Buttercup, and one of the hits of the production was her small daughter's Tommy Tucker. A young and later well known singer, Ida Linn, was Josephine. And in his first role in a Swedish production, Admiral Porter, Knut Schröder scored an immediate success. The choruses were highly praised, and club members considered satisfactory in minor roles. In spite of an increase in ticket prices, the North Side Turner Hall was filled for the first performance. A laurel wreath decked in Swedish colors honoring Gustaf Wicklund for his translation was a well deserved tribute. The manuscript of his translation shows that in it his gifts were at their best. Gilbert's witty, well-turned verses lost little, and the Wicklund songs are as well adapted to the music as are the English originals.[95]

The excellence of the production as well as the welcome variety it offered from the everlasting *Andersson, Pettersson och Lundström* brought *Pinafore* even greater success when it was repeated at McVicker's in January. Never, said *Svenska Amerikanaren*, had this widely performed operetta been better given. All recollections of the performance suggest that the verdict was not unreasonably enthusiastic.[96]

1897-1898

In April 1897 Pfeil directed a Good Templar temperance play, *Kapten Crona,* and that spring the Pfeil Trio was often seen in variety entertainments. But for an unusually long period the Swedish theatre remained dormant. Not until the spring of 1898 were there sporadic efforts to revive it. Then a *Svenska Dramatiska Sällskap,* directed first by Anna Pfeil and for its second play by her husband, offered *Vermländingarne* and *Herr Dardanell och hans upptåg på landet* to both North Side and South Side audiences, with fair success. The company was good—Bolling, Chellman, and the Miltons, Hedman, and Alberg, besides old-timers like Mrs. Hvitfeldt, Sahlin, and Knut Lindstrom—but the scenery and facilities of the Turner Halls were a handicap. So was the audience, *Svenska Amerikanaren* complained. Perhaps many of them came in order to dance, not to watch, but they should at least keep quiet and not throw things in the gallery. Some day, it was to be hoped, the actors would get the audiences they deserved, audiences that could appreciate beautiful dramatic art, and such "literary pearls" as *Vermländingarne.*[97] Only the Pfeils and Alberg attempted any further theatricals in the 1898 spring season. June found Alberg contributing tableaux and a pageant type drama, *Svenskarne på Cuba,* to Swedish patriotic programs in connection with the Spanish-American War, and in July he directed scenes from *Bröllopet på Ulfåsa* for *Svenska National Förbund* festivities at Columbia Park.[98]

1898-1899

Dramatic fare was still rather sparse in the 1898-1899 season, but several productions indicated that the Swedish theatre was coming out of its doldrums. For its renewed progress the Pfeils and the Svithiod Singing Club were chiefly responsible. Wilma Sundborg, too, on her first visit to Chicago, presented *Vermländingarne* at both Turner Halls. Good houses greeted her and a company including Hedman as Erik, Lindhagen as Löpare-Nisse, and Brusell as Anna's father, Jan Hansson. The reviewers were unshaken in their loyalty to Anna Pfeil, but granted that Wilma Sundborg was a capable if somewhat mature Anna, and that she sang better than she acted.[99]

In October Carl Pfeil had opened the season in his popular Lundström role, and from time to time in the following months he presented the operettas and comedies that were his standard repertoire. He also directed the chief production of the season, *Regina von Emmeritz,* acted at the Auditorium in November as part of a Gustaf II Adolf festivity.

The affair was sponsored by the *Svenska Föreningarnas Central För-bund* on behalf of a projected old people's home at Park Ridge; and with an audience of 4,000 paying fifty cents and a dollar, net profits were $800.00. From an artistic standpoint as well, the event was a success. Mrs. Pfeil and Mrs. Hvitfeldt gave excellent performances as Regina and Dorthea, Knut Schröder was an exceptionally good Bertil, and Lindhagen a hitherto unequalled Hieronymus. Of the play's principals only Pfeil, perhaps burdened by his duties as director, was regarded as ineffective, being obviously dependent on the prompter.

The play was almost overshadowed, however, by the preliminary program, and in particular by the speech delivered by the Reverend Mr. Carl A. Ewald of the Augustana Immanuel church—who was also the son-in-law of its first pastor, that implacable foe of the theatre, Erland Carlsson. Ewald's appearance at a play was hailed with rejoicing by *Svenska Ameri-kanaren.* It was a hopeful sign of closer relationships between preachers and people than had generally prevailed. Though there were others in the Augustana Synod as liberal as he, not many Swedish preachers would have spoken at a play, and he was a good example to his brothers. But "only a fanatic could object to *Regina von Emmeritz.*" Johan A. Enander, editor of *Hemlandet,* was another prominent representative of the church who participated in the program, and his newspaper not only gave the play a laudatory review, but urged its readers to give it their support.[100] Support from these sources was not consistent, but the theatre was to benefit by the breaking down of the old divisions.

Less successful but still a hopeful augury of the future was another city performance—the Svithiod Singing Club's *Lilla helgonet,* given at the Studebaker January 12, 1899. Wicklund had provided a good adaptation of *Mam'zelle Nitouche,* Anna Pfeil and Knut Schröder were superb in leading roles, but once more the audience was "not as large as the play deserved." The theatre was not known to the Swedes, the middle of the week was not a good time, and the weather was unfortunate, *Svenska Kuriren* explained. Repetition at the North Side Turner Hall was urged,[101] but the club contented itself with reviving Wicklund's *En afton på "Tre Byttor"* at its summer Bellman Day celebration. This time the play was well performed, with Carl Pfeil as director, John Örtengren in charge of the music, and Mrs. Pfeil again the Ulla.[102]

1899-1900

The 1899-1900 season brought a Swedish American opera from the East for Auditorium performances; there were productions by the Pfeils and by the Svithiod Singing Club; and Alberg made another abortive attempt to establish a company. Another company, also, with the old name, *Svenska Teatersällskap,* made its debut in November. It gave three plays at the North Side Turner Hall, with encouraging success; but there was little reason to suspect that these performances were the beginning of a new and culminating period in the development of the Chicago Swedish theatre.

Christopher Brusell, an accepted leader since the 1880's, was announced as the manager, and it was he and Ernst H. Behmer who formed the new company. Behmer had been an enthusiastic participant in theatrical activities for the last half dozen years, and now he made his bow as a playwright with their first production, *Anna Stina i Chicago.* It was an adaptation of a well known Swedish play, the reviews claimed, but so masterly localized, with such genuine Swedish American types, that Behmer might well be called its author.[103]

The story was the familiar one, a Swedish newcomer's experiences in Chicago. The action, the happy ending and grand finale, are indicated by the titles of the four acts:

I   Just Over
II   A Rich Chicago Family
III   Dining Room on Chicago Avenue
IV   A Picnic in Sharpshooter's Park

Romantic leads were taken by Brusell and Ellen Graf, Anna Francke played a country girl, and Behmer a young Swedish American. Providing local color were Ernest Lindblom[104] as an alderman, Lindhagen as a contractor and coachman, Hedman as a bartender, Ida Anderson-Werner and Mrs. Feltskogh as a boardinghouse keeper and a housewife, and Knut Schröder in two roles, Gus and the snobbish Baron Lejon. Manuscript copies of Schröder's roles show that the Baron who pursues and loses his Swedish sweetheart was first intended to be a British lord, while Gus's part is less conventional, with an amusing mixture of Swedish and English, and references to the wealth he expects when Bryan and Free Silver triumph. The play was thought amusing and had the benefit of gay songs by Gustaf Wicklund; but it was too long, was the final verdict. And, like most of the local plays, *Anna Stina i Chicago* was performed but once.[105]

Alberg made big plans for the company he called the South Side *Svenska Teatersällskap,* and advanced high claims for its inaugural production of Strindberg's *Lycko-Pers resa,* to be given on Christmas Day and New Year's Day. The regular company of twenty young people had

117

been augmented to fifty-three for this play, and its star was a newly arrived comedian, Ernst Ekberg. The America Theatre had been rented for a year of regular performances, prices were to be popular (fifteen to fifty cents), and serving was to be restricted to the room adjoining the theatre. The newspapers ignored the fact that Strindberg was being introduced to Chicago Swedish audiences, and accorded his famous saga play only brief reports of fair houses, beautiful settings, and the genuine comic talent evident in Ekberg's interpretation of Lycko-Per. Of the enterprise as a whole no more was heard.[106]

Other holiday events were joint productions of the Svithiod Singing Club and the Swedish Glee Club: *En afton på "Tre Byttor"* and *Pinafore* at the North Side Turner Hall, and *Pinafore,* "by special request," at the South Side Turner Hall. The performances were somewhat casual but entertained fair audiences.[107] In January, also, the *Svenska Teatersällskap* gave its second production, the reliable *Nerkingarne,* with Brusell and Anna Francke in the leading roles. Newspaper praise was generous, but bitterly cold weather interfered with attendance.[108]

Already Swedish circles were turning their thoughts and efforts to the Swedish American opera that was to be presented at the Auditorium for three evenings in February. *Frithiof och Ingeborg* was the work of a prolific composer of Swedish birth, Carl F. Hanson, of Worcester, Massachusetts, and had received considerable attention after its première there in December 1898. The Chicago performance was sponsored by the *Svenska National Förbund* (underwritten by F. A. Lindstrand), and the society's dynamic secretary, Mrs. Myhrman, left no stone unturned in providing publicity. The majority of the performers came from the East, but the choruses and some of the soloists were from Chicago, Örtengren and Alberg had a share in the direction, and Schoultz supplied the costumes. The opera brought the *Svenska National Förbund* a profit of $848.85. On the whole, however, it was a disappointment. Polite praise was overshadowed by adverse criticism. The libretto, a dramatization of Tegnér's *Fritiofs Saga,* proved undramatic, and the music was neither original nor authentically Swedish, said the Chicago reviewers. A study of *Frithiof och Ingeborg* by the Minneapolis music critic, Hjalmar Nilsson, supports their views, though he defended Hanson's use of Swedish folk melodies and his general approach to a difficult task.[109]

Less pretentious but probably as much enjoyed was the *Svenska Teatersällskap's Vermländingarne,* the one major theatrical effort of the season to follow the opera. Though they pronounced the whole performance ex-

cellent, the reviewers of course found points to criticize. Brusell, playing
Erik for the first time, was thought somewhat passive, and Ernest Lindblom
not well suited to Brusell's usual role of Sven. Behmer's concept of Anders
was questioned, though his acting was not. New members of the cast, Oscar
Sundborg and his wife, Therese, did well, he as Ola i Gyllby and Löpare-
Nisse, and she as Stina. Mrs. Pfeil was as usual a superlative Anna—but on
this occasion Ida Anderson-Werner shared top honors with her. *Svenska
Tribunen* stated flatly that one could not see a better Mor Lisa on Sweden's
most distinguished stage.[110]

1900-1901

Andersson, Pettersson och Lundström, strangely missing the preceding
season, was Carl Pfeil's choice for the celebration of his twenty-fifth anniversary as an actor that opened the 1900-1901 season. At two festive performances, October 6 and 7, at the two Turner Halls, good houses were
kept in ecstasy by Pfeil's Lundström. His "twenty-five years of faithful
service to Thalia" were honored by a laurel wreath presented by Alberg,
"who played Hamlet in the original language before most of us were
born," and there were appropriate verses by the Pettersson of the play,
Leopold Chellman. Pfeil made a "beautiful response," keeping his Lundström character throughout. Behmer played Andersson, and Anna Pfeil,
in a variety of roles, proved again her right to be called "the darling of us
Swedish-Americans."[111]

Not even Anna Pfeil, however, could rescue the third October play,
Alberg's ill fated Auditorium production of the old Börjesson tragedy, *Erik
den fjortonde.* It was a benefit for flood victims at Galveston, Texas, but
the worthiness of the cause did not attract a good audience. Only the parquet was well filled. Alberg himself was ineffectual in the leading role,
making a botch of Erik's most dramatic speeches. The cast was filled with
the city's Swedish American notables, who failed both as drawing cards and
as actors. Among those who trod the boards in *Erik den fjortonde* were
Frans A. Lindstrand, the patron saint of the *Svenska National Förbund*
as well as the publisher of *Svenska Amerikanaren;* such a representative
of the church as Dr. Enander of *Hemlandet;* other journalists, "Kurre"
Johnson, of *Svenska Kuriren,* and Ernst W. Olson; Robert Lindblom, fin-
ancier and civic leader; a prominent doctor, Carl Swensson—not to mention a number of Swedish aldermen and their wives. Presumably, Mrs.
Myhrman and Örtengren gave better performances than these novices, but
only the Pfeils, Ernest Lindblom, and Augusta Milton were credited with

119

able acting. And the whole dragged out to such length that, as *Svenska Kuriren* noted, many spectators left early to catch the last "carsen."[112]

Fortunately, the second Auditorium play of the season, promoted by the *Svenska National Förbund* in February, was a genuine success. This time the play was the popular *Vermländingarne*, the house was filled, and there was a profit of $512.35. A coup for Mrs. Myhrman was the presentation of John Örtengren as Erik, his first but not his last appearance in the role. Ragna Linné, another singer of repute, was Anna, and Mrs. Pfeil was relegated to Stina's comic role, playing opposite Brusell as Per. Carl Pfeil was, except for his exaggerated "getup," a successful Löpare-Nisse. One of the "surprises" popular with Swedish audiences was provided by the Svithiod Singing Club, which sang Söderman's "Wedding March" (from *Bröllopet på Ulfåsa*) at the Maypole festivities in the first act.[113]

The Pfeils gave some of their usual entertainments during the season, and in three April performances introduced a comedy that was to remain popular. This was Uller's old *Kärlek och upptåg,* an absurd tale of misunderstandings developing because a girl and a brig have the same name. Carl Liljegren was a welcome addition to the company for these spring productions. Pfeil had also offered a Christmas novelty, an American localization in English of *Hin och Småländingen* (the play he had tried to keep Liander from producing). Four North Side Turner Hall performances were advertised for the holiday week, and half the profits were to go to the Park Ridge Old People's Home. But *The devil and the Swede*—an ugly title, the papers objected—was acted only once.[114] Undaunted, Pfeil attempted another English adaptation of a Swedish play in May, this time Blanche's *Döden fadder* as *The Wonder Doctor.* The announced week of evening and matinée performances was carried out in part, according to *Svenska Amerikanaren,* with good effect.[115]

Pfeil's December fiasco had been blamed for poor attendance at the *Svenska Teatersällskap's* New Year's Day performance, its third and last of the season. The public had been made suspicious by the cancellation of much advertised plays, said *Svenska Kuriren*—but the *Svenska Teatersällskap* had never cancelled a performance in its "many years of activity" (this in its second season). For its New Year's program, the company revived two long familiar plays, *Bror Jonathan* and *En midsommarnatt i Dalarne,* with, of course, new songs. Behmer was the Jonathan, and Anna Pfeil contributed her talents, as she had in their fall play.[116]

Twice in November the *Svenska Teatersällskap* had acted Geijerstam's recent comedy, *Per Olsson och hans käring,* with unquestioned suc-

cess. The play, in a favorite phrase of the reviewers, "went as if oiled."
Brusell and Ida Anderson-Werner gave outstanding characterizations of the
peasants, Per, and Katrina, his shrewish and greedy wife, and Chellman
seemed born to the role of Fattig-John (Poor-John), Per's brother. Bolling
was Per's son by a previous marriage, and Behmer was Erker, the oafish son
of Per and Katrina. Geijerstam's comedy is no idealized folk picture. Per
discovers that Katrina is trying to poison him to get his money for their son
and to cheat his; and the big scene, that provides a moderately happy ending, comes when Per has pretended to hang himself and by proving Katrina's guilt at last gets the upper hand. The reviewers welcomed the play
for its realistic country types as well as for its comedy, and made sound
prophecies of its future success. The public owed a debt of gratitude, it was
told, to the *Svenska Teatersällskap,* not only for this opportunity to become
acquainted with a dramatist so popular in the homeland, but for the way
in which the company was furthering the cause of the Swedish theatre in
Chicago.[117]

Brusell and Behmer had succeeded in laying the foundation for their
period of leadership. They were ready to move their main productions to
city theatres and to do what the earlier *Svenska Teatersällskap* had failed
to do—make Swedish plays at the North Side Turner Hall old-fashioned.

CHRONOLOGICAL TABLE, CHAPTER IV

Performances, 1891-1892 through 1900-1901

Date	Play	Company	Place
	1891-1892		
Sept. 6, 1891	*Hittebarnet*	S. T.	McVicker's
	Alla möjliga roller		
	Hon både sparkas och bits		
Sept. 6, 1891	*Lustresan från Skåne*	S. D. S.	N. S. T. H
	Sparlakanslexor		
Sept. 13, 1891	*Skal och kärna**	S. T.	McVicker's
	En odåga		
	En midsommarnatt i Dalarne		
Sept. 13, 1891	*Ett resande teatersällskap*	S. D. S.	N. S. T. H.
	(as *Komedianterne*)		
Oct. 3, 1891	*Det skadar inte!*	S. D. S. for Götha Lodge	N. S. T. H.
Nov. 14, 1891	*En domares vedermödor*	S. T. for Balder Lodge	Swedish Music Hall
Nov. 15, 1891	*Hittebarnet**	S. S. S.[118]	Swedish Music Hall
	Bättre aldrig än sent		
Nov. 20, 1891	....	S. S. S.	Swedish Music Hall
Nov. 22, 1891	*Rika Morbror*	S. S. S.	Swedish Music Hall
	Hon både sparkas och bits		
Nov. 29, 1891	....	S. S. S.	Swedish Music Hall
Dec. 5, 1891	*En domares vedermödor*	Svithiod	....
Dec. 13, 1891	*Jernbäraren*	S. S. S.	S. S. Auditorium
Dec. 19, 1891	*De båda rivalerna*	Nordstjernan	Hurbert's Hall, Blue Island
Dec. 26, 1891	*Andersson, Pettersson och Lundström*	S. S. S.	S. S. Auditorium
Jan. 1, 1892	*Andersson, Pettersson och Lundström*	S. D. S.	N. S. T. H.
Mch. 5, 1892	*Vermländingarne*	S. T.	Hooley's
Mch. 13, 1892	*Vermländingarne*	S. T.	Criterion
Mch. 20, 1892	*Jernbäraren*	S. T.	Criterion
	Hon både sparkas och bits		
Mch. 24, 1892	*Vermländingarne*	S. T.	Arcade, Pullman
Apr. 10, 1892	*Vermländingarne*	S. T.	Criterion
May 1, 1892	*Nerkingarne**	S. T.	Hooley's
May 7, 1892	*Hon både sparkas och bits*	S. S. S. for Svithiod	N. S. T. H.
May 8, 1892	*Nerkingarne*	S. T.	Hooley's
May 22, 1892	*Bröllopet på Ulfåsa*	S. T.	Auditorium
May 29, 1892	*Svärfar**	S. T.	Criterion
July 24, 1892	*En afton på "Tre Byttor"*	S. D. S. & Eolus	Ogden's Grove

122

Date	Play		Company	Place
		1892-1893		
Sept. 4, 1892	Vermländingarne		S. T.	Hooley's
Sept. 18, 1892	Bröllopet på Ulfåsa*		S. T.	Hooley's
Oct. 16, 1892	Andersson, Pettersson och Lundström		S. T.	Hooley's
Oct. 23, 1892	Andersson, Pettersson och Lundström		S. T.	Hooley's
Nov. 27, 1892	Carl XII		S. T.	Columbia
Dec. 17, 1892	Pelles första natt i Amerika		Nordstjernan	Uhlich's Hall
Jan. 1, 1893	Andersson, Pettersson och Lundström		S. D. S. for Central Commandery No. 7	N. S. T. H.
Jan. 15, 1893	Jeppe på bjerget		S. T.	McVicker's
Jan. 22, 1893	Jeppe på bjerget		S. T.	Criterion
Jan. 29, 1893	Jeppe på bjerget		S. T.	Criterion
Feb. 9, 1893	Vermländingarne		S. T. Columbia	Marlowe
Feb. 12, 1893	Positivhataren		S. S. S.	Criterion
Feb. 19, 1893	Nerkingarne		S. T.	Hooley's
Mch. 9, 1893	Jeppe på bjerget		S. T.	Arcade, Pullman
Apr. 16, 1893	Den ondes besegrare		S. T.	Columbia
Apr. 23, 1893	Sköflad lycka En Bengalisk tiger		S. D. S. for Mimer Lodge, I. O. of S.	N. S. T. H.
Apr. 30, 1893	Vermländingarne		S. D. S.	N. S. T. H.
May 6, 1893	En natt i Falkenberg		S. D. S. for Svithiod	N. S. T. H.
May 21, 1893	Vermländingarne		S. T.	Columbia
		1893-1894		
Sept. 17, 1893	Bröllopet på Ulfåsa*		S. T.	Hooley's
Sept. 24, 1893	Regina von Emmeritz		Dorsch Co.	Criterion
Oct. 4, 1893	Herr Dardanell och hans upptåg på landet		S. T.	Criterion
Oct. 11, 1893	Balen på Gröna Lund (as Bellman på Gröna Lund)		S. T.	Criterion
Oct. 14, 1893	Mot beräkning		Pfeil Co. for Court Vega No. 34 I. O. F. Pleasure Club	N. S. T. H.
Oct. 15, 1893	Lasse-Maja		Schoultz & Liander Co.	N. S. T. H.
Nov. 12, 1893	Andersson, Pettersson och Lundström		S. D. S.	N. S. T. H.
Dec. 3, 1893	Vermländingarne		S. D. S.	N. S. T. H.
Dec. 25, 1893	Lasse-Maja		Schoultz & Liander Co.	N. S. T. H.

123

Date	Play	Company	Place
Jan. 1, 1894	*Andersson, Pettersson och Lundström*	Pfeil Co. for Central Commandery No. 7	N. S. T. H.
Feb. 2, 1894	*Mot beräkning* *En natt i Falkenberg*	Baltic Society	T. H., Grand Crossing
Mch. 24, 1894	*Sällskapsglaset*	Brusell Co. for Swedish Good Templars	S. S. T. H.
Apr. 7, 1894	*Sällskapsglaset*	Brusell Co. for Swedish Good Templars	Calumet Opera House
Apr. 21, 1894	*Sparlakanslexor*	*Nytta och Nöje* Society	Brand's Hall
Apr. 22, 1894	*Engelbrekt och hans Dalkarlar*	Schoultz & Liander Co.	Hooley's
May 5, 1894	*En brottslig betjent*	Svithiod Lodge No. 1	N. S. T. H.

1894-1895

Date	Play	Company	Place
Aug. 25, 1894	*Lilla helgonet*	S. T.	Criterion
Aug. 26, 1894	*Lilla helgonet*	S. T.	Criterion
Oct. 7, 1894	*Nerkingarne*	S. D. S.	N. S. T. H.
Nov. 4, 1894	*Anna Carlson, Stina Johnson och Lova Petterqvist*	S. D. S.	N. S. T. H.
Dec. 9, 1894	*Döden fadder*	S. D. S.	N. S. T. H.
Dec. 24, 1894	*Doktor Dulcamara*	Swedish Glee Club	N. S. T. H.
Jan. 1, 1895	*Jeppe på bjerget*	S. D. S. for Central Commandery No. 7	N. S. T. H.
Feb. 3, 1895	*Andersson, Pettersson och Lundström*	Pfeil Co.	N. S. T. H.
Feb. 17, 1895	*Chicago nattetid* (as *Nattetid*)	Pfeil Co.	N. S. T. H.
Mch. 3, 1895	*Chicago nattetid* (as *Nattetid*)	Pfeil Co.	S. S. T. H.
Mch. 23, 1895	*En komedi* (as *Två hustrur med endast en stackars man*)	Pfeil Co.	S. S. T. H.
Mch. 24, 1895	*En komedi* (as *Två hustrur med endast en stackars man*)	Pfeil Co.	N. S. T. H.
Mch. 31, 1895	*Doktor Dulcamara*	Swedish Glee Club	N. S. T. H.
Apr. 7, 1895	*Hin och Småländingen*	Brusell & Liander Co.	N. S. T. H.
Apr. 13, 1895	*Fias rivaler*	*Svenska Amatör Klubb*	Gord's Hall, Roseland
Apr. 14, 1895	*Edmond Kean**	Schoultz Co.	Hooley's

124

Date	Play	Company	Place
Apr. 27, 1895	*Fias rivaler*	*Svenska Amatör Klubb*	T. H., Kensington
Apr. 28, 1895	*Vermländingarne*	S. D. S.	N. S. T. H.
May 5, 1895	*Bondbröllopet eller Huru rättarns Erik och nämndemannens Bolla fingo hvarandra*	Svea Quartette of Swedish Good Templars	Phoenix Hall
May 11, 1895	*Fias rivaler*	*Svenska Amatör Klubb*	Linnea Hall, S. Chicago

1895-1896

Date	Play	Company	Place
Sept. 28, 1895	*Hin och Småländingen*	Liander Co.	Criterion
Sept. 29, 1895	*Hin och Småländingen*	Liander Co.	Criterion
Oct. 6, 1895	*Direktör Striese* (as *Sabinskornas bortröfvande*)	S. D. S.	N. S. T. H.
Oct. 13, 1895	*Direktör Striese* (as *Sabinskornas bortröfvande*)	S. D. S.	S. S. T. H.
Oct. 19, 1895	*Gästgifvarmor*	Good Templar Lodge No. 535	Jefferson Hall
Nov. 10, 1895	*Kungen och gatusångerskan*	S. D. S.	N. S. T. H.
Nov. 17, 1895	*Kungen och gatusångerskan*	S. D. S.	S. S. T. H.
Nov. 24, 1895	*En domares vedermödor*	Balder Lodge	S. S. T. H.
Dec. 1, 1895	*Andersson, Pettersson och Lundström*	S. D. S.	N. S. T. H.
Dec. 29, 1895	*Andersson, Pettersson och Lundström*	S. D. S.	S. S. T. H.
Jan. 1, 1896	*Nyårsnatt på Hotell Svea*	....	N. S. T. H.
Feb. 9, 1896	*Jernbäraren*	Donaldson Co.	Lincoln T. H.
Mch. 8, 1896	*Vermländingarne*	S. D. S.	S. S. T. H.
Mch. 15, 1896	*Vermländingarne*	S. D. S.	N. S. T. H.
Apr. 18, 1896	*Sax, taylor på dekis*	Higgins for Nordstjernan	S. S. T. H.
Apr. 26, 1896	*Gustaf Vasa*	S. T.	N. S. T. H.
May 31, 1896	*Ransakningsmålet*	Svenskarne i Illinois Lodge I. O. G. T.	Phoenix Hall

1896-1897

Date	Play	Company	Place
Sept. 26, 1896	*Alderman Swanson*	Lindblom Co.	N. S. T. H.
Oct. 4, 1896	*Herr Dardanell och hans upptåg på landet**	Nya S. T.	Criterion
Oct. 8, 1896	*Herr Dardanell och hans upptåg på landet*	Nya S. T.	South Chicago
Oct. 11, 1896	*De båda döfva* *Balen på Gröna Lund* (as *Bellman på Gröna Lund*)	Nya S. T.	N. S. T. H.

Date	Play	Company	Place
Oct. 18, 1896	Jeppe på bjerget	Hanna von Toyra Co.	N. S. T. H.
Oct. 18, 1896	Valborgsmesso-aftonen	Nya S. T.	Criterion
Nov. 1, 1896	Vermländingarne*	Nya S. T.	Criterion
Nov. 8, 1896	Sparlakanslexor Rika morbror	Nya S. T.	Criterion
Nov. 14, 1896	Grefven af Monte Christo	Nya S. T.	Criterion
Nov. 15, 1896	Grefven af Monte Christo	Nya S. T.	Criterion
Nov. 15, 1896	Pinafore*	Svithiod Singing Club	N. S. T. H.
Nov. 22, 1896	Herr Dardanell och hans upptåg på landet	Nya S. T.	Criterion
Dec. 5, 1896	....	Nya S. T.	Criterion
Dec. 6, 1896	....	Nya S. T.	Criterion
Dec. 12, 1896	Hos fotografen	Nordstjernan	Hoerber's Hall, Blue Island
Dec. 12, 1896	Mottagningstimmen	Svenska National Förbund, No. 2	Spelz Hall
Jan. 1, 1897	Tre förälskade poliskonstaplar Hittebarnet	Central Commandery No. 7	N. S. T. H.
Jan. 10, 1897	Pinafore*	Svithiod Singing Club	McVicker's
Feb. 28, 1897	Andersson, Pettersson och Lundström	S. D. S. for Iduna	S. S. T. H.
Apr. 25, 1897	Kapten Crona	Vårt Hem Lodge, I. O. G. T.	Odd Fellows Hall

1897-1898

Date	Play	Company	Place
Jan. 8, 1898	Sparlakanslexor	Svenska National Förbund, No. 8	Bailey's Opera House, Evanston
Mch. 12, 1898	Vermländingarne	S. D. S.	S. S. T. H.
Mch. 13, 1898	Vermländingarne	S. D. S.	N. S. T. H.
Apr. 9, 1898	Herr Dardanell och hans upptåg på landet	S. D. S.	S. S. T. H.
Apr. 10, 1898	Herr Dardanell och hans upptåg på landet	S. D. S.	N. S. T. H.
Apr. 23, 1898	Rika morbror	Svenska National Förbund, No. 6	Bailey's Opera House, Evanston
May 7, 1898	Hans tredje hustru	Pfeil Co. for Svithiod	N. S. T. H.
June 4, 1898	Svenskarne på Cuba	Alberg Co. for Swedish Volunteer Regiment	Columbia Hall

Date	Play	Company	Place
June 5, 1898	Svenskarne på Cuba	Alberg Co. for Swedish Volunteer Regiment	Columbia Hall
July 3, 1898	Bröllopet på Ulfåsa, scenes	Alberg Co. for Svenska National Förbund	Columbia Park

1898-1899

Date	Play	Company	Place
Oct. 1, 1898	Andersson, Pettersson och Lundström*	S. D. S.	N. S. T. H.
Nov. 3, 1898	Regina von Emmeritz	Pfeil Co. for Svenska Föreningernas Central Förbund	Auditorium
Dec. 3, 1898	....	Pfeil Trio for Svithiod Lodge No. 1	N. S. T. H.
Jan. 1, 1899	Vermländingarne	Wilma Sundborg Co.	N. S. T. H.
Jan. 1, 1899	Den lilla sångfågeln Hans tredje hustru	Pfeil Co. for Iduna	S. S. T. H.
Jan. 12, 1899	Lilla helgonet*	Svithiod Singing Club	Studebaker
Jan. 29, 1899	Vermländingarne	Wilma Sundborg Co.	S. S. T. H.
Mch. 26, 1899	Ett resande teatersällskap	Brage Lodge No. 2, I. O. V.	N. S. T. H.
Apr. 2, 1899	En komedi Prins Pippi och Fröken Fiffi	Pfeil Co.	N. S. T. H.
Apr. 9, 1899	En komedi Prins Pippi och Fröken Fiffi	Pfeil Co.	S. S. T. H.
May 6, 1899	Drilléns operett	Pfeil Co. for Svithiod Lodge No. 1	N. S. T. H.
July 23, 1899	En afton på "Tre Byttor"	Swedish Glee Club & Svithiod Singing Club	Sunnyside Park

1899-1900

Date	Play	Company	Place
Oct. 7, 1899	Prins Pippi och Fröken Fiffi	Pfeil Co.	Hall, Leavitt & 19th
Nov. 5, 1899	Anna Stina i Chicago*	S. T.	N. S. T. H.
Dec. 2, 1899	Misstag på misstag	Pfeil Co. for Svithiod Lodge No. 1	N. S. T. H.

Date	Play	Company	Place
Dec. 25, 1899	Lycko-Pers resa	South Side S. T.	America
Dec. 29, 1899	Pinafore	Swedish Glee Club & Svithiod Singing Club	N. S. T. H.
Dec. 30, 1899	En afton på "Tre Byttor"	Swedish Glee Club & Svithiod Singing Club	N. S. T. H.
Jan. 1, 1900	Lycko-Pers resa	South Side S. T.	America
Jan. 7, 1900	Pinafore	Swedish Glee Club & Svithiod Singing Club	S. S. T. H.
Jan. 28, 1900	Nerkingarne	S. T.	N. S. T. H.
Feb. 12, 1900	Frithiof och Ingeborg	Eastern & Chicago Co. for Svenska National Förbund	Auditorium
Feb. 14, 1900	Frithiof och Ingeborg	Eastern & Chicago Co. for Svenska National Förbund	Auditorium
Feb. 15, 1900	Frithiof och Ingeborg	Eastern & Chicago Co. for Svenska National Förbund	Auditorium
Mch. 18, 1900	Vermländingarne*	S. T.	N. S. T. H.
Apr. 17, 1900	....	Pfeil Co. for Monitor Soc.	S. S. T. H.
May 12, 1900	....	Pfeil Co. for Nordstjernan	Vorwaert's T. H.

1900-1901

Date	Play	Company	Place
Oct. 6, 1900	Andersson, Pettersson och Lundström	Pfeil Co.	S. S. T. H.
Oct. 7, 1900	Andersson, Pettersson och Lundström	Pfeil Co.	N. S. T. H.
Oct. 18, 1900	Erik den fjortonde* (as Erik XIV och Katrina Månsdotter)	Alberg Co.	Auditorium
Nov. 4, 1900	Per Olsson och hans käring*	S. T.	N. S. T. H.
Nov. 25, 1900	Per Olsson och hans käring	S. T.	S. S. T. H.
Dec. 15, 1900	Snarka	Pfeil Trio for Nordstjernan	S. S. T. H.
Dec. 29, 1900	Herr Dardanell och hans upptåg på landet	South Side Swedish Societies	S. S. T. H.

Date	Play	Company	Place
Jan. 1, 1901	Bror Jonathan eller Oxhandlaren från Småland En midsommarnatt i Dalarne	S. T.	N. S. T. H.
Feb. 9, 1901	Vermländingarne*	For Svenska National Förbund	Auditorium
Apr. 6, 1901	Drilléns operett Sparlakanslexor	Pfeil Co.	Spelz Hall
Apr. 13, 1901	Kärlek och upptåg	Pfeil Co.	S. S. T. H.
Apr. 20, 1901	Kärlek och upptåg	Pfeil Co. for Ingeborg Soc.	S. S. T. H.
Apr. 27, 1901	Kärlek och upptåg	Pfeil Co. for Svithiod Singing Club	Svithiod Singing Club Hall

129

CHAPTER V

A CITY THEATRE; BRUSELL AND BEHMER

1901-1902—1917-1918

The performance of *Bröllopet på Ulfåsa* by Brusell and Behmer's *Svenska Teatersällskap* at the Studebaker in October 1901 inaugurated the culminating period in the development of the Chicago Swedish theatre. Now at last major productions in city theatres became the rule, and for the first time there were companies that maintained activities for more than two or three consecutive seasons. Brusell and Behmer went their separate ways in the 1904-1905 season, but the *Svenska Teatersällskap* continued under Brusell, Behmer calling his company the *Svenska Dramatiska Sällskap*. Until the 1917-1918 season, except for one additional season of cooperation under the old name, both companies were active. For four seasons—those immediately after the separation and the 1906-1907 season of united efforts—ten city performances were the norm. Then, gradually, the number of productions decreased. Each company began to limit its city plays to one or two a season, there were fewer performances in outlying halls by the companies or their members, and fewer performances for other organizations. By February 1918 it had become apparent that competitive activity was no longer feasible, and, for the first time since the spring of 1907, Brusell and Behmer gave a joint production.

From 1918 until Brusell's death in 1925, there were intermittent productions in city theatres by the two leaders, together and separately; and Behmer continued his activities with occasional performances in these theatres and with less ambitious productions, until he last appeared in the Eighth Street Theatre *Vermländingarne* of 1946. Even through the years when the *Svenska Teatersällskap* and the *Svenska Dramatiska Sällskap* were giving the public a Swedish theatre on a scale hitherto unknown, there had been minor groups—sporadic and short-lived, as in preceding periods. By the 1920's such movements had come to the fore. New companies, with new, young talents, offering new-fashioned plays, were preparing the way for a new Swedish theatre that was to carry on through the 1930's. The reunion of Brusell and Behmer in 1918 was, in fact, a sign that the old order was not long to survive. The theatre as it had developed since 1868 was thereafter to live more and more in reminiscence, and in revivals that were in themselves reminiscent rather than evidence of a living Swedish theatre.

Though they achieved much, neither the *Svenska Teatersällskap* nor the *Svenska Dramatiska Sällskap* was able to fulfill the old dream of an established Swedish company performing regularly. The situation was not merely the familiar one of divided forces. Many of the difficulties of former years persisted, and more ambitious seasons brought new problems. The actors were still amateurs who had to find time for the theatre in their leisure hours. Though support became more consistent, it could not be relied upon, and costs were increasing. The directors did not have large financial resources—partly because their theatrical activities took precedence over money making—and they had to take financial risks. For a city theatre, rental alone ran into hundreds of dollars for a single performance. Though, as before, prices for city performances were higher than for those at the halls, admission could not ordinarily be set at more than a dollar. Meeting expenses—not to mention making profits—was possible only when the public turned out in force. With a crowd of about 4,000 and a top price of a dollar, there was a net profit of $428.09 when Strindberg's historical drama, *Gustaf Vasa,* was given at the Auditorium in 1912; but expenses beyond $767.90 for rent and a comparable sum given the eminent director and star from Sweden, August Lindberg, amounted to $866.17.[1] For other pretentious productions, deficits of four and five hundred dollars were reported.[2] Many plays, of course, did not require an extensive outlay for settings and costumes, but even with the concessions made by Fritz Schoultz to the Swedish companies, costumes were often a substantial item. Publicity, places for rehearsal, and pay for stage hands, musicians, and actors were all regular expenses. The Swedish theatre was not a profitable enterprise, though Brusell and Behmer could console themselves that over the years losses were pretty well balanced by profits.

City productions offered other hazards as well. Making satisfactory arrangements for the use of theatres was no simple matter. Normally, directors would have to keep watch for theatres that were not to be in use on Sunday afternoons and evenings. These theatres would be rented as far in advance as possible, but the managers would not give contracts, and did not hesitate to rent the theatres more profitably, even after Swedish performances had been advertised. Then, at the last minute, another city theatre would have to be found, or the company would have to get along with the North Side Turner Hall. Often there was no choice but to give a Sunday matinée, though the time was unpopular with Swedish audiences; and the

131

Sunday morning rehearsals that the matinées entailed were no more popular with the actors. In all, it required courage and persistence as well as love of the theatre for Brusell and Behmer and their mainstays to carry on under these conditions for some twenty years.

In Mrs. Othelia Myhrman the theatre of these years had, fortunately, a loyal and capable supporter. She was the secretary of the *Svenska Teatersällskap* for at least the 1901-1902 season, and later served as secretary for Behmer's company; and as the secretary of the *Svenska National Förbund* she exerted herself to gain its backing for the plays. The *Förbund* continued its earlier practice of sponsoring individual performances at the Auditorium and other theatres, and for some seasons maintained a cooperative arrangement with the *Svenska Dramatiska Sällskap*. What the companies lost in assigning a portion of possible profits to the *Förbund* for its charities, they gained in security, and in Mrs. Myhrman's energy as a promoter. She personally took charge of publicity, ticket selling, and the like, and carried through such business with the dynamic generalship she gave to all of the many projects in which she was a leader.[3]

Chicago's Swedish population was growing steadily, though immigration was no longer on the earlier scale, and was sharply reduced after 1914. The passing years were bringing general stability and prosperity, propitious for the Swedish theatre as for other multiplying Swedish organizations. There was, however, more competition for the plays than before, from both Swedish and non-Swedish circles. The taste for Swedish song and comedy continued, but imported talent was more often on hand to satisfy it. Operatic stars, ballad singers and tellers of tales were welcome visitors from the homeland. By 1911, the popular folk comedian, Olle i Skratthult, had made America his home, and was regularly touring the Middle West and making frequent Chicago appearances. The Swedish clubs of Chicago, especially in the early 1900's, devoted much of their energy to bazaars and fairs, some of which, like the Svithiod Singing Club's "Streets of Stockholm," were elaborate affairs, carried on through successive weekends. One-act plays were occasionally features of these fairs, but the talents of the men and women of the theatre were generally employed in variety acts. Lodges and clubs were beginning, too, to give programs and plays in English. And the Swedes, now obviously "Americanized," found much of their entertainment where other Chicagoans found theirs—at American plays and concerts, and at the movies, with their double appeal of novelty and economy.

An audience faithful to the Swedish theatre, had, however, been building through the years. This audience, rather than the newly arrived Swedes, was the main support of the Brusell and Behmer companies. In increasing numbers, also, those Swedes who had scorned the theatre of the "beer halls," or who had followed the dictates of a church now less puritanical, were attracted to the city productions. Never, it seems certain, had the public attending the Swedish plays been so well able to appreciate dramatic art. No longer was there folk play in the audience as well as on the stage, a reviewer noted appreciatively in 1915.[4] Still, criticism of the audience did not cease. Typical was a remark that the spectators enjoyed themselves best when an actor drank and swore;[5] but occasionally there were more caustic comments, like that which appeared in a review of a sentimental play by Jolin: "Persons who understand dramatic act about as well as Zulus appreciate Rafael's Madonna should never be permitted to enter a theatre."[6] Most frequently deplored was the audience habit of laughing when they should have been serious (the critics neglected to point out that in this respect the Chicago Swedes differed little from the audience of any day or place). Of course the public that flocked to *Vermländingarne* laughed at the tragic church scene and at the rescue of Erik and Anna, as they had laughed through the years. That was to be expected. But even the "fairly thick upper crust" of Swedish Americans who saw Ibsen's *A doll's house* in 1907 was, according to one reviewer, too much inclined toward laughter.[7] Of the new plays, those that took the public fancy were rousing comedies. As in the past, the Swedish audiences went to the plays mainly to be amused, and were responsive rather than critical.

The reputation that brought support to the *Svenska Teatersällskap* and the *Svenska Dramatiska Sällskap* was honestly earned. More careful preparation and longer periods of rehearsal than had been customary in preceding years contributed to the improved quality of their main productions. The actors that made up the nucleus of each company were gifted and experienced. Their talents were varied, and chief roles could be well cast. Though in comparison to professional actors these men and women acted infrequently, they benefited from a long period of acting together, and their performances were often of professional quality. All recollections of this period by those who participated in the plays and by those who saw them support this view. As a friend of the theatre pointed out, proof lies in the length of time these companies carried on their city productions with public support.

Similar judgments were frequently expressed in the reviews, which were in general lengthy and encouraging. Still, ironically, the Swedish

133

plays were subjected to unusually severe criticism in this period of generally improved quality. These companies could not expect to have the allowances made for their weaknesses which had been customary when the plays were amateur affairs, said some of the writers, and gave no quarter. Reviews were normally anonymous, but *Svenska Nyheter,* which was a competitor of the older papers from 1898 to 1906, had on its staff for a time a man named Wikman, over whose signature, G. W...n, appeared particularly cutting and personal criticism, apparently intended to display his gift for sarcasm as well as his superior judgment. The producers and actors ordinarily accepted criticism equably, and it was a supporter of the theatre who was roused to written protest against the tone and content of Wikman's reviews. Dr. Anna Windrow Holm was undoubtedly right in stating that his personal remarks gave offense to many, and that the public did not believe the amateurs should be judged as if they were the world's greatest artists: "The Swedish American public is grateful for the merits of their actors and willing to overlook their faults." This view, said Mr. Wikman, showed so little understanding that it called for no reply.[8]

During the years when there were two competing companies, the press maintained a remarkable degree of impartiality. Wikman, it is true, admitted to the grudge against Brusell that was evident in his writing. *Svenska Amerikanaren,* though it dealt kindly with both companies, was thought to favor Behmer, and did give repeated emphasis to his careful directing. One of the most reasonable and capable critics was Theodore Sjöquist of *Svenska Kuriren,* a graduate of Upsala University well acquainted with the theatre of Sweden. He had adapted *Doktor Dulcamara* for performance in the 1890's and in later years acted occasionally.

An excellent statement of the attitudes ordinarily taken by friendly critics and supporters of the theatre that appeared in *Svenska Kuriren* in 1907 was probably the work of Sjöquist. Excessive criticism, the article emphasized, would simply discourage the theatre and interfere with its progress. Stepmotherly treatment had all too often been the fate of the Swedish plays, partly because of the prejudice of the churchly element, partly because of the more general support given to music. One should always consider that for Swedish actors, unless they turned to the American stage, acting must remain an avocation. Only through heroic efforts had Brusell and Behmer been able to give the Chicago Swedes stock companies, and the companies could perform at only too infrequent intervals. Nevertheless, the companies served as schools for actors, many of whom attained more than amateur status. The directors had striven constantly to improve public taste, and with increasing response. Now, perhaps, the day was at hand when the Chicago Swedes, like the Germans, might have a permanent theatre with weekly performances supported by Chicago and by neighboring vicinities.[9] Once again this proved to be wishful thinking, though the companies did achieve unprecedented permanency, and in some seasons took their plays to various Illinois and Minnesota centers. And when a New York *Vermländingarne* had been seen in 1913, the local papers agreed, without a dissenting voice, that Chicago had a Swedish theatre of which it could be proud.[10]

Though there was much conventional praise, and though writers largely interested in amusing their readers often gave undue emphasis to shortcomings, the more numerous and longer reviews of this period give a fairly good idea of the general nature of the performances. Many of the faults that were noted were familiar—like marked reliance on the prompter. In this respect some of the popular actors were notorious sinners; more than once it was considered news that Schycker had learned his role. Long waits and slow performances were still besetting sins, but complaints on this score were balanced on the whole by praise for performances that moved expeditiously. Almost always the musical features of the plays were commended, and for costumes and settings, particularly in the historical and folk plays, when "costumes from Schoultz" were a guarantee of quality, praise was the general rule. Occasionally, however, a lack of authenticity in these respects was noted. An Erik in a white stock and coat was as inappropriate as a sexton in green pantaloons at a funeral; nor should an old-time farmer in national costume wear pincenez—or, perhaps, having just come in from an evening rendezvous with his sweetheart, he had needed them to see her in the dark.[11] Inadequacies and accidents— a transparent tree, the collapse of a prop sword—were described with a relish that may suggest they were exceptional. The audience expected Erik to land on the floor with a resounding thump when he jumped in the water to rescue Anna—but not to find Carl Liljegren as Karl Algotson asleep on the sofa at the home of his dearest enemy when the curtain rose on act three of *Bröllopet på Ulfåsa*. Then the experience of the Birger Jarl, Brusell, stood him in good stead.[12]

The less experienced actors bore the main brunt of the criticism, but the directors and their star performers had to accept their share. Brusell's organ-like voice and the art of his characterizations were ordinarily praised, but for many roles he was considered not sufficiently animated, and he was repeatedly criticized for a peculiar bending knee action that was both ineffective and unromantic.[13] Behmer's strength lay in comedy, reviewers generally agreed. Some of his serious interpretations were highly commended, but he was not thought to be well suited to romantic and heroic roles. In his early career he was often accused of the exaggeration that was considered an unfortunate tendency of many of the Swedish actors, of being too violent in his movements, and noisy when he should have been intense. Lindblom, too, had his characteristic weaknesses; and Wikman, at least, was grateful when he did not growl like a lion and spit through his beard.[14] Of the prominent actors, Ida Anderson-Werner and Augusta Milton were most consistently praised. Mrs. Milton was sometimes considered too citified for country roles, but she was recognized as an actress who could make much of even minor opportunities, and play a comic servant and a haughty queen with equal effectiveness.[15] As for Ida Anderson-Werner, she could be counted on to bring art and finish to each of her wide range of character parts.

Occasionally reviewers admitted that novices showed promise, but more often there was commiseration for the directors who had to rely on them, or a harsh critic might even suggest that they should have been hissed off the stage. They were objected to as awkward and inaudible. A young actor would wear his hat when he embraced his mother, or portray a Swedish lieutenant with such ineptitude that the Swedish army was congratulated at not having to depend on him. Or the suitor of a young actress who had not studied her lines might be advised, "Do not love her, Arthur. She does not understand you."[16] Ensemble scenes that depended on extras often left much to be desired, as in the finale of *Regina von Emmeritz,* when the warriors who marched around the dead heroine were "as gay as newly mustered militia."[17] Chilly love making was a standard topic for humorous comment, whether actors were experienced or inexperienced. And another weakness that at times detracted from the effectiveness of performances— at least for the critical—was the mingling of dialects or use of inappropriate dialects.

Though there were two main companies through most of this period, the distinction between them was, except for the directors, generally more nominal than real. The reason was, of course, that there was not available a supply of actors for two wholly separate troupes,[18] and each director wisely preferred to use the able and experienced actors without being concerned about their acting under his competitor. For a season or two certain actors might be affiliated with Brusell and not with Behmer, or vice versa, but it was common for actors to appear with both companies in the same season. Of the actors who performed regularly in practically each of the seventeen seasons beginning with 1901-1902, Ida Anderson-Werner played with Behmer more frequently than with Brusell, and Mrs. Feltskogh normally took parallel roles for Brusell's *Svenska Teatersällskap*. Chellman and the Miltons acted more often with Brusell than with Behmer. But there were not marked allegiances between certain actors and directors, even when the competition between the companies became actual rivalry and the companies were more formally organized than usual.

Many of the plays given for clubs and lodges and other productions at the popular halls were not company affairs, though advertisements often stressed the fact that the actors were members of a major company. As in earlier years, an actor or two would rent a hall, engage a company, assume financial responsibility, and, if the occasion was profitable, get the main profits. Actors were not always named when *teater* was included at a lodge or club entertainment, but it appears that Chellman and Ekberg often provided the plays, sometimes assisted by only one or two other performers. The Friends of Thalia, or *Folk-Teatern,* a group which acted frequently during the 1906-1907 season, was largely promoted by Chellman. In 1907 a *Svenska Teater Klubb* gave some unpretentious programs, and it may have existed in earlier seasons. Many of the minor productions were given at the Turner Halls, but even before the South Side Turner Hall burned in 1914, other smaller halls were gaining in popularity, notably Belmont Hall, and, until it, too, burned in 1916, Lake View Hall. These two places were fairly satisfactory, but others were criticized as inadequate and unpleasant.

The only representatives of the *Svenska Dramatiska Sällskap* group of the 1880's who were consistently active after 1904 were Christopher Brusell and Mrs. Feltskogh. Mrs. Hvitfeldt continued to act until her death in that year. Mrs. Pfeil's association with the *Svenska Teatersällskap* ended in the fall of 1904, though she returned from her new home in Seattle for welcome appearances with the Behmer company in 1908. Her husband left Chicago at the close of 1902. There were several noteworthy performances by Arthur Donaldson, the last in 1907, but in this period Ovington appeared only in two performances in the spring of 1904, which were also among the last for Littche. Alberg had almost disappeared from the theatrical picture when he was honored by a benefit shortly before his return to Sweden in the spring of 1905.

Most of the regular performers were those who had established their reputations in the 1890's. The men who appeared from season to season were, in addition to the directors, Bolling, Chellman, Liljegren, Lindblom, Schycker, and, until his death in 1909, Lindhagen. Ernst Ekberg acted frequently, but was less consistently affiliated with the major companies. Örtengren appeared from time to time until he returned to Sweden in 1910. Oscar and Therese Sundborg were seen during the first seasons of the period. Carl Milton participated in a large majority of the plays, but acted less than his wife. Mrs. Milton and Ida Anderson-Werner were the mainstays among the women through the years, though the less able Mrs. Feltskogh acted almost as often; and Mrs. Schycker was prominent through half a dozen seasons. In the early seasons Ellen Graf and Anna Nelson continued to act, and during some stays in Chicago Sara Nordstrom renewed her connections with the Swedish companies.

Not until the 1907-1908 season were the local forces of the *Svenska Teatersällskap* and the *Svenska Dramatiska Sällskap* significantly reinforced by new arrivals and additions, but by 1903 a few new actors were appearing. One of them was to have a long and popular career. This was Christopher Brusell's nineteen year old daughter Hedwig, who carried on the tradition of second generation acting in the Swedish plays so happily begun by "little Anna" Pfeil. Others, too, continued the tradition, but for shorter periods and in less important roles. Ida Anderson-Werner's daughter, Magda Anderson, later Magda Anderson Lewis, acted with the *Svenska Dramatiska Sällskap* for several seasons around 1910, and Mr. Behmer's son and daughter, Eric and Lisa, began years of intermittent appearances in 1907, as the children in *A doll's house*. Toward the end of this period Alva Milton, the daughter of Carl and Augusta Milton, occasionally took part in the Swedish plays. Both she and Lisa Behmer also carried on their inherited interest in the theatre in American little theatre groups. A valued member of Behmer's company for many seasons was Sigrid Lindberg, Ida Anderson-Werner's sister, and his niece, Estelle Behmer, acted in some of his plays.

It was as Hedwig Brusell Melinder that Mr. Brusell's daughter was best known to the Swedish audiences. Werner Melinder had come to Chicago in 1904, to pursue his profession of architecture, and had acted with both major companies before his marriage to Hedwig Brusell in 1906 culminated a romance that was neither the first nor the last furthered by associations in the Swedish theatre. Werner and Hedwig Melinder continued their theatrical activities through the 1920's. He was often the Erik to her Anna, and was responsible for several small performances of Strindberg plays. Mr. Melinder was born in Gävle, Sweden, in 1879, and educated at the Chalmerska Institute of Göteborg. From 1908 to 1911 he and his wife lived in Sweden, and they spent part of the 1920's in St. Paul, Minnesota, but during most of the years until his death in 1936 Chicago was their home. Upon Mrs. Myhrman's death in that year, Mrs. Melinder entered the Swedish Employment Bureau, where she was associated with another of the actors of the period, John Ternquist.[19]

Of the many men and women who began acting in the plays during the regimes of Brusell and Behmer, only a few attained prominence, but recurring names among those who took minor roles indicate persistent interest and the enjoyment received from being part of the Swedish theatre. And singers well known in Chicago Swedish circles continued to appear in the popular plays "with song." One of them was Ida Linn, later Ida Linn-Cooley, who had played Josephine in the first *Pinafore*. Another, Signe Mortenson, made the first of a long series of appearances in the 1902-1903 season, and in 1907 young Rosa Pearson, who was to be associated with her in the Northland Trio, began a shorter connection with the plays. The popular Trio travelled for many years through the United States, for a time on the Pantages circuit, and in 1926 made a very successful tour of Sweden under the management of Mrs. Myhrman.[20] In recent years Mrs. Mortenson's continuing interest in the Swedish theatre has expressed itself in her direction of children's plays and programs in Swedish, under lodge auspices. Not new to the Swedish plays, but appearing more frequently in these years than before, was Joel Mossberg, a versatile leader in the Chicago musical world. John Melin, a young singer who had come to Chicago from Sweden in 1902, was repeatedly seen as Erik and in non-singing roles as well; and another singer whose roles included Erik was Carl Lönnerblad.

The formation of two companies brought to the plays for a few seasons a number of men with adequate if not outstanding talent, among them G. Patrick Warner, Frithiof Burgeson, and John Ternquist. These three were business men active in Chicago Swedish affairs. Mr. Warner was employed by the Horlick Company, Mr. Ternquist headed the Swedish Employment Bureau, and Mr. Burgeson's enterprises included the Holmes-Artore Manufacturing Company, of which he was the president. In the 1908-1909 and 1909-1910 seasons three men of greater importance to the plays were added to the rolls of actors: Knut Sjöberg, Oscar Larson, and Carl Stockenberg. Mr. Sjöberg had been a member of the Svea Theatre company in Stockholm, and he later served as director for the popular travelling company of Olle i Skratthult. Most of the years until his accidental death in 1937, at the age of 56, were spent in Chicago, where he became the proprietor of the Van Dorn Pattern Works.[21] Neither Oscar Larson nor Mr. Stockenberg had professional background, but both were talented actors. A third theatrical romance of these years (Frithiof Burgeson and his wife, "songbird" Rosa Pearson Burgeson, also had met while acting in the plays) was that of Oscar Larson and Ruth Johnson, an actress who became increasingly popular after her debut in the 1913-1914 season; their departure for Sweden in 1920 was regarded as a real loss to the Swedish theatre.[22] Mr. Stockenberg's place in the Chicago Swedish theatre was to be unique, for after years of service with the old companies, he continued his activities with the company that dominated the theatre in its closing period, *Svenska Folkteatern,* as one of the company's founders and its director. For many years an employee of the Marshall Field store, Mr. Stockenberg is well known in Swedish circles as a writer of verse and prose. Like Mr. Behmer and others of the theatre group, he has been a moving spirit in the West Side Division of the Swedish Cultural Association, and on a number of occasions has arranged and directed elaborate pageants for Swedish organizations.[23]

A number of other men and women attracted favorable attention for short periods, but of those not already mentioned only Augusta Larson was long associated with the Brusell and Behmer companies. She made her debut in Chicago in 1908, but had received theatrical training and had acted in Sweden.[24] A much more publicized arrival from Sweden, Ebba Kempe, first appeared in Chicago in 1914, but thereafter she acted only intermittently. In Sweden, Miss Kempe had been a member of the Tröbach operetta company and of the *Merry Widow* company headed by Carl Barcklind, who was later to be seen in Chicago.[25] A faithful performer in the early seasons of the century was Mrs. Alice Collini, and in later years Hulda Säfström and Wanja Nauclair were admired. The 1911-1912 season brought to the plays for a number of performances Stellan and Mia Windrow, whose mother was Dr. Anna Windrow Holm, noted earlier as responsible for the letter of protest to critic G. W . . . n. Dr. Holm herself took part in the theatricals, mainly in small Strindberg performances in which her son was interested. A gifted young member of the *Svenska Amerikanaren* staff who had journalistic experience in Sweden, Harold N. Theel, also helped to promote the Strindberg plays and acted in them until his career was cut short by death in 1917.[26] In 1914 Stellan Windrow was acting for the Chicago Essanay moving picture company, and in 1941 he was in Paris as a representative of the Paramount Company.[27] As the

140

period drew to a close, the Brusell and Behmer companies found recruits also within the small acting groups that had been springing up—Elis Gustafson and Gunnar Nordlöf, and two who were to become leaders in the new theatrical developments of the 1920's and 1930's, Nels Carlson and Elna Lilnequist.

The main companies were better supplied with women for character roles and small parts than with leading ladies, Hedwig Brusell being the only Chicago actress available for leading roles over any extended period. For three seasons, however, there was in Chicago an actress of considerable stature, Ida Östergren. She was the star, first of Behmer's *Svenska Dramatiska Sällskap,* then of the *Svenska Teatersällskap* under Brusell and Behmer, and then again of Behmer's company. Behmer introduced her as a "real prima donna" with a successful stage career in Sweden and in the Eastern states. The facts of her earlier experience were left vague, but there is no doubt that she was able and attractive and contributed much to the Chicago Swedish plays. Her debut came at a time of fairly heated rivalry between the two directors, and Brusell's claims for his own leading lady, Wilma Sundborg (now Wilma Sundborg-Stern), led to a law suit against him by Miss Östergren.[28] Madame Sundborg-Stern took leading roles with one or another of the Chicago companies at other times also, during these years.

"Prima donnas" from Sweden of varying degrees of celebrity did appear in the Chicago Swedish plays in this period. Most of them were on concert tours, which, unlike dramatic tours, could be carried through with marked success. A well known singer from the Swedish Royal Opera, Anna Hellström, who made several American tours and was a popular soloist for the American Union of Swedish Singers, played Anna for Brusell in 1905. Madame Emma Wallin-Malm, of the *Svenska* and Vasa Theatres in Stockholm and *Stora Teatern* in Göteborg, spent some time in Chicago in 1907, and participated in one performance, though the directors were unable to induce her to appear in a leading role.[29] In the summer of 1907, Madame Emma Meissner and Miss Rosa Grünberg of Oscar's Theatre, Stockholm, delighted audiences in plays as well as in concerts featuring folk *visor* (ballads). Madame Meissner was the better known; she had begun a successful stage career in her early youth, and had been for a number of years the leading lady at the Vasa Theatre, where her husband was the musical director.[30] An extensive tour that was to take them as far as Australia brought to Chicago in 1910 one of Sweden's most popular light opera stars, Anna Lundberg, and her husband, Otto Lundberg, an actor

141

and director of considerable reputation. They had toured extensively in Scandinavia and elsewhere in Europe, and Madame Lundberg had followed earlier successes at Stockholm's *Södra Teater* with two years at the Folies Bergère in Paris.[31] Less famous but very well received in dramatic appearances and in ballad entertainments were two young women from the *Dramatiska Teater* of Stockholm who visited Chicago in the spring of 1912, Signe Widell and Greta Adamsen.[32]

Among the ballad singers from Sweden were also two sisters who remained in this country, Helga and Ingeborg Sandberg. They had acted at the *Svea Teater* in Stockholm,[33] and in Chicago made a series of appearances with both Brusell and Behmer companies, chiefly in *Vermländingarne.* When Madame Hilda Hellström-Gagnée played Anna in *Vermländingarne* for one of Brusell's productions, her association with Stockholm's *Södra Teater* was emphasized, but she was American born, and much of her varied career was in this country, where she acted in American companies, appeared with dancing troupes, and promoted the Swedish drama in both Swedish and English.[34]

Only in the 1911-1912 season were the men of Sweden's stage prominent in Chicago plays of this period, but that season brought to Chicago a popular Stockholm comedian, Elis Olson, and the most famous of Swedish actors, August Lindberg. Two men who made some appearances in other seasons, Rafael Ramsén of the Swedish theatre of Helsingfors, Finland, and Gustaf Lund of the Stockholm *Folk Teater,* also testify to the relationship between the Swedish theatre of Chicago and that of the homeland.

Ultimate acceptance of August Lindberg as Sweden's leading and most influential actor had come only after a long and controversial career. Three decades of success in the provinces, in Finland and Denmark, preceded admission of his rank by the Stockholm critics. The chief battle centered about his interpretation of Hamlet, the role with which he was most closely identified. Lindberg acted, however, in many Shakespearean roles, and was credited with creating modern Swedish interest in Shakespeare. Even more important was his pioneering in the works of Ibsen, whose plays he introduced in Sweden and Denmark, and also acted in Norway. For Strindberg's plays he did similar yeoman service, and there is, in letters and stories, evidence of the mutual respect of dramatist and actor. To the Chicago Swedes, Lindberg brought their one major production of a Strindberg drama, *Gustaf Vasa,* in which he had acted in its 1899 première.

Anna Almgren Ovington as Kätchen in *Regina
von Emmeritz*, November 3, 1898, Auditorium

Mrs. Hanna Hvitfeldt

August Lindberg as Hamlet

Anna Pfeil

As Anna in *Vermländingarne*

Hedwig Brusell Melinder

Lindberg was born in the Dalarne region in 1846, in humble circumstances, and it was only through his own hard work that he obtained money to enter the Royal Theatre Dramatic School in 1865. After a year of study, his professional career began, tours with well known provincial companies like that of the playwright, Uller, soon being succeeded by tours with his own companies. His first real success came in 1872, at Helsingfors, and there, in 1877, after periods in Stockholm theatres and studies in France, he first essayed the role of Hamlet, and began the struggle to win the approval of the cosmopolitan critics for his interpretation. It was largely his departure from formalism and tradition that made acceptance slow, but unevenness and eccentric mannerisms were charged against his Hamlet and his acting in general. His great virtues, wrote Gustaf af Geijerstam in 1896, when Lindberg was fifty, and enjoying a hard won fame, were his fiery passion and control. At sixty, Lindberg was acting and directing at the Royal Dramatic Theatre, not for the first time, but with unprecedented success. He had also added to his reputation by the readings which he was to continue in his later career, his complete rendition of *The tempest* being thought particularly remarkable. By the time of his death in 1916 there was general agreement with the verdict of Geijerstam some twenty years earlier, that to tell Lindberg's history would be to tell the history of the Swedish theatre. His courage and his devotion to his art and to the drama had brought the theatre of Sweden a renewed life.[35]

With August Lindberg on his American tour was his young son, Per. He made his acting debut in Chicago, to begin a career in the theatre almost as interesting and influential as that of his father. Chiefly known as an experimental director, Per Lindberg was active in London and in Norway and Denmark as well as in Sweden, and extended his interests to the moving picture and radio. He died in 1944, at the age of fifty-four, a leading force in a vital and significant Swedish theatre.[36]

No such significance can be claimed for the other visitor of the 1911-1912 season, but Elis Olson (sometimes called Elis Olson-Elis) was a very successful comedian, before and after his American visit. He celebrated his thirty-third birthday in Chicago, but he had acted since 1900 with companies at the *Folk, Dramatiska*, and *Södra* theatres of Stockholm. From 1925 to 1932, he directed Klippan's open air theatre there. Besides the popular role he played in Chicago, he was particularly identified with that of Lord Bobberly in *Charley's Aunt*. He was also favorably known as a singer and composer of light songs.[37]

143

Relations of the Swedish and Chicago actors were generally very cordial, and the visitors were much feted. For Elis Olson there were particular honors, a banquet, with complimentary speeches and a loving cup, being arranged as a farewell and birthday tribute by his colleagues and their sponsoring *Svenska National Förbund*. Soon, however, his Chicago friends were to be disillusioned. Before leaving Chicago, Olson gave an interview severely criticizing the materialism of America, and on his return to Sweden he not only continued such criticism but accused Mrs. Myhrman of taking money that rightfully belonged to him and to the *Svenska National Förbund,* and of working against the best interests of the Chicago Swedish theatre. The *Förbund* was thoroughly aroused, brought suit against the newspaper that had published the accusation, and sent Mrs. Myhrman to Sweden. There she succeeded in winning a verdict, having, fortunately, the assistance of John Örtengren of the Royal Opera, who had often been associated with her and the plays sponsored by the *Förbund* in Chicago. The whole affair was long drawn out and complicated, and created much interest. Olson, Mrs. Myhrman's friends have said, accepted her hospitality in Chicago without recompense and without gratitude; he was an able actor but did not like America's democratic ways. He was, moreover, disappointed because an American tour could not be arranged, and did not appreciate all Mrs. Myhrman did in the interest of such a tour. She had, as a matter of fact, taken less money than was due her; and of her unselfish interest in the Swedish theatre there could certainly be no question.[38]

Departures from the old repertoire went hand in hand with the increasing stability and prestige of the Swedish theatre. Brusell and Behmer exerted themselves to give the audiences new plays. Many of the plays, it is true, were new only to Chicago, and in type and period did not offer much variety. Others were contemporary; and a number gave support to the often repeated claim that their theatre raised "the cultural level of the Swedes of Chicago." There were in all eighty performances in city or comparable theatres under the direction of Brusell and Behmer, together and separately, in this period, and thirty-five different plays were presented in these performances. Of the thirty-five, twenty-four had not before been seen in Chicago, and one, Geijerstam's rural comedy from 1894, *Lars Anders och Jan Anders och deras barn* (Lars Anders and Jan Anders and their children) had been acted only once, at the North Side Turner Hall, a few years before the *Svenska Teatersällskap* played it at the Garrick in 1911.

Not many of the plays that now had Chicago premières were played often or attained any lasting popularity. The old comedies and sentimental dramas of Jolin—*Barnhusbarnen* (The orphan), *Friaren från Värmland* (The wooer from Värmland), *Löjen och tårar* (Laughter and tears), and *Mäster Smith* (Master Smith)—and the dramatized sensation novels of the 1840's—Blanche's *Flickan i Stadsgården* (The girl in the City Yard) and Emilie Flygare Carlén's *Rosen på Tistelon* (The rose on Thistle Isle)— had outlived their appeal in Chicago as in Sweden. Börjesson's verse drama about Carl XII, from the same period, lacked the theatrical effectiveness that kept some old historical dramas alive. Nor were the ventures into drama of genuine literary quality very encouraging. Notable, nevertheless, as evidence of the interests of the directors and of the advance of the Swedish theatre were single productions by Behmer of *The taming of the shrew* and (in cooperation with Ida Östergren) of *A doll's house,* and Brusell's two performances of Sudermann's *Ära* (Honor). Critics felt that these efforts were worthy but somewhat beyond the capabilities of the actors; the audiences preferred Swedish to Shakespearean comedy, and were not much interested in the somber realism of Ibsen and Sudermann. Not surprisingly, the most successful of the literary dramas was Strindberg's *Gustaf Vasa,* which Lindberg directed as part of the general festivities connected with the dramatist's 63rd birthday. Other plays by Strindberg —who had been seen before only in the slighted *Lycko-Pers resa* of 1899-1900—were several times performed for the "select" few who were increasingly interested in Sweden's great modern dramatist: *Påsk* (Easter), *Pelikanen* (The pelican), and *Paria* (The pariah). There were similar performances also of plays by younger realists, Charlotte Edgren Leffler's *En förlofning (A bethrothal)* and Ernst Ahlgren's *I telefon* (On the telephone).

Non-Swedish plays that had enjoyed marked popularity in Sweden as well as in other countries were among the new plays produced by Behmer, and they were well received, but not ordinarily with the enthusiasm that warranted repetition. One of them was Hedberg's 1903 version of *Gamla Heidelberg* (Old Heidelberg), the German play that furnished the story for Romberg's operetta, *The Student Prince.* Another, *Syrsan* (The cricket), was the Swedish form of Charlotte Birch-Pfeiffer's durable adaptation from George Sand, extensively acted on the American stage as *Fanchon, the cricket.* Behmer himself was responsible for three adaptations: from the French, *Duvals skilsmessa* (Duval's divorce), one of Augustin Daly's big successes as *The lottery of love;* also from the French, the comedy widely known in John Hare's English version, *A pair of spectacles,* and called by Behmer *Farbror Knut från Norrköping* (Uncle Knut from Norrköping); and *Syndabocken* (The scapegoat), from the German play by Lehnhard, *Das opferlamm.* Behmer used the first two of these adaptations again in later years, but only *Farbror Knut från Norrköping,* which was a Swedish localization, was played more than once in this period, and only one of its three performances was in a city theatre.

Not all the characteristically Swedish plays fared much better. With three performances, two in the city, *Ljungby Horn* was a popular addition to the familiar folk plays; but Hedberg's 1884 folk play, *Rospiggarna* (The people of Roslagen), was a near failure. The newer trend to peasant comedy was evident in Geijerstam's *Lars Anders och Jan Anders och deras barn,* acted four times, though only once as a major production, and in a single performance of *Smålandsknekten* (The soldier from Småland) by the well known Swedish folk-lorist and writer of country life sketches, August Bondeson; and, *Sven och liten Anna* (Sven and little Anna), *Anders Jonsa och hans käring* (Anders Jonsa and his woman), and *Jon Ersas piga* (Jon Ersa's girl) were less noteworthy rural plays. *Pelle Grönlunds bryggeri* (Pelle Grönlund's brewery), a farcical picture of provincial life, also represented a type of comedy that was to be increasingly popular. And the play Elis Olson acted three times in Chicago, *Sten Stenson Stéen från Eslöf,* fell largely in the same category.

When new plays caught on with the audiences, directors forgot the need for variety, and gave them repeated performances. Thus two new comedies from the 1880's, *Lifvet på landet* (Life in the country) and *Öregrund-Östhammar,* were acted seven and six times respectively, with all but one of the performances in city theatres. In *Lifvet på landet* Hedberg had transplanted eccentric character types from the German stories by Fritz Reuter, and *Öregrund-Östhammar* was also a farcical localization from the German, the version being credited to a Chicagoan, Algot E. Strand. Mr. Strand was a contributor to various publications in these years, was the compiler of *Hemlandet's* 1909 book premium, *Konung Oscar II, hans lif och verk,* and author of *A history of Norwegians in Illinois* (1905) and *A history of the Swedish-Americans of Minnesota* (1910).[39]

Free cutting and adapting by actors and directors were common practice, and old plays were frequently refurbished with new local songs, but there was little local contribution to repertoire in this period. One local play using familiar materials was given a city performance by the *Svenska Teatersällskap,* newspaperman Carl Atterling's *Kolingarnas lust-*

resa i Amerika (The Kolings' holiday journey in America);[40] an unsuccessful effort of the kind by Chellman, *Pelle Janssons äfventyr* (Pelle Jansson's adventure), was the only other new play of Chicago authorship. Wicklund's *En afton på "Tre Byttor"* was, however, given its two final Chicago performances.

As the period of regular seasons by Brusell and Behmer's companies drew to a close, the directors relied more and more on plays that appealed through familiarity; and first and foremost they relied on *Vermländingarne*. Dahlgren's old folk play had been a feature of most of their seasons, either in city performances or at one of the Turner Halls. In all, during these years, it was given twenty city productions by the major companies; it was played once in the city by the Lundbergs; and five other performances made a total twenty-six. *Andersson, Pettersson och Lundström*, on the other hand, was moving toward oblivion. There were only three city productions of a play that had seemed as imperishable as *Vermländingarne*, though it was played four times at the halls. Next to *Vermländingarne* in popularity among the old folk plays was *Nerkingarne*. It was acted six times, though only once in a city theatre, and it furnished a scene, *Lasse och Stina*, for a number of entertainments. (Others of the old-time plays were also being seen in part on various occasions). The traditional plays were turned to for elaborate and highly publicized productions throughout the period. In 1902 the *Svenska National Förbund* gave Blanche's *Engelbrekt och hans Dalkarlar* on a grand scale. Later, *Regina von Emmeritz* was used three times, Hedberg's folk play, *Valborgsmesso-aftonen*, twice, and his historical drama, *Bröllopet på Ulfåsa*, four times, as high points in Brusell and Behmer seasons.

On the whole, considering public taste, the difficulty and expense that were still involved in obtaining new plays, and the conditions attending theatrical enterprises, the repertoire of the main companies of these years must be considered very respectable. In judging its quality one must remember that the Swedish theatre depended for survival upon its appeal to a general public. The Chicago Swedish audiences were neither more nor less receptive to the new and to the literary drama than were the overall audiences in America or in Sweden; but Brusell and Behmer could not, as could companies that were part of a native theatre, appeal to only certain groups within the general public. The critic who, in reviewing *The taming of the shrew*, pointed out that the transition from *Andersson, Pettersson och Lundström* to Shakespeare should, perhaps, be more gradual was thinking of audience as well as of actors.[41] The plays most given were

147

well suited to the tastes of the public and to the abilities of the companies.

For minor performances old-fashioned types of comedy were still the rule, with Blanche (particularly his *Hittebarnet*), Hedberg, Hodell, and their contemporaries played as before. *En natt i Falkenberg, Tre förälskade poliskonstaplar, Hon både sparkas och bits,* and *En domares vedermödor* were still popular entertainment, and were not to disappear with this period. Many of the comedies now first played in Chicago were published individually in the Swedish series comparable to those of Samuel French in English. They were on sale in Chicago, and a number of those most used were published there also by And. L. Löfström's press, as *Teater-Biblioteket*.[42] Characteristic were the five plays that led the list in number of performances: *Han är inte svartsjuk* (He is not jealous), a farce about the difficulties of a jealous husband; *En orolig natt* (A restless night), the story of a suitor's encounters with his sweetheart's father; *Tosingar* (Lunatics), an amusing picture of the situation developing from the belief that a young man guest is insane; *Karl Sabelträff och hans rivaler* (Karl Sabelträff and his rivals), a Swedish "original" which pits an absurd country suitor against an officer of the artillery and uses a famous Swedish park as a setting; and *En spik i nyckelhålet* (A nail in the keyhole), a French farce in which a young man tries to seduce his neighbor's wife by plugging her keyhole so she must take refuge in his apartment, and is neatly caught by his own trick. A sprinkling of new plays pointed to the growing fondness for rural farce, and the continuing activities of Good Templar groups added temperance plays to those offered in hall programs during these seasons.

1901-1902

As early as July 1901 the *Svenska Teatersällskap* announced plans and personnel for its third season. A new step was to mark its progress, for the company was for the first time to act in a city theatre. Already the Studebaker theatre had been engaged. The company that was listed was later augmented, but there was more definite organization than was ordinarily to obtain. Brusell and Behmer were jointly in charge, Mrs. Myhrman was the secretary, and the actors for the season, in addition to the directors, were: Ida Anderson-Werner, Anna Pfeil, Ellen Graf, Therese Sundborg, Hanna Hvitfeldt, Hulda Feltskogh, Ida Linn, John Lindhagen, Ernest Lindblom, Leopold Chellman, Fred Bolling, John Örtengren, Ernst Schycker, and C. J. Erickson.[43]

The *Svenska Teatersällskap* appeared at least once every month from

October to May, with the exception of January and February, though only three of its seven performances were given at the Studebaker. In February it yielded the spotlight to *Engelbrekt och hans Dalkarlar,* being presented at the Auditorium under the sponsorship of the *Svenska National Förbund.* This also was largely a company affair, however, as it was directed by John Örtengren and included a number of *Svenska Teatersällskap* actors. And with two comedies headed by Carl Pfeil the only other plays of the season, the Brusell and Behmer company had clearly established its position of leadership.

The congratulations and hopes that had greeted the *Svenska Teatersällskap's* "worthy project" did not disappear, but after a promising beginning with *Nerkingarne* at the South Side Turner Hall, criticism began to be mingled with the praise. Detracting from the excellence of the principal actors and the evidence of careful preparation in the first Studebaker play, *Bröllopet på Ulfåsa,* were the length of the performance and inadequate acting in minor roles. Reviewers advised a comedy for the next performance;[44] and November brought one of three new comedies offered in this season, Bondeson's *Smålandsknekten.* There was not the full house which had turned out for *Bröllopet på Ulfåsa*—probably, the newspapers suggested, because the public had found it boring. This time, long waits had been eliminated and the performance could be concluded by 10:30; but Bondeson's play did not live up to expectations. The story was amusing enough, but was slow in getting under way, and the country types were not as satisfactory as those in more familiar plays. Those actors who were experienced and who had studied their lines gave an excellent performance, it was conceded. Appearing for the first time in the season, Anna Pfeil played Inga Fästman with her usual artistry, Ida Anderson-Werner was a skillful Stina på Hägnet, and Chellman made an amusing country fiddler. And music by the *Nordstjernan* singers, introduced as soldiers, was, of course, enjoyed.[45]

Another unfamiliar country comedy followed, at the North Side Turner Hall. *Sven och liten Anna* was a slight affair, but entertaining, with Anna Pfeil and Brusell successful in leading roles, as the daughter of a wealthy farmer and the poor servant who finally won her hand.[46] Thereafter all efforts were directed toward the *Förbund* performance of *Engelbrekt och hans Dalkarlar.* The play's musical features were emphasized, many members of the cast being singers rather than actors, and the whole was not judged according to strict dramatic standards. Director Örtengren was, however, a dignified and impressive folk hero. It was not his fault,

149

Svenska Nyheter noted, that Engelbrekt had to make a long oration after being mortally wounded. Lindblom, too, was able as Sven Ulfsen, and John Lindhagen's Måns Bengston was considered worthy of comparisons with August Lindberg. There was a good audience, but it was not large enough to fill the Auditorium, and with expenses of $2,486.96 and an income of $1,955.66, the *Förbund* incurred a loss of $531.30. Another year a concert supplemented by dramatic tableaux would be less expensive and a better drawing card, it was suggested;[47] and the next season the *Förbund* restricted its theatrical activities to presenting the *Svenska Teatersällskap* in a North Side Turner Hall benefit.

In March, 1902, the Brusell and Behmer company returned to the Studebaker, presenting for the first time a comedy that the public was to enjoy for a number of years, *Öregrund-Östhammar*. It did not draw a good house on this occasion, but was enthusiastically praised; and an April repetition at the North Side Turner Hall (no other theatre being available) helped to establish its popularity. When such an excellent production is taken as a matter of course, wrote complimentary reviewers after the première, one realizes the heights to which the two directors have developed dramatic art among the Swedes.

A manuscript copy of *Öregrund-Östhammar*[48] reveals that the comedy so popular with the Chicago audiences was wildly improbable farce, with a plot almost incredibly complicated. The story may be told in part. The first two of the five acts take place in Östhammar, where three leading citizens, led by a Stockholm engineer, Thorell, have founded a club, Freedom's Brothers, of which their wives disapprove. As Thorell is to move to Stockholm, the Östhammar trio decide to accompany him for a last fling, pretending to their wives that they are going on a business trip to Upsala. The apple cart is upset by young Emil Klint, a *gymnasist* (undergraduate) on vacation in Östhammar. He has found in the papers of his uncle, city treasurer Bratt, a picture of the beautiful Susanna, a Stockholm girl with whom he is love, but tells Bratt's wife that engineer Thorell is to marry Susanna. Actually, Thorell wishes to marry her aunt, Mrs. Söderström, a young widow who owns a Stockholm hotel, secured for her by Bratt, who was a friend of the parents of the orphaned Susanna, whose godfather he is. These connections Bratt has kept a secret from his jealous wife. She and the other wives learn from Emil the true nature of their husbands' journey, and, having founded a club of their own, set out after them, their destination Mrs. Söderström's hotel in Stockholm.

There the rest of the action takes place. Preparations for the reception of Bratt, whom Susanna has never seen, go wrong, as she mistakes a second trio of guests, three men from an Öregrund singing society, come to speed their monarch on a journey, for the Östhammar visitors. The Östhammar men, their wives, and the Öregrund men are shuttled back and forth from room to room, with every conceivable misunderstanding developed. Young Klint arrives and is mistaken by Mrs. Söderström for a newly hired bartender, a situation he regards as humiliating, but which permits a romantic reunion with Susanna. They decide they will marry; Susanna thinks the love letters she has been receiving from Emil were written her by Thorell, and for a time she manages to interfere with the successful culmination of his love affair with her aunt. Another thread of action is the secret correspondence druggist Ortenqvist of Östhammar and his wife have been carrying on, supposedly with unknown affinities, but actually with each other, which leads to a rendezvous at which Bratt and his wife substitute for their friends and develop further suspicions of each other. The Freedom's Brothers do manage to have their Stockholm fling, and Emil uses his knowledge of their night out to gain consent for his romance. Ultimately all the misunderstandings are cleared up, and the visitors are ready to return to their provincial towns, though in the finale they sing the praises of Stockholm, where "one lives well and joyously."

Absurd as the story is, it is undoubtedly lively; the songs with which the whole is larded are amusing; and the characters have been given considerable individuality. A competent *Svenska Teatersällskap* cast did *Öregrund-Östhammar* justice. In Emil Klint Anna Pfeil had a type of role to which she was admirably suited, and her daughter was a delightful ingenue as Susanna. Carl Pfeil was a recruit to the company for this play, with Behmer, Chellman, Schycker, Lindblom, and an unknown, Hjalmar Wessberg, the others in the Öregrund-Östhammar trios. The Orion Quartet, appearing as Upsala students (only talked of in the play MS.), was, of course, welcomed for its songs.[49]

The company made its last appearance of the season at the Svithiod May festival, repeating successfully the play it had presented in the fall, *Nerkingarne*. Much admired were Ida Anderson-Werner as Mamselle Bom, the role made famous by Ovington, and Behmer and Therese Sundborg as Lasse and Stina; but Alberg, in one of his now infrequent appearances, was regrettably weak as the *brukspatron*. To add to the public interest, Svithiod's annual May Queen coronation could be incorporated in the folk festivities of the last act.[50]

The *Svenska Teatersällskap's* three folk plays at the Grand Opera House, two in the fall and one in the spring, constituted the main theatrical season of 1902-1903. There were some comedies by other groups, notably by the Good Templar lodge, Jupiter; the Brusell and Behmer actors also appeared in comedies at club programs, and gave one full length company performance for *Nordstjernan.* The play was *Nerkingarne,* and with a crowd of 2,000 at the South Side Turner Hall, it netted $500.00 for an undesignated charity.[51] This was a season of benefits among the Chicago Swedes, many of the events, like the *Svenska National Förbund* play of May 10, being given on behalf of a Swedish man who was standing trial for murder, John Nordgren. The Swedes of Norrland, who were suffering from catastrophes of flood and fire, were the beneficiaries of the May Grand Opera House play, which made a profit of $352.13.[52]

Limited as it was, the season was successful, in both attendance and enthusiasm. Sell outs were reported for the two fall plays at the Grand Opera House—the old *Vermländingarne,* and *Ljungby Horn,* the new folk play that started off the season. *Ljungby Horn* had been acted hundreds of times in Sweden, the advertisements claimed; this was not, however, the one play of that title that appears in Swedish bibliographies, *Ljungby Horn och Pipa,* by G. L. Silfverstolpe, published in 1858. The Chicago play was the property of Carl Liljegren, and he is said to have written it from memory, after having seen it or acted in it in Sweden. His manuscript copy of the play indicates that if he wrote it from memory his talents were not confined to acting.[53] One is not surprised that *Ljungby Horn,* with its blend of melodrama, comedy, spectacle, legend, and folk festival, in verse and prose and song, pleased the public when introduced in Chicago and in three additional performances.

Ljungby Horn tells a story of trolls and mortals, based on traditional ballad materials. Its heroine is Hildur, the lovely young maiden who was stolen as an infant by the troll woman, Tulla, as vengeance for the theft of troll treasures by her father, the lord of Ljungby. Tulla's daughter was substituted for Hildur, and has grown up as Birgit—a headstrong, trolllike creature who is the despair of the widowed Lady Ingrid of Ljungby (her husband died immediately after his offense against the trolls) and of Birgit's bethrothed, young Junker (nobleman) Olof, who is bound to Birgit only because of a promise made to his dying father. A gay hunting party in the woods introduces Birgit and her followers, among them Måns Kruse, a foolish old knight of the braggart coward type, who is pursuing Birgit and trying to win Olof's property. Olof is left alone, and when Hildur emerges from the troll cave in the background, they immediately fall in love. But Hildur refuses to permit Olof to taste the enchanted drink in a precious beaker she carries, and leaves him in a swoon. The scene changes to the cave, where preparations are under way for the marriage of Hildur and Vidrik, the older of Mother Tulla's two sons. Didrik, the younger (he is only 150 to Vidrik's 356), is his brother's rival, but when Hildur tells him that she has heard from drunken Tulla that she is mortal, he is persuaded to help her escape. And after properly troll-like potions and food have been made ready, the guests of honor—the mountain king, a mermaid, death, and a flittermouse—have made their spectacular appearances and presented their gifts, and the revelry is at its height, Didrik carries out his promise.

On earth, Didrik and Hildur meet Olle Pamp, a one-armed soldier who despises his master, Måns Kruse, and a group of peasants, and then Måns himself, all seeking for the now insane Olof. When Måns presses his attentions on Hildur, Didrik sings a song that casts a temporary spell on the entire company, who flee in panic when the spell breaks. Olof comes, is restored by his reunion with Hildur, and claims her and rejects Birgit. The sorrowing Didrik leaves them, and soon Måns and his people return to capture Hildur, that she may be tried as a witch. Olof valiantly defends her, but is left behind, wounded, after fighting with Olle Pamp.

All of this and more has been presented in three acts. In the two that follow, Hildur undergoes a trial at Ljungby Castle, a scene that is largely farcical until it is interrupted by Olof, Olle Pamp (who has transferred his allegiance to Olof), and by Lady Ingrid, who identifies Hildur as her daughter by means of the Ljungby Horn (the beaker Hildur has brought with her), and a lullaby remembered by Hildur. The defiant Birgit, deprived, as she says, of all but freedom and a will to revenge, leaps out of the window, to make her way, at last, to the troll cave. There Tulla and her sons are preparing to leave, their home being lost to them because the stolen mortal has succeeded in her escape. Birgit refuses to go with them, and cannot be forced, because she was reared in a Christian home. But Tulla insures her daughter's future by giving treasures to Måns Kruse, who has been trying to escape Birgit but now readily agrees to marry her. His joy is short-lived, however, for Birgit harnesses him to the load of treasure, and drives him off with a cracking whip, while he laments that he "took the troll for the gold."

153

Finally, a midsummer festival celebrates the love of Hildur and Olof, with Hildur being crowned May Queen, and Olle Pamp and a servant making another happy couple. Didrik comes to bid farewell, and explains that he has forced Vidrik to join him in good wishes, which include *tomtar* (brownies) to live with them and bring them luck. Happiness and peace of mind they must themselves secure; that is beyond the power of trolls. Hildur grants Didrik his one wish, to kiss her hand, and promises never to forget him; and the play closes with a verse by Olof:

> The ancient kindred from the cave depart
> And only kindly *tomtar* there remain.
> From age to age their mild spirits reach
> When saga writings pale and disappear.

As a matter of fact, except for the absurd and repellent Vidrik, the trolls are presented as having their virtues. As Didrik points out, they do not, like mortals, pretend to be what they are not. And Tulla has only scorn for Måns Kruse, as she buys him for her daughter.

Brusell played Didrik, and his success in making the ugly troll a sympathetic character was considered an outstanding achievement, now and in later performances. The Pfeils, too, were in their element as Birgit and Måns Kruse. Hilma Nelson's sister Anna was Hildur, and Ellen Graf the mermaid, whose dance was an admired feature of an impressive troll wedding. In all, this performance and the promise of Arthur Donaldson's appearance in the forthcoming *Vermländingarne* were taken as indications that the long worked for goal of a Swedish theatre in Chicago had been reached.[54]

The November *Vermländingarne* was joyfully received. The play had, strangely, been missing the previous season, and it presented, besides Donaldson as Erik, Anna Pfeil as Anna. The critics pronounced the performance unsurpassed in Chicago. Donaldson was a charming Erik— elegant without being snobbish, strong without being brutal. As the *provst*, Carl Liljegren was so good that serious scenes ordinarily greeted with laughter were properly effective. Pfeil as Löpare-Nisse, Brusell in a favorite role, Sven Ersson, Behmer as Anders, and, of course, Mrs. Pfeil— all were praised. The use of an inappropriate backdrop in successive scenes could readily be overlooked as a minor shortcoming.[55]

In May, *Valborgsmesso-aftonen* was also accounted excellent. Congratulatory reviews expressed the hope that the company would continue its good work the next season, and distributed praise generously. Again

Carl Liljegren, as the old soldier, Svärd, was thought particularly good; and again Ellen Graf pleased with a dance, this time one characteristic of the Frykdal province. Max Hedman and the Miltons were welcomed as additions to the company. There was a good word for the audience, too: it did one good to hear them applaud the beautiful moral speeches again and again. For the company, there was further gratification, for they took the play to Joliet, and acted for a large and enthusiastic audience.[56]

After appearing in *Vermländingarne,* Carl Pfeil gave a program of old favorites for the Svithiod Singing Club, seemingly his last appearance in Chicago. The circumstances of his departure from Chicago were characteristic of both his versatility and his vicissitudes. A play of his authorship, *The union man,* announced for performance at the North Side Turner Hall on January 1, 1903, was cancelled without notice. The hall was beleaguered by ticket holders and creditors, and Pfeil and his company were next heard of in Hammond, Indiana, where an intended performance was cancelled by its sponsors. Pfeil had been working for the Stromberg-Carlson company and had been active as a labor organizer, and the play, according to a Hammond labor leader, was a sermon on organized labor. It was also reported to be (like Pfeil's *Wonder doctor* of 1901) a version of *Döden fadder.* With so much publicity it should certainly draw, was *Svenska Tribunen's* comment.[57]

1903-1904

The cooperation of Brusell and Behmer in the *Svenska Teatersällskap* ceased in the fall of 1903.[58] The company became Brusell's enterprise, and Behmer limited his activities to one or two independent minor performances. The season was a lively one, though Brusell's company did not act as such after January 1, and gave only two city productions, yielding in the spring to the *Svenska National Förbund's* revival of *Jorden rundt på 80 dagar.* Besides Grand Opera House performances in October and December, however, the *Svenska Teatersällskap* presented *Valborgsmesso-aftonen* and *Vermländingarne* for sponsoring societies, and performed that other hardy folk play, *Nerkingarne,* in Joliet in December. Also, Carl Liljegren restored *Andersson, Pettersson och Lundström* to its old time position as New Year's entertainment, promoting a performance by his colleagues at the North Side Turner Hall. And it was the company's members who acted most of the one-act comedies that entertained different clubs during the season.

Before the *Svenska Teatersällskap* gave its first play in October, the public had been offered what was surely one of the worst plays ever presented at the North Side Turner Hall. With *Pelle Janssons äfventyr,* a melo drama in four acts "after the American fashion," Leopold Chellman made his debut as an author. Supposedly it had already been translated into English and was to be played on the American stage. The newspapers, unimpressed, pronounced it hopelessly confused, impossible to act and to review. *Svenska Teatersällskap* actors did their best: Bolling, Lindblom, and Ekberg were not bad in negro roles. Ellen Graf contributed an effective dance; and even when revolvers emitted feeble clicks, intended victims obliged by dying. Some of the dialogue was witty, but acting, not playwriting, was Chellman's forte, was the kindest comment of the reviewers.[59]

The Turner Halls were full to overflowing with the crowds that turned out for *Valborgsmesso-aftonen* and the two performances of *Vermländingarne*—proof, Brusell was told, that the Swedish theatre could succeed when seriously undertaken. No longer were there scoffing remarks about the quality of the performances. Singer Ida Linn satisfied even in Anna Pfeil's roles, and the company as a whole displayed the skill that comes with experience. The one newcomer, young Hedwig Brusell, making her first appearance in *Valborgsmesso-aftonen,* was given cordial praise for her talent and interests—and for Swedish that was excellent for one American born.[60]

A new play, *Lifvet på landet,* was the *Svenska Teatersällskap* attraction for its two city performances. This time, it was agreed, the proverbial "hundreds of performances in Sweden" had not been misleading publicity. The witty repartee and amusing scenes, the dramatic story and good moral background won immediate success for a comedy that did not have to depend upon songs and variety entertainment. It had been "specially copied" for the company, the press noted gratefully, and, it seems, accurately; for the manuscript copy owned by Hedwig Brusell Melinder comes from the Harald Apelbom *Teateragentur* of Stockholm, and is in two hands, with the signature of the first copyist and the date 10/8/1902 at the close of the second act.[61]

As Louise Haverman, the heroine of *Lifvet på landet,* the then Hedwig Brusell had her first demanding role, for Inspector Haverman, the noble and capable manager of the estate of Baron Axel von Rambow, is dismissed and accused of dishonesty, and Louise joins her father in refusing to marry the Baron's cousin Frans until her father is cleared and the Baron's approval given. Nobility in suffering is the lot also of the Baron's young wife, Frida, who is unable to prevent her husband from mis-

156

treating Haverman and subsequently from mismanaging his estate. The Baron is on the brink of ruin and suicide when salvation for him and happiness for all comes through the good offices of Haverman's faithful friend and the play's chief comic character—the garrulous, eccentric Malaprop, Uncle Bräsig. Earlier, Uncle Bräsig has overheard a villainous social climber, Pomuckelskopp, plotting to gain the Baron's property, but has been unable to get the Baron to take his warnings seriously. Usually associated with Uncle Bräsig in his comedy is the minister's wife, Mrs. Berendsohn, who is also Louise's foster mother. Comedy is provided also by Mrs. Berendsohn's adolescent nephew, Fritz Triddelfitz, who abets the Baron in his folly, is an unwitting factor in the downfall of Haverman, and is smitten by the charms of both Louise and one of the Baron's servants; and the domineering wife of Pomuckelskopp and their silly, affected daughters are presented as comic caricatures. The five-act play includes also scenes with the workers on the Baron's estate, who come to his mansion to protest the sufferings brought on by his conduct of affairs, and, finally, to acclaim the return of Haverman. Among the happier pictures of country life is the Christmas Eve at the parsonage with which the play begins.

Seldom was there such enthusiastic praise for play and actors as greeted *Lifvet på landet,* both when it was first performed, and when it was repeated on December 20, though at that busy time it was, understandably, less well attended. Brusell was considered an admirable Haverman, and his daughter and Max Hedman appealing and competent as the lovers. Schycker and Mrs. Hvitfeldt were excellent as the prattling, well meaning minister and his wife; Lindblom and Ida Anderson-Werner equally good as the pompous Pomuckelskopps. All roles, however, were subordinate to that of Uncle Bräsig, in which Carl Liljegren won a triumph. To most of the audience, then and in later popular performances, Uncle Bräsig was the play; and usually Carl Liljegren was Uncle Bräsig.[62]

A full house for the New Year *Andersson, Pettersson och Lundström* showed that it still kept its old appeal. No fault could be found with Brusell, Liljegren, and Schycker in the name roles, but funny as Schycker's Lundström was, he could not equal Pfeil "of blessed memory." Mrs. Milton was outstanding in the minor role of Andersson's maid, Fia, and was heartily applauded for the scene in which she declared her independence and threw her apron in her mistress's face.[63]

In 1891, *Jorden rundt på 80 dagar* at the North Side Turner Hall had been voted spectacular. In 1904, the resources of the Auditorium and Grand Opera House were available to do justice to its varied scenes and melodramatic action. A host of amateurs and Swedish organizations took part. One of the women's choruses sang in procession around the pyre on which the Rajah's widow was to be burned, and Ellen Graf as the widow did a death dance. The Swedish gymnastic club performed as Indians, and, with Lindblom as their chief, attacked Fort Kearney, ably defended by soldiers from Company I, Second Regiment, of the Illinois National Guard. The Indian attack was considered one of the best scenes, but there was some regret that no Indians were scalped. A number of the principal characters came from the *Svenska Teatersällskap*—Brusell as detective Fixit, and Örtengren as the widely travelled Passepartout. But in the role of Phineas Fogg, Ovington, who originated it in Chicago, returned for his last appearances, and with his earlier success. Fred Littche, too, was one of the actors from the original cast who came out of retirement to participate in the *Svenska National Förbund* entertainment.

The play attracted a good audience at the Auditorium, despite the recent Iroquois Theatre fire, but expenses had mounted into thousands, and there was a deficit of $400.00. Fortunately the repetition at the Grand Opera House was also well attended, and a reasonable sum was realized by the *Förbund* for the unemployed Swedes of Chicago.[64]

1904-1905

In May of 1904, Christopher Brusell and his family went to Sweden for a visit from which they returned in November. His absence brought about a situation that was to exist for most of the remaining seasons of this period: activities by two major companies. In the fall of 1904, Behmer presented two comedies at the Garrick, by the *Svenska Teatersällskap*. Brusell also used the old company name for his first play of the season, a December performance of *Vermländingarne* at the Grand Opera House. Thereafter it became the name of his company, and of the company headed by both directors in the 1906-1907 season, and Behmer adopted the name with which his efforts were long associated, *Svenska Dramatiska Sällskap*. Division did not, to begin with, bring any marked rivalry. There was a general interchange of actors for the productions of the two directors; Behmer himself acted for Brusell, and Hedwig Brusell for Behmer. Behmer, however, had the advantage of the exclusive services of Anna Pfeil and Wilma Sundborg-Stern for several of his plays.

The new development resulted in nine city performances, an unprecedented number; and neither director had recourse to the Turner Halls for full length productions. Four of the nine plays acted in city theatres were

Ida Anderson-Werner as Ingrid

Bröllopet på Ulfåsa, January 28, 1906, Powers Theatre

Hedwig Brusell Melinder as Sigrid the Fair

Fröken Ida Östergren

gifver
HENRIK IBSEN'S

Ett dockhem

å

Music Hall Fine Arts Building

Lördagen den 11te Maj.
kl. 8 e. m.

med benäget biträde af medlemmar af Svenska Teatersällskapet

BILJETTER säljas i Music Hall Biljett Kontor, 203 Michigan Ave.,
från och med Måndagen den 29 April.

1907

SVENSK TEATER

Svenska Dramatiska Sällskapet af Chicago

Gifver å

Grand Opera House
Rockford, Ill.

Fredagen den 24 Nov. 1911
kl. 8 e. m.

Värmländingarne

Lördagen den 25 November
kl. 8 e. m.

Sten Stenson Stéen
från Eslöf

ELIS OLSON

Gästuppträdande af

ELIS OLSON
Från Södra Teatern, Stockholm

ERNST BEHMER, Regissör

BILJETTER (till reserverade platser) tillhandahållas å Tradgardhs
Drug Store, 7th St., J. A. Kron, 111 Kishwaukee St., samt
O. W. Larson, 1239 - 14th Ave.

new. Both men turned to the old Swedish playwright, Jolin, for a novelty, but each also departed from tradition, Behmer with the one serious venture of the Chicago Swedes in Shakespeare, and Brusell with a première of Sudermann's *Ära*. Relatively novel, too, were Geijerstam's *Svärfar*, not acted since its 1892 première, and the comedy introduced in 1902, *Öregrund-Östhammar*, both of which were produced by Behmer; and Brusell presented the latest arrival among the folk plays, *Ljungby Horn*.

The press proudly proclaimed that the Swedish theatre in Chicago was now an established fact. And, except for their two most significant productions, both directors were rewarded by public support as well as by critical encouragement. Behmer made a strong plea for support in the extended program notes for *Svärfar*, his first offering, discussing the importance of the theatre through the ages, and its values in providing recreation for body and spirit, strength for carrying on everyday routine and wearying labor. He expressed gratitude for the interest that had furthered the efforts of the *Svenska Teatersällskap* to win public favor and trust, and regret that, since theatres could not be secured for the evening, he was forced to give matinée performances. But he exerted himself to make the matinées palatable:

> How could Sunday afternoons be more happily, pleasantly, and profitably spent? And then you come home in good and comfortable time and sit and talk a while over a cup of tea—and exchange views about the play and the acting, and still get to bed at a decently early hour—if you wish.

Behmer's first matinée was well attended, and with the director himself in the role of the professor, earlier acted by Björkman, with Ida Anderson-Werner as his wife, Anna Pfeil as their daughter, and Littche playing opposite her as the artist, the performance was accounted expert. The comedy was approved also, but it was Geijerstam's rural pieces that were hereafter to represent him in Chicago. *Svärfar* was seen again only when acted by a company from Rockford in 1925.[65]

Behmer's *The taming of the shrew*, which followed in November, did not have an encouraging house, and the critics, though they appreciated the devotion to dramatic art evident in the choice of play, doubted the advisability of the attempt. Shakespeare's verse offered particular difficulties, and the actors had to compete with memories of Ada Rehan and the Daly Company. Behmer, of course, played Petruchio, and succeeded in a lively and comic characterization, but was criticized for carrying his tyrannical manner into his soliloquies and his final reconciliation with Kate. His star, Wilma Sundborg-Stern, was less satisfactory as the shrew, being,

159

according to *Svenska Nyheter,* more inclined to flee than to fight. Anna Pfeil was the Bianca, and except for two minor roles, the cast was experienced, and its performance creditable. The play was paid the compliment of serious criticism, and recognized as an event in Chicago's Swedish theatrical history. Nevertheless, the reviewers concluded that the company's talents should normally be used in plays of Swedish type, and pointed out that appreciation by a small group would not pay for rent of theatres and costumes.[66]

In contrast, the public flocked to see Brusell's production of its favorite folk play, *Vermländingarne,* in December. A familiar cast was generally approved, but there were the usual strictures: John Örtengren's maturity and operatic style kept his Erik from being convincingly romantic, and his heavy gold wedding band did not add to the illusion. Hedwig Brusell, in the first of many appearances as Anna, attracted most of the critical attention; and, youthful as she was, she came off with honor, fainting before the church like a veteran, and succeeding in an effective mad scene. For her this was a daring venture, undertaken only upon the urging of her father, when a replacement became necessary.[67]

Other popular choices followed. Behmer's *Öregrund-Östhammar* appealed as before, with the director at his best in its burlesque comedy.[68] Brusell's *Ljungby Horn* also repeated its earlier success. The spectacular element of the saga play was well managed; dances which, as often, were under the direction of Fred Bolling, were effective; and Brusell again won praise for his able characterization of Didrik.[69] His production of Jolin's *Löjen och tårar* (Smiles and tears) pleased the public, which enjoyed both the sufferings of the downtrodden servant girl and her unjustly imprisoned father (roles played by Hedwig Brusell and Carl Liljegren) and the comedy of the nagging wife and her husband (played by Christopher Brusell and Augusta Milton). The play was an old-fashioned blend of sentiment, morality, and comedy, said the critics, but they treated it kindly— except G. W...n of *Svenska Nyheter.* It was his vitriolic attack on this performance that called forth Dr. Anna Windrow Holm's letter of protest. Hedwig Brusell he advised to stay home and "help Mamma and Pappa"; as for the director—did he fully recognize the responsibility and care his task involved? And Behmer made his role an inappropriate caricature. In general, the temple of drama should be kept clear of those who misuse it in the name of art. Some roles were well taken, the critic admitted; Liljegren and Schycker possessed real talent. With W...n's concluding indictment, that the performance was slow, his colleagues agreed. Only at midnight, wrote

G. W. . . .n ironically, could he gather up the handkerchief that his sympathetic tears had made as wet as the Kattegat, and battle his way through the departing crowd[70]

Brusell's production of *Ära* was a farewell benefit for Albert Alberg, who was about to return to Sweden, after the ups and downs of his Chicago years. Critics noted appreciatively the opportunity to see the play that Hedberg's adaptation had made so famous in Sweden, and approved the appropriate realism of the performance. But they were chiefly interested in Alberg, in the two laurel wreaths with which he was presented, in the sight—as touching as anything on the stage—of the white-haired, Wotan-bearded old actor kissing the Swedish colors with which they were tied. A happier play, it was pointed out, would doubtless have brought a larger audience to honor him. Once before during this season Alberg had made an appearance, as Baptista in *The taming of the shrew;* in *Ära* he played Counsellor Mühlingh. There was some criticism of Hedwig Brusell and Sara Nordstrom as lacking the strength demanded by their roles—as Alma Heinecke, the laborer's daughter who is victimized by Counsellor Mühlingh's son, and Leonora, the counsellor's daughter, who marries the Heinecke son, Robert, in spite of her father's opposition. And as Robert, whose return from success in the Orient precipitates much of the action, the relatively inexperienced John Fernlundh was considered merely stereotyped. Other important roles were in good hands, with Brusell as Robert's patron, Count von Traft-Saarberg, and Ida Anderson-Werner and Carl Liljegren as old Heinecke and his wife.[71]

If the *Vermländingarne* announced by Behmer for May 14 was acted, the newspapers united in disregarding it. His Jolin comedy, *Friaren från Värmland,* had been found very entertaining. Lindblom was particularly effective as the country suitor of the title, and Wilma Sundborg-Stern good, though, as was bluntly said, she lacked the gift that Anna Pfeil never lost, of creating an illusion of youth.[72] Madame Sundborg-Stern acted with Behmer also in an April comedy given for *Nordstjernan* at the South Side Turner Hall, one of several lesser performances he directed during the season.[73]

1905-1906

Increasingly keen competition between the two companies developed during the 1905-1906 season, with the result that the Swedish public had an otherwise unequalled opportunity to see Swedish plays in seriously undertaken performances. Of the fourteen major productions, twelve were given in city theatres, the *Svenska Dramatiska Sällskap* using the North Side Turner Hall for two of its eight plays. The real rivalry set in during the spring, with each company upholding the claims of its leading lady, and Brusell following the Behmer *Regina von Emmeritz* with the same play two weeks later. Between them, the companies presented two plays a month in January, March, April, and May. If two companies were not what the supporters of the theatre had in mind during the long years of wishing for regular Swedish performances, rivalry did, at any rate, provide performances at approximately the hoped for intervals.

The season had an early start in August, when Brusell took the opportunity to present the visiting prima donna of the Stockholm Royal Opera, Madame Anna Hellström, in *Vermländingarne*. With her as a magnet, he was able to fill the Auditorium. This was no dream, it was actually sold out, said *Svenska Kuriren*. There was not complete agreement as to the merits of the performance or of Madame Hellström's Anna. Her singing was excellent, certainly, but her acting no better than that to which the Chicago Swedish public was accustomed. Brusell measured up well in the role of Erik, which he took over at the last moment, because his second star, Arthur Donaldson, had to rehearse *The Prince of Pilsen*.[74] The usually critical G. W...n was ecstatic about the authentic country pictures, the sunshine atmosphere in which the whole production was bathed. Appropriately festive were laurel wreaths for Brusell and flowers for Madame Hellström; but for too many of the audience the play was merely a festive occasion, G. W...n complained. They talked and laughed aloud, even during Anna's mad song—"Lord forgive them."[75]

Brusell's other production of the fall was also a familiar folk play, *Valborgsmesso-aftonen,* at the Grand Opera House; and though lacking in stellar actors, it drew a good house and was favorably reviewed for individual characterizations, ensemble acting, and lively folk dances. Brusell himself was, as usual, praised for his portrayal of the old man, Tattar-Sven, who helps bring the central romance to a happy conclusion.[76]

In the meantime, Behmer had successfully opened the *Svenska Dramatiska Sällskap* season with two performances of *Farbror Knut från Norrköping,* his own version of *A pair of spectacles*. As in *Lifvet på landet,* Carl Liljegren played the uncle role, this time a selfish and mercenary character. Behmer was his brother, Henrik Brandes, who converts Knut to a new set of values and reconciles him and his son; and Augusta Milton had the third leading role, as the young wife whom Henrik Brandes temporarily suspects. The questions raised by reviewers as to Behmer's success in transforming the characters into true Swedish types evidently did not trouble the audiences, who enjoyed both the Garrick matinée and a North Side Turner Hall evening performance.[77] One of the last gala productions of *Andersson, Pettersson och Lundström* followed as Behmer's December offering—another Garrick matinée. The theatre provided special scenery to enhance the spectacular scenes. Madame Wilma Sundborg-Stern took the principal women's roles, Andersson gave Melinder a new prominence, Liljegren was a capital Pettersson, and, as Lundström, Behmer, who had provided himself with the usual new verses, gave an uncommonly happy characterization. Here was a Lundström who truly sang *dudelandej*, instead of being bowed down by his troubles.[78]

Two sentimental dramas by Jolin not before acted in Chicago were used by Behmer for January and April performances at the Garrick, but did not draw as well as the comedies and had a lukewarm critical reception. *Barnhusbarnen*, "obtained at great expense," was dismissed as a dull domestic story, with chief actors miscast and other amateurs inadequate for Behmer's needs.[79] In *Mäster Smith*, the new star, Ida Östergren was excellent, but the performance as a whole was uneven; and the story of class conflict, with the daughter of the proud, aristocrat-hating Smith falling in love with a member of the aristocracy, now seemed more obvious than tragic.[80] In January, the Behmer company also gave a performance at the North Side Turner Hall. The play was Geijerstam's *Per Olsson och hans käring*—but in these days only city performances received critical attention. There had been minor holiday performances as well, one promoted by Schycker, and one, for the Iduna Society, the *Svenska Teatersällkap* première of *Karl Sabelträff och hans rivaler*.

The first major production by the Brusell company since *Valborgs-messo-aftonen* was its January *Bröllopet på Ulfåsa*. Now Brusell was able to present to the public the star of *The Prince of Pilsen*, Arthur Donaldson. He was considered impressive in the main dramatic role, Birger Jarl, though perhaps not entirely in character. And the feminine audience, the critics feared, were disappointed at seeing him as an old man with a beard. Still he made use of his opportunity at the close of the play to embrace Sigrid the Fair (Hedwig Brusell) with true matinée idol fervor, a contrast to the ordinarily hesitant love making of the Swedish stage, and to the acting in this play of Werner Melinder as her bridegroom, Bengt Lagman.[81] The usual exceptions were taken to some of interpretations, but this was considered one of the good performances of the play[82]

The last of the *Svenska Teatersällskap* plays of the season also had

163

Donaldson as its drawing card, in a role he had played before in Chicago, Asmodeus, the evil spirit, in *Den ondes besegrare*. In the opinion of *Svenska Tribunen*, at least, he gave a striking performance that dominated the play, and was particularly well supported by Ida Anderson-Werner as an old witch. The performance was a benefit for Swedish sufferers in the San Francisco earthquake, but was not specially well attended.[83] The performance of *Nerkingarne* at the Auditorium that closed the *Svenska Dramatiska Sällskap* season a week later was sponsored by the *Svenska National Förbund* for the same cause, but there had probably been too many Swedish plays in the last months. At any rate, the proceeds were disappointing. The leading roles were well taken, was the general opinion, but there were more inexperienced actors than usual.[84]

These performances were, actually, something of an anticlimax. The high point of the season had been reached in the rival productions of *Regina von Emmeritz*, March 18 and April 1. Ida Östergren had been introduced to the public by Behmer on March 4, in *Vermländingarne*, and had been praised, but not as she was to be on further acquaintance. As Anna she was considered no more impressive than many of the splendid actresses Chicago Swedes had been privileged to enjoy, and the performance as a whole was not outstanding.[85] The Behmer *Regina von Emmeritz* with Ida Östergren was announced for March 18 on the 20th of February. On February 27th, the *Svenska Teatersällskap* performance was advertised, its star Wilma Sundborg-Stern of the American *Two orphans* company. This was to be an evening performance because matinées "have proved less popular with our countrymen." Publicity and opposing claims continued, and reached their climax in Miss Östergren's $25,000.00 suit against Brusell. His advertisement that offended her read in part: "The *Svenska Teatersällskap* has never and will never in the future, as long as it is under Brusell's direction, through boastful announcements about appearances of so-called 'prima donnas' from 'Sweden's most distinguished theatres' (to which they never belonged) seek to deceive the public." The slurs were motivated by jealousy, she retorted.[86] And *Hemlandet* commented that if the directors had been Americans, one would suspect a publicity stunt.[87]

Whether or not publicity was the reason (and no more was heard of the suit), both performances—the matinée at the Garrick and the evening performance at the Grand Opera House—had good and enthusiastic houses. The critics dealt out approval and disapproval to the two productions in approximately equal measure, but were somewhat more enthusiastic about Ida Östergren than about Wilma Sundborg-Stern. Even G. W...n called

164

the new actress brilliant in a role that was a real test of her ability, and *Svenska Kuriren* agreed that she was a true artist, making the scenes of inner conflict powerful without undue melodrama. Madame Sundborg-Stern's interpretation was described as capable and technically skilful. Both directors were considered excellent in the same role—the fanatic Jesuit, Hieronymus. For costumes and settings of both companies there was only praise; but neither king was more than adequate, the first, Liljegren, being more dandy than hero, and the second, Melinder, being conscientious but unimpressive. And in both performances there were the expected weaknesses in minor roles.[88]

1906-1907

A popular summer outing sponsored in July of 1906 by the *Svenska Dramatiska Sällskap* naturally included dramatic entertainment, which consisted of scenes from two popular plays. And Brusell took a leading role in a Bellman Day outdoor presentation of *En afton på "Tre Byttor,"* one of the more successful performances of Wicklund's play. Then, with the fall of 1906, came the announcement that the two companies were to merge as the *Svenska Teatersällskap,* with Brusell and Behmer once more joint directors. During their separate activities, there had been little of the advice as to union so freely given when similar situations had existed in earlier years; but the announcement was hailed as meeting the long cherished and often expressed wishes of lovers of the theatre, and the old— and valid—argument was repeated, that the field of the Swedish theatre was not large enough for two companies.[89] The cooperation was, as matters developed, to be temporary, but it was responsible for a successful season, climaxed by a performance of Ibsen's *A doll's house,* presented by Ida Östergren, with the assistance of the *Svenska Teatersällskap.*

Nor was other theatrical entertainment to be missing in the 1906-1907 season. For the first time in several years a new company was playing popular comedy programs, usually at Belmont Hall, at the low prices of 25 and 50 cents. Called both Swedish Friends of Thalia and *Folk-Teatern,* it was, with the exception of its manager, Leopold Chellman, made up chiefly of young people. Members included the Melinders, and actors soon to be playing with the major companies, John Ternquist and Signe Mortenson. Company president Elis Gustafson was also occasionally seen with Brusell and Behmer. The Swedish Friends of Thalia amused the public and themselves, but some of their performances, at least, were so carelessly prepared as to draw the scorn of the reviewers.[90] In the spring, plans for little evening entertainments at Belmont Hall were made by a number of the old guard, also, The formation of the *Svenska Teater Klubb* was announced, with Liljegren and Schycker as directors and Brusell and Behmer among the members; but after two programs the project seems to have been dropped.[91]

From October 1906 to May 1907, at approximately monthly intervals, the Brusell and Behmer *Svenska Teatersällskap* gave eight city productions, including the Ibsen play. Company members also supported Ida Östergren and Wilma Sundborg-Stern in less pretentious experiments in the literary drama, and appeared, with Carl Milton as the promoter, in a New Year première of Geijerstam's *Lars Anders och Jan Anders och deras barn* at the North Side Turner Hall. In October, lovers of the theatre had the opportunity to see Madame Anna Hellström in an act from *The daughter of the regiment,* as part of her Auditorium concert. No such visiting star enhanced this season's two performances of *Vermländingarne,* but they were among the *Svenska Teatersällskap's* outstanding successes. In general, it was the old and not the novel plays that most pleased the season's audiences.

A full house for the opening performance bore witness to the position the Swedish theatre had achieved, but of the newspapers only *Svenska Amerikanaren* was enthusiastic about the play with which the directors marked their reunion. Börjesson's picture of the youthful Carl XII, *Ur Carl XII:s ungdom* (called *Carl XII*), had, in fact, the weaknesses of the pioneer dramatist's other historical plays, being loose in construction, weak in characterization, and more suited to the library than to the stage. Ida Östergren, in the leading feminine role, was generally acclaimed; Behmer, as the king, had a mixed reception. The performance was not helped by the attitude of the audience. They come to laugh, whether the play is serious or comic, *Svenska Kuriren* protested. Small wonder that Ida Östergren occasionally faltered—even Sarah Bernhardt could not have maintained her composure.[92]

There was no questioning the success of the next two plays. In November *Lifvet på landet,* with Liljegren as Uncle Bräsig, delighted another full house, and in December *Andersson, Pettersson och Lundström* gave him another triumph as Lundström. Most of the cast was considered adequate for the careful characterization required in *Lifvet på landet,* though Ekberg's lawyer was damned as a combination of the *bof* of melodrama and a 36th class Mephistopheles, and Patrick Warner as the young lover seemed too ready to devour his sweetheart. To G. W . . . n, writing now in *Svenska Amerikanaren,* the performance as a whole gave the impression of life, not of acting, and was marred only by the behavior of the audience. If they must laugh at the serious, they might at least be more quiet about it.[93] *Andersson, Pettersson och Lundström* attracted an unusually large house for a matinée, but was showing signs of wear, in critical opinion. Liljegren and the directors played the name trio with proper gusto, but the performance as a whole was regarded as rather routine, and was marked by much doubling of roles.[94]

A large audience in holiday spirits gave *Lars Anders och Jan Anders och deras barn* a hearty welcome, but the critics were less happy. Of the play they said little, being occupied with such unauthentic aspects of the production as lovers hanging on each other's necks in a way quite inappropriate for a couple of naive country youngsters, and a cotter garbed in a Texas sombrero and trousers made of American flags.[95] Another new comedy was acted at the Garrick in February, *Pelle Grönlunds bryggeri.* It was the work of Kinmansson, the playwright responsible for the adaptation of *Öregrund-Östhammar* used in Sweden, but its pictures of everyday life and provincial types, with a sprinkling of conniving villains, was considered only moderately funny.[96]

Performances of both *Lifvet på landet* and *Vermländingarne* in Rockford and Moline, Illinois, preceded a March 10 *Vermländingarne* at the Garrick. It was sold out in advance, and a repetition at the Grand Opera House was arranged for the following week. But all was not a bed of roses for the directors. The second performance was followed by an apology for confusion at the box office: at the last minute, too late for adequate publicity, a shift to the Garrick had been necessary. As to the play—the audiences laughed at the same old places, and critics deviated as little from precedent. Was or was not Hedwig Brusell satisfactory in Anna's mad scene? Was Ida Östergren brilliant or too citified as Stina? And so on, through the list of familiar characters.[97]

Wilma Sundborg-Stern, in Chicago between American engagements, had also attracted considerable attention with a semi-public performance on March 16. The play was *En förlofning,* usually known as *Skådespelerskan* (The actress), by the well known novelist of Stockholm's "80ists," Charlotte Edgren Leffler. Madame Sundborg-Stern was thought unusually well suited to the role of the actress whose visit to the bourgeois family of her fiancé upsets their conventional ways, and the audience granted the modern "discussion" play the quiet attention it demanded. The *Doll's house* type of ending, with the heroine returning to her career but hoping not to give up her love, seemed ludicrous to the *Svenska Amerikanaren* reviewer, and characteristic of the psychological weakness of Sweden's women writers.[98] No such modern weaknesses, but old fashioned melodrama and moralizing handicapped the next *Svenska Teatersällskap* play, for which, in its original form, another woman writer was responsible. Emilie Flygare Carlén's *Rosen på Tistelön* had been one of Sweden's popular novels in the 1840's. The 1907 audience wept a little and laughed a little, but the company had a difficult task in trying to give credibility to this story of piracy in the Swedish skerries. Ida Östergren did her best as the housekeeper and daughter-in-law of the old pirate, Haroldson, and Hedwig Brusell as the daughter of the family, the "rose," whose long and involved love story introduces a host of characters. Most successful, however, was Behmer as the younger son, Anton Haroldson, who becomes insane after seeing his father commit murder, and who is eventually responsible for the execution of his reformed older brother for that same murder.[99]

The May presentation of the Chicago Swedish actors' first and only Ibsen play had been prepared for by weeks of publicity, by much praise for Ida Östergren's ability and enterprise, by lengthy discussion of the Chicago Swedish theatre, its aims, progress, and problems. *A doll's house* was a disappointment only in the limited support given it by the public and in the little real understanding displayed by those in attendance. Never had the artistry of Ida Östergren been so thoroughly revealed as in the challenging role of the Ibsen heroine. He had seen Mrs. Dybvad, the famous Norwegian Nora, R. Elfman wrote in *Svenska Amerikanaren,* and Ida Östergren did not suffer by comparison; nothing of Ibsen's intention was lost in the final dramatic scene. For Behmer, too, there was general enthusiasm. His Torvald Helmer was a true characterization. And Lisa and Eric Behmer as Nora and Torvald's children showed inherited dramatic gifts. Only Lindblom's Dr. Rank raised some doubts, but it was conceded that the popular actor had succeeded in avoiding his usual comic burlesque. Without question, this production marked new heights for both Ida Östergren and the *Svenska Teatersällskap.*[100]

Behmer and Miss Östergren won further approval in June, with the second semi-public program of the season, and another play that depended on talk, not scenic effects. Their *Hjärtesorg* (Heart's sorrow) was a version of Theuriet's *Jean-Marie,* which had recently attracted attention as one of the plays acted by the "New Theatre" group that was trying to establish itself as a repertoire company.[101]

For the larger Swedish public, there were summer treats in store. Visiting actresses Emma Meissner and Rosa Grünberg twice appeared with the *Svenska Teatersällskap*. An evening of folk ballads at Powers included the old Danish folk play, *En söndag i Amager* (A Sunday at Amager), welcomed by the *Svenska Kuriren* reviewer for the novelty of its convincing love scenes—even though they raised the already torrid temperature twenty degrees. Also at Powers, *Vermländingarne* was played "just as they do it at home," and Madame Meissner as Anna and Miss Grünberg as Stina were applauded as if the audience needed to keep warm.[102] Similar enthusiasm had greeted another long familiar folk play, *En midsommarnatt i Dalarne*, acted by the *Svenska Teatersällskap* at a June outing in Columbia Park.[103]

1907-1908

In the fall of 1907, Behmer formed an affiliation with the *Svenska National Förbund* that was to continue more or less regularly for half a dozen seasons; and again there were two major companies. The change was accepted by the press with little comment. There were pleas for critical tolerance and public support for the *Förbund* plays by reason of the worthy cause, but unkind references to *"Myhrmanska spektaklet"* indicate the existence of less sympathetic attitudes (Mrs. Myhrman was, of course, the energetic secretary of the *Förbund; spektaklet*, literally the show or spectacle, was used in its derogatory sense). The season was noteworthy as far as the number of city productions was concerned, but performances were uneven, attendance was uncertain, and only one of three new plays was a success. Dividing lines between the companies were more definite than usual, and each company had a good quota of experienced performers and gifted younger recruits; but complaints about inadequate preparation and the use of inexperienced actors increased. The *Svenska Dramatiska Sällskap* made early announcement of the "best dramatic talents" it had engaged: Ida Östergren, Ida Anderson-Werner, Carl Liljegren, Leopold Chellman, Ernest Lindblom, and Fred Bolling, of the older group, and the less familiar John Ternquist, Signe Mortenson, and Sigrid Lindberg.[104] Soon added to the company were Frithiof Burgeson and Rosa Pearson. Acting under Brusell's banner were such able actors as the Melinders, Carl and Augusta Milton, John Lindhagen, and Ernst Schycker, and the talented young Oscar Larson. For his first two productions, Brusell had a powerful attraction in Arthur Donaldson, who, as it turned out, then made his farewell appearances on the Chicago Swedish stage.

Monthly performances in city theatres were the aim of the *Svenska Dramatiska Sällskap*, and though the plan was not completely carried out, the company did give six plays in the city and acted each month from September through April. Financially, however, the season was called a fiasco, and not until January did a performance win whole-hearted critical approval.[105] The play with which the company got its season under way, *Gamla Heidelberg*, might have been expected to have considerable appeal, but only *Svenska Amerikanaren* was loyally enthusiastic. Other papers felt that the performance was not up to standard; it was dull and slow, and gave evidence of careless preparation—a criticism uncommon for plays directed by Behmer. The director himself as the prince and Ida Östergren as Kathi were competent, but measured in terms of Sweden's gay *punsch* drinking university students, the picture of Heidelberg student life seemed tame, even when livened up a bit by Harmoni Glee Club songs.[106]

The company's October choice, *Öregrund-Östhammar*, did not have a much better press, and had lost some of its earlier drawing power. For the first time, too, it was criticized as lacking the fundamental moral concepts that should characterize entertainments appealing for public support. The featured actresses were complimented: Ida Östergren as the young boy, Emil Klint, and Rosa Pearson, in her stage debut, as the ingenue, Susanna.[107] In November the play was acted again in Waukegan, in part as a benefit for the Swedish Tuberculosis Sanatorium of Denver, under the joint sponsorship of the *Förbund* and Vasa Lodge Norden.[108]

Before Behmer's company again acted in Chicago in December, Brusell's *Svenska Teatersällskap* had given two of its four city plays of the season. The first, *Bröllopet på Ulfåsa*, with Donaldson this time in the appropriately romantic role of Bengt Lagman, was welcomed by a sold out house. Donaldson was probably too much the courtier, was *Svenska Kuriren's* comment, and Brusell's Birger Jarl, if less striking than Donaldson's had been, was more historically correct. Reviews were enthusiastic about the performance, but not about an audience that laughed when Sigrid the Fair (again Hedwig Melinder) wept. The only remedy was to give them what should be laughed at.[109] This the next play, the farcical *Sabinskornas bortröfvande*, provided. Donaldson enchanted the audience as the provincial theatre director, John Lindhagen was excellent as the professor-author, and as the professor's wife the Swedish actress, Emma Wallin-Malm, making her one appearance, left the reviewers regretful that there would not be an opportunity to see her in a role really worthy of her gifts. Augusta Milton, the professor's maid, was praised as the company's most genuine talent, and Oscar Larson made a promising debut in a minor part. This was the type of play that gave the actors a legitimate opportunity for the exaggerated comedy to which they were inclined, wrote approving reviewers.[110]

Both companies continued with old plays. December brought the last Chicago performance of Blanche's *Herr Dardanell och hans upptåg på landet,* which Behmer gave its one city production, and January the season's one *Vermländingarne* as a North Side Turner Hall New Year's performance by the *Svenska Teatersällskap,* and Behmer's historical drama for the season, *Regina von Emmeritz.* The Blanche comedy unfortunately had to compete with a memorial program for King Oscar II of Sweden, but the company prefaced the play with a memorial ceremony, and drew a fair house. The performance moved at a lively pace, and the leading actors were warmly lauded—Ida Östergren as the stupid Agapetus (though it was hard for her to conceal her intelligence), Behmer as Herr Dardanell, and Rosa Pearson, "the songbird of the company," as Dorothea.[111] Another royal memorial marked the *Svenska National Förbund's* winter festival production of *Regina von Emmeritz,* a bust of the king being presented to the *Förbund* by the actors. The Auditorium was well if not completely filled, and the play ably acted by the principals: Ida Östergren as Regina, Behmer as Hieronymus, Ida Anderson-Werner as the nurse, and John Örtengren as the king—a role for which his operatic style and impressive appearance made him well suited.[112]

Ida Anderson-Werner's Lisa was one of the high points of a spotty performance of *Vermländingarne,* and Brusell as Sven, Augusta Milton as Stina, and Hedwig Melinder as Anna acted and sang with their usual success. But, said a disgusted *Svenska Amerikanaren* reviewer, singer Carl Lönnerblad, the Erik, had not mastered the rudiments of acting and should never have been permitted to undertake the role; and this time the audience had some excuse for unseemly behavior, with a wretched *provst* marring the serious scenes, and a last scene that had to be interrupted because John Lindhagen as Löpare-Nisse came on the stage drunk and was beyond help from the prompter.[113]

Also in January, a week after *Regina von Emmeritz,* Brusell gave the season's first novelty since the *Svenska Dramatiska Sällskap Gamla Heidelberg.* Not surprisingly, attendance was only fair. And the new Stockholm comedy, *Herrskap och tjenstefolk* (Gentry and servants) proved a weak attraction. It was only the "old sauerkraut warmed up," the ingredients domestic wrangles and a love affair of the daughter of the house (Anna Nelson) and her music teacher. It called for, and was given a burlesque performance, but also, seemingly, a slipshod one, despite publicized

171

authentic servants' costumes from Schoultz and the valiant efforts of Augusta Milton and other experienced actors.[114] Brusell's concluding play, in February, a repetition of Jolin's *Löjen och tårar,* had a better reception, probably in part because it was a farewell for Hedwig Brusell Melinder, who was to join her husband in Sweden. Her loss would be lamented, wrote *Svenska Amerikanaren,* by a public that had watched her grow up on the stage. Comedy by the Schyckers and Mrs. Milton was outstanding in a successful performance; and the assisting Svithiod Singing Club, presenting among other selections an Örtengren setting of a poem by Oscar II, undoubtedly helped attract a good audience.[115] The two groups cooperated also in well received scenes from *Engelbrekt och hans Dalkarlar* at the music club's summer outing. [116]

In the two remaining city productions of the season, the *Svenska Dramatiska Sällskap* reached the high and low points of critical favor with two plays new to the Chicago Swedish stage. The first, *Syrsan,* the familiar story of Fanchon, the cricket, had the advantage of a small cast, which meant that less experienced actors could be dispensed with. The spirited, unconventional young Fanchon gave Ida Östergren one of her best opportunities, and Ida Anderson-Werner was equally outstanding as Fanchon's witch-like but essentially good old grandmother, *Mor Kata på Skogen* (Mother Kate of the Woods). Mrs. Anderson herself named this as her favorite role, and it was the one she acted in celebration of her fiftieth anniversary as an actress. Behmer was competent as the lover whose defiance of his family is rewarded by approval after Fanchon has undergone a transformation, but this was not the type of role in which he was most admired. In two respects the evening was unusual: in the understanding displayed by the audience, and in the entertainment that was introduced in the play as a means of presenting the popular visitor, *Delbostintan* (Madame Ida Gawell-Blumenthal), in folk songs and stories. Her participation probably accounted for a crowd so large that 300 were turned away from the Grand Opera House. Later she wrote with enthusiasm of a performance by a "selected elite troupe" from Chicago's excellent actors, of the responsive audience, and the splendid banquet at which she was honored after the play. In April also she was warmly received when she appeared at the *Svenska National Förbund's* three evening bazaar at the North Side Turner Hall.[117] There, too, the Behmer company concluded its season with two comedies and the familiar Pfeil operetta, *Den lilla sångfågeln.*

When the dramatization of Blanche's old sensation novel, *Flickan i Stadsgården,* was given its one Chicago performance in March, it was played for comedy by actors so convulsed by laughter that they could hardly get through some of its most dramatic episodes. Even the vengeful mason Stork, whose murderous pursuit of the hero, Dr. Axner, is the darkest thread of the long drawn out novel, was called appropriately comic in Liljegren's presentation. As the lovers, Dr. Axner and the mysterious Lalla in whose defense he had as a boy incurred Stork's enmity, Behmer and Ida Östergren seemingly raised the level of performance somewhat, and the intentionally humorous character types, Axner's foster parents, were well portrayed by Ida Anderson-Werner and Bolling. The public accepted willingly a farcical presentation of cholera epidemics and mob scenes in St. Petersburg, but the aesthetic enjoyment of the evening, in the judgment of *Svenska Kuriren,* was provided by the singing of Rosa Pearson and the Linnea quartette.[118]

1908-1909

The *Svenska Dramatiska Sällskap* and *Svenska National Förbund* hit upon a fortunate measure to restore their reputation and recoup their finances in the fall of 1908—they imported "an angel from the West," Anna Pfeil. But after three productions at the Garrick and Grand Opera House, she returned to Seattle; and for the rest of the season the theatre had more in common with that of her early years in Chicago than with recent years of monthly performances in city theatres. The *Svenska Dramatiska Sällskap* ceased activity after a New Year's play at the North Side Turner Hall. Brusell contented himself with a series of old plays at the Turner Halls, and there were unambitious performances under varied leadership there and at the Svithiod Singing Club Hall.

Certainly, however, the season started triumphantly. Never was an actress in the Swedish plays greeted with such joyous enthusiasm as that which now welcomed Anna Pfeil. The Swedish audience might have its faults, said *Svenska Amerikanaren,* but lack of loyalty to its favorites was not one of them. None of the visiting divas and prima donnas had taken the place of their own Anna—the lovable daughter of Suomi land, the most eminent of Swedish American actresses. And in her own particular role of Anna in *Vermländingarne,* in which, of course, she was first presented, she was as superb as she had been twenty years before, as fresh, naive, and moving. The combination of the idolized actress and the favorite folk play was irresistible, and provided an old-fashioned, cozy theatre evening, with wild applause and tributes of flowers. The cast as a whole rose to the occasion with honor. Lindblom, Behmer, Liljegren, Ida Anderson-Werner, Alice Collini, Bolling, Schycker, Oscar Larson, Signe Mortenson, and Sigrid Lindberg were the familiar actors. Only Schycker was criticized for making Anna's father unsuitably comic. Almost overshadowed were the new actor from Sweden, Knut Sjöberg, as Erik, and the visiting Skansen dancers. Sjöberg was recognized as a serious and able artist, though objection was made to his slovenly diction, a criticism he frequently incurred.[119]

A new folk play from the 1880's, the popular Hedberg's *Rospiggarna*, presented a week later, was disappointing, in spite of Mrs. Pfeil and the Skansen dancers. The star had a good opportunity to sing, but her role as the daughter of a farmer was, like the other feminine roles, considered "sublimely colorless." Behmer was the skipper whose betrothal to the heroine was finally celebrated with the customary folk festivities. Carl Liljegren made the most of his part as a soldier. But the play was beyond saving. Its action lacked unity, and the big scenes—the riot at the Stockholm harbor, the comic grounding of a boat, the farm auction—were merely dull. Dialects offered difficulty also, though on the Swedish American stage that should probably not be a matter of criticism, *Svenska Kuriren* observed—with more sarcasm than tolerance.[120]

Once more the *Svenska Dramatiska Sällskap* presented Anna Pfeil, in *Öregrund-Östhammar*, on November 29. As the romantic adolescent, Emil Klint, a role which she had originated in Chicago, she was as delightful as ever, and new members of the cast, Oscar Larson and Knut Sjöberg, as engineeer Thorell and the Öregrund glazier, contributed lively characterizations to a generally expert performance. A backstage fete for Mrs. Pfeil marked the conclusion of her long and valued association with the Chicago Swedish stage. An evening's entertainment at the Svithiod Singing Club Hall, with Mrs. Pfeil appearing in a scene from the now infrequently acted *Nerkingarne*, in the two-character comedy, *Hon vill inte gifta sig* (She will not marry), and in the favorite of the Pfeil company, *Drilléns operett,* had been another happy event in this final visit.[121]

On that same evening, November 8, Brusell had opened his season at the North Side Turner Hall, with the play that had for so long equalled *Vermländingarne* as a box office attraction—*Andersson, Pettersson och Lundström.* A good house saw a satisfactory performance, with Brusell himself as Andersson, Ekberg as Lundström, and a relative newcomer, Walter Jones, as Pettersson. Other familiar members of the cast were Mrs. Milton,

Mrs. Feltskogh, and Chellman.[122] There were sizeable audiences also for the remaining plays of the season. The *Svenska Dramatiska Sällskap's* New Year's offering, *Sven och liten Anna,* was supplied with new comic songs to counteract its sentimentality, and was well acted—though Sjöberg talked as if his mouth were filled with hot potatoes.[123] Brusell's productions of *Ljungby Horn* and *Vermländingarne* and his repetition of *Andersson, Pettersson och Lundström* at the South Side Turner Hall were strengthened by addition of actors from Behmer's company—Sjöberg, Larson, and Lindblom. In the saga play, Brusell's Didrik was admired as before, and Augusta Milton as the spirited Birgit stood out in a cast which had to use many rank amateurs. The guests at the troll wedding were about as animated as plaster figurines, *Svenska Tribunen-Nyheter* complained; and this was a play too dependent on spectacle to be effectively presented at the North Side Turner Hall.[124] No such objections marred the welcome given Brusell's two spring performances of *Vermländingarne,* at the North Side and South Side Turner Halls, and there was cordial praise for a new Anna, the ballad singer from Sweden, Helga Sandberg. Sjöberg again appeared as Erik, but gave less satisfaction than Miss Sandberg and the other experienced members of the cast.[125] And in the summer still another Anna pleased a seemingly insatiable audience, Sara Nordstrom taking the role when Brusell directed the second act of *Vermländingarne* for the outdoor festival of the Svithiod lodges.[126]

1909-1910

The heyday of the Swedish theatre was not past, though hereafter seasons were more limited. All the seven full length plays of the 1909-1910 season were acted in the city, and there was encouragingly consistent support, both for familiar plays and for the novelty with which the visiting Swedish actress, Anna Lundberg, opened the season. She had given a very successful *visafton* (ballad evening), and as she and her husband were visiting Chicago friends for a time they were prevailed upon by the *Svenska National Förbund* to present two plays, with the assistance of the Behmer company. One of the plays, naturally, was *Vermländingarne,* but first Madame Lundberg appeared in the play with which she was most closely identified, *Parispojken,* the Swedish version of the well known *La gamin de Paris.* In *Skådespelarne har ordet,* of 1902, she told of acting *Parispojken* at *Södra Teatern,* before going to Paris, and then of playing it 300 times during a six year tour of Scandinavia, and returning in the same play to Stockholm and the Olympia Theatre. By 1908, she had supposedly acted the role of the mischievous gamin 1,300 times.[127]

Though there had been only a week's notice, a good house greeted *Parispojken* and enjoyed the star's songs and her gay and versatile interpretation of Joseph—his comic escapades, and the courage and goodness of heart he shows in taking up the cause of his sister Elise, after she has been seduced by a general's son. The general, who under Joseph's influence brings about a happy ending, was played by Madame Lundberg's husband, Otto Lundberg, who also served as director. Behmer was the general's son, Miss Karin Lundberg, Elise, and Ida Anderson-Werner, the grandmother of Joseph and Elise. The reviews noted with pleasure the capable performances of the local actors, and particularly the unusual restraint that characterized their acting.[128] A successful performance of *Vermländingarne* was reported without discussion, though the Chicago singer and actor, John Melin, played his first major role as Erik.[129]

Late in October the *Svenska Dramatiska Sällskap* gave its first independent performance of the season, the always successful *Lifvet på landet*. For the first time, Carl Liljegren was not the Uncle Bräsig, his one appearance this season being made with Brusell. But Ernest Lindblom was remarkably successful in the role, and a number of the more recent additions to the acting forces were satisfactory also: Ternquist as the conniving Pomuckelskopp, Stockenberg and Augusta Larson as Pastor Behrendson and his wife, Rosa Pearson as the heroine, Louise, and Sjöberg as her wronged father. Örtengren was again Axel von Rambow, playing one of his last roles in Chicago. *Lifvet på landet* was repeated in March on behalf of the *Svenska National Förbund*, with Behmer in the Baron von Rambow part. Chief compliments on that occasion went to a new actress, Ida Anderson-Werner's young daughter, Magda Lewis, as Marie Möller, Haverman's love-sick servant.[130]

Brusell had given a minor performance the evening of Anna Lundberg's *Vermländingarne*, but the first of his two city productions of the season came the week after the autumn *Lifvet på landet*. The play was *Bröllopet på Ulfåsa*, and the occasion memorable, for it marked Brusell's 25th anniversary as an actor. The company presented him with a laurel wreath—a tribute, wrote *Svenska Tribunen-Nyheter*, in which all the Swedish public interested in genuine Swedish art must join. There were many expressions of gratitude for Brusell's zealous devotion to the Swedish theatre, and for his unselfish endeavors in good times and bad; and his career was recounted in detail. The public turned out in force, practically filling the Garrick. Weaknesses in the performance were passed over lightly, but the usual inadequate amateurs were noted, and it was in this performance that Brusell, playing Birger Jarl, had to call upon the resources long experience had given him to carry off the discovery of his enemy, Karl Algotson (Carl Liljegren) asleep on a sofa at Ulfåsa Hall, Sara Nordstrom was the Sigrid, and her lover and bridegroom the impressive—but mature—John Örtengren. As Sigrid's mother, Mrs. Milton gave a notable performance, and the Prior Botvid of the seldom seen Knut Schröder was also accounted excellent.[131]

The *Svenska Dramatiska Sällskap's Andersson, Pettersson och Lundström* in November 1909 was the last city production of the old Hodell play. Its presentation under favorable conditions was welcomed, but reviewers restricted themselves to general comments—crediting Behmer with carrying most of the performance as Lundström, finding Melin a rather tame Andersson, and Ternquist a satisfactory Pettersson. And new songs by Behmer were, of course, praised. Announcement of the play had been used to counteract some of the publicity recently given to Brusell's "silver wedding with Thalia." Behmer's sixteen years of activity in the Chicago Swedish theatre and the history of the *Svenska Dramatiska Sällskap* since 1904 were reviewed, and there were pointed remarks about the necessity of ruling actors with an iron hand. That Behmer was on the whole a more exacting and careful director than Brusell was often implied in the press, and has been the general opinion of actors of the period.[132]

The March 13 *Lifvet på landet* and a March 20 performance by the *Svenska Teatersällskap* brought the brief season to a successful close. Brusell gave the first city theatre production of Geijerstam's *Lars Anders och Jan Anders och deras barn,* with visiting actors as his attraction—Helga Sandberg, her sister Ingeborg, and the Finnish Rafael Ramsén. The audience was enthusiastic, but reviewers objected that the visitors did not achieve the proper rural tone: in contrast to Brusell as Lars Anders, Ramsén made Jan Anders talk like a Swedish-Finnish clergyman, not a simple cotter.[133]

1910-1911

City productions were limited to two plays by each company in the 1910-1911 season, but with the companies offering rival performances in successive weeks in October and January, competition was lively. A "newly reorganized" *Svenska Dramatiska Sällskap* carried off the honors, at least as far as the reviewers were concerned, Behmer himself providing the two new adaptations with which it won general favor. For the Svithiod Lodge No. 1 he also gave a North Side Turner Hall performance of

Nerkingarne, which had not been seen in full since it was acted at the Auditorium in 1906.

Seldom did any of the plays win such unanimous approval as *Duvals skilsmessa,* Behmer's first offering. The domestic story was well suited to the talents of the company and had the merit of not demanding the elaborate settings that so often made Swedish performances drag. Moreover, the prompter could have stayed at home—even the less experienced and ineffective women of the cast knew their roles, thanks to Behmer's careful direction. The shifting relationships in the familiar *Lottery of love* story gave the leading actors excellent opportunities. Duval, who escapes his domineering mother-in-law when he and her daughter Diane are divorced without regrets, and then acquires the same mother-in-law when she marries druggist Borganeuf, the father of his second wife, was played by Behmer with a pleasing absence of the noisiness and exaggeration to which he had been earlier inclined. Ida Anderson-Werner as the mother-in-law left nothing to be desired, and Liljegren was first-rate as Borganeuf. The role of Diane was skilfully acted by Mrs. Milton, though it lacked the flow of words in which she was inimitable. As an old sailor, Ternquist also contributed a good characterization. The record breaking crowd was considered a tribute to the company's earlier successes, though a more cynical suggestion was that expectation of a sensational divorce story was responsible. Whatever the reason, the success of *Duvals skilsmessa* was regarded as guaranteeing a brilliant future for the company and for the other new plays it promised to present.[134]

But a sold out theatre for Brusell's matinée of *Vermländingarne* the next week showed that the old play had not lost its place in the hearts of the Swedish public. A new Anna, Madame Hilda Hellström-Gagnée, was making her first appearance in Chicago, though she was well known in Swedish circles in the East. The critics were generous with praise, and even paid her the compliment of comparison with Anna Pfeil. Melin, as a last minute substitution in the role of Erik, was forgiven for being a stiff opera singer rather than a Värmland youth. With Brusell giving his usual well considered interpretation of Sven, and Oscar Larson excellent as Anders, minor weaknesses did not interfere with the pleasure of the audience or worry reviewers weary of writing about the play.[135] The *Svenska Dramatiska Sällskap Nerkingarne* in December they also passed over with perfunctory remarks on the durability of the play, the large attendance, and the excellent performance.[136]

178

First of the two city productions in January was Brusell's *Lars Anders och Jan Anders och deras barn,* the Geijerstam comedy he had used the preceding season, with much the same cast. Reviews were polite but lukewarm, emphasizing the prompter's evident desire to win his share of public attention. Helga Sandberg was well received and honored with flowers, but the local actress, Augusta Larson, was considered a more authentic country type. One change from the earlier cast is of interest, for Ramsén was replaced by Nels Carlson, who was to become a leader in dramatic activities and one of the most popular of Chicago's Swedish entertainers. He was accounted a comic Lars Anders, but not one that would have been approved by Geijerstam.[137]

Syndabocken, the play Behmer introduced in January, was only less praised than his *Duvals skilsmessa.* Certainly, reviewers agreed, it presented a highly entertaining situation—a bridegroom palming off as the wife of his friend, Professor Grafstrom, the blackmailing actress who had been his sweetheart, only to have the true Mrs. Grafstrom arrive just as the wedding ceremony is to be performed. With Liljegren as the professor-scapegoat, Behmer as the bridegroom, and Augusta Milton as the actress, less suitable casting in some lesser roles was unimportant. But, unlike *Duvals skilsmessa, Syndabocken* was not played again.[138] This season, the company performed only once more, a February comedy at the Viking Temple for the *Svenska National Förbund,* but in April they honored their director at a banquet, and, with Mrs. Myhrman as spokesman, presented him with a gold watch—a token of their respect and gratitude, and a symbol of the fellowship they had enjoyed.[139]

1911-1912

Four plays by small acting groups and a program at Coffey Hall by the *Svenska Teatersällskap* had followed the February Behmer play to round out the 1910-1911 season—a situation that was to become typical. Not only were Brusell and Behmer, as they cut down the number of city performances, to direct more of the old type comedies in the halls, but such companies as had appeared in the 1910-1911 season—the Norden Amateur Club, the Scandinavian Socialist Club, the Good Templars, and amateurs headed by Ekberg—were to be joined by others, by lodge and labor societies. There were seven productions in the halls, under varied auspices, in the 1911-1912 season. There were also seven city performances—a number not again matched—two actors from Sweden serving to stimulate theatrical activity. Elis Olson, the comedian, was the star of five per-

179

formances, three in city theatres; and August Lindberg, with his production of Strindberg's *Gustaf Vasa,* brought the history of Chicago's Swedish theatre to one of its highest points.

Again the two companies opened the season with favorite plays only a week apart. For the *Svenska Dramatiska Sällskap,* Carl Liljegren returned to his Uncle Bräsig role in *Lifvet på landet,* winning even more acclaim than before. The sometimes hypercritical *Svenska Kuriren* went so far as to say that he would be approved by a far more discriminating audience. Not all the cast, however, was so strong. Sjöberg got through his role of Haverman only with the help of the prompter, and younger additions to the company had little to commend them.[140] Brusell's play was *Vermländingarne;* and the public clearly did not agree with the reviewer who thought the time had come to let the play rest for a few years. The Anna and Erik of Hedwig and Werner Melinder, recently returned from Sweden, were welcomed by an overflow crowd in holiday mood. For the critics, the performance was otherwise chiefly notable in that Schycker, as Löpare-Nisse, had actually learned his lines.[141]

The *Svenska Dramatiska Sällskap* was formally organized for the 1911-1912 season, with Fred Bolling as president, Carl Stockenberg, vice-president, and Mrs. Othelia Myhrman, secretary.[142] The initiative for which Mrs. Myhrman was renowned can be recognized in the extensive publicity that preceded the first appearance of their "guest star," Elis Olson, in November. Never before, said the advertisements, had a ranking Swedish star had such an association with a Swedish American dramatic society as that which gave the Chicago Swedes the opportunity to see Olson in his popular Stockholm success, *Sten Stenson Stéen från Eslöf.* Three hundred times he had made its title role a personal triumph.

Crowded houses saw the play in the first of its three city performances, and in Olson's March farewell, but a second November performance was sparsely attended. Critics and public agreed as to the actor's comic gifts and found the play an entertaining affair. But after their first enthusiasm, the Chicago writers were inclined to agree with Sweden's critic, Carl G. Laurin, who had damned the play with scathing sarcasm after its Stockholm première, though he granted the success of the comedian. The story of Lund University student Sten Stenson Stéen, who visits Skåne and while being tutored there becomes involved with a variety of country characters and summer guests, was, said Laurin, utter trash. Milder Chicago criticism called it inconsequential, and only a reviewer who was a native of the Skåne province was irritated by its farcical caricatures of Skåne types.

At any rate, local audiences, like audiences in Sweden, laughed at the worn out witticisms and stereotyped situations. Olson's role dominated the play, but Ida Anderson-Werner managed to create a good peasant character, Behmer to make something of his role as a tutor, and Augusta Milton to give a lively portrayal of the student, Ameli Andrén. The half drunk sea captain, considered particularly idiotic by Laurin, was played by Liljegren in the fall and Lindblom in the spring.[143]

Another comedy, *Gask på fyra* (A bid of four) served as a vehicle for Elis Olson in two February performances at the South Side Turner Hall and Lake View Hall. It, too, was an absurd mélange, but was accounted funny, and gave Olson an opportunity to show his versatility in the role of old Kladelius, a painter with romantic inclinations. Ida Anderson-Werner and Behmer shared honors with him, she as the painter's wife, who creates an embarrassing situation by returning unexpectedly from a journey, and Behmer as their son, who is in love with a variety actress (played successively by Mia Windrow and Estelle Behmer).[144] *Sten Stenson Stéen från Eslöf* was acted in Rockford, Illinois, November 25, and the evening before, the *Svenska Dramatiska Sällskap* presented *Vermländingarne* there, without the assistance of Olson. Melin was Erik, Gertrud Petterson, a young woman seen mainly in this season, was Anna, and Behmer took the role which he was to make peculiarly his own, Löpare-Nisse.[145] Elis Olson appeared as a singer and entertainer in Chicago and had engagements in Minneapolis and Duluth, Minnesota, but neither Mrs. Myhrman nor Dr. Viktor Nilsson, a leader in Minneapolis musical and Swedish theatre circles, was able to arrange a more extended tour. *Sten Stenson Stéen från Eslöf* was not, Mrs. Myhrman said after trouble with Olson developed, the type of comedy to appeal to Swedish American audiences.[146]

August Lindberg had given successful readings in both London and New York before his tour brought him to Chicago in October of 1911. For his first Chicago appearance, at Handel Hall, October 28, he gave his famous presentation of Shakespeare's *The tempest.* Appreciative critics wrote bitterly of an auditorium only partially filled, and by a mixed crowd, with the "intellectual aristocracy" not in the majority, whereas *Andersson, Pettersson och Lundström* (always cited as the horrible example) could draw full houses. A varied program of Scandinavian readings—Strindberg, Ibsen, and Fröding—at the Swedish Club on November 18 was better attended and even more impressive. And soon the plans that were under consideration for participation in Sweden's celebration of Strindberg's 63rd birthday on January 21 were including the eminent actor. By mid-

181

December, announcement was made that Lindberg, in collaboration with a committee of leading Swedish Americans, had arranged to present Strindberg's historical drama, *Gustaf Vasa,* at the Auditorium, on the birth date itself. Lindberg was to appear as Gustaf Vasa and direct the play, and to be supported by the *Svenska Dramatiska Sällskap.* Fifty per cent of the profits was to go to the Swedish gift to Strindberg, and part of the remaining fifty per cent to the *Svenska National Förbund* charities.[147]

The patriotic appeal of the event as well as the publicity given Lindberg's reputation attracted a crowd of some 4,000 for the *Gustaf Vasa* performance. The occasion was notably festive, many of the audience according it the unusual honor of formal dress. Appropriate ceremonies preceded the play. August Lindberg read a poem in celebration of Strindberg written by the Chicago newspaperman and poet, Jakob Bonggren; the audience sang *Du gamla, du fria* (Thou old, thou free); and librarian Aksel Josephson read the telegram of greeting that had been sent the dramatist. Nevertheless, the reviewers gave the major share of their attention to the play. That is, the performance was extensively discussed, though, except in *Hemlandet,* with a somewhat parochial bias and limited consideration of Strindberg's achievement. The literary merits of *Gustaf Vasa* were acknowledged, but with qualifications. These were not the characters revealed by history, and unless one's taste was highly cultivated, one was likely to find the play somewhat dull. There was little appreciation of Strindberg's development of the king's character, nor was there emphasis on the ways in which the varied characters and episodes contributed to the unity and power of what has often been judged his greatest historical drama.

Lindberg's acting was admired, but in this respect, too, the reviewers permitted themselves to be critical. With pardonable pride, they pointed out that the star was not so superior to the other actors as might have been expected. They repeated the familiar charge that he was somewhat mannered, and they found that he lacked the spirit and physical robustness appropriate to a king who would carry through the execution of traitors who had been his friends.

For Lindberg's direction, however, there was enthusiastic praise. His son, writing later of the Chicago performance, emphasized the difficulties of preparing the play adequately under the circumstances, but six weeks of rehearsal under so skilled a hand brought results that seemed very impressive to the Chicago writers. The role played by Lindberg at the première of *Gustaf Vasa,* that of Olaus Petri, the great religious reformer

182

who was the king's adviser, was taken by Behmer, and he was credited with a masterly performance, showing what he could do when relieved of his usual duties as director. Outstandingly good also was Lindblom as Herman Israel, the Hanseatic Jew who plots against the king whose ally he has been. The tragic role of the Jew's young son, who rejects his father and dies because of his loyalty to the king, was entrusted to John Melin—though it had first been given to the more experienced Knut Schröder—and Schröder played the somewhat priggish Prince John. As the other prince, Erik, August Lindberg's young son Per made a debut that brought general congratulations. Erik is one of the complex and interesting characters of the play, in his seeming irresponsibility and his changing relationships with a father whose domination he resists. His companion, the later traitorous Göran Person, was played by Liljegren, and was thought not sufficiently villainous. Ternquist and Bolling had brief but important roles as miners from Dalarne; and as Engelbrekt, spokesman of the Dalarne men who come to the aid of the king at the climax of the play, Lindblom had a second significant part, which the audience, unfortunately, regarded as comic. Not prominent but effective were Mrs. Milton as the queen and Augusta Larson as the king's strong-minded mother-in-law. Sigrid Lindberg was the tavern girl sweetheart of young Israel, and Mia Windrow played Karins Månsdotter, the flower girl with whom Prince Erik falls in love. In a tense opening scene, Ida Anderson-Werner had a good opportunity to which, of course, she did justice, as the wife of Måns Nilson, the Dalarne leader. For her this was a particularly memorable occasion, for August Lindberg had been her idol in her early acting years in Sweden.

A number of the Chicago actors considered Lindberg somewhat brusque and overbearing; he was overwhelmed by the size of the Auditorium, both they and his son have testified. According to Per Lindberg, his father's enthusiasm carried him through all the obstacles the production offered, and because he was closer to the people than was his son, he was more tolerant. On the tour as a whole Per Lindberg felt keenly the limitations of the public, and he reacted unfavorably to many American ways. In spite of his youth, he carried the burdens of management and finances during the tour (ordinarily they made bare expenses), and with the *Gustaf Vasa* not only made his first appearance on the stage but had his first experience in planning and carrying through the settings—"a real Don Quixote task." His success prophesied his future career. The plans were built with real Strindberg bricks, was his father's comment—"Love gives knowledge and ability." And August Lindberg was satisfied also with his son's acting, which did not, as he had feared, lapse into exaggeration in the more emotional scenes.[148]

Expenses were too high for a large sum to be realized. First reports put Lindberg's share of the profits at $2,500.00, and referred sarcastically to his refusal of the *Svenska National Förbund* offer to make up half the sum needed to bring the gift to Strindberg to $1,000.00, if he would do the same. Actually, the net profits were $428.09, and Lindberg received $687.39. Mrs. Myhrman's complete financial report, as published in *Hemlandet,* was:

Income, ticket sales	$2,749.55
Expenses	2,321.46
Net profits	428.09
To Strindberg	212.93
Förbund charities	215.16

Expenses were: rent, $767.90; to Lindberg (25% of the gross), $687.39; actors, $248.00; Meck orchestra, $85.00; newspaper publicity, $183.06; printing, $75.75; pictures and posters, $16.60; distribution of posters, $37.65; costumes, wigs, etc., $80.95; stage hands, $14.22; rehearsal places, $26.00; express, telephone, etc., $8.17; ticket sellers, $54.16; telegram to Sweden, $19.26; miscellaneous, $17.35.[149]

Continuing festivities contradict any idea of friction. Lindberg was the chief speaker at a Strindberg banquet at the Swedish Club the evening after the play, and he and his son were guests of honor there on March 26, when they returned from a series of readings in the West, Schoultz and Behmer being among the hosts. Soon thereafter Lindberg gave *Ghosts* and Tor Hedberg's most significant play, *Johan Ulfstjerna,* in New York, with Per Lindberg acting for a second time in the Hedberg play. But Lindberg could still go home and, as a January 22 banquet speaker had boasted, tell the Swedes that in Chicago a Swedish play had been presented before an audience larger than anywhere else in the world.[150]

The usual dramatic fare was also being offered the Chicago Swedish public in the later months of the 1911-1912 season. There had been a New Year *Andersson, Pettersson och Lundström* by Brusell's company at the North Side Turner Hall. In spite of the play's reputation as the measure of Swedish audience taste, it was not well attended; but Lindblom made a good Lundström and was ably assisted by Melinder and Brusell as Pettersson and Andersson.[151]

184

In March the *Svenska Teatersällskap* used a new play for its second city production, but *Kolingarnas lustresa i Amerika,* by Carl Atterling of the *Svenska Kuriren* editorial staff, was in many respects an old-time affair. It had the distinction of being the only local play to be performed in a regular city theatre but little else to recommend it. Still, *Kolingarnas lustresa i Amerika* is of interest, because it combines the old immigrant pattern of earlier local plays and the features of the revue, a dramatic type that was to be popular in the Swedish productions of the 1920's and 1930's. The play's absurdities could be forgiven only if it were regarded as a revue, was the verdict of the author's colleagues, who found that it provided little of the entertainment that was Atterling's admitted aim. Its immigrants were two scamps who sneaked past the Ellis Island authorities, and made their way to Rockford, Illinois, where one of them induced the daughter of a Swedish merchant to elope with him to San Francisco, with the father, of course, in hot pursuit. The usual local appeal was furnished by the crowning of a Midsummer Queen in Chicago's Elliott's Park, and by presentation of well known characters, such as "Onkel Ola," publisher of *Svenska Amerikanaren.* But he was not well impersonated, said that paper—he looked as he might in fifteen years, after forty days of starvation and two years of rheumatism. Weak as the whole was, Lindblom, Sjöberg, and the Melinders gave the performance some merit, and the author was honored with the customary laurel wreath.[152]

Other trivial spring performances by the Brusell company had more entertainment value, and served to bring to the Chicago Swedish stage a promising young actress, Ruth Johnson.[153] There were plays by Behmer and his actors with visiting ballad singers, Signe Widell and Greta Adamsen, also; and one of their slight pieces, *I telefon,* has some interest as the work of novelist Ernst Ahlgren.[154]

1912-1913

With Behmer presenting only one play, and that at the Swedish Club, the 1912-1913 season was unusually restricted, but it included some worthy efforts. Brusell gave Sudermann's *Ära* once more, as one of his two city productions, the other being, inevitably, *Vermländingarne.* Strindberg's *Påsk* was acted three times, under Melinder's leadership. More conventional minor productions were plentiful, some by the *Svenska Teatersällskap,* but the majority by a company calling itself the *Svenska Teater Förening* (Society), which performed generally at the Lake View Hall, much used these years in spite of its inadequacy.[155]

Brusell gave novelty to his fall *Vermländingarne* by presenting Inge-borg Sandberg-Settergren in her first Chicago appearance as Anna, but novelty was hardly needed. The public was faithful to the play, and the Garrick could not hold the crowd. The cast included many of the usual old-timers—Brusell as Sven, Melinder as Erik, Schycker as a jovial *provst*, and Chellman as Löpare-Nisse, besides Mrs. Feltskogh, Augusta Larson, and Oscar Larson. Singer Joel Mossberg, as often, played the *brukspatron*, and pleased the audience by his singing of *Du gamla, du fria.* Among the less known actors were Ruth Johnson as Stina and a number who had been serving their apprenticeship with small groups: Thora Kindmark as Britta, Gunnar Nordlöf as Per, and Eric Ericson as Bengt.[156]

Reviewers contented themselves with general praise for this *Verm-ländingarne,* but when a supposedly superior company from the Eastern states brought its production of the play to the Auditorium in the spring—and filled that large theatre—they took the occasion to make extensive comparisons, generally to the advantage of local directors and actors. The visiting company's settings were weak and its costumes at best unauthentic. The boat scene, a favorite even if it was habitually greeted with inappropriate laughter, was omitted. Anna was pretty but her singing so off key that it was agony to listen. Ida Anderson-Werner, Augusta Larson, Melinder, Bolling, Oscar Larson, Brusell, and Behmer were all cited as at least as good as the publicized Eastern actors; and the one Chicago member of the cast, Joel Mossberg, outdid himself, as if to show what kind of amateurs there were in Chicago. The reception was not altogether ungracious, however. There was praise for the dancers, and for Signe Widell, known in Chicago from her appearances the preceding spring; and Elis Person, the Löpare-Nisse, was found worthy of importation.[157]

For his production of *Ära,* Brusell received little encouragement or praise. It was a daring venture for amateurs, was *Svenska Amerikanaren's* judgment, and they were incapable of bringing out the play's fine points. The only paper to discuss the play was *Hemlandet,* which, as part of a changed policy in its last years of existence, was emphasizing the theatre and other arts. One of its editors, Anders Saxon, was a member of the *Ära* cast and acted in other plays from time to time. Sjöberg, in Alberg's former role of Counsellor Mühlingh, and Melinder as young Heinecke were singled out for praise in a company generally identical with that of the October *Vermländingarne.* But this play only half filled the Garrick.[158]

The efforts to present Strindberg were similarly judged. Either the Swedish public was not ready for his "pearls" or did not want to see them in the hands of amateurs, was the conclusion of *Svenska Amerikanaren* after the third performance of *Påsk* had been given at the Swedish Club for a small audience.[159]

The première of *Påsk* (possibly its American première)[160] took place February 13, 1913, at the tiny Intima Theatre, presumably under the sponsorship of Strindbergarna, a society founded the preceding spring to study and present the dramatist's work. Maurice Browne, director of the Intima Theatre, and Melinder were among the members of Strindbergarna, and the group sponsored also the Theatre's performances of two Strindberg one-act plays in English, *The stronger (Den starkare)* and *The creditors (Fordringsägare)*, January 25, 1913.[161] Melinder resigned from Strindbergarna soon after the February performance of *Påsk,* but seemingly continued the presentation of the play as a personal project. Other members of Strindbergarna were in the group that sponsored the play when it was next acted, at the University of Chicago for the American Scandinavian Club of the university: Dr. Anton J. Carlson, Dr. Chester Gould, who was later to head the university's Scandinavian studies, and Henry Goddard Leach, long time president of the American-Scandinavian Foundation.

Svenska Amerikanaren, despite its failure to encourage such enterprises, found some merit in the performance given at the university, and *Hemlandet,* though it felt a less demanding Strindberg work might have been chosen, was enthusiastic. There was agreement that Brusell gave a good characterization as Lindkvist, the victim of frauds earlier committed by the father of Elis Heyst, and, in the final scenes where he frees the Heyst family of its debts, the chief expounder of Strindberg's philosophy. Melinder occasionally did full justice to the part of the jealous and bitter Elis, and his wife was excellent in the difficult role of Eleonora Heyst, whose madness is really unworldly wisdom.[162]

Behmer's revival of his *Farbror Knut från Norrköping* at the Swedish Club in May was favorably reviewed, but a mischance that led to Melinder's reading the role of an absent actor unfortunately interfered with its effectiveness. The announced cast is of interest in that it includes the old time actor, Fred Littche, as the cynical brother, Knut Brander.[163]

1913-1914

The eight plays acted by the *Svenska Teater Förening* in the 1912-1913 season were not reviewed (nor, for that matter, was the Brusell *Nerkingarne* at the South Side Turner Hall); a second season of activity by the *Förening,* however, roused *Svenska Tribunen-Nyheter* to a vigorous attack on "such humbug dramatic presentations" that lure the public with false pretenses and are harmful to the efforts of reputable companies. The *Svenska Dramatiska Sällskap* might well consider bringing suit against these upstarts. But the public, too, was at fault. It should investigate before paying out money for bad performances simply because they were Swedish; and theatre owners should not rent their halls to irresponsible groups. Actually, the company consisted of but two members, said the article, without naming them, but some good actors had made the mistake of associating themselves with its performances: Sjöberg, Melin, Lindblom, and Oscar Larson, of the major companies, and Elna Lilnequist and Gunnar Nordlöf.[164]

The *Svenska Teater Förening* was heard of no more, but the other smaller groups that had been active—the Good Templars, Socialist Clubs, and Norden—supplemented by Englewood and Lake View companies, the South Side Thalia, labor actors, and groups headed by the Melinders, presented plays intermittently throughout the remaining years of the period. Comedy made up their normal repertoire, and if their plays were not carefully produced or of high quality, they still provided entertainment, at low prices, and with the traditional dance after the performance. More serious offerings were Good Templar temperance and propaganda pieces; and evidence of a growing interest in Strindberg is seen in a 1914 Good Templar play, given as a fund raising project for their Strindberg library, and in a successful Strindberg evening carried out by the Scandinavian Socialist Club in 1915.[165]

Meanwhile, the performances of more nearly professional caliber intended for the larger public were continuing, with both Brusell and Behmer presenting their companies in several productions for two more seasons, 1913-1914 and 1914-1915. But city productions were fewer, and there were no new plays. More than ever before, *Vermländingarne* was being relied upon. In the 1913-1914 season, Behmer used it for three of his four main productions, and Brusell for his one city performance. Even with rival performances in successive weeks in September—and Behmer's company acted in the afternoon and evening—both companies turned people away. And the *Svenska Dramatiska Sällskap's* spring performance at the Globe made a profit of $562.31 for the *Svenska National Förbund*.[166] The company's fall performances were for the first time given at the Bush Temple Theatre at Clark and Chicago, described as the North Side's largest and most elegant theatre.[167]

Each director had his quota of experienced actors, and each received his quota of praise for the company *Vermländingarne*. Brusell's Anna was again Ingeborg Sandberg-Settergren (now living in Indiana), and his Erik, John Melin. With customary doubling, Liljegren appeared as both the *provst* and Ola i Gyllby, and Chellman as Anna's father and Löpare-Nisse. There were actors from lesser companies also in Brusell's cast: Elna Lilnequist and Gunnar Nordlöf as Per and Stina, Thora Kindmark and Eric Ericson as Britta and Anders. Hedwig Brusell Melinder and her husband were Behmer's Anna and Erik throughout the season, and other mainstays of his company were Sjöberg, Ida Anderson-Werner, Lindblom, Bolling, Oscar Larson, and Stockenberg. Ruth Johnson was a new and admired Stina. The veteran actors did not escape criticism, and Anders Saxon as Wilhelm drew a scornful comment for failure to wear his student's cap properly; but Behmer's direction and the consequent brisk tempo of the whole were highly commended.[168]

Once more there was a New Year *Andersson, Pettersson och Lundström* at the North Side Turner Hall, a performance by the *Svenska Dramatiska Sällskap* that attracted considerable attention. With Behmer his usual success as Lundström, Sjöberg and Melinder as Pettersson and Andersson, and a generally good cast, the old comedy was given a lively presentation before a good house. And, remarkable indeed, the director's choice was approved by the reviewers as a welcome change from modern dramas of marriage.[169] Chicago's last performance of *Lifvet på landet,* acted at the Globe in March, was Behmer's other ambitious production of the season. The reviewers who remembered Liljegren as Uncle Bräsig felt that Lindblom, though too experienced to spoil the role, lacked the humor necessary to bring out its true values. But "Lill-Carl-Erik," writing in *Hemlandet* of the first Swedish play he had seen in America, thought him incomparable, and was in general very favorably impressed. Ida Anderson-Werner he pronounced "no small theatrical talent"; he praised Behmer, Hedwig Melinder, Augusta Milton, Oscar Larson, and the direction, and found little to criticize. Certainly these amateurs were worthy of all recognition and encouragement.[170]

Brusell gave several plays at Lake View Hall during the first months of the 1913-1914 season, among them *Lars Anders och Jan Anders och deras barn* (which he presented also at the South Side Turner Hall) and *Nerkingarne,* and was forgiven inadequate performances in view of poor facilities. He was again hampered by unfortunate conditions that summer when he directed Wicklund's *En afton på "Tre Byttor"* in its final Chicago

189

performance. The occasion was a Bellman Carnival at Forest Park arranged by a union of ninety Swedish organizations. This union called itself the *Svenska National Förbund,* and was engaged in a conflict with the old organization of that name. A crowd of some 5,000 had trouble in seeing and hearing, and, said "Lill-Carl-Erik," if the blessed "Guck" himself (Wicklund) could have looked down from heaven and seen how incomprehensible his play was, he would have wept great salt tears. An able and well-rehearsed cast of fifty, with Sara Nordstrom as Ulla, Melin as Bellman, and Brusell as Movitz, did as well as possible under the circumstances.[171]

1914-1915

Only the *Svenska Dramatiska Sällskap* played *Vermländingarne* in the 1914-1915 season, but matinée and evening performances on successive September Saturdays at the Bush Temple on the North Side and the Germania in the city must temporarily have satisfied the public appetite. Much of the interest centered in the new Anna from Sweden, Ebba Kempe. If more of an operetta star than a Värmland girl, she was as pretty as any of the role's many interpreters, and pleasing both as singer and actress. Melin, as Erik, sang beautifully, but he had to accept the standard criticism that he had not improved as an actor. On the other hand, the audience had improved, and for once took the serious scenes seriously. The play was enjoyable even for the most blasé, wrote "Lill-Carl-Erik," but he joined his colleagues in lamenting the fact that only this old play seemed able to bring the public out in force.[172]

The other high point of the season was also provided by a folk play —*Ljungby Horn,* given its final production by the *Svenska Teatersällskap* at the Blackstone, as the winter festival of the *Svenska National Förbund* (which of the two organizations using the name this was is not clear). There was an excellent house, and the performance was considered very satisfactory, both in its spectacular settings and in the quality of the acting. Always liked as the self-sacrificing troll, Didrik, Brusell this time made the role a sensation, said *Svenska Kuriren.* Gustaf Lund, formerly of the Stockholm *Folk Teater,* who had been unimpressive in the 1913 *Andersson, Pettersson och Lundström,* was a competent Vidrik. Augusta Milton and Carl Liljegren took the parts created in Chicago by Carl and Anna Pfeil, Birgit and Måns Kruse, and the old troll woman, Tulla, earlier played by Ida Anderson-Werner, was successfully portrayed by Augusta Larson.[173]

With added impetus given by the visit of Madame Frieda Uhl Strind-

190

berg in the early months of 1914, the continuing interest in Strindberg found expression in several performances. At the Scandinavian Socialist Club's Strindberg evening, in which Madame Strindberg participated, there was a repetition of *Paria,* which had been acted by Strindbergarna the preceding summer. Harold Theel and Stellan Windrow were the actors in both performances in this first of Strindberg's experiments with the quarter-hour one-act form.[174] At a similar event, on January 24, Behmer first presented a Strindberg play, choosing one of the best known of his *kammarspelen* (chamber plays), *Pelikanen.* Dr. Anna Windrow Holm appeared in the difficult and characteristically Strindbergian role of the mother who ruins the lives of her son and daughter and is rejected by them and by the man whom she permitted her daughter to marry in order to keep his love for herself. The son, who brings about the fire that destroys the family in a symbolic climax, was played by Harold Theel, Stellan Windrow was the son-in-law, and Lisa Behmer the daughter. The performance was impressive, *Svenska Amerikanaren Hemlandet* reported, and advised repetition in a larger hall. *Pelikanen* was successfully repeated in April at the Swedish Club, with Alice Collini as the mother, and the cast otherwise unchanged;[175] but for city productions there had to be popular drawing cards, the old folk plays and comedies.

1915-1916

Even for the traditional performances, lean days were arriving. The *Svenska Dramatiska Sällskap* itself had presented Swedish movies as the main feature of a Christmas program at Orchestra Hall in 1913; and Denman Thompson's *Old Homestead,* presented by the Svithiod Singing Club in 1914, was but one of a number of plays performed in English by Swedish organizations in these years.[176] Still, as *Svenska Kuriren* remarked, the coming of fall meant the coming of *Vermländingarne,* and in the fall of 1915 there were the usual performances by the two companies, the *Svenska Teatersällskap* acting for the *Svenska National Förbund* at the Garrick, and the *Svenska Dramatiska Sällskap* at the Blackstone two weeks later. The casts were largely the same as in the preceding season, but Hedwig Melinder now acted with her father, opposite Melin as Erik, and Melinder played Anders—a role for which he was thought too elegant. Behmer presented Brusell's former Anna, Ingeborg Sandberg-Settergren, and a new Erik, singer Harry B. Bergstrom. Unfortunately, like other Eriks before and after him, Bergstrom was adjudged to have little ability as an actor. But it is no fun to have to go around looking sad for six acts, was

Svenska Amerikanaren Hemlandet's comment. The theatres were well filled for both performances, but that of the Behmer company was seemingly the better attended; and it was, on the whole, more enthusiastically reviewed, with the usual compliments for the director's "strong guiding hand" and for his Löpare-Nisse, a role with which he had become as closely identified as had "Charlie Chaplin with Biograph movies."[177]

1916-1917

Only a few minor performances followed the two productions of *Vermländingarne* before the 1915-1916 season died out in January; and the 1916-1917 season was not much more extensive. Behmer left the field to Brusell, who provided the public with two city performances of *Vermländingarne* and a revival of *Hittebarnet*. Though acted at Belmont Hall, the old Blanche comedy was a notable success. Chellman was at his best as Konjander, said grateful reviewers, and Brusell, Oscar Larson, Ida Anderson-Werner, and Mrs. Milton were unusually good in the other principal roles.[178]

There was special reason for acting *Vermländingarne* in this season, for the 100th birth date of its author, F. A. Dahlgren, was being celebrated. An appropriate speech by Frithiof Malmquist of *Svenska Amerikanaren* preceded the October performance at Powers, and the company rose to the occasion with honor. Brusell could not complain of the competition of the movies, wrote *Svenska Kuriren,* reporting the numbers that were turned away. The Melinders had never been better in the leading roles, and the other familiar actors outdid themselves. If the settings were better suited to *William Tell,* and if giving the *provst* a toper's red nose was carrying comedy a little too far, these were minor matters. The audience was not critical. It wanted to renew old acquaintances on the stage, to see the ways in which the performance was traditional, and how it varied from tradition. If people still laughed occasionally at the wrong time, that, too, was part of tradition; on the whole, the audience in these days was remarkably dignified. Another full house saw the play at the Blackstone in February, and the occasion was equally happy—for all except the reviewers, who were trying to find something new to write.[179]

1917-1918

Again in the fall of 1917 Brusell gave *Vermländingarne,* in a Powers Theatre performance that was a benefit for the people of Värmland, then suffering from the effects of a drought. Reviewers could only marvel that the

192

old play seemed likely to outlive even that other theatrical phenomenon, Sarah Bernhardt. It was well, if somewhat casually, acted, by a cast largely unchanged from the preceding season. There was a new Lotta, one of the *brukspatron's* "well behaved children," who received a warm welcome: Alva Milton, daughter of Carl and Augusta Milton.[180]

The 1917-1918 season was as a whole the liveliest since that of 1913-1914, though it consisted mainly of comedy performances at the halls. Such entertainment was offered by Brusell, Behmer, and Chellman, as well as by the Good Templars and other groups. In April, *Påsk,* the play by Strindberg most acted in Sweden, was given its fourth and last performance by Chicago Swedish actors, the only play of significance during the season. Melinder headed the performance, and he and his wife took their earlier roles of Elis and Eleonora Heyst. Bolling was a successful replacement for Brusell as Lindkvist, and Ruth Johnson Larson and her husband, Oscar Larson, and Dr. Anna Windrow Holm were the other members of the cast. Butler House Hall, where *Påsk* was acted, held only 200 people, but was well filled, and the performance had an encouraging reception.[181]

There was also a second major production in the 1917-1918 season, and one that aroused great enthusiasm. The Swedish American women of Chicago were engaged in raising funds for the purchase of an ambulance, and they turned to the leaders of the Swedish theatre, Brusell and Behmer, for help in the project. Together the two directors presented *Öregrund-Östhammar* at the Chicago Theatre (the former Globe) in February, amid the acclaim of a congratulatory press: the performance showed what the Chicago Swedes could do in the name of patriotism, and the union of the leaders was a hopeful sign for the future of Swedish dramatic art in Chicago.

With admission at a dollar, a full house, the actors donating their services, and the old friend of the Swedish theatre, Fritz Schoultz, donating the costumes, profits were figured at around $700.00. *Öregrund-Östhammar* was a happy relief from war tensions, reviewers felt, and it was admirably acted. Behmer (made up to resemble Irish comedian Pat Murphy), Brusell, and Melinder were hits as the Öregrund men; Chellman, Lindblom, and Oscar Larson only less good as the trio from Östhammar. Mrs. Hulda Säfström, a more recent addition to the theatrical forces, was an excellent Emil Klint, and the other women, Ida Anderson-Werner, Augusta Milton, Hedwig Melinder, and Ruth Johnson Larson, lived up to their reputations. More such plays by the reunited directors were called for by the press, and the call did not pass unheeded.[182]

193

CHRONOLOGICAL TABLE, CHAPTER V

Performances, 1901-1902 through 1917-1918

Date	Play	Company	Place
	1901-1902		
Oct. 12, 1901	*Nerkingarne*	S. T. for Ingeborg Society	S. S. T. H.
Oct. 26, 1901	*Bröllopet på Ulfåsa*	S. T.	Studebaker
Nov. 23, 1901	*Smålandsknekten**	S. T.	Studebaker
Dec. 7, 1901	*Sven och liten Anna**	S. T. for Lodge No. 1, I. O. S.	N. S. T. H.
Dec. 15, 1901	*Magister Bläckstadius*	Pfeil Co. for Svithiod Singing Club	Svithiod Singing Club Hall
Feb. 6, 1902	*Engelbrekt och hans Dalkarlar**	Örtengren Co. for *Svenska National Förbund*	Auditorium
Mch. 8, 1902	*Öregrund-Östhammar**	S. T.	Studebaker
Apr. 6, 1902	*Öregrund-Östhammar*	S. T.	N. S. T. H.
Apr. 26, 1902	*Bröllopet på Ulfåsa*, scene A comedy	Sveas Döttrar, I. O. S., & Svea Singing Club	Henning's Hall
Apr. 26, 1902	*Svart på hvitt*	Pfeil Trio for *Nordstjernan*	Metropole Hall
May 3, 1902	*Nerkingarne*	S. T. for Lodge No. 1, I. O. S.	N. S. T. H.
	1902-1903		
Oct. 19, 1902	*Ljungby Horn*	S. T.	Grand Opera House
Nov. 9, 1902	*Vermländingarne**	S. T.	Grand Opera House
Dec. 7, 1902	*Sparlakanslexor* *Prins Pippi och Fröken Fiffi*	Pfeil Co. for Svithiod Singing Club	Svithiod Singing Club Hall
Jan. 3, 1903	*Nyårsnatten*	Jupiter Lodge, I. O. G. T.	Phoenix Hall
Feb. 28, 1903	*"I tjenst åstundas"* *De båda döfva*	Kedjan Male Quartette	Belmont Hall
Feb. 28, 1903	*Tre förälskade poliskonstaplar*	S. T. for Monitor Society	S. S. T. H.

Date	Play	Company	Place
Mch. 1, 1903	*En natt i Falkenberg*	S. T. for Monitor Society	S. S. T. H.
Mch. 29, 1903	*Valborgsmesso-aftonen**	S. T.	Grand Opera House
Apr. 4, 1903	*Fem trappor upp*	Jupiter Lodge, I. O. G. T.	Phoenix Hall
Apr. 25, 1903	*Nerkingarne*	S. T. for Nordstjernan	S. S. T. H.
May 2, 1903	*Hon både sparkas och bits*	S. T. for Lodge No. 1, I. O. S.	N. S. T. H.
May 10, 1903	*Han är inte svartsjuk*	S. T. for Svenska National Förbund	N. S. T. H.

1903-1904

Date	Play	Company	Place
Sept. 26, 1903	*Ett friar-äfventyr*	John Nordgren Benefit	Spelz Hall
Oct. 4, 1903	*Pelle Janssons äfventyr*	Chellman Co.	N. S. T. H.
Oct. 5, 1903	*En orolig natt*	For Brage Pleasure Club	Phoenix Hall
Oct. 10, 1903	*En natt i Falkenberg*	Manhem Lodge, I.O.S.	Wicker Park Hall
Oct. 10, 1903	*Valborgsmesso-aftonen*	S. T. for Ingeborg Society	S. S. T. H.
Oct. 17, 1903	*Ett friar-äfventyr* *Fem trappor upp*	John Nordgren Benefit	Kensington T. H.
Oct. 24, 1903	*Vermländingarne*	S. T. for Nordstjernan	S. S. T. H.
Oct. 25, 1903	*Lifvet på landet**	S. T.	Grand Opera House
Nov. 7, 1903	*Tre förälskade poliskonstaplar*	S. T. for Enighet Society	Novotny Hall
Dec. 5, 1903	*Vermländingarne**	S. T. for Svithiod	N. S. T. H.
Dec. 13, 1903	*Hon både sparkas och bits*	For Nordstjernan	S. S. T. H.
Dec. 20, 1903	*Lifvet på landet**	S. T.	Grand Opera House
Dec. 27, 1903	*Han är inte svartsjuk*	For Iduna	S. S. T. H.
Jan. 1, 1904	*Andersson, Pettersson och Lundström*	Liljegren Co.	N. S. T. H.
Jan. 10, 1904	*Han är inte svartsjuk*	For Frithiof Lodge, I.O.V.	Lincoln T. H.
Feb. 20, 1904	*Hon både sparkas och bits*	For Nora Lodge, I.O.S.	Columbia Hall

Date	Play	Company	Place
Feb. 25, 1904	Jorden rundt på 80 dagar*	For Svenska National Förbund	Auditorium
Mch. 5, 1904	Han är inte svartsjuk	For Baltic Society	Grand Crossing Masonic Temple
Mch. 20, 1904	Jorden rundt på 80 dagar	For Svenska National Förbund	Grand Opera House
May 7, 1904	En natt i Falkenberg	Vestgötha Society	Phoenix Hall

1904-1905

Date	Play	Company	Place
Oct. 15, 1904	Sqvallersystrarna	Linnea Singing Society	Wicker Park Hall
Oct. 16, 1904	Svärfar*	S. T.	Garrick
Oct. 22, 1904	En tank-spridd friare	Behmer Co. for Nordstjernan	S. S. T. H.
Oct. 29, 1904	En natt i Falkenberg (as En natt i Falköping)	Vestgötha Society	Phoenix Hall
Nov. 12, 1904	Rum att hyra	S. T. for Monitor Society	N. S. T. H.
Nov. 20, 1904	Så tuktas en argbigga*	S. T.	Garrick
Dec. 4, 1904	Vermländingarne*	S. T.	Grand Opera House
Jan. 15, 1905	Öregrund-Östhammar	S. D. S.	Illinois
Feb. 19, 1905	Löjen och tårar	S. T.	Grand Opera House
Mch. 19, 1905	Ljungby Horn*	S. T.	Grand Opera House
Apr. 15, 1905	Tre förälskade poliskonstaplar	Ingeborg Society	S. S. T. H.
Apr. 16, 1905	Ära*	S. T.	Grand Opera House
Apr. 23, 1905	Friaren från Värmland	S. D. S.	Illinois
Apr. 29, 1905	Han är inte svartsjuk	Behmer Co. for Nordstjernan	S. S. T. H.
May 14, 1905	Vermländingarne	S. D. S.	Powers

1905-1906

Date	Play	Company	Place
Aug. 26, 1905	Vermländingarne*	S. T.	Auditorium
Sept. 23, 1905	Farbror Knut från Norrköping*	S. D. S.	Music Hall
Oct. 29, 1905	Farbror Knut från Norrköping	S. D. S.	N. S. T. H.
Nov. 19, 1905	Valborgsmesso-aftonen	S. T.	Grand Opera House
Dec. 3, 1905	Andersson, Pettersson och Lundström*	S. D. S.	Garrick
Dec. 30, 1905	Pelle Jönsons rivaler	Schycker Co.	Spelz Hall

Date	Play	Company	Place
Jan. 1, 1906	Karl Sabelträff och hans rivaler	S. T. for Iduna	S. S. T. H.
Jan. 7, 1906	Barnhusbarnen*	S. D. S.	Garrick
Jan. 14, 1906	Per Olsson och hans käring	S. D. S.	N. S. T. H.
Jan. 28, 1906	Bröllopet på Ulfåsa*	S. T.	Powers
Mch. 4, 1906	Vermländingarne	S. D. S.	Garrick
Mch. 18, 1906	Regina von Emmeritz	S. D. S.	Garrick
Apr. 1, 1906	Regina von Emmeritz	S. T.	Grand Opera House
Apr. 8, 1906	Mäster Smith	S. D. S.	Garrick
May 13, 1906	Den ondes besegrare*	S. T.	Grand Opera House
May 19, 1906	Nerkingarne*	S. D. S. for Svenska National Förbund	Auditorium
July 3, 1906	Andersson, Pettersson och Lundström, scene Nerkingarne, scene	S. D. S.	Santa Fé Park
July 29, 1906	En afton på "Tre Byttor"*	Swedish Singers Union & I. O. S.	Elliott's Park

1906-1907

Date	Play	Company	Place
Sept. 23, 1906	A. B. C. Han hyr rum af hans betjent	Swedish Friends of Thalia[183]	Belmont Hall
Oct. 7, 1906	Han hyr rum af hans betjent	Swedish Friends of Thalia	Belmont Hall
Oct. 14, 1906	Ur Carl XII:s ungdom (as Carl XII)	S. T.	Grand Opera House
Oct. 21, 1906	A. B. C. Kärleken på sommarnöje Min gamla hatt	Swedish Friends of Thalia	Belmont Hall
Oct. 28, 1906	Regementets dotter, II	Anna Hellström Co.	Auditorium
Nov. 11, 1906	Hittebarnet Civilklädd	Swedish Friends of Thalia	Belmont Hall
Nov. 18, 1906	Lifvet på landet*	S. T.	Grand Opera House
Dec. 9, 1906	Andersson, Pettersson och Lundström	S. T.	Grand Opera House
Dec. 30, 1906	De båda döfva Grannarne Hittebarnet	Swedish Friends of Thalia	Belmont Hall

Date	Play	Company	Place
Jan. 1, 1907	Lars Anders och Jan Anders och deras barn*	S. T. for Carl Milton	N. S. T. H.
Jan. 27, 1907	Han är inte svartsjuk	Schycker Co.	Svithiod Singing Club Hall
Feb. 3, 1907	Pelle Grönlunds bryggeri*	S. T.	Garrick
Feb. 9, 1907	En spik i nyckelhålet Den lilla sångfågeln	Swedish Friends of Thalia	Belmont Hall
Mch. 10, 1907	Vermländingarne	S. T.	Garrick
Mch. 16, 1907	En farlig kommission En orolig natt	Phoenix Amateur Club	Kensington T. H.
Mch. 16, 1907	En förlofning	Wilma Sundborg-Stern Co.	Y. M. C. A. Auditorium
Apr. 6, 1907	Tre förälskade poliskonstaplar	S. T. Klubb	Claremont Hall
Apr. 14, 1907	Rosen på Tistelön*	S. T.	Grand Opera House
May 11, 1907	Ett dockhem*	Ida Östergren & S. T.	Music Hall
June 2, 1907	Hjärtesorg* Hon vill inte gifta sig*	Ida Östergren Co.	Castberg Shop
June 23, 1907	En midsommarnatt i Dalarne*	S. T. for Swedish Singers Union & I. O. S.	Columbia Park
July 14, 1907	En Söndag på Amager	S. T.	Powers
July 21, 1907	Vermländingarne*	S. T.	Powers

1907-1908

Date	Play	Company	Place
Sept. 22, 1907	Gamla Heidelberg*	S. D. S. for Svenska National Förbund	Garrick
Oct. 13, 1907	Öregrund-Östhammar*[184]	S. D. S. for Svenska National Förbund	Garrick
Oct. 26, 1907	Mot beräkning	S. T. Klubb	Claremont Hall
Nov. 24, 1907	Bröllopet på Ulfåsa*	S. T.	Grand Opera House
Nov. 27, 1907	Värfningen	Lodge No. 3, I. O. S.	....
Dec. 8, 1907	Direktör Striese* (as Sabinskornas bortröfvande)	S. T.	Grand Opera House

Date	Play	Company	Place
Dec. 15, 1907	*Herr Dardanell och hans upptåg på landet**	S. D. S. for *Svenska National Förbund*	Grand Opera House
Jan. 1, 1908	*Vermländingarne**	S. T.	N. S. T. H.
Jan. 19, 1908	*Regina von Emmeritz**	S. D. S. for *Svenska National Förbund*	Auditorium
Jan. 26, 1908	*Herrskap och tjenstefolk*	S. T.	Grand Opera House
Feb. 16, 1908	*Löjen och tårar*	S. T. & Svithiod Singing Club	Grand Opera House
Feb. 23, 1908	*Syrsan*	S. D. S. for *Svenska National Förbund*	Grand Opera House
Mch. 22, 1908	*Flickan i Stadsgården**	S. D. S. for *Svenska National Förbund*	Grand Opera House
Apr. 2, 1908	*Han är inte svartsjuk* (as *En svartsjuk äktaman*)	S. D. S. for *Svenska National Förbund*	N. S. T. H.
Apr. 3, 1908	*Den lilla sångfågeln*	S. D. S. for *Svenska National Förbund*	N. S. T. H.
Apr. 4, 1908	*En tank-spridd friare*	S. D. S. for *Svenska National Förbund*	N. S. T. H.
June 6, 1908	*I första klassens väntsal*	Ida Östergren Co.	Y. M. C. A. Auditorium
Aug. 16, 1908	*Engelbrekt och hans Dalkarlar*, scene	S. T. S. for Svithiod Singing Club	Alton Park

1908-1909

Date	Play	Company	Place
Oct. 4, 1908	*Vermländingarne*	S. D. S. for *Svenska National Förbund*	Garrick
Oct. 11, 1908	*Rospiggarna**	S. D. S. for *Svenska National Förbund*	Garrick

199

Date	Play	Company	Place
Nov. 8, 1908	Drilléns operett Hon vill inte gifta sig Nerkingarne, scene	Anna Pfeil & S. D. S.	Svithiod Singing Club Hall
Nov. 8, 1908	Andersson, Pettersson och Lundström	S. T.	N. S. T. H.
Nov. 29, 1908	Öregrund-Östhammar	S. D. S. for Svenska National Förbund	Grand Opera House
Dec. 6, 1908	Han är inte svartsjuk	For Svithiod Singing Club	Svithiod Singing Club Hall
Jan. 1, 1909	Sven och liten Anna	S. D. S.	N. S. T. H.
Jan. 3, 1909	Civilklädd	Chellman Co. for Yngve Lodge, I.O.V.	Lincoln T. H.
Mch. 7, 1909	Andersson, Pettersson och Lundström	S. T.	S. S. T. H.
Mch. 14, 1909	Ljungby Horn*	S. T.	N. S. T. H.
Mch. 28, 1909	Vermländingarne	S. T.	S. S. T. H.
Apr. 4, 1909	Vermländingarne	S. T.	N. S. T. H.
Apr. 11, 1909	Tre friare och en älskare (as Värdshuset Gröna Åsnen)	Oscar Larson Co.	Svithiod Singing Club Hall
May 1, 1909	Karl Sabelträff och hans rivaler	S. T. for Lodge No. 1, I. O. S.	N. S. T. H.
July 18, 1909	Vermländingarne, II	Brusell Co. for I. O. S.	Brand's Park

1909-1910

Date	Play	Company	Place
Sept. 19, 1909	Pariserpojken* (as Parispojken)	Lundberg Co.	Grand Opera House
Oct. 3, 1909	Tre förälskade poliskonstaplar	Brusell Co.	Svithiod Singing Club Hall
Oct. 3, 1909	Vermländingarne	Lundberg Co.	Grand Opera House
Oct. 24, 1909	Lifvet på landet*	S. D. S.	Garrick
Oct. 31, 1909	Bröllopet på Ulfåsa*	S. T.	Garrick
Nov. 28, 1909	Andersson, Pettersson och Lundström*	S. D. S. for Svenska National Förbund	Garrick
Dec. 26, 1909	Han är inte svartsjuk Nerkingarne, scene	Behmer Co. for Thor Society	Lincoln T. H.
Jan. 2, 1910	Bättre aldrig än sent	For Yngve Lodge, I.O.V.	Lincoln T. H.
Jan. 9, 1910	Han hyr rum af hans betjent	For Frithiof Lodge, I.O.V.	Lincoln T. H.

Date	Play	Company	Place
Mch. 13, 1910	Lifvet på landet*	S. D. S. for Svenska National Förbund	Grand Opera House
Mch. 20, 1910	Lars Anders och Jan Anders och deras barn	S. T.	Garrick

1910-1911

Date	Play	Company	Place
Oct. 23, 1910	Duvals skilsmessa*	S. D. S.	Grand Opera House
Oct. 30, 1910	Vermländingarne	S. T.	Garrick
Dec. 3, 1910	Nerkingarne	S. D. S. for Lodge No. 1, I. O. S.	N. S. T. H.
Dec. 11, 1910	Tosingar* Nerkingarne, scene	S. D. S.	S. S. T. H.
Dec. 26, 1910	Den lilla sångfågeln*	S. T.	S. S. T. H.
Jan. 1, 1911	Bättre aldrig än sent	S. D. S. for Vikingarna No. 1, I.O.V.	N. S. T. H.
Jan. 1, 1911	En domares vedermödor	Ekberg Co. for Yngve Lodge, I.O.V.	Lincoln T. H.
Jan. 8, 1911	Hon både sparkas och bits	Behmer Co. for Thor Society	Viking Temple
Jan. 22, 1911	Lars Anders och Jan Anders och deras barn	S. T.	Garrick
Jan. 29, 1911	Syndabocken*	S. D. S.	Grand Opera House
Feb. 5, 1911	Hon både sparkas och bits	S. D. S. for Svenska National Förbund	Viking Temple
Feb. 12, 1911	En domares vedermödor	Ekberg Co. for Gustaf II Adolf Society	Viking Temple
Mch. 25, 1911	Hittebarnet	Norden Amateur Club	Lake View Hall
Apr. 2, 1911	Andersson, Pettersson och Lundström, II Vermländingarne, II	S. T.	Coffey Hall
Apr. 30, 1911	Mottagningstimmen	Scandinavian Socialist Club	Viking Temple
May 14, 1911	De båda direktörerna	Svenskarne i Illinois Lodge I. O. G. T.	Verdandi Hall

1911-1912

Date	Play	Company	Place
Oct. 1, 1911	Lifvet på landet*	S. D. S.	Powers

201

Date	Play	Company	Place
Oct. 8, 1911	*Vermländingarne*	S. T.	Lyric
Nov. 5, 1911	*Hon både sparkas och bits*	S. D. S.	Lake View Hall
Nov. 12, 1911	*Sten Stenson Stéen från Eslöf**	S. D. S.	Chicago Opera House
Nov. 23, 1911	*De båda direktörerna*	Lake View Division of S. S. *Arbetar Förbund*	Lake View Hall
Nov. 26, 1911	*Sten Stenson Stéen från Eslöf*	S. D. S.	Powers
Nov. 30, 1911	*Tre friare och en älskare*	Norden Amateur Club for Enighet Society	Belmont Hall
Dec. 10, 1911	*Det skadar inte!*	S. T. for Illinois Lodges, V. O. A.	S. S. T. H.
Jan. 1, 1912	*Andersson, Pettersson och Lundström*	S. T.	N. S. T. H.
Jan. 21, 1912	*Gustaf Vasa**	August Lindberg & S. D. S. with *Svenska National Förbund*	Auditorium
Feb. 4, 1912	*Gask på fyra*	S. D. S.	Lake View Hall
Feb. 16, 1912	*Gask på fyra*	S. D. S.	S. S. T. H.
Mch. 3, 1912	*Sten Stenson Stéen från Eslöf*	S. D. S.	Powers
Mch. 10, 1912	*Civilklädd*	Melin & Liljegren	Svithiod Singing Club Hall
Mch. 30, 1912	*I telefon*	Widell & Adamsen	S. S. T. H.
Mch. 31, 1912	*Kolingarnas lustresa i Amerika*	S. T.	Lyric
Mch. 31, 1912	*En natt i Falkenberg*	S. T. Group	Lake View Hall
Apr. 14, 1912	*Han är inte svartsjuk* (as *En svartsjuk äktaman*)	Adamsen Co.	Lake View Hall
Apr. 28, 1912	*Kärlek och upptag*	S. T.	Lake View Hall

1912-1913

Date	Play	Company	Place
Sept. 29, 1912	*Tre förälskade poliskonstaplar*	S. T.	Lake View Hall
Oct. 6, 1912	*Vermländingarne*	S. T.	Garrick
Oct. 27, 1912	*En farlig kommission*	S. T. F.[185]	Lake View Hall
Nov. 10, 1912	*En orolig natt*	Englewood Scandinavian Socialist Club	Lake View Hall

Date	Play	Company	Place
Nov. 24, 1912	Civilklädd	S. T. F.	Lake View Hall
Dec. 8, 1912	Nerkingarne	S. T. for District Lodge Illinois No. 8, V. O. A.	S. S. T. H.
Feb. 1, 1913	Påsk*	Melinder Co.	Intima Theatre
Feb. 2, 1913	De båda direktörerna	S. T. F.	Lake View Hall
Feb. 16, 1913	De båda direktörerna	S. T. F.	Coffey Hall
Feb. 23, 1913	Löftet	Norman Lodge, I.O.G.T.	....
Feb. 23, 1913	Civilklädd	S. T. F.	Coffey Hall
Feb. 28, 1913	Påsk	Melinder Co.	Reynolds Club, University of Chicago
Mch. 2, 1913	Tre förälskade poliskonstaplar	S. T. F.	Coffey Hall
Mch. 9, 1913	Tre friare och en älskare	S. T. F.	Coffey Hall
Mch. 16, 1913	Tre friare och en älskare	S. T. F.	Lake View Hall
Mch. 30, 1913	Ära*	S. T.	Garrick
Apr. 5, 1913	Anders Jonsa och hans käring	Trofast Lodge, I.O.G.T.	....
Apr. 6, 1913	Påsk	Melinder Co.	Swedish Club
Apr. 20, 1913	Kometen	Lake View & Englewood Scandinavian Socialist Clubs	Lake View Hall
Apr. 27, 1913	Andersson, Petterson och Lundström, II	S. T. F.	Lake View Hall
Apr. 27, 1913	Vermländingarne	Eastern Co.[186]	Auditorium
May 18, 1913	Farbror Knut från Norrköping*	S. D. S.	Swedish Club
June 1, 1913	Döbeln vid Jutas	....	Gardner's Park

1913-1914

Date	Play	Company	Place
Sept. 21, 1913	Vermländingarne*	S. T.	Blackstone
Sept. 28, 1913 (matinée and evening)	Vermländingarne*	S. D. S.	Bush Temple
Sept. 28, 1913	Döbeln vid Jutas	S. T. F.	Lake View Hall
Oct. 19, 1913	Tre förälskade poliskonstaplar	S. T. F.	Lake View Hall

Date	Play	Company	Place
Oct. 25, 1913	För tidigt	Melinder Co. for Nordstjernan	S. S. T. H.
Nov. 9, 1913	Han är inte svartsjuk	S. T.	Lake View Hall
Nov. 22, 1913	Husvill för sista gången	Jupiter Lodge, I. O. G. T.	Arcade Hall
Nov. 27, 1913	Tre friare och en älskare	Norden Amateur Club for Enighet Society	Belmont Hall
Dec. 7, 1913	Lars Anders och Jan Anders och deras barn	S. T. for District Lodge Illinois No. 8, V. O. A.	S. S. T. H.
Dec. 7, 1913	Andersson, Pettersson och Lundström, II	S. T. F.	Lake View Hall
Dec. 14, 1913	Nerkingarne	S. T.	Lake View Hall
Dec. 28, 1913	Lars Anders och Jan Anders och deras barn	S. T.	Lake View Hall
Dec. 28, 1913	En domares vedermödor	Ekberg Co. for Angantyr Lodge, I.O.V.	S. S. T. H.
Dec. 31, 1913	Sällskapsglaset Lars Johnson och hans hustru	Trofast Lodge, I. O. G. T.	S. S. Good Templar Hall
Jan. 1, 1914	Andersson, Pettersson och Lundström	S. D. S.	N. S. T. H.
Jan. 4, 1914	En spik i nyckelhålet	S. T.	Lake View Hall
Jan. 18, 1914	Bröderna	Svenskarne i Illinois Lodge I. O. G. T.	Verdandi Hall
Feb. 22, 1914	Vermländingarne*	S. D. S. for Svenska National Förbund	Globe
Mch. 15, 1914	Numero ett, rundt om hörnet	Brage Pleasure Club	Viking Temple
Mch. 29, 1914	Lifvet på landet*	S. D. S.	Globe
Apr. 18, 1914	Hon vill inte gifta sig	Behmer Co.	Swedish Club
May 16, 1914	Han är inte svartsjuk[187]	Behmer Co.	Swedish Club
July 26, 1914	En afton på "Tre Byttor"*	S. T. for Svenska National Förbund	Forest Park
Aug. 2, 1914	Paria*	Strindbergarna, private performance	Jensen home Ravinia

204

Date	Play	Company	Place
	1914-1915		
Sept. 20, 1914 (matinée and evening)	*Vermländingarne**	S. D. S.	Bush Temple
Sept. 27, 1914 (matinée and evening)	*Vermländingarne*	S. D. S.	Germania
Sept. 27, 1914	*En orolig natt Vermländingarne*, II	Melinder & Liljegren Co.	Lake View Hall
Oct. 4, 1914	*Han är inte svartsjuk*	Melinder Co.	Lake View Hall
Oct. 18, 1914	*Gask på fyra*	S. D. S. for Swedish Ladies Club, S. F. A.	Lake View Hall
Oct. 29, 1914	*Rådhusrätten i Farvalla*	Swedish-American League	Jackson Hall
Nov. 1, 1914	*Ljungby Horn**	S. T. for *Svenska National Förbund*	Blackstone
Nov. 8, 1914	*Mot beräkning*	Brage Pleasure Club	Viking Temple
Nov. 22, 1914	*En svartsjuk tok*	Melinder Co.	Lake View Hall
Dec. 27, 1914	*En natt i Falkenberg*	Angantyr Lodge, I.O.V.	Carpenter's Hall
Jan. 24, 1915	*Pelikanen**	Behmer Co.	Brunt Hall, Bush Temple
Feb. 7, 1915	*Paria**	Strindbergarna Co. for Scandinavian Socialist Club	Good Templar Hall
Feb. 14, 1915	*En farlig kommission*	*Svenskarne i Illinois* Lodge I. O. G. T.	Verdandi Hall
Mch. 18, 1915	*En natt i Falkenberg* (as *Min hustru*)	Jupiter Lodge, I. O. G. T., Study Circle	Good Templar Hall
Apr. 10, 1915	*När bojorna brista*	Jupiter Lodge, I. O. G. T., Study Circle	Good Templar Hall
Apr. 10, 1915	*Pelikanen*	Behmer Co.	Swedish Club
Apr. 25, 1915	*Konjaksagenten Karl Sabelträff och hans rivaler*	Jupiter Lodge, I. O. G. T., Study Circle	Good Templar Hall

Date	Play	Company	Place
July 25, 1915	*Gask på fyra*	S. D. S. for Swedish National Day	White City

1915-1916

Date	Play	Company	Place
Sept. 26, 1915	*Vermländingarne**	S. T. for Svenska National Förbund	Garrick
Oct. 10, 1915	*Vermländingarne**	S. D. S.	Blackstone
Oct. 17, 1915	*Oraklet i Grönköping*	Jupiter Lodge, I. O. G. T., Study Circle	Good Templar Hall
Nov. 7, 1915	*Rusets fånge*	Svenskarne i Illinois Lodge I. O. G. T., Study Circle	Verdandi Hall
Dec. 12, 1915	*Mot beräkning*	S. D. S. for Norden Singing Club	Knights of Pythias Hall, Roseland
Jan. 15, 1916	*När bojorna brista*	Lake View Amateur Co.	Lake View Hall
Jan. 23, 1916	*Kärleken på sommarnöje*	....	Good Templar Hall

1916-1917

Date	Play	Company	Place
Aug. 20, 1916	*Punkt för punkt*	Strindbergarna, private performance	Jensen home, Ravinia
Oct. 29, 1916	*Vermländingarne**	S. T.	Powers
Nov. 11, 1916	*En natt i Falkenberg*	Balder Lodge, I. O. S.	Dania Hall
Nov. 18, 1916	*Punkt för punkt*	Strindbergarna for Chicago Aid Soc.	Swedish Club
Feb. 25, 1917	*Vermländingarne*	S. T.	Blackstone
Mch. 10, 1917	*Hittebarnet*	Lyra Lodge, V. O. A.	Belmont Hall
Apr. 7, 1917	*Mottagningstimmen*	Amateur Club Thalia	Rosalie Hall

1917-1918

Date	Play	Company	Place
Aug. 15, 1917	*En svartsjuk tok*	Idoghet Lodge, I. O. G. T.	Good Templar Hall
Aug. 25, 1917	*Sparlakanslexor*	S. T.	Svithiod Singing Club Hall

206

Date	Play	Company	Place
Oct. 21, 1917	*Vermländingarne**	S. T.	Powers
Oct. 21, 1917	*En tank-spridd friare*	Behmer Co.	Viking
	Nerkingarne, scene	for Brage Lodge, I. O. V.	Temple
Nov. 10, 1917	*Lars Anders och Jan Anders och deras barn*	Södra T. for Bessemer Lodge,V.O.A.	Strummel's Hall
Nov. 15, 1917	*Ett rum att hyra*	Framåt Lodge, I. O. G. T.	Good Templar Hall
Nov. 17, 1917	*Kärleken på sommarnöje*	Amateur Club Thalia	Rosalie Hall
Nov. 17, 1917	*En spik i nyckelhålet*	Brusell Co. for Lyra Lodge, V. O. A.	Belmont Hall
Nov. 18, 1917	*Konjaksagenten*	Jupiter Lodge, I. O. G. T.	Good Templar Hall
Dec. 2, 1917	*De båda döfva*	Chellman Co. for District Lodge Illinois No. 8, V. O. A.	Hyde Park Masonic Temple
Dec. 6, 1917	*Tosingar*	Idoghet Lodge, I. O. G. T.	Belmont Hall
Dec. 29, 1917	*Tre friare och en älskare*	Behmer Co. for Rogers Park Lodge, S. F. A.	Belmont Hall
Jan. 9, 1918	*De båda döfva*	Chellman Co. for Lyra Lodge, V. O. A.	Yondorf Hall
Jan. 26, 1918	*Jan Ersas piga*	Amateur Club Thalia	Rosalie Hall
Feb. 17, 1918	*Öregrund-Östhammar**	Brusell and Behmer Co.	Chicago
Feb. 28, 1918	*När bojorna brista*	Lake View Swedish Socialist Club	Belmont Hall
Mch. 2, 1918	*De båda döfva*	Chellman Co. for Verdandi Lodge, I.O.S.	Verdandi Hall
Mch. 17, 1918	*Kärleken jå sommarnöje*	Amateur Club Thalia	Knights of Pythias Hall, Roseland
Apr. 13, 1918	*Påsk**	Melinder Co.	Butler House

207

CHAPTER VI

NEW GODS ARRIVE

1918-1919—1950-1951

For nine seasons after 1917-1918, the traditional city performances continued. Rarely were there as many as four in a single season, but a fall *Vermländingarne* could generally be counted upon, and there were a number of performances in other Illinois communities and in Minnesota, as there had been through the years. It was Brusell and Behmer who carried on, sometimes separately but often together, until, in May 1925, some six months after he had made his last appearance, in *Vermländingarne,* death brought to a close the career Christopher Brusell had begun in Chicago's Swedish theatre forty-one years before. The last plays initiated by Behmer were slight affairs in the spring of 1936, but his activities had become increasingly irregular, and after an October 1928 *Vermländingarne* he had directed only two city performances. Of his contemporaries, Ekberg was the only one who occasionally presented plays in those last years. Clearly, the day of the old gods and the old Swedish theatre was past.

Accompanying the decline of the old, however, was the rise of a new Swedish theatre. Its arrival was marked by the organization of the company calling itself *Svenska Folkteatern,* in the fall of 1929, but the young men and women who were its leaders had been acting for several years. They had headed short-lived companies, had appeared with lodge groups; some of them had acted in Sweden, and some had been associated with Brusell and Behmer companies. A member of the old companies since 1909, Carl Stockenberg, was also a founder of *Svenska Folkteatern,* its director, and for a number of years its president. The company did not act in city theatres, but for its main productions used the North Side Victoria Theatre and large North Side halls. The plays it presented had ordinarily no literary pretensions, but most of them were modern, and many were current Swedish successes. For fourteen seasons *Svenska Folkteatern* remained active, and in popularity as well as in longevity it rivalled the companies that it succeeded.

Over almost as long a span of years, but less regularly and for a more restricted public, plays were given by the *Arbetar Teater* (labor theatre). And from 1931 through 1935, *Vikingarnas Teatersällskap,* the Viking Theatre Company, affiliated with the Independent Order of Vikings,

208

succeeded with a series of small performances, often at weekly intervals. Other Swedish lodges and societies also gave a host of performances in the 1920's and 1930's. This was not, of course, a novel development; but whereas the minor performances of earlier years had interest as stepping stones toward a more stable Swedish theatre, the chief significance of the majority of the distinctly amateurish productions by these miscellaneous groups is the proof they furnish of how firmly the tradition of plays in Swedish had been established. In these minor performances are seen, too, the new as well as the old trends in repertoire, particularly the fashion of the local revue that was characteristic of the period; and a few societies presented plays of interest for their social or literary values. But the story of only three new companies needs to be told in any detail—*Svenska Folkteatern,* the *Arbetar Teater,* and the Viking Company. Even when their activities ceased in the early 1940's, however, theatrical performances in Swedish did not entirely disappear. There were minor performances, though trivial and infrequent, throughout the decade; and two notable revivals in 1946 and 1950 indicate the hold of *Vermländingarne* on the affections of both actors and public.[1]

Changed as the Chicago Swedish theatre was, and unimportant as were many of its manifestations, its persistence seems nothing short of amazing. Not that the continued interest in plays in Swedish was restricted to Chicago; the reception of Chicago companies in Rockford, Moline, and Joliet, Illinois, and in Minneapolis, Minnesota, and visits to Chicago by actors from Minnesota and Rockford show that the interest survived in other Swedish centers also. Moreover, travelling Swedish companies were successful in the Middle West through the 1920's and early 1930's. These companies served to stimulate interest, but they also competed with local performances. And there was new competition from the movies—Swedish pictures. For many years they were regularly offered at North Side movie houses. Swedish comedies starring Edvard Persson provided just the type of entertainment Chicago Swedish audiences liked best. There were film versions of the plays the audiences had enjoyed through the earlier years of the Swedish theatre: in 1922, of *Vermländingarne;* in 1925, of *Andersson, Pettersson och Lundström;* and, as late as 1945 and 1949, of *Lifvet på landet.* Carl XII and Lasse Maja were subjects of moving pictures, as they had been of stage plays, and in the 1940's plays acted by *Svenska Folkteatern* were reaching the screen. One point is clear—popular taste in Sweden and Chicago did not vary widely.

It was not the influx of immigrants that accounted for the lasting interest in Swedish plays. World War I had, of course, sharply reduced immigration, and legislation continued to keep the number of immigrants low. After 1915, fewer than 10,000 Swedes were entering the United States yearly, and by the 1930's the number was more often in the hundreds.[2] Chicago was still an attractive center for these immigrants, and the new arrivals supplemented both the audience and the theatrical forces to some degree. An increasing number of the actors, however, were second generation Swedish Americans, and American born Swedes made up a considerable proportion of a surprisingly youthful audience. But while the Swedish theatre enjoyed a decade of rebirth in the 1930's and the Swedish lodges flourished and some dozen regional clubs attracted members from the various provinces of Sweden, the fate of the Swedish press was a striking reflection of changing conditions in the colony. In 1914, the oldest Swedish weekly, *Hemlandet,* was absorbed by *Svenska Amerikanaren.* In 1929, *Svenska Tribunen,* which had bought out *Svenska Nyheter* in 1906, took over *Svenska Kuriren.* And in 1936, the two papers from the 1870's, *Svenska Tribunen* and *Svenska Amerikanaren,* merged as *Svenska Amerikanaren Tribunen,* which still survives, but as a small paper compared to its predecessors.

The story of the old type Swedish theatre in Chicago during this period is largely the story of the directors who had dominated it since 1899 and of a succession of performances of *Vermländingarne.* There were new and younger actors in the Brusell and Behmer companies, but there was a goodly representation of the directors' old associates. Ida Anderson-Werner, the Miltons, Lindblom, Mrs. Feltskogh, Sigrid Lindberg, Chellman, Ekberg, Sjöberg, and, of course, Stockenberg continued to act almost as long as there were plays directed by Behmer. Schycker and Ebba Kempe appeared, but less frequently, and Behmer's son and daughter and Alva Milton acted occasionally. The Melinders were less prominent than before, partly because they lived in Minnesota for a time. Several actors were lost to the theatre because they returned to Sweden: Augusta Larson first, then Oscar Larson and his wife in 1920, and Hulda Säfström in 1921. By 1921, Carl Liljegren was living in Cleveland, but he returned for some appearances that year, and Ludwig Lundgren, well known in the 1880's, made one appearance during a 1918 visit.

Then, too, there were still some visiting actors from Sweden to give impetus to the Chicago Swedish theatre. A number of those who acted with the old group were from the Royal Opera: Signe Schillander, Samuel Ljungkvist, and Ernst Svedelius (who had been seen in North Side Turner

Hall plays of the 1890's). From Stockholm's popular Ranft's theatre came Gunhild Sjöstedt-Fallberg, and from the Royal Theatre, Siri Hård. One of Sweden's most popular musical comedy stars and directors, Carl Barcklind, was in Chicago with his actress wife Hilma, for much of the 1927-1928 season, and headed four performances. Barcklind had directed Ranft's touring company and had, in the early 1900's, been especially successful as the hero of *The merry widow*—a type of romantic role he had become too rotund to play effectively. In the 1930's, Barcklind acted with the excellent *Dramatiska Teater* company of Stockholm, and was much admired in such roles as Jupiter in *Amphitryon 38,* and Falstaff, and the famous leading roles of revived Blanche comedies, Director Sjövall in *Ett resande teatersällskap* and Konjander in *Hittebarnet.*[3]

In the eleven seasons from 1918-1919 through 1928-1929, there were eighteen city performances by Swedish companies—and for thirteen of these performances the play was *Vermländingarne.* But the other trends that had characterized the repertoire since the 1860's were also represented. When Brusell left Chicago in 1922 (temporarily, as it developed), he presented *Bröllopet på Ulfåsa* as his farewell—and gave the historical drama its farewell production. Under Carl Barcklind's direction, *Regina von Emmeritz* was last acted in Chicago. Together Brusell and Behmer gave again the modern comedy, *Öregrund-Östhammar.* Behmer used another, *Duvals skilsmessa,* to celebrate his 25th anniversary on the stage, and also presented the old Uller comedy, *Kärlek och upptåg. Andersson, Pettersson och Lundström, Vermländingarne's* long time rival in popularity, was not used in Chicago by Brusell and Behmer, but they played it in Minnesota. Its one Chicago performance after 1914 came in 1935, under Ekberg's direction. The preceding year, Behmer had directed a third venerable historical drama, *Engelbrekt och hans Dalkarlar,* at the Blackstone, in its last performance. For the performances in halls by these actors during the 1920's it was old comedies, naturally, that were acted. Chellman was active in providing such entertainments, usually making one play, such as *Den lilla sångfågeln* or *De båda döfva,* serve for a series of performances. Behmer also relied almost altogether on familiar comedy for the smaller productions with which he later tried to keep the old theatre alive.

1918-1919

A Butler House performance sponsored by the Swedish Women's Club in September 1918 is of more interest than most of these minor productions by the older group of actors, for the play was Blanche's *Hit-*

211

tebarnet, and the Konjander was Ludwig Lundgren—Sigyn. On the whole, though the actors were well known and Ida Anderson-Werner gave an exceptionally capable characterization of the housekeeper, Blanche, and not the performance, was considered responsible for an entertaining evening. Lundgren's earlier acting years were recalled with pleasure, but now he was unprepared and too clownish. Announcement was made that he had written a "very funny" comedy called *Vernamo Marknad* in which he would shortly appear, but the plan was apparently not carried out.[4]

Theatrical activities were few in this war time season, but November found *Vermländingarne* being presented as a benefit for the Swedish Women's Patriotic Fund, and scoring its usual success. Except for the Anna, who was a young singer, Elvira Anderson, the cast was experienced and familiar. Melinder was a stately Erik, noticeably older than Anna, wrote reviewers, as they had when Örtengren played the role opposite the youthful Hedwig Brusell. Congratulations went particularly to Brusell as Sven and to Behmer as Anders and Löpare-Nisse: certainly they seemed professional, not amateur.[5]

1919-1920

The 1919-1920 season was more eventful. There were three performances of *Vermländingarne,* two in the fall and one in the spring, and they were made notable by the New York singer, Greta Torpadie, and Samuel Ljungkvist of the Swedish Royal Opera. Seldom had such brilliant artists played Erik and Anna, reviewers reported after the fall matinée and evening performances; and a cast not burdened by inexperienced members made the most of the other roles. Full houses were enthusiastic, welcomed Anna with flowers, and rose when the Chicago singer, Joel Mossberg, as the *brukspatron,* sang *Du gamla, du fria.* The March performance and an appearance at Rockford the preceding evening were made possible by a spring concert engagement of the stars.[6]

In November of 1919 Behmer followed a jointly produced *Vermländingarne* with his 25th anniversary celebration, which had been delayed a year by the war. The press recounted his career with high and deserved praise for his faithful labors and many contributions to the Chicago Swedish theatre. As he said in his program notes, since October 1893, when he made an obscure debut in *Andersson, Petterson och Lundström,* he had played some forty-odd roles, and he had doubled as Anders and Löpare-Nisse in *Vermländingarne* more than twenty times. Behmer had not had the foresight to buy himself a laurel wreath, *Svenska Amerikanaren*

212

noted ironically, so the ceremonies suitable to the occasion were missing—but a good house and an excellent performance of the comedy he had himself adapted, *Duvals skilsmessa,* were in themselves proper tributes. Brusell's role was that of the bluff sailor, Corbulon, and Ida Anderson-Werner was again the mother-in-law of Duval—acted, of course, by Behmer. Hulda Säfström was Diane, Duval's wife; and both Eric and Lisa Behmer acted with their father for his silver jubilee.[7]

The Chicago company also appeared in Minneapolis this season, Brusell presenting *Vermländingarne* there in September, and the two directors heading a performance of *Andersson, Pettersson och Lundström* in January.[8] *Vermländingarne* was given again in part at the May benefit for Oscar Larson at the Svithiod Singing Club with which the company concluded its 1919-1920 activities. *Civilklädd,* which Chellman had presented three times earlier in the season, was also acted on this occasion.

1920-1921

Not only *Vermländingarne,* but *Öregrund-Östhammar* was played at the Aryan Grotto Temple (the former Globe and Chicago, now commonly used for city productions of Swedish plays) in the 1920-1921 season; and Brusell and Behmer took *Vermländingarne* on a successful pre-season tour to nearby Joliet, Moline, and Rockford. The singing of the widely known Northland Trio (including former actresses Signe Mortenson and Rosa Pearson Burgeson) and dances by the Skansen Dance Club helped to make the production of the folk play attractive, and the company's combination of old favorites and rising young actors was generally appreciated. Hedwig Melinder, who had not appeared as Anna since 1917, was given a warm welcome, and there was praise for a young Minneapolis singer, August Loring, as Erik. Ernst Schycker, not often seen in these seasons, was enjoyed as the *provst,* but criticized for his characteristic tendency to turn the role to comedy. The *brukspatron* attracted particular interest because Theodore Sjöquist of *Svenska Kuriren* made him "for once" properly aristocratic in appearance and speech. Younger members of the cast were Otto Benson, Maja Dejenberg, and Werner Norén (later commonly spelled Noreen) as Per, Stina, and Wilhelm.[9]

Öregrund-Östhammar was presented by Behmer in January as a benefit for the *Rädda Barnen* (Save the children) fund; and with the actors performing gratis, and the Northland Trio again an attraction, it netted the unusual sum of $1,100.00. One of two performances of *Hittebarnet,*

213

Chellman's project for the season, realized $200.00 for the same cause when sponsored in February by the Swedish Club's Women's Auxiliary. A factor in the success of *Öregrund-Östhammar* was Carl Liljegren, who came from Cleveland "at his own expense" to play one of the Öregrund trio, and called forth many happy memories of his Uncle Bräsig role. Hulda Säfström was an outstanding hit as the boy, Emil Klint, and the whole was thought to be excellently acted. This was Mrs. Säfström's last appearance, as the April 16 farewell benefit given for her did not include a play.[10]

1921-1922

Vermländingarne, still "as necessary to Chicago Swedes as salt to soup," opened a 1921-1922 season in which the older forces were more active than was now common. Again there were illustrious visiting actors to attract a packed house and make the occasion festive. Royal Opera singer Signe Schillander was an excellent Anna, and reviewers were tolerant about her being more the opera star than the country girl. Gunhild Sjöestedt-Fallberg of Ranft's Theatre was liked as Stina; and Svedelius's rendition of the *brukspatron's* song, *Du gamla, du fria,* was one of the high points of the evening. Honors were shared, however, by the local actors, particularly by Brusell as Sven, Behmer as Anders, and Ida Anderson-Werner as Lisa. Melin, too, rose to the occasion as Erik. And the audience enjoyed the novelty of country dances performed by children.[11]

Gunhild Sjöestedt-Fallberg also acted with Behmer in *Kärlek och upptåg* at the Aryan Grotto Temple in December. The old Uller piece was well received, Ida Anderson-Werner's love-sick widow being particularly liked, but the attendance was not encouraging.[12] In February, Behmer twice repeated the play, at Belmont Hall and the Calumet Club House; and in January, he had given the Hedberg comedy, *Majorens döttrar,* to launch a new enterprise, a dramatic company sponsored by the Swedish Club.

The prospects of the new company were promising. The club house included a small theatre that was suitable and attractive, and, as a further advantage, rent free. Members of the club were leading Swedish Americans of Chicago, genuinely interested in the arts, who had on a number of occasions included plays in their activities. Fritz Schoultz, prominent in the Swedish Club, showed his continued interest in Swedish theatricals by assuming the presidency of its dramatic company. The treasurer was C. S. Peterson. And an "interested countryman" had offered to make up possible deficits, so the company would not be hampered, as the Swedish actors had been so often, by an income too small to cover expenses. The company was to present new plays, "to make dramatic art really popular," and promised truly artistic performances. Members included such well known actors as Ida Anderson-Werner, Bolling, Stockenberg, and Sjöberg, and the newly-arrived Signe Rosén, who had received dramatic training in Sweden.

Only three of the anticipated four performances were carried out, however, and the plays were not new, with the exception of one of the comedies in the concluding April program, *Tillfälligheter* (Chances). It had been seen earlier only in an English version by Behmer, *Just by chance,* acted at the Swedish Club in 1914. *Majorens döttrar* was accounted good and entertaining, and poor attendance was laid to inadequate publicity. *Duvals skilsmessa* had its usual success as the February play, with Liljegren in the role of Duval's father-in-law a welcome addition to the company. The April program offered, besides two comedies, Liljegren and Behmer in Strindberg's *Paria,* which had not been acted in Chicago since 1914. Behmer played Mr. X., a Swedish archeologist, and Liljegren the second character in the dramatic debate, Mr. Y., an ex-convict who has returned from America, and whose attempted blackmail fails because Mr. X. does not regard as murder an accidental killing for which he was responsible.[13]

The company was not revived in the fall, nor was Behmer himself again active in the Swedish theatre until the fall of 1924. An annual exhibit of Swedish American art became the special project of the Swedish Club, and its only later connection with this history is an indirect one. There the famous Swedish actor, Anders de Wahl, gave readings from Strindberg and Shakespeare in September, 1922—but he was not seen in a play in Chicago.[14]

1922-1923

The popularity of a screen *Vermländingarne* the preceding spring may have prompted Brusell to choose *Bröllopet på Ulfåsa* for his supposedly final production before going to St. Paul, Minnesota, to make his home with the Melinders in the fall of 1922. He had celebrated his twenty-fifth anniversary with the same Hedberg drama, presenting as his star Arthur Donaldson in the role of Bengt Lagman. Now his Sigrid the Fair was a visitor of reputation, Madame Siri Hård of Segerstad, from the Royal Theatre. An overflowing house "in this day of films" was reported

215

by *Svenska Amerikanaren,* with a question as to whether the farewell or Madame Hård accounted for it. She was admired, but considered better suited to Ibsen roles than to the young, romantic Sigrid (she did appear in Strindberg's *Miss Julia* and Leighton Osman's *The fortune teller,* acting in English with the Gunn Players, but not again in a Swedish play). Melinder, somewhat shaky in his lines, played Bengt Lagman, and Mrs. Melinder was Inga, the daughter of Knut Algotson's faithful follower, Björn. Excellent performances were credited to Brusell's long time associates, Ida Anderson-Werner and Augusta Milton, as Sigrid's mother and the wife of Birger Jarl. The play itself, however, seemed outmoded, and some inappropriately comic makeups were deprecated. For Brusell, "the Nestor of Swedish actors," and his impressive Birger Jarl, there were only praise, and thanks for his "good work and true guardianship in Thalia's temple."[15]

1923-1924

The following fall Brusell was recalled to Chicago, to assist the Swedish Glee Club, then sponsoring *Vermländingarne* in two city performances, the first since his *Bröllopet på Ulfåsa,* and the only ones of the season. The director brought with him from Minnesota not only the Melinders but also several other actors with whom he had been associated there. Hedwig Melinder gave her best performance in nineteen years of playing Anna, said *Svenska Amerikanaren* enthusiastically. And, surprisingly, the young Chicagoan, Gunnar Sund, who had been the Swedish Glee Club soloist on its tour of Sweden the preceding summer and was making the first of several appearances in the role of Erik, showed himself able to act as well as to sing: his farewell scene with Anna was sufficiently sublime to make the audience cry instead of laugh. Other familiar Chicago actors were Chellman as Löpare-Nisse, Stockenberg as Jan Hansson, and Ebba Kempe as Stina. They appeared with the company in spring performances in Minneapolis and Duluth also. Unfortunately for the Swedish Glee Club, which was attempting to make up a deficit incurred on its tour, the second Chicago performance drew a small crowd. This was once too many times, concluded the *Svenska Amerikanaren* reviewer. Maybe the movies were at fault—as for him, he preferred flesh and blood. But no longer could *Vermländingarne* be counted on as a box office success for more than one performance a year.[16]

Even that statement seemed over optimistic in the fall of 1924. Brusell and the Melinders had returned to Chicago, and Brusell and Behmer again joined forces to present *Vermländingarne*. The cast was little changed, except for Behmer's resumption of his Löpare-Nisse role, and the performance was accounted excellent. A performance in Rockford was well attended, but in Chicago the audience filled only the parquet of the Eighth Street Theatre (the Aryan Grotto Temple once more re-christened). Again the movies were blamed. This was a season of many Swedish films, including *Andersson, Pettersson och Lundström*—heartily welcomed in the new medium.[17]

1925-1926

The story of *Vermländingarne* in Chicago had not, however, been told. Both 1925 and 1926 found the traditional fall performances, directed now by Behmer, attracting the traditional full houses. The Swedish theatrical situation seemed in general to be looking up, wrote *Svenska Tribunen* early in 1926. Not only had there been favorable response to *Vermländingarne*, but the young company calling itself Norden had been giving promising performances, and several plays by a company from Rockford had been enthusiastically supported.[18] A number of newly arrived Swedes could be counted among the friends of the theatre. Old theatre friends should not conclude that the Swedish theatre in Chicago, as in other Swedish centers, was on the downgrade, and shake their heads thoughtfully at suggestions that this or that well known play should be presented.[19]

The 1925 *Vermländingarne* had been sponsored by the Swedish Glee Club, and Gunnar Sund had repeated his success as Erik. The Anna was new—American born Mrs. Elsa Söderstrom, member of a popular ladies' trio. Like a number of her predecessors, she was thought a little coquettish and artificial. As for Löpare-Nisse, Behmer was unrivalled, it was generally agreed, though the old objection to his being over noisy was revived. Again a number of the older actors were seen in favorite roles—the Miltons, Ida Anderson-Werner, Sjöberg; and again Schoultz furnished excellent costumes. The Swedish Glee Club sang, and its hymn, "A mighty fortress is our God," was credited with preventing some of the usual laughter at the church scene. Only the orchestra and a few inexperienced actors were below standard. And if the actors faltered, it mattered little, for the audience knew the roles by heart.[20]

Behmer's last production of *Duvals skilsmessa*—at the Midway Masonic Temple in the spring of 1926—was less encouraging. Behmer, as Duval, was supported by Carl Liljegren, Ida Anderson-Werner, Sjöberg, Ternquist, and a sprinkling of unknown actors; and the performance was called generally good. But the audience was slim—why, it was hard to tell. Reasons suggested were public suspicion of amateurs or lack of interest in the play, though *"Duvals skilsmessa* had been given hundreds of times in Sweden and but seldom in Chicago."[21]

Still Behmer and his associates retained their enthusiasm, and in the spring of 1926 laid their plans for a resuscitated *Svenska Teatersällskap* and a regular schedule of performances for the following season. The reorganization was announced with proud recollections of forty years of unbroken activity by Chicago's Swedish actors, and regrets for the recent retrogression of their theatre. The actors were not willing to admit that the time had come when laurels were all for which a director could hope. There were enough Swedes in Chicago to restore the theatre to its earlier vigor if the project were undertaken seriously by both the young and the old. Actors—old and young—were invited to join the society, and other interested persons urged to become inactive members. Organizations were told that the company would be available for entertainments. Behmer was, of course, the director. The chairman was Werner Melinder, the vice-chairman, Carl Stockenberg. Mrs. Melinder was the secretary, and Lisa Behmer her assistant.[22]

1926-1927

Talented new actors were recruited, and early in the fall *Vermländingarne* was being rehearsed for an October 24 performance at the Auditorium—where no Swedish play had been acted since 1913. Those earlier days were relived, and, presumably, some of their spirit revived, at a banquet given by Mr. Ternquist at the Swedish Club on October 2. Werner Melinder acted as toastmaster, and spoke in honor of Behmer and the other veterans, Augusta Milton and Ida Anderson-Werner; and Behmer responded with an account of his years in the Chicago Swedish theatre.[23]

The performance was an unqualified success. The Auditorium was filled "from floor to ceiling," and both new and old actors proved highly satisfactory. Praise was generous for Sjöberg as Sven, Ida Anderson-Werner as Lisa, Behmer as Löpare-Nisse, and Stockenberg as the *brukspatron.* Only one untoward incident occurred, Carl Milton, the *provst,* almost losing his mustaches at a serious moment; and that mishap gave the public

218

a welcome opportunity for laughter. Most of the critical attention was directed to the new actors: Folke Anderson, the Erik, an operatic singer who had made a splendid impression in earlier concerts; Helen Anderson, the Anna, a young Minneapolis singer about to embark upon operatic studies in the East; and two experienced actors from Sweden, Thora Wiberg, the Britta, and Thore Österberg, seen in a role he had acted in Sweden, Anders. Thora Wiberg came from Selander's Stockholm company, and Thore Österberg had acted at Karlskoga and with Tröback's operetta company. He was credited also with having written some musical revues.[24]

Vermländingarne was repeated in Rockford the following week, and the outlook for the *Svenska Teatersällskap* seemed bright. But the clock could not be turned back. The attempt to build a company that would bring together old and new forces collapsed after one more production in the 1926-1927 season and two appearances—without Behmer—under the direction of Carl Barcklind in the fall of 1927. In part, the failure grew out of disagreement within the executive group as to offices, casting, and salaries. The young actors, too, were ready to take the initiative, and resented being kept in the background and relegated to subordinate roles. And new types of plays were attracting them, the types to which they were soon to turn with the founding of *Svenska Folkteatern*.[25]

Except in attendance, the second 1926 production of the *Svenska Teatersällskap* was a notable event. The play was *Syrsan,* and it was acted at the Goodman Theatre (the small non-commercial theatre east of the Art Institute), to celebrate the fiftieth anniversary on the stage of one of the most admired and best loved women of the Chicago Swedish theatre, Ida Anderson-Werner. The sixty-four year old actress played her favorite role, Fadette, the old grandmother. Thora Wiberg, as the granddaughter heroine, shared honors with her. Behmer played the lover, and did not escape criticism for assuming so youthful a role. Several other old-time colleagues of Mrs. Anderson were in the cast: her sister, Sigrid Lindberg, Carl and Augusta Milton, Carl Stockenberg, and Knut Sjöberg. To say *Syrsan* was old was not to say that it was unsuitable for modern performance, *Svenska Amerikanaren* pointed out, indicating that it was not an altogether popular choice. But play and performance were overshadowed by the tributes to Ida Anderson-Werner. To the best of his knowledge, wrote the *Svenska Amerikanaren* reviewer, she was the only Swedish American actress who could celebrate such an anniversary, a fact not surprising in view of the obstacles that always stood in the way of the Swedish theatre, and the

219

limited opportunities for its actors to gain anything but glory. Flowers and a poem by Carl Stockenberg in honor of "the evening's heroine . . . the true servant of art" were reported, with hearty praise for her talents, her willing cooperation, her spirit of comradeship—notes Behmer was to echo in the memoir he wrote after her death in 1945.[26]

1927-1928

Since the spring of 1927 the visit of Carl and Hilma Barcklind and their appearance in Swedish plays had been anticipated, and they were much feted upon their arrival in September. The Barcklinds came to America mainly to show a moving picture of Swedish life and to prepare a similar film about America for the Swedish public. They made Chicago their headquarters until the following spring, and Mrs. Barcklind appeared in concerts as well as in the four plays directed by her husband.

The first of the plays was the last Swedish production at the Auditorium and the last Chicago performance of *Regina von Emmeritz*. The theatre was filled—thanks, said Mr. Barcklind, to the energetic management of Mrs. Myhrman. Gustaf II Adolf day had been selected for the performance, to give the play a double patriotic appeal, but *Regina von Emmeritz och Gustaf II Adolf* (the old Chicago version of the title was used) could no longer impress critics and audience as when it was first acted by the Pfeils in 1888. It was too heavy to be popular, said the reviews, and had the disadvantage of being unfamiliar. Still the Barcklinds lived up to their reputation as Regina and the king, Ida Anderson-Werner was successful as the nurse Dorthea, a role she had often played, and other *Svenska Teatersällskap* actors—Sjöberg, Ternquist, Österberg—gave capable performances. The lights and settings managed by Melinder and Bolling, Schoultz's costumes, and songs by the Swedish Glee Club also did much to make the play enjoyable. But at the Auditorium, even as at the old North Side Turner Hall, things could go wrong; and the big scene of storming the castle did not come off properly— the king's horse was recalcitrant, and the wall refused to fall.[27]

This performance was specifically mentioned by Barcklind when he was interviewed after his return to Sweden. Because it would have cost dollars to have even a single prop moved, there had been no real dress rehearsal, and still the première, including even the mob scenes, had been skilfully handled. As for *Vermländingarne*, the company knew it so well that only two rehearsals had been necessary. In all, Barcklind was generous

220

with praise for the Chicago actors and what they achieved under difficult conditions.[28]

He had followed the tradition of the Royal Theatre, if not Chicago tradition, in presenting *Vermländingarne* as Christmas entertainment. And a large holiday audience had found the production at the Victoria, a North Side theatre that was the home of a German company, quite as satisfactory as the usual city performance. Hilma Barcklind was a first-rate Anna, and her husband an admirable Sven, though the role was considered too small for an actor of his ability. Of the *Svenska Teatersällskap* actors, Ida Anderson-Werner was, of course, a good Lisa, and Chellman a comic Löpare-Nisse. Melinder played Erik capably, though his singing suffered somewhat in comparison with that of recent interpreters of the role. Young Thore Österberg again made an excellent impression as Anders, and Elna Lilnequist Kronberg and Maja Dejenberg-Anderson won their share of commendation as Britta and Stina.[29]

Seemingly there were plans for a performance of *Lifvet på landet* by this group,[30] but the two spring performances that Barcklind directed were projects of a youthful company that called itself the *Svenska Teaterensemble;* it had performed only once before, at the Goodman in December 1926. Now advertisements pointing out that this company was not to be confused with the *Svenska Teatersällskap* emphasized the independence of the young actors who were striking out for themselves: Thore Österberg, Maja Dejenberg-Anderson, and Elna Lilnequist Kronberg, who had been associated with the Behmer company; and others who had made their start in Norden and varied small groups, Ragnhild Lindstrom, Arvid Nelson, Carl Lambert, and Greta Ohlman. With these two performances, the *Svenska Teaterensemble* ended its brief history, but soon these actors were to become a part of *Svenska Folkteatern* and the new theatrical developments for which it was responsible.

These young people were promising, even if some of them lacked polish, was the critical verdict, and they were congratulated on having had the guidance of so careful and experienced a director. Their play was *Hin och Smålandingen*, which had given Liander and Lindhagen popular roles, and seemed as entertaining as ever. The performances brought back recollections of Pfeil and his attempt to prevent Liander from presenting the new Hedberg comedy at the North Side Turner Hall.[31] Now, too, it was first given at the North Side Turner Hall, but the place was the same in name only. The long time home of the Swedish plays had been turned to other uses in 1926, and was to be razed in 1937.[32]

221

1928-1929

In the October 1928 *Vermländingarne* that was Behmer's one production for the season (and his first since *Syrsan* in 1926), several of the
Svenska Teaterensemble actors appeared, as well as veterans Ida Anderson-
Werner, Stockenberg, Ternquist, and Sjöberg. The Swedish Glee Club
again sponsored the performance, and singer Gunnar Sund returned to the
role of Erik, with Ragnhild Lindstrom as a new Anna. Thore Österberg
was Anders once more, and the press did not hesitate to ask why he had
not yet been seen as Erik. There was a good house at the Victoria, but in
spite of a generally competent performance, a lack of audience enthusiasm
was noted. Criticism was directed particularly against setting and costumes:
Sven Ersson's home was too modern and elegant; and Anna in knee length
dresses and ballet slippers made one wonder if one was in Värmland or on
Belmont Avenue.[33]

Again in 1928 a Christmas folk play was given at the Victoria, but
this time it was *Nerkingarne*. It was advertised as having more popular
appeal than *Vermländingarne,* because it was more modern—a statement
which, if a bit misleading, was literally true, as *Vermländingarne* dates
from 1846 and *Nerkingarne* from 1872. The fact that *Vermländingarne*
had been seen earlier in December in a very successful performance by the
popular touring comedian, Olle i Skratthult, and a company including
Chicago actors[34] was probably a factor in the shift to *Nerkingarne*. Head
of the *Nerkingarne* company was Paul Norling, who had been winning
recognition in smaller productions since coming from Sweden some two
years before; and acting with him were, beside *Svenska Teaterensemble*
members Ragnhild Lindstrom, Arvid Nelson, Thore Österberg, Greta Ohlman, and Elna Kronberg, two representatives of earlier theatrical circles,
Carl Stockenberg and Alva Milton. A male chorus, *De Svenske,* sponsored
the performance, and was rewarded with a reasonably good house. The
actors did well, said the reviewers, except when they were upset by an
audience that reverted to its traditional behaviour and laughed at the most
dramatic scenes. *Svenska Tribunen-Nyheter* was moved to stern words of
reproof: if the public wanted a good Swedish theatre, it must show more
cultivation and understanding.[35]

Once more the group acted together before forming *Svenska Folkteatern* in the fall of 1929. In June of that year, under the leadership of
Stockenberg and Norling, they gave an outdoor performance of *Vermländingarne* for the annual *Svenskarnas Dag* outing of the Good Templars at

222

Standing, Knut Sjöberg, Fred Bolling, Carl Stockenberg, Florence Johnston, John Ternquist; Seated, Ida Anderson-Werner, Carl Liljegren, Ernst Behmer, Director, Mrs. Othelia Myhrman

Svenska Dramatiska Sällskap, 1910-1911

Front, Werner Melinder as Olof, Hedwig Brusell Melinder (kneeling) as Hildur, Mrs. Hulda Feltskogh as Lady Ingrid of Ljungby, Augusta Milton as Birgit, Carl Liljegren as Måns Kruse, Ernest Lindblom as court chaplain, Christopher Brusell as country judge

Svenska Teatersällskap in scene from Ljungby Horn, November 1, 1914, Blackstone Theatre

their Geneva park. Ragnhild Lindstrom was Anna, and at last Thore Österberg was Erik instead of Anders. The papers limited themselves to general
comments on a successful performance, but other participants agree with
Stockenberg, whose 1933 account of *Svenska Folkteatern* called it an un-
forgettable memory for the actors, and surely also for the thousands who
were present. What other Anna had been able to pick flowers in a real
forest dell? And what Anders had, like Arvid Nelson, revived the heroine
from her swoon in the church scene with water actually fetched from a
nearby brook?[36]

1930-1931

There was no other local production of *Vermländingarne* until
Behmer directed it at the Victoria for the Swedish Relief Committee in
February 1931, though Olle i Skratthult had given a series of popular performances of the play in the winter of 1929, with Knut Sjöberg as his
director and, again, a number of Chicago actors in the cast. In Behmer's
Vermländingarne, advertisements claimed, there would be "only the old
guard that can really act."[37] And the old guard was well represented, if not
exclusively used. Mrs. Melinder, who had first played Anna twenty-six
years before, made her final appearance in the role, with Gunnar Sund
as Erik. These were the last stage appearances in *Vermländingarne* for Ida
Anderson-Werner and Augusta Milton, playing Lisa and Annika, and for
Sjöberg and Carl Stockenberg, the Sven and Jan Hansson. All due honor
was paid to the veteran actors, and there was rejoicing because the old
play could still attract a good audience.[38]

A span of forty-seven seasons, in forty-two of which *Vermländingarne*
had been presented, came to a close with this 1931 performance. From
1908 through 1928, except when Brusell had substituted *Bröllopet på Ulfåsa* in 1922, the play had been a regular fall feature of the Swedish theatre.
When it was next seen, in 1946, Behmer was the only representative of the
old group. Some of his long time colleagues had given their farewell performances in *Vermländingarne* in a radio version of the last act, in 1936.
In this program, the Swedish Glee Club sang, and one of its members, Ivar
Johnson, was Erik. Alva Milton was Anna, and Otto Benson, Anders.
But truly reminiscent of the days that were gone were the *brukspatron,*
the *provst,* Annika, and Lisa—Knut Sjöberg, Carl Milton, Augusta Milton,
and Ida Anderson-Werner. [39]

1934-1935

Before the 1946 revival of *Vermländingarne, Svenska Folkteatern* had also ceased its activity. During the years when the new company constituted the main Swedish theatre, Behmer produced plays in only two more seasons. For the West Side Division of *Svenska Kultur Förbundet* (Swedish Cultural Association), of which he was a moving spirit, he directed *Engelbrekt och hans Dalkarlar* at the Blackstone in November 1934, almost sixty-four years after the play had been given its first Chicago production. The five hundredth anniversary of the folk hero's deeds was being celebrated, and a commemorative prologue was delivered by Dr. Gottfrid Nelson of the Swedish Trinity Church (such a stamp of clerical approval had long since ceased to be a topic of discussion). The Harmoni Glee Club and the National Dance Company cooperated, and the music was furnished by Meck's orchestra, as it had been so often throughout the years of Swedish plays. Behmer played Engelbrekt, and his daughter Lisa the queen. But, strangely, the performance was passed by without reviews.[40]

1935-1936

Within a few months the Chicago Swedish public was offered also the last revival of a play even older in its theatrical history, the long popular if often derided *Andersson, Pettersson och Lundström.* Though so frequently seen since its 1869 première, it had not been acted since 1914. Ernst Ekberg headed the final February 1935 performance, and played Lundström, with the traditional local verses for his *dudelandej* song provided by Stockenberg.[41] And in the spring of 1936, Ekberg closed his theatrical career with a single performance of a comedy he had often presented in the preceding years, *En domares vedermödor.*

In the 1935-1936 season, too, Behmer presented his old adaptation, *Farbror Knut från Norrköping,* in two performances. In November, it was acted at the Chicago Woman's Club theatre. This was a theatre, the advertisements pointed out, not a dance hall with movable chairs. There would be no dance after the play. Attendance was meagre, and the old explanation of an unfamiliar place was offered. The New Year's performance was given at the popular South Side Viking Temple, with the traditional dance restored. Whatever the reason, the house was excellent. Play and actors—among them, Sjöberg and, from the second generation, Alva Milton and Lisa Behmer—were enthusiastically praised, and other repetitions were urged.[42] But Behmer left the field to the younger groups, and in 1944 he

224

moved to the West. His name continued, however, to be synonymous with the Swedish theatre, and, inevitably, when plans to revive *Vermländingarne* developed in 1946, he was summoned to Chicago to direct it.

The first half dozen seasons following the founding of *Svenska Folk-teatern* in October 1929, were the culminating period in the resurgence of theatrical activity of which there had been signs since the years when Brusell and Behmer were maintaining separate companies. Each of the three new companies that now came to the fore had its forerunners. *Folkteatern* actors came from Norden, which had been active in 1925-1926, as well as from the *Svenska Teaterensemble*. The labor theatre that began extensive activity as early as the 1928-1929 season had been anticipated by plays acted by socialist and labor clubs; and before the Viking Theatrical Company was formed in the spring of 1931, various Viking lodges had been producing and sponsoring plays.

A variety of other independent companies, lodges, and clubs were also offering theatrical entertainment in the early 1930's, and so frequently that there were more amateur performances than ever before. About the majority of these affairs there is little information, the newspapers ordinarily reporting them without discussion, when choosing to report them at all.[43] But they, as well as the more publicized plays, contributed to a revival that takes on added interest when one considers that it developed in the years of economic depression. Entertainment, and inexpensive entertainment, was particularly needed in those years, both for the established residents and for the young Swedes who were coming to Chicago from a depression ridden Sweden. The Swedish plays were performing a social function, as they had in the days of the first rapid growth of the Swedish colony.

At the same time, the revival reflects the progress that had enabled a number of Swedish organizations to obtain their own buildings, buildings in which halls suitable for small theatrical performances were readily available. There were three Swedish Good Templar buildings, two on the South Side and a third on the North Side. The Independent Order of Vikings had built "temples" on both the North Side and South Side. Verdandi Hall, headquarters of the Verdandi Lodge of the Independent Order of Svithiod, was also used, though less frequently. Belmont Hall retained some of its earlier popularity, but minor theatrical events, when not housed in Swedish halls, now commonly took place in halls belonging to the Masonic lodges or the Knights of Pythias.

The Swedish lodges had, of course, a long record of interest in theatricals, and both the Svithiod and Vasa orders continued their old custom of including Swedish plays on their programs. The Brage Pleasure Club, originally associated with Viking lodge Brage, still acted intermittently, and there were scattered performances by other Viking lodges, besides those of the Viking Theatrical Company. Occasionally, also, plays were seen by lodges of the Scandinavian Fraternal Association. Club Idrott, made up of young people from Good Templar lodges on the North Side, was one of many Good Templar groups presenting plays. From the 1935-1936 through the 1940-1941 season, a Good Templar company acted with fair frequency. Its plays were ordinarily directed by Hugo Ottoson, and his wife, Stina Ottoson, was generally one of the actors. Mr. Ottoson came to the United States in 1929, a young man of twenty, and carried on in Chicago the art of glass etching which he had learned at the famous Kosta glass works in Sweden.[44] High point of this company's activities, perhaps, was a performance of *Miss Person från U. S. A.,* June 20, 1937, at *Svenskarnas Dag* at Good Templar Park—an occasion at which dramatic entertainment was traditional.

It was a Good Templar lodge also—the Jupiter—that was responsible for the founding of *Svenska Studie Förbundet* (Swedish Study Association), one of the most interesting among the organizations presenting Swedish plays. Since its beginnings in 1916, with the well known librarian, Aksel Josephson, as president, it has carried out a program of unusual value, including lectures by eminent speakers, debates and discussions, as well as a series of plays. In 1926 it united with a similar study circle, that of the Svithiod lodge, Verdandi,[45] and took a new name, *Svenska Bildnings Förbundet* (Swedish Educational Association). Scandinavian labor organizations replaced Verdandi in 1928, and when that affiliation ceased, other Good Templar lodges began a cooperation with the society that still continues.[46]

Musical organizations maintained their long standing interest in the theatre in these years, though the productions in which they were concerned were more likely to be revues of local authorship than plays or operettas of the traditional type. The Swedish Glee Club, of course, headed major productions of *Vermländingarne.* Other choruses that presented or sponsored dramatic entertainment were *Nordstjernan,* the Viking Male Chorus, *De Svenske,* and the Harmoni and Bellman Glee Clubs. And when the last three united as the Swedish Male Chorus, their former interest continued.

Several of the *hembygd* (home province) societies that mushroomed during the 1920's also played a considerable part in the revival of Swedish theatricals. *Värmlandsklubben,* founded in 1926, gave a number of plays in the 1930's, largely on the initiative of one of its members who was prominent in acting and entertainment circles, Einar Carlson. In 1928, three years after its organization, *Värmlands Nation* began occasional theatrical activity, and was eventually to undertake the 1946 revival of *Vermländingarne*. *Ölandsklubben*, dating from 1928, and *Hälsingarna*, founded in 1926, engaged in theatricals from time to time during the early 1930's. Eric J. Ericson was responsible for the plays given by *Norrlänningarna*, another of the regional clubs, with beginnings in 1926, and he also directed the North Side Amateur Company, which gave performances for many organizations throughout the 1930's.[47] One of the first projects of *Klubben Norrskenet*, was the establishment of an amateur company, *Myggan* (The gnat). *Myggan* was active from the spring of 1929 until December, 1930, and gave at least eight comedies, as well as many variety programs. The leading spirit and director was Oscar Renman, and he made the company a main attraction of the club's meetings—with the support of a fifty dollar fund for a theatrical library, make-up, and the like.[48]

Of the independent groups, Norden,[49] with such later *Svenska Folkteatern* leaders as Arvid Nelson, Ragnhild Lindstrom, and Carl Lambert among its members, attracted a good deal of attention. Its 1925-1926 performances included *Nerkingarne* as well as a series of ably acted comedies, and occasional appearances in Rockford. A company calling itself Skansen was acting in 1929 and 1930, but with less success, if publicity is the criterion. This was a period of travelling companies, and one of them was headed by two Chicago actors, Otto Benson and Werner Noreen. They had become known through appearances with various groups, and had occasionally headed performances before taking a company on tour in the Middle Western and Eastern states during seasons from 1928-1929 through 1931-1932. Chicago audiences also welcomed two other touring companies that offered Swedish plays: the Bert Leman Company, which played a number of engagements from 1926 through the early 1930's; and the Olle i Skratthult Company, which ordinarily visited Chicago once or twice a year for a dozen seasons after Olle turned from variety to plays in 1920.[50]

Brief and inconsequential comedies were the usual offerings of these varied groups. There were, in all, a good many performances of old favorites: of plays that had been seen since the 1870's, like *Oxhandlaren från Småland, Kärleken på sommarnöje, Hans tredje hustru;* and plays that had been popular in the 1890's and later, like *Tre förälskade poliskonstaplar, Tosingar,* and *En orolig natt.* There was an occasional Blanche comedy, *Hittebarnet* or *Rika Morbror,* for instance. But the historical plays were absent from

227

this repertoire, as, with rare exceptions, were the old folk plays. Locally written revues were popular,[51] and there were a few local plays of other types. The majority of the plays, however, were modern comedies from Sweden, many of them intended for amateur performance. Typical of the plays written for amateurs were the series of comedies with descriptive titles, such as *När Klickens tös fick fästman* (When Klicken's girl got a sweetheart), acted by *Myggan* in 1930; *När Tekla i Finnbygda äntlitt blev gift* (When Tekla of Finnbygda finally got married), acted by the Värmlands Club in 1938; and *När Svensson skulle köpa ångtröskverk* (When Svensson was going to buy a threshing machine), presented by Skansen in 1929.

Though not restricting themselves to serious drama, Idrott and the *Svenska Studie Förbund* were responsible for most of the plays with values beyond light entertainment presented by the groups that acted intermittently. Each society presented one of Strindberg's one-act plays that had not been acted in Swedish in Chicago. As early as December 1918, the study circle gave *Den starkare,* a tour de force with only one speaking part, that of a woman who tries to persuade her husband's mistress that she, the betrayed wife, is the stronger and happier of the two. In 1932, *Moderskärlek* (Mother's love) was acted by Idrott. It is a bitter and ironic picture of a mother, a former prostitute, who selfishly succeeds in keeping her daughter away from the opportunities her newly discovered father wishes to give her. A three-act drama from 1920, *Örnarna* (The eagles), by Ernst Didring, which was played by both groups, also reflects their social interests. Its central situation is the dilemma of a statesman who is trying to carry through a liberal reform program and has promised his political opponents that he will not commute the death sentence of a number of labor leaders. Didring (1868-1931) was best known for his novel, *Malm* (Silver), but had a considerable reputation also for his naturalistic and proletarian drama.[52] Another three-act drama of social theme, *Stridbar ungdom,* (Fighting youth), dating from 1907, was acted by *Svenska Studie Förbundet* in 1923; it was the work of a reputable writer on feminist and social topics, Harold Gote (Helga F. M. Steenhof).[53]

Good Templar lodges twice played one of their older temperance plays, *Konjaksagenten,* and departed from the usual comedy fare on other occasions also. In 1925, District Lodge No. 2 gave a performance of *Svenskt folk, eller Myllans krafter* (Swedish people, or The power of mould), a three-act drama from 1921 by a Stockholm journalist with theatrical connections, Ivar Thore Thunberg. It was commended for its good teachings, but *Svenska Tribunen-Nyheter* suggested that a change of title would have been advisable, with an audience so largely born in America.[54] In 1934, a sentimental melodrama by the popular Henning Ohlson-Sörby, *Fädernearf* (Paternal inheritance), was several times acted by Good Templar groups. Sentimental also, certainly, but of interest as a reflection of the times were the two sketches, one with a Swedish and the other with an American setting, presented by the Idrott Club for Christmas performances in 1932 and 1933. Both were written by club members. *Julafton hos Henning Svenson* (Christmas Eve at Henning Svenson's) pictured lonely parents in Sweden visited and helped by children who had emigrated, and *Julafton i en fattig Svensk-Amerikansk familj* (Christmas Eve in a poor Swedish-American family) showed parents whose hopes were rewarded when their father obtained work, after a Christmas with neither food nor gifts.[55] The Skansen company, too, presented a thesis play, in 1929: *Krig* (War), a 1914 presentation of pacifist views through the story of a Swedish farm boy in the Russo-Swedish war of 1789-1790. The author was Fridolf (E. Henning Lind), a Swedish business man with a number of plays to his credit.[56]

Of the acting groups with histories demanding fuller consideration, the *Arbetar Teater* (sometimes called the Chicago *Arbetar Teater)* was the least publicized; only the director, Paul E. Fröjd (1898-1949), received mention in the brief notices accorded its plays. But both in the extent of its activities and in the nature of its repertoire it is one of the most interesting developments in the history of the Chicago Swedish theatre. The *Arbetar Teater* began as the project of a South Side division of the *Skandinaviska Arbetarnas Bildningsförbund af Illinois* (Educational League), apparently in the fall of 1928.[57] From that time on, at any rate, there were notices of frequent performances, given sometimes for the West Side and Lake View sections of the *Förbund,* sometimes without special auspices. By the spring of 1940, the company had acted thirty-four plays in fifty-four performances, About one-third of the plays were comedies of the old type; they were ordinarily not repeated, and only Blanche's *Rika morbror* had as many as three performances. Typical contemporary comedy was also acted on occasion. But the majority of the company plays that can be identified and those that were most frequently acted dealt, though not always seriously, with social topics. Twenty of the *Arbetar Teater* plays were new to Chicago, and most of these new plays were not acted by other companies.

Two of the labor company's *tendens* plays had been given earlier performances: *Tjuven* (The thief), announced as an adaptation from Upton Sinclair, was acted by the Lake View Amateurs for the Scandinavian

Socialist Society in 1923; and the temperance drama, *Rusets fånge* (The slave of drink), by a Good Templar company in 1915. The *Arbetar Teater* acted *Tjuven* twice and *Rusets fånge* three times. The author of *Rusets fånge* was the famous radical journalist and agitator of Sweden, Hinke Bergegren (1861-1936); and his *Skökan rättvisan* was another success, being acted four times in 1935 and 1936. *Skökan rättvisan* told a story of everyday life in Stockholm, involving the labor movement, a sympathetic clergyman, and a romance. A misreading of the title to mean *The harlot brought to justice* instead of *Harlot justice* was suggested as the probable reason for its popular appeal. Hinke (Bernhard Henrik) Bergegren was a prolific writer in varied fields; he was attacked and imprisoned for his beliefs, and in 1924 was not permitted to make an anticipated trip to the United States. But in his later years he was highly esteemed by those who disagreed with him as well as by his followers.[58]

Besides *Skökan rättvisan*, the two plays most frequently acted by the *Arbetar Teater* were *Godsägarens dotter* (The landowner's daughter), with six performances, and *Immigrant liv*, with five. Both plays were blends of comedy and serious themes, and both may have been written locally. *Immigrant liv* was a picture of Chicago life attributed to a Werner Wenberg or Wiberg. *Godsägarens dotter* was the work of Allan Wallenius, who wrote under the pen name of Per Olson. A leftist journalist, he had been a refugee from Finland at the time of the first World War, had come to America from Sweden, and went eventually to Russia. In 1927 he was in Chicago, writing for the Scandinavian labor press, and as the play was first acted in 1928, and was published in Stockholm (in the *Arbetar Teater* series) in 1929, the probability is that he wrote it in Chicago.[59] Two three-act dramas imported from Sweden were of the same general type: *Slavarna på Molokstorp* (The slaves at Moloks farm), by Wilfrid Schober, published in 1907; and *Mot ljuset* (Toward the light), an *Arbetar Teater* publication of 1927, by Harald Henriksson. Henriksson's play depicted the life of the Swedish workers, and was based on the Sundvall strikes of 1922, during which, the announcement recalled, "one striker paid with his life."[60]

An interesting item in the *Arbetar Teater* repertoire is *Vilse i lifvet* (Astray in life), a 1920 dramatization by Harald Haraldsson (Per O. Hansell) of Geijerstam's brief novel of the same title. Geijerstam's book is a study of a laborer, whose murder of his child is presented as an indictment of fate and society. *Fädernearf*, the melodrama introduced by Good Templar actors, was twice acted by the labor company in the 1936-1937 season.

230

The comedies from Sweden used by the company included *Timmerflottarens son* (The river logger's son), by Emil Juhlin, a worker from Kalmar, and author of many amateur plays; *Sjömansliv* (Sailors' life); and, presumably, *Den stora uppståndelsen i Kråkemåla* (The big excitement at Kråkemåla).[61] Some of the company's locally written plays were comedies—*Chicago Kronikle,* and the *Arbetar Teater's* contribution to the popular musical revue type, *Storstädning på Snusboulevarden* (The big cleanup on Snuff Boulevard). But there is no clue as to what kind of treatment was given the pictures of Chicago life in *Prosperitetsveckan* (Prosperity week) and *Andy på nödhjälp* (Andy on relief).

A total of eight appearances, including the four performances of *Skökan Rättvisan,* made the 1935-1936 season a high point in the history of the *Arbetar Teater,* and it was the last season in which the company acted frequently. From then until they gave their last play on record, in the spring of 1940, there were only seven scattered performances, and the plays acted had, in general, less "social significance" than those of earlier years. The *Arbetar Teater* had, on the whole, few connections with the other Swedish theatrical developments in Chicago, but Paul Fröjd acted with the Viking Company in 1939; and in 1946, when *Vermländingarne* brought together the acting forces of the Chicago Swedes, he took the role of the *provst.*

In contrast to both the *Arbetar Teater* and *Svenska Folkteatern,* the Viking Theatre Company used a generally old-fashioned repertoire. During the six years of its regular activity, beginning December 14, 1930, the company presented twelve plays in thirty-three performances, not including some appearances in nearby communities. Six of the plays were new, but they accounted for only eleven of the performances. And only one play was not a comedy. The choice of plays—and it seemed to please the audiences very well—is not surprising when one considers that the company director, Nels Carlson, was somewhat older than the actors of the other new companies then flourishing, and had served his acting apprenticeship in the earlier Swedish theatre. He appeared first with Swedish groups in Boston, where he spent seven years after his arrival in the United States. Upon coming to Chicago in 1910, at the age of twenty-three, he acted with Brusell occasionally, and acquired a reputation as a writer of witty dramatic sketches. Mr. Carlson made his living as an upholsterer.[62] *Vikingarnas'* repertoire was well suited to the talents of the company, which, with the exception of Carlson, and of Nils Linde, who often appeared with *Svenska Folkteatern,* was made up of actors not otherwise known. Most frequently mentioned as appearing in the plays were, in addition to Carlson and Linde: Paul Anderson, Arthur Chellberg, Arthur Noren, Walter Walters, Mrs. Emma Alfredson, and Frida Hagberg.

The old plays acted by the Viking Company included not only the time tried one-act comedies, like *En natt i Falkenberg,* which was given five times, but longer comedies like Hodell's *Kärleken på sommarnöje,* seen in four performances, and the more modern *Per Olsson och hans käring* by Geijerstam, which was acted twice. One of the novelties was *En dag under smekmånaden* (A day on the honeymoon), by the early playwright, Uller; another was an unidentified trifle, *När cirkusen kom till sta'n* (When the circus came to town). Two of Carlson's new plays were by Alfred Ebenhard, a popular and profilic contemporary writer for the amateur stage. And one of them gave the company its biggest success—a comedy called *När Smed-Erik och Pligg-Jan fick Amerikafrämmande* (When Smith-Erik and Peg-Jan got visitors from America), dating from 1932, and introduced at that year's *Svenskarnas Dag* at the Good Templar Park. It was given five additional performances in the next seasons. Ebenhard's sentimental melodrama from 1929, *Tänk på mor* (Think of mother) began the 1934-1935 season; and to offer such a play to the comedy loving Swedish public was considered a daring experiment. *Tänk på mor* ends happily, but concerns a blind woman and her sufferings as an unhappy wife, widow, and mother. It was, as a matter of fact, well received in three performances.[63]

In 1939, after a lapse of four years, the Viking Theatre Company was briefly revived, and gave three performances of a typical comedy from 1932, by another much acted author—*Karlsson får Amerika-arv* (Karlsson gets an America-inheritance), by Kurt Göransson. Carlson was again the director, and two of his former actors, Chelberg and Paul Anderson, appeared with him, but leading roles were taken by Paul Fröjd of the labor company, the well known Maja Dejenberg-Anderson, and by American born Elsa Appelgren and Helen Johnson, who were popular radio singers and entertainers and members of a trio called *De Tre Gnistorna* (The three sparks). The welcome given the play was proof, said *Svenska Amerikanaren Tribunen,* that even in these days of radio and films, a Swedish play could be a success. There were good, if not crowded, houses, and the story of the servant temporarily cheated out of an inheritance was thoroughly enjoyed.[64] That had been true, in general, of the Viking Theatre Company plays. They could not be called significant, and no such claims were made for them, but they were welcome entertainment.

A distinctive feature of the new theatrical developments that reached their height in the 1930's—the Viking company repertoire notwithstanding —was the extent to which contemporary plays were used. With most of the actors in their twenties or thirties, the trend to the plays of their own day was a natural one. The actors themselves wrote the majority of the local comedies and revues that were widely acted. And all the playwrights extensively played by the acting groups already discussed and by *Svenska Folkteatern* were modern. Of the twenty-odd authors for whom some biographical facts can be secured, nine were born in the 1880's, eight in the 1890's, and three after 1900. Dates of plays indicate that most of the other writers were at least as young; and older authors whose plays were acted were, as a rule, still living.

Svenska Folkteatern used many plays that were popular on the professional stage of Sweden as well as the pieces provided by its own members. A large number of the plays acted by other groups had been written for amateur performance. Unlike the light comedy of the preceding decades, these latter plays were not ordinarily the work of men and women closely associated with the theatre. Many of the authors were journalists and business men; a few, including two of the most productive, were publishers. Alfred Ebenhard, who headed the Kristdala publishing house, and Knut S. Haglöf, founder and owner of *Teaterförlaget Borlänge* (Theatrical publishing house Borlänge), [65] were represented by the largest number of plays, ten each. Kurt Göransson and Gunnar Erlind (Ernst G. Lind) each furnished six plays. The plays by Göransson and by another author used in Chicago, E. R. Hedin, were among the many published by Haglöf. Fridolf (Henning Lind) and Gunnar Erlind (Ernst G. Lind) were published in the *Amatör-Teater* series. Other plays commonly acted were available in other popular "theatre libraries." Most of the authors were prolific, many of them turning out plays at the rate of at least one a year. Their comedies about Lars Jonsa and Kalle Svensson and the rest tended to be both trite and trivial, but they were good choices for the Chicago amateurs, from the point of view of economy, availability, audience taste, and equipment, as well as the limitations of the actors.

Only two plays of the amateur type by authors popular with the other groups were acted by *Svenska Folkteatern,* one by Göransson and one by Haglöf. The company made a modest beginning in the fall of 1929 with comedies that had proved their popularity through the years, and used such plays several times later when acting for other organizations. But the plays from Sweden it used for its main productions were secured through a Stockholm agent, to whom they were returned after the roles had been copied, and regular royalties were paid.[66] Never before, *Svenska Folkteatern* boasted, had this been the practice, or had current stage successes been offered to Chicago Swedish audiences. Seven of the company's plays, the largest number by a single author, were by Henning Ohlson-Sörby (also called Henning Ohlson), already mentioned in connection with his *Fädernearf*. His long and successful career included acting and the direction of motion pictures as well as the authorship of some forty plays, most of them for the professional stage.[67] The company acted three plays by Björn Hodell, one by the versatile actor, painter, and dramatist, Ernst Fastbom,[68] and one by Sigge Fischer, a director of one of the Stockholm summer theatres,[69] where many of the *Svenska Folkteatern* plays were originally produced. Dramatist and novelist Vilhelm Moberg, whose latest novel was recently written in the United States, was represented by a one-act comedy. As the account of the company will show, its repertoire was almost exclusively light, but the literary drama was not altogether neglected. A serious one-act piece by Birger Mörner, an able writer in the fields of poetry and literary criticism as well as a dramatist, was presented as part of one program,[70] and Strindberg's *Hemsöborna* was the high point of the 1936-1937 season.

Gradually, through the 1920's, the local musical revue had been establishing itself as a popular type of entertainment in Chicago's Swedish theatrical groups, and in the increased activities of the 1930's it loomed large. A series of revues given by *Svenska Folkteatern* were outstanding examples of the type and were among the company's most successful productions, but some of the earlier revues also were both elaborate and successful. On the whole, the new fashion stimulated local authorship to an unprecedented degree. The revue had few links with the earlier local plays, though the plays had ordinarily included songs and dances, and the revues continued the traditional use of topical references and impersonations of identifiable Chicagoans. Essentially, the revues had the same characteristics as American musical comedy, particularly of the "Follies" type: a series of loosely related scenes, the combination of broad comedy and the beautiful and spectacular, and extensive use of song and dance. Since the early 1900's, however, such revues, generally New Year's productions, had been increasingly popular in Sweden. By 1930, Sweden's New Year revues were running until midsummer, and critics who preferred drama of some literary merit were pondering the unreasonable enthusiasm they aroused and the degree to which they dominated the theatre. The Vasa,

Södra, and Folk theatres as well as the many summer theatres were devoting themselves to the type, and France was sending revues to Sweden.[71]

Two, at least, of the Chicago revues were written in whole or in part by men who had experience with revues in Sweden—Ernst Hägerström and Thore Österberg[72]—and undoubtedly the Swedish fondness for such entertainment influenced the Chicago actors. The custom of holiday productions, at any rate, was followed to some extent. Just as in the old days *Andersson, Pettersson och Lundström* had been standard North Side Turner Hall New Year's entertainment, now the revue, or the "cabaret" evening that approximated it, was the accepted feature of New Year's Eve festivities. Seven of the fourteen revues known to have been performed in Chicago were introduced during or near the winter holiday season, and two were presented soon after Easter.

Chicago critics did not at first welcome the revues more enthusiastically than did those of Stockholm; Atterling's *Kolingarnas lustresa* of 1912 had been rather contemptuously dismissed for its revue characteristics, and in 1923 *Utan yab* (Without job), the first full blown example of the type, had a mixed reception.

Utan yab and its 1925 successor, *Fattiga riddare, eller När bubblan sprack* (Poor knights, or When the bubble burst) were presented by the Harmoni Glee Club, and were written by one of its members, Dr. Einar Fabian Söderwall. Before returning to Sweden, where he died some years ago, Dr. Söderwall was known as one of the most versatile and picturesque figures among the Chicago Swedes. Educated at the University of Lund, he had come to America in 1904, and in 1908, after studies at the University of Illinois Library School, had become the assistant librarian of the Elbert H. Gary Law Library of Northwestern University's Chicago Law School. He was active in musical circles, being for a time director of the Swedish Glee Club; he wrote poetry with some success; he lectured; he was a talented painter, organized a society of Swedish artists and was its first president, and was instrumental in establishing the Swedish Club's annual exhibits of Swedish American art; he was a founder of Strindbergarna, and a member and officer of the Verdandi Club. He was not, obviously, a retiring individual, and there were those who did not appreciate his activities and personality.[73]

Newspaper accounts indicate, and recollections bear them out, that Dr. Söderwall made his revues vehicles for personal prejudices and animosities. He should, it was suggested, have been hissed rather than applauded for the biting satire of *Utan yab*. But on the whole this revue was welcomed as a kind of novelty needed in Swedish organizational life, and it attained a record of seven performances over a two months period. The central character of *Utan yab,* against whom much of Söderwall's satire was directed, was Mrs. M . . . hm!—Mrs. Myhrman—well played by Fred Bolling, and pictured in characteristic activities, as the manager of a summer excursion to Göteborg who secures "yabs" for the tourists. To recognize all the characters—a chameleon, a "hypocritic hipocrat" called Hix Flux, and a snobbish student, among others—one would, as *Svenska Amerikanaren* said, have to be a diligent reader of Chicago's Swedish press; but a number of them, like a congressman representing the Honorable Carl R. Chindblom, and specific newspapermen, are readily identified. Far removed from the central situation were some of the popular spectacular scenes, such as a moonlight fantasy on the Sahara.[74]

Perhaps because it was less of a novelty, Dr. Söderwall's second revue was presented only twice. But large audiences enjoyed its varied settings and fantastic characters. Supposedly some of the satire was again personal, but there is no suggestion of identities in its Count of No Account, living ancestral portraits, four gallows birds, fireproof knight, and Perpetuum Mobile—"a phenomenon in skirts," proud of her ability to paint on oil cloth.[75]

Skördekalaset i Nickebo (The harvest festival at Nickebo), with which the *Svenska Teaterensemble* made its bow to the public in 1926 (at the Goodman, shortly after the *Svenska Teatersällskapet Syrsan* there) was unique among the Chicago revues in using Swedish materials, though it contained the usual local allusions. The author was Ernst Hägerström, a young man recently come from Sweden, where, it was said, he had successfully produced his own revues. As the description of its three acts indicates, *Skördekalaset i Nickebo* had something in common with the folk plays: I. The Nickebo farm, with a festival concluded by a ballet of peasant girls; II. A country fair, concluding with a ballet of sailors from Göteborg; III. A magician's theatre at Tivoli Fair, visited by well known Swedish characters. Reviewers, judging in terms of the folk play, condemned the lack of central action and continuity. With its twenty-three elaborate scenes, chorus girls more or less (mostly more) shapely, and songs Mr. Hägerström had brought with him from Sweden, *Skördekalaset i Nickebo* was, however, admitted to be good entertainment.[76] It remained his one contribution to the Chicago Swedish stage.

In 1930, the revue came into its own as popular entertainment. Both the *Arbetar Teater* and *Nordstjernan* gave spring revues: *Storstädning på*

Snusboulevarden, mentioned earlier, and *Sånglunds födelsedagskalas* (Sånglund's birthday party). New Year's Eve brought the first *Svenska Folkteatern* revue, which was acted twice with great success. Three more New Year's revues by *Svenska Folkteatern,* in 1933, 1935, and 1940, were enthusiastically received.[77] The Swedish Glee Club gave a New Year's Eve revue, *Pytt i panna* (Hash), in 1934. The I.O.G.T. Male Chorus had in October 1933 celebrated the success of the Century of Progress with an amusing revue by Nels L. Lindquist, *Pepparkorn i grynvällingen, eller Vad som plockas upp i mörkret* (Pepper in the rice porridge, or What is picked up in the dark). Its outstanding feature was "Rally Sand" in a dance begun in Eskimo costume.[78] In 1936 and 1940 there were other Good Templar revues for New Year's Eve watch parties: *Vill du veta vad som hände dig igår?* (Do you want to know what happened to you yesterday?), and *Svenska Amerikanaren Tribunen* editor E. Einar Andersson's *Flickorna från gamla sta'n* (The girls from the old town). And one of the last Swedish dramatic entertainments in Chicago was a Good Templar New Year's revue, *Ett folk i kö* (A people in line), in 1946. Besides some reminiscences of the recent revival of *Vermländingarne,* it employed the usual topical appeals, satirizing John L. Lewis, and concluding with a house hunting couple taking refuge in a window display bedroom.[79]

Ett folk i kö was written and produced by the man who took the initiative in founding *Svenska Folkteatern,* Paul Norling. He arranged for a meeting at his home on October 6, 1929, of a nucleus of the actors with whom he had been associated in the *Nerkingarne* and *Vermländingarne* productions of the preceding season. At once the new organization was decided upon, and two weeks later *Svenska Folkteatern* presented its first play. Present at the October 6 meeting were, besides Mr. Norling, Carl Stockenberg, Arvid Nelson, Thore Österberg, Ragnhild Lindstrom, and Elna Lilnequist Kronberg. Mr. Stockenberg, who was the oldest and most experienced of the group, was made president and director, and remained the director for the entire period of the company's activities. Thore Österberg was the secretary until, after three seasons, he returned to Sweden. In May 1935 the officers were: Mr. Norling, president; Ragnhild Lindstrom, vice president; Oscar Ahlstrand, protocol secretary; Yngve Jancke (also spelled Yancke), corresponding secretary; Harold Swanson, treasurer; and Arvid Nelson, business manager.[80]

Though the leaders of *Svenska Folkteatern,* except Mr. Stockenberg, were young people, they had backgrounds of acting experience. Many of them had acted together, in the *Svenska Teaterensemble* and in other companies. Elna Lilnequist Kronberg (Mrs. Herbert Kronberg) and Arvid Nelson had been members of the Olle i Skratthult and Noreen and Benson companies, and Mrs. Kronberg had acted in Minneapolis before coming to Chicago. Arvid Nelson and Ragnhild Lindstrom had been associates in the Norden company, and Ragnhild Lindstrom had appeared with Brusell and Behmer. Paul Norling as well as Thore Österberg had done professional acting in Sweden (and Österberg continued his stage career for a short time after returning there). Mr. Norling had acted since childhood in Gävle in his native Norrland, and as a young man had taken leaves from his work to act with touring companies. He had come to Chicago in 1923, because of poor business conditions in Sweden, and was soon gaining recognition in Good Templar performances. In Chicago as in Sweden he has worked as a printer, and he is at present employed by the System Press. Arvid Nelson, by occupation a mail carrier, contributed much to *Folkteatern,* not only as an actor, but as a writer of plays and revues. For many years he has been a popular entertainer in Chicago Swedish circles, the trio which he has headed, *De Glada Våghalsarna* (The merry sailors), continuing its activities into the present.

Besides the founders, the men and women most consistently active in *Svenska Folkteatern* were Einar Carlson, Oscar Ahlstrand and his wife, Viola Ahlstrand, Greta Ohlman, Yngve Jancke, and Carl Yngve. For at least three seasons, other regular performers were Maja Dejenberg-Anderson, Nils Linde, Anna-Lisa Lambert (later Anna-Lisa Ryman), Anna Österberg (Mrs. Thore Österberg), Carl and Ivar Lambert, Harold Swanson, Carl Wennerstrand, Karin Sjöberg, Engla Hulström, and Clara Hammar.

Of these actors, Greta Ohlman and Ivar Lambert had also been members of Norden. Nils Linde was a mainstay of the Viking Theater Company, and he, Carl Wennerstrand, and Harold Swanson were, at different times, members of the *Glada Våghalsarna* trio. Maja Dejenberg-Anderson (Mrs. Arvid Anderson) was, of course, widely known. Since coming from Värmland in 1906, she had acted with Brusell and Behmer and with Olle i Skratthult as well as with smaller companies, and had often appeared as a singer. Carl Yngve was also born in Värmland; he had made his first appearances in Swedish plays in Minneapolis, in 1919, some ten years after coming to America. Yngve Jancke was one of many actors with musical interests, and an active member of the chorus *De Svenske.* Both he and Carl Yngve worked as painters, and Oscar Ahlstrand was a cabinet maker. One of the most gifted of *Folkteatern* actors was Einar Carlson (1892-1949). He had been in Chicago since 1912, and was a toolmaker

Lifvet på Landet

Genomrolig, skrattretande folkkomedi i 5 akter
af Frans Hedberg

gifves å

Grand Opera

House

87 S. CLARK STREET

Onkel Bräsig

Söndagen den 13 Mars

Kl. 8 e. m.

af

Svenska Dramatiska Sällskapet

Ernst Behmer, Regissör

Biljetter $1.00, 75c och 50c

Ernest Lindblom as Onkel Bräsig, 1910

ERNST BEHMER

firar sitt

25-ÅRS-JUBILEUM

SÅSOM SVENSK-AMERIKANSK SKÅDESPELARE

med uppförande af

DUVALS SKILSMESSA

LUSTSPEL I TRE AKTER AF ALEXANDRE BISSON

å ARYAN GROTTO TEMPLE

WABASH AVENUE AND EIGHTH STREET

SÖNDAGEN DEN 9 NOVEMBER 1919

KLOCKAN 8 E. M.

Biljetter @ $1.00, 75c och 50c (plus War Tax) till salu hos Mrs.
Myhrman, 143 N. Dearborn St.; Youngberg, 3210 N. Clark St.;
Peterson, 5938 S. Halsted St.; Helander, 7442 Cottage Grove Ave.;
Sommanson, 10846 Michigan Avenue; sant C. E. Anderson,
10500 Avenue J.

Back row, center Otto Benson as Per, Helen Johnson as Stina. Second row, Ernest Magnuson as the *provst*, David Nordquist as the *bruks-*

by trade. His nickname bespoke his native province: as Värmlands-Kalle he was known throughout most of his Chicago years as an extremely popular entertainer. He was a valued member of the Värmlands Club and the Orphei Singing Society, and participated in the dramatic activities of these and other organizations. A dreamer who gave true life to his stage creations and spread joy with his comedy, a genuine Swede and *ur-Värmlander* Paul Norling called him after his death—one whose services to the preservation of Swedish language and culture were great, if uncelebrated.[81]

There were many participants in the *Svenska Folkteatern* plays besides those who have been named. Several well known actors appeared with the company from time to time: Otto Benson and Werner Noreen; Nels Carlson, the director of the Viking Theater Company; Hilma Lindblom and Sigrid Wollertz, from Olle i Skratthult's company. Others who were seen for relatively short periods or in lesser roles were Linnea Anderson (later Linnea Vik), Florence Ruden, Herta Larson, Gurli Nelson, Sonja Boström (a singer, who returned to Sweden), Elsa Appelgren of *De Tre Gnistorna,* and Allan Nyberg.

On the whole, as was true of the Brusell and Behmer Companies, major roles in *Svenska Folkteatern* plays were taken by actors with talent and experience, and minor roles by inexperienced amateurs who might or who might not have talent; and the new company had in large measure the advantage of continuity of personnel enjoyed by its 20th century predecessors. Its main handicap was that which had always confronted Swedish actors in Chicago: no matter how ardent their interest was, acting had to remain an avocation, time for rehearsals and other preparations had to be found in limited leisure hours. Now as before, there were among the actors those whose talents and interest might, under different circumstances, have led to successful careers on the professional instead of the amateur or semi-professional stage. As it was, these young people, like those who preceded them, devoted themselves to the theatre for the pleasure it gave them and the pleasure their plays gave to others. Profits they thought of in terms of being able to carry on their activities. And in these activities the most prominent of the companies in this latest phase of the Chicago Swedish theatre continued to serve the old needs—keeping the newer immigrants from loneliness and giving them a sense of contact with the life they had left behind.

No longer, however, was the practice of using city theatres for main productions possible. Costs had become prohibitive, and the movies had reduced the number of legitimate theatres available. One of the outlying

239

theatres that was converted to a movie house was the North Side Victoria, or "Vic's," also called the German theatre, which had been used for Swedish plays in the late 1920's and housed three *Svenska Folkteatern* productions in the early seasons of the company.[82] The majority of its regular productions—specifically, thirty-five out of a total of sixty-nine—were presented in two North Side halls, the Lincoln Auditorium and the North Side Auditorium. These two halls were smaller than the Victoria, with its seating capacity of some 1,500, but they could accommodate an audience of eight or nine hundred, and had, on the whole, fairly adequate facilities. The North Side Auditorium was, in general, a center for Swedish organizations and events.[83] A few of the company plays, those given for other organizations usually, or South Side performances of plays that had been acted on the North Side, were presented at the popular smaller halls. Five of the seasons included the outdoor performances in which there was a renewed interest in this period. Occasionally, also, the company performed outside the city.

The time honored custom of dances and refreshments after the plays was regularly followed by *Svenska Folkteatern*—largely as a means of attracting young people and of providing needed income. As *Svenska Amerikanaren Tribunen* said, after raising the question of the appropriateness of turning from a Strindberg play to a dance, it was necessary, in order to balance debit and credit; and when one had spent evening after evening in rehearsal, making up a deficit was not much fun.[84]

In costs of production the *Svenska Folkteatern* plays did not mark a return to the simpler North Side Turner Hall days; often, in fact, their plays required expenditures on the scale of the elaborate city productions of the past. With the addition of royalties to rent and other routine expenses, and with plays that frequently required a variety of settings, an outlay of over one thousand dollars was normal for their main productions. Expenses for the company's first new play from Sweden, *Styrman Karlssons flammor* (Mate Karlsson's flames), acted in the spring of 1930, amounted to $1,300.00. Fortunately, since the treasury contained only $35.00, the income was $1,700.00. They were young and daring, the leaders say in retrospect, and did not worry about the financial risk. This was not a new situation in the Swedish theatre of Chicago, certainly, but the amounts expended had often been more modest. Admission to *Svenska Folkteatern* plays ranged from seventy-five cents to a dollar and a half—more than the fifty cents that was standard for most of the performances of this period, but less than had been charged in the city in recent years. If the company had not played almost consistently to crowded houses, it could not, of course, have continued to present its imported hits. But the plays pleased the public and were usually acted on Saturday nights, a popular time; and more than once the theatre was sold out so early that the performance began well in advance of the scheduled curtain time.[85]

The Swedish press gave *Svenska Folkteatern* plays the support that was traditional for the chief productions of the Chicago Swedish theatre. Writers normally shared the enthusiasm of the audience, and frequently expressed gratitude to the new company for keeping the Swedish theatre alive and providing good entertainment—entertainment that was especially welcome in depression times. There was much praise for capable performances; and when the settings were not so successful as usual or the plays not so well rehearsed, the public was reminded that the scenery was largely home made and that the actors had to work hard all day.[86] The plays themselves were considered highly amusing, and well suited to the tastes of the audience. Publicity emphasized the success of the plays in Sweden, the fact that these were the plays that were being enjoyed at Sweden's popular summer theatres, and in Stockholm's old, established *Södra Teater*. Evidence of the popularity of the summer theatres was supplied, in advertisements and articles: in 1905, *Folkets Park* (People's Park), the first Stockholm open air theatre, had been established; in the summer of 1939, there were 800 summer performances by sixteen companies.[87] At the *Södra Teater*, plays used by *Svenska Folkteatern*, like *Styrman Karlssons flammor* and *Ebberödsbank* (The Ebberöd bank), had long runs, and their gay comedy won critical approval as well as public support.[88]

On March 15, 1930, after four performances of old comedies, *Svenska Folkteatern* gave its first première, *Styrman Karlssons flammor*. Two more new plays completed its first season. The next fall there were two performances of one of these plays and two of another new play, and on New Year's Eve the first of the company revues was presented. Then five repetitions of the season's new plays preceded two premières that brought this second season to a close. For five more seasons this general pattern was followed, with a range of from six to twelve performances a season. By the spring of 1932, there had been twenty-nine performances, and twelve of the plays acted had been new. Director Stockenberg did not exaggerate when he stated in the 1933 *Hembygden:* "never before has any Swedish theatre company acted so many different plays in so short an existence."[89] After the 1935-1936 season the number of performances was sharply reduced, with only two seasons having as many as three, but then too there

241

were new plays; and in its flourishing years *Svenska Folkteatern* normally offered four or five new plays a season.

Though most of the new plays were of Swedish origin, there were, out of a total of sixty-nine performances of forty-two plays, nine local works seen in thirteen performances. Four of the Chicago "originals" were revues, two were straight comedies, and the others were comedies with musical features. Arvid Nelson wrote or had a hand in almost all of these Chicago pieces.[90] Only eight times after the first season were plays from earlier periods used. Four times the play was Geijerstam's *Lars Anders och Jan Anders och deras barn,* which, though dating from 1894, was the type of peasant comedy now at the height of its popularity.

Regardless of origin or age, what *Svenska Folkteatern* offered the public was, almost without exception, light entertainment. Still the repertoire was not without variety. The revues and the operetta and musical comedy type of musical pieces presented a wide range of settings and characters. Comedies with few musical features or none were broadly farcical, with plots ordinarily centering about domestic difficulties related to money or social position. Certain character types and settings were used repeatedly. But seashore, farm, and provincial village, sailors, farmers, fishermen, and, for some reason, tailors, entertained the audiences in turn.

The first two of the company's four revues were rousing successes, and they were the only ones to be given more than one performance. The 1930 revue was ironically entitled *"Måtte våra barn få rika föräldrar",* eller *Svenska folkets underbara öden* (May our children get rich parents, or The remarkable destiny of the Swedish people); its sub-title seems to have been a reference to a nine volume history of Sweden published not many years before.[91] This revue bore some resemblance to the traditional local play, its scenes—a club, the corner of Belmont and Clark, and Lincoln Park, with the Linné statue—being reminiscent of Ernst Lindblom's *Pelle Pihlqvists Amerika-resa.* And there were the local characters found in the old plays as well as in the revues. In Adrian Södervalv, Dr. Söderwall got some of his own medicine, and *Svenska Amerikanaren* editor Frithiof Malmquist figured as Ivar Malmsten. Both these roles were taken by Carl Yngve. Fred Bolling, the Mrs. . . . hm! of Söderwall's *Utan yab,* had his turn, too, with Paul Norling's impersonation of Frid Bowling. Einar Carlson was one of the hits of the evening as Olle i Skratthult. A representative of *Svenska Folkteatern* was acted by Thore Österberg, who, with Carl Stockenberg, "cooked up" the revue. Policemen, bricklayers, painters, and a landlady were others in a grand confusion of characters. There was, of course, a ballet; and, to add to the fun, texts were provided for some of the songs, so the audience could join in.[92]

In the title of the 1933 revue, *Den förgylda kaffegöken, eller Gudar på awager, eller Vassego, det är serverat* (The drunken coffee addict, or Gods on the loose, or Come to the table, you are served), there was also it seems, an allusion—to a play called *Den förgylda lergöken* (The drunken clay cuckoo), in which the earlier Chicago actor, John Liander, had made a reputation in Sweden.[93] It was the Norse gods of Valhalla who were on the loose, and visited a favorite Chicago Swedish restaurant, Idrott, and then the Swedish pavilion of the Century of Progress, on its Swedish Day. A triumphant closing tableau, with Svea and Columbia as the central figures, followed the inevitable glimpse of Sally Rand and an encounter with Hitler at the Oriental village.[94]

Another revue in 1935, *Arbetslösa Amoriner, eller Ledighetskommittén får semester* (Unemployed Cupids, or The committee on leisure gets a vacation), was a big drawing card, but found less favor with reviewers. Its chief scenes took place in a forest preserve and the Black Cat cabaret.[95] And the 1940 revue, *En omgång till, eller Fram på småtimmarna* (One more swing around, or In the small hours), was a less elaborate production and received little attention.[96] The halcyon days of *Svenska Folkteatern* were then past; this was the second performance of the season, and the next to the last in the history of the company.

On New Year's Eve of 1931, *Svenska Folkteatern* did not present a revue, but an operetta by Arvid Nelson, *Söder om Rio Grande*. A romantic tale of a Mexican rancher and a reformed robber chieftain, it had picturesque costumes and settings and gay songs—and even an audience with a predilection for the characteristically Swedish greeted it with enthusiasm.[97] *Luffarbaron* (Tramp baron), which the company imported from Sweden for its fifth anniversary performance on October 14, 1934, was another operetta. Its plot was typically absurd—the tramp who assumes the role of a baron fools the parents of a bridegroom who has tried to keep them from interrupting his honeymoon by a tale of the baron who is his guest —but leaders of *Folkteatern* agree that this was outstanding among their productions, in scenery and in performance. Arvid Nelson played the tramp baron, with his usual success.[98]

More characteristic entertainment than either *Luffarbaron* or *Söder om Rio Grande* were the several plays about Swedish sailors and their adventures—chiefly amorous—of which the 1930 *Styrman Karlssons flammor* was the first example. Not all of these plays, however, had its musical

243

comedy features. With scenes at sea, at Barbados, in a Chinese opium den, a sailor's saloon, in the South Seas and at the harbor of Sidney, and with a corresponding variety of characters, songs, and dances, *Styrman Karlssons flammor* was an ambitious undertaking. The production as a whole was considered less finished than that given a second Karlsson piece in the fall of 1931, but the round the world love affairs were found very amusing. Thore Österberg was successful in the leading role, and his wife was enjoyed as the pert cabin boy, Jonas. Ragnhild Lindstrom was Bessie Doring, the last of Karlsson's flames, whom he meets in Sidney, and who accompanies him on another journey round the world in *Styrman Karlssons bröllopsresa* (Mate Karlsson's wedding journey). Thore Österberg again played Karlsson, but Ragnhild Lindstrom was Jonas, and the young singer, Sonja Boström, Bessie. Scenery by Yngve Jancke was an important factor in the warm welcome given this production on two successive evenings.[99]

One of the Ohlson-Sörby plays, *Flottans lilla fästmö* (The little sweetheart of the fleet), given at Riverview Park in June 1933, was another gay story of sailor romance. The center of its action was the Golden Anchor Inn, of which a retired sailor was the proprietor. Einar Carlson took this role, Ragnhild Lindstrom was his daughter, the sweetheart of the fleet, and *De Svenske's* singing sailors contributed to a lively performance.[100] A more melodramatic story of a wandering sailor was acted in 1935, *Vi gå ilann i Spanien* (We go ashore in Spain), a play with music that had been locally adapted from a story in a Swedish magazine.[101] And, further evidence of the popularity of the sailor type, the title character of *Svenska John går i land* (Swedish John goes ashore), twice performed in 1936 and repeated in 1940, was a sailor, though the play was in general typical rural farce.[102]

The one entirely serious play presented by *Svenska Folkteatern*, Mörner's one-act *Nummer 39* (Number 39), was acted with *Vi gå ilann i Spanien*. *Nummer 39* was a dramatic story of the Foreign Legion, and was, said *Svenska Amerikanaren*, ably acted but a little too somber for public taste.[103] This was the only occasion when the company performed more than one play on the same evening.

In the domestic comedies with a small town background that made up a considerable portion of the *Svenska Folkteatern* repertoire, tailors figure more frequently than representatives of other occupations. They were important in two new plays introduced in 1930 and 1931 that were among the few attaining as many as four performances: *När byskräddaren och byskomakaren gifte bort sin pojke* (When the town tailor and town

244

shoemaker marry off their boy) and *Ebberödsbank* (The Ebberöd bank). Björn Hodell, who had written the Styrman Karlsson plays, had made *När byskräddaren och byskomakaren gifte bort sin pojke* rollicking comedy, and Einar Carlson and Paul Norling made the most of their roles as the tailor and shoemaker who succeed in thwarting a charlatan preacher and marrying off to the belle of the village the foundling they have brought up. [104] The originally Danish *Ebberödsbank* had been a hit in all three Scandinavian countries, and its Chicago success was no surprise. Satirical wit and timeliness combined to make amusing its story of the tailor who starts a bank after being impressed by the money his brother has brought back to Sweden from America, and the comic character types were much enjoyed—particularly the tailor and his brother, acted by Carl Yngve and Paul Norling. [105]

The troubled relations of husbands and wives was the central theme of the Ohlson-Sörby play, *Aktiebolaget Strid och Frid* (Joint stock company Strife and Peace), acted once in April 1931; and both husbands were tailors, one old-fashioned, the other with new-fangled notions. [106] A more involved plot and more varied character types characterized Sigge Fischer's *Hur ska' det gå för Petterson?* (How will things go for Petterson?), introduced in a 1936 New Year's Eve performance and repeated as the final *Svenska Folkteatern* performance on New Year's Eve 1941. The central character is a soldier, but the girl whom he temporarily believes to be his illegitimate daughter knows him as tailor Petterson, and the real tailor Petterson is called upon to impersonate him. The untangling of a triangle situation and of the girl's romance with the soldier's son provided lively comedy, and both performances were successful. Paul Norling was the soldier in 1936 and Nels Carlson in 1941, with Arvid Nelson playing tailor Petterson on each occasion. [107]

Elaborate intrigue of similar type characterized *Trötte Theodor* (Tired Theodor), one of the few plays acted by *Svenska Folkteatern* that did not rely at least in part on the appeal of Swedish character types and local color. *Trötte Theodor* was an adaptation from the German, and had been seen in Chicago in a popular screen version before being performed in Swedish in the fall of 1935. Theodor, who does not dare explain to his wife that he is tired because he is working nights in order to help a young singer who is his protegée, provided Paul Norling with one of his favorite roles, and he and the play were considered extremely funny. [108] But audiences could also enjoy plays with simpler plots. Two slight comedies by Arvid Nelson had the added interest of Chicago settings. His *Handlarns första piga* (The tradesman's first maid servant), which was twice successfully acted, used the popular *nouveau riche* theme in a picture of a Swedish American family adjusting themselves to the maid they considered necessary for social prestige.[109] In *Hemma hos Karlsons* (At home at Karlsons) the romance of a boarder and the daughter of the family furnished the comedy.[110] No more modern in situation was the company's last new play from Sweden, *Jansson, jag älskar dej* (Jansson, I love you), acted on New Year's Eve, 1937, but the comedy of boarding house life, with a lovesick old maid pursuing a young man and being persuaded by him to advertise for a husband, proved entertaining enough.[111] *Edla Hansons friare* (Edla Hanson's suitors), which was concerned with a widow pursued by rival suitors, was considered a good choice when it was acted at Belmont Hall in the spring of 1938, because it required little scenery—and was a welcome change from rural comedies.[112]

The *allmogen* or peasant comedy that had been growing in popularity since the days of Geijerstam and Bondeson was, naturally, well represented in the repertoire of *Svenska Folkteatern*. Besides the four performances of Geijerstam's *Lars Anders och Jan Anders och deras barn,* there were single performances of seven more recent plays of the type. Two were one-act plays presented at Belmont Hall: *Sommarnöje på Skönlunda* (Summer pleasure at Beautiful Grove) and Moberg's *En marknadsafton* (An evening at the fair). Also acted at Belmont Hall was the company's one Haglöf comedy, already familiar to Chicago audiences, *Lars Jonsa och hans käring* (Lars Jonsa and his wife). It told a typical story of country parents disagreeing as to whom their daughter shall marry.[113]

For the 1930 *Svenskarnas Dag* at Good Templar Park, where the same actors had so successfully presented *Vermländingarne* the year before, the play was Ohlson-Sörby's *Kopparslagargreven* (The coppersmith count), one of several country plays with music acted by *Svenska Folkteatern.* This was the company's second ambitious production, and a real success, twice repeated the next season. There were Värmland scenes and songs (the songs by Elis Olson, the Chicago visitor of 1911-1912) in *Kopparslagargreven,* and a story combining comedy and romance. The difficulties of the lovers reversed the problem of *Vermländingarne,* a young nobleman having to masquerade as a coppersmith to win the hand of a coppersmith's daughter. Carl Stockenberg, who often limited himself to the duties of director, played the father, Thore Österberg the hero, Sigrid Wollertz the heroine, and Elna Kronberg a comic servant. There was praise for all the cast; and writing of the performance later, Stockenberg emphasized the masterful acting of Paul Norling as the journeyman copper- smith, Hans, particularly in the moving episode when Hans and his bride set out from their old home.[114] Two years later, another of Ohlson-Sörby's musical pieces, *Rallare* (Railroad workers), was given an outdoor produc- tion for a 1932 *Sångarnas Dag* (Singers' Day). It was enjoyed especially for the acting of Einar Carlson as Kalle-Värmland, one of several regional characters in the country life picture.[115] Pure farce were both *När Bengt och Anders bytte hustrur* (When Bengt and Anders trade wives), acted at Riverview Park in 1931, and the March 1933 *Torpar-Petter säljer sin kä- ring* (Cotter-Petter sells his wife). Arvid Nelson made Torpar-Petter one of his many successful comic roles, and the modern twist given the plot by the cotter's trying to sell his wife because he needed money for a movie career was considered amusing.[116]

Country plays distinguished by sea coast settings and with fishermen as a prominent character type were among the most popular of *Svenska Folkteatern* productions. Some were typical farce, some farce spiced with melodrama. One of the farce-comedies, *Bröderna Östermans huskors* (The Österman brothers' household cross), was most frequently acted, with four performances in 1932 and 1933. The efforts of three old fishermen to get rid of a housekeeper with reforming ways and to disappoint a brother-in-law who was hopefully waiting to inherit their property delighted audiences then, and had not lost its appeal when a movie version was shown on Chi- cago's North Side in 1948 and 1950. *Svenska Folkteatern* actors were thought to do the play full justice—Einar Carlson, Arvid Nelson, and Carl Yngve as the Österman brothers, and Elna Kronberg as the housekeeper.[117] Twice successfully acted by the *Folkteatern* company, in 1933 and 1938, was another long-lived comedy of life in the Swedish skerries, Fastbom's *Halta Lena och vindögda Per* (Lame Lena and cross-eyed Per). It had been introduced by the Leman Company in 1928, and was seen again in a film version in 1949—with the title characters transformed into lazy Lena and blue-eyed Per. Their love affair, more comic than romantic, and rival claims as to an inheritance by two half-brothers provided the main action of the play.[118] A sea coast piece by Ohlson-Sörby was used also, for the 1934 New Year's Eve performance. It was entitled *Äktenskapsbolaget U.P.A.* (Joint stock Company, Marriage U.P.A.), and its ingredients were those of *Bröderna Östermans huskors,* except that Ohlson-Sörby's fishermen were young.[119]

Plays with this setting in which there was a dramatic element include Strindberg's *Hemsöborna* (The people of Hemsö), the one play in which

247

Svenska Folkteatern identified itself with the literary drama;[120] and two that were more representative of the usual repertoire: *För fulla segel* (Sail on), another Ohlson-Sörby product, and *Dansen på Brottskär* (The dance at Brott Skerry), by Hjalmar Harriston. *Dansen på Brottskär* dealt with the persecution of a humble young suitor by his old and wealthy rival, its climax being the dance at which the young hero narrowly escapes arrest and disgrace. The spectacle and musical features were admired, particularly the pier scene which was the setting for the dance.[121] In *För fulla segel* another wealthy suitor was thwarted, this time in a plot to cheat his sweetheart's father, and there was the usual quota of character types of which audiences seemed never to tire, the omnipresent love-sick spinster among them. Both of these plays were twice acted, Harriston's in 1932 and 1933, and Ohlson-Sörby's in 1935.[122]

Strindberg's *Hemsöborna* was presented May 16, 1937, in commemoration of the 25th anniversary of the dramatist's death, and was jointly sponsored by *Svenska Folkteatern* and the Scandinavian Labor Societies. There was a full house at Lincoln Auditorium to hear an impressive memorial program, and to enjoy the play in its only Chicago performance. The novel of the same title on which the play was based is one of Strindberg's most admired works, but is a marked contrast to much of his writing. He had happy memories of the skerries and their people, and the book is characterized by a humor that is often warm and sympathetic. Remarkably blended with this tone in the background pictures is the uncompromising realism of the central story. But there is ironic humor, also, in the characterization of Carlsson, who comes from Värmland to the coastal farm of the widow Flod, marries her to obtain ownership of her farm, and then, through philandering with her servant, brings about her death and his own. Unfortunately, many of the novel's good qualities were lost in the play. Strindberg himself made the dramatization, though reluctantly, because he was in need of money; and when the première was a fiasco said it was proof of what happens when one is untrue to one's self.[123] Strindberg scholar Martin Lamm calls the play a vandalization, and critics have generally agreed with him.[124]

Hemsöborna was, however, a good choice for an audience that could not be expected to enjoy more representative Strindberg naturalism. The character types were admirably suited to the talents of the *Svenska Folkteatern* actors, and the play was given a good performance. Arvid Nelson had the most demanding role, that of Carlsson; Oscar Ahlstrand was Gusten, the son of Widow Flod, who opposed her marriage to Carlsson;

and Elna Kronberg played the widow. Specially commended was Director Carl Stockenberg's characterization of the unconventional and humorous clergyman, Nordstrom, who shows another side of his nature at the climax of the story, when Carlsson has perished in the wintry storm as he and Gusten are trying to bring the body of the widow to church for burial.[125]

In the fall of 1938, shortly after *Svenska Folkteatern* had given a performance of *Halta Lena och vindögda Per,* a letter appeared in *Svenska Amerikanaren Tribunen* over the signature Pelle. Much of the letter was a lament for the good old days and a nostalgic celebration of the Swedish theatre of the 1890's, when Pelle had first come to Chicago and joined the devotees of Thalia. Regretfully, he looked back to performances by such actors as Pfeil, Schycker, and Brusell, and to plays such as *Bröllopet på Ulfåsa, Regina von Emmeritz,* and *Jernbäraren,* produced in city theatres. How wretched, in contrast, was the stuff now being offered the public: *Styrmannens skelögda dotter* (The mate's squint-eyed daughter), *Johnsons låghalta Lotta* (Johnson's limping Lotta), *Madame Karlsons snuskige pojk* (Madame Karlson's slovenly boy)—"or whatever they are." *Svenska Folkteatern* was not mentioned, but the reference to its plays was unmistakable.[126]

Pelle was Carl Stockenberg's former colleague, Leopold Chellman— and it is certain that he did not speak for himself alone. The views he expressed were not, however, left unchallenged. The following week the paper carried Mr. Stockenberg's reply to Pelle, a letter notable for its blend of friendliness, humorous satire, and good sense. Paying tribute to the older actors and their achievements and referring to his own participation in their plays, Mr. Stockenberg said that he, too, remembered with pleasure the earlier productions, "which are the best loved conversational topics when the old associates get together, now too infrequently." But the achievements of the past do not, he continued, give Pelle the right to criticize the exceedingly funny and entertaining comedies of *Svenska Folkteatern*—which, moreover, he has not seen. The new plays are those that have been popular in Sweden in recent years. Many of them were produced at *Folkets Park* theatre. Their titles are funny even when they are not twisted and ridiculed. These plays are suited to theatres without much stage equipment, such as *Svenska Folkteatern* must use. The company has maintained the Swedish theatre in Chicago in spite of hard times, often at the cost of great sacrifices, when others were unwilling to do so; and the financial risks are even greater than they were in the past.

As far as the earlier actors are concerned, they too gave trivial plays —*En spik i nyckelhålet, De båda döfva, En natt i Falkenberg, Kärleken på sommarnöje,* for instance—and under the most primitive conditions. Undoubtedly, if the present day plays had then been available, Pelle, with his love for the merry and lively, his fondness for comic, even grotesque, roles, would have acted in them.

Past performances grow better in recollection, Stockenberg concluded, and only by seeing one of these new plays can fair comparisons be made. "To come and see *Flottans lilla fästmö* would perhaps show lack of intelligence—and I would be the last to wish you to descend from the heights on which you think you stand. But, Pelle, 'May the old gods still live.' Hurrah for you, old comrade."[127]

The points made by Mr. Stockenberg about the relationship between the old Swedish theatre and that of *Svenska Folkteatern* days—in difficulties, in the spirit with which those difficulties were met, and in the plays that were acted—cannot be questioned, and they need not be belabored. True, the more recent repertoire included fewer attempts to present literary drama; but Brusell and Behmer's experiences with Ibsen and Sudermann and Strindberg had not been encouraging. It must be admitted, also, that the historical dramas and many of the folk plays and comedies acted by the older companies had a higher standing in their own day than did *Svenska Folkteatern* plays in terms of contemporary standards; but not many of the older plays stood the test of stricter literary judgments and changing fashions, nor could they continue to hold the stage except in occasional revivals. Furthermore, novelty had been the cry of press and public, and farcical comedy had been used to provide the novelty in earlier times also.

The differences between the old comedies and the new were certainly more apparent than real. The new comedies about sailors, tailors, and country types that loomed large in the *Svenska Folkteatern* repertoire, though many of them had distinctly modern features showing the influence of the revue, were clearly descended from traditional Swedish comedy— from the sailor uncle in *Rika morbror;* from tailor Pettersson in *Andersson, Pettersson och Lundström,* whose fortune went to his head; from the comic servants in folk plays like *Vermländingarne* and *Nerkingarne* and the folk pictures in innumerable plays, including *Andersson, Pettersson och Lundström.* The domestic comedies had their earlier parallels as well. *Jansson, jag älskar dej,* with its *pension* background and love-sick old maid, had its links with Hodell's *Ett rum att hyra* and Jonason's *Mot beräkning,* to mention just two from a host of old comedies. And the "comedy with song" that was as old as the native drama of Sweden was appearing in new guise in many *Folkteatern* productions.

The general Chicago Swedish public gained from these *Folkteatern* plays and from others acted in the same period what they had always wanted from the Swedish theatre—amusement and reminders of their homeland. And now the sons and daughters of immigrants gained an interest in their parents' backround, its language and way of life. Whether the plays were idealized or farcical, whether they had literary values or were merely entertaining, they served the same purposes. It was after the performance of such "wretched stuff" as *När Smed-Erik och Pligg-Jan fick Amerikafrämmande* that a white-haired old man came to the director of the Viking Theatre Company, and, with tears in his eyes, expressed his gratitude for the opportunity to relive his youth.[128] Not only tradition-hallowed *Vermländingarne* brought memories of home.

When *Svenska Folkteatern* gave *Hur ska' det gå för Petterson?* on New Year's Eve of 1941, after a year of inactivity, the company's return was welcomed, with prophecies of renewed popularity. But this was only its eighth appearance since presenting *Hemsöborna* in the spring of 1937, and it did not act again. For the next few years only a scattering of lodge performances (usually initiated by *Folkteatern* actors) carried on the tradition of the Swedish theatre. When clubs and lodges wanted Swedish entertainment, they generally turned to music and comic monologues. Their amateur plays—and there were a good many—were in English. Or, on festive occasions, there might be pageants, like the "America marches on," directed by Mr. Stockenberg for the Independent Order of Svithiod in 1942.[129] Especially before Mr. Behmer moved from Chicago, Swedish plays and the Chicago Swedish theatre were frequent topics at the programs of the West Side Division of the Swedish Cultural Association in which he and Mr. Stockenberg were active. Occasionally, too, there would be talk of reviving *Vermländingarne*. The old-timers wanted to act in it again, and many of those who remembered the yearly performances wanted to see it. In 1942 a plan for a *Svenska Folkteatern* performance of *Vermländingarne* as a Red Cross benefit was broached. A committee, including Hedwig Brusell Melinder and a number of leading Chicago Swedes, was set up. But the project was dropped.[130] The Swedish theatre—the old gods and the new ones that supplanted them—had, it seemed, succumbed at last to changing times.

251

And still there were to be noteworthy episodes in the history of the Swedish theatre and of *Vermländingarne* in Chicago. On October 27, 1946, Dahlgren's old folk play was acted again, sixty-two years after its first Chicago performance, and almost eighty years after the city's Swedish theatre had its beginnings. This was, in all respects, an historic occasion. The year marked the 100th anniversary of the play itself, an anniversary widely celebrated in Sweden, with a series of gala performances. And the Chicago production, now, as often before, at the Eighth Street Theatre, was directed by Ernst Behmer, more than fifty years after he had begun his association with the Swedish plays. There were no other members of the old guard in the 1946 *Vermländingarne*, but Behmer, at seventy-four, played the sprightly Löpare-Nisse with the practised art that had made him a favorite in the role.

The revival of *Vermländingarne* was, appropriately, the project of the *Värmlands Nation* society.[131] For months in advance of the performance, the club carried on an active publicity campaign. *Svenska Amerikanaren Tribunen* ran feature articles about the Swedish centennial events, about Dahlgren, about the play and its long popularity in Chicago, a popularity even more remarkable than the position of the play as a favorite in Sweden. Advertisements for the matinée and evening performances listed prices higher than had been asked for a Swedish play, $1.25 to $4.00. And once more, said *Svenska Amerikanaren Tribunen*, reporting two well filled houses, *Vermländingarne* proved that it was imperishable, that the old gods still lived.

The veterans in this performance had been young recruits to the stage in the old Behmer and Brusell days, and the new recruits, including the Erik and Anna, were from a younger generation. Some members of the company had been associated with Behmer before: Maja Dejenberg-Anderson and Werner Noreen, who were Lisa and Jan Hansson, and Otto Benson, who, as Per, played a role he had taken in several of Behmer's productions since 1920. Mr. Behmer's son Eric acted Wilhelm, the role in which his father had first appeared in *Vermländingarne*. Paul Norling of *Svenska Folkteatern* was Sven Ersson; Paul Fröjd of the *Arbetar Teater* was the *provst;* Elsa Appelgren Flodin and Helen Johnson, who sometimes appeared with the *Folkteatern* company, were seen as Britta and Stina. In the leading roles were young Chicago singers, Inga Maye Nordquist and Waldemar E. Walberg. *Danslaget National,* a company that had been active since 1925, presented the dances. And costumes came from the company that still bore the name of Fritz Schoultz.

Now there was only one paper to pass judgment on the performance. *Svenska Amerikanaren Tribunen* was complimentary if not uncritical, pronouncing this *Vermländingarne* a credit to all concerned, to the sponsoring *Värmlands Nation*, to the director, and to the actors. Singing and dancing were excellent, and settings good. All the veteran actors were competent and Anna was properly young and pretty. Costumes and make-up were a different matter: the wealthy farmer, Ola i Gyllby, was outfitted like a gipsy, and Löpare-Nisse looked as if he were on his way to a Hallowe'en party. There were traditional weaknesses, also. Erik, like many a singer before him, was called a somewhat chilly lover. As usual, the boat went aground, and it may be assumed, though it was not reported, that the audience laughed. More enthusiastic reports come from those who participated in the play—of its general success, and of Behmer's ability as director. A story is told, also, of two engineers from Sweden who chanced to be in the city and came to the matinée performance, where they told the audience how much they were impressed, not only by the way the play was given, but by the fact that it was being given.[132]

Behmer and his old theatre friends had a happy reunion at the home of Augusta Milton before he returned to his new home in Colorado.[133] The cast enjoyed a Christmas party.[134] There were echoes of the *Vermländingarne* performance at lodge and club meetings: in November, Anna and Erik reenacted some of their scenes; Paul Norling used bits of the play in his New Year's revue, and in January gave the entire play as a dramatic reading.[135] But thereafter the Swedish theatre seemed indeed to exist only—in Stockenberg's words—as "the best loved topic of conversation" for those who had been associated with it.

Still no friend of Chicago's Swedish theatre would admit that it was dead. To be sure, plans for presenting a Strindberg play as part of the 1949 centennial were not carried out; but there was a Strindberg program at which Mr. Norling gave readings from *Hemsöborna*.[136] In May 1949, two Swedish comedies were acted in Chicago. At a Vasa lodge meeting, Mr. Norling presented *När Kalle på Nabben friade* (When Kalle of Nabben went wooing), which he had written for a Good Templar performance of 1944; and at the South Side Viking Temple, Maja Dejenberg-Anderson and the Värmlands Club amateur actors gave *Mot beräkning*, which had its first Chicago performance in 1876.[137]

A year elapsed, with some appearances by Olle i Skratthult in September 1949[138] the only reminder of earlier Swedish theatre days. Then rumors that *Vermländingarne* would be acted again became, in the fall of 1950, definite announcements. The Värmland Clubs of the North Side and the South Side and *Värmlands Nation* were sponsoring two Sunday matinées, October 22 and October 29, at Lindblom High School on the South Side and Amundsen High School on the North Side. There was less fanfare than for the 1946 revival, but there was favorable publicity in *Svenska Amerikanaren Tribunen,* and its reviews were, if brief, warmly cordial.

There were relatively few changes from the 1946 cast. Inga Maye Nordquist and Waldemar Walberg were again the Erik and Anna, and most of the character roles were carried by the experienced men and women who had played them in 1946: Paul Norling as Sven Ersson, Maja Dejenberg-Anderson as Lisa, Otto Benson and Helen Johnson as Per and Stina, and Werner Noreen as Jan Hansson. But Mr. Behmer's long time colleague, Carl Stockenberg, replaced him as director, and Nils Linde, of Viking Company and *Svenska Folkteatern* fame, was the new Löpare-Nisse. As in 1946, the dances were performed by *Danslaget National.* Limited musical support was provided by the Alenius Ensemble. To this revival the reviewer gave general praise—for music, dances, acting, costumes, and make-up. Mr. Hugo Ottoson (earlier leader of Good Templar plays) was credited with the excellence of costumes and make-up. All of the chief actors were commended, with some of the special tributes going to a lovely Anna and a Löpare-Nisse of undoubted talent. For Erik there was the traditional remark that he sang well, and that was what was expected of him. And Mr. Stockenberg received hearty thanks for the enthusiasm and energy with which he made the whole a success.

Both matinées were well attended, the second drawing a packed house, and being marked also by a more finished and more swiftly moving performance. On this occasion, Mr. Stockenberg delivered a memorial tribute to King Gustaf V of Sweden, whose death had occurred that day—just as, in 1907, performances had included tributes to King Oscar II. Also reminiscent of older days in the Swedish theatre was the limited equipment available on the high school stages. Accordingly, the often troublesome boat scene was relegated to the wings. Otherwise, the play was acted without cutting. In general, ensemble acting as well as individual performances balanced limitations, and gave evidence of the quality of the *Svenska Folkteatern* productions with which many of the actors had been associated.

It is a pity, wrote the *Svenska Amerikanaren Tribunen* reviewer after the October 29 performance, to drop the play, after so much work has been expended on it, and when there is so much evidence of interest. His suggestion that the Stockholm tradition of presenting *Vermländingarne* on

Second Christmas Day (December 26) be followed was not acted upon.[139] But one would hesitate to predict that there will not be another *Vermländingarne* in Chicago.

To see this *Vermländingarne,* to observe the genial, festive mood that filled the auditorium—from the old members of the audience, who could not count on their fingers the number of times they had seen the play, to the children, who had to have the story explained to them—and to see the joyful gusto and art with which the veteran actors performed was to become convinced even more thoroughly than before that the story of which this production was a part is worthy to be known and remembered. When one has come to know the men and women of Chicago's Swedish plays, directly or indirectly, and has felt a sense of participation in their hopes and struggles, their disappointments and successes, objectivity becomes difficult. What they achieved in creating a Swedish theatre and in keeping it alive through more than eight decades has, however, a significance entirely independent of sentiment. If their aims were never fully attained, if their repertoire and performances were not always impressive, what they accomplished far outweighs weaknesses that were dictated by circumstances. In the history of the social and cultural life of the Swedish immigrant and in the history of the foreign language theatre of America, the Chicago Swedish theatre has earned a place of honor.

CHRONOLOGICAL TABLE, CHAPTER VI

Main Performances, 1918-1919 through 1946-1947

Date	Play	Company	Place
	1918-1919		
Sept. 21, 1918	Hittebarnet	Lundgren Co. for Swedish Women's Club	Butler House
Sept. 26, 1918	En spik i nyckelhålet	S. T. actors for Verdandi Lodge, I.O.S.	Verdandi Hall
Nov. 3, 1918	Vermländingarne*	S. T.	Aryan Grotto Temple
Nov. 7, 1918	En spik i nyckelhålet	S.T. actors for Lyra Lodge,V.O.A.	Yondorf Hall
Nov. 30, 1918	En spik i nyckelhålet	S.T. actors for Verdandi Lodge, I.O.S.	Verdandi Hall
	1919-1920		
Oct. 5, 1919 (matinée and evening)	Vermländingarne*	S.T.	Aryan Grotto Temple
Oct. 18, 1919	De båda döfva	Chellman Co. for Irving Park Lodge, I.O.S.	Myrtle Masonic Temple
Nov. 9, 1919	Duvals skilsmessa*	Behmer & S.T.	Aryan Grotto Temple
Nov. 27, 1919	De båda döfva Civilklädd	Chellman Co.	Knights of Pythias Hall
Nov. 30, 1919	Civilklädd	Chellman Co. for Illinois Lodge, V.O.A.	Viking Temple
Mch. 21, 1920	Vermländingarne*	S.T.	Aryan Grotto Temple
Mch. 27, 1920	Civilklädd	Chellman Co. for Sveas Döttrar, I.O.S.	Belmont Hall
Apr. 17, 1920	En natt i Falkenberg	Behmer Co. for Rogers Park Lodge, S. F. A.	Belmont Hall
May. 8, 1920	Vermländingarne, II Civilklädd	S.T. actors for Oscar Larson	Svithiod Singing Club Hall

256

Date	Play	Company	Place
		1920-1921	
Oct. 10, 1920	*Vermländingarne**	S.T.	Aryan Grotto Temple
Oct. 31, 1920	*Den lilla sångfågeln*	Chellman Co. for Lyra Lodge,V.O.A.	Good Templar Hall
Dec. 18, 1920	*Han är inte svartsjuk* (as *En svartsjuk äktaman*)	S.D.S. for Rogers Park Lodge, S.F.A.	Belmont Hall
Jan. 30, 1921	*Öregrund-Östhammar*	S.D.S.	Aryan Grotto Temple
Feb. 26, 1921	*Hittebarnet*	Chellman Co. for Swedish Club Women's Auxiliary	Swedish Club
Mch. 12, 1921	*Hittebarnet*	Chellman Co.	Butler House
		1921-1922	
Nov. 3, 1921	*Vermländingarne**	S.T.	Aryan Grotto Temple
Dec. 4, 1921	*Kärlek och upptåg**	S.D.S.	Aryan Grotto Temple
Dec. 4, 1921	*Den lilla sångfågeln*	Chellman Co. for N. S. lodges, I.O.S.	Belmont Hall
Jan. 6, 1922	*Majorens döttrar**	Swedish Club Dramatic Co.	Swedish Club
Jan. 7, 1922	*Den lilla sångfågeln*	Chellman Co. for I.O.V.	Viking Temple
Feb. 4, 1922	*Kärlek och upptåg*	S.D.S.	Belmont Hall
Feb. 5, 1922	*Kärlek och upptåg*	S.D.S.	Calumet Club House
Feb. 12, 1922	*Duvals skilsmessa*	Swedish Club Dramatic Co.	Swedish Club
Apr. 2, 1922	*Tillfälligheter* *Paria** *Hon både sparkas och bits*	Swedish Club Dramatic Co.	Swedish Club
		1922-1923	
Oct. 1, 1922	*De båda döfva*	Chellman Co. for Engelbrecht Lodge, I.O.V.	Grace Hall

257

Date	Play	Company	Place
Nov. 5, 1922	Tre förälskade poliskonstaplar	S.T. actors for S. S. lodges, I.O.V.	Carpenter's Hall
Nov. 19, 1922	Bröllopet på Ulfåsa*	Brusell & S. T.	Powers
Dec. 9, 1922	Kärlek och upptåg*	Stockenberg Co. for Svithiod Lodge, I.O.S.	Belmont Hall
May 6, 1923	Tre förälskade poliskonstaplar	S.T. actors for lodges, I.O.S.	Belmont Hall

1923-1924

Date	Play	Company	Place
Oct. 28, 1923	Vermländingarne*	S. T. & Swedish Glee Club	Studebaker
Nov. 25, 1923	Vermländingarne	S. T. & Swedish Glee Club	Aryan Grotto Temple
Dec. 1, 1923	Kärleken på sommarnöje	Chellman Co. for Lyra Lodge,V.O.A.	Svithiod Singing Club Hall
Feb. 24, 1924	Kapten Frakassa	Ekberg Co.	Viking Temple

1924-1925

Date	Play	Company	Place
Oct. 26, 1924	Vermländingarne*	S.T.	Eighth Street
Nov. 30, 1924	En domares vedermödor	Ekberg Co. for S.S. lodges,I.O.V.	Carpenter's Hall
Dec. 13, 1924	En domares vedermödor	Ekberg Co. for Vestgötha Society	Viking Temple

1925-1926

Date	Play	Company	Place
Oct. 11, 1925	Vermländingarne*	Behmer & Swedish Glee Club	Studebaker
Mch. 14, 1926	Duvals skilsmessa*	S.D.S.	Midway Masonic Temple

1926-1927

Date	Play	Company	Place
Oct. 24, 1926	Vermländingarne*	S.T.	Auditorium
Nov. 28, 1926	Syrsan*	S.T.	Goodman
Dec. 5, 1926	Skördekalaset i Nickebo	Svenska Teaterensemble	Goodman

1927-1928

Date	Play	Company	Place
Oct. 23, 1927	Regina von Emmeritz* (as Gustaf II Adolf)	S.T. & Barcklinds	Auditorium

258

Date	Play	Company	Place
Dec. 26, 1927	Vermländingarne*	S.T. & Barcklinds	Victoria
Mch. 4, 1928	Hin och Småländingen	Barcklinds & Svenska Teaterensemble	N.S.T.H. (new)
Apr. 7, 1928	Hin och Småländingen	Barcklinds & Svenska Teaterensemble	Midway Masonic Temple

1928-1929

Date	Play	Company	Place
Oct. 7, 1928	En farlig kommission	A.T.[140]	S.S.V.T.[141]
Oct. 31, 1928	Vermländingarne*	Behmer & Swedish Glee Club	Victoria
Nov. 11, 1928	Mot beräkning*	A.T.	Maccabee Temple
Dec. 2, 1928	Godsägarens dotter	A.T.	Viking Temple
Dec. 9, 1928	En svartsjuk tok	A.T.	Maccabee Temple
Dec. 26, 1928	Nerkingarne*	Norling Co. for De Svenske	Victoria
Dec. 31, 1928	En svartsjuk tok	A.T.	Maccabee Temple
Mch. 3, 1929	Rusets fånge	A.T.	Viking Temple
Mch. 10, 1929	Rika morbror*	A.T.	Maccabee Temple
Mch. 30, 1929	Godsägarens dotter	A.T.	Grand Crossing Masonic Temple
Mch. 31, 1929	En natt i Falkenberg (as Min hustru)	A.T.	Maccabee Temple
Apr. 14, 1929	Mottagningstimmen	A.T.	Maccabee Temple
Apr. 20, 1929	Rusets fånge	A.T.	S.S.V.T.
June 23, 1929	Vermländingarne	Stockenberg & Norling Co.	Good Templar Park

1929-1930

Date	Play	Company	Place
Oct. 20, 1929	Det skadar inte!*	S.F. [142]	N.S.A.[143]
Nov. 16, 1929	Alida-Isabelle	A.T.	S.S.V.T.
Nov. 30, 1929	Rika morbror	A.T.	S.S.V.T.
Dec. 1, 1929	Rika morbror	A.T.	Maccabee Temple
Dec. 8, 1929	Tosingar*	S.F.	Belmont Hall

259

Date	Play	Company	Place
Dec. 31, 1929	Fem trappor upp	A.T.	Viking Temple
Jan. 18, 1930	Det skadar inte!	S.F.	S.S.V.T.
Jan. 19, 1930	Tre förälskade poliskonstaplar	S.F.	N.S.A.
Feb. 16, 1930	Tjuven	A.T.	S.S.V.T.
Mch. 2, 1930	Mrs. Nilsons hyresgäster	A.T.	Good Templar Hall
Mch. 2, 1930	Storstädning på Snusboulevarden	A.T.	Viking Temple
Mch. 15, 1930	Styrman Karlssons flammor*	S.F.	Victoria
Mch. 16, 1930	Chicago krönika	A.T.	Ivar Temple
Mch. 30, 1930	Den stora uppståndelsen i Kråkemåla	A.T.	Belmont Hall
Apr. 6, 1930	Mot ljuset	A.T.	Viking Temple
Apr. 19, 1930	Immigrant liv	A.T.	S.S.V.T.
May 25, 1930	Immigrant liv	A.T.	Viking Temple
June 22, 1930	Kopparslagargreven*	S.F.	Good Templar Park
Aug. 10, 1930	När byskräddaren och byskomakaren gifte bort sin pojke*	S.F.	Good Templar Park

1930-1931

Date	Play	Company	Place
Oct. 19, 1930	När byskräddaren och byskomakaren gifte bort sin pojke	S.F.	N.S.A.
Oct. 19, 1930	Immigrant liv	A.T.	Maccabee Temple
Oct. 26, 1930	Immigrant liv	A.T.	Viking Temple
Nov. 9, 1930	Sme-Olas stora synd	A.T.	Maccabee Temple
Nov. 16, 1930	En domares vedermödor	Ekberg Co.	S.S.V.T.
Nov. 16, 1930	Ebberödsbank*	S.F.	N.S.A.
Nov. 23, 1930	När byskräddaren och byskomakaren gifte bort sin pojke	S.F.	S.S.V.T.
Nov. 30, 1930	Ebberödsbank	S.F.	Maccabee Temple
Nov. 30, 1930	Prosperitetsveckan	A.T.	Viking Temple
Dec. 14, 1930	Mottagningstimmen	V.T.C.[144]	S.S.V.T.
Dec. 31, 1930	"Måtte våra barn få rika föräldrar"*	S.F.	L.A.[145]
Jan. 10, 1931	Den stora uppståndelsen i Kråkemåla	A.T.	S.S.V.T.
Jan. 17, 1931	"Måtte våra barn få rika föräldrar"	S.F.	Victoria
Feb. 1, 1931	Ebberödsbank	S.F.	Maccabee Temple
Feb. 5, 1931	Vermländingarne*	S.D.S.	Victoria
Feb. 8, 1931	Ebberödsbank	S. F.	S.S. Masonic Temple

Date	Play	Company	Place
Feb. 22, 1931	Kopparslagargreven	S. F.	N.S.A.
Mch. 8, 1931 (matinée and evening)	Kopparslagargreven*	S. F.	N.S.A.
Mch. 29, 1931	Kärlek och upptåg	V.T.C.	S.S.V.T.
Apr. 5, 1931	Vilse i lifvet	A.T.	Viking Temple
Apr. 12, 1931	A:B Strid och Frid*	S.F.	Victoria
May 31, 1931	När Bengt och Anders bytte hustrur	S.F. for De Svenske	Riverview Park
June 20, 1931	Mottagningstimmen	V.T.C.	S.S.V.T.
June 21, 1931	Majorens döttrar*	Behmer Co.	Good Templar Park

1931-1932

Date	Play	Company	Place
Oct. 3, 1931	Styrman Karlssons bröllopsresa*	S.F.	L.A.
Oct. 4, 1931	Styrman Karlssons bröllopsresa*	S.F.	L.A.
Oct. 6, 1931	En natt i Falkenberg	V.T.C.	S.S.V.T.
Oct. 18, 1931	Lustresan från Skåne* (as Familjen Trögelin)	V.T.C.	S.S.V.T.
Nov. 8, 1931	En natt i Falkenberg	V.T.C.	Belmont Hall
Nov. 15, 1931	En natt i Falkenberg	V.T.C.	S.S.V.T.
Nov. 21, 1931	En natt i Falkenberg	V.T.C.	Ivar Temple
Dec. 5, 1931	De båda direktörerna	V.T.C.	S.S.V.T.
Dec. 6, 1931	En brottslig betjent	S.F.	Belmont Hall
Dec. 31, 1931	Tosingar	V.T.C.	S.S.V.T.
Dec. 31, 1931	Söder om Rio Grande	S.F.	N.S.A.
Jan. 14, 1932	Lars Jönsa och hans käring	S.F.	Belmont Hall
Feb. 21, 1932	Tosingar	V.T.C.	Good Templar Hall
Mch. 3, 1932	Mottagningstimmen (as Doktor Hjälplös)	V.T.C.	S.S.V.T.
Mch. 6, 1932	Lars Anders och Jan Anders och deras barn*	S. F.	Belmont Hall
Apr. 16, 1932	En brottslig betjent	S. F.	Pythian Temple
Apr. 17, 1932	Per Olsson och hans käring	V.T.C.	S.S.V.T.
Apr. 23, 1932	En brottslig betjent (as Piperman i knipan)	S.F.	Rainbo Gardens
May 1, 1932	Tosingar	V.T.C.	S.S.V.T.
May 8, 1932	Civilklädd	V.T.C.	S.S.V.T.
June 5, 1932	Bröderna Östermans huskors	S.F. and De Svenske	Erhardt's Grove
June 19, 1932	Rallare	S.F.	Riverview Park
June 19, 1932	När Smed-Erik och Pligg-Jan fikk Amerikafrämmande	V.T.C.	Good Templar Park
Aug. 7, 1932	Per Olsson och hans käring	V.T.C.	Good Templar Park

261

Date	Play	Company	Place
	1932-1933		
Oct. 30, 1932	Bröderna Östermans huskors*	S.F.	L.A.
Nov. 20, 1932	Bröderna Östermans huskors	S.F.	L.A.
Dec. 8, 1932	En natt i Falkenberg	V.T.C.	Good Templar Hall
Dec. 31, 1932	Dansen på Brottskär*	S.F.	L.A.
Jan. 22, 1933	Sånt händer	S.F.	Belmont Hall
Jan. 29, 1933	Handlarns första piga*	S.F.	N.S.A.
Feb. 5, 1933	En orolig natt	A.T.	Good Templar Hall
Feb. 11, 1933	Bröderna Östermans huskors	S.F.	S.S.V.T.
Feb. 12, 1933	Kärlek och upptåg	V.T.C.	S.S.V.T.
Feb. 25, 1933	Mottagningstimmen	V.T.C.	S.S.V.T.
Feb. 26, 1933	Mottagningstimmen	V.T.C.	S.S.V.T.
Mch. 5, 1933	Torpar-Petter säljer sin käring*	S.F.	L.A.
Mch. 26, 1933	När Smed-Erik och Pligg-Jan fikk Amerikafrämmande	V.T.C.	S.S.V.T.
Apr. 16, 1933	Anton i Amerika	A.T.	Viking Temple
June 11, 1933	Flottans lilla fästmö*	S.F.	Riverview Park
	1933-1934		
Nov. 18, 1933	Halta Lena och vindögda Per*	S.F.	L.A.
Nov. 21, 1933	Kärlek och upptåg	V.T.C.	S.S.V.T.
Dec. 9, 1933	Giftermålsbyrån	S.F. for De Svenske	Verdandi Hall
Dec. 31, 1933	Den förgylda kaffegöken	S.F.	L.A.
Jan. 20, 1934	Den förgylda kaffegöken	S.F.	L.A.
Jan. 28, 1934	Den förgylda kaffegöken	S.F.	S.S.V.T.
Feb. 4, 1934	Lars Anders och Jan Anders och deras barn	S.F.	Belmont Hall
Feb. 11, 1934	När Smed-Erik och Pligg-Jan fikk Amerikafrämmande	V.T.C.	S.S.V.T.
Mch. 10, 1934	När Smed-Erik och Pligg-Jan fikk Amerikafrämmande	V.T.C.	Pythian Hall
Mch. 11, 1934	Godsägarens dotter	A.T.	S.S.V.T.
Apr. 1, 1934	När Smed-Erik och Pligg-Jan fikk Amerikafrämmande	V.T.C.	N.S.A.
May 13, 1934	Den stora uppståndelsen i Kråkemåla	A.T.	Pythian Hall
Aug. 12, 1934	Godsägarens dotter	A.T.	Linné Woods
	1934-1935		
Sept. 16, 1934	Tänk på mor	V.T.C.	Viking Temple
Sept. 23, 1934	När Smed-Erik och Pligg-Jan fikk Amerikafrämmande	V.T.C.	Belmont Hall
Oct. 14, 1934	Tänk på mor	V.T.C.	S.S.V.T.
Oct. 14, 1934	Slavarna på Molokstorp	A.T.	Viking Temple

Date	Play	Company	Place
Oct. 14, 1934	Luffarbaron*	S.F.	L.A.
Nov. 11, 1934	Kärlek och upptåg	V.T.C. for Värmlands Nation	S.S.V.T.
Nov. 25, 1934	Engelbrekt och hans Dalkarlar	Behmer Co. for W. S. Svenska Kulturförbund	Blackstone
Dec. 9, 1934	Sommarnöje på Skönlunda	S.F.	Belmont Hall
Dec. 9, 1934	När cirkusen kom til sta'n	V.T.C.	S.S.V.T.
Dec. 16, 1934	Immigrant liv	A.T.	Pythian Hall
Dec. 16, 1934	Handlarns första piga	S.F.	Belmont Hall
Dec. 31, 1934	Äktenskapsbolaget U. P. A.	S.F.	L.A.
Feb. 2, 1935	Dansen på Brottskär	S.F.	L.A.
Feb. 15, 1935	Andersson, Pettersson och Lundström*	Ekberg Co. for Viking Athletic Association	Belmont Hall
Feb. 17, 1935	Vi gå ilann i Spanien Nummer 39	S.F.	Belmont Hall
Feb. 17, 1935	Andy på nödhjälp	A.T.	Pythian Hall
Feb. 24, 1935	Tänk på mor	V.T.C.	Belmont Hall
Mch. 17, 1935	Tre förälskade poliskonstaplar	S.F. for Värmlands Club	Belmont Hall
Mch. 24, 1935	Edla Hansons friare	S.F. for De Svenske	Belmont Hall
Apr. 21, 1935	Tjuven (as Inbrottstjuven) Karolina	A.T.	Pythian Hall
June 2, 1935	Banken	A.T.	Linné Woods
June 16, 1935	För fulla segel*	S.F.	Good Templar Park
July 21, 1935	Karolina	A.T.	Linné Woods

1935-1936

Date	Play	Company	Place
Oct. 13, 1935	Trötte Theodor*	S.F.	N.S.A.
Nov. 10, 1935	När byskräddaren och byskomakaren gifte bort sin pojke	S.F.	N.S.A.
Nov. 17, 1935	Farbror Knut från Norrköping*	S.D.S.	Chicago Woman's Club
Nov. 28, 1935	Skökan rättvisan*	A.T.	S.S.V.T.
Dec. 8, 1935	För fulla segel	S.F.	N.S.A.
Dec. 15, 1935	En marknadsafton	S.F. for Swedish Athletic Association	Belmont Hall
Dec. 31, 1935	Arbetslösa Amoriner	S.F.	N.S.A.
Jan. 1, 1936	Farbror Knut från Norrköping	S.D.S.	S.S.V.T.

Date	Play	Company	Place
Feb. 16, 1936	Godsägarens dotter	A.T.	Lundquist's Hall
Mch. 1, 1936	Skökan rättvisan	A.T.	Viking Temple
Mch. 29, 1936	Skökan rättvisan	A.T.	Strummel's Hall
Apr. 5, 1936	Han hyr rum af sin betjent (as Pettersons betjent)	S.F. for De Svenske	Belmont Hall
Apr. 11, 1936	Svenska John går i land	S.F.	N.S.A.
Apr. 12, 1936	Sjömansliv	A.T.	Viking Temple
Apr. 17, 1936	En domares vedermödor*	Ekberg Co. for Brage Lodge, I.O.V.	Viking Temple (?)
May 10, 1936	Rusets fånge	A.T.	Good Templar Hall
May 17, 1936	Godsägarens dotter	A.T.	S.S.V.T.

1936-1937

Date	Play	Company	Place
Oct. 25, 1936	Svenska John går i land*	S.F.	L.A.
Nov. 26, 1936	Fädernearf	A.T.	S.S.V.T.
Dec. 31, 1936	Hur ska' det gå för Petterson?*	S.F.	L.A.
Mch. 28, 1937	Fädernearf	A.T.	Viking Temple
May 16, 1937	Hemsöborna*	S.F. with Scandinavian Labor Societies	L.A.

1937-1938

Date	Play	Company	Place
Nov. 25, 1937	Timmerflottarens son	A.T.	Viking Temple
Dec. 31, 1937	Jansson, jag älskar dej*	S.F.	N.S.A.

1938-1939

Date	Play	Company	Place
Oct. 23, 1938	Halta Lena och vindögda Per*	S.F. for N.S. Boosters Club	N.S.A.
Nov. 24, 1938	Sara vinner på lotteri	A.T.	Viking Temple
Feb. 19, 1939	Sara vinner på lotteri	A.T.	Holter's Hall
Mch. 12, 1939	Karlsson får Amerika-arv*	V.T.C.	S.S.V.T.
May 14, 1939	Karlsson får Amerika-arv	V.T.C.	Ivar Temple

1939-1940

Date	Play	Company	Place
Nov. 12, 1939	Karlsson får Amerika-arv	V.T.C. for Nordstjernan	Belmont Hall
Nov. 23, 1939	Ett tragiskt misstag	A.T.	S.S.V.T.
Dec. 31, 1939	Hemma hos Karlsons*	S.F. for Chicago Swedish Male Chorus	N.S.A.

Date	Play	Company	Place
Feb. 11, 1940	Lars Anders och Jan Anders och deras barn	S.F.	Belmont Hall
Feb. 18, 1940	Lars Anders och Jan Anders och deras barn	S.F.	S.S.V.T.
Apr. 20, 1940	Skomakar-Jacke	A.T.	10413 Michigan

1940-1941

Date	Play	Company	Place
Nov. 23, 1940	Svenska John går i land*	S.F.	L.A.
Dec. 31, 1940	En omgång till	S.F. for Chicago Swedish Male Chorus	N.S.A.

1941-1942

Date	Play	Company	Place
Dec. 31, 1941	Hur ska' det gå för Petterson?*	S.F.	L.A.

1946-1947

Date	Play	Company	Place
Oct. 27, 1946 (matinée and evening)	Vermländingarne*	Behmer Co. for Värmlands Nation	Eighth Street

1950-1951

Date	Play	Company	Place
Oct. 22, 1950	Vermländingarne*	Stockenberg Co. for Värmland Clubs	Lindblom High School
Oct. 29, 1950	Vermländingarne*	Stockenberg Co. for Värmland Clubs	Amundsen High School

265

SUPPLEMENT TO CHAPTER VI

Dates of performance and names of performing groups are given for these plays acted by groups (including travelling companies) whose performances are not included in the chronological table for the chapter. Companies are designated when possible by the name of the company or of the director; for other performances, the sponsoring organization is named. Plays not designated by number were acted also by other groups in this or a preceding period, and are listed in Section I of the Appendix, with bibliographical information. For the numbered plays, which are not listed in Section I of the Appendix, available information as to type of play, author, and date, precedes the facts of performance. Abbreviations used to indicate types of plays are explained in Section I of the Appendix.

1. *Akta er för änkor,* c. 3; Apr. 9, 1932, Swedish Club
2. *Alldeles som man tar det,* c. 1, E. R. Hedin, 1923; Apr. 27, 1929, *Myggan* Co.
   Alida-Isabelle; Mch. 4, 11, 1934, Noreen & Benson Co.; Apr. 6, 1935, Brage Lodge, I.O.V.
3. *Amanda i Lerbo ser spöken,* c.; Jan. 25, 28, 29, 1933, Leman Co.
4. *Argsinta Hans och småsinta Stina,* c. 2, Knut S. Haglöf, 1924; 1930, *Myggan* Co.
5. *August och Karolina och deras barn,* burlesque c. 1, Fridholm (Karl Reigin); Feb. 7, 8, March 13, 19, 20, 1932, Noreen & Benson Co.
6. *Auktion på manfolk,* c. 1, H. Antonius (Harald N. Andersson), 1934; Mch. 14, 1937. Värmlands Club
7. *Axéns dubbelgångare,* f. 3, Kurt Göransson, 1928; Mch. 22, 1930, Skansen Co.
8. *Barberar'n i Skrålköping,* c; Nov. 25, 1921, Brage Pleasure Club
9. *Barndop i Värmland,* c. 1, Yngve Jancke; May 21, 1932, S.F. actors
10. *Bondbröllop,* burlesque c. 1, Yngve Jancke & Einar Carlson; Feb. 21, 1932, Värmlands Club women; Apr. 28, 1932, Skansen Lodge Co., S.F.A.; Dec. 10, 1938, *Värmlands Nation*[146]
    Bror Jonathan, as *Oxhandlaren från Småland;* Mch. 18, May 13, 1934, Viking Male Chorus.
    Brottslig betjent, En; as *Piperman i knipan,* Mch. 6, 13, 1920, Olle i Skratthult Co.; Apr. 17, 1926, I.O.G.T. Co.
    Bröderna; Dec. 30, 1928, Venus Lodge, I.O.G.T.
11. *Bönder och fint folk,* c. 3, Kurt Göransson, 1927; Dec. 31, 1929, Skansen Co.
12. *Cigarr, En,* f. 1, Frans Hodell, 1860; Dec. 31, 1924, District Lodge No. 2, I.O.G.T.; as *Polykarpus Osts frieri,* Mch. 29, 1945, Stora Tuna Club
    Civilklädd; Oct. 12, 1932, Trohet Lodge, S.F.A.
    Det skadar inte!; Mch. 8, Apr. 11, 1925, Norden Co.
13. *Doktor Bloms första mottagning,* f. 1, Knut S. Haglöf, 1913; Oct. 26, 1929, *Myggan* Co.
    Domares vedermödor, En; May 18, 1932, Brage Lodge, I.O.V.
14. *Ensam,* d., Henning von Melsted, 1917; Nov. 10, 1921, Lake View Amateur Co.

266

15. *Envis käring, En,* c. 3, Kurt Göransson, 1926; Apr. 26, 1930, *Myggan* Co.

16. *Erssons pojke,* c. 3, Alfred Ebenhard, 1927; Mch. 24, 1929, Venus Lodge, I.O.G.T.; Dec. 31, 1932, Illinois Scandinavian Grand Lodge

Farlig Kommission, En; Mch. 6, 1932, Noreen & Benson Co.; Mch. 19, 1933,—

17. *Fattiga riddare, eller När bubblan sprack,* r., Einar F. Söderwall; Feb. 15, 22, 1925, Harmoni Glee Club.

18. *Fiskare Östermans sommargäst,* c. 3, Kurt Göransson, 1926; Dec. 3, 1936, Idrott Club Co.

19. *Fisket vid Valhalla Båtbiggar,* c.; Nov. 25, 1920, Brage Pleasure Club

20. *Flickorna från gamla sta'n,* r., E. Einar Andersson; Dec. 31, 1940, District Lodge No. 5, I.O.G.T.

21. *Folk i kö, Ett,* r., Paul Norling; Dec. 31, 1946, District Lodge No. 2, I.O.G.T.

22. *Folket på Sörgården,* c. 3, Kurt Göransson, 1929; June 21, 1936, N.S. I.O.G.T. Amateur Co.

23. *Friare-annons, En,* c.; Feb. 22, 1944, Tuna Club women

24. *Frithiof och Carmencita,* c. w. song, Arvid Nelson; Apr. 2, 1938, *De Svenske*

Fädernearf; Nov. 13, 1920, District Lodge No. 2, I.O.G.T.; Dec. 31, 1921, Lake View Amateur Co.; Mch. 2, 30, 1924, Jupiter Lodge, I.O.G.T.

25. *Fädernegården,* flk. play 2, Robert Bernskog, 1923; Dec. 31, 1931, District Lodge No. 2, I.O.G.T.; Mch. 20, 1932, District Lodge No. 2, I.O.G.T. and Eric Ericson Co.

26. *Fru Pett'son har blitt goodtemplare,* c. 1, Hjalmar Wernberg, 1911; Nov. 13, 1932, I.O.G.T. Co.

27. *Gamla hänger i, De,* c. 3, Kurt Göransson, 1927; Mch. 22, 1928, I.O.G.T. Amateur Co.; Feb. 2 (2), 3, 8, Mch. 8, 9, 1930, Olle i Skratthult Co.; Apr. 27, 1930, Hilma Lindblom Co.; Apr. 26, 1934, Benson Co.; Oct. 27, 1934, Vasa Society

28. *Giftermålsannonsen;* possibly a new play of the title, c. 1, by Gunnar Erlind (Ernst G. Lind), 1915; Mch. 15, 1931, Noreen & Benson Co.

Giftermålsbyrån, May 2, 1931, *De Svenske;* Dec. 9, 1933, S. F. members and *De Svenske*

29. *Glada Svensson,* f. 1, Knut S. Haglöf, 1930; Feb. 16, 1939, Framåt Lodge, I.O.G.T.

30. *Gubben Manssons testamente,* c. 3; Jan 25, 26 (2), 30, 1930, Olle i Skratthult Co.

Halta Lena och vindögda Per; Oct. 28, Nov. 4, 1928, Leman Co.

31. *Han heter August,* c. 3, Alfred Ebenhard, 1923; Apr. 25, 1937, Ankaret Lodge, I.O.G.T.

Hans tredje hustru; Feb. 7 (2), 10, 14, 1926, Leman Co.

32. *Hej svejs i lingonskogen,* c. w. song, Arvid Nelson; Oct. 15, 1933, *De Glada Våghalsarna* Co.

33. *Herre utan frack, En,* f. w. song, Richard Gustafsson, 1869; Mch. 25, 1926, *De Svenske*

34. *Hulda på Holmen och Farbror Kagge,* c. 2; Mch. 3, 13, 1935, *Värmlands Nation*

35. *Hur August lurade Lotta,* f., Knut Lövgren; May 16, 1937, Vasa Children's Club.

36. *Hårda tider;* Jan. 1, 1942, Lodbrok Lodge, I.O.V.

267

37. *Informatorn,* c., Al Cederoth; May 21, 1927, Swedish Youth Club; May 24, 1930, Alma Mater Society Amateur Co.

Jan Ersas piga; Nov. 21, 1920, Noreen & Benson Co.; Jan. 30, 1926, Noreen & Benson Co.

38. *Julafton hos Henning Svenson;* Dec. 22, 1932, Idrott Club

39. *Julafton i en fattig Svensk-Amerikansk familj;* Dec. 21, 1933, Idrott Club

40. *Järnvägsagenten och skådespelerskan;* July 2, 1926,—

41. *Kalle Pettersson No. 1 & 2,* c. 3, Knut S. Haglöf, 1914; Jan. 29, Feb. 23, 1930, *Myggan* Co.

42. *Kamraterna från landsvägen,* c. 2, Gunnar Erlind (E. G. Lind), 1934; Jan. 30, 1938, N.S. I.O.G.T. Amateur Co.; June 18, 1939, I.O.G.T. Co.

Kometen; Mch. 22, 1934, I.O.G.T. Amateur Club

43. *Kommunalstämma,* f.; May 1, 1924, Youth Club Ideal, I.O.G.T.

Konjaksagenten; Dec. 31, 1926, I.O.G.T. Amateur Co.; Mch. 12, 1927, I.O.G.T. Amateur Co.

44. *Konsten att få körkort,* c.; Feb. 16, 1939, Framåt Lodge, I.O.G.T.

45. *Krig,* d. 3, Fridolf (E. Henning Lind), 1914; May 26, 1929, Skansen Co.; Dec. 28, 1935, *Förgät-mig-ej* Lodge, I.O.G.T.

46. *Kvinnans list övergår mannens förstånd,* c. 5 scenes, 1925; 1930, *Myggan* Co.

47. *Käringa mi' kusin,* c. 3, Alfred Ebenhard, 1929; Jan. 10, 11, 18, 1931, Olle i Skratthult Co.

48. *Kärlek och affärer,* c. 3, Jean Sibelius (Tage Nilsson) 1934; Mch. 10, 1935, Einar Carlson Co.

Kärlek och upptåg; Mch. 2, 1924, I.O.G.T. Amateur Co.; Apr. 13. 1924, I.O.G.T. Amateur Co.

Kärleken på sommarnöje; July 19, 1928, Venus Lodge women, I.O.G.T.; as *Sara ljuger för sin kärlighets skull* and *Saras kärlek,* Feb. 2, 22, Mch. 8 (2), Mch. 15, 1931, Noreen & Benson Co.

49. *Kärleksäfventyr på Fälla,* c. 4; Nov. 12, 1931, Svea Lodge, I.O.S. Co.

50. *Kryckestât,* c. w. song, Paul Norling; June 18, 1944, Paul Norling Co.

Lars Anders och Jan Anders och deras barn; Mch. 6, 16, 1920, Olle i Skratthult Co.; Nov. 4 (2), 11, 18, 1923, Olle i Skratthult Co.; Mch. 1, 2, 6, 1927, Olle i Skratthult Co.; Mch. 17, 1929,—

Lars Jonsa och hans käring; Jan. 20, 1929, W.S. Amateur Co.; Mch. 2, 1929, *Värmlands Nation;* Oct. 25, 1931, Värmlands Club

51. *Lars Persa och Per Anners,* c. 3, Kurt Göransson, 1925; July 11, 1929, Skansen Co.

52. *Lefve fåfängan,* c. w. song, 2, Carl J. Moquist, 1855; Feb. 20, 1926, Norden Co. and *De Svenske*

Lilla sångfågeln, Den; Mch. 14, 1926, W. S. Lodges, V.O.A.

Liten satunge, En; Mch. 22, 1934, I.O.G.T. Amateur Co.

53. *Lustiga barberaren, Den,* c.; Apr. 24, 1932, Tuna Lodge, V.O.A.

Mamsell Sundblad vill gifta sig; as *Mamsell Lundblom . . .,* Feb 9, 11, 12 (2), 1928, Olle i Skratthult Co.; Mch. 29, 1931, N.S. Amateur Co.

54. *Mannen som ville säga sanningen,* c.; Nov. 10, 1932, Framåt Lodge Co. I.O.G.T.; May 11, 1933, I.O.G.T. Male Chorus; May 6, 1934, Norrskenet Club Amateur Co.

55. *Meklamenterna,* c. 1, Gunnar Erlind (E. G. Lind), 1920; Feb. 21, 1926, I.O.G.T. Amateur Co.

Min hustrus affärer; Nov. 29, 1925 (2), Norden Co.; Jan. 30, 1926, Norden Co.

56. *Miss Persson från U.S.A.,* c. 3, Kurt Göransson, 1934; June 20, 1937, I.O.G.T. Co.

57. *Misslyckat frieri, Ett,* c. 1, Gunnar Erlind (E. G. Lind), 1915; Nov. 26, 1931, *Förgät-mig-ej* Lodge Co., I.O.G.T.

58. *Moderskärlek,* d. 1, August Strindberg, 1894; Apr. 21, 1932, Idrott Club Co.

59. *Mor Emmas pojke ska' bortgiftas, eller No. 3333,* c. w. song, 3; Nov. 3, 6, 9, 13, 1927, Leman Co.

Mot beräkning; Nov. 28, 1928, *Värmlands Nation;* May 17, 1930, Maja Dejenberg-Anderson & Otto Benson Co.; Oct. 30, 1932, Maja Dejenberg-Anderson & Benson Co.; as *Madame Anderssons hyresgäster,* May 1, 1949, Maja Dejenberg-Anderson and Värmlands Club Co.

Mottagningstimmen; Nov. 23, 1924, Oscar II Lodge Co., I.O.G.T.; Mch. 8, 1936, Einar Carlson Co.

Natt i Falkenberg, En; Mch. 22, 1933, Trohet Lodge, S.F.A.

Nerkingarne; Dec. 6, 1925, Norden Co.; Jan. 10, 1926, Norden Co.; Dec. 26, 1929, Paul Norling Co.

60. *No. 444,* c. 3, Alfred Ebenhard, 1925; Feb. 20, Mch. 1, Apr. 26, 1936, N. S. I.O.G.T. Co.

61. *När bröllopsklockorna ringa,* f.; Nov. 1, 1930, Diana Lodge, S.F.A.

62. *När Efraim döptes,* c., possibly *Tyst Efraim,* by Gunnar Perrson, 1930; Dec. 31, 1935, Swedish Male Chorus

63. *När Kalle på Nabben friade,* c., Paul Norling; Apr. 30, Nov. 18, Dec. 31, 1944, Paul Norling Co.; May 24, 1949, Paul Norling Co.

64. *När Klickens tös fick fästman,* f. 2 scenes, Knut S. Haglöf, 1925; Dec. 27, 1930, *Myggan* Co.

65. *När Pettersonskans Frasse fungerar som hembiträde,* c. 1, Harald N. Andersson, 1934; as *Pettson fungerar som hembiträde,* Jan. 13, 1935, Einar Carlson Co.

66. *När Stulta-Nils skulle ha måg,* c. 3, Knut S. Haglöf, 1911; June 11, 1931, I.O.G.T. Co.

67. *När Svensson skulle köpa ångtröskverk,* c. 2, K—m, 1916; Nov. 30, 1929, Skansen Co.

68. *När svärmor kom,* c. 1, E. R. Hedin, 1923; Oct. 18, 1930 *Värmlands Nation*

69. *När Tekla i Finnbygda äntlit blev gift,* c.; Mch. 20, 1938, Värmlands Club

70. *När två blir ett,* c. 3, Alfred Ebenhard, 1928; Jan. 29, 1934, Ankaret Lodge, I.O.G.T.

Orolig natt, En; Feb. 6, 1932, Stjerna Lodge, S.F.A.; Mch. 12, 1932, Sundsvalls Club

71. *Pelles misslyckade frieri, eller Sven fick Svea,* c. 3; Nov. 21 (2), 24, 28 29, 1926, Apr. 7, 1927, Olle i Skratthult Co.

72. *Pepparkornen i grynvällingen, eller Vad som plockas upp i mörkret,* r., Nels L. Lindquist; Oct. 12, 1934, I.O.G.T. Male Chorus

73. *Per Hansas låta dräng,* c., Joel Järnstrom; Nov. 8, 15, 1931, Noreen & Benson Co.; Apr. 25, 1935, Highland Park Co.

Per Olsson och hans käring; Feb. 13, 17 (2), Mch. 24, 1929, Olle i Skratthult Co.

269

74. *Peter Jönssons huskors,* c. 2; Apr. 2, 1941, Chicago Swedish Male Chorus

75. *Pytt i panna,* r.; Dec. 2, 1934, Swedish Glee Club

76. *På friarstråt i Lincoln Park,* c.; Dec. 31, 1945, *De Glada Våghalsarna* Co.

77. *På Johanssons platsbyrå,* c. 1, Harald N. Andersson, 1934; Apr. 16, 1939, Stora Tuna Club

Rika morbror; Apr. 19, 1924, Venus Lodge Co., I.O.G.T.; Feb. 20, 1932, S.S. lodges, I.O.S.; Mch. 17, 1935, Viking Male Chorus

78. *Riktig kanalje, En,* f. 2 scenes, Knut S. Haglöf, 1913; Jan. 24, 1929, S.S. Amateur Co.

79. *Rättvisa. Domstolsscen,* c., Gunnar Erlind (E. G. Lind), 1920; 1930, *Myggan* Co.

80. *Sjöbergs Louisa,* c. 2, Alfred Ebenhard, 1933; Feb. 17, 18, 1934, Olle i Skratthult Co.

81. *Skoldar,* c., Paul Norling; Nov. 21, 1948, Paul Norling Co.

82. *Skottårsresonemang, Ett,* c. 1; Mch. 18, 1928, Venus Lodge women, I.O.G.T.

83. *Skådespelare sökas,* f. 1, Ossiander (Gunnar Persson), 1928; as *Artister sökas,* Feb. 19 (3), 26, 1928, Leman Co.

84. *Sköna Adolfina,* c., Paul Norling; May 25, 1946, Paul Norling Co.; and later unrecorded performances.

85. *Skördefest i Sverige,* c. 1; Aug. 16, 1941, *Svenska Klubb,* I.O.G.T.

Sme-Olas stora synd; Nov. 2, 3, Dec. 9, 11, 1927, Olle i Skratthult Co.; Apr. 27, 1933, Ankaret Lodge Co., I.O.G.T.; Nov. 24, 1934, Feb. 10, 1935, *Förgät-mig-ej* Lodge Amateurs, I.O.G.T.

86. *Snöbollskrig,* c. 1; Jan. 1936, Idrott Club

87. *Stackars karlar,* f. 1, Hedvig Nenzén-Haquinius, 1934; Mch. 7, 1937, Jupiter Lodge, I.O.G.T.

88. *Stackars Karlsson,* f. 3, Josef Karlsson, 1931; Feb. 5, 1933, Olle i Skratthult Co.

89. *Starkare, Den,* d. 1, August Strindberg, 1889; Dec. 27, 1918, *Svenska Studie Förbund.*

90. *Stora sensation, Den,* c.; Mch. 15, 1931, District Lodge No. 2, I.O.G.T.

Stora uppståndelsen i Kråkemåla, Den; Feb. 2, 1932, Linden Park Lodge, I.O.S.

91. *Stridbar ungdom,* d. 3, Harold Gote (Helga F. M. Steenhof), 1907; Apr. 28, 1923, *Svenska Studie Förbund.*

92. *Stråk-John,* d. 1, "Halvard," 1916; Feb. 20, 1927, S.S. I.O.G.T. Co.

93. *Svenskt folk, eller Myllans krafter,* d. 3, Ivar T. Thunberg, 1921; Dec. 31, 1925, District Lodge No. 2, I.O.G.T.

94. *Syföreningen,* c.; Dec. 11, 1938, Victory Lodge, I.O.V.; May 11, 1941, Stora Tuna Club women.

95. *Sånglunds födelsedagskalas,* r.; Apr. 12, 1930, *Nordstjernan* Song Club

Tjuven; Sept. 22, 1923, Lake View Amateur Co.

Tosingar; Dec. 31, 1923, I.O.G.T. Co.

Tre förälskade poliskonstaplar; Oct. 25 (2), Nov. 5, 6, 8, 1925, Olle i Skratthult Co.; Mch. 13, 1935, S. F. members; May 5, 1945, Paul Norling Co.

96. *Träffa hans käring,* c.; Apr. 24, 1943, Paul Norling Co.

97. *Två sjömän och en vacker flicka,* f.; Oct. 24, 26, 27 (2), 1929, Olle i Skratthult Co.

Tänk på mor; May 10, 1936, Nils Linde Co.

98.   *Upp och nedvände världen, Den,* d. burlesque 1, Fridholm (Karl Reigin), 1930; Nov. 5, 1932, Diana Lodge, S.F.A.

99.   *Utan yab,* r., Einar F. Söderwall; Feb. 27, 28 (2), Mch. 24, 31, Apr. 8 (2), 1923, Harmoni Glee Club
   Vermländingarne; Dec. 15, 16, 1928, Nov. 17, 1929, Olle i Skratthult Co.

100.   *Vill du veta vad som hände dig igår?* r. 1936; Dec. 31, 1936, District Lodge No. 2, I.O.G.T.

101.   *Älskogskranka och giftaslystna,* c. 2; Oct. 21, 27, 28, 1928, Olle i Skratthult Co.

102.   *Örnarna,* d. 3, Ernst Didring, 1920; Apr. 16, 1925, *Svenska Studie Förbund* and Lake View Amateur Co.; Apr. 4, 1931, Idrott Club and Lake View Dramatic Co.

APPENDIX

I. PLAYS.

This alphabetical list of plays includes all the plays for which performances are recorded in the chronological tables following Chapters II through VI, but not the 102 plays for which performances are recorded only in the alphabetical list that is a supplement to Chapter VI. For plays acted under more than one title or under a sub-title, all titles are listed, with cross references. In parentheses, after the bibliographical information, the year or years when each play was acted in Chicago are given, with the number of performances when a play was acted more than once during a year. Performances recorded in the supplement to Chapter VI for 36 of these plays are included, but not, ordinarily, performances of scenes or acts only, or performances outside Chicago. Any detailed discussion of a play in the text accompanies the account of its first performances, and some plays are briefly considered in the discussion of repertoire for the period when they were first acted.

The type of play and number of acts, when known, follow the title and precede the facts of authorship, being indicated by the following abbreviations: c.—comedy or comic; d.—drama or dramatic; dial.—dialogue; e.—epilogue; f—farce; flk.—folk; h.—historical; m.—melodrama; mon.—monologue; o.—opera; o.b.—opera bouffe; opt.—operetta; p.—play; pro.—prologue; r.—revue; rom.—romantic; t.—tableaux; trag.—tragedy or tragic; v.—vaudeville. Additional abbreviations used are: ad.—adaptation or adapted; tr.—translation or translated; w.—with.

For adaptations, the author of the Swedish version acted is normally first named, with other adaptors and original authors next given. When known, the date of the first performance of the Swedish play, original or adapted, follows. For plays known to have been published, facts as to one edition, as a rule the first edition, are then given. Bibliographical data have been obtained from sources included in the Bibliography, Section III, and, for local plays, from Chicago Swedish newspapers and persons active in the Swedish theatre. Changing usage and variant forms in sources account for inconsistencies in the spelling of Swedish titles. Spelling in earliest available bibliographical listing has ordinarily been used.

1. *A.B.C., eller En man åt Berta*, c. w. song, 1, by Johan Flodmark, from German *E.S.S.*, by C. Juin; 1866. Stockholm: Flodin, 1863 (1906, 2).

2. *Afton på "Tre Byttor", En*, c. w. song, 1, by Gustaf Wicklund. Stockholm: Bonnier, 1893 (1892; 1899, 2; 1906; 1914).

3. *Aftonsången.* Possibly *Under aftonsången*, c. w. song, 1, by Frans Hodell. Stockholm: 1865 (1870).

4. *Aktiebolaget Strid och Frid, eller Kraschen i Krångelköping*, c., 3, by Henning Ohlson-Sörby (1931).

5. *Alderman Swanson*, c. w. song, by Ernst Lindblom (1896).

6. *Alida-Isabelle, eller Tvisten om den spruckna båten*, c., 2, by Alfred Ebenhard. Vimmerby: Kristdala Tryckeri, 1926 (1929; 1934, 2; 1935).

7. *Alla möjliga roller*, c. w. song, by August Säfström, from *Alle mulige roller*, ad. by Erik Bögh, from *Froisine, ou La dernière venue*, by Jean B. Radet; 1860 (1891).

8. *Allt för guld*, m., 5, by A. B. Holson and Gustaf Wicklund; 1885 (1885).

9. *Alpflickan, eller Skatten bakom spiseln*, Alpine idyll w. song, 2. Possibly *Skatten i Jumafjellet*, d. picture in verse, by A. H. Ölander. Stockholm: O. L. Lamm, 1882 (1888).

10. *Anders Jonsa och hans käring*, c. (1913).

11. *Andersson, Pettersson och Lundström,* flk. c. w. song, 7 t., by Frans Hodell, from *Der böse geist Lumpaci Vagabundus,* by Johannes Nestroy. Stockholm: Bonnier, 1866. Also an infrequently used version, with the same title, by Gustaf Engström, 1869 (1869; 1870; 1879, 2; 1885; 1886; 1889; 1890, 2; 1891, 2; 1892, 3; 1894; 1895, 3; 1897; 1898; 1900, 2; 1904; 1905; 1906, 2; 1908; 1909, 2; 1912; 1914; 1935).

12. *Andy på nödhjälp* (1935).

13. *Anna Carlson, Stina Johnson och Lova Petterqvist,* flk. c., 7 t., by Sigyn (Ludwig Lundgren); 1894 (1894).

14. *Anna Stina i Chicago,* flk. c. w. song & dance, 4, by Ernst H. Behmer; 1899 (1899).

15. *Anton i Amerika* (1933).

16. *Arbetslösa Amoriner, eller Ledighetskommittén får semester,* r., by Arvid Nelson, Carl Stockenberg, and Oscar Ahlstrand; 1935 (1935).

17. *Arfvingen till en million!* f. w. song, 1, by Johan Flodmark, from German ad. by C. F. Tietz of *Trois gobe-mouches,* by Honoré; 1862. Stockholm: Flodin, 1862 (1870).

18. *Balen på Gröna Lund, eller Ulla skall på bal,* c. w. song & dance, 1, by August Säfström, from *Ulla skal paa bal,* by Johan L. Heiberg; 1860. Also a version by Jonas Philipsson. Stockholm: Bonnier, 1861 (1889; 1891; 1893; 1896). Acted also as *Bellman på Gröna Lund.*

19. *Banken* (1935).

20. *Barnhusbarnen, eller Verldens dom,* d., 5, by Johan Jolin; 1849. Stockholm: Bonnier, 1849 (1906).

Bellman på Gröna Lund. See *Balen på Gröna Lund.*

21. *Bengalisk tiger, En, eller Ett odjur,* c., 1, by Fredrik N. Berg, from *Et uhyre, eller Den hvite Othello,* ad. by Erik Bögh from *Un tigre du Bengal,* by Edouard Brisebarre and Marc-Michel; 1850. Stockholm: Bonnier, 1850 (1893).

22. *Bildning och natur,* May jest w. song, 1. Possibly *Konst och natur,* c., 4, by Jeanette C. G. Stjernström, from *Kunst und natur,* by Albini, 1857 (1889).

23. *Bondbröllopet, eller Huru rättarns Erik och nämndemannens Bolla fingo hvarandra,* c. (1895).

24. *Bror Jonathan, eller Oxhandlaren från Småland,* c. w. song, 2, by August Säfström, from *L'Oncle Baptiste,* ad. by Emile Souvestre from *Stadt und land,* by F. Kaiser; 1859. Stockholm: Bonnier, 1860 (1878; 1888; 1901; 1934).

25. *Brottslig betjent, En,* c., 1, by Richard Gustafson, from *Les forfaits de Pipermans,* by Alfred Duru and Henri Chivot. Stockholm: Flodin, 1869 (1885; 1894; 1920, 2; 1926; 1931; 1932, 2).

Acted also as *Piperman i knipan.*

26. *Bröderna,* 1, by E. K. (Ernest Klein) and K.E. (Karl-Erik Forsslund). Malmö, 1908 (1914, 1928).

27. *Bröderna Östermans huskors,* c., by Oscar Wennersten (1932, 3; 1933).

28. *Bröllopet på Ulfåsa,* h.d., 4, by Frans Hedberg, with music by J. A. Söderman; 1865. Stockholm: Bonnier, 1865 (1891, 2; 1892, 2; 1893; 1901; 1906; 1907; 1909; 1922).

29. *Båda direktörerna, De,* c. w. song, 1, by Frans Hodell, from *Monsieur Hercules,* ad. by Axel Bosin from *Monsieur Hercules,* by G. Belly. Stockholm: Flodin, 1866 (1869; 1887, 2; 1911, 2; 1913, 2; 1931).

30. *Båda döfva, De,* c., 1, by Bertha Spanier, from *Les deux sourds,* by Jules Moinaux and Anicet Bourgeois. Stockholm: Flodin, 1867 (1882, 2; 1896; 1903; 1906; 1917; 1918; 1919, 2; 1922).

31. *Båda rivalerna, De,* c., 1, from *Les rivaux amis,* by M. Fargeot (1891).
32. *Bättre aldrig än sent,* c. w. song, 1, by Uller (Johan F. Lundgrén); 1859; Stockholm: Flodin, 1861 (1868, 2; 1891; 1910; 1911).
Carl XII. See *Ur Carl XII:s ungdom.*
33. *Carl XII, eller Lejonet vaknar,* h.d., 3, w. e., by Frans Hedberg; 1868. Stockholm: Bonnier, 1868 (1892).
34. *Chicago krönika,* c., 1 (1930).
35. *Chicago nattetid,* c. w. song, 4, by Carl Pfeil; 1889 (1889); as *Nattetid* (1895, 2).
36. *Civilklädd,* c., 1, by Carl O. Wijkander, from German of Gust Kudelberg. Stockholm: Bonnier, 1901 (1906; 1909; 1912, 2; 1913; 1919, 2; 1920, 2; 1932, 2).
37. *Dag under smekmånaden, En,* c., 1, by Uller (Johan F. Lundgrén), from *Glüchliche flitterwochen,* by Georg Horn. Stockholm: Flodin, 1864 (1933).
38. *Dansen på Brottskär,* c. w. song, by Hjalmar Harriston (1932, 1935).
39. *"Det har jag gjort en visa om,"* c. w. song, 2, by Frans Hodell, from *"Herr Grille och hans nyeste viser,"* ad. by Erik Bögh, from *M. Jovial, ou L'Huissier chansonnier,* by M. E. G. M. Théaulon de Lambert and Adolphe Choquart. Stockholm: Flodin, 1866 (1889).
40. *Det skadar inte!* c., 3, by Frans Hedberg. Stockholm: Bonnier, 1870 (1888, 2; 1890; 1891; 1911; 1925; 1929; 1930).
41. *Direktör Striese, eller Sabinskornas bortröfvande,* c., 4, from *Der raub der Sabinerinnen,* by Franz von Schönthan (1889, 2; 1895, 2; 1907).
42. *Dockhem, Ett,* d., 3, tr. of *Et dukkehjem,* by Henrik Ibsen. Tr. by Rafaël Hertzberg, Helsingfors: Edlund, 1880; by Harald Molander, Stockholm: Loostrom & K:o., 1895 (1907).
43. *Doktor Dulcamara, eller Konsten att af basar göra tenorer,* c. o., 3, by Theodore Sjöquist, from German of Kuntze; 1894 (1894; 1895).
Doktor Hjälplös. See *Mottagningstimmen.*
44. *Domares vedermödor, En, eller Sjåarens fataliteter,* c., 1 (1891, 2; 1895; 1911, 2; 1913; 1924, 2; 1930; 1932; 1936).
45. *Drilléns operett,* c. w. song, 1, by O. Leman and G. A. Gottman, from *Aus liebe zu kunst,* by Gustav von Moser. Stockholm: Flodin, 1867 (1888; 1889; 1899; 1901; 1908).
46. *Duvals skilsmessa,* c., 3, by Ernst H. Behmer, from *Les surprises du divorce,* by Alexandre Bisson and Antony Mars; 1910 (1910; 1919; 1922; 1926).
47. *Döbeln vid Jutas,* scene, from *Döbeln vid Jutas,* poem by Johan L. Runeberg (1913, 2).
48. *Döden fadder,* saga c. w. song, 3, by August Blanche, from tr. by Wilhelm Malm of *Der töd und der wunder-doktor,* legend by Karl Haffner; 1850. Stockholm: Bonnier, 1850 (1894).
Ad. by Carl Pfeil as *The wonder doctor,* 1901, and as *A union man,* 1903.
49. *Ebberödsbank,* f. w. song, from *Ebberöd banke,* by Axel Breidahl and Axel Frische; 1923 (1930, 2; 1931, 2).
50. *Edla Hansons friare,* c., 3, by Theodore Berthel (1935).
51. *Edmond Kean,* d., 5, from *Kean,* by Alexandre Dumas, *père,* M. E. G. M. Théaulon, and F. de Courcy. By Magnus E. C. Pontin, 1840; by Gustaf af Geijerstam (1895).
52. *Emigration 1871—nyårspjes,* f., 2; 1871 (1871, 2).
53. *Engelbrekt och hans Dalkarlar,* h.d. w. music, 5, by August Blanche; 1846. Stockholm: Bonnier, 1846 (1870; 1886; 1894; 1902; 1934).

54. *Erik den fjortonde,* h. trag., 5, by Johan Börjesson; 1846. Stockholm: C. A. Bagge, 1846 (1869, Act II; 1900).

55. *Exekutionsbetjenten-poet,* c., 2, by Frans Hodell (1888). *Familjen Trögelin.* See *Lustresan från Skåne.*

56. *Farbror Knut från Norrköping,* c., 3, by Ernst H. Behmer, from *A pair of spectacles,* ad. by Sidney Grundy, from *Les petits oiseaux,* by Eugène Labiche and Delacour; 1905 (1905, 2; 1913; 1935; 1936).

57. *Farlig kommission, En,* f. w. song, 1, by Frans Hodell, from *En hemmelig lidenskab,* Danish ad. of *Pas de fumée sans feu,* by J. F. A. Bayard. Stockholm: Flodin, 1868 (1907; 1912; 1915; 1928; 1932; 1933).

58. *Fem trappor upp,* v., 1, by Frans Hodell, from *Millioner paa quisten,* Danish ad. of *Risette, ou Les millions de la mansarde,* by Edmond V. F. About; 1860. Stockholm: Flodin, 1860 (1903, 2; 1929).

59. *Fias rivaler,* c. w. song, 1, by Edward Holmer; 1895 (1895, 3).

60. *Flickan i Stadsgården,* d. w. song, 6 t., from *Flickan i Stadsgården,* novel by August Blanche (1908).

61. *Flottans lilla fästmö,* song-c., 3, by Henning Ohlson-Sörby (1933). *Folktalaren.* See *Nationaldagen.*

62. *Friare i lifsfara, En,* f. w. song, 1, by Johan Flodmark, from German of A. Hopf. Stockholm: Flodin, 1863 (1870).

63. *Friaren från Värmland,* c. w. song & dance, 3, by Johan Jolin, Stockholm: Bonnier, 1894 (1905).

64. *Friaräfventyren,* c. Credited to Uller (Johan F. Lundgrén) (1903, 2).

65. *Frithiof och Ingeborg,* o., by Carl F. Hanson, from *Frithiofs saga,* by Esaias Tegnér; 1898 (1900, 3).

66. *Fädernearf,* d., 2, by Henning Ohlson, Falköping: *Ny folkets hus dramatik,* 1918 (1920; 1921; 1924; 1936; 1937).

67. *Fäktaren i Ravenna,* o. (1876). Seemingly not *Fäktaren från Ravenna,* trag., 5, by M. A. Goldschmidt, from *Der fechter von Ravenna,* by F. Halm, 1862.

68. *För fulla segel,* song-c., by Henning Ohlson-Sörby (1935, 2).

69. *För tidigt,* c., 1, by Anders de Wahl. Stockholm: *Svenska teatern,* 1902 (1913).

70. *Förgylda kaffegöken, Den, eller Gudar på awager, eller Vassego, det är serverat,* r., by Arvid Nelson, Yngve Jancke, and Einar Carlson; 1933 (1933, 3).

71. *Förlofning, En, eller Skådespelerskan,* d., 2, by Charlotte Edgren Leffler; 1880. Stockholm: Häggstrom, 1883 (1907).

72. *Gamla Heidelberg,* d., w. song, 3, by Frans Hedberg, from *Alt Heidelberg,* by Wilhelm Meyer-Förster. Stockholm: Bonnier, 1903 (1907).

73. *Gask på fyra,* c., by "Ack" (1912, 2; 1914; 1915). *Giftermålsannonsen.* See *Magister Bläckstadius.*

74. *Giftermålsbyrån,* c. 1, by John Edström. *Amatörteater,* 1926 (1933).

75. *Godsägarens dotter,* d., 1, by Per Nelson (Allan Wallenius). Stockholm: *Arbetarteatern,* 1929 (1928; 1929; 1934, 2; 1936, 2).

76. *Grannarne,* scenic dial., 1, by August Blanche, from French idea; 1850. Stockholm: Bonnier, 1853 (1870, in Galesburg and Princeton, Ill.; 1906).

77. *Grefven af Monte Christo,* d., from *Monte Cristo,* by Alexandre Dumas, *père* (1896, 2).

Gustaf II Adolf och Regina von Emmeritz. See *Regina von Emmeritz.*

78. *Gustaf Vasa,* h.d. (1896). Possibly *Gustaf Eriksson Wasa,* h.d., 5, by O. U. Torsslow, from *Gustaf Wasa,* by A. F. von Kotzebue, 1837; or *Gustaf Wasa,* lyric trag., 3, by J. H. Kellgren, 1786 (1896).

275

79. *Gustaf Vasa,* h.d., 5, by August Strindberg; 1899. Stockholm: Gernandt, 1899 (1912).

80. *Gästgifvarmor,* c., by Bruno E. Höckert; 1895 (1895).

81. *Halta Lena och vindögda Per,* flk. c., 4, by Ernst Fastbom (1928; 1933; 1938).

82. *Hamlet,* trag., 5, by William Shakespeare. Possibly Per A. Granberg's ad. of tr. by G. F. Åkerhjelm, 1819; or Nils Arfvidsson's ad. of tr. by Carl A. Hagberg, 1853 (1885).

83. *Han hyr rum af sin betjent, eller Pettersons betjent,* c., 1, by Uller (Johan F. Lundgrén), from *Zur miethe beim bedienten,* ad. by Theodor Gassman, from *En pension chez son groom,* by Marc-Michel and Eugène Labiche. Stockholm: Flodin, 1863 (1869; 1906, 2; 1910).

84. *Han är inte svartsjuk,* c., 1, by J. F. I. Högfeldt, from tr. by Louise G. Stjernström of *Er ist nicht eifersüchtig,* by Alexander Elsz, from *Pas jaloux,* by Laurencin and Lubize; 1862, (1903, 2; 1904, 2; 1905; 1907; 1908, 2; 1909; 1912; 1913; 1914, 2; 1920).

Acted also as *En svartsjuk äktaman.*

85. *Handlarns första piga,* c., 3, by Arvid Nelson; 1933 (1933; 1934).

86. *Hans tredje hustru,* c. w. song, 1, by Johan Flodmark, from *Seine dritte! oder Amerika und Spandau,* by E. Pohl; 1862 (1870, 2: 1889; 1898; 1899; 1926, 4).

87. *Hemma hos Karlsons,* c., by Arvid Nelson and Yngve Jancke; 1939 (1939).

88. *Hemsöborna,* d., 4, by August Strindberg, from *Hemsöborna,* novel by August Strindberg; 1889 (1937).

89. *Herr Dardanell och hans upptåg på landet,* c. w. music, 4, by August Blanche, from tr. by Lars A. Malmgren of *Eulenspiegel, oder Schabernack über schabernack,* by Johannes Nestroy; 1846. Stockholm: Bonnier, 1847 (1879; 1893; 1896, 3; 1898, 2; 1900; 1907).

90. *Herr Larssons resa till landtbruksmötet,* c. w. song, 2, by Frans Hodell. Stockholm: Flodin, 1868 (1887, 2).

91. *Herr Petter Jönsons resa till Amerika,* c. Possibly by Magnus Elmblad (1875).

92. *Herrskap och tjenstefolk,* c. w. song, 3, by Ludwig Josephson, from *Les domestiques,* by Grangé and Raimond Deslandes; 1863 (1908).

93. *Hin och Småländingen,* saga c., pro. & 4, by Frans Hedberg. Stockholm: Bonnier, 1906 (1895, 3; 1928, 2).

Ad. by Carl Pfeil as *A devil and a Swede,* 1900.

94. *Hittebarnet,* c. w. song, 2, by August Blanche, from *Roquelain à la recherche d'un père,* by J. F. A. Bayard and A. F. Varner; 1847. Stockholm: Bonnier, 1848 (1884; 1891, 2; 1897; 1906, 2; 1911; 1917; 1918; 1921, 2).

95. *Hjärtesorg,* d., 1, by Alfred Stenhagen, from *Jean-Marie,* by André Theuriet. Norrköping: Stenhagen, 1899 (1907).

96. *Hon både sparkas och bits,* f., 1, by Sartoris. Credited to W. T. Strand in 1922 (1891, 2: 1892, 2; 1903; 1904; 1911, 3; 1922).

97. *Hon vill inte gifta sig,* c., 1, by Gustaf Fredrikson, from German of Otto Möller. Stockholm: Bonnier, 1892 (1907; 1908; 1914).

98. *Hos fotografen,* c., 1 (1896).

99. *Hur ska' det gå för Petterson?* c., 3, by Sigge Fischer (1936; 1941).

100. *Husvill för sista gången,* c. w. song, 3, by Gustaf Engström. Stockholm: Flodin, 1866 (1868, 2; 1913).

101. *Hvita halsdukan, Den,* c., 1, by Frans Hedberg, from *La cravate blanche,* by Edmond Gondinet; 1868. Stockholm: Bonnier, 1884 (1887).

102. *I första klassens väntsal,* c., 1, by Nathalia and Bertha Spanier, from *Im wartesalon I klasse,* by Hugo Müller. Stockholm: Flodin, 1866 (1908).

103. *I klädlogen,* f. w. song, 1, by Karl J. Warburg, from *Skrädderens debut,* by Erik Bögh. Stockholm: Flodin, 1875 (1882).

104. *I telefon,* bagatelle, 1, Ernst Ahlgren. *Illustrerad Svensk Familj-Journal,* 1887 (1912).

105. *"I tjenst åstundas,"* f., 1, by Robert H. Bachmann, from *On demande des domestiques,* by Henri Chivot and Alfred Duru; 1863 (1868; 1881, 2; 1903). *Inbrottstjuven.* See *Tjuven.*

106. *Immigrant liv,* c., 2, by Werner Wenberg (or Wiberg) (1930, 4; 1934).

107. *Jag känner till politiken, jag!* f. w. song, 1, by Frans Hodell, from *Cabinetssecretæren* by Erik Bögh. Stockholm: Flodin, 1865 (1885).

108. *Jan Ersas piga,* c., 1, by Werner Noreen and Otto Benson (1918; 1920; 1926).

109. *Jansson, jag älskar dej,* c., 3, by Fritiof Hedvall (1937).

110. *Jeppe på bjerget, eller Den förvandlade bonde,* c., 5, by Ludvig Holberg, 1722. Tr. by Albert Alberg; (1893, 4; 1895; 1896).

111. *Jernbäraren,* d., 3, by August Blanche, from *Jernbäraren,* novel by August Blanche; 1866. Stockholm: Bonnier, 1877 (1885; 1891; 1892; 1896).

112. *Jorden rundt på 80 dagar,* d. travel adventure, 14 t., by Birger Schöldström, from ad. by Erik Bögh of *Le tour du monde en 80 jours,* by Jules Verne and d'Ennery. Stockholm: Associations Boktryckeri, 1876 (1891, 2; 1894, 2).

113. *Kapten Crona,* d., 2, by Henrik Molander. Stockholm: Edm. Janse och Co., 1893 (1897).

114. *Kapten Frakassa,* opt., 1, by Ernst Ekberg (1924).

115. *Karl Sabelträff och hans rivaler,* c. w. song, 1, by Herman Martinsson. Stockholm: Bonnier, 1861 (1906; 1909; 1915).

116. *Karolina,* c. (1935, 2).

117. *Karlsson får Amerika-arv,* c., 3, by Kurt Göransson, Borlänge, 1932 (1939, 3).

118. *Kolingarnas lustresa i Amerika,* c. w. song, by Carl Atterling; 1912 (1912).

119. *Komedi, En, eller Två hustrur med endast en stackars man,* c., 3, by Johan Jolin; 1845. Stockholm: Abr. Lundquist, 1845 (1888; 1895; 1899, 3). *Komedianterna.* See *Resande teatersällskap, Ett.*

120. *Kometen,* c., 1, by Karl-Erik Forsslund. Malmö: *Folkets Hus Dramatik,* 1909 (1913, 1934).

121. *Konjaksagenten,* d., 2, by Sten (J. G. Danielsson). Stockholm, 1897 (1915; 1917; 1926; 1927).

122. *Kopparslagargreven,* c. w. song, by Henning Ohlson-Sörby (1930; 1931, 3).

123. *Kronjuvelerna på Nordsidan,* c. w. song, 4, by Gustaf Wicklund; 1883 (1883).

124. *Kungen och gatsångerskan,* o.b., 2, by Richard A. Gustafson, from *Perichole,* by Henri Meilhac and Ludovic Halévy w. music by Jacques Offenbach, Stockholm: Bonnier, 1869 (1895, 2). Acted as *Kungen och gatusångerskan.*

125. *Kärlek och upptåg,* c. w. song, 3, by Uller (Johan F. Lundgrén) 1860. Stockholm: *Bibliothek för Teatervänner,* 1860 (1901, 3; 1912; 1921; 1922, 3; 1924, 2; 1931; 1933, 2; 1934).

126. *Kärleken på sommarnöje,* c. w. song, 1, by Frans Hodell. Stockholm: Bonnier, 1862 (1878; 1906; 1916; 1917; 1918; 1923; 1928; 1931, 5). Acted also as *Sara ljuger för sin kärleks skull* and *Saras kärleksäfventyr.*

127. *Lars Anders och Jan Anders och deras barn,* flk. c., 3, by Gustaf af Geijerstam; 1894. Stockholm: Bonnier, 1894 (1907; 1910; 1911; 1913, 2; 1917; 1920, 2; 1923, 4; 1927, 3; 1929; 1932; 1934; 1940, 2).

128. *Lars Johnson och hans hustru,* c. (1913).

129. *Lars Jonsa och hans käring,* c., 2, by Knut S. Haglöf. Borlänge: Hasselkvist & C:os Tryckeri, 1911 (1929, 2; 1931; 1932).

Lasse och Stina. See *Nerkingarne.*

130. *Lasse-Maja,* flk. c. w. song and dance, 7 t., by M. Ringh (1893, 2).

131. *Lifvet på landet,* c., 5, by Frans Hedberg, from *Ur meine stromtid (Abendteuer des Entspekter Bräsig),* fiction by Fritz Reuter (1903, 2; 1906; 1909; 1910; 1911; 1914).

132. *Lilla helgonet,* opt., 3, from *Mam'zelle Nitouche,* by Henri Meilhac and Moiser P. Millaud. Unknown adaptor, 1894; ad. by Gustaf Wicklund, 1899 (1894, 2; 1899).

133. *Lilla sångfågeln, Den,* c. w. song, 1, by A. E. Hellgren, from *Singvögelchen,* by Eduard Jacobsen. Stockholm, 1869 (1888; 1899; 1907; 1908; 1910; 1920; 1921; 1922; 1926).

134. *Liten satunge, En,* v., 1, by Ludwig Josephson, from *Une fille terrible,* by Eugène Deligny; 1862. Stockholm: *Bibliothek för Teatervänner,* 1862 (1869, 2; 1934).

135. *Ljungby Horn,* saga d. w. song, 5. Possibly related to *Ljungby Horn och pipa,* rom. d. w. song, 3, by A. G. Silfverstolpe, 1858 (1902; 1905; 1909; 1914).

Lotte. See *Mot beräkning.*

136. *Luffarbaronen,* opt. (1934).

137. *Lustresan från Skåne, eller Familjen Trögelin,* c. w. song, 2, by Frans Hodell. Stockholm, 1870 (1876; 1886; 1891; 1931).

138. *Lycko-Pers resa,* saga d., 5, by August Strindberg; 1883. Stockholm: Bonnier, 1882 (1899; 1900).

139. *Löftet,* d., 3, by Rose Carlson (1913).

140. *Löjen och tårar,* flk. c. w. song, 3, by Johan Jolin, from *Das volk, wie's weint und lacht,* ad. by Ottaker Frans Ebergsberg and David Kalisch from *Paris qui pleure et Paris qui rit,* by Laurencin and Cormon; 1862. Stockholm: C. M. Thimgren, 1862, (1905; 1908).

Madame Anderssons hyresgäster. See *Mot beräkning.*

141. *Magister Bläckstadius, eller Giftermålsannonsen,* c. w. song, 2, by August Blanche, from *Aprilsnarrene, eller Intriguen i skolen* and *Et eventyr i Rosenborghave,* by Johan L. Heiberg; 1844. Stockholm: Hierta, 1846 (1901; 1931).

142. *Majbruden,* c. w. song, 1, by Gustaf Wicklund; 1888 (1888).

143. *Majdag i det gamla hemmet, En* (1868).

144. *Majorens döttrar,* c., 3, by Frans Hedberg. Stockholm: Bonnier, 1871 (1880; 1922; 1931).

145. *Malins korgar,* v. mon. w. song, 1, by August Säfström, from a Danish idea; 1850 (1870, in Galesburg and Princeton, Ill.).

146. *Mamsell Garibaldi, eller Inga herrar! Inga herrar!* f. w. song, 1, by Rudolf Wall and August Säfström, from *Valeur et Compagnie,* by Jean Bayard and Devorme; 1859. Stockholm: Bonnier, 1859 (1876).
Mamsell Lundblom vill gifta sig. See *M:ll Sundblad vill gifta sig.*

147. *M:ll Sundblad vill gifta sig,* c., 1, by Bertha Spanier, from the French. Stockholm: Flodin, 1865 (1870; 1928, 4; 1931).
Acted also as *Mamsell Lundblom vill gifta sig.*

148. *Marknadsafton, En,* flk. c., 1, by Vilhelm Moberg. Stockholm: *Svenska Teatern,* 1930 (1935).

149. *Menniskovän, En,* c., 2 t., by Uller (Johan F. Lundgrén), from *Jeremias Grille,* by E. Pohl. Stockholm: Flodin, 1866 (1869).

150. *Midsommarnatt i Dalarne, En,* d. idyll w. song, by August Kloo and Elis W. Lindblad, from *Huldrebakken,* by Erik Bögh; 1854. Stockholm: Bonnier, 1854 (1869, 2; 1891; 1901; 1907).

151. *Min gamla hatt,* c. mon. w. song, 1, by Frans Hodell; 1862. Stockholm: Flodin, 1862 (1906).
Min hustru. See *Natt i Falkenberg, En.*

152. *Min hustrus affärer,* c. w. song, 1, by Frans Hodell, from *Ein toilettengeschichtchen,* ad. by C. A. Görner, from the French; 1861. Stockholm: Flodin, 1862 (1862, 2; 1888; 1925, 2; 1926).

153. *Misstag på misstag,* c., 1, by Herman A. Kullberg, from *Missverständnisse,* by Ernst A. von Steigentesch; 1817 (1899).

154. *Mjuka tjenare! eller Halfidioten,* c. w. song, 2, by Frans Hodell, from *Eine fixe idée,* by Moritz A. Grandjean. Stockholm: Flodin, 1865 (1887).

155. *Mot beräkning, eller Lotte, eller Madame Anderssons hyresgäster,* c. w. song, 1, by Aron Jonason, from *Store Bededagsaften,* ad. by F. Jansen, from the French. Stockholm: Flodin, 1871 (1876, 2; 1889; 1893; 1894; 1907; 1914; 1915; 1928, 2; 1930; 1932; 1949).

156. *Mot ljuset,* d., 2, by Harald Henriksson. Stockholm: *Arbetarteatern.* 1927 (1930).

157. *Mottagningstimmen,* f., 1, by Bertha Spanier, from *Die sprechstunde,* by A. Reich. Stockholm: Flodin, 1868 (1896; 1911; 1917; 1924; 1929; 1930; 1931; 1932; 1933, 2; 1936).
Acted also as *Doktor Hjälplös.*
Piperman i knipan. See *Brottslig betjent, En.*

158. *Mrs. Nilsons hyresgäster,* c. (1930).

159. *Mäster Smith, eller Aristokrater äro vi alla,* d., 5, by Johan Jolin; 1847. Stockholm: Bonnier, 1847 (1906).

160. *"Måtte våra barn få rika föräldrar," eller Svenska folkets underbara öden,* r., 3, by Thore Österberg and Carl Stockenberg; 1930 (1930; 1931).

161. *Nationaldagen, eller Den importerade älskaren,* c. w. song, 3 t., by Ville Åkerberg; 1889 (1889).
Also called *Folktalaren.*

162. *Natt i Falkenberg, En, eller Min hustru,* f. w. song, 1, by Jonas Philipsson, from *En nat i Roeskilde,* ad. by Hans Christian Andersen, from *Une chambre à deux lits,* by Charles V. Varin and Louis Lefèvre; 1850. Göteborg: Ph. Meijer, 1851 (1886; 1893; 1894; 1903, 2; 1904, 2; 1912; 1914; 1915; 1916; 1920; 1929; 1931, 4; 1932; 1933).
Acted also as *En natt i Falköping.*
Natt i Falköping, En. See *Natt i Falkenberg, En.*
Nattetid. See *Chicago nattetid.*

279

163. *Nerkingarne,* flk. d. w. song, 3, by Axel Anrep. Stockholm: Skoglund, 1872 (1888; 1890; 1892, 2; 1893; 1894; 1900; 1901; 1902; 1903; 1906; 1910; 1912; 1913; 1925; 1926, 2; 1928).
Scenes from *Nerkingarne* acted as *Lasse och Stina* and *Stina och Lasse.*

164. *Numero ett, rundt om hörnet, eller En mörkblå rock med perlemor-knappar,* f., 1, by Karl J. Warburg, from *Number one, round the corner,* by W. Brough. Stockholm: Flodin, 1875 (1914).

165. *Nummer 39,* e., 1, by Birger Mörner. Stockholm, in *Iduns Julnisse,* 1901 (1935).

166. *Nyårsnatt på Hotell Svea,* New Year's jest w. song (1896).

167. *Nyårsnatten,* d., 1, by Axel Bosin, from *Die neujahrsnacht,* by Julian R. Benedix. Stockholm: Flodin, 1875 (1903).

168. *Nyårsnatts dröm i Chicago, En,* f. w. song, by Calle Dunkel (Charles Eklund), from *Söndags-Nisse;* 1870 (1870).

169. *När Bengt och Anders bytte hustrur,* c. (1931).

170. *När bojorna brista,* d., 3, by G. Adolv Olsson. Gävle: Hudiksvall, 1908 (1915, 2; 1918).

171. *När byskräddaren och byskomakaren gifte bort sin pojke,* c., 3, by Björn Hodell (1930, 3; 1935).

172. *När cirkusen kom till sta'n,* c. (1934).

173. *När Smed-Erik och Pligg-Jan fick Amerikafrämmande,* flk. c., 3, by Alfred Ebenhard. Vimmerby: Kristdala Tryckeri, 1932 (1932; 1933; 1934, 4).

174. *Obrottslig tystlåtenhet,* v., 1, by Birger Schöldström, from *Cousine Lotte,* by C. M. Wengel. Stockholm: Flodin, 1868 (1870).

175. *Odåga, En,* c., 4, by Frans Hedberg, from *Le tourbillon,* by Michel Carré and Raimond Deslandes. Stockholm: Bonnier, 1867 (1891).

176. *Omgång till, En, eller Fram på småtimmarne,* r., 4 t., by Arvid Nelson and Yngve Jancke; 1940 (1940).

177. *Ondes besegrare, Den,* flk. c. w. song, 5, by Jeanette C. G. Stjernström, from *Fandens overmand,* ad. by Thomas Overskou, from *Le fils de la vierge,* by Mélesville; 1855. Stockholm: Bonnier, 1857 (1888; 1893; 1906).

178. *Oraklet i Grönköping,* c. (1915).

179. *Orolig natt, En,* c., 1, by Isidor Lundström. Stockholm: Flodin, 1871 (1903; 1907; 1912; 1914; 1932, 2; 1933).

180. *Paria,* d., 1, by August Strindberg, from *Paria,* story by Ola Hansson. Stockholm, 1889 (1914; 1915; 1922).

181. *Pariserpojken,* c. w. song, 2, by Fredrik N. Berg, from *Le gamin de Paris,* by J. F. A. Bayard and Emile L. Vanderburch; 1837. Stockholm: Typograf-förening, 1837 (1909).
Acted as *Parispojken.*

182. *Pelikanen,* d., 1, by August Strindberg, 1907. Stockholm: Aktiebolaget Ljus, 1907 (1915, 2).

183. *Pelle Grönlunds bryggeri,* c., 4 (1907).

184. *Pelle Janssons äfventyr,* m., 4, by Leopold Chellman (Kjellman); 1903 (1903).

185. *Pelle Jönsons rivaler,* c., 1 (1905).

186. *Pelle Pihlqvists Amerika-resa,* c. w. song, 3, by Ernst Lindblom; 1890 (1890, 2).

187. *Pelles första natt i Amerika,* c., 1, by Carl Wennberg; 1892 (1892).

188. *Per Olsson och hans käring*, flk. c., 3, by Gustaf af Geijerstam; 1894. Stockholm: Bonnier, 1894 (1900, 2; 1906; 1929, 4; 1932, 2).

Pettersons betjent. See *Han hyr rum af sin betjent.*

189. *Pinafore*, c. op., 2, by Gustaf Wicklund, from *H.M.S. Pinafore, or The lass that loved a sailor*, by W. S. Gilbert and A. S. Sullivan; 1896 (1896; 1897; 1899; 1900).

Piperman i knipan. See *Brottslig betjent, En.*

190. *Positivhataren*, c. w. song, 4, by August Blanche; 1843. Stockholm: Hörbergska Tryckeri, 1843 (1893).

191. *Preciosa*, rom. d. w. song & dance, 4, by Per Ad. Granberg, from *Preciosa*, ad. by P. A. Wolff, w. music by Carl Maria von Weber, from *Gitanilla Preciosa*, by Miguel de Cervantes; 1824. Stockholm, 1824 (1887; 1888).

192. *Prins Pippi och Fröken Fiffi*, opt., 1, by Birger Schöldström, from *Prins Pipi och Fröken Titi*, ad. by Erik Bögh, from *L'Ile Tulipan*, by Henri Chivot and Alfred Duru, w. music by Jacques Offenbach and C. R. Littmarck. Stockholm: Flodin, 1871 (1899, 3; 1902).

193. *Prosperitetsveckan*, d. (1930).

194. *Punkt för punkt*, c., 1, by Bertha and Nathalia Spanier, from *Le serment d'Horace*, by Henri Murger; 1861. Stockholm: Flodin, 1862 (1869; 1916, 2).

195. *På första Maj*, c. w. song, 1, by Gustaf Wicklund; 1886 (1886).

196. *Påsk*, d., 3, by August Strindberg; 1901. Stockholm: Gernandt, 1901 (1913, 3; 1918).

197. *Rallare*, c., by Henning Ohlson-Sörby (1932).

198. *Ransakningsmålet*, c., 1, by W. Styrlander, Gefle: Ahlström och Cederbergs Tryckeri, 1893 (1896).

199. *Regementets dotter*, c.o., 2, by Niklas af Wetterstedt, from *La fille du régiment*, by J. H. V. de Saint-Georges and J. A. F. Bayard, w. music by Gaetano Donizetti; 1845. Stockholm: Abr. Hirsch, 1845 (1906, Act II).

200. *Regina von Emmeritz*, h.d., 5, by Zacharias Topelius, w. music by J. A. Söderman; 1853. Stockholm: Bonnier, 1854 (1889; 1890; 1893; 1898; 1906, 2; 1908; 1927).

Acted also as *Gustaf II Adolf och Regina von Emmeritz.*

201. *Resande teatersällskap, Ett, eller En tragedi i Vimmerby, eller Komedianterna*, f. w. music, 2, by August Blanche, in part from *Le roman comique*, ad. by d'Ennery, Cormon, and Romain, from *Le roman comique*, by Paul Scarron; 1848. Stockholm: Bonnier, 1881 (1881; 1891).

202. *Rika morbror*, c. w. song, 2, by August Blanche; 1845. Stockholm: Bonnier, 1846 (1878; 1891; 1896; 1898; 1924; 1929, 3; 1932; 1935).

203. *Rochus Pumpernickel*, f. w. song, 3, by J. J. Askenbom, from *Rochus Pumpernickel*, by Matthias Stegmayer; 1842. Stockholm: Gust. Rahms Förlag, 1857 (1879).

204. *Rosen på Tistelön*, d., 5, ad. by Mauritz Cramaer, as *Brottslingarne*, from *Rosen på Tistelön*, novel by Emilie Flygare Carlén. Stockholm: Hörbergska Tr., 1843 (1907).

205. *Rospiggarna*, flk. c. w. song and dance, 4, by Frans Hedberg. Stockholm: Bonnier, 1884 (1908).

206. *Rum att hyra*, c., 1, from *"Furnished Apartment,"* by Cormon and Grangé. Ad. by Jeanette G. Stjernström, 1855; by Axel Bosin, Stockholm: Flodin, 1863 (1904).

207. *Rum att hyra, Ett*, c. w. song, 1, by Frans Hodell; 1860. Stockholm: Flodin, 1860 (1876; 1917).

208. *Rum för resande, Ett,* c., 1, by Lars A. Malmgren, from *Eine meublırte wohnung,* by C. A. Görner; 1859 (1871, 3).

209. *Rusets fånge,* d., 1, by Hinke (Bernhard Henrik) Bergegren. Stockholm: Södertelje Tryckeri, 1911 (1915; 1929; 1936).

210. *Rådhusrätten* (1914).

Sabinskornas bortröfvande. See *Direktör Striese.*

211. *Samhällsdanaren,* c., by Magnus Elmblad (1870's).

Sara ljuger för sin kärleks skull. See *Kärleken på sommarnöje.*

212. *Sara vinner på lotteri,* flk. c. (1938; 1939).

Saras kärleksäfventyr. See *Kärleken på sommarnöje.*

213. *Sax, taylor på dekis,* c., 1, by Gus Higgins; 1896 (1896).

214. *Sjömansliv,* 2 (1936).

215. *Skal och kärna, eller En man af verld och en man af värde,* d., 1, by Johan Jolin; 1846. Stockholm: Bonnier, 1866 (1891).

Skomakar-Jacke. See *Skomakar-Kalle.*

216. *Skomakar-Kalle, eller Prästen,* c., 1, by Knut S. Haglöf. Borlänge: *Dalarnes Tidnings* Boktryckeri, 1921 (1940).

Acted as *Skomakar-Jacke.*

Skådespelerskan. See *Förlofning, En.*

217. *Sköflad lycka.* Credited to Victorien Sardou (1893).

218. *Skökan rättvisan,* d., 4, by Hinke (Bernhard Henrik) Bergegren. In *Hinke 65 år,* Stockholm: Fram, 1926 (1935; 1936, 2).

219. *Skördekalaset i Nickebo,* r., 3, by Ernst Hägerström (1926).

220. *Slavarna på Molokstorp,* d., 3, by Wilfred Schober (V. Schöberg). Karlskrona: Tryckeri Föreningen "Blekinges" Tryckeri, 1907 (1934).

221. *Sme-Olas stora synd,* c., 3, by Alfred Ebenhard. Vimmerby: Kristdala Tryckeri, 1926 (1927, 4; 1930; 1933; 1934; 1935).

222. *Smålandsknekten,* flk. c., 3, by August Bondeson; 1894. Stockholm: Bonnier, 1894 (1901).

223. *Snarka,* c., 1 (1900).

224. *Sockenskräddaren,* mon. w. song, 1, by G. Bothén (Nétob); 1866 (1868).

225. *Sommarnöje på Skönlunda,* c., 1 (1934).

226. *Sparlakanslexor,* c., 1, by Knut Almlöf, from *Kandels gardinenspredigten,* by Gustaf von Moser. Stockholm: Bonnier, 1872 (1888; 1891; 1894; 1896; 1898; 1901; 1902; 1917).

227. *Spik i nyckelhålet, En,* c., 1, by Bertha Spanier Straube, from *La clé sous le paillasson,* by Eugène Grangé, Emile de Najac, and Edmond F. V. About. Stockholm: Bonnier, 1867 (1907; 1914; 1917; 1918, 3).

228. *Sqvallersystrarne,* d. sketch, 3, by Johan Jolin. In *Linnea,* 1864 (1904).

229. *Sten Stenson Stéen från Eslöf,* c., 3, by John Wigfors; 1903 (1911, 2; 1912).

Stina och Lasse. See *Nerkingarne.*

230. *Stockholms-mamsell, En,* c. mon. w. song, 1, by Frans Hodell; 1863. Stockholm: Flodin, 1864 (1868).

231. *Stora uppståndelsen i Kråkemåla, Den,* c. Possibly related to *Kråkemåla marknad, eller Rosen från herregården,* c., 3, by Fridolf (Henning Lind), Falun, 1923 (1930; 1931; 1932; 1934).

232. *Storstädning på Snusboulevarden,* c. (1930).

233. *Styrman Karlssons bröllopsresa,* c. w. song, by Björn Hodell, from *Styrman Karlssons bröllopsresa,* novel by Sigge (Sigfrid) N. Strömberg (1931, 2).

234. *Styrman Karlssons flammor*, c. w. song, by Björn Hodell, from *Styrman Karlssons flammor*, novel by Sigge (Sigfrid) N. Strömberg (1930).

235. *Svart på hvitt, eller Fruntimmerna på öfverblefna chartan*, c., 2, by Carl Envallsson, from *Le dédit*, by C. R. Dufresny; 1791 (1902).

236. *Svartsjuk tok, En*, c. w. song, 1, by Uller (Johan F. Lundgrén); 1859. Stockholm: Bonnier, 1859 (1878; 1914; 1917; 1928, 2).
Svartsjuk äktaman, En. See *Han är inte svartsjuk.*

237. *Sven och liten Anna*, flk. c. w. song, 3, by Herman Martinsson; 1858. Stockholm, Bonnier, 1861 (1901; 1909).
Svenska folkets underbara öden. See *"Måtte våra barn få rika föräldrar."*

238. *Svenska John går i land*, c., by Henning Ohlson-Sörby, (1936, 2; 1940).

239. *Svenskarne på Cuba*, d., 4 t., by Albert Alberg; 1898 (1898, 2).

240. *Svärfar*, c., 4, by Gustaf af Geijerstam; 1888. Stockholm: Bonnier, 1888 (1892; 1904).

241. *Syfröknarna*, flk. c. w. song, 8 t., by Frans Hodell, from *Eine leichte person*, by Ant. Bittner. Stockholm: Bonnier, 1869 (1884).

242. *Syndabocken*, c., 3, by Ernst H. Behmer, from *Das opferlamm*, by Paul R. Lehnhard; 1911 (1911).

243. *Syrsan*, c., 4, from *Fanchon, oder Die grille*, ad. by Charlotte Birch-Pfeiffer, from *La petite Fadette*, novel by George Sand. Tr. by W. Swenson, 1858; credited to August Blanche and to Frans Hodell (1908; 1926).

244. *Så tuktas en argbigga*, c., 5, from *The taming of the shrew*, by William Shakespeare. Ad. by Louise G. Stjernström, from tr. by Carl A. Hagberg, 1860; by Wilh. Bolin, from tr. by Carl A. Hagberg, ca. 1880 (1904).

245. *Sånt händer*, f., 2, t., credited to Uller (Johan F. Lundgrén) (1933).

246. *Sällskapsglaset*, d., 5, from *The social glass*, by T. Trask Woodward (1894, 2; 1913).

247. *Sätt att fria, Ett*, f., 1, by L. Drowtey (1884).

248. *Söder om Rio Grande*, c. w. song, by Arvid Nelson; 1931 (1931).

249. *Söndag i det gröna, En*, c. w. song, 1, by Frans Hodell; 1861. Stockholm: Flodin, 1861 (1878).

250. *Söndag på Amager, En*, c. w. song, 1, from *En Söndag på Amager*, by Johanne L. Heiberg. Tr. by August Säfström, 1852; by John F. I. Högfeldt, 1854 (1907).

251. *Tank-spridd friare, En*, c. Possibly *Den tankspridde*, c. mon. w. song, 1, by Frans Hedberg; 1859. Stockholm, 1859 (1904; 1908; 1917).

252. *Tillfälligheter*, c., 1, by Gustaf Fredrikson, from *Surrogat*, by Otto Benzon. Stockholm: Bonnier, 1892 (1922).
Ad. by Ernst H. Behmer as *Just by chance*, 1914.

253. *Timmerflottarens son*, flk. c., 2, by Mille (Emil Juhlin). Falun: *Amatörteatern*, 1931 (1937).

254. *Tjuven*, d., from Upton Sinclair. Possibly *Sjungande fängelsefåglar*, by Upton Sinclair, tr. by Ture Newman. Stockholm: Axel Holmstrom, 1892 (1923; 1930; 1935).
Acted also as *Inbrottstjuven*.

255. *Torpar-Petter säljer sin käring*, f. w. song, 3, by Hjalmar Harriston (1933).

256. *Tosingar*, f., 1, by Wurm Junior; ca. 1867. Stockholm: Flodin, 1883 (1910; 1917; 1923; 1929; 1931; 1932, 2).

257. *Tragiskt misstag, Ett*, c. (1939).

258. *Tre friare och en älskare, eller Värdshuset på Gröna Åsnan,* c., 1, by Uller (Johan F. Lundgrén), from *Zum Grünen Esel,* ad. by R. Hahn, from *Les prétendus de Gimblette,* by Paul Dandré, P. C. J. A. Lefranc, Marc-Michel, and Senneif. Stockholm: Flodin, 1861 (1869; 1878; 1909; 1911; 1913, 3; 1917).

259. *Tre förälskade poliskonstaplar,* c. w. song, 1, by Johan Jolin, from *Trois amours de pompiers,* by Moreau, Paul S. de Sancy, and Alfred C. Lartigue; 1858. Stockholm: Flodin, 1870 (1897; 1903, 2; 1905; 1907; 1909; 1912; 1913, 2; 1922, 2; 1925, 5; 1930; 1935, 2; 1945).

260. *Trötte Theodor,* f., 3, from *Der müde Theodor,* by Max Neal and Max Ferner (1935).

Två hustrur med endast en stackars man. See *Komedi, En.*

261. *Tänk på mor,* d., 3, by Alfred Ebenhard. Oskarshamn: Kristdala Tryckeri, 1929 (1934, 2; 1935; 1936).

Ulla skall på bal. See *Balen på Gröna Lund.*

262. *Ur Carl XII:s ungdom,* d., 5, by Johan Börjesson; 1858 (1906). Acted as *Carl XII.*

263. *Valborgsmesso-aftonen,* flk. d. w. song, 4, by Frans Hedberg, w. music by J. W. Söderman; 1855. Stockholm: 1865 (1890; 1896; 1903, 2; 1905).

264. *Vermländingarne,* "tragi-comic talk-song-and dance-play," 2 parts, 6 t., by Fredrik August Dahlgren, w. music by A. Randel; 1846. Stockholm: Hörbergska Tryckeri, 1846 (1884, 2; 1886; 1888; 1890, 2; 1892, 5; 1893, 4; 1895; 1896, 3; 1898, 2; 1899, 2; 1900; 1901; 1902; 1903, 2; 1904; 1905, 2; 1906; 1907, 3; 1908, 2; 1909, 3; 1910; 1911; 1912; 1913, 4; 1914, 5; 1915, 2; 1916; 1917, 2; 1918; 1919, 2; 1920, 2; 1921; 1923, 2; 1924; 1925; 1926; 1927; 1928, 3; 1929, 2; 1931; 1946, 2; 1950, 2).

265. *Vi gå ilann i Spanien,* c., from story from French in Swedish periodical (1935).

266. *Vildsinte Mexikanaren, Den,* c., 1 (1886).

267. *Vilse i lifvet,* d., by Harald Haraldsson (Per T. Hansell), from *Vilse i lifvet,* novel by Gustaf af Geijerstam. Stockholm, 1920 (1931).

268. *Vår förening,* f. w. song, 2, by Gustaf Wicklund; 1883 (1883).

Värdshuset på Gröna Åsnan. See *Tre friare och en älskare.*

269. *Värfningen,* d. picture of bird life w. song, 1. In *Flygskriften Stadsbudet,* Stockholm, 1864 (1884; 1907).

270. *Äktenskapsbolaget U.P.A.,* c., by Henning Ohlson-Sörby (1934).

271. *Ära,* d., 4, by Frans Hedberg, from *Die ehre,* by Hermann Sudermann. Stockholm: Bonnier, 1890 (1905; 1913).

272. *Öregrund-Östhammar,* f., 3, by Herman Kinmansson, from *Kyritz-Pyritz,* by H. Wilken. Ad. by Algot E. Strand (1902, 2; 1905; 1907; 1908; 1918; 1921).

273. *Överraskning, En,* f. w. song, 2, by Gustaf Wicklund; 1883 (1883).

II. AUTHORS.

Authors of plays are listed under two categories: A. Swedish, and B. Non-Swedish. The lists include authors of original sources and of intermediate versions as well as of the plays in Swedish, but non-Swedish authors are given for the plays in the Appendix, Section I, only; not for plays listed only in the supplement to Chapter VI, almost all of which were originally written in Swedish. For authors in section B. the nationality is indicated by the following abbreviations: A.—American; D.—Danish; E.—English; F.—French; G—German; N.—Norwegian; S.—Spanish. Authors in both A. and B. are listed also under pseudonyms, variant spellings, etc., with cross references. Known dates of birth and death are given, and Chicago authors are indicated by asterisks. After the dates, cross references to plays in the Appendix, Section I, are given by number, and to plays in the supplement to Chapter VI by number, followed by the letter a.

II. A. SWEDISH.

"Ack"; 73.
Ahlgren, Ernst; pseud. of Victoria Benedictsson.
Ahlstrand, Oscar, *; 16.
Alberg, Albert, *, 1838- ca. 1928; 110.
Almlöf, C. A. Knut, 1829-1899; 226.
Andersson, E. Einar, *, 1902-   ; 20a.
Andersson, Harald N.; pseud., H. Antonius 1898-   ; 6a, 65a, 77a.
Anrep, Axel, 1835-1897; 163.
Antonius, H.; pseud. of Harald N. Andersson.
Arfvidsson, Nils, 1802-1880; 82 (?).
Askenbom, J. J.; 203.
Atterling, Carl, *; 118.
Bachman, Robert H.; 105.
Behmer, Ernst Hugo, *, 1872-   ; 14, 46, 56, 242, 252 (Eng.).
Benedictsson, Victoria; pseud., Ernst Ahlgren, 1850-1888; 104.
Benson, Otto, *, 1892-   ; 108.
Berg, Fredrik N., 1802-1884; 21, 181.
Bergegren, Hinke (Bernhard Henrik), 1861-1936; 209, 218.
Bernskog, Robert; 25a.
Berthel, Theodore; 50.
Blanche, August, 1811-1868; 48, 53, 60, 76, 89, 94, 111, 141, 190, 201, 202, 243 (?).
Bolin, Wilhelm, 1835-1924; 244 (?)
Bondeson, August, 1854-1906; 222.
Bosin, Axel, 1840-1910; 29, 167, 206 (?).
Bothén, G.; pseud., Nétob; 224.
Börjesson, Johan, 1790-1866; 54, 262.
Carlén, Emilie Flygare, 1809-1892; 204.
Carlson, Einar,*, 1892-1949; 70, 10a.
Carlson, Rose, *; 139.
Cederoth, Al, *; 37a.
Chellman (Kjellman), Leopold, *; 1872-1940; 185.
Cramaer, Mauritz, 1818-1848; 204.
Dahlgren, Fredrik August, 1816-1849; 264.
Danielsson, Johan G.; pseud., Sten, 1863-1938; 121.
Didring, Ernst, 1868-1931; 102a.
Drowtey, L. (*?); 247.
Dunkel, Calle; pseud. of Charles Eklund.
Ebenhard, Alfred, 1877-   ; 6, 173, 221, 261, 16a, 31a, 47a, 60a, 70a, 80a.
Edgren, Charlotte. See Leffler, A. Charlotte Edgren.
Edström, John, 1903-   ; 74.
Ekberg, Ernst, *, 1870-   ; 114.
Eklund, Charles; pseud., Calle Dunkel, *; 1830 -   ? ; 168.
Elmblad, Magnus, *, 1848-1888; 91 (?), 211.
Engström, Gustaf; 11, 100.

Kinmansson, Herman; 272.
Kjellman, Leopold. See Chellman, Leopold.
Klein, Ernest, 1887-1937; 26.
Kloo, August, 1815-1862; 150.
Kullberg, Herman A., 1772-1834; 153.
K . . . m; 70a.
Leffler, A. Charlotte Edgren, 1849-1892; 71.
Leman, O.; 45.
Lind, E. Henning, R.; pseud., Fridolf, 1886-   ; 231 (?), 45a.
Lind, Ernst G.; pseud., Gunnar Erlind, 1885-   ; 28a (?), 42a, 55a, 57a, 79a.
Lindblad, Elis W., 1828-1878; 150.
Lindblom, Ernst,*, 1865-1925; 5, 186.
Lindquist, Nels L.,*; 72a.
Lundgrén, Johan Fredrik; pseud., Uller, 1821-1885; 32, 37, 64 (?), 83, 125, 149, 236, 245 (?), 258.
Lundgren, Ludwig; pseud. Sigyn,*, 1872-1931; 13.
Lundström, Isidor, 1843 -   ? ; 179.
Lövgren, Knut; 35a.
Malm, Wilhelm, 1811 -   ? ; 48.
Malmgren, Lars A., 1813-1861; 89, 208.
Martinsson, Herman, 1834 -   ? ; 115, 237.
Melsted, Henning von, 1875-   ; 14a.
Mille; pseud. of Emil Juhlin.
Moberg, Vilhelm, 1898-   ; 148.
Molander, Harald, 1858-1900; 42 (?).
Molander, Henrik; 113.
Moquist, Carl J., 1825-1869; 52a.
Mörner, Birger, 1867-1930; 165.
Nelson, Arvid,*, 1888-   ; 16, 70, 85, 87, 176, 248, 24a, 32a.
Nelson, Per; pseud. of Allan Wallenius.
Nenzén-Haquinius, Hedvig, 1880-   ; 87a.
Nerman, Ture, 1886-   ; 254.
Nilsson, Tage; pseud., Jean Sibelius; 48a.
Noreen, Werner,*, 1893-   ; 108.
Norling, Paul,*, 1897-   ; 21a, 50a, 63a, 81a, 84a.
Ohlson, Henning Olof, or Henning Ohlson-Sörby, 1884-1941; 4, 61, 66, 68, 122, 197, 238, 270.
Olsson, G. Adolv, 1886-   ; 170.
Ossiander; pseud. of Gunnar Persson.
Persson, Gunnar; pseud., Ossiander; 62a, 83a.
Pfeil, Carl,*, 1853-1924; 35, 48 (Eng.), 93 (Eng.).
Philipsson, Jonas; 18 (?), 162.
Pontin, Magnus E. C., 1819-1852; 51 (?).
Reigin, Karl; pseud., Fridholm, 1895-   ; 5a, 98a.
Ringh, M.; 130.
Runeberg, Johan L., 1804-1877; 47.
Sartoris; 96.
Schober, Wilfred; pseud. of V. Schöberg.
Schöberg, V.; pseud., Wilfred Schober; 220.
Schöldström, Birger F., 1840 -   ? ; 112, 174, 192.
Sibelius, Jean; pseud. of Tage Nilsson.

287

Sigyn; pseud. of Ludwig Lundgren.
Silfverstolpe, Axel, 1762-1816; 135 (?).
Sjöquist, Theodore, *; 43.
Spanier, Bertha, or Bertha S. Straube, 1839 -   ? ; 30, 102, 147, 157, 194, 227.
Spanier, Nathalia, ?   -1866; 102, 194.
Steenhof, Helga, F. M.; pseud., Harold Gote, 1865 -   ? ; 91a.
Sten; pseud. of Johan G. Danielsson.
Stenhagen, Alfred; 95.
Stjernström, Jeanette C. G., 1825-1857; 22 (?), 177, 206 (?).
Stjernström, Louise E. G., 1827 -   ? ; 84, 244 (?).
Stockenberg, Carl, *, 1878-   ; 6, 160.
Strand, Algot E.,*; 271.
Strand, W. T. (*?); 96 (?).
Straube, Bertha S. See Spanier, Bertha.
Strindberg, August, 1849-1912; 79, 88, 138, 180, 182, 196, 58a, 89a.
Strömberg, Sigge (Sigfrid N.), 1885-1920; 233, 234.
Styrlander, W.; 198.
Swenson, W.; 243.
Säfström, August, 1813-1888; 7, 18 (?), 24, 145, 146, 250 (?).
Söderwall, Einar Fabian, *, 1869 -   ? ; 17a, 99a.
Sörby-Ohlson, Henning. See Ohlson, Henning Olof.
Tegnér, Esaias, 1782-1846; 65.
Thunberg, Ivar T., 1888-   ; 93a.
Topelius, Zacharias, 1818-1898; 200.
Uller; pseud. of Johan Fredrik Lundgrén.
Wahl, Anders de, 1869-   ; 69.
Wall, Rudolf, 1825-1893; 146.
Wallenius, Allan; pseud., Per Nelson, 1890-   ; 75.
Warburg, Karl Johan, 1852-1918; 103, 164.
Wenberg or Wiberg, Werner (*?); 106.
Wennberg, Carl,*; 187.
Wennersten, Oscar; 27.
Wernberg, Hjalmar, 1867-1924; 26a.
Wetterstedt, Niklas af, 1780-1855; 199.
Wicklund, Gustaf,*, 1852-1905; 2, 8, 123, 132, 142, 189, 195, 268, 273.
Wigfors, Sten, 1872-1909; 229.
Wijkander, Carl O., 1826-1899; 36.
Wurm Junior; 256.
Yancke, Yngve. See Jancke, Yngve.
Åkerberg, Ville,*, 1864-1894; 161.
Åkerhjelm, G. F., 1776-1853; 82.
Ölander, A. H.; 9 (?).
Österberg, Thore,*; 160.

II. B. NON-SWEDISH.

About, Edmond F. V., 1828-1885, F.; 58, 227.
Albini; pseud. of Albin J. B. von Meddlhammer.
Andersen, Hans Christian, 1805-1875, D.; 162.
Basté, Pierre E.; pseud., Grangé, 1810-1887, F.; 92, 206.
Bayard, J. F. A., 1796-1853, F.; 57, 94, 146, 181, 199.
Belly, G., F.; 29.

289

Horn, Georg, 1831-1897, G.; 37.
Ibsen, Henrik, 1828-1906, N.; 42.
Jacobsen, Eduard, 1833-1897, G.; 133.
Jansen, F., D.; 155
Juin, C., G.; 1.
Justinius, O.; pseud. of Ernst Heinrich Wilken.
Kaiser, Friedrich, 1814-1874, G.; 24.
Kalisch, David, 1820-1872, G.; 140.
Kotzebue, August Friedrich von, 1761-1819, G.; 78(?).
Kudelberg, Gust, G.; 36.
Kuntze; G.; 43.
Labiche, Eugène; pseud., Dandré, 1815-1888, F.; 56, 83, 258.
Lartigue, Alfred C.; pseud., Delacour, 1815-1883, F.; 259.
Laurencin; pseud. of Paul-Aimée Chapelle.
Lefèvre, Louis, Lfébure-Wely or Lefébure, Louis Janen Alfred, 1817-1870, F.; 162
Lefranc, P. C. J. August, 1814-1878, F.; 258.
Lehnard, Paul R., G.; 242.
Lemoine, L. I. E.; pseud., Moreau, 1806-1876, F.; 259.
Lubize; pseud. of Pierre H. Martin.
Marc-Michel; pseud. of Michel, Marc A. A.
Mars, Antony, 1862-1915, F.; 46.
Martin, Pierre H., 1800-1863, F.; 84.
Meddlhammer, Albin J. B. von; pseud., Albini, 1777-1838, G.; 22 (?).
Meilhac, Henri, 1831-1897, F.; 124, 132.
Mélesville; pseud. of A. H. J. Duveyrier.
Meyer-Förster, Wilhelm, 1862-1934, G.; 72.
Michel, Marc A. A.; pseud., Marc-Michel, 1812-1868, F.; 21, 83, 258.
Millaud, Moiser Polydire, 1813-1871, F.; 132.
Moinaux, Jules, 1815-1895, F.; 30.
Moreau; pseud. of Lemoine, L. I. E.
Moser, Gustav von, 1825-1903, G.; 45, 226.
Murger, Henri, 1822-1861, F.; 194.
Möller, Otto, G.; 97.
Müller, Hugo, 1871-   , G.; 102.
Münch-Bellinghausen, Eligius Franz Joseph von; pseud., Friedrich Halm, 1806-1871,
    G.; 67(?).
Najac, Emile de, 1828-1889, F.; 222.
Neal, Max, 1865 -   ? , G.; 260.
Nestroy, Johannes, 1802-1862, G.; 11, 89.
Overskou, Thomas, 1798-1873, D.; 177.
Philippe, Eugène; pseud., d'Ennery or Dennery, 1811-1899, F.; 112, 201.
Piestri, Pierre E.; pseud., Eugène Cormon, 1811-1903, F.; 140, 201, 206, 227.
Pohl, Emil, 1824-1901, G.; 86.
Radet, Jean B., 1751-1830, F.; 7.
Reich, Albert, 1881-   , G.; 157.
Remy, Charles H.; pseud., Honoré, 1792-1858, F.; 17.
Reuter, Fritz, 1810-1874, G.; 131.
Romain; pseud. of Chapelain.
Saint-Georges, Jules H. Vernay de, 1801-1875, F.; 199.
Sand, George; pseud. of Amantine L. A. Dudevant.
Sardou, Victorien, 1831-1908, F.; 217 (?).

290

Scarron, Paul, 1610-1660, F.; 201.
Schönthan, Frans, von, 1849-1913, G.; 41.
Senneif; pseud. of Charles M. de Fiennes.
Shakespeare, William, 1564-1616, E.; 82, 244.
Sinclair, Upton, 1878-   , A.; 254.
Siraudin de Sancy, Paul, 1813-1883, F.; 259.
Souvestre, Emile, 1805-1854, F.; 24.
Stegmayer, Matthias, ?   -1820, G.; 203.
Steigentesch, Ernst A. von, 1774-1826, G.; 153.
Sudermann, Hermann, 1857-1928, G.; 271.
Théaulon de Lambert, Marie E. G. M., 1787-1841, F.; 39, 51.
Theuriet, André, 1833-1907, F.; 95.
Tietz, Christ. Friedrich, G.; 17.
Vanderburch, Emile Louis, 1794-1862, F.; 181.
Varin, Charles V., 1798-1869, F.; 162.
Varner, Antoine F., 1789-1854, F.; 94.
Verne, Jules, 1828-1905, F.; 112.
Wailly, Augustin J. de; pseud., Devorme, 1806-1866, F.; 146.
Wengel, C. M., G.; 174.
Wilken, Ernst Heinrich; pseud., O. Justinius, 1846 -   ? , G.; 272.
Wolff, Pius A., 1784-1828, G.; 191.
Woodward, T. Trask, A.; 246.

III.   THEATRES AND HALLS.

Included in this alphabetical list of places in Chicago and its suburbs at which Swedish plays are known to have been presented are the locations, when known, and seasons of use. The new system of street numbering adopted in 1909 makes the addresses for places used only before that time somewhat misleading. For a few places used both before and after the change, the successive street numbers are given. Avenues and halls are designated, but for streets and theatres such specific designation is omitted.

1. Alton Park, Lemont, Ill.; 1908-1909.
2. America, 459 E. 31st; 1899-1900.
3. Amundsen High School, W. 61st and Walcott; 1950-1951.
4. Anderson Hall, 810-812 W. 69th; 1931-1932.
5. Arcade Hall, 3351 N. Clark; 1913-1914.
6. Arcade, Pullman; 1891-1892, 1892-1893.
7. Aryan Grotto (earlier Globe, later Chicago, Eighth Street), 741 S. Wabash Ave.; 1918-1919, 1919-1920, 1920-1921, 1921-1922, 1923-1924.
8. Aurora Turner Hall, Milwaukee Ave., N.E. Corner of W. Huron; 1875-1876.
9. Auditorium, Wabash Ave. and Congress; 1891-1892, 1898-1899, 1899-1900, 1900-1901, 1901-1902, 1903-1904, 1905-1906, 1906-1907, 1907-1908, 1911-1912, 1912-1913, 1926-1927, 1927-1928.
10. Bailey's Opera House, Evanston; 1896-1897.
11. Banner Blue Masonic Temple, 6734 S. Wentworth Ave.; 1923-1924.
12. Batavia; 1931-1932.
13. Baum's Pavilion, Corner of Cottage Grove and Indiana Aves.; 1884-1885.
14. Belmont Hall (earlier Spelz Hall), 1682-1684 N. Clark, 3205-3207 N. Clark; 1906-1907, 1911-1912, 1916-1917, 1917-1918, 1919-1920, 1920-1921, 1921-1922, 1922-1923, 1923-1924, 1924-1925, 1925-1926, 1926-1927, 1928-1929, 1929-1930, 1930-1931, 1931-1932, 1932-1933,

1933-1934, 1934-1935, 1935-1936, 1936-1937, 1937-1938, 1939-1940.
1944-1945, 1945-1946.

15. Binz Hall, Corner of Cottage Grove Ave. and 27th; 1883-1884.
16. Blackstone, 60 E. 7th, 60 E. Balbo Ave.; 1913-1914, 1914-1915, 1915-1916, 1916-1917, 1934-1935.
17. Brand's Hall, 170 N. Clark;1893-1894.
18. Brand's Park, 3261 N. Elston Ave.; 1908-1909.
19. Bryn Mawr, 1125 W. Bryn Mawr Ave.; 1925-1926.
20. Bush Temple, 108 W. Chicago Ave.; 1913-1914, 1914-1915.
21. Butler House, 3212 Broadway; 1917-1918, 1918-1919, 1920-1921, 1924-1925.
22. Calumet Club Hall, Cottage Grove Ave. and 62nd; 1920-1921.
23. Calumet Opera House, 9202 South Chicago Ave.; 1893-1894.
24. Carpenter's Hall, 7427 South Chicago Ave.; 1914-1915, 1920-1921, 1922-1923, 1923-1924, 1924-1925, 1938-1939, 1940-1941.
25. Castberg Shop, 185 Michigan Ave.; 1906-1907.
26. Central Hall, 2139 S. Wabash Ave.; 1882-1883, 1885-1886.
27. Chicago Norwegian Club, 2350 N. Kedzie Ave.; 1929-1930.
28. Chicago Opera House, 118 Washington; 1891-1892.
29. Chicago Theatre (earlier Globe, Aryan Grotto, later Eighth Street), 741 S Wabash Ave.; 1917-1918.
30. Chicago Woman's Club, 410 S. Michigan Ave.; 1935-1936.
31. Claremont Hall, 1630 N. Clark; 1906-1907.
32. Coffey Hall, 311 E. 58th; 1910-1911, 1912-1913.
33. Colonial Hall, 5436 S. Wentworth Ave.; 1919-1920.
34. Columbia, 5322-5326 S. State; 1892-1893, 1897-1898, 1903-1904.
35. Columbia Park; 1897-1898.
36. Criterion, 274 N. Sedgwick; 1891-1892, 1892-1893, 1893-1894, 1894-1895, 1895-1896.
37. Eighth Street (earlier Globe, Aryan Grotto, Chicago), 741 S. Wabash Ave.; 1924-1925, 1946-1947.
38. Englewood Masonic Temple, 6730 S. Wentworth Ave.; 1922-1923, 1929-1930.
39. Elliott's Park; 1905-1906.
40. Erhardt's Grove, Park Ridge; 1931-1932.
41. Finnish Theatre, Waukegan; 1930-1931.
42. Forest Park, end of Garfield elevated, West; 1913-1914.
43. Freiberg's Hall, 180-184 22nd; 1889-1890.
44. Gardner's Park; 1911-1912.
45. Garrick, 107 E. Randolph; 1904-1905, 1905-1906, 1906-1907, 1907-1908, 1908-1909, 1909-1910, 1910-1911, 1912-1913, 1915-1916.
46. German Hall, 94 N. Wells; 1867-1868, 1868-1869, 1869-1870, 1870-1871.
47. Germania, 64 E. Van Buren; 1914-1915.
48. Globe (later Aryan Grotto, Chicago, Eighth Street), 741 S. Wabash Ave.; 1913-1914.
49. Good Templar Hall, 1041 W. Newport Ave.; 1919-1920, 1920-1921, 1923-1924, 1931-1932, 1932-1933, 1933-1934, 1935-1936, 1936-1937, 1944-1945, 1946-1947.
50. Good Templar Hall, 647 E. 61st; 1927-1928, 1928-1929, 1929-1930, 1930-1931, 1931-1932, 1932-1933, 1933-1934, 1934-1935, 1935-1936, 1940-1941.

51. Good Templar Hall, 10156 Ave. M., S. Chicago; 1922-1923, 1923-1924, 1928-1929.
52. Good Templar Park, Geneva, Ill.; 1928-1929, 1929-1930, 1930-1931, 1931-1932, 1933-1934, 1934-1935, 1935-1936, 1936-1937, 1938-1939, 1940-1941, 1943-1944.
53. Goodman, S. Michigan Ave., foot of E. Adams; 1926-1927.
54. Gord's Hall, Roseland; 1894-1895.
55. Grace Hall; 1922-1923.
56. Grand Crossing Masonic Temple, 7443 Ingleside; 1903-1904.
57. Grand Crossing Turner Hall, 75th and S.W. Corner of Dobson Ave.; 1893-1894.
58. Grand Opera House, 87 S. Clark; 1890-1891, 1902-1903, 1903-1904, 1904-1905, 1905-1906, 1906-1907, 1907-1908, 1908-1909, 1909-1910, 1910-1911, 1911-1912.
59. Henning's Hall, Corner, North and Spaulding Aves.; 1901-1902.
60. Highland Park Masonic Hall; 1934-1935.
61. Hillinger's Park, 1357 Belmont Ave.; 1888-1889, 1890-1891.
62. Hoerber's Hall, 712 Blue Island Ave.; 1891-1892, 1896-1897.
63. Holter's Hall, 633 N. Cicero Ave.; 1931-1932, 1938-1939.
64. Hooley's, 149 E. Randolph; 1889-1890, 1890-1891, 1891-1892, 1892-1893, 1893-1894, 1894-1895.
65. Houston Street Hall, 46-48 E. Houston; 1869-1870.
66. Hyde Park Masonic Temple, 102 E. 51st; 1917-1918.
67. Illinois, 20 E. Jackson Blvd.; 1904-1905.
68. Imperial Hall, 2409 N. Halsted; 1924-1925.
69. Intima (or Little), 4th floor, Fine Arts Building, 410 S. Michigan Ave.; 1912-1913.
70. Ivar Temple, I.O.V., 4146 N. Elston Ave.; 1925-1926, 1929-1930, 1931-1932, 1932-1933, 1937-1938, 1938-1939.
71. Jackson Hall, 1465 E. 55th; 1914-1915.
72. Jefferson Hall, 190 E. 55th, 1895-1896.
73. Jensen home, Ravinia; 1913-1914, 1914-1915.
74. Kensington Turner Hall, 2507 Kensington Ave.; 1894-1895, 1899-1900, 1903-1904, 1906-1907.
75. Lake View Hall, 3143 N. Clark; 1910-1911, 1911-1912, 1912-1913 1913-1914, 1914-1915, 1915-1916.
76. Leavitt Street Hall, Leavitt and 19th; 1899-1900.
77. Lincoln Auditorium, 4219 N. Lincoln Ave.; 1930-1931, 1931-1932, 1932-1933, 1933-1934, 1934-1935, 1936-1937, 1940-1941, 1941-1942, 1946-1947.
78. Lincoln Turner Hall, 1019 Diversey Ave.; 1895-1896, 1908-1909, 1909-1910.
79. Lindblom High School, Damen and Foster Aves.; 1950-1951.
80. Linné Woods; 1933-1934, 1934-1935.
81. Linnea Hall, 8743 Buffalo Ave.; 1894-1895.
82. Lundquist's Hall, 6058 S. Morgan; 1935-1936.
83. Lyric, 83 E. Jackson Blvd., 1911-1912.
84. Maccabee Temple, 5711 W. Chicago Ave.; 1923-1924, 1925-1926, 1926-1927, 1927-1928, 1928-1929, 1929-1930, 1930-1931, 1931-1932, 1932-1933.
85. Mannos Hall, 7447 Cottage Grove Ave.; 1924-1925.
86. Marlowe, 6254 Stewart Ave.; 1892-1893.

87. McVicker's, 82 E. Madison; 1891-1892, 1892-1893, 1896-1897.
88. Metropole Hall, 456 31st.; 1901-1902.
89. Midway Masonic Temple, 6107 Cottage Grove Ave.; 1925-1926, 1927-1928.
90. Music Hall, 203 S. Michigan Ave.; 1905-1906, 1906-1907.
91. Myrtle Masonic Temple, N. Tripp Ave. and Irving Park Rd.; 1919-1920.
92. North Side Auditorium, 3730 N. Clark; 1927-1928, 1928-1929, 1929-1930, 1930-1931, 1932-1933, 1933-1934, 1935-1936, 1937-1938, 1938-1939, 1939-1940, 1940-1941, 1943-1944, 1944-1945.
93. North Side Turner Hall, 259 N. Clark, 826 N. Clark; 1870-1871, 1877-1878, 1878-1879, 1879-1880, 1881-1882, 1882-1883, 1883-1884, 1884-1885, 1885-1886, 1886-1887, 1887-1888, 1888-1889, 1889-1890, 1890-1891, 1891-1892, 1892-1893, 1893-1894, 1894-1895, 1895-1896, 1896-1897, 1897-1898, 1898-1899, 1899-1900, 1900-1901, 1901-1902, 1902-1903, 1903-1904, 1904-1905, 1905-1906, 1906-1907, 1907-1908, 1908-1909, 1910-1911, 1911-1912, 1913-1914, 1924-1925, 1925-1926.
94. North Side Turner Hall, 820 E. Chicago Ave.; 1926-1927, 1927-1928.
95. Novotny Hall, 1566-1568 W. 22nd; 1903-1904.
96. Odd Fellows Hall, 406-408 Milwaukee Ave.; 1896-1897.
97. Odd Fellows Hall, 6316 S. Yale Ave.; 1943-1944, 1944-1945.
98. Oden Club Hall, 6853 Stewart Ave.; 1930-1931, 1932-1933.
99. Ogden's Grove, 415 Clybourne Ave.; 1891-1892.
100. Orphei Hall, 3541 N. Clark; 1935-1936.
101. Phoenix Hall, 324 E. Division; 1895-1896, 1902-1903, 1903-1904, 1904-1905.
102. Powers, 149 E. Randolph; 1905-1906, 1906-1907, 1911-1912, 1916-1917, 1917-1918, 1922-1923.
103. Pythian Hall, 7439 Cottage Grove Ave.; 1917-1918, 1918-1919, 1919-1920, 1923-1924, 1926-1927, 1931-1932, 1934-1935.
104. Pythian Hall, Roseland, 11037 S. Michigan Ave.; 1915-1916, 1922-1923, 1933-1934.
105. Pythian Temple, 9231 Cottage Grove Ave.; 1919-1920, 1926-1927.
106. Rainbo Gardens, 4810-4834 N. Clark; 1931-1932.
107. Reynolds Club, University of Chicago, 57th and University Ave.; 1912-1913.
108. Riverview Park, Belmont and Western Aves.; 1930-1931, 1931-1932, 1932-1933.
109. Rosalie Hall, 57th and Harper Ave.; 1916-1917, 1917-1918.
110. Santa Fé Park; 1899-1900, 1905-1906.
111. Schwartz, Waukegan; 1907-1908.
112. Social Turner Hall, 1651 Belmont Ave.; 1924-1925.
113. South Chicago Opera House; 1886-1887.
114. South Side Auditorium, 77 31st; 1891-1892.
115. South Side Masonic Temple, 6400 S. Green; 1925-1926.
116. South Side Turner Hall, 3143-3147 S. State; 1893-1894, 1894-1895, 1895-1896, 1897-1898, 1898-1899, 1899-1900, 1900-1901, 1901-1902, 1902-1903, 1903-1904, 1904-1905, 1905-1906, 1907-1908, 1908-1909, 1910-1911, 1911-1912, 1912-1913, 1913-1914.
117. South Side Viking Temple, 6855 S. Emerald Ave.; 1928-1929, 1929-1930, 1930-1931, 1931-1932, 1932-1933, 1933-1934, 1934-1935, 1935-1936, 1936-1937, 1937-1938, 1938-1939, 1939-1940, 1943-1944.
118. Spelz Hall (later Belmont Hall), 1630 N. Clark; 1896-1897, 1900-1901, 1903-1904, 1905-1906.

119. Strummel's Hall, 158 E. 107th; 1917-1918, 1935-1936.
120. Studebaker, 203 S. Michigan Ave.; 1898-1899, 1901-1902, 1923-1924, 1925-1926.
121. Sunnyside Park; 1898-1899.
122. Svea Hall, Corner of Wells and Superior; 1875-1876, 1876-1877.
123. Svithiod Fraternity Temple, 4332 N. Kedzie Ave.; 1931-1932.
124. Svithiod Singing Club Hall, 1768 Wrightwood Ave., 624 Wrightwood Ave; 1900-1901, 1901-1902, 1902-1903, 1906-1907, 1908-1909, 1909-1910, 1911-1912, 1916-1917, 1919-1920.
125. Swedish Club, 1258 N. La Salle; 1912-1913, 1913-1914, 1914-1915, 1916-1917, 1920-1921, 1921-1922, 1926-1927, 1931-1932, 1933-1934.
126. Swedish Engineers Club, 503 Wrightwood Ave.; 1938-1939.
127. Swedish Music Hall, 456 31st; 1891-1892.
128. Uhlich's Hall, 27-29 N. Clark; 1892-1893.
129. Verdandi Hall, 5015-5017 N. Clark; 1910-1911, 1913-1914, 1914-1915, 1915-1916, 1917-1918, 1918-1919, 1931-1932, 1933-1934.
130. Victoria (also called Vic's and German), 3143 N. Sheffield Ave.; 1927-1928, 1928-1929, 1929-1930, 1930-1931.
131. Viking Temple, Sheffield Ave. and School; 1910-1911, 1913-1914, 1914-1915, 1917-1918, 1919-1920, 1920-1921, 1921-1922, 1922-1923, 1923-1924, 1924-1925, 1928-1929, 1929-1930, 1930-1931, 1931-1932, 1932-1933, 1934-1935, 1935-1936, 1936-1937, 1937-1938, 1938-1939, 1942-1943, 1943-1944.
132. Viking Valhalla, Gurnee, Ill.; 1944-1945.
133. Vorwaert's Turner Hall, 1168-1170 W. 12th; 1899-1900.
134. White City, 63rd and South Park Ave.; 1914-1915.
135. Wicker Park Hall, 501-507 North Ave.; 1903-1904, 1904-1905.
136. Yondorf's Hall, 163-165 North Ave.; 1917-1918, 1918-1919.
137. Young Men's Christian Association Auditorium, 153-155 La Salle; 1906-1907, 1907-1908.

IV. CASTS.

Casts that are sufficiently complete to give an idea of the play or company have been included. Actors in leading roles are often named in the discussion of other performances in Chapters II—VI.

Rochus Pumpernickel, Feb. 29, 1880 (Moline, Ill.).
Herr von Borthal—Hjalmar Hopp
Margareta, his wife—Miss J. Strömberg
Sophie, his daughter by his first marriage—Mrs. Erika Hopp
Captain Borthal, his brother—A. Lehnberg
Herr von Littau, Sophie's suitor—E. Lundgren
Herr Rochus Pumpernickel, son of a wealthy country squire—Fritz Schoultz
Purgantius, a doctor—C. Freeburg
Bombastus, a doctor—Herman Hagström
Schreyer, a surgeon—John Höglund
Henrik, Littau's servant—H. Johnson
Babette, Sophie's maid—Mrs. Anna Lundgren
Sebastian, servant—Charles Nelson
Philippina and Dorothea, two men—J. Johnson and A. Hagström
(*S.T.,* Feb. 25, 1880)

295

De båda döfva, Apr. 29, 1882.
Damoisian—Knut Lindstrom
Placidi, his servant—Andrew Johnson
Boniface—Hjalmar Hopp
Gardener—Charles Nelson
Forester—C. O. Carlson
(*S.T.,* Apr. 12, 1882)

En överraskning, Feb. 3, 1883 (Moline, Ill.).
Wahlström, mining speculator—Andrew Johnson
Mälvina, his wife—Mrs. A. Roberts
Wahlström's servants,
    Lina—Anna Palmberg
    Springer—Knut Lindstrom
Rullan, bricklayer, former notary—Christopher Brusell
Kulstedt, hack reporter, former lieutenant—William Carlson
Ilström, expressman, former postal official—Gustaf Wicklund
Pank, lamplighter, former cashier—Emil Ahlberg
Solenros, misunderstood poet—Andrew Johnson
Kalle Peterson, present and former ne'er-do-well—C. Berg
Coachman—Otto Pallin
    In Metamorphoses:
Figaro—Rullan
Manufacturor of St. Jacob's Oil—Kulstedt
Storm, Stockholm soldier—Ilström
Gustana, a devotee from Rock Island—Otto Pallin
A boxer—George C. Sherman
Lundström, of the firm of Andersson, Pettersson och Lundström—Springer
(*S.T.,* Jan. 24, 1883)

Vår förening, May 5, 1883
    D.S.T., *De Skinande Trättorne* (The Brilliant Wranglers)
Peter Klubbman, president of D.S.T.—Knut Lindstrom
Emma, his daughter—Anna Palmberg
Axel Stone, artist—Christopher Brusell
Lungqvist, treasurer of D.S.T.—Emil Ahlberg
Bladman, protocol secretary of D.S.T.—Gustaf Wicklund
Finberg, master of ceremonies and corresponding secretary of D.S.T.—Otto Pallin
Protehm, quarrelsome society member—G. Ljungberg
(*S.T.,* May 2, 1883)

Kronjuvelerna på Nordsidan, Dec. 16, 1883
Klunk, tailor—Knut Lindstrom
Knappholm, presser—C. Cederlöf
Klingstedt, former musical director—Christopher Brusell
Kalle Karlson, former emigrant—Robert Olson
Kikbom, book agent—Fritz Schoultz
Kornman, farmer from Kansas—Emil Ahlberg
Konrad, his nephew, Fritz Schoultz
Kalsohmin, fresco painter—F. Lysell
Kuningkunda, Klunk's wife—Miss C. Söderbäck
Klara, Klunk's daughter—Miss T. Peterson

296

Kajsa Kacklander, hotel waitress—Mrs. Weidenhavn
Korsmessa Anderson—A. Lagerström
Karolina—Miss F. Nilsson
Koralie—Miss M. Palmberg
Kalospintero—Miss L. Larson
    In masked ball:
Admiral from *Pinafore*—Klunk
Mefistopheles from Faust—Klingstedt
Mother Hubbard from memory—Kikbom
A dude from ?—Kalle Karlson
(*S.T.*, Dec. 5, 1883).

Syfröknarna, Jan. 20, 1884
Eberling, general—Otto Pallin
Theodore, his son—E. Almgren
Pelle Lungqvist—A. Lindeberg
Spratt, notary—C. Nilson
Snobb, wholesale merchant—O. Hedlund
Betty, Marie, Louise, Charlotte, seamstresses—The Misses A. Boije, A. Jockum, M.
    Palmberg, J...
Miss Hoppenrath—Matt Ovington
Madame Lindberg—Mrs. A. Weidenhavn
Mrs. Spitzig, dressmaker—Mrs. L. Nordgren
Fina, her maid—Mr. A....
Ström, police constable—S. Sandberg
Hammarberg, Smith from Örebro—Christopher Brusell
Fiolin, instrument maker—Gunnar Sahlin
Mrs. Linnander—Miss A. Bjurlin
Fanny, her daughter—Miss E. Bjurlin
Julia, her foster daughter—Anna Palmberg
Judge—N. Crona
City messenger—C. Nordgren
Watchman—O. Zanteson
(*S.T.*, Jan. 16, 1884).

Hittebarnet, May 18, 1884.
Konjander, a rich old bachelor—Knut Lindstrom
Mrs. Wahlstrom, his housekeeper—Mrs. Louise Nordgren
Kattong, wholesale merchant—Gustaf Wicklund
Amanda, his wife—Anna Palmberg
Bällin, young painter—Fritz Schoultz
Alenberg, Konjander's nephew—Robert Olson
(*S.T.*, May 14, 1884).

Vermländingarne, Nov. 16, 1884.
Brukspatron (proprietor of iron works)—Christopher Brusell
Wilhelm, his son—E. Lönnquist
Lotta, his daughter—Anna Palmberg
Provst (clergyman, dean)—A. Eckerberg
Sven Ersson i Hult, juryman—R. Holmes
Lisa, his wife—Miss A. Boije
Erik, their son—Axel Lundgren

Ola i Gyllby, wealthy farmer—J. Stone
Britta, his daughter—Miss Lindquist
Jan Hansson vid sjön, cotter—P. F. Ekenberg
Annika, his wife—Mrs. A. Weidenhavn
Anna, their daughter—Miss M. Björlin
Anders, their servant—Fred Littche
Per, Sven Ersson's servant—George E. Holmes
Stina, Sven Ersson's maid—Ottilie Mörk
Bengt på Åsen—Matt Ovington
Henrick i Backa—N. Berg
Nils Jonsson, called Löpare-Nisse—J. Stone
Brukspatron's servant—J. Johnson
(*S.T.*, Nov. 12, 1884).

Jernbäraren, Feb. 1, 1885.
General, a hunter—Knut Lindstrom
Dahl, *brukspatron*—Gunnar Sahlin
Axelson, *jernbäraren* (iron bearer)—Christopher Brusell
Felman, smith—J. F. Johnson
Anna, Axelson's daughter—Mrs. Louise Nordgren
Mrs. Strömquist, tavern keeper—
Karin, waitress—Miss J. Söderbeck
Coachman—Fritz Schoultz
Carter—F. Larson
Vintner—Fred Littche
Dalcarlian—Matt Ovington
Brig worker—A. Norborg
Police assistant—Fred Littche
Chimney sweep—Otto Nordgren
Country man—Fred Littche
Country woman—Miss M. Söderbeck
Country girl—Ottilie Mörk
(*S.T.*, Jan. 21, 1885)

En brottslig betjent, Feb. 1, 1885.
Chalomel, doctor—Fritz Schoultz
Suzanne, his wife—Mrs. Louise Nordgren
Piperman, his servant—Knut Lindstrom
(*S.T.*, Jan. 21, 1885).

Jag känner till politiken, jag, Dec. 26, 1885.
Grönbom, alderman from Borås, former coppersmith—George E. Holmes
Ingeborg, his daughter—Anna Palmberg Brusell
Sillström, merchant and alderman from Upsala—Gusten Myhrman
Agnes, his daughter—. . .
Hedin, student and writer—Christopher Brusell
Burkman, distributor—Otto Pallin
Professor Falsenpatter, wax works owner—C. Fagerlund
Grewe, his assistant—M. Engdahl
Minnie, maid—Miss G. Spångberg
Lundquist, porter—J. Holmes
(*S.A.*, Dec. 19, 1885).

En midsommarnatt i Dalarne, Dec. 26, 1885
Matts—George E. Holmes
Britta, his wife—Miss M. Björlin
Göran—M. Engdahl
Hakan—C. Fagerlund
Lisa—Miss G. Spångberg
Karin—Anna Palmberg Brusell
Baron Axel—Christopher Brusell
Karl, artist—Otto Pallin
Gustaf—P. Petterson
(*S.A.,* Dec. 19, 1885)

På första Maj, May 1, 1886.
Hallman, old widower—Fritz Schoultz
Annie, his daughter—Amelie Peterson
Sharp, a corn doctor. Hallman's boarder—Otto Pallin
Kalle Frisk, clerk—Christopher Brusell
(Program)

En komedi, Oct. 7, 1888.
Major Wapensköld—Fred Littche
His wife—Miss Enbom
Axel, their son, who appears as:
    Calle Wallin, sailor
    Von Wilken, toll collector
    Angelica, housekeeper   } Carl Pfeil
    Anders, farmer
    Grip, coastal sergeant
Von Wilken, toll collector, major's boyhood friend—Gunnar Sahlin
Mathilda, his daughter—Anna Pfeil
First coast guard—Fritz Schoultz
Second coast guard—Ville Åkerberg
(Program)

Andersson, Pettersson och Lundström, Jan. 1, 1889.
Infernalis, protector of frivolity—Gunnar Sahlin
Andersson, journeyman joiner—Gunnar Sahlin
Pettersson, journeyman tailor—Fritz Schoultz
Lundström, journeyman shoemaker—Carl Pfeil
Pluggstedt, school teacher—Matt Ovington
Hasselqvist, master joiner—Albin Smith
Three roles—Anna Pfeil
Newspaper editor—Ville Åkerberg
(*S.T.,* Jan. 5, 1889)

Hans tredje hustru, May 25, 1889.
Carolina Petterson, washerwoman—Anna Pfeil
Svante Flax, watchmaker—Matt Ovington
Polykarpus Widman, tavern keeper from Arboga—Carl Pfeil
Calle, shoemaker's servant—Ville Åkerberg
(*S.T.,* May 18, 1889)

Ulla skall på bal, July 28, 1889.
Ulla—Anna Pfeil
Corporal Mollberg—Carl Pfeil
Father Berg—Matt Ovington
Father Mowitz—Gus Higgins
(*S.T.,* Aug. 1, 1889)

Pelle Pihlqvists Amerika-resa, Nov. 2, 1890.
Bergström, merchant on Townsend Street—Albin Smith
Louise, his wife—Anna Almgren
Mary, their daughter—Hilma Nelson
Frida Eklund, Bergström's sister-in-law—Mrs. Hanna Hvitfeldt
Pelle Pihlqvist, perpetual undergraduate from Upsala—Ville Åkerberg
Bohmansson, literary man from Stockholm—Matt Ovington
Hjulström, director of Linné monument association—Fritz Schoultz
Westergren, saloon keeper—Gus Higgins
Sophie, servant at Bergströms—Anna Åkerberg
(*S.T.,* Oct. 30, 1890)

Skal och kärna, Sept. 13, 1891.
Rameau, Parisian artist—Albert Alberg
Baron Göran—Olaf Colldén
Baron Adolf—Emil Thimgren
Ebba—Hilma Nelson
(*H.,* Sept. 17, 1891)

Hittebarnet, Sept. 6, 1891.
Konjander a rich old bachelor—Olaf Colldén
Mrs. Wahlstrom, his housekeeper—Mrs. Hanna Hvitfeldt
Kattong, wholesale merchant—Albert Alberg
Amanda, his wife—Hilma Nelson
Bällin, young painter—Emil Thimgren
(*S.A.,* Sept. 10, 1891)

Nerkingarne, May 1, 1892.
Stål, *brukspatron*—Albert Alberg
Selma, his daughter—Anna Almgren
Mamsell Bom, governess—Matt Ovington
Sven Jonsson i Lekhyttan, official—Gunnar Sahlin
Sven, his son, student—Max Hedman
Mother Katarina, Sven Jonsson's sister, rich widow—Mrs. Hanna Hvitfeldt
Lasse, her son—Olaf Colldén
Olle Lek, her son, student—Ernst Schycker
Östing, former soldier, now sexton and fiddler—Gus Higgins
Ingeborg, country girl—Hilma Nelson
Stina, Mother Katarina's servant—Selma Stäckig
(*S.T.,* Apr. 27, 1892)

Svärfar, May 29, 1892.
Theodor Klint, zoology professor—Edwin Björkman

300

Cecilia, his wife—Mrs. Hanna Hvitfeldt

Elizabeth   —Hilma Nelson
Karin   their daughters   —Beda Lindquist
Elsa   —Olga Thebom

Mrs. Louisa Engström, Cecilia's mother—Jenny Gustafson
Axel Fahrström, lieutenant, Elizabeth's fiancé—Guido Walter
Otto Norstedt, artist—Gus Higgins
Agaton Pumpendal, assessor—Emil Thimgren
Amanda, model—Miss Börgquist
Strange gentleman—Mr. Petrie
Emilie, Klints' servant—Miss Ekstrand
(S.T., June 8, 1892)

Bröllopet på Ulfåsa, Sept. 18, 1892.
Knut Algotson—Gunnar Sahlin
Ingrid, his wife—Mrs. Hanna Hvitfeldt
Sigrid the Fair, their daughter—Hilma Nelson
Björn, squire—Ernst Schycker
Bengt Lagman—Fred Littche
Birger Jarl—Albert Alberg
His wife—Ragnhild Hedman
Härved Boson—Max Hedman
(S.T., Sept. 21, 1892)

Bröllopet på Ulfåsa, Sept. 17, 1893.
Knut Algotson—John Liander
Ingrid, his wife—Mrs. Hanna Hvitfeldt
Sigrid the Fair, their daughter—Augusta Nyström
Björn, squire—Ernst Schycker
Bengt Lagman—Fred Littche
Birger Jarl—Arthur Donaldson
His wife—Anna Almgren
Härved Boson—Albert Alberg
Prior Botvid—Matt Ovington
(S.A., S.T., Sept. 20, 1893)

Edmond Kean, Apr. 14, 1895.
George, Prince of Wales—Ernst Svedelius
Count Coefeld, Danish ambassador—Gunnar Sahlin
Countess Helena, his wife—Augusta Milton
Lord Melville, English peer—Albert Alberg
Countess Amy Goswill—Mrs. Hanna Hvitfeldt
Sir Arthur Neville—Ernst Schycker
Lord Hamptoncourt—John Grundström
Marquis de Beauvoir—Carl Milton
Anna Danby, rich heiress—Anna Pfeil
Edmond Kean—Emil von der Osten
Director of Covent Garden Theatre—Carl Milton
Bardolph and Tom, actors—John Grundström and Carl Milton
Darius, theatre hairdresser—Ernst Schycker
Salomon, prompter—Carl Pfeil
Pistol, rope dancer—Ludwig Lundgren

Peter Patt, host at sailors' tavern, "The Coal Mine"—Ernst Schycker
Louise, lady in waiting—Mrs. Hanna Hvitfeldt
(Program)

Herr Dardanell och hans upptåg på landet, Oct. 4, 1896.
Herr Dardanell—Carl Pfeil
Mrs. Hedda Fox—Ida Anderson-Werner
Agapetus, her son—Anna Pfeil
Miller Wädersten—John Lindhagen
Baron Lejonkula—Albert Alberg
Henrik Strand—Carl Milton
Krok—Matt Ovington
Servant—Ellen Graf
(*S.K.,* Oct. 6, 1896)

Vermländingarne, Nov. 1, 1896.
Provst—Carl Pfeil
Sven Ersson i Hult—Gunnar Sahlin
Lisa, his wife—Mrs. Hanna Hvitfeldt
Erik, their son—Max Hedman
Britta—Ellen Graf
Jan Hansson vid sjön—Matt Ovington
Annika, his wife—Ida Anderson-Werner
Anna, their daughter—Anna Pfeil
Per, Sven Ersson's servant—Carl Milton
Stina, Sven Ersson's maid—Augusta Milton
Nils Jonsson, called Löpare-Nisse—Carl Pfeil
(*S.K.,* Nov. 4, 1896)

Pinafore, Nov. 15, 1896.
Sir Joseph Porter—Knut Schröder
Captain Corcoran—Christopher Brusell
Ralph Rackstraw—Gust. Lindquist
Dick Deadeye—Fred R. Franson
Bill Bobstaye—Herman Sundean
Bob Becket—Th. Johnson
Tom Tucker—Little Anna Pfeil
Josephine—Ida Linn
Hebe—Breda Schoeninger
Little Buttercup—Anna Pfeil
(Program)

Pinafore, Jan. 10, 1897.
Same cast as above, with one change:
Hebe—Margaret Dahlström
(Program)

Andersson, Pettersson och Lundström, Oct. 1, 1898
Hocus Pocus, ruling monarch—Fred Bolling
Mystifax, his high priest—Carl Milton
Hilaris, son of Mystifax—Little Anna Pfeil
Fortuna, fortune's fairy—Ellen Graf
Brillantin, her daughter—Bessie Nelson

302

Amorosa, true love's fairy—Anna Pfeil
Lumpacius, protector of frivolity—John Lindhagen
Andersson, journeyman joiner—Leopold Kjellman
Pettersson, journeyman tailor—Knut Schröder
Lundström, journeyman shoemaker—Carl Pfeil
Mother Pehrson—Mrs. Hanna Hvitfeldt
Pluggstedt, school teacher—Fred Bolling
Olle, country boy—Anna Pfeil
Lisa, country girl—Ellen Graf
Hasselqvist, master joiner—Fred Bolling
Lotta, his daughter—Anna Pfeil
Janne, joiner's apprentice—Carl Milton
Fia, maid at Hasselqvists—Mrs. Hanna Hvitfeldt
Stryker, portait painter—Carl Milton
Balance, merchant—Leopold Kjellman
Baron von Luftig—John Lindhagen
Camille—Anna Pfeil
Isabella—Ellen Graf
Annette, maid—Marie Connelly
Hammarlund, coppersmith—Carl Pfeil
(Program)

Lilla helgonet, Jan. 12, 1899.
Prioress—Mrs. Hanna Hvitfeldt
Denise de Falvigny, the little saint—Anna Pfeil
Célestin, organist—Knut Schröder
Sister—Anna Almgren Ovington
Count Chateau Gibus, major—Fred R. Franson
Fernaud de Champlatreux—Siegfried Franson
Lariat, corporal on leave—Gust. Lindquist
Gustave—Aug. Anderson
Robert—Albert Andren
Theatre director—C. J. Erickson
Stage manager—Patrick Warner
Corinne ⎰ —Anna Almgren Ovington
Gimblette ⎱ actresses —Linnea Hultman
Lydia ⎰ —Emma Nyberg
Sylvia ⎱ —Jennie Warner
Corporal—Axel Anderson
First student—Clara Billquist
Second student—Greta Hvitfeldt
Third student—Little Anna Pfeil
(Program)

Anna Stina i Chicago, Nov. 5, 1899.
Country girl—Mrs. Anna Francke
Alderman-saloon keeper—Ernest Lindblom
Contractor—John Lindhagen
Coachman—John Lindhagen
Gus—Knut Schröder
Baron Lejon—Knut Schröder

303

Bartender—Max Hedman
Young Swedish-American—Ernst Behmer
Lover—Christopher Brusell
Fiancée—Ellen Graf
Landlady—Mrs. Hanna Hvitfeldt
Cook—Ida Anderson-Werner
(S.T., Nov, 8, 1899; roles)

Vermländingarne, Mch. 18, 1900.
Sven Ersson i Hult—Ernest Lindblom
Lisa, his wife—Ida Anderson-Werner
Erik, their son—Christopher Brusell
Ola i Gyllby, wealthy farmer—Oscar Sundborg
Jan Hansson vid sjön—Leopold Kjellman
Annika, his wife—Mrs. Hanna Hvitfeldt
Anna, their daughter—Anna Pfeil
Anders, their servant—Ernst Behmer
Stina, Sven Ersson's maid—Therese Sundborg
Nils Jonsson, called Löpare-Nisse—Oscar Sundborg
(S.T., Mch. 21, 1900)

Erik den fjortonde, Oct. 18, 1900.
Oxenstjerna—Robert Lindblom
Duke Carl—"Kurre" Johnson
Johan III—Alderman Larson
Erik XIV—Johan Erickson
Stenbocker—Frans A. Lindstrand
Gustaf II Adolf—Johan A. Enander
Dr. Bruselius—Sam Carlson
Katarina Månsdotter—Ottilie Mörk Myhrman
Carl XII—Gusten Myhrman
Gustav III—Jakob Bonggren
Oscar II—Albert Alberg
Fredrik I—Gus Broberg
Carl XIV—Dr. Carl Swensson
Bellman—John Örtengren
Lejonshufvud—Ernst W. Olson
Ulrika Eleonora—Mrs. Frank Lundin
Queen Louisa—Mrs. Edvall
Carl XIII—Alderman Olson
Gustav IV—Alderman Petterson
Göran Persson—Alderman Hallström
Fredrik VII—Carl Netterström
Gustaf Vasa's court brewer—Mr. Wennersten
Carl XIII's court brewer—Frank Lundin
King Erik's court tailor—Johan Rydell
(S.A., Oct. 9, 1900)

Per Olsson och hans käring, Nov. 4, 1900.
Per Olsson, farmer—Christopher Brusell
Katrina, his wife—Ida Anderson-Werner
Erker, their son—Fred Bolling

304

Olof, Per's son by his first marriage—Ernst Behmer
Jöns i Nöbbelöf, farmer—Ernest Lindblom
Lisa, his daughter—Anna Pfeil
Fattig-Johan, Per's brother—Leopold Kjellman
Anders, peddler from West Gothland—Oscar Sundborg
Sanna, Per's servant—Therese Sundborg
(*S.T.*, Nov. 28, 1900)

Vermländingarne, Feb. 9, 1901.
Sven Ersson i Hult—Ernest Lindblom
Lisa, his wife—Ida Anderson-Werner
Erik, their son—John Örtengren
Ola i Gyllby, wealthy farmer—Adolf Paulson
Britta, his daughter—Therese Sundborg
Jan Hansson vid sjön—Leopold Kjellman
Annika, his wife—Mrs. Hanna Hvitfeldt
Anna, their daughter—Ragna Linné
Anders, their servant—Christopher Brusell
Stina, Sven Ersson's maid—Anna Pfeil
Nils Jonsson, called Löpare-Nisse—Carl Pfeil
(*S.K.*, Feb. 12, 1901)

Smålandsknekten, Nov. 23, 1901.
Nisse i Stangård—John Lindhagen
Inga, his daughter—Anna Pfeil
Juryman—Ernest Lindblom
Anna Brita, his wife—Therese Sundborg
Lasse, their son—Fred Bolling
Hurtig—Christopher Brusell
Standard-bearer—Ernst Schycker
Spel-Ola, fiddler—Leopold Kjellman
Corporal Rask—Ernst Behmer
Stina på Hägnet—Ida Anderson-Werner
Håkon—Ernst Ekberg
(*S.N.*, Nov. 26, 1901)

Sven och liten Anna, Dec. 7, 1901.
Lars Hanson—John Lindhagen
Anna Hanson—Anna Pfeil
Sven—Christopher Brusell
Striding, sheriff—Ernest Lindblom
Jon Jonson, miller—Leopold Kjellman
Erik Olafson, miner—Ernest Lindblom
Minister—Fred Bolling
Per, servant—Ernst Behmer
Karin, servant—Therese Sundborg
(*S.N.*, Dec. 10, *S.T.*, Dec. 11, 1901)

Engelbrekt och hans Dalkarlar, Feb. 6, 1902.
Engelbrekt—John Örtengren
Ingrid, his wife—Mrs. Hanna Hvitfeldt

Ingeborg, their daughter—Agnes Hedström
Sven Ulfsen—Ernest Lindblom
Jösse Erickson—Ernst Schycker
Abilgard, his son—Mr. Leonard
Måns Bengtson—John Lindhagen
Erik XIII—Mr. Erickson
Filippa, Queen—Therese Sundborg
Cecilia, lady-in-waiting—Ellen Graf
Abbess—Selma Tidblom
Danish knight—Leopold Kjellman
Bishop of Linköping—Hjalmar Wessberg
Erik—Mr. Westerberg
Monk—Ernst Ekberg
Märta—Signe Mortenson
Karin—Ida Linn
Troubador—C. F. Martens
(S.T., Feb. 12, 1902)

Öregrund-Östhammar, Mch. 8, 1902.
Östhammar residents:
    Filip Bratt, city treasurer and merchant—Hjalmar Wessberg
    Mathias Grönberg, dyer—Carl Pfeil
    Lars Erik Örtenquist, druggist—Ernst Schycker
    Mathilda, Bratt's wife—Therese Sundborg
Öregrund residents:
    Ringdahl, sexton and organist—Ernst Behmer
    Rutberg, glazier—Ernest Lindblom
    Frisén, wig maker—Leopold Kjellman
Emil Klint, Bratt's nephew, undergraduate at Upsala—Anna Pfeil
Mrs. Söderström, hotel keeper—Ellen Graf
Susanna, her relative—Little Anna Pfeil
(S.N., Mch. 11, 1902, play MS.)

Vermländingarne, Nov. 9, 1902.
Brukspatron—Ernest Lindblom
Provst—Carl Liljegren
Sven Ersson i Hult—Christopher Brusell
Lisa, his wife—Ida Anderson-Werner
Erik, their son—Arthur Donaldson
Jan Hansson vid sjön—Ernst Schycker
Annika, his wife—Mrs. Hulda Feltskogh
Anna, their daughter—Anna Pfeil
Anders, their servant—Ernst Behmer
Per, Sven Ersson's servant—Fred Bolling
(S.A., Nov. 11, 1902)

Valborgsmesso-aftonen, Mch. 29, 1903.
Tattar-Svens—Christopher Brusell
Svärd, old soldier—Carl Liljegren
Waxelin, sexton—Leopold Kjellman
Ola Manson, farmer—Ernst Schycker

Rydquist—Ernest Lindblom
Mother Elin—Ida Anderson-Werner
Lotta—Anna Nelson
Pehr—Max Hedman
Nils i Kroken—Carl Milton
Britta—Augusta Milton
Servants—Fred Bolling, Oscar Sundborg
Servants—Ellen Graf, Magda Anderson
(*S.N.*, Mch. 31, 1903)

Lifvet på landet, Oct. 25, 1903
Baron Axel von Rambow, estate owner—John Örtengren
Frida, his wife—Ellen Graf
Frans von Rambow, his cousin—Max Hedman
Pomuckelskopp, landed proprietor—Ernest Lindblom
Mrs. Pomuckelskopp—Ida Anderson-Werner
Salla and Malla, their daughters—Signe Mortenson and Hildur Levin
Pastor Behrendsohn—Ernst Schycker
Karolina, his wife—Mrs. Hanna Hvitfeldt
Fritz Tiddelfitz, her nephew—Leopold Kjellman
Haverman, inspector—Christopher Brusell
Louise, his daughter—Hedwig Brusell
Marie Möller, his servant—Augusta Milton
Bräsig—Carl Liljegren
Knifving, lawyer—Carl Milton
Daniel, Rambow's old servant—Fred Bolling
Kristian Dasel and Peter Wasel, laborers—Oscar Sundborg and Ernest Lindblom
Katarina, Dasel's wife—Signe Mortenson
(*S.A., S.K.*, Oct. 27, 1903, play MS.)

Vermländingarne, Dec. 5, 1903.
Brukspatron—Ernest Lindblom
Wilhelm, his son—Robert Johnson
Lotta, his daughter—Hedwig Brusell
Provst—Carl Milton
Sven Ersson i Hult—Carl Liljegren
Lisa, his wife—Ida Anderson-Werner
Erik, their son—Max Hedman
Ola i Gyllby, wealthy farmer—Carl Milton
Britta, his daughter—Ellen Graf
Jan Hansson vid sjön—Leopold Kjellman
Annika, his wife—Augusta Milton
Anna, their daughter—Ida Linn
Anders, their servant—Christopher Brusell
Per, Sven Ersson's servant—Fred Bolling
Bengt på Åsen—Ernst Schycker
Nils Jonsson, called Löpare-Nisse—Ernst Schycker
(*S.T.*, Dec. 9, 1903)

Lifvet på landet. Dec. 20, 1903
Same cast as Oct. 25, 1903.

307

Jorden rundt på 80 dagar, Feb. 25, 1904.
Phineas Fogg—Matt Ovington
Passepartout—John Örtengren
Detective Fixit—Christopher Brusell
Corsican—Fred Littche
Englishman—Ernst Schycker
German saloon keeper—Ernst Schycker
Police chief at Port Said—Fred Bolling
Indian chief—Ernest Lindblom
Margareta—Hedwig Brusell
Rajah's widow—Ellen Graf
Rajah's sister—Alice Collini
(*S.A.,* Mch. 1, 1904)

Svärfar, Oct. 16, 1904.
Theodor Klint, zoology professor—Ernst Behmer
Cecilia, his wife—Ida Anderson-Werner
Elisabeth ⎫   ⎧ —Anna Pfeil
Karin   ⎬ their daughters ⎨ —Mabel Runberg
Elsa   ⎭   ⎩ —Magnhild Runberg
Mrs. Louisa Engström, Cecilia's mother—Alice Collini
Axel Fahrström, lieutenant—C. Sheldon
Otto Norstedt, artist—Fred Littche
Agaton Pumpendal, assessor—Carl Liljegren
Amanda, model—Helga Håkanson
Strange gentleman—Ernest Lindblom
Emilie, Klints' servant—Augusta Milton
(Program)

Så tuktas en argbigga, Nov. 20, 1904.
Kate—Wilma Sundborg-Stern
Petruchio—Ernst Behmer
Gremio—Carl Liljegren
Curtis—Ida Anderson-Werner
Bianca—Anna Pfeil
Baptista—Albert Alberg
Hortensio—C. Sheldon
Grumio—Fred Bolling
Tailor—Ernest Lindblom
Servants—John Melin and Ernest Lindblom
(*S.N.,* Nov. 22, 1904)

Vermländingarne, Dec. 4, 1904.
Sven Ersson i Hult—Ernest Lindblom
Lisa, his wife—Ida Anderson-Werner
Erik, their son—John Örtengren
Jan Hansson vid sjön—Ernst Schycker
Annika, his wife—Alice Collini
Anna, their daughter—Hedwig Brusell
Anders, their servant—Christopher Brusell
Stina, Sven Ersson's maid—Augusta Milton
Nils Jonsson, called Löpare-Nisse—Ernst Schycker
(*S.A.,* Dec. 6, 1904)

Ljungby Horn, Mch. 19, 1905.
Didrik, troll—Christopher Brusell
Tulla, troll woman—Ida Anderson-Werner
Birgit—Augusta Milton
Måns Kruse of Månstorp, knight—Carl Liljegren
Olle Pomp, soldier, follower of Måns—John Fernlundh
Olof, nobleman—John Örtengren
Hildur—Hedwig Brusell
Ivar Munk, magistrate—Ernest Lindblom
Mountain king—Ernest Lindblom
Court chaplain—Ernest Lindblom
Country judge—Carl Milton
Vidrik, troll—Carl Milton
Lady Ingrid of Ljungby—Mrs. Hulda Feltskogh
Mother Greta—Alice Collini
Per, country boy—Fred Bolling
Mermaid—Helen Håkanson
Flittermouse—Alice Collini
Servants—Alice Collini and Helga Håkanson
(*S.T.,* Mch. 22, 1905, play MS.)

Ära, Apr. 16, 1905.
Counsellor Mühlingh—Albert Alberg
Kurt Mühlingh, his son—Max Hedman
Lenore Mühlingh, his daughter—Sara Nordstrom
Lothar Brandt—Carl Milton
Count von Traft-Saarberg—Christopher Brusell
Robert Heinecke—John Fernlundh
Old Heinecke—Carl Liljegren
His wife—Ida Anderson-Werner
Alma, their daughter—Hedwig Brusell
Augusta, their daughter—Sigrid Lindberg
Michalski, Augusta's husband—Ernest Lindblom
Mrs. Hebenstreit—Augusta Milton
(*S.T.,* Apr. 19, 1905)

Vermländingarne, Aug 26, 1905.
Brukspatron—Joel Mossberg
Wilhelm, his son—Axel Hulten
Lotta, his daughter—Anna Nordstrom
Provst—Carl Liljegren
Sven Ersson i Hult—Ernest Lindblom
Lisa, his wife—Ida Anderson-Werner
Erik, their son—Christopher Brusell
Ola i Gyllby, wealthy farmer—Adolf Paulson
Britta, his daughter—Maria Schycker
Anna—Madame Anna Hellström
Anders—Richard Rosengren
Per, Sven Ersson's servant—Fred Bolling
Stina, Sven Ersson's maid—Sara Nordstrom
Bengt på Åsen—John Melin

309

Nils Jonsson, called Löpare-Nisse—Ernst Schycker
(*S.T.*, Aug. 30, 1905)

Farbror Knut från Norrköping, Sept. 23, 1905.
Henrik Brander, chamberlain—Ernst Behmer
Ellen, his wife—Augusta Milton
Arthur, his son—Werner Melinder
Knut Brander, manufacturer, Henrik's brother—Carl Liljegren
Rickard, his son—Leopold Chellman
Ahlengren, merchant—C. Sheldon
Elise, his daughter—Anna Anderson
Johan, servant—John Melin
(*S.T.*, Sept. 27, 1905)

Andersson, Pettersson och Lundström, Dec. 3, 1905.
Hocus Pocus, ruling monarch—Ernest Lindblom
Filiocus, his high priest—Carl Milton
Mystifax, son of Filiocus—C. Sheldon
Fortuna, fortune's fairy—Wilma Sundborg-Stern
Koketta, her daughter—Sigrid Lindberg
Amorosa, true love's fairy—Sara Nordstrom
Infernalis, protector of frivolity—Werner Melinder
Andersson, journeyman joiner—Werner Melinder
Pettersson, journeyman tailor—Carl Liljegren
Lundström, journeyman shoemaker—Ernst Behmer
Jan Pehrson, wealthy peasant—Ernst Ekberg
Pluggstedt, school teacher—Carl Milton
Olle, country boy—John Melin
Lisa, country girl—Sara Nordstrom
Hasselqvist, master joiner—Ernest Lindblom
Fiken, his daughter—Sara Nordstrom
Janne, joiner's apprentice—Carl Milton
Fia, maid at Hasselqvist's—Wilma Sundborg-Stern
Plank, portrait painter—Carl Milton
Balance, merchant—John Melin
Oxelqvist, butcher—Ernest Lindblom
Baron von Luftig—C. Sheldon
Jew—Ernst Ekberg
Countrywoman—Sigrid Lindberg
Camille—Wilma Sundborg-Stern
Isabella—Sigrid Lindberg
(Program)

Barnhusbarnen, Jan. 7, 1906.
Colonel Melcher—Ernst Behmer
His valet—Carl Milton
Mathias Bertel—Carl Liljegren
Sara, his wife—Augusta Milton
Fanny } orphans { —Anna Anderson
Herman } orphans { —Werner Melinder
Countess Leonora—Ida Anderson-Werner

310

Jacob, sailor—Ernest Lindblom
Army officer—Elis Gustafson
(*S.T.*, Jan. 9, 1906)

Bröllopet på Ulfåsa, Jan. 28, 1906.
Knut Algotson—John Lindhagen
Ingrid, his wife—Ida Anderson-Werner
Sigrid, the Fair, their daughter—Hedwig Brusell
Björn, squire—Ernst Schycker
Bengt Lagman—Werner Melinder
Kol Tynnelson, his groom—Ernest Lindblom
Birger Jarl—Arthur Donaldson
His wife—Augusta Milton
Härved Boson—Christopher Brusell
Prior Botvid—Leopold Kjellman
Inga—Sigrid Lindberg
Sune—M. Hägg
(*S.T.*, Jan. 30, 1906)

Den ondes besegrare, May 13, 1906.
Asmodeus—Arthur Donaldson
Oswald, farmer—Ernst Schycker
Maria—Hedwig Brusell
Joseph, her betrothed—Werner Melinder
Old woman—Ida Anderson-Werner
Nepomak Blaisus, love-sick sexton—Lopold Chellman
Batli—Augusta Milton
Damian—Christopher Brusell
(*S.T.*, May 15, 1906)

Nerkingarne, May 19, 1906
Stål, *brukspatron*—Carl Liljegren
Selma, his daughter—Sara Nordstrom
Mamsell Bom, governess—Ida Anderson-Werner
Sven Jonsson i Lekhyttan, official—C. Sheldon
Sven, his son, student—Max Hedman
Mother Katarina, Sven Jonsson's sister, rich miner's widow—Alice Collini
Lasse, official, her son—Ernst Behmer
Olle Lek, student, her son—Patrick Warner
Östing, former soldier, now sexton and fiddler—Ernest Lindblom
Ingeborg, shepherdess—Ellyn M. Swanson
Stina, Mother Katarina's servant—Ida Östergren
(Program)

En afton på "Tre Byttor," July 29, 1906
Gustaf III—Christopher Brusell
Elis Schröderheim—Carl Nielson
Carl Michael Bellman—Joel Mossberg
Ulla Winblad—Sara Nordstrom
Movitz, constable and alehouse fiddler—Max Hedman
Mollberg, corporal—Fred R. Franson

311

Father Berg—Pelle Westerberg
Christian Wingmark—Ernst Ekberg
Mother Maja Lena, alehouse keeper at "Tre Byttor,"—Mrs. Sara Nordstrom
Lisa, her barmaid—Wanja Nauclair
Bredström—Mauritz Hultin
Cajsa Stina—Maria Schycker
Jergen Puckel, of German birth—Ernst Schycker
Miss Lona—Mrs. Nauclair
Grip ⎱ palace servants ⎰—William Dahlen
Hummer ⎰ ⎱—Mr. Boström
(*S.T.N.,* July 24, 1906)

Lifvet på landet, Nov. 18, 1906.
Baron Axel von Rambow, estate owner—John Örtengren
Frida, his wife—Ida Östergren
Frans von Rambow, his cousin—Patrick Warner
Pomuckelskopp, landed proprietor—Ernest Lindblom
Mrs. Pomuckelskopp—Maria Schycker
Pastor Behrendsohn—Ernst Schycker
Karolina, his wife—Mrs. Sara Nordstrom
Fritz Tiddelfitz, her nephew—Ernst Behmer
Haverman, inspector—Christopher Brusell
Louise, his daughter—Sara Nordstrom
Bräsig—Carl Liljegren
Knifving, lawyer—Ernst Ekberg
(*S.A.,* Nov. 20, *S.K.,* Nov. 24, 1906)

Lars Anders och Jan Anders och deras barn, Jan. 1, 1907.
Lars Anders—Carl Liljegren
Jan Anders—Christopher Brusell
Britta Stina—Ida Anderson-Werner
Karolina—Maria Schycker
Lena—Sara Nordstrom
Karl Johan—Ernst Behmer
Anna Mansson, young widow—Augusta Milton
Jonas, servant—Ernest Lindblom
(*S.T.N.,* Jan. 8, 1907)

Pelle Grönlunds bryggeri, Feb. 3, 1907.
Baron Hugo Lindencrantz—Christopher Brusell
Adele von Löwenancker—Ida Östergren
Mrs. Hedwig Grönlund—Ida Anderson-Werner
Aurora, her daughter—Sara Nordstrom
Daniel Isaacson—Carl Liljegren
Meyer—Ernst Behmer
Blomquist, ale connoisseur—Ernest Lindblom
Anderson, shoemaker—Ernest Lindblom
Stina—Signe Mortenson
Mats—Walter Jones
Maria—Hedwig Brusell Melinder
Olson, shoemaker—John Ternquist

312

Zetterberg, brewmaster—Werner Melinder
Vesterlund—Ernst Schycker
(*S.K.*, Feb. 9, 1907)

Rosen på Tistelön, Apr. 14, 1907.
Anton Haroldson—Ernst Behmer
Birger Haroldson—Carl Liljegren
Haroldson—Christopher Brusell
Gabriella Haroldson, the rose—Hedwig Brusell Melinder
Erika, Birger's wife—Ida Östergren
Lieutenant Arnman—Werner Melinder
Askenberg, shoemaker—Ernest Lindblom
His wife—Augusta Milton
Rydquist, sheriff—Ernst Schycker
Märtan—Walter Jones
(*S.T.N.*, Apr. 9, 1907)

Ett dockhem, May 11, 1907.
Torvald Helmer—Ernst Behmer
Nora, his wife—Ida Östergren
Emmy, their daughter—Lisa Behmer
Ivar, their son—Eric Behmer
Doctor Rank—Carl Liljegren
Mrs. Linde—Ida Anderson-Werner
Krogstad, lawyer—Ernest Lindblom
Anne-Marie, nurse maid—Signe Mortenson
City messenger—Walter Jones
(Program)

Hjärtesorg, June 2, 1907.
Joel—John Fernlundh
Therese—Ida Östergren
Jean Marie—Ernst Behmer
(Program)

Hon vill inte gifta sig, June 2, 1907.
He—Ernst Behmer
She—Ida Östergren
(Program)

En midsommarnatt i Dalarne, June 23, 1907.
Matts—Carl Liljegren
Britta—Ellyn Swanson
Göran—Carl Lönnerblad
Håkan—Leopold Kjellman
Lisa—Signe Mortenson
Karin—Wanja Nauclair
Baron Axel—Werner Melinder
Karl, artist—Christopher Brusell
Gustaf—Ernest Lindblom
(*S.K.*, June 15, 1907)

Vermländingarne, July 21, 1907.
Brukspatron—Joel Mossberg
Wilhelm, his son—M. Hägg
Lotta, his daughter—Wanja Nauclair
Provst—Carl Liljegren
Sven Ersson i Hult—Ernest Lindblom
Lisa, his wife—Ida Anderson-Werner
Erik, their son—Werner Melinder
Ola i Gyllby, wealthy farmer—Carl Liljegren
Britta, his daughter—Sigrid Lindberg
Jan Hansson vid sjön—Ernst Schycker
Annika, his wife—Augusta Milton
Anna, their daughter—Rosa Grünberg
Anders, their servant—Christopher Brusell
Stina, Sven Ersson's maid—Madame Emma Meissner
Bengt på Åsen—Carl Sterner
Nils Jonsson, called Löpare-Nisse—Leopold Chellman
(*S.T.N.,* July 23, 1907)

Gamla Heidelberg, Sept. 22, 1907.
Karl Henrik, crown prince of Sachsen-Karlsburg—Ernst Behmer
His Excellency von Haugk, minister of state—Patrick Warner
Von Passarge, court marshal—Ernest Lindblom
Counsellor von Breitenberg—L. Swanström
Jüttner, doctor of philosophy—Carl Liljegren
Lutz, valet—Leopold Kjellman
Rüder, innkeeper—Fred Bolling
Mrs. Rüder—Signe Mortenson
Mrs. Dörffel, her aunt—Ida Anderson-Werner
Käthie—Ida Östergren
Count Detlef von Asterberg—Ernest Lindblom
Karl Bilz — Frithiof Burgeson
Kurt Engelbrecht ⎱ Heidelberg ⎰ —L. Swanström
Von Wedell ⎰ students ⎱ —C. Werner
Kellerman, students' waiter—John Ternquist
Schölerman, lackey—Hilding Alarik
Glanz, lackey—Fred Bolling
(Program)

Öregrund-Östhammar, Nov. 23, 1907 (Waukegan, Ill.)
Östhammar residents:
    Filip Bratt, city treasurer and merchant—Ernest Lindblom
    Mathias Grönberg, dyer—Ernst Behmer
    Lars Erik Örtenquist, druggist—Leopold Kjellman
    Mathilda, Bratt's wife—Ida Anderson-Werner
    Dorothea, Grönberg's wife—Signe Mortenson
    Evelina, Örtenquist's wife—Alice Collini
Öregrund residents:
    Ringdahl, sexton and organist—Carl Liljegren
    Rutberg, glazier—John Ternquist
    Frisén, wig maker—Fred Bolling

Emil Klint, Bratt's nephew, undergraduate at Upsala—Ida Östergren
Karl Thorell, engineer—David Luthers
Mrs. Söderström, hotel keeper—Sigrid Lindberg
Susanna, her relative—Rosa Pearson
Fritz, hotel employee—Frithiof Burgeson
Josephine, chambermaid—Ella Eklund
(Program)

Bröllopet på Ulfåsa, Nov. 24, 1907.
Knut Algotson—John Lindhagen
Sigrid the Fair, his daughter—Hedwig Brusell Melinder
Björn, squire—Ernst Schycker
Bengt Lagman—Arthur Donaldson
Kol Tynnelson, his groom—Carl Lönnerblad
Birger Jarl—Christopher Brusell
Härved Boson—Walter Jones
Prior Botvid—Ernst Berg
Mechthild—Maria Schycker
(*S.K.,* Nov. 30, 1907)

Sabinskornas bortröfvande, Dec. 8, 1907.
Direktor Striese—Arthur Donaldson
Professor Gallen—John Lindhagen
His wife—Madame Emma Wallin-Malm
Karl Gross—Ernst Schycker
Emil Gross—Oscar Larson
Paula—Hedwig Brusell Melinder
Maria—Edla Wikström
Augusta—Karin Crok
Meissner—Walter Jones
Servant—Augusta Milton
Dr. Nyman—Carl Lönnerblad
(*S.T.N.,* Dec. 10, 1907)

Herr Dardanell och hans upptåg på landet, Dec. 15, 1907.
Herr Dardanell—Ernst Behmer
Mrs. Hedda Fox—Ida Anderson-Werner
Agapetus, her son—Ida Östergren
Miller Wädersten—Ernest Lindblom
Jacob, his servant—Frithiof Burgeson
Servant—Sigrid Lindberg
Baron Lejonkula—John Ternquist
Johan, his servant—Fred Bolling
Henrik Strand—Leopold Kjellman
Krok—Carl Liljegren
Dorothea—Rosa Pearson
Lena—Signe Mortenson
(*S.A.,* Dec. 17, 1907)

Vermländingarne, Jan. 1, 1908.
Brukspatron—Joel Mossberg
Provst—Ernst Berg

315

Sven Ersson i Hult—Christopher Brusell
Lisa, his wife—Ida Anderson-Werner
Erik, their son—Carl Lönnerblad
Jan Hansson vid sjön—Ernst Schycker
Anna, his daughter—Hedwig Brusell Melinder
Anders, his servant—Oscar Larson
Nils Jonsson, called Löpare-Nisse—John Lindhagen
(S.A., Jan. 7, 1908)

Regina von Emmeritz, Jan. 19, 1908.
King Gustaf II Adolf—John Örtengren
Prince of Emmeritz—Carl Liljegren
Regina von Emmeritz—Ida Östergren
Axel Lilje, Colonel for Österbottning men—John Ternquist
Larson, Swedish officer of Finnish cavalry—Ernest Lindblom
Bertil, Finnish officer of Finnish cavalry—Gunnar Brandt
Father Hieronymus, head of Jesuits—Ernst Behmer
First monk—William Larson
Second monk—Leopold Chellman
Von Alten, German colonel in Swedish service—B. Brady
Swedish herald—Fred Bolling
Dorthe, Regina's nurse—Ida Anderson-Werner
Kätchen, chambermaid—Signe Mortenson
First nun—Sigrid Lindberg
Second nun—Rosa Pearson
Swedish riding master—Leopold Chellman
Swedish lieutenant—Will Aronson
Swedish soldier—J. Hermelin
Prince's adjutant—John Melin
(Program)

Flickan i Stadsgården, Mch. 22, 1908.
Brundström, coppersmith—Fred Bolling
His wife—Ida Anderson-Werner
Grönqvist, coppersmith—Ernest Lindblom
Madame Svensson—Sigrid Lindberg
Sergeant Hök—Leopold Chellman
Gustaf Pauli—Gunnar Brandt
Countess Urusoff—Signe Mortenson
Stork, bricklayer—Carl Liljegren
Laura—Ida Östergren
Dr. Adolf Axner—Ernst Behmer
(S.A., Mch. 24, 1908)

Rospiggarna, Oct. 11, 1908.
Lars Österman, home owner—Knut Sjöberg
Hanna, his daughter—Anna Pfeil
Westerbom, fisher—Ernst Schycker
Lina, his wife—Alice Collini
Kalle, steamboat man, their son—Oscar Larson
Anna, servant girl, their daughter—Sigrid Lindberg

316

Mrs. Österberg, fish buyer's widow—Ida Anderson-Werner
Laura, her daughter—Signe Mortenson
Blommen, chief officer of fleet—Tryggve Kling
Sheriff Söderholm—Ernest Lindblom
Janne Boman, skipper—Ernst Behmer
Anders, member of his crew—Fred Bolling
Berg, sheriff's secretary—Carl Svensson
Hulting, former soldier—Carl Liljegren
Victor—John Melin
Police constable—Ernst Schycker
Soldier—E. Herrmelin
Laborers—Ernest Lindblom and Knut Sjöberg
(Program)

Ljungby Horn, Mch. 14, 1909.
Didrik, troll—Christopher Brusell
Tulla, troll woman—Augusta Larson
Birgit—Augusta Milton
Måns Kruse of Månstorp, knight—Carl Liljegren
Olle Pomp, soldier, follower of Måns—Knut Sjöberg
Olof, nobleman—Oscar Larson
Hildur—Gerda Peterson
Ivar Munk, magistrate—Ernest Lindblom
Court chaplain—Ernest Lindblom
Vidrik, troll—Leopold Chellman
(*S.A.,* Mch. 18, 1909)

Parispojken, Sept. 19, 1909.
General de Morin—Otto E. Lundberg
Mrs. de Morin, general's sister-in-law—Augusta Larson
Mrs. Meunier—Ida Anderson-Werner
Joseph, her grandson—Anna Lundberg
Elise, her granddaughter—Karin Lundberg
Amédée, general's son—Ernst Behmer
Hilaire, general's valet—Fred Bolling
Bizot, pawnbroker—Ernest Lindblom
General's servants—Carl Svensson and John Melin
(Program)

Lifvet på landet, Oct. 24, 1909.
Baron Axel von Rambow, estate owner—John Örtengren
Frida, his wife—Sigrid Lindberg
Frans von Rambow, his cousin—Frithiof Burgeson
Pomuckelskopp, landed proprietor—John Ternquist
Mrs. Pomuckelskopp—Ida Anderson-Werner
Their daughter—Effie Rosander
Pastor Behrendsohn—Ernst Schycker
Karolina, his wife—Augusta Milton
Fritz Tiddelfitz, her nephew—John Melin
Haverman, inspector—Ernst Behmer
Louise, his daughter—Rosa Pearson

Bräsig—Ernest Lindblom
Knifving, lawyer—Fred Bolling
Kristian Dasel and Peter Wasel, laborers—Ernst Schycker and Fred Franzen
(*S.A.*, Oct. 28, 1909)

Bröllopet på Ulfåsa, Oct. 31, 1909.
Knut Algotson—Carl Liljegren
Ingrid, his wife—Mrs. Hulda Feltskogh
Sigrid the Fair, their daughter—Sara Nordstrom
Björn, squire—Leopold Chellman
Bengt Lagman—John Örtengren
Kol Tynnelson, his groom—Oscar Larson
Birger Jarl—Christopher Brusell
His wife—Augusta Milton
Härved Boson—C. J. Erickson
Prior Botvid—Knut Schröder
Inga—Karin Crok
Sunne—Axel Jones
(*S.A.*, Nov. 4, 1909)

Andersson, Pettersson och Lundström, Nov. 28, 1909.
Hocus Pocus, ruling monarch—Ernest Lindblom
Fortuna, fortune's fairy—Augusta Larson
Andersson, journeyman joiner—John Melin
Pettersson, journeyman tailor—John Ternquist
Lundström, journeyman shoemaker—Ernst Behmer
Pluggstedt, schoolteacher—Carl Stockenberg
Hasselqvist, master joiner—Ernest Lindblom
Fiken, his daughter—Sigrid Lindberg
Janne, joiner's apprentice—Fred Bolling
Fia, maid at Hasselqvist's—Ida Anderson-Werner
Balance, merchant—Fred Bolling
Baron von Luftig—Carl Stockenberg
Camille—Augusta Larson
(*S.A.*, Nov. 25, *S.K.*, Nov. 27, 1909)

Lifvet på landet, Mch. 13, 1910.
Baron Axel von Rambow, estate owner—Ernst Behmer
Frida, his wife—Sigrid Lindberg
Frans von Rambow, his cousin—Frithiof Burgeson
Pomuckelskopp, landed proprietor—John Ternquist
Mrs. Pomuckelskopp—Ida Anderson-Werner
Salla, their daughter—Anna Matsson
Malla, their daughter—Nanny Hellström
Pastor Behrendsohn—Carl Stockenberg
Karolina, his wife—Augusta Larson
Fritz Tiddelfitz, her nephew—John Melin
Haverman, inspector—Knut Sjöberg
Louise, his daughter—Rosa Pearson
Bräsig—Ernest Lindblom
Knifving, lawyer—Fred Bolling

318

Marie Möller, Haverman's maid—Magda Anderson Lewis
Daniel, Rambow's old servant—Helge Blomdal
Kristian Dasel, laborer—Carl Stockenberg
Peter Wasel, laborer—Frank Lundberg
Katharina, Dasel's wife—Carolina Wibeck
(Program)

Duvals skilsmessa, Oct. 23, 1910.
Henri Duval—Ernst Behmer
Mrs. Bonivard—Ida Anderson-Werner
Diane—Augusta Milton
Corbulon, sea captain—John Ternquist
Champeaux, capitalist—Knut Sjöberg
Borganeuf, former druggist—Carl Liljegren
Gabrielle, his daughter—Florence Johnston
Mariette, chambermaid—Estelle Behmer
Victor, servant—Carl Stockenberg
(S.K., Oct. 29, 1910)

Tosingar, Dec. 11, 1910.
Professor Confucius Wurm, retired head of insane asylum—Carl Liljegren
Thore Wurm, his nephew, medical student—Knut Sjöberg
Inga Griller, professor's granddaughter—Florence Johnston
Brukspatron Zakarias Fikonqvist—Carl Stockenberg
Barbara, his wife, professor's niece—Ida Anderson-Werner
Amedé, their son—Fred Bolling
Hampus Stolling, artist—Ernst Behmer
(S.K., Dec. 17, 1910)

Den lilla sångfågeln, Dec. 26, 1910.
Netchen, flower girl—Ingeborg Sandberg-Settergren
Lord Mickleby—Christopher Brusell
Lover—Leopold Chellman
Friedel, gardener's apprentice—Leopold Chellman
Box, servant—Ernst Ekberg
(S.K., Dec. 31, 1910)

Syndabocken, Jan. 29, 1911.
Rudolf Svennerstedt, rich landowner—John Ternquist
Constance, his wife—Ida Anderson-Werner
Adele, their daughter—Florence Johnston
Hans, Svennerstedt's nephew—Fred Bolling
Lieutenant Erik Liljenstråhle—Ernst Behmer
Lehman, lumber merchant—Knut Sjöberg
Hildegard, his daughter—Mia Windrow
Miss von Igelhoff—Magda Anderson Lewis
Vanda Belinski, equestrienne—Augusta Milton
Professor Otto Grafström—Carl Liljegren
Elise, his wife—Estelle Behmer
Svante Drakenborg—Carl Stockenberg
Frans, servant—F. O. Franzen
(Program)

319

Lifvet på landet, Oct. 1, 1911.
Baron Axel von Rambow, estate owner—Ernst Behmer
Frida, his wife—Sigrid Lindberg
Frans von Rambow, his cousin—Stellan Windrow
Pomuckelskopp, landed proprietor—John Ternquist
Mrs. Pomuckelskopp—Augusta Milton
Pastor Behrendsohn—Carl Stockenberg
Karolina, his wife—Ida Anderson-Werner
Haverman, inspector—Knut Sjöberg
Louise, his daughter—Mia Windrow
Bräsig—Carl Liljegren
Knifving, lawyer—Fred Bolling
Marie Möller, Haverman's maid—Magda Anderson Lewis
(*S.K.,* Oct. 7, 1911)

Sten Stenson Stéen från Eslöf, Nov. 12, 1911.
Ludvig Strand, artist—Stellan Windrow
Hildegard, his sister—Sigrid Lindberg
Anette Strand, their cousin—Gertrud Petterson
Löfman, proprietor, her fiancé—John Melin
Falkengren, merchant from Stockholm—John Ternquist
Theodor, his son, tutor in civil law—Ernst Behmer
Elvira, Falkengren's daughter—Mia Windrow
Ameli Andrén, candidate in philosophy, Falkengren's ward—Augusta Milton
Sten Stenson Stéen, student in law—Elis Olson
Sandbergh, steam ship captain—Carl Liljegren
Froman, engineer—Carl Stockenberg
Anders Person, farmer—Carl Stockenberg
Kjersti, his wife—Ida Anderson-Werner
Martha, their daughter—Estelle Behmer
Truls, Anders Person's servant—Fred Bolling
(*S.K.,* Nov. 18, 1911, and program, Rockford, Ill., for Nov. 25, 1911)

Vermländingarne, Nov. 24, 1911 (Rockford, Ill.).
Brukspatron—Frank Lundberg
Wilhelm, his son—Stellan Windrow
Lotta, his daughter—Mia Windrow
Provst—John Ternquist
Sven Ersson i Hult—Carl Liljegren
Lisa, his wife—Ida Anderson-Werner
Erik, their son—John Melin
Ola i Gyllby, wealthy farmer—John Ternquist
Britta, his daughter—Sigrid Lindberg
Jan Hansson vid sjön—Carl Stockenberg
Annika, his wife—Sigrid Lindberg
Anna, their daughter—Gertrud Petterson
Anders, their servant—Ernst Behmer
Per, Sven Ersson's servant—Fred Bolling
Stina, Sven Ersson's maid—Estelle Behmer
Bengt på Åsen—Fred Bolling
Nils Jonsson, called Löpare-Nisse—Ernst Behmer
(Program)

Gustaf Vasa, Jan. 21, 1912.
King Gustaf I—August Lindberg
Queen Margareta Lejonhufvud—Augusta Milton
Ebba Karlsdotter, nun in Wresta convent, king's mother-in-law—Augusta Larson
Prins Erik—Per Lindberg
Prins Johan—Knut Schröder
Magister Olaus (Olaus Petri)—Ernst Behmer
Herman Israel, counsellor from Lübeck—Ernest Lindblom
Jacob Israel, his son—John Melin
Göran Person, Erik's secretary—Carl Liljegren
Måns Nilson i Aspeboda, miner from Dalarne—John Ternquist
Anders Person på Rankhyttan, miner from Dalarne—Fred Bolling
Ingel Hanson, miner from Dalarne—Carl Stockenberg
Nils i Söderby, miner from Dalarne—Carl Liljegren
Magister Stig, priest at Kopparberg—Frank Lundberg
Måns Nilson's wife—Ida Anderson-Werner
Barbro, her daughter—Estelle Behmer
Two small girls—Elsa Lindblom and Lisa Behmer
Agda, barmaid—Sigrid Lindberg
Karin Månsdotter, flower girl—Mia Windrow
Kristina, Magister Olaus's wife—Anna Matsson
Marcus, clerk—Carl Stockenberg
Stenbock, commander of the guard—Stellan Windrow
Engelbrecht, former miner in Dalarne, ski-runner—Ernest Lindblom
(Program, and interview with Mrs. Knut Schröder)

Påsk, Feb. 1, 1913.
Mrs. Heist—Mrs. Hulda Feltskogh
Elis, her son—Werner Melinder
Eleonora, her daughter—Hedwig Brusell Melinder
Kristina, Elis's fiancée—Ruth Johnson
Benjamin—Oscar Larson
Lindquist—Christopher Brusell
(*H.,* Jan. 28, 1913)

Ära, Mch. 30, 1913.
Counsellor Mühlingh—Knut Sjöberg
Amalie, his wife—Mrs. Hulda Feltskogh
Kurt Mühlingh, their son—Anders Saxon
Lenore Mühlingh, their daughter—Ruth Johnson
Lothar Brandt—Oscar Larson
Count von Traft-Saarberg—Christopher Brusell
Robert Heinecke—Werner Melinder
Old Heinecke—Carl Liljegren
His wife—Augusta Larson
Augusta, their daughter—Thora Kindmark
Alma, their daughter—Hedwig Brusell Melinder
Michalski, Augusta's husband—Gunnar Nordlöf
Mrs. Hebenstreit—Mrs. Hulda Feltskogh
Wilhelm Mühlingh's servant—C. E. Erickson
Johan, Mühlingh's coachman—C. Johnson
Hugo Stengel—John Melin
(*H.,* Mch. 20, 1913)

Farbror Knut från Norrköping, May 18, 1913.
Henrik Brander, chamberlain—Ernst Behmer
Ellen, his wife—Christine Chindblom
Arthur, his son—John Melin
Knut Brander, manufacturer, Henrik's brother—Fred Littche
Rickard, Knut's son—Knut Sjöberg
Ahlengren, merchant—Clarence Ongman
Elise, his daughter—Lisa Behmer
Johan, servant—Edgar von Melen
Sundquist, shoemaker—Anders Saxon
(Program)

Vermländingarne, Sept. 21, 1913.
Brukspatron—Frank Lundberg
Wilhelm, his son—Stellan Windrow
Lotta, his daughter—Thyra Ericson
Provst—Carl Liljegren
Sven Ersson i Hult—Christopher Brusell
Lisa, his wife—Augusta Larson
Erik, their son—John Melin
Ola i Gyllby, wealthy farmer—Carl Liljegren
Britta, his daughter—Thora Kindmark
Jan Hansson vid sjön—Leopold Chellman
Anna, his daughter—Ingeborg Sandberg-Settergren
Anders, their servant—Eric J. Ericson
Per, Sven Ersson's servant—Gunnar Nordlöf
Stina, Sven Ersson's servant—Elna Lilnequist
Nils Jonsson, called Löpare-Nisse—Leopold Chellman
(*S.K.,* Sept. 25, 1913)

Vermländingarne, Sept. 28, 1913.
Brukspatron—Ernest Lindblom
Wilhelm, his son—Anders Saxon
Provst—Oscar Larson
Sven Ersson i Hult—Knut Sjöberg
Lisa, his wife—Ida Anderson-Werner
Erik, their son—Werner Melinder
Anna—Hedwig Brusell Melinder
Anders—Ernst Behmer
Per, Sven Ersson's servant—Fred Bolling
Stina, Sven Ersson's servant—Ruth Johnson
Nils Jonsson, called Löpare-Nisse—Ernst Behmer
(*S.A.,* Oct. 2, 1913)

Vermländingarne, Feb. 22, 1914.
Brukspatron—Ernest Lindblom
Wilhelm, his son—Sten S... son Ödmann
Lotta, his daughter—Lisa Behmer
Provst—John Ternquist
Sven Ersson i Hult—Knut Sjöberg
Lisa, his wife—Ida Anderson-Werner

Erik, their son—Werner Melinder
Ola i Gyllby, wealthy farmer—John Ternquist
Britta, his daughter—Sigrid Lindberg
Jan Hansson vid sjön—Carl Stockenberg
Annika, his wife—Sigrid Lindberg
Anna, their daughter—Hedwig Brusell Melinder
Anders, their servant—Ernst Behmer
Per, Sven Ersson's servant—Oscar Larson
Stina, Sven Ersson's maid—Ruth Johnson
Bengt på Åsen—Gustaf Lund
Nils Jonsson, called Löpare-Nisse—Ernst Behmer
(Program)

Lifvet på landet, Mch. 29, 1914.
Baron Axel von Rambow, estate owner—Werner Melinder
Frida, his wife—Hedwig Brusell Melinder
Frans von Rambow, his cousin—Oscar Larson
Pomuckelskopp, landed proprietor—John Ternquist
Mrs. Pomuckelskopp—Ida Anderson-Werner
Pastor Behrendsohn—Carl Stockenberg
Karolina, his wife—Augusta Larson
Haverman, inspector—Ernst Behmer
Louise, his daughter—Ruth Johnson
Bräsig—Ernest Lindblom
Knifving, lawyer—Carl Milton
Marie Möller, Haverman's maid—Magda Anderson Lewis
Daniel, Rambow's old servant—N. Erikson
Kristian Dasel, laborer—Carl Stockenberg
Peter Wasel, laborer—Frank Lundberg
(*H.,* Mch. 19, *S.A.,* Apr. 2, 1914)

En afton på "Tre Byttor," July 26, 1914.
Gustaf III—Carl Lönnerblad
Carl Michael Bellman—John Melin
Ulla Winblad—Sara Nordstrom
Movitz, constable and alehouse fiddler—Christopher Brusell
Mollberg, corporal—Fred Bolling
Father Berg—Gunnar Nordlöf
Mother Maja Lena, alehouse keeper at "Tre Byttor"—Carl Liljegren
Bredström—Ernest Lindblom
Jergen Puckel, of German birth—Ernst Schycker
(*S.K.,* July 30, 1914)

Paria, Aug. 2, 1914.
Mr. X—Harold Theel
Mr. Y—Stellan Windrow
(*S.A.,* July 30, 1914)

Vermländingarne, Sept. 20, 1914
Brukspatron—Ernest Lindblom
Lotta, his daughter—Lisa Behmer

323

Provst—Oscar Larson
Sven Ersson i Hult—Knut Sjöberg
Lisa, his wife—Ida Anderson-Werner
Erik, their son—John Melin
Ola i Gyllby, wealthy farmer—Oscar Larson
Britta, his daughter—Augusta Milton
Jan Hansson vid sjön—Carl Stockenberg
Annika, his wife—Augusta Milton
Anna, their daughter—Ebba Kempe
Anders, their servant—Ernst Behmer
Per, Sven Ersson's servant—Gunnar Nordlöf
Stina, Sven Ersson's servant—Ruth Johnson Larson
Bengt på Åsen—Werner Svensson
Nils Jonsson, called Löpare-Nisse—Ernst Behmer
(*S.A.*, Sept. 24, 1914)

Ljungby Horn, Nov. 1, 1914.
Didrik, troll—Christopher Brusell
Tulla, troll woman—Augusta Larson
Birgit—Augusta Milton
Måns Kruse of Månstorp, knight—Carl Liljegren
Olle Pomp, soldier, follower of Måns—John Liljeström
Olof, nobleman—Werner Melinder
Hildur—Hedwig Brusell Melinder
Ivar Munk, judge—Ernest Lindblom
Court chaplain—Ernest Lindblom
Country judge—Christopher Brusell
Vidrik, troll—Gustaf Lund
Lady Ingrid of Ljungby—Mrs. Hulda Feltskogh
Per, country boy—Gunnar Nordlöf
(*S.A.H.*, Nov. 5, 1914)

Pelikanen, Jan. 24, 1915.
Mother, Elise, widow—Dr. Anna Windrow Holm
Son, Fredrik, law student—Harold Theel
Daughter, Gerda—Lisa Behmer
Son-in-law, Axel, Gerda's husband—Stellan Windrow
Margaret, servant—Alice Collini
(*S.A.H.*, Jan. 28, 1915).

Paria, Feb. 7, 1915.
Mr. X—Harold Theel
Mr. Y—Stellan Windrow
(*S.A.H.*, Feb. 4, 1915)

Vermländingarne, Sept. 26, 1915.
Brukspatron—Joel Mossberg
Provst—Carl Liljegren
Sven Ersson i Hult—Christopher Brusell
Lisa, his wife—Augusta Larson
Erik, their son—John Melin

Jan Hansson vid sjön—Ernst Schycker
Annika, his wife—Mrs. Hulda Feltskogh
Anna, their daughter—Hedwig Brusell Melinder
Anders, their servant—Werner Melinder
Per, Sven Ersson's servant—Fred Bolling
Stina, Sven Ersson's servant—Thora Kindmark
Nils Jonsson, called Löpare-Nisse—Leopold Chellman
(*S.A.H.,* Sept. 23, 1915)

Vermländingarne, Oct. 10, 1915.
Brukspatron—Ernest Lindblom
Provst—Carl Milton
Sven Ersson i Hult—Knut Sjöberg
Lisa, his wife—Ida Anderson-Werner
Erik, their son—Harry B. Bergstrom
Ola i Gyllby, wealthy farmer—Carl Milton
Jan Hansson vid sjön—Carl Stockenberg
Annika, his wife—Augusta Milton
Anna, their daughter—Ingeborg Sandberg-Settergren
Anders, their servant—Ernst Behmer
Per, Sven Ersson's servant—Oscar Larson
Stina, Sven Ersson's servant—Ruth Johnson Larson
Nils Jonsson, called Löpare-Nisse—Ernst Behmer
(*S.T.N.,* Oct. 12, 1915)

Vermländingarne, Oct. 29, 1916.
Brukspatron—Ernest Lindblom
Provst—Ernst Schycker
Sven Ersson i Hult—Christopher Brusell
Lisa, his wife—Augusta Milton
Erik, their son—Werner Melinder
Jan Hansson vid sjön—Leopold Chellman
Annika, his wife—Mrs. Hulda Feltskogh
Anna, their daughter—Hedwig Brusell Melinder
Anders, their servant—Oscar Larson
Per, Sven Ersson's servant—Gunnar Nordlöf
Stina, Sven Ersson's servant—Hulda Säfström
Nils Jonsson, called Löpare-Nisse—Leopold Chellman
(*S.A.,* Oct. 19, 1916)

Vermländingarne, Oct. 21, 1917.
Brukspatron—Joel Mossberg
Wilhelm, his son—Nils Peterson
Lotta, his daughter—Alva Milton
Provst—Ernest Lindblom
Sven Ersson i Hult—Christopher Brusell
Lisa, his wife—Augusta Milton
Erik, their son—Werner Melinder
Annika—Mrs. Hulda Feltskogh
Anna, her daughter—Hedwig Brusell Melinder
Anders, their servant—Oscar Larson

Per, Sven Ersson's servant—Gunnar Nordlöf
Stina, Sven Ersson's servant—Ruth Johnson Larson
Nils Jonsson, called Löpare-Nisse—Leopold Chellman
(*S.A.*, Oct. 11, 1917)

Öregrund-Östhammar, Feb. 17, 1918.
Östhammar residents:
  Filip Bratt, city treasurer and merchant—Christopher Brusell
  Mathias Grönberg, dyer—Ernst Behmer
  Lars Erik Örtenquist, druggist—Werner Melinder
  Wives—Ida Anderson-Werner, Augusta Milton
Öregrund residents:
  Ringdahl, sexton and organist—Oscar Larson
  Rutberg, glazier—Ernest Lindblom
  Frisén, wig maker—Leopold Chellman
Emil Klint, undergraduate at Upsala, Bratt's nephew—Hulda Säfström
Karl Thorell, engineer—Carl Stockenberg
Mrs. Söderström, hotel keeper—Ruth Johnson Larson
Susanna, her relative—Hedvig Brusell Melinder
Fritz, hotel employee—Fred Bolling
Josephine, chambermaid—Magda Anderson Lewis
(*S.A.*, Feb. 21, 1918)

Påsk, Apr. 13, 1918.
Mrs. Heist—Dr. Anna Windrow Holm
Elis, her son—Werner Melinder
Eleonora, her daughter—Hedwig Brusell Melinder
Kristina, Elis's fiancée—Ruth Johnson Larson
Benjamin—Oscar Larson
Lindquist—Fred Bolling
(*S.A.*, Apr. 18, 1918)

Vermländingarne, Nov. 3, 1918.
Brukspatron—Ernest Lindblom
Wilhelm, his son—Eric Behmer
Lotta, his daughter—Alva Milton
Provst—Oscar Larson
Sven Ersson i Hult—Christopher Brusell
Lisa, his wife—Ida Anderson-Werner
Erik, their son—Werner Melinder
Ola i Gyllby, wealthy farmer—Oscar Larson
Britta, his daughter—Augusta Milton
Jan Hansson vid sjön—Carl Stockenberg
Annika, his wife—Mrs. Hulda Feltskogh
Anna, their daughter—Elvira Anderson
Anders, their servant—Ernst Behmer
Per, Sven Ersson's servant—Fred Bolling
Stina, Sven Ersson's servant—Ruth Johnson Larson
Bengt på Åsen—Gunnar Nordlöf
Nils Jonsson, called Löpare-Nisse—Ernst Behmer
(*S.A.*, Nov. 7, 1918)

Vermländingarne, Oct. 5, 1919.
Provst—Oscar Larson
Sven Ersson i Hult—Christopher Brusell
Lisa, his wife—Ida Anderson-Werner
Erik, their son—Samuel Ljungkvist
Ola i Gyllby, wealthy farmer—Ernest Lindblom
Britta, his daughter—Augusta Milton
Jan Hansson vid sjön—Carl Stockenberg
Annika, his wife—Mrs. Hulda Feltskogh
Anna, their daughter—Greta Torpadie
Per, Sven Ersson's servant—Fred Bolling
Stina, Sven Ersson's servant—Ruth Johnson Larson
Nils Jonsson, called Löpare-Nisse—Leopold Chellman
(*S.A.,* Oct. 9, 1919)

Duvals skilsmessa, Nov. 9, 1919.
Henri Duval—Ernst Behmer
Mrs. Bonivard—Ida Anderson-Werner
Diane—Hulda Säfström
Corbulon, sea captain—Christopher Brusell
Champeaux, capitalist—Knut Sjöberg
Borganeuf, former druggist—Oscar Larson
Gabrielle, his daughter—Lisa Behmer
Mariette, chamber maid—Marie Boehm
Victor, servant—Eric Behmer
Country man—Eric Anderson
(Program)

Vermländingarne, Mch. 21, 1920.
Brukspatron—Ernest Lindblom
Wilhelm, his son—Eric Behmer
Lotta, his daughter—Alva Milton
Provst—Carl Liljegren
Sven Ersson i Hult—Christopher Brusell
Lisa, his wife—Ida Anderson-Werner
Erik, their son—Samuel Ljungkvist
Ola i Gyllby, wealthy farmer—Carl Milton
Britta, his daughter—Anna Nordenfelt
Jan Hansson vid sjön—Carl Stockenberg
Annika, his wife—Augusta Milton
Anna, their daughter—Greta Torpadie
Anders, their servant—Ernst Behmer
Per, Sven Ersson's servant—Gunnar Nordlöf
Stina, Sven Ersson's servant—Maja Dejenberg
Nils Jonsson, called Löpare-Nisse—Ernst Behmer
(*S.T.N.,* Mch. 24, 1920)

Vermländingarne, Oct. 10, 1920.
Brukspatron—Theodore Sjöquist
Wilhelm, his son—Werner Noreen
Lotta, his daughter—Signe Anderson

327

Provst—Ernst Schycker
Sven Ersson i Hult—Christopher Brusell
Lisa, his wife—Ida Anderson-Werner
Erik, their son—August Loring
Ola i Gyllby, wealthy farmer—Ernst Schycker
Britta, his daughter—Ellen Anderson
Jan Hansson vid sjön—Carl Stockenberg
Annika, his wife—Mrs. Hulda Feltskogh
Anna, their daughter—Hedwig Brusell Melinder
Anders, their servant—Ernst Behmer
Per, Sven Ersson's servant—Otto Benson
Stina, Sven Ersson's servant—Maja Dejenberg
Nils Jonsson, called Löpare-Nisse—Ernst Behmer
(*S.K.,* Oct. 14, 1920)

Vermländingarne, Nov. 3, 1921.
Brukspatron—Ernst Svedelius
Wilhelm, his son—Eugene Bremer
Lotta, his daughter—Lisa Behmer
Provst—Ernest Lindblom
Sven Ersson i Hult—Christopher Brusell
Lisa, his wife—Ida Anderson-Werner
Erik, their son—John Melin
Ola i Gyllby, wealthy farmer—Ernest Lindblom
Britta, his daughter—Stella Johnson
Jan Hansson vid sjön—Carl Stockenberg
Annika, his wife—Mrs. Hulda Feltskogh
Anna, their daughter—Signe Schillander
Anders, their servant—Ernst Behmer
Per, Sven Ersson's servant—Gunnar Nordlöf
Stina, Sven Ersson's servant—Gunhild Sjöestedt-Fallberg
Nils Jonsson, called Löpare-Nisse—Ernst Behmer
(*S.A.,* Oct. 27, 1921)

Kärlek och upptåg, Dec. 4, 1921.
Holmström, rich corn trader—Ernest Lindblom
Karolina, his daughter—Margit Ahrenlöf
Amelie, his daughter—Gunhild Sjöestedt-Fallberg
Svenson, his bookkeeper—Carl Stockenberg
Widow Stenquist, his housekeeper—Ida Anderson-Werner
Sven, his servant—Fred Bolling
Fredrik Holm, young employee—Eugene Bremer
Thornborg—Ernst Behmer
(Program)

Majorens döttrar, Jan. 6, 1922.
Major Grip—Ernst Behmer
Stafva—Ida Anderson-Werner
Lilly—Signe Rosén
Blenda, her sister—Lisa Behmer
Lieutenant Arvid—Eugene Bremer

328

Harald—Knut Sjöberg
Träff—Fred Bolling
Johannes, miller—Eric Behmer
(*S.T.N.*, Jan. 11, 1922)

Paria, Apr. 22, 1922.
Mr. X—Ernst Behmer
Mr. Y—Carl Liljegren
(*S.A.*, Mch. 30, 1922)

Bröllopet på Ulfåsa, Nov. 19, 1922.
Knut Algotson—Carl Stockenberg
Ingrid, his wife—Ida Anderson-Werner
Sigrid the Fair, their daughter—Siri Hård of Segerstad
Bengt Lagman—Werner Melinder
Kol Tynnelson, his groom—Ernest Lindblom
Birger Jarl—Christopher Brusell
His wife—Augusta Milton
Härved Boson—Knut Sjöberg
Prior Botvid—Leopold Chellman
Inga—Hedwig Brusell Melinder
Sune—M. Husing
(*S.A.*, Nov. 25, 1922)

Kärlek och upptåg, Dec. 9, 1922.
Holmström, rich corn trader—Ernest Lindblom
Karolina, his daughter—Augusta Milton
Amelie, his daughter—Alva Milton
Svenson, his book keeper—Carl Milton
Widow Stenquist, his housekeeper—Ida Anderson-Werner
Sven, his servant—Fred Bolling
Fredrick Holm, young employee—Leopold Chellman
Thornborg—Carl Stockenberg
(*S.T.N.*, Dec. 13, 1922)

Vermländingarne, Oct. 28, 1923
Sven Ersson i Hult—Christopher Brusell
Erik, his son—Gunnar Sund
Ola i Gyllby, wealthy farmer—Frank Lundberg
Jan Hansson vid sjön—Carl Stockenberg
Anna, his daughter—Hedwig Brusell Melinder
Anders, his servant—Werner Melinder
Per, Sven Ersson's servant—Werner Noreen
Stina, Sven Ersson's servant—Ebba Kempe Chellgren
Nils Jonsson, called Löpare-Nisse—Leopold Chellman
(*S.A.*, Nov. 1, 1925)

Vermländingarne, Oct. 26, 1924.
Brukspatron—Joel Mossberg
Wilhelm, his son—Hans Hagman
Lotta, his daughter—Signe Erickson

Provst—Carl Milton
Sven Ersson i Hult—Christopher Brusell
Lisa, his wife—Ida Anderson-Werner
Erik, their son—Gunnar Sund
Ola i Gyllby, wealthy farmer—E. Linde
Britta, his daughter—Augusta Milton
Jan Hansson vid sjön—Carl Stockenberg
Annika, his wife—Emma Strand
Anna, their daughter—Hedwig Brusell Melinder
Anders, their servant—Ernst Behmer
Per, Sven Ersson's servant—Werner Noreen
Stina, Sven Ersson's servant—Hilma Wikström
Bengt på Åsen—Eric Behmer
Nils Jonsson, called Löpare-Nisse—Ernst Behmer
(*S.A.*, Oct. 30, 1924)

Vermländingarne, Oct. 11, 1925.
Brukspatron—Frank Lundberg
Wilhelm, his son—H. W. Kellerman
Lotta, his daughter—Lisa Behmer
Sven Ersson i Hult—Knut Sjöberg
Lisa, his wife—Ida Anderson-Werner
Erik, their son—Gunnar Sund
Ola i Gyllby, wealthy farmer—Carl Milton
Britta, his daughter—Augusta Milton
Jan Hansson vid sjön—Carl Stockenberg
Annika, his wife—Augusta Milton
Anna, their daughter—Elsa Söderstrom
Anders, their servant—Ernst Behmer
Per, Sven Ersson's servant—Werner Noreen
Stina, Sven Ersson's servant—Maja Dejenberg
Bengt på Åsen—W. E. Wahlberg
Nils Jonsson, called Löpare-Nisse—Ernst Behmer
(*S.A.*, Oct. 12, 1925)

Min hustrus affärer, Jan. 30, 1926.
Lukas Trotte—Arvid Nelson
Simon Bratt—William Johnson
Rebekka Bratt—Gurli Nelson
Kastun—Earl Lindberg
Lotta—Ragnhild Lindstrom
Sven—Erik Berglind
(*S.T.N.*, Feb. 3, 1926)

Duvals skilsmessa, Mch. 14, 1926.
Henri Duval—Ernst Behmer
Mrs. Bonivard—Ida Anderson-Werner
Diane—Lisa Behmer
Corbulon, sea captain—John Ternquist
Champeaux, capitalist—Knut Sjöberg
Borganeuf, former druggist—Carl Liljegren

Gabrielle, his daughter—Hilma Wikström
Victor, servant—E. Whalberg
(S.A., Feb. 25, 1926)

Vermländingarne, Oct. 24, 1926.
Brukspatron—John Ternquist
Wilhelm, his son—Waldemar Walberg
Lotta, his daughter—Hilma Wikström
Provst—Carl Milton
Sven Ersson i Hult—Knut Sjöberg
Lisa, his wife—Ida Anderson-Werner
Erik, their son—Folke Anderson
Ola i Gyllby, wealthy farmer—Werner Noreen
Britta, his daughter—Thora Jacobson-Wiberg
Jan Hansson vid sjön—Carl Stockenberg
Annika, his wife—Sigrid Lindberg
Anna, their daughter—Helen Anderson
Anders, their servant—Thore Österberg
Per, Sven Ersson's servant—Otto Benson
Bengt på Åsen—Erik Larson
Nils Jonsson, called Löpare-Nisse—Ernst Behmer
(S.T.N., Oct. 27, 1926)

Syrsan, Nov. 28, 1926.
Fadette—Ida Anderson-Werner
Syrsan, her granddaughter—Thora Jacobson-Wiberg
Jean Barbaud—Werner Melinder
Mother Barbaud—Maja Dejenberg
Didier Barbaud—Otto Benson
Landry Barbaud—Ernst Behmer
Caillard—Carl Milton
Madelon—Sigrid Lindberg
Susette—Hedwig Brusell Melinder
Mariette—Lisa Behmer
Manon—Augusta Milton
Peasants—Carl Stockenberg, Knut Sjöberg, Thore Österberg
(S.A., Dec. 2, 1926)

Regina von Emmeritz, Oct. 23, 1927.
King Gustaf II Adolf—Carl Barcklind
Prince of Emmeritz—John Ternquist
Regina von Emmeritz—Hilma Barcklind
Larson, Swedish officer of Finnish cavalry—Knut Sjöberg
Bertil, Finnish officer of Finnish cavalry—Thore Österberg
Father Hieronymus, head of Jesuits—Werner Melinder
First monk—C. H. Hedlund
Second monk—S. Mjörner
Von Alten, German colonel in Swedish service—Carl Stockenberg
Dorthe, Regina's nurse—Ida Anderson-Werner
Kätchen, chambermaid—Thora Jacobson-Wiberg
Prince's adjutant—August Nordmand

331

King's doctor—Arthur Carlson
Swedish officers—Gunnar Sund, John Melin
(S.A., Oct. 27, 1927)

Vermländingarne, Dec. 26, 1927.
Sven Ersson i Hult—Carl Barcklind
Lisa, his wife—Ida Anderson-Werner
Erik, their son—Werner Melinder
Ola i Gyllby, wealthy farmer—A. T. Paulson
Britta, his daughter—Elna Lilnequist Kronberg
Anna—Hilma Barcklind
Anders—Thore Österberg
Stina, Sven Ersson's servant—Maja Dejenberg-Anderson
Nils Jonsson, called Löpare-Nisse—Leopold Chellman
(S.K., Dec. 29, 1927)

Vermländingarne, Oct. 31, 1928.
Brukspatron—Frank Lundberg
Wilhelm, his son—Sigurd Berg
Lotta, his daughter—Anna Danielson
Provst—Carl Milton
Sven Ersson i Hult—Knut Sjöberg
Lisa, his wife—Ida Anderson-Werner
Erik, their son—Gunnar Sund
Ola i Gyllby, wealthy farmer—John Ternquist
Jan Hansson vid sjön—Carl Stockenberg
Anna, his daughter—Ragnhild Lindstrom
Anders, his servant—Thore Österberg
Per, Sven Ersson's servant—Otto Benson
Stina, Sven Ersson's servant—Maja Dejenberg-Anderson
Bengt på Åsen—Gustaf Johnson
Nils Jonsson, called Löpare-Nisse—Ernst Behmer
(S.A., Sept. 27, Oct. 11, 1928)

Mot beräkning, Nov. 11, 1928.
Madame Andersson—Maja Dejenberg-Anderson
Lotta Tråd, seamstress—Elvy Johnson
Tobias Sikt, baker—K. Frölander
(S.T.N., Nov. 7, 1928)

Nerkingarne. Dec. 26, 1928.
Selma—Alva Milton
Mamsell Bom, governess—Elna Lilnequist Kronberg
Sven Jonsson i Lekhyttan, miner—Paul Norling
Sven, his son, student—Thore Österberg
Mother Katarina, Sven Jonsson's sister, rich miner's widow—Greta Ohlman
Lasse, her son—Arvid Nelson
Ingeborg—Ragnhild Lindstrom
Stina, Mother Katarina's servant—Anna-Lisa Lambert Ryman
(S.A., Nov. 22, 28, Dec. 13, 1928)

Rika Morbror, Mch. 10, 1929.
Kummelund, city major and merchant—Gustaf Johnson
Matilda, his daughter—Esther Andreason
Mamselle Rosennase, her governess—Ruth Nelson
Westerkvist, vice justice—Paul Fröjd
Job Kurk, Kummelund's brother-in-law—Carl Benson
Tomas, Kummelund's servant—Erik Carlson
Brita, Kummelund's maid—Ruth Olenius
Bookkeeper—Bernt Johnson
Sailor—Carl Gustafson
(*S.T.N.,* Mch. 6, 1929)

Det skadar inte! Oct. 20, 1929.
Körner, assessor—Carl Stockenberg
His unmarried sister—Elna Lilnequist Kronberg
Pilehn—Arvid Nelson
Körner's niece—Ragnhild Lindstrom
Counsellor Groth—Paul Norling
His son—Thore Österberg
Körner's stepson—Ivar Lambert
Körner's cook—Greta Ohlman
Servant—Harold Swanson
(*S.T.N.,* Oct. 2, 1929)

Tosingar, Dec. 8, 1929.
Professor Confucius Wurm, retired head of insane asylum—Paul Norling
Thore Wurm, his nephew, medical student—Ivar Lambert
Inga Griller, professor's granddaughter—Ragnhild Lindstrom
Brukspatron Zakarias Fikonqvist—Carl Stockenberg
Barbara, his wife—Elna Lilnequist Kronberg
Amedé, their son—Carl Yngve
Hampus Stolling, artist—Thore Österberg
Lotta, servant—Anna-Lisa Lambert Ryman
(*S.A.,* Dec. 5, 1929)

Styrman Karlssons flammor, Mch. 15, 1930.
Kalle Karlsson, mate—Thore Österberg
Wolf, commissioner—Paul Norling
Sjögren, captain—Carl Stockenberg
Augustsson, boatswain—Arvid Nelson
Jonas, cabin boy—Anna Österberg
Berentz, clerk—Gunnar Kassman
Miss Lundgren, cashier—Elna Lilnequist Kronberg
Jönsson, waiter—Carl Yngve
Nina, called Nanette—Ragnhild Lindstrom
French Creole innkeeper—Paul Norling
Pete, negro—Carl Yngve
Englishman—Gustaf Johnson
Creole—Harold Swanson
Hop Lung, owner of opium den—Carl Lambert
Mimosa San—Florence Ruden

333

Brogren, ship owner—Ivar Lambert
Miss Jantrisos, bar maid—Signe Johnstone
Mamie Swansson—Elna Lilnequist Kronberg
Bartender—Gustaf Johnson
Kid Hallaren, athlete and boxer—Paul Norling
First warrant officer—Ivar Lambert
Second warrant officer—Sven Gustafson
Police constable—Alphonso Carlson
Sammi, negro comedian—Anna-Lisa Lambert Ryman
Benson, doctor—Paul Norling
Tamuto, emperor—Arvid Nelson
Naomo, his daughter—Ragnhild Lindstrom
First cannibal—Gustaf Johnson
Mrs. Doring—Elna Lilnequist Kronberg
Bessie, her daughter—Ragnhild Lindstrom
(Program)

Kopparslagargreven, June 22, 1930.
Herman Hofdik, master coppersmith—Carl Stockenberg
Hendrike, his daughter—Sigrid Wollertz
Juliana, his servant—Elna Lilnequist Kronberg
Hans Heij, Hofdik's journeyman coppersmith—Paul Norling
Carl, Hofdik's apprentice—Anna Österberg
Count Gregori van Werwel—Paul G. Pohlson
Wilhelmine van Werwel, his countess—Margit Pettersson
Fredrik, their son—Thore Österberg
Hermine, their daughter—Ida Hilding
Jost, count's servant—Carl Yngve
Pieter Pieterwijk, wandering journeyman—Arvid Nelson
(S.A., June 26, 1930)

När byskräddaren och byskomakaren gifta bort sin pojke, Aug. 19, 1930.
City tailor—Einar Carlson
City shoemaker—Paul Norling
Karlson, country boy—Arvid Nelson
Love-sick girl—Elna Lilnequist Kronberg
Tok-Jan—Carl Stockenberg
Skytte—Carl Stockenberg
Lay preacher Göranson—Carl Yngve
Mother Anna—Hilma Lindblom
Maid—Sigrid Wollertz
Servant—Thore Österberg
Pettersson, postman—Yngve Jancke
Farm boy—Harold Swanson
(S.A., Aug. 7, 1930)

Ebberödsbank, Nov. 16, 1930.
Vingelin, tailor—Carl Yngve
His wife—Elna Lilnequist Kronberg
His brother—Paul Norling
Toddens, apprentice—Arvid Nelson

334

Vingelin's maid—Sigrid Wollertz
Bank inspector—Thore Österberg
Shareholders in bank—Hilma Lindblom, Einar Carlson, Ragnar Melander
(*S.T.N.,* Nov. 12, 1930)

"Måtte våra barn få rika föräldrar," Dec. 31, 1930.
Kalle Wallin, bricklayer—Arvid Nelson
Oscar Grönlund, painter—Allan Nyberg
Rask, policeman—Paul Norling
Frid Bowling, Knight of the Vasa Order—Paul Norling
Charles Isaksson, contractor—Einar Carlson
His cross wife—Elna Lilnequist Kronberg
Representative of *Svenska Folkteatern*—Thore Österberg
Ivar Malmsten, editor—Carl Yngve
Adrian Södervalv, artist—Carl Yngve
Olle, peasant comedian—Einar Carlson
Ida Göransson, landlady—Hilma Lindblom
Maids—Ragnhild Lindstrom, Anna Österberg
(*S.A.,* Dec. 5, 1930)

Vermländingarne, Feb. 5, 1931.
Provst—Carl Milton
Sven Ersson i Hult—Knut Sjöberg
Lisa, his wife—Ida Anderson-Werner
Erik, their son—Gunnar Sund
Jan Hansson vid sjön—Carl Stockenberg
Annika, his wife—Augusta Milton
Anna, their daughter—Hedwig Brusell Melinder
Anders, their servant—Werner Noreen
Per, Sven Ersson's servant—Otto Benson
Stina, Sven Ersson's maid—Maja Dejenberg-Anderson
Nils Jonsson, called Löpare-Nisse—Ernst Behmer
(*S.A.,* Feb. 12, 1931)

Kopparslagargreven, Mch 8, 1931.
Herman Hofdik, master coppersmith—Carl Stockenberg
Hendrike, his daughter—Sigrid Wollertz
Juliana, his servant—Elna Lilnequist Kronberg
Hans Heij, Hofdik's journeyman coppersmith—Paul Norling
Carl, Hofdik's apprentice—Anna Österberg
Count Gregori van Werwel—Carl Yngve
Wilhelmine van Werwel, his countess—Clara Hammar
Fredrik, their son—Thore Österberg
Hermine, their daughter—Ida Hilding
Jost, count's servant—Allan Nyberg
Pieter Pieterwijk, wandering journeyman—Arvid Nelson
(Program)

A:B Strid och Frid, Apr. 12, 1931.
Petter Strid, tailor of the new school—Carl Yngve
Isabella, his wife—Maja Dejenberg-Anderson
Fritiof, their son, Chalmer student—Allan Nyberg

335

Niklas Frid, tailor of the old school—Paul Norling
Amalia, his wife—Elna Lilnequist Kronberg
Ingeborg, their daughter—Viola Ahlstrand
Nelson, the whole show—Arvid Nelson
Märgström, half the police force—Thore Österberg
Björnbom, merchant—Einar Carlson
Rector's wife—Lydia Hegelfelt
Mayor—Yngve Jancke
(Program)

Majorens döttrar, June 11, 1931.
Major Grip—Ernst Behmer
Stafva—Maja Dejenberg-Anderson
Lilly—Alva Milton
Blenda, her sister—Viola Ahlstrand
Lieutenant Arvid—Nils Linde
Harald—Oscar Ahlstrand
Träff—Einar Carlson
Birger Holm—Ragnar Reimer
(*S.A.,* June 11, 1931)

Styrman Karlssons bröllopsresa, Oct. 3, 4, 1931.
Captain Sjögren—Paul Norling
Mate Karlsson—Thore Österberg
Augustsson, boatswain—Arvid Nelson
Jonas, cabin boy—Ragnhild Lindstrom
Mr. Hunt—Carl Yngve
Mr. Jones—Allan Nyberg
Bessie—Sonja Boström
Governor—Yngve Jancke
Servant—Einar Carlson
Felip Roya, leader of band of highway robbers—Allan Nyberg
Isabella, his sister—Florence Ruden
Robertson, employee of American mining company—Carl Stockenberg
Lawson, employee of American mining company—Carl Yngve
Joe—Paul Norling
Zebata—Einar Carlson
Smith—Arvid Nelson
Sammy—Yngve Jancke
Flossy—Elna Lilnequist Kronberg
Big Joe, captain of whaling vessel, Brixton Bell—H. Harlington
Brigg, boatswain—Einar Carlson
Waipa, South Sea girl—Sonja Boström
First whaler—Arvid Nelson
Second whaler—Harold Swanson
Webber—Allan Nyberg
Bronson—Carl Yngve
Jack Bloomer—H. Harlington
Miss Dolly—Ragnhild Lindstrom
Tramp—Arvid Nelson
Emperor—Yngve Jancke

336

Summers, South Sea skipper—Carl Stockenberg
Paamu—Yngve Jancke
Paamuta, his favorite wife—Elna Lilnequist Kronberg
Olson, mate at Bornito—Einar Carlson
O'Brien, boatswain—Paul Norling
(Program)

Familjen Trögelin, Oct. 18, 1931.
Tralling, merchant—Paul Anderson
His wife—Agnes Olson
Brukspatron Trögelin—Nels Carlson
His wife—Agda Frisell
Their daughter—Margaret Lundell
Trippee, notary—Walter Walters
Trapp, policeman—Arthur Noren
Truls, Trögelin's servant—Arthur Chellberg
(*S.A.,* Oct. 15, 1931)

Lars Anders och Jan Anders och deras barn, Mch. 6, 1932.
Lars Anders—Einar Carlson
Jan Anders—Carl Yngve
Britta Stina—Elna Lilnequist Kronberg
Karolina—Nita Ohlin
Lena—Karin Sjöberg
Karl Johan—Allan Nyberg
Anna Mansson, young widow—Sonja Boström
Jonas, servant—Arvid Nelson
(*S.T.N.,* Mch. 9, 1932)

Bröderna Östermans huskors, Oct. 30, 1932.
Österman brothers—Einar Carlson, Carl Yngve, Arvid Nelson
Jan Westman—A. Rönn
Helena Westman, his wife—Mrs. V. Rönn
Ella, their daughter—Karin Sjöberg
Axel Olson, sailor—Harold Swanson
His mother—Herta Larson
Constable—Otto Bolling
Count von Leijonflyckt—Yngve Jancke
Countess von Leijonflyckt—Clara Hammar
Westman—Hugo Anderson
Housekeeper—Elna Lilnequist Kronberg
(*S.A.,* Oct. 27, *S.T.N.,* Oct. 19, 1932)

Dansen på Brottskär. Dec. 31, 1932.
August på Nidskär, wealthy fisherman—Einar Carlson
Lydia, his sister—Greta Ohlman
Anna Svensson, widow—Elna Lilnequist Kronberg
Sonja, her daughter—Linnea Anderson
Johan Bergsten, former skipper—Carl Yngve
Claes-Erik, his son—Harold Swanson
Fikas Fia, mad woman—Beatrice Burgeson

Kalle Spira, sailor, employed by Bergsten—Arvid Nelson
Constable—Yngve Jancke
(Program)

Handlarns första piga, Jan. 29, 1933.
Chauffeur—Arvid Nelson
Miss Johanna Asp—Greta Ohlman
Newsbureau—Karin Sjöberg
Her son—Gunnar Bäckström
Doctor of law—Carl Yngve
Employees— {Einar Carlson, Harold Swanson
{Linnea Anderson, Elna Lilnequist Kronberg
(*S.T.N.*, Jan. 18, 1933)

Torpar-Petter säljer sin käring, Mch. 5, 1933.
Torpar-Petter—Arvid Nelson
Louisa, his wife—Greta Ohlman
Jons, business man—Einar Carlson
Simonson, auctioneer—Carl Yngve
Miss von Holliday, summer guest—Ragnhild Lindstrom
(*S.A.,* Mch. 2, 1933)

Flottans lilla fästmö, June 11, 1933.
Host of the Golden Anchor, former boatswain—Einar Carlson
Majken, his daughter, sweetheart of the fleet—Ragnhild Lindstrom
Gunnar Hjelm, marine lieutenant—Oscar Ahlstrand
His sister—Elsa Appelgren
Ada Karlson, servant—Greta Ohlman
Kalle Person, sailor—Arvid Nelson
Tor von Stangenburg, roisterer and rascal—Carl Yngve
Acke Svensson—Anna-Lisa Ryman
Sheriff—Yngve Jancke
(*S.A.,* June 1, 1933)

Halta Lena och vindögda Per, Nov. 18, 1933.
Algot Söderman, home owner—Carl Yngve
Hilda, his wife—Herta Larson
Lena, their daughter—Elna Lilnequist Kronberg
Magda, their daughter—Millie Espling
Johan Söderholm, rich farmer—Otto Bolling
Karl Henrik, his son—Lars Larson
Österberg, old fisherman—Yngve Jancke
Per, his son—Arvid Nelson
Larson, fisherman—Oscar Carlson
Emelie, his wife—Karin Sjöberg
Anders, Larson's employee—Sampa Garbo
Viktor, Söderholm's servant—Harold Swanson
Maja, peasant woman—Mary Dahlin
Selma, peasant girl—Martha Hedberg
(Program)

Luffarbaron, Oct. 14, 1934.
Groborn, wealthy margarine manufacturer—Carl Yngve
His wife—Elna Lilnequist Kronberg
Their daughter—Elsa Appelgren
Tramp baron—Arvid Nelson
Stanville, his friend—Nils Linde
Baron—Yngve Jancke
Doctor—Oscar Carlson
Druggist—Carl Wennerstrand
Servant—Harold Swanson
Maid—Mary Dahlin
(*S.A.,* Oct. 4, 1934)

Andersson, Pettersson och Lundström, Feb. 15, 1935.
Fortuna, fortune's fairy—Viola Sellberg
Infernalis, protector of frivolity—Nels Gustafson
Andersson, journeyman joiner—J. Lindholm
Pettersson, journeyman tailor—Otto Benson
Lundström, journeyman shoemaker—Ernst Ekberg
Pluggstedt, school teacher—Theodor Thorselius
Fiken—Maja Dejenberg-Anderson
Lisa, country girl—Theresa Lind
Plank, portrait painter—Waldemar Ekström
(*S.A.,* Feb. 14, 1935)

För fulla segel, June 16, 1935.
Lighthouse keeper—Paul Norling
Eva, his daughter—Ragnhild Lindstrom
Ramner, merchant, an imposter—Lars Larson
Harry—Oscar Ahlstrand
Nicke—Carl Yngve
Gura Person—Nils Linde
Rulle Loch—Arvid Nelson
Housekeeper—Elna Lilnequist Kronberg
(*S.A.,* June 13, 1935)

Trötte Theodor, Oct. 13, 1935.
Tired Theodor—Paul Norling
His wife—Elna Lilnequist Kronberg
Jenny, their daughter—Linnea Anderson Vik
Felix, her cousin—Oscar Ahlstrand
Kajser—Carl Stockenberg
Wolfgang, his son—Carl Yngve
Lydia Lydi, young singer—Ragnhild Lindstrom
Director Janse—Yngve Jancke
Assistant—Arvid Nelson
Servant—Maja Björkegren
Chambermaid—Greta Ohlman
Bellboy—Anna-Lisa Ryman
(*S.A.,* Oct. 3, 1935)

339

Farbror Knut från Norrköping, Nov. 17, 1935.
Henrik Brander, chamberlain—Ernst Behmer
Ellen, his wife—Lisa Behmer
Arthur, his son—Lars Larson
Knut Brander, manufacturer, Henrik's brother—Knut Sjöberg
Ahlengren, merchant—Nels Carlson
Elise, his daughter—Alva Milton
Sundquist, shoemaker—Ragnar Reimer
Housekeeper—Maja Dejenberg-Anderson
(*S.A.,* Nov. 21, 1935)

Skökan rättvisan, Nov. 28, 1935.
Hellman—Fred Oberg
His wife—Helga Wennerström
Evert—Paul Fröjd
Vendla—Eleanor Pearson
Pastor Akerberg—Thorvald Johnson
Mayor—Knut Berglund
Public prosecutor—W. Gustafson
Neighbor—Elly Edquist
(*S.T.N.,* Dec. 4, 1935)

En domares vedermödor, Apr. 17, 1936.
Judge—Knut Sjöberg
Notary—Emil Thörnblom
Accused—Ernst Ekberg
Business man—Fred Wahlberg
Policeman—Sixtén Hillström
Servant—Ellis Kullberg
(*S.A.,* Apr. 23, 1936)

Svenska John går i land, Oct. 25, 1936.
Svenska John—Oscar Ahlstrand
Finska Kalle—Arvid Nelson
Faithful Marie—Elna Lilnequist Kronberg
Blom, her admirer—Carl Yngve
Ulla, her niece—Engla Hulström
Folke Johanson, her fiancé—Allan Wennerstrand
De Bourg—Paul Norling
Anna Josefina Persdotter—Ragnhild Lindstrom
Swindler's accomplice—Anna-Lisa Ryman
(*S.A.T.,* Oct. 15, 1936)

Hur ska' det gå för Petterson? Dec. 31, 1936.
Furir Jönsson, Skånsk soldier—Carl Yngve
Amadus Philen, tailor who poses as Petterson—Arvid Nelson
Fair Fina, his housekeeper—Ragnhild Lindstrom
Alfredsson, navy corporal—Carl Wennerstrand
Rulle Järnhammar, soldier—Paul Norling
Maja, his wife—Elna Lilnequist Kronberg
Herbert, their son—Oscar Ahlstrand

Ingrid, Järnhammar's daughter—Viola Ahlstrand
Mandal—Carl Stockenberg
Blända Krok—Millie Espling
(S.A.T., Jan. 7, 1937)

Hemsöborna, May 16, 1937.
Carlsson—Arvid Nelson
Widow Flod—Elna Lilnequist Kronberg
Gusten, her son—Oscar Ahlstrand
Violin professor—Eric Wangelin
Ida, his daughter—Engla Hulström
Rundquist—Einar Carlson
Pastor Nordstrom—Carl Stockenberg
Norman, boatswain on leave—Carl Wennerstrand
Inspector—Carl Yngve
Madame Styv, fish buyer—Millie Espling
Mrs. Lyk, midwife—Anna Meyers
Traveller—Nils Linde
(S.A.T., May 13, 1937)

Jansson, jag älskar dej, Dec. 31, 1937.
Olle Rask—Carl Yngve
Arne, his son—Carl Wennerstrand
Malin—Maja Dejenberg-Anderson
Miss Blom, love-sick spinster—Elna Lilnequist Kronberg
Mrs. Vinter, man hater—Millie Espling
Karin Vinter—Engla Hulström
Klassen, travelling salesman—Oscar Ahlstrand
Jansson, travelling salesman—Arvid Nelson
(S.A.T., Jan. 6, 1938)

Halta Lena och vindögda Per, Oct. 23, 1938.
Mrs. Hilda Söderman—Maja Dejenberg-Anderson
Lena, her daughter—Elna Lilnequist Kronberg
Johan Söderholm, rich farmer—Einar Carlson
Karl Henrik, his son—Carl Yngve
Per Österberg—Arvid Nelson
(S.A.T., Oct. 13, 1938)

Karlsson får Amerika-arv, Mch. 12, 1939.
Karlsson—Paul Fröjd
Lina, his haughty wife—Maja Dejenberg-Anderson
Fanny, their proud and love-sick daughter—Helen Johnson
Count Klohök—Paul Anderson
His daughter—Elsa Appelgren
Lieutenant Spansk—Nils Linde
Jonason, inspector—Arthur Chellberg
Edvard Persson, cattle trader from Tomelilla—Sam Anderson
(S.A.T., Mch. 2, 1939)

341

Hemma hos Karlsons, Dec. 31, 1939.
Karlson—Einar Carlson
His wife—Elna Lilnequist Kronberg
Elvira, their daughter—Millie Espling
Annie, their daughter—Edna Johnson
Samuel Bolinder, her music teacher—Tage Carlson
Fred Malm, boarder at Karlsons—Arvid Nelson
Nels Ek—Carl Wennerstrand
Selma Peterson, neighbor—Alida Ahlberg
Johan Svärd, agent—Gunnar Johanson
(*S.A.T.,* Jan. 4, 1940)

Svenska John går i land, Nov. 23, 1940.
Same cast as Oct. 25, 1936, with one change:
Anna Josefina Persdotter—Mary Blomskog
(*S.A.T.,* Nov. 14, 1940)

Hur ska' det gå för Petterson? Dec. 31, 1941.
Furir Jönsson, Skånsk soldier—Carl Yngve
Amandus Philen, tailor who poses as Petterson—Arvid Nelson
Fair Fina, his housekeeper—Mary Blomberg
Alfredsson, navy corporal—Nils Linde
Rulle Järnhammar, soldier—Nels Carlson
Maja, his wife—Elna Lilnequist Kronberg
Herbert, their son—Oscar Ahlstrand
Ingrid, Järnhammar's daughter—Viola Ahlstrand
Blända Krok—Millie Espling
Love-sick woman—Clara Hammar
(*S.A.T.,* Dec. 18, 1941)

Vermländingarne, Oct. 27, 1946.
Brukspatron—David Nordquist
Wilhelm, his son—Eric Behmer
Lotta, his daughter—Alice Carlson
Sven Ersson i Hult—Paul Norling
Lisa, his wife—Maja Dejenberg-Anderson
Erik, their son—Waldemar Walberg
Provst—Paul Fröjd
Ola i Gyllby, wealthy farmer—Gustaf Ekman
Britta, his daughter—Elsa Appelgren Flodin
Jan Hansson vid sjön—Werner Noreen
Annika, his wife—Signe Jansson
Anna, their daughter—Inga Maye Nordquist
Anders, their servant—Albin Nordström
Per, Sven Ersson's servant—Otto Benson
Stina, Sven Ersson's maid—Helen Johnson
Bengt på Åsen—Paul Johnson
Nils Jonsson, called Löpare-Nisse—Ernst Behmer
(Program)

Vermländingarne, Oct. 22 and 29, 1950.
Brukspatron—David Nordquist
Wilhelm, his son—Raymond Lundberg

342

Lotta, his daughter—Alice Carlson
Sven Ersson i Hult—Paul Norling
Lisa, his wife—Maja Dejenberg-Anderson
Erik, their son—Waldemar Walberg
Provst—Ernst Magnuson
Ola i Gyllby, wealthy farmer—Sigfrid Erickson
Britta, his daughter—Aina Johanson
Jan Hansson vid sjön—Werner Noreen
Annika, his wife—Signe Jansson
Anna, their daughter—Inga Maye Nordquist
Anders, their servant—Albin Nordström
Per, Sven Ersson's servant—Otto Benson
Stina, Sven Ersson's maid—Helen Johnson
Bengt på Åsen—Kenneth Olson
Nils Jonsson, called Löpare-Nisse—Nils Linde
(Program)

V.   CHICAGO SWEDISH ACTING COMPANIES

This list does not include companies headed by an actor for one or two performances, or companies made up of members of a social or musical organization
for an occasional performance. The lists of organizations and actors in the index
will provide information on these points. Listed here are organizations more or
less formally organized, and, ordinarily, giving a series of performances. References
are to the chapters for the periods in which they were active.

Amateur Club Thalia, V
Arbetar Teater, VI
Behmer Company. V, VI. See also *Svenska Dramatiska Sällskap* (C) and *Svenska
      Teatersällskap* (B).
Brusell Company, III, IV, V. See also *Svenska Teatersällskap* (B).
Chellman Company, V, VI
Ekberg Company, V, VI
Enbom Company, II
Fahlbeck Company, II
Figaro, III
Folkteatern. See Swedish Friends of Thalia.
I.O.G.T. Amateur Company, VI
Lake View Amateur Company, V, VI
Leman Company (travelling), VI
Liander Company, IV
Lindstrom and Nordgren Company, III
Melinder Company, V
Myggan Company, VI
Norden Amateur Club (A), V
Norden Amateur Club (B), VI
Noreen and Benson Company (travelling), VI
North Side Amateur Company, VI
Nya Svenska Teatersällskap, IV
Olle i Skratthult Company (travelling), VI
P. W. Nelson Company, II

BIBLIOGRAPHY

I. NEWSPAPERS.

The newspapers listed are weekly Swedish language newspapers published in Chicago and *Skandia,* published in Moline, Illinois. English language newspapers have been cursorily examined to note the extent of attention they gave to the Swedish performances, but were not of value as sources. The Chicago Swedish language newspapers used include known extant files in this country. The chief collections are in the Augustana College Library, Rock Island, Illinois, and in the University of Chicago libraries; they have been supplemented by the files owned by the late G. Patrick Warner of Chicago and the collection at the Minnesota Historical Society, St. Paul, Minnesota. The history of the Swedish press in Chicago is sketched in the text, and a diagram on the following page indicates the periods of publication and the relationships of the principal newspapers.

1. *Fäderneslandet.* Published Dec. 1877 - Dec. 1880. Used:
   1879, with these issues missing: Feb. 15, 22, Mch. 1.
   1880, Jan. 3, 10, 17.

2. *Hemlandet (Den Gamla och Nya*—varying titles). Published (in Chicago), Jan. 1859 - Sept. 1914. Used:
   1867: June 4, 11, 18, 25, July 2, 9, 16, 23, 30.
   1870 through Sept. 1914, with these issues missing: 1871, June 6, Dec. 12; 1872, Aug. 13, Sept. 10, 17, Oct. 15; 1876, Jan. 14, Feb. 4, 11, 18, 24, Mch. 3, Sept. 8, Oct. 6, Nov. 24; 1877, Apr. 18, May 23, June 6, July 11, 18, Sept. 5, Oct. 3; 1878, Jan. 23, May 1, Sept. 4, 25, Oct. 2, 23, Nov. 6, 13, 20, Dec. 18; 1881, Aug. 24, Nov. 2, 30, Dec. 21, 28; 1882, June 7, 21, July 26, Aug. 16, 30; 1885, Mch. 4, 18, Apr. 8, 15, 22, 29, May 6, 13, 20, 27, June 3, 17, 24, July 1, 8, 15, 22, Aug. 19, Sept. 2, 9, 16, Oct. 14, 21, Nov. 4, 18, 25, Dec. 2; 1886, Feb. 24, Apr. 14, May 5, July 7, 28, Aug. 4, 18, 25, Sept. 1, 8; 1887, June 4, 11, 18, 25, July 2, 9, 16, 23, 30, Aug. 13, 27, Sept. 3, 10, Oct. 22, 29; 1889, Feb. 7, May 23, 30, June 6, 20, July 18, Aug. 8, 15, 22, Sept. 5, 19, 26, Oct. 3, 17, Nov. 7, 14, 21; 1891, May 21; 1897, May 12.

3. *Nya Svenska Amerikanaren.* Published Apr. 1873 - Sept. 1877. Used:
   1876, with these issues missing: Jan. 6, Dec. 21, 28.

4. *Skandia.* Published Dec 1876 - Apr. 1878. Used:
   1877; 1878, through April 24.

5. *Svenska Amerikanaren* (A). Published Sept. 1866 - Mch. 1873. Used:
   1866, Sept. 8, 19; 1867, Jan. 2, Sept. 18, Oct. 9, Nov. 6, Dec. 18, 25.
   1868 through 1871, with these issues missing: 1868, Jan. 15, May 14, June 3, July 1, 29, Sept. 2, 30, Nov. 11, Dec. 1, 16, 30; 1869, Jan. 19, Mch. 16, 30, Apr. 20, May 11, 18, June 8, Aug. 3, 10, 31, Dec. 7; 1870, May 24, Sept. 13, Oct. 4, 11, Dec. 13; 1871, Jan. 3, 10, Mch. 14, 21, Apr. 11, May 2, 30, June 6, 13, 20, 27, Aug. 1, Sept. 12, Oct. 4 on.

6. *Svenska Amerikanaren* (B). Published Oct. 1877 - May 1936 (Oct. 1914 - Dec. 1915 as *Svenska Amerikanaren Hemlandet).* Used:
   1881, June 16; 1884, Oct. 28; 1885, Dec. 5, 19, 26; 1886, Jan. 2.
   1891 through May 1936, with these issues missing: 1891, Jan. 8, Mch. 26, May 14, 21, 28, June 25, Oct. 22; 1892, Feb. 4, 11, May 19, Oct. 25, Nov. 8, 22, 29; 1894, June 12, 26, July 10, 17, 24, Aug. 7, 14, Sept. 11, 18, Nov. 27, Dec. 18, 25; 1923, May 31; 1934, Oct. 18, Nov. 1; 1936, Feb. 27.

7. *Svenska Amerikanaren Tribunen.* Published May 1936 on. Used:
   May 1936 through December 1950.

345

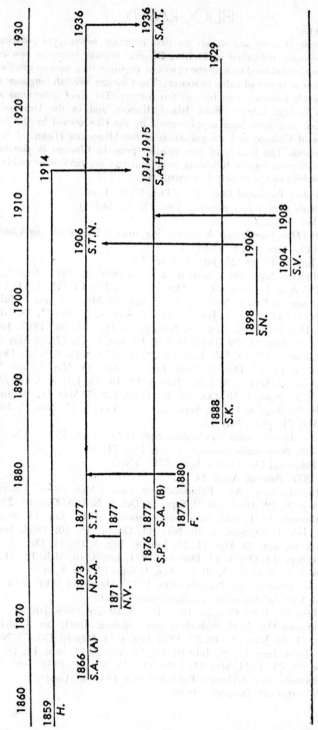

DIAGRAM OF PRINCIPAL CHICAGO SWEDISH NEWSPAPERS[1]

| 1859 | 1860 | 1870 | 1880 | 1890 | 1900 | 1910 | 1920 | 1930 |

1859
H.

1866
S.A. (A)

1873
N.S.A.

1871
N.V.

1876 1877
S.P. S.A. (B)

1877
F.

1877
S.T.

1877

1880

1888
S.K.

1898
S.N.

1904
S.V.

1906

1906
S.T.N.

1908

1914

1914-1915
S.A.H.

1929

1936

1936
S.A.T.

[1]Key to abbreviations: F.—Fäderneslandet; H.—Hemlandet; N.S.A.—Nya Svenska Amerikanaren; N.V.—Nya Verlden; S.A. (A)—Svenska Amerikanaren (A); S.A. (B)—Svenska Amerikanaren (B); S.A.H.—Svenska Amerikanaren Hemlandet; S.A.T.—Svenska Amerikanaren Tribunen; S.K.—Svenska Kuriren; S. N.—Svenska Nyheter; S.P.—Svenska Posten; S.T. —Svenska Tribunen; S.T.N.—Svenska Tribunen-Nyheter; S.V.—Svenska Världen.

8. *Svenska Kuriren.* Published Jan. 1888 - Sept. 1929. Used:
1889, Dec. 21, 28.
1890 through 1892, with these issues missing: 1890, June 26, July 3, 10, 17, 31, Aug. 7; 1891, July 22, Aug. 12; 1892, June 15, July 20, Aug. 3, Sept. 7, 14, 21, 28, Oct. 12.
1893, Mch. 7.
1894 through Sept. 1929, with these issues missing: 1894, Mch. 13, July 31, Oct. 2, Nov. 13; 1895, Sept. 3, 24, Oct. 15; 1896, Jan. 14, Mch. 17, June 9, July 7, Aug. 11, Oct. 27, Dec. 15; 1897, Jan. 26, May 11, 25, June 29, July 20; 1899, Aug. 15, Dec. 26; 1900, June 26, July 3, 17, Sept. 4, Dec. 25; 1902, Apr. 29; 1904, Mch. 15; 1907, Mch. 23, Apr. 27; 1909, Jan. 2, Oct. 30; 1911, July 15, Oct. 21; 1912, May 11, July 6, 13, 20, 27.

9. *Svenska Nyheter.* Published Dec. 1898 - July 1906. Used:
1901 through July 1906, with these issues missing: 1901, Jan. 1 through Sept. 24.

10. *Svenska Tribunen.* Published Sept. 1877 - May 1936 (July 1906 on as *Svenska Tribunen-Nyheter*). Used:
1877, Sept. 20, 27, Oct. 4, 11, 18, 25, Nov. 1, 8, 14, 21, 28, Dec. 5, 12, 19, 26; 1878, Feb. 13, May 22, Sept. 7, 14.
1879 through May 1936, with these issues missing: 1879, Jan. 1, Sept. 3, 10, Dec. 3, 10, 17, 24, 31; 1882, Jan. 4; 1928, Jan. 4; 1930, July 9; 1931, Apr. 2.

11. *Svenska Världen.* Published Mch. 1904 - Mch. 1908. Used:
1904 through 1907.

II. BOOKS AND PERIODICALS relating to immigration, Chicago, Swedes in Chicago and in the United States.

Andersson, E. Einar, ed., *Hembygden. Historisk festskrift för Chicagos Svenska hembygdsföreningar.* Chicago: Hembygdens Förlag, 1933.

Andreas, A. T., *History of Chicago.* Chicago: A. T. Andreas Company, 1884-1886. 3 vols.

Babcock, Kendrick C., *The Scandinavian element in the United States. University of Illinois Studies in the Social Sciences,* Vol. III, No. 3. Urbana, Ill.: University of Illinois, 1914.

Beckman, Ernst, *Amerikanska studier.* Stockholm: Z. Häggströms Förlagsexpedition, 1883.

Benson, Adolph B., and Naboth Hedin, *Swedes in America, 1638-1938.* New Haven, Conn.: Yale University Press, 1938.

Berger, Vilhelm (Felix Vivo), *Hundår och lyckodagar.* New York: Nordstjernans Boktryckeri, 1905.

Berger, Vilhelm, *Svenska folklynnet i förskingringen.* Brooklyn, N. Y.: Paragon Press, 1924.

Berger, Vilhelm, *Svensk-Amerikanska meditationer.* Rock Island, Ill.: Augustana Book Concern, 1916.

Björkman, Edwin, *Gates of life.* New York: Alfred A. Knopf, 1923.

Björkman, Edwin, *The soul of a child.* New York: Alfred A. Knopf, 1922.

Björkman, Edwin, *Voices of tomorrow: Critical studies of the new spirit in literature.* New York and London: Mitchell Kennedy, 1913.

Blegen, Theodore C., *Norwegian migration to America. The American transition.* Northfield, Minn.: Norwegian-American Historical Association, 1940.

Blegen, Theodore C., *Norwegian migration to America, 1825-1860.* Northfield, Minn.: Norwegian-American Historical Association, 1931.

Bläckfisken. Årsbok Svenska Journalistförbundet i Amerika, 1920-1921. Chicago: J. V. Martenson Printing Company, 1921.

Boissy, Tancred (H. A. Peters), *Svenska nationaliteten i Förenta Staterna.* Göteborg: Charles A. Berglunds Förlag, 1862.

Bokstugan. Organ för Studieförbundet Verdandi. Chicago. No. 36, Vol. VII (Mch. 1925); No. 44, Vol. X (Jan. 1928).

Bowers, David D., ed., *Foreign influences in American life.* Princeton, N. J.; Princeton University Press, 1944.

Broder Lustig. Illustrerad skämttidning för Svenskarne i Amerika. Chicago. Vols. I, 1 - II, 37 (Mch. 7, 1896 - Nov. 13, 1897).

Brodin, Knut, ed., *Emigrantvisor och andra visor.* Stockholm: Åhlén & Åkerlunds Förlag, 1938.

Chicago blue book. For the year ending 1895. Chicago: Chicago Directory Company, c. 1894.

Chicago business directory, 1890 and 1891. Chicago: Rand, McNally and Company, 1890, 1891.

Dalkullan. Almanak och kalender. 1903, 1907, 1910, 1921. Chicago: Capt. And. L. Löfström.

Edwards' thirteenth annual directory of the city of Chicago for 1870. Chicago: Chicago Directory Company, 1870.

Elmblad, Magnus, *Samlade arbeten.* Minneapolis, Minn.: *Svenska Folkets Tidnings Förlag,* 1890.

Elmblad, Magnus, *Samlade dikter.* Chicago: C. J. Stenquists Förlag, 1878.

Elmblad, Magnus, *Samlade dikter.* Stockholm: Boktr. Aktiebolag Acknert, 1889.

Faust, Albert B., *The German element in the United States.* Boston and New York: Houghton Mifflin Company, 1909. 2 vols., II.

Gawell-Blumenthal, Ida, *Stintans Amerika färd.* Stockholm: Fr. Skoglunds Förlag, 1908.

Gladt humör. Lifvade humoresker på vers och prosa med roliga gubbar af Gus Higgins. New enlarged ed. Chicago: And. L. Löfström, 1903.

Halpin and Bailey's Chicago city directory for the year 1861-1862. Chicago: Halpin and Bailey, 1861.

Hamilton, Joseph G., *Bror Erik. En bild ur Chicagolifvet.* 2nd. ed. Chicago: Hamilton Press, 1932.

Hansen, Marcus L., *The immigrant in American history.* Cambridge, Mass.: Harvard University Press, 1940.

Hansen, Marcus L., *The problem of the third generation immigrant. Augustana Historical Society Publications.* Rock Island, Ill.: Augustana Book Concern, 1938.

Hedberg, Lydia *(Bergslagsmor), Reseminnen från U.S.A.* Sköfde: Isaksonska Boktryckeri-Aktiebolaget, 1925.

Hessel, Theodore *(Farbror* Slokum), *Farbror Slokums memoarer.* Chicago: Theodore A. Hessel Förlag, n.d.

Hildebrand, Karl, and Axel Fredenholm, eds., *Svenskarna i Amerika.* Stockholm: A.-B. Historiska Förlaget, 1924. 2 vols., II.

Historical review, 1908-1943, District Lodge No. 8, Vasa Order of America. Carl Stockenberg, ed. Chicago: District Lodge Illinois No. 8, Vasa Order of America, n.d.

Historik öfver Vasa Orden af Amerikas 25-åriga verksamhet, 1896-1921. Chicago: J. V. Martenson Company, 1921.

History of Verdandi Lodge No. 3, I.O.S., 1931-1940. Chicago, 1940.

Humoristen, Gustaf Wicklund, ed. Chicago. Vol. VIII, No. 52 (Dec. 26, 1897), Vol. IX, No. 1 (Jan. 1, 1898).

Iduna. Illustrerad vecko-tidning. Chicago. Continuation of *Broder Lustig*, with no Vol. I published. Vols. II-IV (Nov. 20, 1897 - Feb. 18, 1899).

Janson, Florence E., *The background of Swedish immigration, 1840-1930*. Chicago: University of Chicago Press, 1931.

Johnson, Eric, and Charles F. Peterson, *Svenskarna i Illinois*. Chicago: W. Williamson, 1880.

Johnson, Gustav E., *The Swedes of Chicago*. Unpublished doctoral dissertation, The University of Chicago, 1940.

Koch, G. H. von, *Emigranternas land. Studier i Amerikanskt samhällslif*. Stockholm: Aktiebolaget Ljus, 1910.

Kurre Kalender för 1899, 1900, 1901, 1903. Chicago: *Svenska Kurirens* Förlag, 1899, 1900, 1901, 1903.

Lakeside annual directory of the city of Chicago. 1874-1875, 1885, 1891, 1899, 1903, 1906, 1910. Chicago: Williams, Donnelly & Company, 1875; Chicago Directory Company, 1885, 1891, 1899, 1903, 1906, 1910.

Larson, Fredrik, *Statistik öfver Svenskarna i Förenta Staterna intill året 1910*. 2nd. ed. Chicago: Författarens Förlag, 1914.

Larson, Oscar W., *Främlingsland. Skisser och berättelser ur emigrantlifvet*. Chicago: Scandinavian Workers Publ. Soc., n.d.

Leuchs, Fritz A. H., *The early German theatre in New York, 1840-1872*. New York: Columbia University Press, 1928.

Lewis, Lloyd, and Henry J. Smith, *Chicago. The history of its reputation*. New York: Harcourt, Brace & Company, 1929.

Linder, Oliver A., *Svensk-Amerikanska pseudonymer. Ur Nya Verlden*, 1899. With MS. notes by author.

Lindhagen, Carl, *På Vikingastråt i västerled. En Amerikaresa*. Stockholm: Wahlström och Widstrand, 1926.

Lindstrand, Frans A. (*Onkel Ola*), *Pennteckningar och reseskildringar*. Chicago: *Svenska Amerikanarens* Förlag, 1898.

Moses, John, and Joseph Kirland, eds., *The history of Chicago, Illinois*. Chicago and New York: Munsell and Company, 1895. 3 vols.

Nelson, Helge, *Nordamerika, natur, bygd och Svenskbygd*. Stockholm: Á.-B. Mag. Bergvalls Förlag, 1926.

Nisbeth, Hugo, *Två år i Amerika (1872-1874). Reseskildringar*. Stockholm: *Aftonbladets* Aktiebolags Tryckeri, 1874.

Norlander, Emil, *Anderssonskans Kalle. Pojkprat och käringsqvaller . . . med originalteckningar af Gus Higgins*. Chicago: And. L. Löfströms Förlag, n.d.

Olson, Ernst W., *History of the Swedes in Illinois*. Chicago: Engberg-Holmberg Publishing Company, 1908.

Osland, Birger, "Norwegian clubs in Chicago," *Norwegian-American Studies and Records*, XII (1941), 105 - 127.

Park, Robert E., *The immigrant press and its control*. New York: Harper and Brothers, 1922.

Park, Robert E., and Herbert A. Miller, *Old world traits transplanted*. New York: Harpers, for Society for Sociological Research, University of Chicago, 1925.

Person, Johan, *I Svensk-Amerika. Berättelser och skisser*. Worcester, Mass.: Knutson och Persons Förlag, 1900.

Peterson, Charles F., *Sverige i Amerika*. Chicago: Royal Star Company, 1898.

Pierce, Bessie L., *A history of Chicago*. New York: Alfred A. Knopf, 1937, 1940. 2 vols., II.

Prärieblomman. Kalender. Anders Schön, ed. For 1900 and 1902-1913. Rock Island, Ill.: Augustana Book Concern, 1900, 1902-1913.

Ranie (E. Einar Andersson), *Bland Norrlänningar i Chicago.* Chicago: System Press, 1942.

Runristningar. Independent Order of Vikings, 1890-1915. Chicago: J. V. Martensons Tryckeri, 1915.

Schick, Joseph S., *The early theater in Eastern Iowa.* Chicago: University of Chicago Press, 1939.

Skarstedt, Ernst, *Pennfäktare. Svensk-Amerikanska författare och tidningsmän.* Stockholm: Åhlén och Åkerlunds Förlag (for *Publicistklubben*), 1930.

Skarstedt, Ernst, *Svensk-Amerikanska folket i helg och söcken.* Stockholm: Björck och Börjesson, 1917.

Skarstedt, Ernst, *Vagabond och redaktör. Lefnadsöden och tidsbilder.* Seattle, Wash.: Washington Printing Company, 1914.

Statistical review of immigration, 1820-1910. Distribution of immigrants, 1850-1910. Reports of the Immigration Commission. Washington: Government Printing Office, 1911.

Stephenson, George M., *A history of American immigration, 1820-1924.* New York: Ginn and Company, 1926.

Stephenson, George M., "The background of the beginnings of Swedish immigration, 1850-1875," *American Historical Review,* XXXI (1925-1926), 708-723.

Stephenson, George M., *The religious aspects of Swedish immigration.* Minneapolis, Minn.: University of Minnesota Press, 1932.

Stephenson, George M., "The stormy years of the Swedish colony in Chicago before the great fire," *Transactions of the Illinois State Historical Society,* XXXVI (1929), 166-184.

Strand, Algot E., *A history of the Swedish-Americans of Minnesota.* Chicago: Lewis Publishing Company. 3 vols., I.

Sundbeck, Carl, *Svensk-Amerikanerna. Deras materiella och andliga sträfvanden. Anteckningar från en resa i Amerika.* Rock Island, Ill.: Augustana Book Concern, 1904.

Sundbeck, Carl, *Svenskarna i Amerika.* Stockholm: F. C. Askerbergs Bokförlag, 1900.

Svenska Klubben, 1870-1916. A brief resume [sic] of forty-six years of history. Chicago: Peterson Linotyping Company, 1916.

Swedish blue book, The. A Swedish-American directory and yearbook of Chicago. 1927 and 1928. Chicago: Swedish American Publishing Company, n.d.

Söderström, Alfred, *Blixtar på tidnings-horisonten.* Warroad, Minn., 1910

Söderström, Alfred, *Minneapolis minnen. Kulturhistorisk axplockning från qvarnstaden vid Mississippi.* No place or date.

Thompson, Warren S., and P. K. Whelpton, *Population trends in the United States.* New York and London: McGraw-Hill Book Company, 1933.

Valkyrian. Illustrerad månadsskrift. Edward Sundell, ed. New York: Charles K. Johansen. Vols. I-XIII (1897-1909).

Värmland vår hembygd. Chicago: *Värmlands Nation.* Vol. V (1930).

Wennerberg, Gunnar, *Gluntarne, med inledning.* Stockholm: Hugo Gebers Förlag, 3d. ed., 1908.

Westman, Erik G., ed., *The Swedish element in America.* Chicago: Swedish-American Biographical Society, 1931-1934. 4 vols.

Wicklund, Gustaf, *Gnistor från rimsmedjan.* Minneapolis, Minn., 1906.

Wilt, Napier, and Henriette C. K. Naeseth, "Two early Norwegian dramatic societies in Chicago," *Norwegian-American Studies and Records,* X (1938), 44-75.

Wittke, Carl, *We who built America. The saga of the immigrant.* New York: Prentice Hall, Inc., 1939.

Wærner, Ninian (C.A. Tollèn), *Mina hundår i Amerika. Humoristiska berättelser.* Stockholm: C. & E. Gernandts Förlagsaktiebolag, 1900.

Wærner, Ninian, *Pennstreck. Humoresker, skisser och berättelser.* Minneapolis, Minn.: *Svenska Folkets Tidnings* Förlag, 1896.

III. SOURCES relating to the Swedish theatre in Sweden and in Chicago.

A. Bibliographical, critical, and historical works.

Allgemeiner bücher-lexikon . . . von 1700 . . . 1892 erschienener bücher, Wilhelm Heinsius and others, eds. Leipzig: J. F. Gledistch, 1812-1928; F. A. Büchaus, 1836-1896. 19 vols.

August Lindberg. En monografi. Den Svensk-Amerikanska pressen tillägnad. Stockholm: Albert Bonniers Boktryckeri, 1911.

Biografiskt lexikon öfver namnkunnige Svenske män. Vols. I-VIII, new revised ed., Stockholm, F. & G. Beijers Förlag, 1874-1876; Vols. IX-XXIII, Örebro and Upsala: N. M. Lindhs Förlag, 1845-1857.

Blanc, Tharald H., *Norges förste nationale scene (Bergen, 1850-1865); et bidrag til den Norske dramatiske kunsts historie.* Kristiania: Alb. Cammermeyer, 1884.

Bok om Per Lindberg, En. Stockholm: Wahlström & Widstrand, 1944.

Brown, Thomas A., *A history of the New York stage from . . . 1732 to 1901.* New York: Dodd, Mead & Company, 1903. 3 vols.

Browne, Walter, and E. De Roy Koch, *Who's who on the stage.* New York: B. W. Dodge & Company, 1908.

Bæckstrom Oscar, and others, *Skådespelarne har ordet.* Stockholm: Albert Bonniers Förlag, 1902.

Clarence, Reginald (Eldredge, H. J.), *The stage cyclopedia; a bibliography of plays.* London: "The stage," 1909.

Collin, Edgar, and Arthur Aumont, *Det Danske nationalteater, 1748-1889.* Köbenhavn: J. Jörgenson og Companie, 1896-1900.

Dahlgren, Fredrik A., *Förteckning öfver Svenska skådespel uppförda på Stockholms theatrar 1737-1863.* Stockholm: P. A. Norstedt och Söner, 1866.

Dansk biografisk haandleksikon, Svend Dahl and Povl Engelstoft, eds. Köbenhavn: Gyldendalske Bogh., 1923-1926. 3 vols.

Dansk biografisk leksikon, Povl Engelstoft, ed. Köbenhavn: J. H. Schultz Forlag, 1933-1944. 27 vols., IV.

Dansk bogfortegnelse . . . samt fortegnelse over musikalier, 1841-1929. Kjöbenhavn: G. E. C. Gad & O. H. O. Delhanco, 1861-1929. 79 vols.

Deutsches bücherverzeichnis; eine zusammenstellung der im Deutschen buchhandel erscheinende bücher, 1911-1935. Leipzig: Leipzig Börsenverein der Deutschen Buchhändler zu Leipzig, 1916-1917. 18 vols.

Erdmann, Nils, *August Blanche och hans samtid.* Stockholm: Albert Bonniers Förlag, 1892.

Erslev, Thomas H., *Almindeligt forfatter-lexicon for Kongeriget Danmark med tilhörende bilande, fra 1814 til 1840.* Kjöbenhavn: Forlagsforeningens Forlag, 1843-1853. 3 vols. Supplement, 1858-1868. 3 vols.

Goedeke, Karl, and Edmund Goetze, *Grundriss zur geschichte der Deutschen dichtungen der quellen von Karl Goedeke,* 3d. ed. Dresden and Hanover: L. Ehlerman, 1859-1881, 1884-1913. 12 vols.

Grethlein, Konrad, *Allgemeiner Deutscher theaterkatalog.* Münster i West.: Adolph Verlag, 1894.

Gustafson, Alrik, ed., *Scandinavian plays of the twentieth century. First series.* Princeton, N. J.: Princeton University Press, for the American-Scandinavian Foundation, 1944.

Hansen, Peter, *Den Danske skueplads. Illustrert theater-historie.* Kjöbenhavn: E. Bojesen, 1889-1896. 3 vols.

Hansen, Peter, *Illustrert Dansk litteraturhistorie,* 2nd. ed. Kjöbenhavn: Den Nordiske Forlag, 1889-1896. 3 vols. in 2.

Hedberg, Frans, *Svenska skådespelare. Karakteristiker och porträtter.* Stockholm: C. E. Fritzes Hofbokhandel, 1884.

Hedberg, Tor, *Ett decennium. Uppsatser och kritiker i litteratur, konst, teater m.m.* Stockholm: Albert Bonniers Förlag, 1913. 3 vols., III.

Henriques, Alf, *Svensk litteratur efter 1900* Tr. from Danish by Herbert Friedländer. Stockholm: Forum. Albert Bonniers Boktryck., 1945.

Huitfeldt-Kaas, Henrik J., *Christiania theater historie.* Kjöbenhavn: Gyldendalske Boghandel, 1876.

Johnsson, Melker, *En åttitalist. Gustaf af Geijerstam, 1858-1895.* Göteborg: Elanders Boktryckeri Aktiebolag, 1934.

Klemming, Gustaf E., *Sveriges dramatiska litteratur till och med 1875. Bibliographie.* Stockholm: P. A. Norstedt och Söner, 1863-1879. Parts 40, 55, 67, 71, 72. Vol. 19, *Samlingar utgifna af Svenska Fornskrift Sällskapet.*

Lamm, Martin, *August Blanche som Stockholms-skildrare.* Stockholm: Hugo Gebers Förlag, 1931.

Lamm, Martin, *August Strindberg.* Stockholm: Bonniers, 1940. Del I.

Levertin, Oscar I., ed. *Sveriges national-litteratur, 1500-1920.* Stockholm: Albert Bonniers Förlag, 1907-1922. 30 vols., XXV.

Lindberg, Per, and Sten af Geijerstam, *Anders de Wahl.* Stockholm: Wahlström & Widstrand, 1944.

Lindblom, Ernst, *Svenska teaterminnen från Chicago.* Stockholm: C. I. Gullbergs Förlag, 1916.

Linnström, Hjalmar, *Svenskt boklexicon, åren 1830-1865.* Stockholm: Hjalmar Linnströms Förlag, 1883-1884. 2 vols.

Lorenz Otto H., ed., *Catalogue général de la librairie Française depuis 1840.* Paris: O. Lorenz, 1867-1877; Librairie Nilsson, 1878-1912. 23 vols.

Mason, Hamilton, *French theatre in New York. A list of plays, 1899-1939.* New York: Columbia University Press, 1940.

Nordensvan, Georg G., *I rampljus.* Stockholm: Albert Bonniers Förlag, 1900.

Norlander, Emil, *August Blanche. Minnesteckning i breda drag.* Stockholm: Åhlén och Åkerlunds Förlag A.-B., 1918.

Ny illustrerad tidning, D. Weber, ed. Stockholm: *Ny serie. Vols.* XIX-XXII (1883-1886).

Ny Svensk tidskrift. R. Geijer, ed. Stockholm: P. A. Norstedt och Söners Förlag. Vols. I-XI (1880-1890).

Odell, George C. D., *Annals of the New York stage.* New York: Columbia University Press, 1927-1949. 15 vols.

Ollén, Gunnar, *Strindbergs dramatik. En handbok.* Stockholm: Ronzo Boktryckeri A.-B., 1949.

Ord och bild. Illustrerad månadsskrift, Karl Wåhlin, Sven Rinman, eds. Stockholm: A.-B. Wahlström & Widstrand. Vols I-XLVIII (1892-1939).

Overskou, Thomas. *Den Danske skueplads, i dens historie, fra de förste spor...indtil vor tid*. Kjöbenhavn: Thieles Bogtrykkeri, 1854-1876. 7 vols. in 6.

Overskou, Thomas, *Overskous haandbog for yndere och dyrkere af Dansk dramatisk literatur och kunst, indeholdende de Kongelige Theatres repertoire fra 18 Dec'br. 1848, indtil begyndelsen af saisonen 1879-1880*. Kjöbenhavn: J. H. Schubothes Boghandel, 1879.

Personne, Nils, *Svenska teatern*. Stockholm: Wahlström och Widstrand, 1913-1927. 8 vols.

Quérard, Joseph M., *La France littéraire, ou Dictionnaire bibliographique . . . des XVIIIe et XIXe siécles*. Paris: Firmin Didot Père et Fils, 1827-1864. 12 vols.

Rydell, Gerda, *Adertonhundratalets historiska skådespel i Sverige före Strindberg*. Stockholm: P. A. Norstedt och Söner, 1928.

Schneider, Max, *Deutsches titelbuch; ein hilfsmittel zum nachweis von verfassern Deutsches litteratur werke*, 2nd. ed. Berlin: Hande und Spenersche Büchhandlung, 1927.

Schück, Henrik, and Karl Warburg, *Illustrerad litteraturhistoria*, 3d revised ed. Stockholm: Hugo Gebers Förlag, 1932. 7 vols., VI and VII.

Selander, Sten, and Sigurd Westberg, eds., *Levande Svensk litteratur*. Stockholm: Albert Bonniers Förlag, 1936-1938. 22 vols.

Strömberg, Kjell, *Modern Svensk litteratur*. Stockholm: Bokförlaget Natur och Kultur, 1932.

Svea. Folk kalender. Stockholm: Albert Bonniers Förlag. Vols. XXVI-LXIV (1870-1908).

Svensk bok-katalog för åren 1866-1905. Stockholm, 1878-1908, 5 vols.

Svensk litteratur historisk bibliographie, 1900-1935. Uppsala: Svenska Litteratursällskapet, 1939.

Svensk tidskrift, Eli K. Hekscher and Gösta Bagge, eds., Stockholm: Centraltryckeriet. Vols. III-XII (1913-1922).

Svensk uppslagsbok, 2nd, rev. ed. Malmö: Fölagshuset Norden A.-B., 1947-1949. 10 vols.

Svenskt biografisk handlexicon, Herman Hofberg, ed. Stockholm: Albert Bonniers Förlag, 1906. 2 vols.

Svenskt biografiskt lexicon, Berthil Boëthius, ed. Stockholm: Albert Bonniers Förlag, 1918-1931. 11 vols.

Svenskt biografiskt lexicon. Ny följd. Örebro: N. M. Lindhs Boktryckeri; Stockholm: Beijers Förlag, 1857-1890. 10 vols.

Svenskt författarlexikon, 1900-1940. Bibliografisk handbok till Sveriges moderna litteratur. Bengt Åhlén, ed. Stockholm: Svenskt Författarlexikons Förlag Raben och Sjögren, 1942. 3 vols.

Svenskt litteratur tidskrift, C. R. Nyblom, ed. Uppsala: W. Schultz. Vols. II-XII (1866-1876).

Thieme, Hugo P., *Guide bibliographique de la litterature Française de 1800 à 1906*. Paris: H. Welter, 1907.

Thilo, Ernst (E. Olith), *Vadmecum dramatischer werke*. Hanover: Lüdeman, 1895-1896.

Ur dagens krönika, Arvid Ahnfelt, ed. Stockholm: Oscar L. Lamms Förlag. Vols. I-XI (1881-1891).

Vollständiges bücher-lexicon, 1750-1910. Christian G. Kayser and others, eds. Leipzig, 1834-1911. 36 vols. in 27.

Wingren, G., *Svensk dramatisk litteratur under åren 1840-1913. Bibliografisk förteckning.* Uppsala: F. C. Askerbergs Bokförlagsaktiebolag, 1914.

Witkowski, Georg, *Das Deutsche drama des neunzehnten jahrhunderts in seiner entwicklung dargestellt,* 3d. ed. Leipzig: B. G. Teubner, 1910.

Årskatalog för Svenska bokhandeln. Stockholm: Svenska Bokförläggareföreningen, 1901-1925. 54 vols.

B. Plays acted in Swedish in Chicago, including sources, and adaptations in English. Descriptions of the plays and original dates are given in the Appendix, I, and are omitted here.

Blanche, August. *Flickan i Stadsgården.* Stockholm: Albert Bonniers Förlag (1847), 1928. Novel.

Blanche, August. *Samlade arbeten, teaterstycken.* Stockholm: Albert Bonniers Förlag, 1892. 2 vols.
  I. *Positivhataren; Magister Bläckstadius, eller Giftermålsannonsen; Rika morbror.* II. *Engelbrekt och hans Dalkarlar; Jernbäraren; Herr Dardanell och hans upptåg på landet; Hittebarnet; Ett resande teatersällskap; Döden fadder; Grannarene.*

Bondeson, August, *Smålandsknekten.* Stockholm: Bonniers Förlag, 1894.

Börjesson, Johan, *Valda skrifter, med författarens biografi af N. Arfvidsson.* Stockholm: Bonniers Förlag, 1873. 2 vols.
  I. *Erik den fjortonde.*

Carlén, Emilie Flygare, *The rose of Tistelön. A tale of the Swedish coast.* Tr. from Swedish. London: Longman, Brown, Green and Longmans, 1844. 2 vols.

Dahlgren, Fredrik A., *Vermländingarne,* 5th ed. Stockholm: Albert Bonniers Förlag, 1890.

Daly, Augustin, *A night off.* New York: Dick and Fitzgerald. First acted, 1885. Copyright date, 1897 *(Sabinskornas bortröfvande).*

Daly, Augustin. *The lottery of love.* Privately printed. First acted, 1888 *(Duvals skilsmessa).*

Flodmark, Johan, *En friare i lifsfara. Teater-biblioteket No. 15.* Chicago: And. L. Löfströms Förlag, n.d.

Geijerstam, Gustaf af, *Svenska bondepjeser.* Stockholm: Bonniers Förlag, 1894.
  Per Olsson och hans käring; Lars Anders och Jan Anders och deras barn.

Geijerstam, Gustaf af, *Svärfar.* Stockholm: Bonniers Förlag, 1888.

Geijerstam, Gustaf af, *Vilse i lifvet.* Stockholm: Albert Bonniers Förlag, 1897. Novel.

Grundy, Sidney, *A pair of spectacles.* Typed copy, Morton Collection, University of Chicago *(Farbror Knut från Norrköping).*

Gustafson, Richard, *En brottslig betjänt. Teater-biblioteket No. 5.* Chicago: And. L. Löfströms Förlag, n.d.

Hedberg, Frans, *Bröllopet på Ulfåsa,* 2nd. ed. Stockholm: Albert Bonniers Förlag, 1876.

Hedberg, Frans, *Carl XII, eller Lejonet vaknar.* Stockholm: Albert Bonniers Förlag, 1868.

Hedberg, Frans, *Lifvet på landet.* Harald Apelboms Teateragentur, Stockholm, 1902, MS.

Hodell, Frans, *Andersson, Pettersson och Lundström.* Chicago: And. L. Löfströms Förlag, 1912.

Hodell, Frans, *En cigarr. Teater-biblioteket No. 3.* Chicago: And. L. Löfströms Förlag, n.d.

Hodell, Frans, *Ett rum att hyra. Teater-biblioteket No. 19.* Chicago: And. L. Löfströms Förlag, n.d.

Hodell, Frans, *Kärleken på sommarnöje. Teater-biblioteket No. 14.* Chicago: And. L. Löfströms Förlag, n.d.

Holberg, Ludvig von, *Ludvig Holbergs comoedier i urval,* Carl R. and Helena Nyblom, eds. Stockholm: Fahlcrantz & Co., 1888-1890. 12 vols. in 1.
Jeppe paa bierget.

Holson, A.B., and Wicklund, Gustaf, *Allt för guld.* Mr. Wicklund's original MS., 1885.

Ibsen, Henrik. *Samlede værker. Mindeudgave.* Kristiania: Gyldendalske Bogh., 1906-1907. 5 vols.
IV. *Et dukkehjem.*

Jolin, Johan, *Teaterstycken.* Stockholm: Bonnier, 1895. 3 vols.
I. *En komedi; Skal och kärna; Mäster Smith, eller Aristokrater äro vi alla.*
III. *Löjen och tårar.*

Jolin, Johan, *Tre förälskade poliskonstaplar. Teater biblioteket No. 9.* Chicago: And. L. Löfströms Förlag, n.d.

Jonason, Aron, *Mot beräkning. Teater-biblioteket No. 11.* Chicago, And. L. Löfströms Förlag, n.d.

Leffler, A. Charlotte Edgren, *Skådespelerskan.* Stockholm: Z. Hæggströms Förlagsexpedition, 1883.

Ljungby Horn. MS., originally owned by Carl Liljegren.

Lundgrén, Johan F. (Uller), *En dag under smekmånaden. Teater-biblioteket No. 6,* Chicago: And. L. Löfströms Förlag, n.d.

Lundgrén, Johan F. (Uller), *En menniskovän. Teater-biblioteket No. 22,* Chicago: And. L. Löfströms Förlag, n.d.

Lundgrén, Johan F. (Uller), *En svartsjuk tok. Teater-biblioteket No. 7,* Chicago: And. L. Löfströms Förlag, n.d.

Lundgrén, Johan F. (Uller), *Han hyr rum af sin betjent. Teater-biblioteket No. 25.* Chicago: And. L. Löfströms Förlag, n.d.

Lundström, Isidor, *En orolig natt. Teater-biblioteket No. 4.* Chicago: And. L. Löfströms Förlag, n.d.

Martinsson, Herman, *Karl Sabelstraff [sic] och hans rivaler. Teater-biblioteket No. 2.* Chicago: And. L. Löfströms Förlag, n.d.

Möller, Otto, *Hon vill inte gifta sig. Teater-biblioteket No. 26.* Chicago: And. L. Löfströms Förlag, n.d.

Müller, Hugo, *I första klassens väntsal. Teater-biblioteket No. 12.* Chicago: And. L. Löfströms Förlag, n.d.

Philipsson, Jonas, *Min hustru, eller En natt i Falkenberg. Teater-biblioteket No. 1.* Chicago: And. L. Löfströms Förlag, n.d.

Spanier, Bertha, *Mamsell Sundblad vill gifta sig. Teater-biblioteket No. 10.* Chicago: And. L. Löfströms Förlag, n.d.

Spanier, Bertha, *Mottagningstimmen. Teater-biblioteket No. 18.* Chicago: And L. Löfströms Förlag, n.d.

Strand, Algot E., *Öregrund-Östhammar.* MS.

Straube, Bertha Spanier, *En spik i nyckelhålet. Teater-biblioteket No. 30.* Chicago: And. L. Löfströms Förlag, n.d.

Strindberg, August, *Hemsöborna. Skärgårdsberättelse.* Stockholm: Albert Bonniers Förlag, 1907. Novel.

Strindberg, August, *Kammarspel. Opus 4.* Stockholm: Aktiebolaget Ljus, 1907.
Pelikanen.

Strindberg, August, *Påsk.* Stockholm: Albert Bonniers Förlag, 1921.

Strindberg, August, *Samlade dramatiska arbeten*. Stockholm: Hugo Gebers Förlag, 1903-1904. 6 vols.

I. *Lycko-Pers resa*. II. *Paria; Moderskärlek; Den starkare*. V. *Gustaf Vasa*.

Sudermann, Hermann, *Die ehre*, 7th ed. Stuttgart: Verlag der J. G. Cotta'schen Buchhandlung, 1896.

Säfström, August, *Bror Jonathan, eller Oxhandlaren från Småland. Teater-biblioteket No. 21*. Chicago: And. L. Löfströms Förlag, n.d.

Topelius, Zacharias, *Dramatiska dikter*. Stockholm: Albert Bonniers Förlag, 1881. *Regina von Emmeritz*.

Waldauer, August, *Fanchon, the cricket*. French's Standard Drama, acting ed., No. 334. New York: Samuel French, n.d. *(Syrsan)*.

Warburg, Karl J., *Numro ett, rundt om hörnet. Teater-biblioteket* No. 17. Chicago: And. L. Löfströms Förlag, n.d.

Wicklund, Gustaf, *En afton på "Tre Byttor."* Stockholm: Albert Bonniers Förlag, 1893.

Wicklund, Gustaf, *Pinafore*. Original MS., 1896.

Woodward, T. Trask, *The social glass; or Victims of the bottle*. French's Standard Drama, No. 385. New York: Samuel French, n.d. *(Sällskapsglaset)*.

Wurm Junior, *Tosingar*, 9th ed. *Bibliotek för teatervänner No. 148*. Stockholm: Sigfrid Flodins Förlag, 1912.

Österberg, Thore, and Stockenberg, Carl, *Kupletter ur Svenska folkets underbara öden, eller "Måtte våra barn få rika föräldrar."*

C. Clippings, and materials other than plays provided by persons connected with the Swedish theatre of Chicago.

1. Clippings.
   Linder, Oliver A., Clipping Collection (from newspapers, periodicals, correspondence). Augustana College Library, Rock Island, Illinois.
   Pfeil, Mrs. Anna, scrap book and other clippings, 1890-1929. From Mrs. Alex Engström.
   Svea, Worcester, Massachusetts, Apr. 4, 1896. From Arthur Donaldson collection, American Swedish Historical Museum of Philadelphia.

2. Manuscript roles from plays, from Mrs. Knut Schröder.
   Anna Stina i Chicago: Baron Lejon, Gus.
   Andersson, Pettersson och Lundström: Andersson.
   Bröllopet på Ulfåsa: Prior Botvid.
   Gustaf Vasa: Prins Johan.
   Lilla Helgonet: Célestin.
   Nerkingarne: Olle.
   Pinafore: Sir Joseph Porter.
   Regina von Emmeritz: Bertil.
   Vermländingarne: Provst.

3. Pictures. From Mr. Arthur Donaldson, Mrs. Alex Engström, Mrs. Werner Melinder, Mr. Paul Norling, Mrs. Anna Nylund, Mrs. Knut Schröder, Mr. Carl Stockenberg, Mrs. Gustaf Wicklund.

4. Posters. From Mr. Ernest H. Behmer and Mrs. Gustaf Wicklund.

5. Programs. From Mr. Ernst H. Behmer, Mrs. Alex Engström, Mrs. Elna L. Kronberg, Mr. Paul Norling, Mr. Carl Stockenberg, Mrs. Knut Schröder, Mrs. Gustaf Wicklund.

NOTES

FOREWORD

[1]Marcus L. Hansen, *The immigrant in American history* (Cambridge, Mass., 1940), pp. 206-208.

[2]Carl Wittke, *We who built America* (New York, 1939), pp. 378-385.

[3]Theodore C. Blegen, *Norwegian migration to America. The American transition* (Northfield, Minn., 1940), pp. 560-563.

[4]Robert E. Park and Herbert A. Miller, *Old world traits transplanted* (New York, 1925), pp. 129-131.

[5]See Napier Wilt and Henriette C. K. Naeseth, "Two early Norwegian dramatic societies in Chicago," *Norwegian-American Studies and Records,* X (1938), 44-75.

[6]The one general account of the Swedish theatre in the United States, in addition to a brief paragraph in Carl Sundbeck's *Svenskarne i Amerika* (Stockholm, 1900), 279, is Ernst H. Behmer's "Seventy years of Swedish theatre in America," in *The Swedish element in America,* Erik G. Westman, ed. (Chicago, 1931-1934), IV, 111-120. Considerable information about the Minneapolis Swedish theatre is given in Alfred Söderström's *Minneapolis minnen* (no place, or date), pp. 267-276.

CHAPTER I

[1]Representative figures are: in 1870, 6,154 native born Swedes and 59,299 native born Germans; in 1900, 100,155 Swedes, both native born and of Swedish parentage, and 416,663 Germans, in the two categories. Bessie L. Pierce, *A history of Chicago* (New York, 1940), II, 482; *Statistical review of immigration, 1820-1910* (Washington, 1911), p. 16.

[2]Florence E. Janson, *The background of Swedish immigration, 1840-1930* (Chicago, 1931), pp. 9-13, 133, 501.

[3]Gustav E. Johnson, *The Swedes of Chicago* (unpublished doctoral dissertation, University of Chicago, 1940), p. 15 .

[4]Janson, *op. cit.,* pp. 504-505.

[5]Johnson, *op. cit.,* p. 15.

[6]Johan A. Enander, "Chicago-Branden," *Valkyrian,* V (Dec. 1901), 631-640; Charles F. Peterson, "Några Svenska Chicagominnen; ett mycket lifliga re skede," *Valkyrian,* III (1899), 286-288; Ernst W. Olson, *History of the Swedes in Illinois* (Chicago, 1908), pp. 310-312. Numbers designating location of streets are those adopted in 1909.

[7]Johnson, *op. cit.,* p. 15.

[8]See Appendix, III, for a list of places where plays were performed, with addresses and seasons. Adoption of a new system of street numbering in 1909 confuses the locations somewhat. The present system is followed here, except for the German Hall and Criterion; for the North Side Turner Hall both addresses are given.

[9]George M. Stephenson, *The religious aspects of Swedish immigration* (Minneapolis, Minn., 1932), p. 148.

[10]Vilhelm B e r g e r, *Svensk-Amerikanska meditationer* (Rock Island, Ill., 1916), pp. 22-27; Ernst W. Olson, *op. cit.,* pp. 356-624; Charles F. Peterson, "Blickar mellan kulisserna i Chicagos Svenska verld för 35 år sedan," *Valkyrian,* V (Jan. 1901), 34-46, and *Sverige i Amerika* (Chicago, 1898), pp. 42-44, 73; George M. Stephenson, *op. cit.,* pp. 5-9, 104-105, 131-132, 171-174, 196-205, and "The stormy years of the Swedish colony in Chicago before the great fire," *Transactions of the Illinois State H i s t o r i c a l Society,* XXXVI (1929), 166-184.

[11]Alfred Söderström, *Blixtar på tidnings-horisonten* (W a r r o a d, Minn., 1910), pp. 72-73.

[12]Johan A. Enander, "En Svensk-Amerikansk tidnings 50-års jubileum," *Prärieblomman,* VI, (1906), 228-248; Olson, *op. cit.,* pp. 771-772; Ernst Skarstedt, *Svensk-Amerikanska folket i helg och söcken* (Stockholm, 1917), p. 182, and *Vagabond och redaktör* (Seattle, Wash., 1914), pp. 158-160, 211-240, 386-394; Söderström, *Blixtar på tidnings-horisonten, passim;* Westman, *op. cit.,* II, 328-334. See Bibliography, I, for

diagram presenting the development of the Swedish press in Chicago.

[13]Vilhelm Berger, *Hundår och lyckodagar* (New York, 1905), pp. 13-27; Otto Croelius, "Ett bröllop som ej blef af," *Kurre-Kalender*, 1901, pp. 79-93. 188; Ninian Wærner, *Mina hundår i Amerika* (Stockholm, 1900), pp. 79-93. See also Stephenson, *Religious aspects of Swedish immigration*, pp. 397 ff.

[14]Tancred Boissy, *Svenska nationaliteten i Förenta Staterna* (Göteborg, 1862), p. 5.

[15]Croelius, *op. cit.*, p. 179.

[16]Wærner, *op. cit.*, pp. 5-11; Johan Person, *I Svensk-Amerika* (Worcester, Mass., 1900), pp. 49-51, 132-133.

[17]Magnus Elmblad, *Samlade arbeten* (Minneapolis, Minn., 1890), pp. 195-196.

[18]Person, *op. cit.*, p. 130.

[19]*Kurre Kalender*, 1899, pp. 30-31. *Du-skål*: drinking healths on terms of intimacy indicated by familiar pronoun.

[20]Vilhelm Berger, *Svenska folklynnet i förskingringen* (Brooklyn, N. Y., 1924), pp. 13-21; Skarstedt, *Svensk-Amerikanska folket i helg och söcken*, pp. 7-11.

[21]Berger, *Svensk-Amerikanska meditationer*, pp. 89-97; Peterson, *Sverige i Amerika*, pp. 409-914; Westman, *op. cit.*, II, 306; *et al.*

[22]Eric Johnson and Charles F. Peterson, *Svenskarne i Illinois* (Chicago, 1880), pp. 256-258; *et al.*

[23]*H.*, Feb. 23, Apr. 23, 1875.

[24]E. Einar Andersson, ed., *Hembygden* (Chicago, 1933); O. A. Linder, "Svenska föreningernas i Chicago alderdomshem," *Valkyrian*, XIII (Oct. 1909), 514-516, and "Svenska National-förbundet i Chicago," *Valkyrian*, XIII (Apr. 1909), 188-191; Olson, *op. cit.*, pp. 705-759, 888-915; Peterson, *Sverige i Amerika*, pp. 256-260; *Runristningar* (Chicago, 1915); *Svenska Klubben, 1870-1916* (Chicago, 1916); Westman, *op. cit.*, II, 396-496; Swedish newspapers, *et al.*

[25]Lindstrand, *Pennteckningar och reseskildringar* (Chicago, 1898), pp. 51-56.

[26]Interviews; Ernst Lindblom, *Svenska teaterminnen från Chicago* (Stockholm, 1916), p. 114. See. p. 53.

[27]These points apply in general to the Swedish theatre elsewhere in America also. See Berger, *Svensk-Amerikanska meditationer*, pp. 102-116, and Skarstedt, *Svensk-Amerikanska folket i helg och söcken*, pp. 140-141.

[28]F. A. Dahlgren was for a time *litteratör* at the Royal Theatre, and wrote and adapted a good many plays, overshadowed by *Vermländingarne*. He was also a distinguished linguistic scholar, writer and collector of folk songs, and author of a valuable theatrical record.

[29]*August Lindberg. En monografi* (Stockholm, 1911); Gustaf af Geijerstam, "Teater," *Ord och Bild*, V (1896), 523-528; Gustaf Linden, "August Lindberg," *Ord och Bild*, XXVI (1917), 365-372; *et al.*

[30]*Ibid.;* George Nordensvan, "Shakespeare i Sverige. Några anteckningar," *Ord och Bild*, XXV (1916), 225-232.

[31]Gunnar Ollén, *Strindbergs dramatik. En handbok* (Stockholm, 1949), *et al.*

[32]Books and periodicals listed in the Bibliography, III, are general sources for this discussion of the theatre and drama of Sweden.

[33]Gunnar Ollén, in *Strindbergs dramatik*, which lists chief Swedish performances and many performances outside Sweden, calls the February 1913 *Påsk* (Easter) the American première, and for *Gustaf Vasa* names no American performance except that in Chicago in 1912. For *Lycko-pers resa* (Lucky Per's journey), *Paria* (The pariah), and *Pelikanen* (The pelican), Ollén refers to American performances later than those in Chicago; for *Den starkare* (The stronger), to a performance earlier than that in Chicago; and for two other plays acted in Chicago, *Hemsöborna* (The people of Hemsö) and *Moderskärlek* (Mother love), he mentions no American performances. Full records of other Swedish acting groups in the United States would doubtless supplement and in some cases supersede these Chicago performances.

[34]Olson, *op. cit.*, p. 305; Carl Sundbeck, *Svensk-Amerikanerna* (Rock Island, Ill., 1904), pp. 385-389.

[35]Peterson, *Sverige i Amerika*, p. 300.

[36]*S. T.*, Mch. 30, 1892.

CHAPTER II

[1]*H.,* July 16, 1867.

[2]*S. A.,* July 24, 1867.

[3]*H.,* June 18, 1867.

[4]*Skandia,* Mch. 9, 1877.

[5]*H.,* Mch. 16, 1877. This exchange was part of a larger dispute concerning *Skandia,* and the relation to the Augustana Synod of its editor, who had been for a time a member of the Augustana College faculty.

[6]"Då Christina Nilsson kom till Chicago," *Prärieblomman* (1900), pp. 50-61.

[7]*S. A.,* May 5, 1868.

[8]*S. A.,* Mch. 2, 1869. The reference in "presten spår" (the minister prophesies) is probably to the outspoken pastor of the Augustana Immanuel Church, Erland Carlsson.

[9]This was customary at German and Norwegian plays also.

[10]*S. A.,* Feb. 15, 1869. Such a reference in 1869 may be interpreted as suggesting performances earlier than those for which there are records.

[11]*S. A.,* Jan. 3, 1871.

[12]Johnson and Peterson, *op. cit.,* p. 410; Charles F. Peterson, "Chicago minnen. Efter branden," *Valkyrian,* V (July 1889), 407-411; *S. A.,* Mch. 2, 1869.

[13]*S. A.,* Dec. 6, 1870.

[14]*S. A.,* Jan. 19, 1871.

[15]*S. A.,* Apr. 9, 1870.

[16]See pp. 45 and 59.

[17]Johnson and Peterson, *op. cit.,* p. 415.

[18]*Ibid.,* p. 412; *N. S. A.,* Nov. 30, 1876.

[19]*S. A.,* Jan. 10, 1871.

[20]Johnson and Peterson, *op. cit.,* p. 403; *S. T.,* Jan. 16, 1878. *Svenska Tribunen* began publication in 1877, but only a few issues are available for the years before 1879.

[21]*S. T.,* Jan. 16, Mch. 27, 1878.

[22]With the 1909 change in numbering, the address became 826 N. Clark.

[23]Information in part from Mrs. Hedwig Brusell Melinder (Mrs. Werner Melinder).

[24]A. T. Andreas, *History of Chicago* (Chicago, 1884-1886), I, 494; Enan-der, "Då Christina Nilsson kom till Chicago," *loc. cit.;* Olson, *op. cit.,* pp. 888-892; *N. S. A.,* Nov. 23, 1876.

[25]*H.,* May 4, 1875; *S. A.,* Mch. 2, 1869; *S. T.,* Jan. 30, 1878.

[26]The benefit m i g h t indicate that Fahlbeck had made earlier appearances or simply that he was promoting the entertainment.

[27]*S. A.,* Mch. 2, 1869.

[28]Of some interest is the inclusion of a speech on Börjesson by Magnus Elmblad in a series of lectures at Svea Hall in the spring of 1874. *H.,* Mch. 31, 1874.

[29]There were other Swedish adaptations of the Nestroy play, both before and after the Hodell version. It was, however, the most popular, both in Sweden and in Chicago.

[30]*S. A.,* Jan. 18, Feb. 1, 1870.

[31]*S. A.,* Jan. 4, 1870.

[32]This may have been Freja, which had been organized in the fall of 1869, with both Norwegian and Swedish members, but a majority of Swedes. Olson, *op. cit.,* p. 174.

[33]*S. A.,* Nov. 29, Dec. 6, 1870, Jan. 3, 1871.

[34]A possible exception was *Fäktaren i Ravenna,* acted early in 1876. It was advertised as an opera, but the only work listed under that title is a five act tragedy. F. A. Dahlgren, *Förteckning öfver Svenska skådespel* (Stockholm, 1866), p. 215; *N. S. A.,* Feb. 24, 1876.

[35]*S. A.,* Jan. 3, 10, 1871.

[36]Charles F. Peterson, "Svensk-Amerikanska banbrytare å pressens fält. Magnus Elmblad," *Valkyrian,* I (June 1897), 2-4; Skarstedt, *Vagabond och redaktör,* pp. 113-128, 162-163, *et al.*

[37]Knut Brodin, ed., *Emigrantvisor och andra visor* (Stockholm, 1938), pp. 38-40; Magnus Elmblad, *Samlade arbeten* (Minneapolis, Minn., 1890), p. 111-113; Magnus Elmblad, *Samlade dikter* (Chicago, 1878), pp. 125-127; Magnus Elmblad, *Samlade d i k t e r* (Stockholm, 1889), pp. 90-92; unidentified clipping from Swedish newspaper, June 7, 1938.

[38]*S. T.,* Feb. 27, 1878.

[39]*N. S. A.,* Nov. 16, 1876.

[40]Norwegian actors cooperated, and *List och flegma* was acted in Norwegian.

[41]This and the April 30, 1870, performance by the New York company are included because of the limited record for this early period. Later performances by visiting groups are included only when of some importance.

[42]A scene from *Macbeth*, in English, was also played.

[43]This is referred to as a second performance, but there is no available record of a first performance. *N. S. A.*, Feb. 24, 1876.

[44]A comedy in English, *The colored tragedian*, was also played.

[45]*Samhällsdanaren*, by Magnus Elmblad, was acted in the 1870's, but no facts of performance are known.

CHAPTER III

[1]Helge Nelson, *Nordamerika, natur, bygd och Svenskbygd* (Stockholm, 1926), p. 327.

[2]See pp. 9-10 for further discussion of the plight of the educated immigrant.

[3]*Bläckfisken* (Chicago, 1921), pp. 183 ff.; Skarstedt, *Vagabond och redaktör*, pp. 211 ff.; Alfred Söderström, *Blixtar på tidnings-horisonten; et al.*

[4]From interviews with Mrs. Gustaf Wicklund, who acted at this time, and was closely associated with the leading figures of the 1880's.

[5]See p. 15 for "Onkel Ola's" account of such disturbances.

[6]Lindblom, *Svenska teaterminnen från Chicago*, p. 18. See p. 53.

[7]Skarstedt, *Vagabond och redaktör*, p. 393, refers specifically to Torsell as writer of a review. Lindblom, *op. cit.*, pp. 20-27; Charles F. Peterson, "Svensk-Amerikanska banbrytare å pressens fält. Valdemar Torsell," *Valkyrian*, I (Nov. 1897), 25-27; Söderström, *Blixtar på tidnings-horisonten*, pp. 93-95. Like many of his colleagues, Torsell died young and penniless.

[8]Lindblom, *op. cit.*, pp. 112-113.

[9]Johnson and Peterson, *op. cit.*, p. 427; Skarstedt, *Vagabond och redaktör*, pp. 147-151; *S. A.*, May 23, 1912; *S. T.*, May 11, 1889; interview with Mrs. Gustaf Wicklund.

[10]It was during this visit that he learned from his father that he could legitimately add *von* to his name. *S. T.*, Aug. 2, 1889, May 27, 1903.

[11]Olson, *op. cit.*, Part 2, p. 129; Anders Schön, "En Svensk-Amerikansk konstsamlare," *Prärieblomman*, 1911, pp. 205-221; Skarstedt, *Vagabond och redaktör*, pp. 167-169; *S. A.*, Oct. 30, 1913, Dec. 9, 1926, Mch. 26, 1931; *S. T.*, May 27, 1903, *et al.*

[12]Lindblom, *op. cit.*, pp. 139-143; Skarstedt, *Vagabond och redaktör*, pp. 169-170; interviews with Mrs. Gustaf Wicklund.

[13]*Gnistor från rimsmedjan* (Minneapolis, Minn., 1906), p. 213.

[14]Wicklund, *op. cit.*, p. 6.

[15]Another translation, *Teblommen* (The tea blossom), mentioned by Skarstedt and other sources that use his information, was seemingly not acted in Chicago, nor does Mrs. Wicklund have information about it. Skarstedt, *Pennfäktare. Svensk-Amerikanska författare och tidningsmän* (Stockholm, 1930), pp. 202-203.

[16]*H.*, Oct. 17, 1905; Olson, *op. cit.*, p. 882; Schön, *Prärieblomman*, 1906, pp. 292-296; *S. A.*, Oct. 13, 1905; Skarstedt, introduction to *Gnistor från rimsmedjan*, pp. 1-10, *Pennfäktare*, pp. 202-203, *Vagabond och redaktör*, pp. 147-151; *Valkyrian*, IX (Nov. 1905), 550-554; interviews with Mrs. Gustaf Wicklund.

[17]Olson, *op. cit.*, pp. 372-373; *S. A.*, Aug. 4, 1921, May 28, 1925, *S. K.*, May 28, 1925; *S. T.*, Nov. 9, 1904; interviews.

[18]Unidentified clipping, Linder Clipping Collection, Augustana College Library, Rock Island, Illinois.

[19]Elmblad was one of those whose self-ruin was a matter of weakness, not choice, wrote newsman Oliver A. Linder, in a discussion of the Bohemians of the Chicago Swedish colony which

has provided material concerning Higgins and Åkerberg. Elmblad left Chicago for Sweden in 1884, and died there four years later, only forty years old. Bound newspaper clippings, Linder Clipping Collection.

[20]Skarstedt, *Pennfäktare*, pp. 208-209; *S. K.*, June 12, 1894; *S. T.*, June 13, 1894. A note Åkerberg appended to a photograph of himself gives a good idea of his situation and his nature. "I look angry, but I am not. The clothes are new and fine, and therefore naturally not paid for. My Irish upper lip was somewhat too heavy, so I had a hard time keeping my jaw shut. I took the picture only two buttons down the vest, to avoid showing that I have no watch. My cravat was sewed by my wife. That is evident. My hair is in artistic disarray. In contrast, I have brushed my teeth, but that does not show. If you find it appropriate to mention this to a larger reading public, I have no objection, but if so, add that the coat was bought at G. on Chicago Avenue, so perhaps I'll get a pair of trousers in the bargain, for sake of the advertisement." Skarstedt, *Pennfäktare*, p. 208. See also verses by Åkerberg, p. 11.

[21]Among the explanations are: a. after the death of an Irish girl with whom he fell in love, he took her name. Lindblom, *op. cit.*, p. 49; b. an Irish fellow-boarder forced him to make the change. Schön, *Prärieblomman*, 1910, p. 256; c. an Irish family named Higgins with whom he lived honored him with their name because of his prowess in drinking. Linder, *Valkyrian*, XIII (1909), 341-343; d. not enthusiasm for the Irish but disgust with the pronunciation of Lindstrom was his reason. *Broder Lustig,* I (Nov. 14, 1896), 524-525.

[22]I (Nov. 14, 1896), 524-525. Higgins was at this time a regular contributor to the weekly periodical *Broder Lustig* (Brother Mirth).

[23]Linder, bound newspaper clippings, Linder Clipping Collection; Schön, *Prärieblomman*, 1910, pp. 253-266; *S. K.*, July 16, 1904; *et al.*

[24]An episode from McKeesport told by Ludwig Lundgren, another Chicago actor who moved there, shows Higgins as having, on occasion, more will power

than his Good Templar friends. They agreed that he should be permitted to paint a mural in a saloon, and then, when they went to admire the Swedish Christmas scene he painted, broke their pledges. Higgins himself resisted temptation, he said, because of the poor quality of the liquor. Sigyn, "Julsupen," *Bläckfisken*, pp. 60-65.

[25]*S. T. N.*, May 18, 1909.

[26]*Broder Lustig,* I (July 25, 1896), 268; Lindblom, *op. cit.,* p. 46.

[27]Lindblom, *op. cit.*, pp. 46-62.

[28]Söderström, *Blixtar på tidnings-horisonten,* p. 121.

[29]Lindblom, *op. cit.,* pp. 32-35; Schön, *Prärieblomman,* 1905, pp. 221-222; Skarstedt, *Pennfäktare,* pp. 146-147; *S. T.,* May 25, 1904. *Gluntarne* may be translated as the boys, but the title came from the nickname of one of the students who originally sang the songs and became a character in the picture they give of Upsala student life in the 1840's. Gunnar Wennerberg, *Gluntarne* (Stockholm, 1908), Introduction, pp. 60-61.

[30]His death and that of Wicklund were almost simultaneous, and brought many reminiscences of their friendship and of the early carefree days. *H.*, Oct. 24, 1905; Olson, *op. cit.,* pp. 829-831; Schön, *Prärieblomman,* 1906, pp. 288-290; Skarstedt, *Pennfäktare,* pp. 195-197; Söderström, *Blixtar på tidnings-horisonten,* pp. 107-108, 243-244; *Valkyrian,* IX (Nov. 1905), 550-554; interviews.

[31]Skarstedt, *Pennfäktare,* pp. 108-109; *S. A.,* Apr. 27, 1897, Nov. 12, 1925; *S. T.,* May 23, 1894; *S. T. N.,* Nov. 11, 1925.

[32]Interview with Mrs. Gustaf Wicklund.

[33]*Ibid.; S. K.,* May 15, 1919.

[34]*Broder Lustig,* I (Dec. 12, 1896), 41; *H.,* Jan. 1, 1891; *S. A.,* Oct. 31, 1899; *S. T.,* Sept. 5, 1883; Söderström, *Blixtar på tidnings-horisonten,* p. 268.

[35]*S. A.,* June 16, 1892.

[36]*S. A., S. K.,* Mch. 9, 1922; interviews.

[37]Mr. Herbert Hedman, letter; *S. A.,* Sept. 25, 1924; *S. A. T.,* Jan. 17, 1946, Westman, *op. cit.,* III, 502; Ernst H. Behmer's "Seventy years of Swedish

theatre in America," in Westman, op. cit., IV, 111-120, has provided material concerning a number of the actors here discussed.

[38]An engagement in the spring of 1891 was with Ben Hendricks of "Ole Olson" fame. Another engagement with an American t o u r i n g company was undertaken in the late spring of 1899. S. A., Mch. 28, 1899, S. T., May 28, 1891. Interview with Mrs. Pfeil in Seattle Star, May 18, 1911. Clipping provided by Betty Pfeil Engström (Mrs. Alex Engström).

[39]Söderström, Blixtar på tidnings-horisonten, p. 108.

[40]F i n s k a Amerikanaren, Brooklyn, n. d. Clipping provided by Mrs. Alex Engström.

[41]Seattle Star, May 18, 1911; S. T., Mch. 10, 31, 1888; S. T. N., Apr. 30, 1924; programs and unidentified clippings in Swedish and English supplied by Mrs. Alex Engström; interviews.

[42]Facts from Mrs. Hvitfeldt's daughter, Mrs. Anna Nylund, and a clipping supplied by her: Birger Schöldström, Idun, June 22, 1905; S. T., Aug. 31, 1904; interviews.

[43]He may have been the Adolf Linde-berg referred to as a famous tragedian (one suspects irony) in a Hemlandet story of his resentment of the scanty publicity given his 1890 visit to Western cities by Ninian Wærner, then with Svenska Korrespondenten of Denver. H., Jan. 1, 1891.

[44]Behmer, loc. cit., p. 111; Lindblom, op. cit., pp. 28-30. See p. 71.

[45]Hubert Carter was one of his students who became well known. Alberg saw him in London in 1905 and left with him manuscripts he hoped to get published. S. T., Nov. 14, 1905. Pamphlet, Linder Clipping Collection.

[46]S. A., Dec. 27, 1892.

[47]Pamphlet, Linder Clipping Collection.

[48]Iduna, III (Jan. 29, 1898), 2-3.

[49]Ibid.; Einar Adamson, article in unidentified Swedish publication, Linder Clipping Collection; H., Apr. 2, 1891; Skarstedt, Pennfäktare, pp. 15-16; S. K., Mch. 13, 1890.

[50]These figures do not include two advertised productions for which no plays

were named or the play by Åkerberg for which no newspaper record has been found. See Chronological T a b l e, pp. 80 ff.

[51]F., Feb. 1, Mch. 15, S. T., Jan. 28, Feb. 12, 1879.

[52]F., Apr. 26, 1879.

[53]F., Sept. 20, S. T., Oct. 1, 1879.

[54]F., Nov. 29, S. T., Nov. 26, 1879.

[55]Ibid.; S. T., Feb. 25, 1880. Performances in Moline, in Rockford, and more extensive tours will be referred to throughout this account, though there were certainly m o r e performances out of the city than were reported. Writing of his years in Chicago, 1885-1894, Ernst Lindblom emphasizes what every account, oral or written, tells of the fun derived from these trips. He describes the travelling itself, with the troupe riding for half fare, the way the actors took over the car and entertained themselves by singing, and the support in Moline, which usually made these expeditions profitable. He may or may not be correct in saying that the performances ordinarily took place between Christmas and New Year; he wrote from memory and hearsay, and he makes the inaccurate statement that in these years there was as a rule only one Chicago performance a year, near Christmas. There is, at any rate, no Chicago r e c o r d of a Moline visit between the two holidays. Svenska teaterminnen från Chicago, pp. 114-115.

[56]S. T., Sept. 1, 1880.

[57]S. T., Nov. 9, 1881.

[58]Martin Lamm, August Blanche som Stockholms-skildrare (S t o c k h o l m, 1931), pp. 42 ff.; Carl G. Laurin, Ord och Bild, XXVII (1918), 118; Lindblom, op. cit., p. 113; S. T., Nov. 23, 1881; et al.

[59]S. T., Sept. 20, 1882.

[60]S. T., Jan. 31, Feb. 14, 1883.

[61]S. T., Jan. 24, 31, May 2, 1883.

[62]S. T., Dec. 5, 19, 1883. Photographs owned by Mrs. Gustaf Wicklund.

[63]Lindblom, op. cit., pp. 93-99; S. T., Dec. 19, 1883. One of Lindblom's entertaining tales recounts his first Chicago reunion with his old friend, whom he discovered playing Swedish melodies in an Irish saloon on the West Side, shortly after Becker's arrival in Chicago.

[64]*S. T.*, Jan. 16, 23, 1884. Of interest is the possible presence in the cast of Nils J. Crona, an army man from Scandinavia who had won recognition as an officer in the Civil War. Johnson and Peterson, *op. cit.*, p. 146.

[65]*S. T.*, May 14, 21, 1884.

[66]*S. T.*, Jan. 21, Feb. 4, 1885.

[67]*S. T.*, Oct. 29, Nov. 19, 26, 1884.

[68]*S. T.*, Nov. 19, Dec. 17, 24, 1884.

[69]*S. T.*, Apr. 15, May 13, 1885. The reference is to *Rudolf, eller blodbadet på Sicilien*, an 1863 tragedy by Lorentz A. Hedin.

[70]Fulfillment of ambition of a different kind may be indicated by a reference in 1901 to A. B. Holson as a well known Swedish-American i n v e n t o r, whose most recent invention was a two-wheeled electric automobile. *H.*, Mch. 27, 1901.

[71]Lindblom, *op. cit.*, pp. 38-42.

[72]*Ibid.*, pp. 44-45.

[73]Interviews with Mr. John Ternquist, Mrs. Gustaf Wicklund.

[74]Available street car service was explained in the advertisements, an indication that the location was unfamiliar. *S. T.*, June 24, 1885.

[75]*Ibid.*, *S. T.*, July 1, 1885.

[76]*S. A.*, Dec. 19, 1885, Jan. 2, 1886; *S. T.*, Dec. 19, 1885, Feb. 20, 1886.

[77]Program, gift of Mrs. Gustaf Wicklund.

[78]*S. T.*, Oct. 16, 1886.

[79]*S. T.*, Jan. 28, Mch. 12, Apr. 2, 1887.

[80]Another tale describes repercussions following local references in songs written by Lindblom for one of Sandgren's musical *soirées*. Lindblom, *op. cit.*, pp. 5-10; *S. T.*, Nov. 6, 20, 1886.

[81]*S. T.*, Jan. 14, 28, 1888.

[82]*S. T.*, Jan. 7, Feb. 11, 1888.

[83]*S. T.*, Apr. 7, 1888.

[84]*S. T.*, Mch. 17, 1888.

[85]*S. T.*, Feb. 25, 1888.

[86]*S. T.*, Apr. 14, Sept. 8, 1888.

[87]*S. T.*, May 12, 1888.

[88]*S. T.*, Apr. 14, 1888. See p. 48.

[89]*S. T.*, Oct. 13, 27, Nov. 3, 1888. Complaints, frequently playing on the name of director Biorn (bear), continued, and the following season Gustavus Norlander's orchestra w a s welcomed as a replacement for the "bear garden." *S. T.*, Sept. 26, 1889. Biorn was a well known artist and musician, for many years the director of the male chorus called the Norwegian Quartet Club. Birger Osland, "Norwegian clubs in C h i c a g o," *Norwegian-American Studies and Records*, XII (1941), 113.

[90]*S. T.*, Nov. 10, Dec. 22, 1888.

[91]*S. T.*, Jan. 19, 1889.

[92]Skarstedt, *Vagabond och redaktör*, pp. 392-393. The other plays Skarstedt saw, but on which he did not comment, were *Nerkingarne* and *Andersson, Pettersson och Lundström*.

[93]This may have been the Fredrik Hedlund of later Swedish reputation, and it is possible he played in the November *Vermländingarne*, which was unreviewed. The M c C a u l l Company with which he is said to have been associated was in Chicago, but American newspapers did not list him in the company's personnel. See p. 56.

[94]*S. T.*, Dec. 22, 1888.

[95]*S. T.*, Jan. 5, 1889.

[96]*S. T.*, Apr. 6, 1889.

[97]*Ibid.*

[98]The theatre had been rebuilt by Mr. Richard Hooley on its Randolph Street site after the fire, in 1872, and remodelled in 1885. Andreas, *op. cit*, III, 665.

[99]Skarstedt, *Pennfäktare*, p. 209; *S. T.*, Sept. 5, 19, 1889.

[100]*S. T.*, Sept. 26, 1889.

[101]It was often called *Gustaf II Adolf och Regina von Emmeritz* in Chicago, evidently to gain the appeal of the national hero's name.

[102]Translated. Scrapbook supplied by Mrs. Alex Engström.

[103]*S. K.*, Jan. 16, 1890; *S. T.*, Oct. 17, Nov. 7, 1889.

[104]*S. T.*, Nov. 7, 1889.

[105]*H.*, Dec. 5, 1889; Lindblom, *op. cit.*, pp. 11-12. The incident is known to Mrs. Gustaf Wicklund.

[106]*S. K.*, Jan. 2, 1890.

[107]*S. K.*, *S. T.*, Feb. 6, 1890.

[108]*Ibid.*; *S. K.*, Feb. 13, *S. T.*, Feb. 13, Apr. 24, 1890.

[109]*S. T.*, Mch. 27, 1890.

[110]*S. T.*, Apr. 3, 1890.

[111]*S. T.*, Apr. 24, 1890.

[112]*S. T.*, Apr. 24, May 1, 1890. See n. 38, p. 362 re. the tour.

[113]*S. K.*, Apr. 8, 15, *S. T.*, Apr. 2, 1891. The admiral from *Pinafore* had already made his appearance in Wicklund's *Kronjuvelerna på Nordsidan,* and in a few years his Swedish *Pinafore* was to be acted. See p. 62 and pp. 114 ff.

[114]Lindblom, *op. cit.,* pp. 15-19.

[115]*S. A.,* Mch. 12, 1891; *S. T.,* Nov. 6, 1890.

[116]*S. K.,* Oct. 9, Nov. 6, 20, *S. T.,* Oct. 23, 30, Nov. 6, 20, 27, Dec. 4, 1890.

[117]Alberg, pamphlet in Linder Clipping Collection; *Iduna,* III (Jan. 29, 1898), 2-3; Lindblom, *op. cit.,* pp. 30-31;*Ord och Bild,* IV (1895), 53.

[118]*S. K.,* Jan. 8, 1891; *S. T.,* Dec. 25, 1890, Jan. 8, Feb. 26, 1891.

[119]*S. T.,* Oct. 2, 23, 1890.

[120]*S. A., S. T.,* Apr. 23, 30, 1891.

[121]*S. K.,* May 13, *S. T.,* May 14, 1891.

[122]*S. T.,* May 21, 28, 1891. Minneapolis papers include no record of subsequent appearances by the company.

[123]S. A. S.—*Svenska Amatör Sällskap.*

CHAPTER IV

[1]*S. A.,* Feb. 21, 1893.

[2]*S. T.,* Sept. 23, 1891.

[3]*S. T.,* Sept. 10, 17, 1891, Feb. 22, 1893, *et al.*

[4]*S. T.,* Feb. 22, 1893.

[5]*S. K.,* Apr. 16, 1895.

[6]*S. A.,* Jan. 9, 1894.

[7]*S. K.,* Oct. 23, 1900; *S. T.,* Sept. 20, 1893; *et al.*

[8]*S. T.,* Mch. 30, 1892.

[9]Her roles included Marie in *The circus girl,* produced Apr. 22, 1897, and Juliette in *The geisha,* produced Sept 2, 1896. She danced a gypsy dance with Isadora Duncan and one or two others in *Much ado about nothing,* produced Dec. 21, 1897, and in Daly's adaptation of Scott's *Meg Merrilies,* produced Mch. 12, 1897. T. Allston Brown, *A history of the New York stage* (New York, 1903), II, 579-582; Joseph F. Daly, *The life of Augustin Daly* (New York, 1917), p. 606.

[10]Skarstedt, *Pennfäktare,* p. 132; *S. A.,* June 16, 1896, Sept. 19, Oct. 24, Nov. 14, 1899, June 12, 1900, July 28, 1927; *S. T.,* July 6, 1892, June 6, 1894, Oct. 11, 1899; *Valkyrian,* I (February, 1897), 23.

[11]Program, *Duvals skilsmessa,* Nov. 9, 1919. Gift of Mr. Ernst H. Behmer.

[12]*Ibid.; S. A.,* Oct. 23, 1919, July 6, 1927, July 7, 1932; *S. A. T.,* July 2, 1942; Westman, *op. cit.,* II, 140; interviews.

[13]*S. A.,* June 14, Sept. 9, 1934; *S. K.,* Nov. 11, 1926; *S. T.,* Apr. 13, 1944, July 26, 1945; interviews.

[14]Behmer, *loc. cit.,* p. 114; interviews.

[15]*H.,* Oct. 20, 1908, June 11, 1914; *S. A.,* May 10, 1917; *S. T.,* June 25, 1907; *S. V.,* Nov. 11, 1904; interviews.

[16]*Bokstugan,* VII (May, 1926), 14; *Ny Svensk Tidskrift,* VIII (1887), 329-341; *S. A.,* July 29, 1909; *S. A. T.,* Aug. 2, 1945, Mch. 21, 1946; *S. K.,* Sept. 24, 1925; *S. T. N.,* Aug. 3, 1909; *Ur Dagens Krönika,* VII (1887), 982; Harald Wieselgren, "Claes Albert Lindhagen," *Svea,* XLIV (1888), 237-240; interviews. Carl Lindhagen visited the United States in the interest of world peace in 1925, spoke in many cities, including Chicago, and published an interesting account of his experiences and purposes, *På Vikingastråt i Västerled* (Stockholm, 1926).

[17]*S. A.,* May 24, 1928; *S. T.,* Dec. 11, 1911; interviews.

[18]*S. A.,* Feb. 6, 1913, Feb. 10, 1921; *S. A. T.,* Jan. 31, 1936, May 5, 1949, Jan. 19, 1950.

[19]*S. A.,* Mch. 23, 1922; *S. A. T.,* July 25, 1940, Jan. 3, 1946; interviews.

[20]*S. A.,* July 12, 1917, Sept. 25, 1919, June 19, 1924; *S. T.,* Aug. 8, 1900; information from Mrs. Ernest Lindblom; interviews.

[21]*Broder Lustig,* I (Nov. 1896), 508-509; *H.,* Apr. 8, 1896, Oct. 6, 1906; Olson, *op. cit.,* II, 230-231; *Ord och Bild,* XXX (1921), 396; *S. A. T.,* Jan. 25, 1940; *S. T.,* June 25, 1907; *Ur Dagens Krönika,* V (1885), 505-525; *et al.*

[22]*S. T.,* Aug. 31, 1892.

[23]*S. K.,* Dec. 12, 1899; interview with Mrs. Knut Schröder.

²⁴*Broder Lustig*, the humorous and literary periodical published in 1896 and 1897 by A. F. Lindstrand, owner of *Svenska Amerikanaren*, directed its attacks against the editor of *Svenska Kuriren*, Alexander or "Kurre" Johnson, and against Sigyn.

²⁵Söderström, *Blixtar på tidningshorisonten*, p. 280.

²⁶See n. 24, p. 361.

²⁷*Bläckfisken*, p. 240; Skarstedt, *Pennfäktare*, p. 119; *S. A.*, Sept. 3, 1914; *S. A. T.*, Oct. 21, 1931; Söderström, *Blixtar på tidnings-horisonten*, p. 122.

²⁸Edwin Björkman, letter to O. A. Linder, Linder Clipping Collection; Karl Hellbeg, "Two Swedish-American writers," *Scandinavia*, 79-92, in Linder Clipping Collection; *H.*, May 21, 1914; *Iduna*, III (Jan. 1898), 7; Skarstedt, *Pennfäktare*, p. 34.

²⁹Edwin Björkman, *Gates of life* (New York, 1923), p. 329.

³⁰*Ibid.*, p. 384.

³¹*Svenska teaterminnen från Chicago*, p. 31.

³²Oscar Bæckstrom and others, *Skådespelarne har ordet* (Stockholm, 1902), pp. 85-97.

³³*S. T.*, Aug. 27, 1891, Oct. 4, 1893; Söderström, *Blixtar på tidnings-horisonten*, p. 239.

³⁴Walter Browne & E. D. Koch, eds., *Who's who on the stage* (New York, 1908), pp. 133-134; Arthur Donaldson, letters, Aug. 21, 24, 1950; *S. A.*, Aug. 11, 1903, Apr. 14, 1910; *S. A. T.*, Mch. 21, May 5, 1949; *S. K.*, Apr. 24, 1924; *S. T.*, Mch. 22, 1893, Aug. 30, Sept. 6, 1899, Feb 21, 1900, Aug. 11, 12, 1903; *S. T. N.*, Oct. 6, 1920; *Svea*, Worcester, Mass., Apr. 4, 1896; *Valkyrian*, III (Sept., 1899), 470-472.

³⁵Olson, *op. cit.*, p. 753; *S. A.*, Sept. 12, 1905, Mch. 19, 1907; *S. A. T.*, Oct. 13, 1938; *S. K.*, Dec. 13, 1898.

³⁶Behmer, *loc. cit.*, V, 113; Frans Hedberg, *Svenska skådespelare* (Stockholm, 1884), pp. 240-246; *Ny Illustrerad Tidning*, VI (1885), 25; *Ny Svensk Tidskrift*, X (1889), 588-602; *S. A.*, Sept. 22, 1908; *S. T.*, Aug. 9, 1893; *Ur Dagens Krönika*, II (1882), 1 ff., and VI (1886), 427.

³⁷*Ny Illustrerad Tidning*, VI (1885), 143; *Ord och Bild*, II (1893), 238; *S. T.*, Apr. 3, 1895; *Ur Dagens Krönika*, VIII (1888), 545-547, and X (1890), 415.

³⁸There may have been additional performances in the 1892-1893 season, when the *Svenska Teatersällskap* was said to have acted twenty-one times, though only twelve productions appear in the newspaper records. *S. T.*, May 17, 1893. See p. 103.

³⁹The number of performances omits six for which plays were not named, and does not include the unrecorded *Svenska Teatersällskap* performances of the 1892-1893 season. As several of the new plays were seen in combination with plays introduced earlier, the number of performances for which they accounted must be approximate.

⁴⁰O. A. Linder, *Svensk-Amerikanska pseudonymer. Ur Nya Verlden*, 1899, p. 22; Skarstedt, *Pennfäktare*, p. 84.

⁴¹*S. T.*, July 5, 1899.

⁴²Plays of local authorship in this period that have not been named are: Gus Higgins, *Sax, taylor på dekis* (Tailor on the downward path); Edward Holmer, *Fias rivaler* (Fia's rivals); Carl Wennberg, *Pelles första natt i Amerika* (Pelle's first night in America); and the anonymous *Nyårsnatt på Hotell Svea* (New Year's night at Hotel Svea).

⁴³*H., S. A.*, Sept. 10, 17, 1891; *S. T.*, Aug. 27, Sept. 9, 16, 23, 1891.

⁴⁴*S. A.*, Nov. 19, *S. T.*, Dec. 17, 31, 1891.

⁴⁵*S. K.*, Jan. 6, 1892.

⁴⁶Jan. 10, *Ett odjur* (A monster), by Erik Bögh; *Alla möjliga roller* (All possible roles); *Hon både sparkas och bits;* February 7, *Mer än pärlor och guld* (More than pearls and gold), by Hans Christian Andersen.

⁴⁷From *Efter femtio år. H.*, Feb. 11, *S. A.*, Mch. 3, *S. T.*, Feb. 17, 1892.

⁴⁸*S. A.*, Jan. 14, 1892.

⁴⁹*S. A.*, Apr. 21, *S. T.*, Apr. 20, 27, 1892.

⁵⁰*S. T.*, Mch. 30, 1892. See p. 85. The cast varied somewhat for the different performances, and was not given completely for any of them.

⁵¹*S. T.*, May 18, 25, 1892.

⁵²*S. T.*, May 25, June 1, 8, 1892.

⁵³*S. A.*, July 19, *S. T.*, July 13, 27, 1892.

[54]Arthur Donaldson, letter, August 24, 1950.

[55]*S. A.*, Jan. 31, May 16, *S. T.*, Feb. 1, May 17, 1893.

[56]*Skådespelarne har ordet*, pp. 95-96.

[57]*S. A.*, May 2, *S. T.*, May 3, 1893.

[58]*S. A.*, Feb. 14, 1893.

[59]*S. A.*, Feb. 14, *S. T.*, Feb. 15, 1893.

[60]*S. A.*, Feb. 21, 1893.

[61]*S. K.*, Nov. 29, *S. T.*, Nov. 30, 1892.

[62]*Runristningar. Independent Order of Vikings, 1890-1915* (C h i c a g o, 1915), pp. 85-86.

[63]*S. A.*, Jan. 10, Feb. 21, Apr. 18, May 23, *S. T.*, May 24, 1893.

[64]*S. A.*, Sept. 20, *S. T.*, Aug. 10, 16, Sept. 13, 19, 1893, *Bröllopet på Ulfåsa*, first announced for September 10, was postponed a week because of the death of Mr. Richard Hooley, owner of the theatre.

[65]*S. T.*, Sept. 6, 13, 27, 1893.

[66]*S. K.*, May 1, 1894.

[67]*S. A.*, Jan. 9, *S. T.*, Jan. 3, 1894; Wicklund, *op. cit.*, pp. 198-200.

[68]*S. T.*, Nov. 15, Dec. 6, 1893

[69]See p. 13.

[70]*S. A., S. K.*, Mch. 27, 1894.

[71]*S. A.*, Oct. 17, *S. T.*, Oct. 18, 1893.

[72]*S. K.*, Apr. 24, *S. T.*, Apr. 25, 1894.

[73]*S. A.*, Aug. 28, *S. T.*, Aug. 29, 1894.

[74]*S. A.*, Sept. 25, *S. K.*, Oct. 9, *S. T.*, Oct 10, 1894. See also Lindstrand's account of the evening's events, p. 15.

[75]*S. A., S. K.*, Dec. 11, 1894.

[76]*S. K.*, Nov. 6, *S. T.*, Nov. 7, 1894.

[77]*S. A.*, Feb. 19, *S. K.*, Feb. 5, 19, *S. T.*, Feb. 6, 13, 20, 1895.

[78]*S. A.*, Apr. 16, 1895.

[79]*S. A.*, Mch. 19, 1895.

[80]*Skådespelarne har ordet*, pp. 95-97; *S. T.*, Apr. 10, 1895.

[81]*S. A.*, Apr. 23, *S. K.*, Apr. 9, 30, *S. T.*, Apr. 10, 1895.

[82]*S. A.*, Apr. 16, *S. T.*, Apr. 17, 1895.

[83]*S. A.*, Oct. 1, *S. T.*, Sept. 11, Oct. 2, 1895.

[84]*S. K.*, Nov. 12, 1895.

[85]*S. T.*, Feb. 12, 1896.

[86]*S. A.*, Dec. 17, 1895, Jan. 7, 1896; Mr. Ernst H. Behmer, letter, Aug. 31, 1940.

[87]*S. A.*, Apr. 28, *S. K.*, Apr. 26, *S. T.*, Apr. 29, 1896.

[88]*S. K.*, Sept. 1, *S. T.*, Aug. 19, 1896, etc.

[89]*S. A.*, Sept. 29, *S. K.*, Sept. 22, *S. T.*, Sept. 23, 1896.

[90]*S. A., S. K.*, Oct. 6, *S. T.*, Sept. 30, Oct. 7, 14, 1896.

[91]*S. K.*, Oct. 13, *S. T.*, Oct. 14, 1896.

[92]*S. K.*, Nov. 3, *S. T.*, Nov. 4, 1896.

[93]*S. A.*, Dec. 15, *S. T.*, Nov. 18, Dec. 15, 23, 1896.

[94]*S. A., S. K.*, Oct. 20, *S. T.*, Oct. 21, 1896.

[95]*S. K.*, Nov. 17, *S. T.*, Nov. 18, 1896. The *Pinafore* manuscript was given by Mrs. Gustaf Wicklund to the Augustana College Library, Rock Island, Ill.

[96]*S. A.*, Jan. 12, *S. T.*, Jan. 13, 1897; interviews.

[97]*S. A.*, Mch. 15, Apr. 12, *S. K.*, Mch. 15, *S. T.*, Apr. 13, 1898. Carl Pfeil was in January 1898 manager of the tavern, *Flaggen*, at 67 E. Kinzie. Advertisement in *Humoristen*, Jan. 1, 1898.

[98]*H.*, May 18, June 1, 8, July 6, *S. T.*, June 8, 22, 1898.

[99]*S. A.*, Jan. 31, *S. T.*, Jan. 4, 1899.

[100]*H.*, Oct. 12, Nov. 9, *S. A., S. K.*, Nov. 8, *S. T.*, Nov. 9, 1898.

[101]*S. K.*, Jan. 17, *S. T.*, Jan. 18, 1899.

[102]*S. T.*, July 26, 1899.

[103]The play was advertised as an adaptation (*S. A.*, Oct. 24, 1899), but Mr. Behmer has vouched for its originality. Letter, Aug. 31, 1940.

[104]This was not the journalist, Ernst Lindblom, but the singer, who was from now on increasingly prominent.

[105]*S. A.*, Oct. 24, Nov. 7, *S. K.*, Nov. 7, *S. T.*, Oct. 11, Nov. 8, 1899. Mr. Schröder's roles were supplied by Mrs. Schröder.

[106]*S. A.*, Dec. 5, 12, 1899, Jan. 2, 1900; *S. T.*, Dec. 6, 1899, Jan. 3, 1900.

[107]*S. K.*, Jan. 9, *S. T.*, Jan. 3, 1900.

[108]*S. A.*, Jan. 30, *S. T.*, Jan. 31, 1900.

[109]*H.*, Feb. 14, 21, 1900; Hjalmar Nilsson, "Den första Svensk-Amerikanska operan," *Valkyrian*, III (Jan. 1899), 18-22; *S. A.*, Aug. 8, Nov. 8, 1899, Jan. 24, Feb. 13, 1900; *S. K.*, Jan. 16, Feb. 13, *S. T.*, Feb. 14, 1900.

[110]*S. K.*, Mch. 20, *S. T.*, Mch. 21, 1900.

[111]*S. A.*, Oct. 9, *S. T.*, Oct. 10, 1900.

[112]*S. A.*, Oct. 9, 23, *S. K.*, Oct. 23, *T.*, Oct. 17, 1900.

[113]*S. K.*, Feb. 12, Mch. 5, *S. T.*, Feb. 13, 1901.

[114]Pfeil claimed that the play was original, and it was also said to be based on *Döden fadder*, which he used in May and later. *S. A.*, Nov. 27, Dec. 11, 18, 1900; *S. K.*, Nov. 27, 1900, Jan. 1, 8, 1901; *S. T.*, Nov. 28, Dec. 19, 1900.

[115]*S. A.*, May 21, *S. T.*, May 21, 1901.
[116]*S. A.*, *S. K.*, Jan. 8, 1901.
[117]*S. A.*, Oct. 16, Nov. 26, 27, *S. K.*, Oct. 16, Nov. 6, *S. T.*, Nov. 14, 28, 1900.
[118]*Svenska Skådespelare Sällskap.*

CHAPTER V

[1]*H.*, Oct. 9, 1901, Jan. 30, 1912; *S. A.*, Jan. 25, *S. T. N.*, Jan. 30, 1912. See p. 184.
[2]*S. A.*, *S. K.*, *S. T.*, Mch. 1, 1904; *S. K.*, Mch. 4, 1902; *et al.*
[3]Lydia Hedberg (*Bergslagsmor*), *Reseminnen från U. S. A.* (Sköfda, 1925), pp. 50 ff.; interviews.
[4]*S. K.*, Sept. 30, 1915.
[5]*S. K.*, Dec. 15, 1907
[6]*S. N.*, Apr. 10, 1906.
[7]*S. K.*, May 18, 1907.
[8]*S. N.*, Feb. 28, 1905.
[9]*S. K.*, Mch. 30, 1907.
[10]*S. A.*, *S. K.*, May 1, *S. T. N.*, Apr. 29, 1913.
[11]*S. K.*, Oct. 2, 1913, Nov. 25, 1905.
[12]*S. K.*, Apr. 7, 1906; *S. T.*, Oct. 8, 1912, Aug. 30, 1904; *S. A.*, Nov. 9, 1909.
[13]*S. K.*, Oct. 20, 1906, Mch. 26, 1910, *et al.*
[14]*S. N.*, Dec. 6, 1904.
[15]*S. K.*, Jan. 15, 1903.
[16]*S. A.*, Oct. 23, 1906, Feb. 12, 1907; *S. N.*, Oct. 31, Jan. 9, 1906.
[17]*S. K.*, Apr. 7, 1906.
[18]Letter from Mr. Ernst H. Behmer, Aug. 21, 1940.
[19]*S. A.*, Jan. 2, 1936, *S. T. N.*, Sept. 19, 1911.
[20]Interview with Rosa Pearson Burgeson, *et al.*
[21]*S. A.*, Feb. 9, 1928, Mch. 4, 19, 1937.
[22]*S. A.*, *S. K.*, May 13, 1920.
[23]*S. A.*, Mch. 15, 1928; *S. A. T.*, Nov. 11, 1943, Mch. 23, 1944, Sept. 25, 1947, *et al.*
[24]Behmer, *loc. cit.*, p. 114.
[25]*H.*, *S. A.*, Aug. 20, 1914.
[26]Skarstedt, *Pennfäktare*, p. 190; *S. T. N.*, Jan. 9, 1917.
[27]*S. A.*, July 30, 1914; *S. A. T.*, Feb. 5, 1941.
[28]*S. A.*, Mch. 27, *S. K.*, Mch. 10, *S. T.*,

Feb. 20, *S. V.*, Feb. 16, Mch. 30, 1906. See p. 164.
[29]*S. A.*, *S. T. N.*, Dec. 10, 1907; interviews.
[30]Emma Meissner, "Mina första debuter," in *Skådespelarne har ordet*, pp. 127-131; Herman Hofberg, ed. *Svenskt biografisk håndlexicon* (Stockholm, 1903), II, 134; *S. K.*, July 6, 1907.
[31]*H.*, Mch. 19, June 22, *S. A.*, July 1, 1910. Madame Lundberg's article in *Skådespelarne har ordet* is mainly an amusing account of her happy and successful period in Paris. Pp. 115-124.
[32]*S. K.*, Mch. 23, 1912.
[33]*S. T. N.*, Mch. 23, 1909.
[34]Behmer, *loc. cit.*, p. 117; *S. A.*, *S. K.*, Oct. 8, 1910.
[35]Gustaf af Geijerstam, "Teater," *Ord och Bild*, V (1896), 523-528; Tor Hedberg, *Ett Decennium* (Stockholm, 1913), III, 24-27, 125-129; *August Lindberg. En Monografi* (Stockholm, 1911); Gustaf Linden, "August Lindberg," *Ord och Bild*, XXVI (1917), 365-372; *Ny Illustrerad Tidning*, V (1884), 401; *Ny Svensk Tidskrift*, VI (1885), 275 ff.; *Ollén, op. cit., passim.*; *Ord och Bild*, IV (1895). 385-389, X (1901), 385-386, XIV (1905), 410, XVI (1907), 61; *Svenskt biografisk håndlexikon*, II, 65; *Ur Dagens Krönika*, IX (1889), 88-101. See also pp. 92-93 as to Edwin Björkman's account of Lindberg.
[36]*En bok om Per Lindberg* (Stockholm, 1944); *Ord och Bild*, XXXI (1922), 120, XXXVI (1927), 36, XXXVII (1928), 111; Per Lindberg, *Anders de Wahl* (Stockholm, 1944), and *Gösta Ekman* (Stockholm, 1942).
[37]*Ord och Bild*, XII (1903), 611-612; *Svensk uppslagsbok* (Malmö, 1947-1949), VIII, 513-514; *S. T. N.*, Nov. 14, 1911. A book of songs by

Elis Olson was given as a premium by *Svenska Amerikanaren* in 1913. Advertisement, *S. A. T.,* Apr. 7, 1949.

[38]*H.,* Mch. 26, Oct. 1, Nov. 12, 1912, Jan. 7, Oct. 16, 1913; *S. A.,* Mch. 28, May 22, 1912, Feb. 5, Oct. 16, 1913; *S. K.,* May 25, *S. T. N.,* May 26, 1912.

The path of the impressario for Swedish artists was often far from smooth, and others besides Olson were ready to criticize America's democratic Swedes. The book written by *Bergslagsmor,* a ballad singer, about her travels is a case in point. She writes appreciatively of receptive audiences, and of Mrs. Myhrman's efforts on her behalf, undertaken as a favor after she had "sworn off" because of the Elis Olson affair, but the account is frequently satirical about the way of life in Swedish America. *Delbostintan,* another popular folk entertainer, wrote with far more kindliness and understanding. L y d i a Hedberg, *Reseminnen från U. S. A.;* Ida Gawell-Blumenthal, *Stintans A m e r i k a färd* (Stockholm, 1908).

[39]Program, Nov. 23, 1907; manuscript copy of the play; *Kurre-Kalender,* 1903; *S. N.,* 1904; *S. T.,* Dec. 31, 1902. See n. 48, p. 368, and n. 108, p. 369.

[40]The word *k o l i n g e n,* meaning drunken good-for-nothing, was popularized by cartoonist Albert Engström of Sweden.

[41]*S. K.,* Nov. 26, 1904.

[42]The *Dalkullan Almanak* from 1910 to 1921 (and probably both earlier and later) a d v e r t i s e d twenty-odd plays, chiefly comedies, at prices from ten to sixty cents. Löfström's *Teater-Biblioteket* plays are still available at the Dalkullan shop in Chicago.

[43]*S. A.,* Oct. 15, 19, *S. K.,* July 16, 1901.

[44]*S. K., S. N.,* Oct. 29, 1901. *S. N.* characteristically took exception to Behmer's interpretation of Prior Botvid, with eyes rolling "as if he were a cannibal chief in pursuit of missionaries."

[45]*S. A., S. K., S. N.,* Nov. 26, *S. T.,* Nov. 27, 1901.

[46]*S. N.,* Dec. 10, *S. T.,* Dec. 11, 1901.

[47]*H.,* Feb. 12, Mch. 5, *S. A.,* Feb. 11, *S. K.,* Feb. 11, Mch. 4, *S. T.,* Feb. 12, 1902.

[48]The copy owned by Mr. Melinder,

with Mr. Strand named as author, kindly lent by Mrs. Melinder. Of interest is the fact that directions for settings that precede the play are given in English.

[49]*S. A.,* Mch. 11, Apr. 8, *S. K.,* Feb. 18, Mch. 11, 18, *S. N.,* Apr. 8, *S. T.,* Mch 12, 1902.

[50]*S. A., S. N.,* May 6, 1902. A sign of changing times may be noted in the fact that a performance of *Pinafore* by the John E. Young Opera Company was the feature of the Swedish Glee Club's Bellman Day celebration July 27. *S. K.,* July 22, 1902.

[51]*S. T.,* Apr. 25, 1903. *Nerkingarne* was also acted in Joliet, Ill., December 2. *S. N.,* Dec. 1, 1902.

[52]*S. A.,* Apr. 7, 1903.

[53]Interviews with Mr. Ernst H. Behmer, Mrs. Werner Melinder, and Mr. and Mrs. Carl Milton. Mrs. Melinder has lent the *Ljungby Horn* MS. There is seeming correspondence between the handwriting in the text and Mr. Liljegren's signature on the cover.

[54]*S. A.,* Oct. 21, *S. K.,* Aug. 5, Sept. 16, Oct. 21, *S. N.,* Oct 28, *S. T.,* Sept. 17, 1902.

[55]*S. A., S. K., S. N.,* Nov. 11, 1902.

[56]*S. A.,* Mch. 31, Apr. 7, *S. K.,* Mch. 31, *S. T.,* Apr. 1, 1903.

[57]*S. A.,* Dec. 23, 1902; *S. K., S. N.,* Jan. 6, *S. T.,* Jan. 7, 14, 1903.

[58]An announcement of the season's plans on September 15 named Brusell and Behmer as company directors, but from October 6 on the *Svenska Teatersällskap* was referred to as Brusell's. Emphasis was given, however, to its fifth year of activity. *S. A.,* Sept. 15, Oct. 6, 1903.

[59]*S. A.,* Sept. 22, Oct. 6, *S. K., S. N.,* Oct. 6, 1903.

[60]*S. A.,* Oct. 13, Dec. 8, *S. N.,* Oct. 27, Dec. 8, *S. T.,* Oct. 28, Dec. 9, 1903.

[61]This play, too, has been lent by Mrs. Werner Melinder.

[62]*S. A.,* Sept. 15, Oct. 27, *S. K.,* Sept. 29, Oct. 27, *S. N.,* Oct. 27, *S. T.,* Dec. 23, 1903.

[63]*S. A., S. K.,* Jan. 5, 1904.

[64]*S. A.,* Feb. 9, Mch. 1, Mch. 22, *S. K.,* Mch. 1, 22, *S. N.,* Mch. 1, *S. T.,* Mch. 2, 23, 1904. The March performance probably replaced a *Svenska Teater-*

368

sällskap production planned for that month. *S. T.*, Dec. 9, 1903.

65*S. A.*, Oct. 18, 1904, Mch. 12, 26, Apr. 19, 1925; *S. N.*, Oct. 18, *S. T.*, Oct. 19, 1904.

66*S. A.*, *S. N.*, Nov. 22, *S. K.*, Nov. 26, *S. T.*, Nov. 23, 1904.

67*S. A.*, *S. N.*, Dec. 5, *S. K.*, Dec. 10, *S. T.*, Dec. 7, 1904; interview with Mrs. Werner Melinder.

68*S. A.*, Jan. 24, *S. K.*, Jan. 21, *S. N.*, Jan. 17, 1905.

69*S. A.*, Mch. 21, *S. K.*, Mch. 25, *S. T.*, Mch. 22, 1905.

70*S. A.*, *S. N.*, Feb. 21, *S. T.*, Feb. 22, 1905. See p. 134.

71*S. K.*, Apr. 22, *S. N.*, Apr. 18, *S. T.*, Apr. 19, 1905.

72*S. A.*, May 9, *S. K.*, Apr. 22, 29, *S. T.*, Apr. 26, 1905.

73*S. A.*, May 2, 1905.

74This situation was exceptional. As Mr. Donaldson has written, "During my long engagement under Col. Henry W. Savage management, he kindly gave me permission to appear on Sunday evenings with the Swedish Theater Company whenever I came to Chicago and played *The Prince of Pilsen* at the Studebaker Theater." Letter, Aug. 8, 1950.

75*S. A.*, Aug. 29, *S. K.*, Sept. 2, *S. N.*, Aug. 29, *S. T.*, Aug. 30, 1905.

76*S. A.*, Nov. 28, *S. K.*, Nov. 25, *S. N.*, *S. T.*, Nov. 21, 1905.

77*S. K.*, Sept. 30, *S. N.*, Sept. 26, *S. T.*, Sept. 27, 1905.

78*S. A.*, Dec. 5, *S. K.*, Dec. 9, *S. N.*, *S. T.*, Dec. 5, 1905.

79*S. K.*, Dec. 23, 1905; *S. N.*, *S. T.*, Jan. 9, 1906.

80*S. A.*, Apr. 10, *S. K.*, Apr. 14, *S. N.*, *S. T.*, Apr. 10, 1906.

81The comment w a s probably intended to carry some implications, as the engagement of Hedwig Brusell and Werner Melinder was shortly announced. *S. T.*, Feb. 6, 1906.

82*S. K.*, Feb. 3, *S. N.*, *S. T.*, Jan. 30, 1906.

83*S. A.*, May 15, *S. K.*, May 19, *S. T.*, May 15, 1906.

84*S. A.*, May 22, *S. K.*, May 26, *S. N.*, *S. T.*, May 22, 1906.

85*S. A.*, Mch. 13, *S. N.*, Mch. 6, 1906.

86*S. K.*, Mch. 10, 1906, *et al.*

87*H.*, Mch. 13, 1906.

88*S. A.*, Feb. 27, Mch. 20, Apr. 3, *S. K.*, Mch. 20, 24, Apr. 7, *S. N.*, Mch. 20, *S. T.*, Feb. 20, 27, Mch. 20, Apr. 3, *S. V.*, Mch. 30, 1906.

89*S. K.*, Sept. 22, *S. T. N.*, Sept. 18, 1906.

90*S. A.*, Sept. 25, Oct. 23, 1906, Jan. 8, 1907; *S. T. N.*, Oct. 2, 9, 30, 1906, *et al.*

91This is the story in *S. V.*, Apr. 6, 1907. In direct contradiction, *S. T. N.*, Apr. 2 and Oct. 22, 1907, called the programs given celebrations of a fifth anniversary. I have found no earlier mention of such a company, though these actors had presented similar entertainment on many occasions.

92*S. A.*, Oct. 16, *S. K.*, Oct. 20, *S. T. N.*, Oct. 16, 1906.

93*S. A.*, Nov. 20, *S. K.*, Nov. 24, 1906.

94*S. A.*, Dec. 11, *S. K.*, Dec. 12, *S. T. N.*, Dec. 11, 1906.

95*S. A.*, *S. T. N.*, Jan. 8, 1907.

96*S. K.*. Feb. 9, *S. T. N.*, Feb. 12, *S. V.*, Feb. 8, 1907.

97*S. A.*, Mch. 12, 26, *S. K.*, Mch. 9, 16, 23, *S. T. N.*, Mch. 12, 1907.

98*S. A.*, *S. T. N.*, Mch. 19, 1907.

99*S. A.*, Apr. 23, *S. K.*, Apr. 20, *S. T. N.*, Apr. 16, 1907.

100*S. A.*, May 14, *S. K.*, Mch. 30, May 18, *S. T. N.*, Apr. 2, May 14, 1907. See material from *S. K.* article, p. 133.

101*S. A.*, June 4, *S. K.*, June 8, 1907.

102*S. A.*, July 16, 23, *S. K.*, July 20, *S. T. N.*, July 23, 1907.

103*S. A.*, *S. T. N.*, June 25, 1907.

104*S. A.*, Sept. 17, Aug. 17, 1907.

105*S. A.*, Oct. 8, 1908.

106*S. A.*, Sept. 24, *S. K.*, Sept. 28, *S. T. N.*, Sept. 24, 1907.

107She had only a week in which to learn the role and prepare for her first appearance, Mrs. Burgeson (the former Rosa Pearson) tells.

108*S. A.*, *S. T. N.*, Oct. 15, 1907; program, W a u k e g a n, Nov. 23, 1907, Schwartz's Theatre. In connection with the October performance, Algot E. Strand was first mentioned as responsible for the adaptation, but there was no indication that this was not the same play acted earlier.

109*S. A.*, Nov. 26, *S. K.*, Nov. 30, 1907.

[110]S. A., Dec. 10, S. K., Dec. 14, S. T. N., Dec. 10, 1907.

[111]S. A., S. K., Dec. 17, 1907.

[112]S. A., Jan. 21, S. K., Jan. 25, 1908.

[113]S. A., S. T. N., Jan. 7, 1908.

[114]S. A., Jan. 28, S. K., Feb. 1, S. T. N., Jan. 28, 1908.

[115]S. A., Jan. 28, S. K., Feb. 18, 22, 1908.

[116]S. A., Aug. 18, 1908.

[117]Ida Gawell-Blumenthal, op. cit., pp. 91, 93-94, 178; S. A., Feb. 25, S. K., Feb. 29, 1908.

[118]S. A., Mch. 10, 17, 24, S. K., Mch. 28, 1908.

[119]S. A., Sept. 1, 22, 29, Oct. 8, S. K., Oct. 3, 10, 1908.

[120]S. A., Oct. 15, S. K., Oct. 18, 1908.

[121]S. A., Nov. 12, Dec. 3, S. K., Dec. 5, 1908.

[122]S. A., Nov. 12, 1908.

[123]S. A., Jan. 7, 1909.

[124]S. A., Mch. 18, S. T. N., Mch. 16, 1909.

[125]S. A., Apr. 1, 8, S. T. N., Apr. 6, 1909. An appearance of Miss Sandberg with Behmer's company in a March 7 production of Vermländingarne at the Grand Opera House had been announced, but seems to have been cancelled. S. A., Feb. 11, 1909.

[126]S. A., July 15, 22, S. T. N., July 20, 1909.

[127]Skådespelarne har ordet, pp. 115-124; S. A., July 1, Sept. 16, 1909. The shortened form of the title, Pariserpojken, was used in Chicago.

[128]S. A., Sept. 23, S. T. N., Sept. 21, 1909.

[129]S. T. N., Oct. 5, 1909.

[130]S. A., Oct. 28, 1909, Mch. 17, 1910, S. K., Mch. 19, 1910, S. T. N., Nov. 2, 1909.

[131]S. A., Oct. 28, Nov. 4, S. K., Nov. 6, S. T. N., Oct. 26, Nov. 2, 1909.

[132]S. A., Nov. 18, 25, S. K., Nov. 20, 27, 1909.

[133]S. K., Mch. 5, 26, S. T. N., Mch. 22, 1910.

[134]S. A., Oct. 27, S. K., Oct. 29, 1910.

[135]S. A., Nov. 3, S. K., Nov. 5, S. T. N., Nov. 1, 1910.

[136]S. A., Dec. 8, S. T. N., Dec. 13, 1910.

[137]S. A., Jan. 26, S. K., Jan. 28, S. T. N., Jan. 24, 1911.

[138]S. A., Feb. 2, S. K., Feb. 4, S. T. N., Jan. 31, 1911.

[139]S. K., Apr. 15, 1911.

[140]S. A., Oct. 5, S. K., Oct. 7, S. T. N., Oct. 3, 1911.

[141]S. K., Oct. 14, S. T. N., Oct. 10, 1911.

[142]S. T. N., Sept. 19, 1911.

[143]Carl G. Laurin, "Från Stockholms teatrar," Ord och Bild, XII (1902), 611-612; program, Rockford; S. A., Nov. 16, 30, 1911, Mch. 7, 1912; S. K., Oct. 28, Nov. 4, 18, 25, 1911, Mch. 9, 1912; S. T. N., Nov. 7, 14, 28, 1911.

[144]S. A., Feb. 8, S. K., Feb. 10, 24, S. T. N., Feb. 6, 1912.

[145]Program.

[146]S. K., May 25, 1912. See p. 144.

[147]S. A., Oct. 26, Nov. 2, 23, S. K., Oct. 14, 28, Nov. 4, 18, Dec. 23, S. T. N., Oct. 17, 31, Nov. 21, Dec. 12, 19, 1911.

[148]En bok om Per Lindberg, pp. 18-24; Ollén, op. cit., pp. 290-298; H., Jan. 23, S. A., Jan. 25, S. K., Jan. 13, 27, S. T. N., Jan. 23, 1912; program; interviews with Ida Anderson-Werner, Carl and Augusta Milton, Mrs. Knut Schröder.

[149]H., Jan. 30, S. A., Jan. 25, S. T. N., Jan. 30, 1912.

[150]En bok om Per Lindberg, pp. 20-26; H., Jan. 30, Apr. 12, 1912.

[151]S. K., Jan. 6, S. T. N., Jan. 9, 1912.

[152]S. A., Apr. 4, S. K., Mch. 16, Apr. 6, 1912.

[153]S. A., May 2, S. T. N., Apr. 30, 1912.

[154]S. K., Apr. 20, 1916.

[155]Occasional references show that there were more minor performances by such groups than were advertised or reported.

[156]H., Oct. 8, S. A., Oct. 10, S. T. N., Oct. 8, 1912.

[157]H., S. A., S. K., May 1, S. T. N., Apr. 29, 1913.

[158]H., S. A., Apr. 3, 1913.

[159]S. A., Apr. 10, 1913.

[160]See n. 33, p. 358.

[161]H., Jan. 21, Chicago Tribune, Jan. 20, 1913.

[162]H., Apr. 30, 1912, Jan. 28, Feb. 4, Apr. 10, 1913; S. A., Mch. 5, 1912, Feb. 13, Apr. 10, 1913.

^{163}S. A., S. K., May 22, S. T. N., May 27, 1913; program.
^{164}S. T. N., Mch. 17, 1914.
^{165}H., Jan. 15, 1914, S. A. H., Feb. 4, 11, 1915.
^{166}S. A., Mch. 5, 1914.
^{167}S. A., Sept 2, 11, 1913.
^{168}S. A., S. K., Sept. 25, Oct. 2, 1913, Feb. 26, 1914, S. T. N., Sept. 23, 30, 1913.
^{169}S. A., S. K., Jan. 8, S. T. N., Jan. 6, 1914.
^{170}H., S. A., S. K., Apr. 2, S. T. N., Mch. 31, 1914.
^{171}H., July 30, S. A., July 23, 30, S. K., July 30, S. T. N., July 28, 1914.
^{172}H., Aug. 20, Sept. 24, S.A.H., Oct. 1, S. K., Sept. 24, Oct. 1, S. T. N., Sept. 22, 29, 1914.
^{173}S. A. H., S. K., Nov. 5, S. T. N., Nov. 3, 1914.
^{174}S. A. H., Feb. 4, 11, 1915.
^{175}S. A. H., Jan. 28, Apr. 15, 1915.

^{176}H., Dec. 25, 1913, Feb. 26, 1914.
^{177}S. A. H., Sept. 23, 30, Oct. 21, S. K., Sept. 30, Oct. 14, S. T. N., Sept. 28, Oct. 12, 1915.
^{178}S. A., Mch. 15, S. T. N., Mch. 13, 1917
^{179}S. A., Nov. 2, 1916, Mch. 1, 1917, S. K., Nov. 2, S. T. N., Oct. 31, 1916, Feb. 27, 1917.
^{180}S. A., S. K., Oct. 25, S. T. N., Oct. 23, 1917.
^{181}Ollén, op. cit., p. 155; S. A., S. K., Apr. 18, S. T. N., Apr. 16, 1918.
^{182}S. A., Feb. 7, 21, S. K., Feb. 21, S. T. N., Feb. 19, 1918.
^{183}Also called Folk-Teatern.
^{184}Cast for November performance in Waukegan, Illinois.
^{185}S. T. F.—Svenska Teater Förening.
^{186}Visiting company of actors from Boston, New York, etc.
^{187}Just by chance, Behmer's translation of Tillfälligheter, was also acted.

CHAPTER VI

^{1}The chronological t a b l e for this chapter is limited to plays headed by the old actors, those presented by these three companies a n d the Svenska Teater-ensemble that preceded Svenska Folk-teatern, and the two late revivals of Vermländingarne. A supplement to the chapter, f o l l o w i n g the chronological table, lists alphabetically all the other plays recorded for the period, with main facts of performance.
^{2}Adolph B. Benson a n d Naboth Hedin, Swedes in America, 1638-1938 (New Haven, Conn., 1938), pp. 116-117.
^{3}Ord och Bild, XVI (1907), 293; XLI (1932), 107; XLIII (1934), 121; XLIV (1935), 384-385; XLV (1936), 116-117.
^{4}S. A., Sept. 12, 26, S. K., Sept. 26, S. T. N., Sept. 25, 1918.
^{5}S. A., Nov. 17, S. K., Nov. 14, 1918.
^{6}S. A., S. K., Oct. 9, 1919, Mch. 25, 1920, S. T. N., Oct. 8, 1919, Mch. 24, 1920.
^{7}S. A., S. K., Nov. 13, 1919.
^{8}S. A., Aug. 28, Sept. 21, 1919, S. T. N., Jan. 28, 1920.
^{9}S. A., Sept. 9, Oct. 21, S. K., Sept. 23, Oct. 14, S. T. N., Oct. 13, 20, 1920.
^{10}S. A., Jan. 6, Feb. 17, Mch. 2, S. K., Feb. 3, Mch. 10, S. T. N., Feb. 2, Apr. 13, 1921.
^{11}S. A., S. K., Oct. 27, S. T. N., Oct. 26, 1921.
^{12}S. A., Dec. 8, S. T. N., Dec. 7, 1921.
^{13}S. A., Jan. 12, Apr. 6, S. K., Jan. 12, Mch. 20, Apr. 6, 1922, S. T. N., Nov. 2, 1921, Jan. 11, 1922.
^{14}S. A., Aug. 31, S. T. N., Sept. 27, 1922.
^{15}S. A., Nov. 2, 23, 30, Dec. 7, S. K., Nov. 23, S. T. N., Nov. 15, 22, 1922.
^{16}S. A., S. K., Nov. 1, 29, 1923, S. K., May 7, 1924.
^{17}S. A., Oct. 16, 30, 1924, Apr. 23, 1925, S. K., Oct. 30, 1924.
^{18}On April 18 and 19, 1925, a Rockford company acted Svärfar; and on November 15, 1925, and February 21, April 17, and June 20, 1926, presented Nerkingarne. S. A., Mch. 12, 1925, Feb. 4, 25, Apr. 8, 22, 1926, S. K., June 24, 1926, S. T. N., Nov. 18, 1925.
^{19}S. T. N., Jan. 20, Mch. 10, 1926.
^{20}S. A., S. K., Oct. 15, S. T. N., Oct. 14, 1925.
^{21}S. A., S. K., Mch. 25, 1926.

[22]S. A., Apr. 11, S. K., Apr. 8, S. T. N., Mch. 31, 1926.

[23]S. K., Oct. 7, 1926.

[24]S. A., Sept. 23, 30, Oct. 7, 14, 27, S. T. N., Oct. 27, 1926.

[25]Interviews.

[26]S. A., Oct. 28, Dec. 2, 1926, S. A. T., Aug. 30, 1945, S. K., Nov. 18, S. T. N., Dec. 1, 1926.

[27]S. A., Apr. 7, Aug. 11, Sept. 8, Oct. 27, S. K., Oct. 27, S. T. N., Oct. 26, 1927.

[28]S. K., May 24, 1928.

[29]S. A., Dec. 8, 15, S. K., Dec. 29, 1927.

[30]On a loose sheet in the manuscript copy of Lifvet på landet there is a cast for the play, written in an unidentified hand.

[31]See pp. 110-111.

[32]S. A., Aug. 26, 1926, Feb. 23, Mch. 8, 1928, S. A. T., Mch. 4, 1937, S. K., Mch. 28, 1928.

[33]S. A., S. K., Nov. 8, S. T. N., Nov. 7, 1928.

[34]Sjöberg played Sven; Maja Dejenberg-Anderson, Stina; Werner Norén, Per; and Thore Österberg, Anders. Olle was Löpare-Nisse, and the well known Hilda Hellstrom-Gagnée, Mor Lisa. S. A., Dec. 6, 13, 20, S. K., Dec. 20, 1928.

[35]S. A., Nov. 22, Dec. 13, 1928, Jan. 3, 1929, S. T. N., Jan. 2, 1929.

[36]Carl Stockenberg "Svenska Folkteatern," Hembygden, p. 104; S. A., June 6, 27, S. K., July 4, 1929.

[37]When Behmer returned briefly to theatrical activity in June 1931, presenting Majorens döttrar for Svenskarnas Dag at the Good Templar Park, his actors were drawn mainly from Svenska Folkteatern forces. S. A., June 11, 25, S. T. N., June 24, 1931.

[38]S. A., Feb. 12, S. T. N., Jan. 21, Feb. 11, 1931.

[39]S. T. N., Jan. 29, 1936. Behmer gave a Swedish recitation on a Swedish Glee Club radio program in February 1936, and in March of that year the Miltons, Sjöberg, Paul Norling, and Herta Larson presented a radio sketch, En spelemansägen (A fiddler story). Svenska Folkteatern had given a Swedish radio program in June 1935, also. S. A., June 27, 1935, Feb. 20, 1936, S. T. N., Mch. 18, 1936.

[40]S. A., Oct. 31, S. T. N., Sept. 19, 1934.

[41]S. A., Feb. 7, 14, 1935.

[42]S. A., Oct. 24, 31, Nov. 14, 21, Dec. 26, 1935, S. T. N., Nov. 20, 1935, Jan. 8, 1936.

[43]For instance, not all the plays listed as given by the company called Myggan in an account in Hembygden (p. 43) appear in the newspaper records. Nor are references to the number of performances of a specific play within a season always borne out by newspaper records.

[44]S. A. T., Aug. 9, 1949.

[45]The Verdandi Club, also, has had a long history, and for many years published an excellent periodical, Bokstugan.

[46]Hembygden, pp. 101-103.

[47]E. Einar Andersson, clipping from Good Templar publication, Linder Clipping Collection; Bland Norrlänningar i Chicago (Chicago, 1942), p. 9; S. A. T., Mch. 3, 1938.

[48]Hembygden, p. 43, and passim.

[49]The name Norden had been used by an amateur company in 1911, but there is no evidence of connection with the 1925-1926 Norden.

[50]Hjalmar Peterson (Olle i Skratthult) was born in Värmland in 1885, came to Minneapolis in 1906, and immediately became a success on the stage with his comic Swedish characterizations and songs. He toured Sweden with a Swedish American quartette in 1909, returned to the United States in 1911, and began the extensive tours that continued into the 1930's and have been recently revived. For a number of years his wife, Olga Peterson, was his leading lady. Sångarfest album, n.d., Linder Clipping Collection, et al.

[51]See pp. 234-237 and 242-243.

[52]Alf Henriques, Svensk litteratur efter 1900 (Stockholm, 1945), pp. 115-116; Carl G. Laurin, Ord och Bild, XXV (1916), 108, XXVI (1917), 396-397, XXVII (1918), 120-121; Svenskt författarlexikon, 1900-1940, Bengt Åhlén, ed. (Stockholm, 1942), I, 154-155; S. A., Apr. 19, 25, 1925.

[53]Svenskt författarlexikon, II, 756-757.

[54]Svenskt författarlexikon, II, 826; S. T. N., Jan. 6, 1926.

⁵⁵*S. A.,* Dec. 29, 1932; Dec. 14, 1933, *S. T. N.,* Dec. 28, 1932.

⁵⁶*Svenskt författarlexikon,* I, 473; *S. A.,* May 23, 1929.

⁵⁷There had been a performance by the Lake View Division of the South Side *Arbetar Förbund* as early as November, 1911, and other performances by related groups may have been given without newspaper record.

⁵⁸*Bokstugan,* no. 39, Jan. 29, 1926, p. 19; *Svenskt författarlexikon,* I, 65-66; *S. A.,* Feb. 27, May 14, 28, 1936, *S. K.,* Jan. 31, 1924. Three performances of *Skökan rättvisan* were recorded in the press, but the Mch. 29, 1936, performance was the fourth of the season, according to *S. T. N.,* Mch. 25.

⁵⁹*Svenskt författarlexikon,* II, 860-861.

⁶⁰*S. A.,* Apr. 3, 1930.

⁶¹This may be related to the play by Fridolf, *Kråkemåla marknad eller Rosen från herregården.* (Kråkemåla fair or the rose of the manor). *Författarlexikon,* I, 473.

⁶²*S. A. T.,* Apr. 1, 1937.

⁶³*S. A. T.,* Feb. 28, 1935.

⁶⁴*S. A. T.,* Mch. 2, 16, 1939; *Värmland vår hembygd,* V (1930), 39.

⁶⁵*Svenskt författarlexikon,* I, 160-162, 273-274, and *passim.*

⁶⁶Interview with Mr. Paul Norling.

⁶⁷*Svenska författarlexikon,* II, 620; *S. A. T.,* Feb. 13, 1941.

⁶⁸*Svenska författarlexikon,* I, 209.

⁶⁹*S. A. T.,* Dec. 10, 1936.

⁷⁰*Svenska författarlexikon,* II, 567-568.

⁷¹Carl G. Laurin, *Ord och Bild,* XIV (1905), 410; XXXIX (1930), 335; XL (1931), 415-416.

⁷²See pp. 219 and 236.

⁷³Skarstedt, *P e n n f ä k t a r e,* p. 189; "Svensk Amerikanska konstnäre," Linder Clipping Collection; Westman, *The Swedish element in the United States,* III, 280; interviews.

⁷⁴*S. A.,* Mch. 1, Apr. 12, *S. K.,* Feb. 1, Mch. 1, 1923.

⁷⁵*S. A.,* Feb. 12, 19, *S. K.,* Feb. 19, *S. T. N.,* Feb. 18, 1925.

⁷⁶*S. A.,* Dec. 9, *S. K.,* Oct. 2, 7, Nov. 4, 9, Dec. 8, *S. T. N.,* Dec. 9, 1926.

⁷⁷Similar in type was Arvid Nelson's *Hej svejs i lingonskogen* (We'll be seeing you), presented by *Svenska Folketeatern* actors at Belmont Hall in October 1933. *S. A.,* Oct. 5, 19, 1933.

⁷⁸*S. A.,* Oct. 19, *S. T. N.,* Sept. 13, 1933.

⁷⁹*S. A.,* Dec. 19, 1946; interview with Mr. Paul Norling.

⁸⁰Interviews; *S. A.,* May 30, 1935.

⁸¹Interviews; programs, Linder Clipping Collection; *S. A. T.,* Mch. 27, 1941, Mch. 31, 1949; *Värmland vår hembygd,* IV (1929), 16.

⁸²Not unnaturally, in view of its Belmont Avenue location, the Victoria has from time to time s h o w n Swedish movies. Among its Swedish pictures in 1949 w e r e *Lifvet på landet* and a modern version of a comedy acted by *Svenska Folketeatern, Halta Lena och vindögda Per.*

⁸³In 1945 the North Side Auditorium was purchased by members of Svithiod lodges organized as the Svithiod Club. *S. A. T.,* Jan. 19, 1950.

⁸⁴*S. A. T.,* May 20, 1937.

⁸⁵Interviews with Arvid Nelson, Paul Norling, and Carl Stockenberg; Stockenberg, *loc. cit.*

⁸⁶*S. T. N.,* Jan. 8, 1936, *et al.*

⁸⁷*S. A.,* June 5, July 3, 1930, May 7, 1931, Feb. 1, 1934, *S. A. T.,* Aug. 24, 1939.

⁸⁸Carl G. L a u r i n, *Ord och Bild,* XXXIV (1925), 427; XXXIII (1924), 173-172.

⁸⁹*Hembygden,* p. 106.

⁹⁰Nelson wrote two comedies for the c o m p a n y, *Hemma hos Karlsons* and *Handlarns första piga;* the musical play, *Söder om Rio Grande;* and was part author of their revues of 1933, 1935, and 1940. Two of his musical plays were acted by other groups: *Frithiof och Carmencita* and *Hej svejs i lingonskogen.*

⁹¹Carl Grimberg, *Svenska folkets underbara öden* (Stockholm, 1916-1924).

⁹²*S. A.,* Dec. 11, 25, 1930, Jan. 8, 15, 1931, *S. T. N.,* Dec. 24, 1930, Jan. 14, 1931.

⁹³Lindblom, *op. cit.,* p 33; *S. A. T.,* Feb. 13, 1941.

⁹⁴*S. A.,* Dec. 14, 1933, Jan. 4, 1934, *S. T. N.,* Jan. 3, 10, 1934.

⁹⁵*S. A.,* Dec. 26, 1935, Jan. 9, 1936, *S. T. N.,* Dec. 25, 1935, Jan. 8, 1936.

⁹⁶*S. A. T.,* Dec. 12, 26, 1940.

⁹⁷Stockenberg, *loc. cit.*, p. 106; *S. A.*, Dec. 31, 1941.

⁹⁸Interviews; *S. A.*, Oct. 24, 1934.

⁹⁹*S. A.*, Feb. 13, 20, Mch. 20, 1930, Aug. 20, Sept. 3, Oct. 8, 1931, *S. T. N.*, Jan .1, 1930, Oct. 7, 1931; programs.

¹⁰⁰*S. A.*, June 1, 1933.

¹⁰¹*S. A.*, Feb. 15, 1935; interviews.

¹⁰²*S. A.*, Mch. 5, Oct. 15, 1936.

¹⁰³*S. A.*, Feb. 14, 1935.

¹⁰⁴*S. A.*, July 30, Aug. 7, 14, Oct. 23, *S. T. N.*, Aug. 13, 1930, *et al.*

¹⁰⁵*S. T. N.*, Nov. 5, 12, 1930; interviews. Of interest is the fact that a Finnish performance of the play was given the evening after the *Folkteatern* première, and in the same hall.

¹⁰⁶*S. T. N.*, Apr. 1, 15, 1931.

¹⁰⁷*S. A.*, Dec. 14, 1936, Jan. 7, 1937, *S. A. T.*, Dec. 18, 1941, Jan. 8, 1942.

¹⁰⁸*S. A.*, Oct. 3, 17, 1935.

¹⁰⁹*S. A.*, Jan. 26, 1933, Dec. 20, 1934.

¹¹⁰*S. A. T.*, Dec. 7, 28, 1939, Jan. 4, 1940.

¹¹¹*S. A. T.*, Dec. 23, 1937, Jan. 6, 1938.

¹¹²*S. A.*, Mch. 21, *S. T. N.*, Mch. 20, 1935.

¹¹³*S. A.*, June 14, 1932.

¹¹⁴Stockenberg, *loc. cit.*, p. 105; *S. A.*, June 5, 26, *S. T. N.*, June 25, 1930.

¹¹⁵*S. A.*, June 16, 23, 1932

¹¹⁶*S. A.*, Mch. 2, 9, 1933.

¹¹⁷*S. A.*, May 26, Oct. 27, Nov, 3, 24, 1932, *S. A. T.*, June 17, 1948, May 4, 1950, *S. T. N.*, Oct. 19, 26, 1932.

¹¹⁸*S. A.*, Oct. 26, 1933, *S. A. T.*, Oct. 13, 1938.

¹¹⁹*S. T. N.*, Dec. 26, 1934. The same pattern undoubtedly characterized these two plays also: Kurt Göransson's *Fiskarne Östermans sommargäst* (Fishermen Östermans' summer guest), acted by Idrott in 1936; and *Peter Jonssons huskors*, presented by the Chicago Swedish Male Chorus in 1941.

¹²⁰The Belmont Hall performance of *Nummer 39* cannot be so regarded.

¹²¹*S. A.*, Jan. 17, 24, 31, Feb. 7, *S. T. N.*, Feb. 6, 1935.

¹²²*S. A.*, June 13, 20, *S. T. N.*, June 19, 1935.

¹²³Strindberg was urged by August Lindberg to make the adaptation, and his comment on the 1889 première was made in a letter to Lindberg. Lindberg gave a more successful production of *Hemsöborna* in Helsingfors in 1890. Ollén, *op. cit.*, pp. 94-96.

¹²⁴Martin Lamm, *August Strindberg, Del 1* (Stockholm, 1940), pp. 377-399.

¹²⁵*S. A. T.*, Apr. 29, May 6, 13, 20, 1937.

¹²⁶*S. A. T.*, Nov. 10, 1938.

¹²⁷*S. A. T.*, Nov. 17, 1938; interview with Mr. Carl Stockenberg.

¹²⁸*S. A. T.*, Feb. 7, 1934.

¹²⁹Mr. Stockenberg directed similar pageants for the Svithiod Order in 1935 and 1938, and Mr. Behmer had charge of the elaborate historical pageant depicting the history of the Swedes of the United States at the Century of Progress Swedish Day, in September 1934.

¹³⁰*S. A. T.*, May 19, 1942.

¹³¹Of interest is the fact that attorney Carl H. Lundquist, president of *Värmlands Nation*, had married Wanja Nauclair, who acted with Brusell and Behmer companies.

¹³²*S. A. T.*, Jan. 26, Feb. 21, Aug. 1, ff., Oct. 3, 10, 24, 31, 1946; interview with Mr. Paul Norling.

¹³³Other persons p r e s e n t included Mrs. Werner Melinder, of Milwaukee, Fred Bolling, John Melin, Magda Lewis, and Ebba Kempe. Mr. Stockenberg was kept away by an illness which had also prevented his acting in *Vermländingarne*. *S. A. T.*, Dec. 5, 1946.

¹³⁴*S. A. T.*, Jan. 16, 1947.

¹³⁵*S. A. T.*, Nov. 14, Dec. 19, 1946, Jan. 23, 1947.

¹³⁶*S. A. T.*, Nov. 25, 1948, Mch. 3, 1949.

¹³⁷*S. A. T.*, Apr. 28, May 19, 1949. *Mot beräkning* was acted under its subtitle, *Madame Anderssons hyresgäster* (Mrs. Andersson's boarders).

¹³⁸These appearances were part of a longer tour. *S. A. T.*, Sept. 8, Nov. 24, 1949, Feb. 16, 1950.

¹³⁹*S. A. T.*, Oct. 5, 12, 19, 26, Nov. 2, 1950; the October 22 performance seen.

¹⁴⁰A. T.—*Arbetar Teater.*

¹⁴¹S. S. V. T.—South Side Viking Temple.

¹⁴²S. F.—*Svenska Folkteatern.*

¹⁴³N. S. A.—North Side Auditorium.

¹⁴⁴V. T. C.—Viking Theatrical Company.

[145]L. A.—Lincoln Auditorium.
[146]Performances of a tableau or sketch of similar title were given by children's groups in recent years: Apr. 16, 1944, Stora Tuna Club; June 11, 1944, Vasa children's meeting; Mch. 21, 1946, Beacon Lodge, I. O. V. They may have been related to Richard Gustafsson's *Ett bondbröllop*, 1876.

INDEX

The three sections of the Index do not in general duplicate materials in the Appendix: plays, authors (except local authors), places of performance, and acting companies are not indexed. The index of Persons, Section I, A, includes references to Appendix, IV, Casts. A supplementary list under B names persons not referred to elsewhere but mentioned in newspaper accounts as having appeared in a play or plays, with chapter references to indicate periods. Section II indexes Chicago Swedish organizations referred to in the text, chronological tables, and the supplement to Chapter VI. Section III, a limited subject index, does not, except for a few topics, give references to materials in the chronological accounts.

I. Persons. A.

Some names found only in casts may be stage names used when there was doubling in roles, and variations in spelling or inadequate identification may have caused some duplication in listings. Visiting actors from Sweden are indicated by asterisks. Pages referred to inclusively indicate, as a rule, mention rather than extended discussion.

Adamsen, Greta*, 142, 185, 202.
Ahlberg, Alida, 342.
Ahlberg, Emil, 296.
Ahlstrand, Oscar, 237, 238, 248, 336, 338, 340, 341, 342.
Ahlstrand, Viola (Mrs. Oscar Ahlstrand), 238, 336, 339, 341, 342.
Ahrenlöf, Margit, 328.
Alarik, Hilding, 314.
Alberg, Albert, 16, 57, 59, 76-79, 83, 88, 89, 98-101, 103-106, 112-115, 117-119, 126-128, 137, 151, 161, 186, 300-302, 304, 308, 309.
Alfredson, Emma, Mrs., 232.
Almgren, Anna (Mrs. Matt Ovington), 56, 73, 75-78, 86, 99, 101, 105, 300, 301, 303.
Almgren, E., 297.
Anderson, Anna, 310.
Anderson, August, 303.
Anderson, Axel, 303.
Anderson, Ellen, 328.
Anderson, Eric, 327.

Anderson, Elvira, 212, 326.
Anderson, Folke, 219, 331.
Anderson, Helen, 219, 331.
Anderson, Hugo, 337.
Anderson, John, 113.
Anderson, Linnea. See Vik, Linnea Anderson, Mrs.
Anderson, Magda. See Lewis, Magda Anderson, Mrs.
Anderson, Maja (Maria) Dejenberg-. See Dejenberg-Anderson, Maja, Mrs.
Anderson, Paul, 232, 337, 341.
Anderson, Sam, 341.
Anderson, Signe, 327.
Anderson, Yngve. See Yngve, Carl.
Anderson-Werner, Ida (Mrs. Werner Anderson), 16, 88, 111, 113, 117, 119, 121, 136-138, 148, 149, 151, 157, 159, 161, 164, 169, 171-174, 176, 178, 181, 183, 186, 189, 190, 192, 193, 210, 212-223, 302, 304-332, 335.
Andersson, E. Einar, 237.
Andreason, Esther, 333.
Andren, Albert, 303.
Appelgren, Elsa (Mrs. Flodin), 232, 239, 252, 338, 339, 341, 342.
Aronson, Will, 316.
Atterling, Carl, 146, 185, 235.

Barcklind, Carl*, 17, 140, 211, 219-221, 258, 259, 331, 332.
Barcklind, Hilma (Mrs. Carl Barcklind)*, 211, 220, 221, 331, 332.
Barron, D., 31.
Becker, Emil, 62, 362n.
Behmer, Ernst Hugo, 2, 3, 16, 49, 56, 57, 76, 84, 87, 88, 98, 99, 107, 111, 112, 114, 117, 119-121, 130-134, 136-142, 144, 145, 147-152, 154, 155, 158-179, 181, 183-189, 191-193, 196, 200, 201, 204, 205, 207, 208, 210-215, 217-220, 223-225, 238, 239, 250-254, 256, 258, 259, 261, 263, 265, 304-306, 308, 310-332, 335, 336, 340, 342, 372n, 377n.
Behmer, Eric. 138, 168, 210, 213, 252, 313, 326, 327, 329-331, 342.
Behmer, Estelle, 138, 181, 319-321.
Behmer, Lisa, 87, 138, 168, 191, 210, 213, 218, 223, 313, 321-324, 327, 328, 330, 340.

Hanson, Carl F., 98, 118.
Harlington, H., 336.
Hasselquist, T. N., 28.
Hazalius, Mrs., 31.
Hedberg, Lydia (*Bergslagsmor*), 368n.
Hedberg, Martha, 338.
Hedberg, Tor, 24, 184.
Hedlund, C. H., 331.
Hedlund, Fredrik*, 56, 71 (?), 363n.
Hedlund, O., 297.
Hedman, Herbert, 54, 361n.
Hedman, Max (Carl Maximus), 54, 75, 76, 78, 86, 101, 103, 104, 113, 115, 117, 155, 157, 300-302, 304, 307, 309, 311.
Hedman, Ragnhild Fosmark (Mrs. Max Hedman), 86, 104, 301.
Hedström, Agnes, 306.
Hegelfelt, Lydia, 336.
Hellström, Anna, Madame*, 17, 141, 162, 166, 197, 309.
Hellström, Hilda. See Gagnée, Hilda Hellström-, Madame.
Hellström, Nanny, 318.
Hermelin, J., 316.
Herrmelin, E., 317.
Higgins, Gus (Gustaf Lindstrom), 49-51, 71, 72, 75, 77, 86, 92, 101, 102, 110-112, 125, 300, 301, 361 notes.
Hilding, Ida, 334, 335.
Hillström, Sixtén, 340.
Holm, Anna Windrow, 134, 140, 160, 191, 193, 324, 326.
Holm, Mr., 31.
Holmes, Edward, 110.
Holmes, George E., 298, 299.
Holmes, J., 298.
Holmes, John, 74.
Holmes, R., 297.
Holson, A. B., 65-67, 80, 363n.
Hooley, Richard, 363n, 366n.
Hopp, Erika (Mrs. Hjalmar Hopp), 45, 60, 295, 296.
Hopp, Hjalmar, 45, 60, 295.
Hulström, Engla, 238, 340, 341.
Hultén, Axel, 309.
Hultin, Mauritz, 312.
Hultman, Linnea, 303.
Husing, M., 329.
Hvitfeldt, Greta, 303.
Hvitfeldt, Hanna Holmquist (Mrs. Robert Hvitfeldt), 16, 55, 72, 73, 75, 76, 86, 99, 101, 102, 104, 107, 108, 113, 115, 116, 137, 148, 157, 300-305, 307.
Hvitfeldt, Robert (Sr.), 56.

Hvitfeldt, Robert (Jr.), 56.
Håkanson, Helga, 308, 309.
Hård, Siri, af Segerstad, Madame*, 17, 211, 215, 216, 329.
Hägerström, Ernst, 235, 236.
Hägg, M., 311, 314.
Höckert, Bruno E., 98, 112.
Höglund, John, 295.

Ivendorff, Euphemia, 30.

Jacobson-Wiberg, Thora, Mrs. 219, 331.
Jancke (Yancke), Yngve, 237, 238, 244, 334, 336-339.
Jansson, Signe, 342, 343.
Jennings, Mr., 113.
Jockum, Miss A., 297.
Johanson, Aina, 343.
Johanson, Gunnar, 342.
Johnson, Alex. J. (Kurre), 119, 304, 365n.
Johnson, Alfred, 31, 61.
Johnson, Andrew, 296.
Johnson, Bernt, 333.
Johnson, C., 321.
Johnson, Edna, 342.
Johnson, Elvy, 332.
Johnson, Gustaf, 332-334.
Johnson, H., 295.
Johnson, Helen, 232, 252, 254, 341-343.
Johnson, Ivar, 223.
Johnson, J., 295, 298.
Johnson, J. F., 298.
Johnson, Paul, 342.
Johnson, Robert, 307.
Johnson, Ruth (Mrs. Oscar Larson), 140, 185, 186, 189, 193, 210, 321-327.
Johnson, Stella, 328.
Johnson, Th., 302.
Johnson, Thorvald, 340.
Johnson, William, 330.
Johnston, Florence, 319.
Johnstone, Signe, 334.
Jones, Axel, 318.
Jones, Walter, 174, 312, 313, 315.
Josephson, Aksel, 182, 226.
Josephson, Ludvig, 96.

Kassman, Gunnar 333.
Kellerman, H. W., 330.
Kempe, Ebba (Mrs. E. V. Chellgren), 140, 190, 210, 216, 324, 329, 374n.
Kindmark, Thora, 186, 189, 321, 322, 325.
Kling, Tryggve, 317.

379

380

381

Anderson, Hanna, VI.
Anderson, Herman, VI.
Anderson, Karin, VI.
Anderson, Karl, VI.
Anderson, Knut, VI.
Anderson, Louis, VI.
Anderson, Martin, VI.

Backlund, A., VI.
Bastman, Mr., III.
Beckman, Anna, V.
Berg, Gottfred, VI.
Berg, Karin, VI.
Berg, L., III.
Bergman, A., VI.
Bergman, Stina, VI.
Bergsten, Hjalmar, VI
Bergston, Ed., VI.
Bergstrand, Åke, VI.
Blomgren, Gösta, IV.
Blücher, Ruth, VI.
Bolinder, Selma, VI.
Borg, Hildur, VI.
Borg, O., VI.
Brogren, Pauline, VI.
Bäckström, Harold, VI.
Bäckström, Ragnhild, VI.

Carlén, David, VI.
Carlson, Ellen, V.
Carlson, Gertrude, VI.
Carlson, Gustav, VI.
Celinder, David, VI.
Celinder, Douglas, VI.
Chellman, Velma, VI.
Clauson, Mr., IV.
Clauson, Mrs., IV.

Dahlblom, Waldemar, IV.
Dahlen, Nils, VI.
Danielson, Bert, VI.
Davis, Edward, IV.
Demar, Florence, IV.
Dillner, P. W., VI.

Edwinson, J. E., VI.
Edwinson, Richard, VI.
Elfström, Miss., IV.
Engström, Albert, VI.
Engström, Carl, VI.
Engström, Herbert, VI.
Erickson, Otto, VI.
Erickson, Pete, VI.
Erickson, Evald, VI.
Erickson, Gottfred, VI.
Ericson, Helen Näslund, Mrs., VI.

Ericson, Victor, VI.
Evert, Maria, VI.

Felldén, Gösta, V.
Fornell, Evy, VI.
Fornell, Hilding, VI.
Forström, F., VI.
Franzen, Arvid, VI.
Friberg, Herbert, V.

Gabrielson, Olaf, VI.
Giljam, C., IV.
Grönquist, Mr., IV.
Gustafson, Thure, VI.

Haglund, Paul, VI.
Halberg, Anna, V.
Hall, Ella, VI.
Hanson, Olga, V.
Harlington, Ragnar, VI.
Hedberg, Frida, Mrs., VI.
Hede, Anna, VI.
Hedelin, Alice, VI.
Hedström, Mr., V.
Hegg, Manna, V.
Higgins, Mrs. Gus, IV.
Hoffman, Hans, VI.
Holmquist, Gottfred, III.
Holmstrom, Ludwig, VI.
Hult, Amanda, V.
Hultman, G., VI.
Höckert, Magna, IV.

Janson, Erik, VI.
Jehander, Albert, VI.
Johanson, Alice, VI.
Johnson, Alexis, VI.
Johnson, C. Albert, IV.
Johnson, Edvin, VI.
Johnson, Ernest, VI.
Johnson, Fred, VI.
Johnson, Gottfred, IV.
Johnson, Gunborg, VI.
Johnson, Henning, VI.
Johnson, Hilma, Mrs., VI.
Johnson, Oscar, VI.
Johnson, Ragna, VI.
Johnson, Signe, VI.
Jonason, Elsa, V.
Jonsson, Elsa, VI.

Karlsson, Anna, VI.
Koch, Mr., IV.
Kohlen, Mr., VI.
Kullenberg, Mathilda, IV.
Kullenberg, Mr., IV.
Kunert, George, VI.

II. Chicago Swedish Organizations.

Names now commonly used in translation have been given in English, or in Swedish and English with cross references. The type of organization is commonly given in English.

Sundsvalls Club, 269.
Svea Singing Club, 194.
Svea Society, 1, 4, 12, 27-32 *passim*, 37, 39, 40, 41.
Svenska Bildnings Förbund, 226.
Svenska Förbund, 12, 37.
Svenska Föreningarnas Central Förbund, 13, 14, 116, 127.
Svenska Kultur Förbund, 14; West Side Division, 140, 224, 251, 263.
Svenska National Förbund (A.), 13, 16, 56, 84, 115, 118, 119, 120, 126, 127, 129, 132, 144, 147, 149, 150, 152, 155, 158, 169, 171, 172, 175, 176, 179, 182, 184, 188, 190, 194-206 *passim*.
Svenska National Förbund (B.), 190, 204.
Svenska Studie Förbund, 226, 228, 270, 271.
Svenska Sångarförbund, 13, 90, 105, 141, 197, 198.
Svenska Sångförbund, 12.
Svithiod Club (A.), 12, 31, 37, 41.
Svithiod Club (B.), 373n.
Svithiod Singing Club, 5, 13, 73, 99, 113, 114, 116, 117, 118, 120, 126, 127, 128, 129, 132, 155, 172, 191, 194, 199, 200.
Swedish-American League, 205.
Swedish Athletic Association, 263.
Swedish Club, 5, 12, 13, 181, 184, 214, 215, 235, 257; Swedish Club Women's Auxiliary, 214, 257. See also Swedish Glee Club.
Swedish Dragoon Regiment, 101, 104.
Swedish Glee Club, 13, 54, 99, 104, 118, 124, 128, 216, 217, 220, 222, 223, 226, 235, 237, 258, 259, 270, 368n.
Swedish Gymnastic Club, 158.
Swedish Male Chorus, 226, 264, 265, 269, 270.
Swedish National Association. See *Svenska National Förbund*.
Swedish Odd Fellows Lodge, 12, 31, 41.
Swedish Old People's Home Association. See *Svenska Föreningernas Central Förbund*.
Swedish Relief Committee, 223.
Swedish Social Club, 80.
Swedish Societies Central Association. See *Svenska Föreningernas Central Förbund*.

Swedish Study Association or Circle. See *Svenska Studie Förbund*.
Swedish Volunteer Regiment, 126, 127.
Swedish Women's Club, 211, 256.
Thor Society, 200, 201.
Vasa Order of America (V.O.A.), 14, 202, 225; lodges: Bessemer, 207; District Lodge Illinois, No. 8, 203, 204, 207; Illinois, 256; Norden, 170; Lyra, 206, 207, 256, 257, 258; Tuna, 268; West Side lodges, 268; Vasa Children's Club, 267, 375n.
Vasa Society, 267.
Verdandi Club, 5, 235, 372n.
Vestgötha Society, 196, 258.
Viking Athletic Association, 263.
Värmlands Club, 226, 228, 239, 253, 263, 266, 268, 269; North Side and South Side, 254, 265.
Värmlands Nation, 227, 252, 253, 254, 263, 265-269 *passim*.
Ölandsklubben, 227.

III. Subject.

Chicago, center of Swedish immigration, 3, 4, 132, 210.
Chicago Swedish colony:
  Assimilation, 8-12, 132. See also Chicago Swedish colony: Economic situation; organizations and social life; and Chicago Swedish theatre: Actors; Audience, type and support; Social aspects.
  Church, 5-7, 10. See also Chicago Swedish theatre: Relations with church.
  Conflicting attitides, 5-7, 12, 27, 28.
  Economic situation, 8-11, 42, 87. See also Chicago Swedish theatre: Actors; Audience, type and support.
  Growth, 3-5, 42, 83, 84, 132, 210.
  Increasing unity, 13, 28, 29, 43, 84, 116.
  Linné monument, 26, 69, 77, 79, 242.
  Location, 4, 5, 27, 83.
  Organizations and social life, 10-13, 16. See also Chicago Swedish theatre: Relations with organizations; Social aspects.
  Press, 7, 8, 27, 42, 43, 210, 346. See also Chicago Swedish theatre: Actors; Relations with press.
  Types of immigrants, 9-11, 42, 43.